What They Said
in 1970

What They Said In 1970

The Yearbook of Spoken Opinion

•

Compiled and Edited by

ALAN F. PATER

and

JASON R. PATER

MONITOR BOOK COMPANY, INC.

To

The Newsmakers of the World . . .

May they never be at a loss for words

Preface to the First Edition (1969)

Wᴏʀᴅs can be powerful or subtle, humorous or maddening. They can be vigorous or feeble, lucid or obscure, inspiring or despairing, wise or foolish, hopeful or pessimistic . . . they can be fearful or confident, timid or articulate, persuasive or perverse, honest or deceitful. As tools at a speaker's command, words can be used to reason, argue, discuss, cajole, plead, debate, declaim, threaten, infuriate, or appease; they can harangue, flourish, recite, preach, discourse, stab to the quick, or gently sermonize.

When casually spoken by a stage or film star, words can go beyond the press-agentry and make-up facade and reveal the inner man or woman. When purposefully uttered in the considered phrasing of a head of state, words can determine the destiny of millions of people, resolve peace or war, or chart the course of a nation on whose direction the fate of the entire world may depend.

Until now, the *copia verborum* of well-known and renowned public figures—the doctors and diplomats, the governors and generals, the potentates and presidents, the entertainers and educators, the bishops and baseball players, the jurists and journalists, the authors and attorneys, the congressmen and chairmen-of-the-board—whether enunciated in speeches, lectures, interviews, radio and television addresses, news conferences, forums, symposiums, town meetings, committee hearings, random remarks to the press, or delivered on the floors of the United States Senate and House of Representatives or in the parliaments and palaces of the world—have been dutifully reported in the media, then filed away and, for the most part, forgotten.

The editors of ᴡʜᴀᴛ ᴛʜᴇʏ sᴀɪᴅ believe that consigning such a wealth of thoughts, ideas, doctrines, opinions and philosophies to interment in the morgues and archives of the Fourth Estate is lamentable and unnecessary. Yet the media, in all their forms, are constantly engulfing us in a profusion of endless and increasingly voluminous news reports. One is easily disposed to disregard or forget the stimulating discussion of critical issues embodied in so many of the utterances of those who make the news and, in their respective fields, shape the events throughout the world. The conclusion is therefore a natural and compelling one: the educator, the public official, the business executive, the statesman, the philosopher—everyone who has a stake in the complex, often confusing trends of our times—should have material of this kind readily available.

These, then, are the circumstances under which ᴡʜᴀᴛ ᴛʜᴇʏ sᴀɪᴅ was conceived. It is the culmination of a year of listening to the people in the public eye; a year of scrutinizing, monitoring, reviewing, judging, deciding—a year during which the editors resurrected from almost certain oblivion those quintessential elements of the year's *spoken* opinion which, in their judgment, demanded preservation in book form.

ᴡʜᴀᴛ ᴛʜᴇʏ sᴀɪᴅ is a pioneer in its field. Its *raison d'etre* is the firm conviction that presenting, each year, the highlights of vital and interesting views from the lips of prominent people on virtually every aspect of contemporary civilization fulfills the need to give the *spoken* word the permanence and lasting value of the *written* word. For, if it is true that a picture is worth 10,000 words, it is equally true that a verbal conclusion, an apt quote or a candid comment by a person of fame or influence can have more significance and can provide more understanding than an entire page of summary in a standard work of reference.

The editors of WHAT THEY SAID did not, however, design their book for researchers and scholars alone. One of the failings of the conventional reference work is that it is blandly written and referred to primarily for facts and figures, lacking inherent "interest value." WHAT THEY SAID, on the other hand, was planned for sheer enjoyment and pleasure, for searching glimpses into the lives and thoughts of the world's celebrities, as well as for serious study, intellectual reflection and the philosophical contemplation of our multifaceted life and mores. Furthermore, those pressed for time, yet anxious to know what the newsmakers have been saying, will welcome the short excerpts which will make for quick, intermittent reading— and rereading. And, of course, the topical classifications, the speakers' index, the subject index, the place and date information—documented and authenticated and easily located—will supply a rich fund of hitherto not readily obtainable reference and statistical material.

Finally, the reader will find that the editors have eschewed trite comments and cliches, tedious and boring. The selected quotations, each standing on its own, are pertinent, significant, stimulating—above all, relevant to today's world, expressed in the speakers' own words. And they will, the editors feel, be even more relevant tomorrow. They will be re-examined and reflected upon in the future by men and women eager to learn from the past. The prophecies, the promises, the "golden dreams," the boastings and rantings, the bluster, the bravado, the pleadings and representations of those whose voices echo in these pages (and in those to come) should provide a rare and unique history lesson. The positions held by these luminaries, in their respective callings, are such that what they say today may profoundly affect the future as well as the present, and so will be of lasting importance and meaning.

ALAN F. PATER

JASON R. PATER

Beverly Hills, California

x

Table of Contents

About the 1970 Edition . . .

Uɴʟɪᴋᴇ other annual reference books, which are merely "updated" each year, ᴡʜᴀᴛ ᴛʜᴇʏ ꜱᴀɪᴅ is totally new with each edition, and so it is readily adaptable for added features and changes. We hope any improvements that may be made from edition to edition will aid the reader to better understand the people, the issues and the events that make the news each year.

New for 1970, and of special interest particularly to researchers, scholars and students, is the inclusion of complete source information with every quotation, consisting of name of source, date and page number. Thus, the reader may quickly refer to the original press report of the quotation in question to verify authentication or to obtain more material. This new feature has been added at the request of numerous librarians who appreciate the value of ᴡʜᴀᴛ ᴛʜᴇʏ ꜱᴀɪᴅ and are anxious to extend its usefulness. We are pleased to incorporate the source information as a permanent addition to ᴡʜᴀᴛ ᴛʜᴇʏ ꜱᴀɪᴅ and would, as always, welcome suggestions for subsequent editions.

The State of the Union address, delivered annually by the President of the United States, is perhaps the single most significant political address of the year. Besides being an indication of the overall views of the President on numerous national issues, it is also a summary of where the nation stands at the start of the year and is frequently a barometer of things to come. Because of the importance of this speech, as both an historical document and as a tradition, ᴡʜᴀᴛ ᴛʜᴇʏ ꜱᴀɪᴅ, beginning with this edition, will present the full text of the President's State of the Union address each year.

Readers of last year's ᴡʜᴀᴛ ᴛʜᴇʏ ꜱᴀɪᴅ will note some category changes in the 1970 volume. In line with the new vocabulary of today, "Conservation and Pollution" has been renamed "The Environment." "Taxes" has been incorporated into the "Labor/Economy" section, and "Patriotism" has been combined into a totally new category, "The American Scene." Another new category, "The Arts," has been added and includes, among other subjects, quotations on censorship of the arts in general. "Space" has been transformed into "Space/Science/Technology," which reflects both a diminution in the importance of space in 1970 and a combining of related subjects into one cohesive section.

Since ᴡʜᴀᴛ ᴛʜᴇʏ ꜱᴀɪᴅ is a reflection of the constantly-changing world scene, the issues and voices raised from year to year are bound to vary in importance. By comparing each year's edition with those before it, the reader will find some topics receiving either more or less attention, according to their relevance in a given year, and some individuals, more than others, speaking out on the issues. With no intention of being a news summary of 1970, following are some of the happenings reflected in many of this year's quotations:

Student Dissent:

The Kent State and Jackson State University shootings were the two major events involving campus protests and dissent, along with the report of the President's Commission on Student Unrest. Many of the pro and con arguments about these issues are contained in WHAT THEY SAID in 1970.

Labor/Economy:

Inflation was the big subject in 1970 as far as the economy was concerned. The incumbent Nixon Administration defended its measures to curb price rises, preferring not to employ wage-price controls. The opposition contended that the Administration was not doing enough, or was employing the wrong measures. Both sides are amply represented in this issue of WHAT THEY SAID.

Journalism:

Vice President Spiro T. Agnew propelled the news media into prominence in 1969 by strongly criticizing their presentation of news. His protests stirred both agreement and strong opposition, which continued at even greater strength in 1970. Under this category will be found arguments from both sides—those charging media bias and distortion of news, and those citing (and denouncing) media harassment and government intimidation of the press.

Politics:

The 1970 elections predictably brought political rhetoric from Republicans and Democrats, liberals and conservatives, left-wing and right-wing factions—as well as from moderates—and provided a fertile field for WHAT THEY SAID editors. Political speeches and oratory can be—and usually are—very colorful, and our Politics section provides an insight into this—at times vitriolic—aspect of American political life. Vice President Agnew was 1970's most frequent political speaker and thus is well represented in the current issue of WHAT THEY SAID. His critics and defenders are legion, and the repartee makes for stimulating reading.

The Environment:

This subject continued to be, in 1970, one of the most controversial of the year, culminated by an "Earth Day" observance around the country.

Foreign Affairs:

The "Nixon Doctrine" was the subject of a great deal of speculation in 1970. And the terms "policeman of the world" and "neo-isolationism" were much talked about. All seemed to agree that the future of American foreign policy was being formulated, and readers will probably find that the words and views in WHAT THEY SAID's Foreign Affairs section will reflect the course of American diplomatic trends in coming decades.

Law and Order:

Some said this was *the* main issue in the 1970 elections. Arguments centered around those who felt that strong—in some cases, drastic—measures were necessary to deal with violence, and those who viewed such actions as dangerous and repressive.

National Defense:

Two of the big topics in this category during 1970 were the ABM and a voluntary armed force to supplant the draft system.

Transportation:

Most controversial in the field of transportation was the SST, and whether the Federal government should allocate funds for its development. The British-French and the Russian SST's, already developed and flight-tested, stirred hot debates in and out of Congress.

Law/Judiciary:

Congress' rejection of Judge G. Harrold Carswell, President Nixon's nominee for the Supreme Court, was the biggest story in this category in 1970.

The Middle East:

Major events during 1970, and reflected in WHAT THEY SAID's Middle East section for this year, were the death of Egyptian President Nasser, the continued actions by Palestine commando organizations climaxed by a costly war in Jordan, the hijack and destruction of civilian aircraft by the commandos, the U.S.-initiated cease-fire along the Suez Canal—with counter-charges of violations by both Arabs and Israelis—and, as the year ended, the imminent commencement of peace talks between the parties under the aegis of Gunnar Jarring, United Nations mediator.

Europe:

Big news in Europe in 1970 was the signing of diplomatic pacts and treaties by West Germany with the Soviet Union, East Germany and Poland; rioting in Poland and the subsequent resignation of Polish Communist Party leader Gomulka; the death of French President de Gaulle; the Labor Party's upset defeat in Britain; and the continuing controversy over NATO.

The Americas:

The election of a Marxist President in Chile—Salvador Allende—was Latin America's major event. Canadian Prime Minister Trudeau's implimentation of the War Measures Act to deal with Quebec militant separatists was North America's big story.

ABOUT THE 1970 EDITION...

Asia and the Pacific:

The war in Vietnam became known as the Indochina war, as fighting increased in Cambodia and Laos. Controversy over what part the United States should take in the intensified battle area makes up a large portion of the Indochina section of WHAT THEY SAID IN 1970.

Editorial Treatment

ORGANIZATION OF MATERIAL

(A) The categories are arranged alphabetically within each of three major sections—

Part I: "National Affairs"
Part II: "International Affairs"
Part III: "General"

In this manner, the reader can quickly locate quotations pertaining to particular fields of interest. It should be noted that some quotations contain a number of thoughts or ideas—sometimes on different subjects—while some are vague as to exact subject matter and thus do not fit clearly into a specific topic classification. In such cases, the judgment of the editors has determined the most appropriate category.

(B) Within each category, the speakers' names are in alphabetical order.

(C) Where there are two or more entries by one speaker within the same category, they appear chronologically by date spoken or date of source.

SPEAKER IDENTIFICATION

The rank, position, occupation, profession or title of the speaker is given as it was *at the time the statement was made*. Thus, due to possible changes in status during the year, a speaker may be shown with different identifications in various portions of the book, or even within the same category. In the case of speakers who hold more than one position or occupation simultaneously, the judgment of the editors has determined the most appropriate identification to use with a specific quotation.

THE QUOTATIONS

All quotations are printed verbatim, as they were originally spoken and reported by the media, except in those cases where the editors of WHAT THEY SAID have eliminated extraneous or overly-long portions. In such cases, *ellipses* (. . .) are always inserted—and in no case has the meaning or intention of any quotation been altered.

DOCUMENTATION AND SOURCES

Documentation (circumstance, place, date) of each quotation is provided as fully as could be obtained, and the sources are furnished with all quotations. In some instances, no documentation details were available, and in these cases only the sources are given. Following are the sequence and style for this information—

> Circumstance of quotation, place, date/Name of source, date: section number (if applicable), page number.

> Example: *Before the Senate, Washington, Dec. 4/The New York Times, 12–6:(4)13.*

The above example indicates that the quotation was delivered before the Senate in Washington on December 4. It was taken from *The New York Times,* issue of December 6, section 4, page 13. (In cases where a newspaper publishes more than one edition on the same date, it should be noted that page numbers may vary from edition to edition.)

THE INDEXES

(A) Arranged alphabetically in the *Speakers' Index,* with their respective page numbers, are the names of all speakers whose quotations appear in this volume. This index will be of use to readers wishing to locate *all* quotations of a particular speaker, regardless of topic.

(B) For detailed study and research, the *Subject Index* provides an in-depth listing of all subjects, places, institutions, individuals, etc., mentioned or discussed in the quotations throughout the book, along with page numbers of their locations.

ABOUT FAIRNESS

The editors of WHAT THEY SAID realize that much of the value of a book of this kind rests in its objectivity. As a result, there has been no conscious editorial bias or influence in the selection of the quotations, the choice of speakers or the manner of editing. Relevance of the statements and the status of the speakers remain the exclusive criteria for inclusion, without any regard whatsoever to the personal beliefs and views of the editors.

Furthermore, every effort has been made to include a multiplicity of opinions and ideas from a wide cross-section of speakers on each topic. Nevertheless, should there appear to be, on some controversial subjects, a preponderance of material favoring one point of view over another, it is simply the result of there having been a preponderance of those views expressed during the year. Also, since persons in politics and government account for a large percentage of the speakers in WHAT THEY SAID, there may exist a heavier weight of opinion favoring the political philosophy of those in office at the time, whether in the United States Congress, the Administration, or foreign capitals. This is natural and to be expected and should not be construed as a reflection of agreement or disagreement with that philosophy on the part of the editors of WHAT THEY SAID.

Abbreviations

Following are abbreviations commonly used by the speakers in this book. Rather than spelling them out in full each time they appear in the quotations, this list will avoid such unnecessary repetition.

ABC: American Broadcasting Company (United States)
ABM: Antiballistic missile
AFL: American Football League (United States)
AFL-CIO: American Federation of Labor-Congress of Industrial Organizations (United States)
CAB: Civil Aeronautics Board (United States)
CATV: Cable television
CBS: Columbia Broadcasting System (United States)
FAA: Federal Aviation Agency (United States)
FBI: Federal Bureau of Investigation (United States)
FCC: Federal Communications Commission (United States)
GNP: Gross national product
HEW: Department of Health, Education and Welfare (United States)
HUD: Department of Housing and Urban Development (United States)
ICBM: Intercontinental ballistic missile
MIRV: Multiple independently-targetable re-entry vehicle (missile)
NAACP: National Association for the Advancement of Colored People (United States)
NATO: North Atlantic Treaty Organization
NBC: National Broadcasting Company (United States)
NFL: National Football League (United States)
NLF: National Liberation Front (Viet Cong/South Vietnam)
OAS: Organization of American States
POW: Prisoner of War
ROTC: Reserve Officers Training Corps (United States)
SST: Supersonic transport
TV: Television
UN: United Nations
USIA: United States Information Agency
WPA: Works Progress Administration (United States)

Party affiliation of United States Senators and Congressmen—
     D: Democrat
     R: Republican
     C: Conservative

The Quote of the Year

"Poor peace! So abandoned, so necessary, so acclaimed; and still, today, so feigned, offended and betrayed."

—POPE PAUL VI

PART ONE

National Affairs

The State of the Union Address

Delivered by Richard M. Nixon, President of the United States, in the House of Representatives, Washington, January 22, 1970.

Mr. Speaker, Mr. President, members of the Congress, our distinguished guests and my fellow Americans:

To address a joint session of the Congress in this great chamber, where I was once privileged to serve, is an honor for which I am deeply grateful.

The State of the Union address is traditionally an occasion for a lengthy and detailed account by the President of what he has accomplished in the past, what he wants the Congress to do in the future, and, in an election year, to lay the basis for the political issues which might be decisive in the fall.

Occasionally there comes a time when profound and far-reaching events command a break with tradition.

This is such a time.

I say this not only because 1970 marks the beginning of a new decade in which America will celebrate its 200th birthday. I say it because new knowledge and hard experience argue persuasively that both our programs and our institutions need to be reformed.

Unfinished Work

The moment has arrived to harness the vast energies and abundance of this land to the creation of a new American experience, an experience richer and deeper and more truly a reflection of the goodness and grace of the human spirit.

The seventies will be a time of new beginnings, a time of exploring both on the earth and in the heavens, a time of discovery. But the time has also come for emphasis on developing better ways of managing what we have and of completing what man's genius has begun but left unfinished.

Our land, this land that is ours together, is a great and good land and also an unfinished land. The challenge of perfecting it is the summons of the seventies.

It is in that spirit that I address myself to those great issues facing our nation which are above partisanship.

When we speak of America's priorities the first priority must always be peace for America and the world.

End of Viet War

The major immediate goal of our foreign policy is to bring an end to the war in Vietnam in a way that our generation will be remembered, not so much as the generation that suffered in war, but more for the fact that we had the courage and character to win the kind of a just peace that the next generation was able to keep.

We are making progress toward that goal.

The prospects for peace are far greater today than they were a year ago.

A major part of the credit for this development goes to the members of this Congress who, despite their differences on the conduct of the war, have overwhelmingly indicated their support of a just peace. By this action, you have completely demolished the enemy's hopes that they can gain in Washington the victory our fighting men have denied them in Vietnam.

No goal could be greater than to make the next generation the first in this century in which America was at peace with every nation in the world.

I shall discuss in detail the new concepts and programs designed to achieve this goal in a separate report on foreign policy, which I shall submit to the Congress at a later date.

Today, let me describe the directions of our new policies.

We have based our policies on an evaluation of the world as it is, rather than as it was 25 years ago at the end of World War II. Many of the policies which were necessary and right then are obsolete today.

Then, because of America's overwhelming military and economic strength, the weakness of other major free world powers and the inability of scores of newly independent nations to defend—let alone govern—themselves, America had to assume the major burden for the defense of freedom in the world.

In two wars, first in Korea and then in Vietnam, we furnished most of the money, most of the arms and most of the men to help others defend their freedom.

Europe Restored

Today the great industrial nations of Europe, as well as Japan, have regained their economic strength, and the nations of Latin America—and many of the nations that acquired their freedom from colonialism after World War II in Asia and Africa —have a new sense of pride and dignity, and a determination to assume the responsibility for their own defense.

That is the basis of the doctrine I announced at Guam.

Neither the defense nor the development of other nations can be exclusively or primarily an American undertaking.

The nations of each part of the world should assume the primary responsibility for their own well-being; and they themselves should determine the terms of that well-being.

We shall be faithful to our treaty commitments, but we shall reduce our involvement and our presence in other nations' affairs.

Insistence by U.S.

To insist that other nations play a role is not a retreat from responsibility, but a sharing of responsibility.

The result of this new policy has been not to weaken our alliances, but to give them new life, new strength and a new sense of common purpose.

Relations with our European allies are once again strong and healthy, based on mutual consultation and mutual responsibility.

We have initiated a new approach to the nations of Latin America, in which we deal with them as partners rather than patrons.

The new partnership concept has been welcomed in Asia. We have developed an historic new basis for Japanese-American friendship and cooperation, which is the linchpin for peace in the Pacific.

If we are to have peace in the last third of the 20th Century, a major factor will be the development of a new relationship between the United States and the Soviet Union.

I would not underestimate our differences, but we are moving with precision and purpose from an era of confrontation to an era of negotiation.

Russia, China Talks

Our negotiations on strategic arms limitations and in other areas will have far greater chance for success if both sides enter them motivated by mutual self-interest rather than naive sentimentality.

It is with this same spirit that we have resumed discussions with Communist China in our talks at Warsaw.

Our concern in our relations with both these nations is to avoid a catastrophic collision and to build a solid basis for peaceful settlement of our differences.

I would be the last to suggest that the road to peace is not difficult and dangerous, but I believe our new policies have contributed to the prospect that America may have the best chance since World War II to enjoy a generation of uninterrupted peace. That chance will be enormously increased if we continue to have a relationship between Congress and the executive in which, despite differences in detail, where the security of America and the peace of mankind are concerned, we act not as Republicans or Democrats—but as Americans.

Material Wealth

As we move into the decade of the 70s, we have the greatest opportunity for progress of any people in world history.

Our Gross National Product will increase by $500 billion in the next 10 years. This increase is greater than the entire growth of the American economy from 1790 to 1950.

The critical question is not whether we will grow, but how we will use that growth.

The decade of the sixties was also a period of great growth economically. But in that same 10-year period we witnessed the greatest growth of crime, the greatest increase in inflation and the greatest social unrest in America in 100 years. Never has a nation seemed to have had more and enjoyed it less.

At heart, the issue is the effectiveness of government.

Ours had become as it continues to be—and should remain—a society of large expectations. Government helped to generate these expectations and undertook to meet them. Yet, increasingly, it proved unable to do so.

As a people, we had too many visions—and too little vision.

Now, as we enter the seventies, we should enter also a great age of reform of the institutions of American government.

Our purpose in this period should not be simply better management of the programs of the past. The time has come for a new quest—a quest not for a greater quantity of what we have—but for a new quality of life in America.

Priority Matters

A major part of the substance for an unprecedented advance in this nation's approach to its problems and opportunities is contained in more than twoscore legislative proposals which I sent to the Congress last year and which still await enactment.

I will offer at least a dozen more major programs in the course of this session.

At this point I do not intend to go through a detailed listing of what I have proposed or will propose, but I would like to mention three areas in which urgent priorities demand that we move:

—We cannot delay longer in accomplishing a total reform of our welfare system. When a system penalizes work, breaks up homes and robs recipients of dignity, there is no alternative to abolishing that system and adopting in its place the program of income support, job training and work incentives which I recommended to the Congress last year.

—The time has come to assess and reform all of our institutions of government at the federal, state and local level. It is time for a new federalism, in which, after 190 years of power flowing from the people and local and state governments to Washington, it will begin to flow from Washington back to the states and to the people.

—We must adopt reforms which will expand the range of opportunities for all Americans. We can fulfill the American dream only when each person has a fair chance to fulfill his own dreams. This means equal voting rights, equal employment opportunity and new opportunities for expanded ownership. In order to be secure in their human rights, people need access to property rights.

Reforms Needed Now

I could give similar examples of the need for reform in our programs for health, education, housing, and transportation, as well as in other critical areas which directly affect the well-being of millions of Americans.

The people of the United States should wait no longer for these reforms that would so deeply enhance the quality of their life.

When I speak of actions which would be beneficial to the American people, I can think of none more important than for the Congress to join this Administration in the battle to stop the rise in the cost of living.

It is tempting to blame someone else for inflation.

Some blame business for raising prices.

Some blame unions for asking for higher wages.

Heavy Federal Spending

But a review of the stark fiscal facts of the 1960s clearly demonstrates where the primary blame for rising prices must be placed.

In the decade of the sixties the federal government spent $57 billion more than it took in in taxes.

In that same decade the American people paid the bill for that deficit in price increases which raised the cost of living for the average family of four by $200 per month.

Millions of Americans are forced to go into debt today because the federal government decided to go into debt yesterday. We must balance our federal budget so that American families will have a better chance to balance their family budgets.

Only with the cooperation of the Congress can we meet this highest priority objective of responsible government.

We are on the right track.

We had a balanced budget in 1969.

This Administration cut more than $7 billion out of spending plans in order to produce a surplus in 1970.

In spite of the fact that Congress reduced revenues by $3 billion, I shall present a balanced budget for 1971.

Balanced Budget

But I can assure you that not only to present but to stay within a balanced budget requires hard decisions. It means rejecting spending programs which would benefit some of the people when their net effect would result in price increases for all the people.

It is time to quit putting good money into bad programs. Otherwise we will end up with bad money as well as bad programs.

I recognize the political popularity of spending programs, particularly in an elec-

tion year. But unless we stop the rise in prices, the cost of living for millions of American families will become unbearable and government's ability to plan programs for progress for the future will become impossible.

In referring to budget cuts, there is one area where I have ordered an increase rather than a cut—the requests of those agencies with the responsibility for law enforcement.

We have heard a great deal of over-blown rhetoric during the sixties in which the word "war" has perhaps too often been used—the war on poverty, the war on misery, the war on disease, the war on hunger. If there is one area where the word "war" is appropriate it is in the fight against crime. We must declare and win the war against the criminal elements which increasingly threaten our cities, our homes and our lives.

We have a tragic example of this problem in the nation's capital, for whose safety the Congress and the executive have the primary responsibility. I doubt if there are many members of this Congress who live more than a few blocks from here who would dare leave their cars in the Capitol Garage and walk home alone tonight.

13 Crime Bills

Last year this Administration sent to the Congress thirteen separate pieces of legislation dealing with organizd crime, pornography, street crime, narcotics and crime in the District of Columbia.

None of these bills has reached my desk for signature.

I am confident that the Congress will act now to adopt the legislation I placed before you last year. We in the executive have done everything we can under existing law, but new and stronger weapons are needed in this fight.

While it is true that state and local law enforcement agencies are the cutting edge in the effort to eliminate street crime, burglaries, and murder, my proposals to you have embodied my belief that the federal government should play a greater role in working in partnership with these agencies.

Federal spending in 1971 for aiding local law enforcement will double that budgeted for 1970.

Special Responsibility

The primary responsibility for most crimes that affect individuals is with local and state rather than with federal government. But in the field of organized crime, narcotics and pornography, the federal government has a special responsibility it should fulfill. And we should make Washington, D.C., where we have the primary responsibility, an example to the nation and the world of respect for law rather than lawlessness.

I now turn to a subject which, next to our desire for peace, may well become the major concern of the American people in the decade of the seventies.

In the next 10 years we shall increase our wealth by 50%. The profound question is—does this mean that we will be 50% richer in a real sense, 50% better off, 50% happier?

Or, does it mean that in the year 1980 the President standing in this place will look back on a decade in which 70% of our people lived in metropolitan areas choked by traffic, suffocated by smog, poisoned by water, deafened by noise and terrorized by crime?

Everyday Experience

These are not the great questions that concern world leaders at summit conferences. But people do not live at the summit. They live in the foothills of everyday experience. It is time for us all to concern ourselves with the way real people live in real life.

The great question of the seventies is, shall we surrender to our surroundings, or shall we make our peace with nature and begin to make reparations for the damage we have done to our air, our land and our water?

Restoring nature to its natural state is a cause beyond party and beyond factions. It has become a common cause of all the people of America. It is a cause of particular concern to young Americans—because they more than we will reap the grim consequences of our failure to act on programs which are needed now if we are to prevent disaster later.

Clean Air, Water

Clean air, clean water, open spaces—these should once again be the birthright of every American. If we act now they can be.

We still think of air as free. But clean air is not, and neither is clean water. The price tag on pollution control is high. Through our years of past carelessness we incurred a debt to nature, and now that debt is being called.

The program I shall propose to Congress will be the most comprehensive and costly program in this field ever in the nation's history.

It is not just a program for the next year. A year's plan in this field is no plan at all. This is a time to look ahead not a year, but five or ten years—whatever time is required to do the job.

I shall propose to this Congress a $10 billion nation-wide clean waters program to put modern municipal waste treatment plants in every place in America where they are needed to make our waters clean again, and do it now.

We have the industrial capacity, if we begin now, to build them all within five years. This program will get them built within five years.

Open Spaces, Parks

As our cities and suburbs relentlessly expand, those priceless open spaces needed for recreation areas accessible to their people are swallowed up—often forever. Unless we preserve these spaces while they are still available, we will have none to preserve. Therefore, I shall propose new financing methods for purchasing open space and park lands, now, before they are lost to us.

The automobile is our worst polluter of the air. Adequate control requires further advances in engine design and fuel composition. We shall intensify our research, set increasingly strict standards and strengthen enforcement procedures — and we shall do it now.

We no longer can afford to consider air and water common property, free to be abused by anyone without regard to the consequences. Instead, we should begin now to treat them as scarce resources, which we are no more free to contaminate than we are free to throw garbage in our neighbor's yard.

This requires comprehensive new regulations. It also requires that, to the extent possible, the price of goods should be made to include the costs of producing and disposing of them without damage to the environment.

Redirected Growth

Now I realize the argument is often made that a fundamental contradiction has arisen between economic growth and the quality of life, so that to have one we must forsake the other.

The answer is not to abandon growth, but to redirect it. For example, we should turn toward ending congestion and eliminating smog the same reservoir of inventive genius that created them in the first place.

Continued vigorous economic growth provides us with the means to enrich life itself and to enhance our planet as a place hospitable to man.

Each individual must enlist if this fight is to be won.

It has been said that no matter how many national parks and historical monuments we buy and develop, the truly significant environment for each of us is that in which we spend 80% of our time—that is, our homes, our places of work and the streets over which we pass.

Street litter, rundown parking strips and yards, dilapidated fences, broken windows, smoking automobiles, dingy working places, all should be the object of our fresh view.

Everyone Must Help

We have been much too tolerant of our surroundings and too willing to leave it to others to clean up our environment. It is time for those who make massive demands on society to make some minimal demands on themselves. Each of us must resolve that each day he will leave his home, his property and the public places of his city or town a little cleaner, a little better, a little more pleasant for himself and those around him.

With the help of people we can do anything. Without their help we can do nothing. In this spirit, together, we can reclaim our land for ours and generations to come.

Between now and the year 2000, over 100 million children will be born in the United States. Where they grow up—and how—will, more than any one thing, measure the quality of American life in these years ahead.

This should be a warning to us.

For the past 30 years our population has also been growing and shifting. The result is exemplified in the vast areas of rural America emptying out of people and of promises —a third of our counties lost population in the 1960s.

Decayed U.S. Cities

The violent and decayed central cities of our great metropolitan complexes are the most conspicuous area of failure in American life.

I propose that before these problems become insoluble, the nation develop a national growth policy.

In the future, decisions as to where to build highways, locate airports, acquire land or sell land should be made with a clear objective of aiding a balanced growth.

In particular, the federal government must be in a position to assist in the building of new cities and the rebuilding of old ones.

At the same time, we will carry our concern with the quality of life in America to the farm as well as the suburb, to the village as well as the city. What rural America most eeds is a new kind of assistance. It needs to e dealt with, not as a separate nation, but as art of an overall growth policy for all America. We must create a new rural environment that will not only stem the migration to urban centers but reverse it. If we eize our growth as a challenge, we can make he 1970s an historic period when by concious choice we transformed our land into what we want it to become.

Use Science Properly

America, which has pioneered in the new abundance and in the new technology, is called upon today to pioneer in meeting the concerns which have followed in their wake -in turning the wonders of science to the ervice of man.

In the majesty of this great chamber we ear echoes of America's history, of debates hat rocked the Union and those that repaired it, of the summons to war and the earch for peace, of the uniting of the peo le and the building of a nation.

Those echoes of history remind us of our oots and our strengths.

They remind us also of that special genius f American democracy, which at one crital turning point after another has led us to oot the new road to the future and given us he wisdom and courage to take it.

As I look down that new road which I ave tried to map out today, I see a new merica as we celebrate our 200th birthday ust six years from now.

I see an America in which we have abolhed hunger, provided the means for every mily in the nation to obtain a minimum ncome, made enormous progress in provid g better housing, faster transportation, imroved health and superior education.

I see an America in which we have hecked inflation, and waged a winning war gainst crime.

I see an America in which we have made eat strides in stopping the pollution of our r, cleaning up our water, opening up new arks, and continuing to explore in space.

Most important, I see an America at peace with all the nations of the world.

This is not an impossible dream. These goals are all within our reach.

In times past, our forefathers had the vision but not the means to achieve such goals.

Let it not be recorded that we were the first generation that had the means but not the vision to make that dream come true.

But let us, above all, recognize a fundamental truth. We can be the best clothed, best fed, best housed people in the world, enjoying clear air, clean water and beautiful parks, but we could still be the unhappiest people in the world without that indefinable spirit—the lift of a driving dream which has made America from its beginning the hope of the world.

Spiritual Needs

Two hundred years ago this was a new nation of three million people, weak militarily, poor economically. But America meant something to the world which could not be measured in dollars, something far more important than military might.

Listen to President Thomas Jefferson in 1802: "We act not for ourselves alone but for the whole human race."

We had a spiritual quality which caught the imagination of millions of peoples of the world.

Today, when we are the richest and strongest nation in the world, let it not be recorded that we lack the moral and spiritual idealism which made us the hope of the world at the time of our birth.

The demands on us in 1976 are even greater than in 1776.

It is no longer enough to live and let live. Now we must live and help live.

We need a fresh climate in America, one in which a person can breathe freely and breathe in freedom.

Our recognition of the truth that wealth and happiness are not the same thing requires us to measure success or failure by new criteria.

RICHARD M. NIXON

Inspiration to Youth

Even more important than the programs I have described today, this nation needs the example of its elected leaders in providing the spiritual and moral leadership which no programs for material progress can satisfy.

Above all, let us inspire young Americans with a sense of excitement, a sense of destiny, a sense of involvement in meeting the challenges we face in this great period of our history. Only then are they going to have any sense of satisfaction in their lives.

The greatest privilege an individual can have is to serve in a cause bigger than himself. We have such a cause.

How we seize the opportunities I have described today will determine not only our future, but the future of peace and freedom in this world in the last third of this century.

May God give us the wisdom, the strength and, above all, the idealism to be worthy of that challenge, so that America can fulfill its destiny of being the world's best hope for liberty, for opportunity, progress and peace for all peoples.

Spiro T. Agnew
Vice President of the United States

Let us never forget what the dignity of work can do for a human being. One reason the silent majority is so silent is this: They're too busy working to make a lot of noise. All too often today, we see some young people—by no means all, but some—who take refuge in postgraduate study not to get a better education, not to prepare themselves for productive lives, not even to evade the draft—but to avoid going to work. We see some welfare-rights organizations denouncing our family-assistance plan, not because it doesn't help the helpless, but because it requires able-bodied people to go to work. We see some employes arriving at work in the morning with their minds fixed on the coffee break; we see people starting their careers with one goal in mind—early retirement; we see some union leaders promising their membership a golden era of a 20-hour week. I submit that the people with a phobia about working are missing one of the great satisfactions of life. The quality of life will not be determined by how much time off we have; it will be determined by the quality of the work we do.

Before Order of American Hellenic Educational Progressive Association, Washington, March 9/U.S. News & World Report, 3-23:85.

We must look to how we are raising our children. They are, for the most part, the children of affluent, permissive, upper-middle-class parents who learned their Dr. Spock and threw discipline out the window—when they should have done the opposite . . . Today, by the thousands—without a cultural heritage, without a set of spiritual values and with a moral code summed up in that idealistic injunction, "Do your own thing," Junior—his pot and *Portnoy* secreted in his knapsack—arrives at "the Old Main" and finds there a smiling and benign faculty even less demanding than his parents.

Fort Lauderdale, Fla., April 28/Time, 5-11:20.

I feel this way, that it is necessary for the frustrations of the American people, as they sit back and observe the steady erosion of the fabric of our society taking place, with hardly a word raised in its defense, to have a strong spokesman. When a fire takes place, a man doesn't run into a room and whisper, "Would somebody please get the water?"; he yells, "Fire!" And I am yelling "Fire!" because I think "Fire!" needs to be called here.

Interview, Washington/Face the Nation, Columbia Broadcasting System, 5-3.

This is a time when application, achievement and success are derided as callous, corrupt and irrelevant. This is a time when criminal misfits are glamorized while our best men die in Asian rice paddies to preserve the freedoms those misfits abuse. This is a time when the charlatans of peace and freedom eulogize foreign dictators while desecrating the flag that keeps them free.

At United States Military Academy commencement/Life, 6-19:26.

There are people in our society who should be separated and discarded. I think it's one of the tendencies of the liberal community to feel that every person in a nation of over 200 million people can be made into a productive citizen. I'm realist enough to believe this can't be. We're always going to have our prisons; we're always going to have our places of preventive detention for psychopaths; and we're always going to have a certain number of people in our community who have no desire to achieve or who have no desire to even fit in an amicable way with the rest of society. And these peo-

(SPIRO T. AGNEW)

ple should be separated from the community —not in a callous way, but they should be separated as far as any idea that their opinions shall have any effect on the course we follow.

Television interview, London, June 30/
The Dallas Times Herald, 7–1:A4.

As we go forward in our attack against what's *wrong* with America, we should never forget what's *right* with America. Let us see and treat the blemishes, but never let them blind us to the beauty.

Before Education Commission of the States,
Denver, July 9/The New York Times, 7–10:21.

America hasn't survived for nearly two centuries and become the world's richest nation, and its strongest, because we were weak or dispirited or because we had a "system" that didn't work. The other free nations of the world haven't turned to us time and again to help preserve their freedom because we held freedom lightly. When we have poured out our resources to help the poor and the disadvantaged, it hasn't been because we didn't care. As we have erected new batteries of legal safeguards for the rights of minorities, it hasn't been because we were racist or bent on oppression. We have done all these things because the heart of America is good, and because its arm is strong, and because we believe in liberty and justice— not just for a favored few but for all. We have done them because our "system" is good; and we have been able to do them because it works.

Before American Legion, Portland, Ore.,
Sept. 2/Los Angeles Herald-Examiner, 9–2.

Before we can properly address ourselves to any national issue, each one of us must address himself to this personal issue: How can we reinstill a sense of discipline in our thinking? Discipline is a harsh word. But . . . there is no greater need in the American body politic today than the need for discipline. During the last generation, a philosophy of permissiveness has permeated American life. In our schools, the ability to adjust became more important than the ability to excel. In our courts, the rights of the accused became more important than the rights of the victims. In our legislatures, the temptation to spend exceeded the willingness to tax. In our culture, the need to protect free expression overrode the need to restrain bad taste and outrageous vulgarity. In our society, the need to escape was exalted and the need to cope was demeaned.

Milwaukee, Sept. 25/
San Francisco Chronicle, 9–26:1.

The competitive, ambitious, aggressive side of our outlook is under attack. The businessman's drive for profit is labeled "money grubbing"; the politician's joust with his opponent is branded as "vicious and divisive"; the military commander's desire for victory is mocked (as) "jingoistic heroics" . . . It is because freedom requires vigilance and effort to survive that I am worried about the "anti" culture of today. I fear that those who espouse this way of life do not realize how quickly a massive individual rejection of responsibility and power could snuff out the freedom that makes their style of life possible.

Before board of directors, Boys' Clubs
of America, New York, Dec. 7/
Los Angeles Herald-Examiner, 12–8:A4.

W.H. Auden
Poet

About America I feel optimistic. I think it's the young people who worry me most; and those drugs. Heavens, we could be unhappy and confused in the Thirties. But we were never bored; there was a life to live . . . They don't understand that life has a rhythm; that there is work and what I call "carnival." You must never get them muddled.

Interview/The Washington Post, 8–19:B5.

Helen Delich Bentley

Chairman, Federal Maritime Commission

This is a great nation, this America of ours. If it is not Utopia, it is the closest approach to it that man has achieved throughout the whole history of his existence.

Quote, 9–6:218.

Leonard Bernstein

Composer, Conductor

Thank God you're impatient, because impatience is a certain signal of hope. What is this despair we keep hearing about? The answer is it's not despair—it's impatience, frustration, fury. Nothing comes instantly except death, and every generation has to learn that anew. Good Lord, our own country is not yet 200 years old! There's still hope for everything. Even patriotism—a word which is being defiled every day—even patriotism can be rescued from the flagwavers and bigots. It's true that we have to work faster and harder if we're going to take our next social step before the overkill stops us dead in our tracks. But if anybody can do it, faster and harder and better, it's you—the best generation in history.

Before students, Berkshire Music Center/
The New York Times, 11–25:37.

Leon B. Blair

Member, history faculty, University of Texas at Arlington

The pessimists see nothing but the nation on the verge of revolution: two societies (black and white) separate, but unequal; universities in turmoil; constant peril from Communist pressures; debilitated and debauched by drugs; and inundated with sex . . . But let's talk about some positive Americanism. Let's understand the healthy body before we examine the sick one. After all, 196,459,483 people did *not* commit a criminal offense in this country last year; 201,489,-710 did *not* use illegal drugs; 4,896,720 college students did *not* participate in a campus demonstration.

At meeting of American Heritage Program,
Abilene, Texas, Aug. 14/
The Dallas Times Herald, 8–14:A10.

Edward L. Bond, Jr.

Chairman, Young & Rubicam, Inc.

I shall not apologize for my pursuit of profit. For the profit motive has led to innovation, greater efficiency and to a gross national product that increased by $411 billion between 1961 and 1969; that *gain* is larger than the *total* output of any other nation in the world, except the Soviet Union. Nor shall I apologize for my country's wealth. This wealth has made possible the growth of a vast middle class that enjoys—and let there be no question about it: they *do* enjoy it—more comforts, more vacations, more education, more security, than any people, anywhere else. Thirty-seven million American families own their own homes; seven out of ten homes have washing machines; 99.8 per cent have refrigerators; half the people in this country have finished secondary school—more than in any other country; this year, 7.4 million students are enrolled in colleges and universities—although not all of them will spend their time in the pursuit of knowledge; more people buy and read books in the U.S.A. than anywhere else; our Broadway shows—*Fiddler, Mame, Dolly, Cactus Flower,* even *Hair,* are playing to standing-room-only in more countries than I have time to list; you can call San Francisco from New York during the daytime for only $1.35; you can dial a number and hear a prayer, get the weather, learn the time, or reach someone who will stop you from taking a drink—if that happens to be your hangup. No; I shall not apologize for our country's wealth or the pursuit of the profit motive. Show me a country without a free-enterprise system, and I will show you a country without free art, free elections, free speech. The wealth of our society—much of which we give away in foreign aid and in assistance to developing nations—is due to the ingenuity found in such profusion in the marketplace.

Before National Industrial Conference
Board Marketing Conference, New York,
Oct. 15/Vital Speeches, 12–1:125.

Julian Bond
Georgia State Legislator

We must reject this stupid idea of patriotism that has made us first in war, last in peace and last in the hearts of our countrymen.

Daily World, 9–12:7.

Daniel J. Boorstin
Director, National Museum of History and Technology, Washington

. . . our society has always tended to lead us away from drawing distinctions of all kinds: between rich and poor, between citizen and newcomer, between Protestant and Catholic. The Women's Liberation Front wants common toilets that will blur the distinction between men and women. Air conditioning and central heating thin out climatic distinctions. You can eat the same food at one Holiday Inn as at another. We are evening out the distribution of the Negro population. The South and the West are catching up with the rest of the country in industrialization, and so on. Whether or not I consider them bad or good, I suggest that they may be depriving people of something they want and perhaps need; namely, a sense of hills and valleys and variety in their existence, to the benefit of their minds and their lives. So some turn to things which offer poignancy, or which hit their sensations. They try to remind themselves that they are alive by taking drugs, by throwing rocks, by screaming obscenities, by burning—anything to remind them that they are there. I suggest that one reason why racism is becoming voguish—why people are saying that "black is beautiful" or "white is beautiful"—is that they are desperate for some kind of distinction.

Interview, Washington/
U.S. News & World Report, 10–19:65.

Henry A. "Red" Boucher
Mayor of Fairbanks, Alaska

I think that some of the very frustrations that American youth is experiencing are due to the feeling of our young people that there are no more rivers to cross, no more frontiers to explore and settle. American youth needs the kind of challenge and opportunity that Alaska has to offer . . . Alaska offers our youth the opportunity to fulfill ideals, to develop the kind of community life that meets those ideals. There are only 300,000 people in this state. Alaska gives a person a chance to reach outward, to escape the claustrophobia of the big cities, and it stimulates an invigorating spirit. It is not a place that allows anyone to feel lazy. It is the state of the future for the American youth who longs for adventure, success and a clean way of life.

Interview, Fairbanks/
Los Angeles Herald-Examiner, 6–26:A14.

Kingman Brewster, Jr.
President, Yale University

The problems raised by the young, the questions they ask, are not going to be solved speedily, or even in the time of your generation and mine. But the chance of our children to solve them, to answer them, will depend greatly on two things. First, whether or not the younger generation feel that the critic, the skeptic, the heretic are still welcome, even honored and respected, in the United States. Second, whether or not they feel that the channels of communication, persuasion and change are truly open, as the Bill of Rights intended they should be. The ability of universities and newspapers to defend and to utilize their freedom will have much to do with the ability of the young to keep their faith in freedom.

Before American Newspaper Publishers
Association Bureau of Advertising, April 21/
The Washington Post, 4–25:A14.

Edward W. Brooke
United States Senator, R-Mass.

. . . a patriot is one who knows that his nation is its people and who works to preserve and advance the precious community on which their well-being depends.

Interview/Parade, 7–5:5.

Warren E. Burger
Chief Justice of the United States

In the annals of history, our country is still a very young country, and all our claims to pre-eminence and greatness in many fields of human endeavor cannot hide this fact. It is good that we are in our youth as a nation, because the young can adjust more readily than the old. Our resiliency and flexibility is a great national resource that makes revolution, in the violent sense, irrelevant and unnecessary. One aspect of our being a young nation accounts for a national attitude—not universal, but wide-spread—that whatever is American is *best* and that we probably invented it.

Nov. 14/The Washington Post, 11–20:A26.

Bill Chappell, Jr.
United States Representative, D-Fla.

America has never cradled a more permissive society than she does now. Parental, educational and religious guidance and governmental enforcement have all permitted and encouraged the individual to "do his own thing," even to the extent of participating in civil disorders and selecting the laws which they will or will not obey . . . Our society leans over backward in an apparent effort not to influence and discipline our young people toward our ideals and hopes, lest we spoil their personalities. How alienated and unloved many of them must feel . . . permissiveness by the parents of America spreads its tentacles into the courts, into our churches and embeds itself deeply in our schools. It encourages our young people to form revolutionary groups, stimulates illegal sales and uses of drugs, fosters organized criminal activity and heightens every area of crime.

Before Kiwanis and Rotary Clubs, Ocala, Fla., March 30/Vital Speeches, 5–1:424.

Mark Clark
General, United States Army, Retired

At the risk of sounding like an old-fashioned flag waver, it is evident that many of our young people have rebelled at a permissive society. It is one thing to question the policies of your country, but to actively plot its downfall and support its enemies is little less than treason.

Before Knife and Fork Club, Dallas, March 17/ The Dallas Times Herald, 3–18:A37.

Henry Steele Commager
Historian

It's easier to say what patriotism isn't than what it is. It is not conformity. It is not passive acceptance of the status quo. It is not preference for everything American over everything foreign. It is not a particular creed, version of history or philosophy. It is willingness to subordinate every private advantage to the larger good. It is an appreciation for the rich and diverse contributions that come from the most varied sources. It is allegiance to the traditions that have guided our greatest statesmen and inspired our poets—traditions of freedom, of equality, democracy and tolerance. Every effort to confine patriotism to a single pattern or constrain it to a single formula is disloyal to everything that is valid in Americanism.

Interview/Parade, 7–5:4.

Clifton Daniel
Associate editor, "The New York Times"

Don't imagine that, if our present system is demolished, you will necessarily inherit the wreckage. History tells us that, all too often, dictators and tyrants pick up the pieces . . . I know the processes of democracy are painfully slow. We have reason to be impatient with them, but we abandon them at our peril. Our institutions have not failed us. We have failed them. We do not need new ideals. We need to be more devoted to the old ones.

At University of North Carolina commencement/The New York Times, 6–9:24.

Sebastian de Grazia
Professor of Political Science, Rutgers University

It's asking for trouble to keep a large num-

(SEBASTIAN DE GRAZIA)

ber of post-puberty youth in a dependent status. The mark of independence and taking your place in our society has always been the job. After puberty, youth becomes restless to take their place. When you spread out the interval of uncertainty about what their place will be, you find profound discontent arises.

St. Paul, Minn./The New York Times, 3–18:66.

Federico Fellini
Motion picture director

. . . America holds endless fascination for a European Latin like myself. In a way, it is dangerous to be an ancient man with thousands of years in one's veins and come from a place where the past is all around you. When walking around Rome, you ignore the ruins of the past, the ancient monuments; you think it is only for the tourists. But no; the past is in your subconscious, and there is a danger that it makes you slightly indifferent about the future. It makes you say deep down: "Look how futile life is. It comes and goes. Nothing is really important." And then you go to America, where maybe the oldest monument is a gasoline station erected five years ago, and suddenly you must come to terms with the future. You feel the rhythm of life around you and with a watch in your hand suddenly realize that you live in a world where the clock is backwards. Yes, America, with its contradictions, with its Establishment, its hippies, its astronauts— with its innocence, with the eagerness of its people—is truly fantastic!

Interview, Rome/Los Angeles Times (Calendar), 6–7:19.

Fred C. Foy
Chairman, Koppers Company

You (adults) are a bunch of bums. Your characters and morals are questionable. Your achievements have contributed mostly to discontent and confusion. You have been weighed and found wanting. The report is in, and it says that you are a pack of money-grabbing hyenas. Your hearts—if you have

hearts—pump to the rhythm of the cash register. You are interested only in your own petty selves. You have no use for your neighbors, except as consumers in an over-stimulated economic system. If the human race survives into the twenty-first century—which is not at all certain—it will be in spite of your efforts. You are outmoded and old fashioned, guilty of such stupidities as ambition, competitiveness and patriotism . . . I hope I don't have to tell you that this is not my assessment. It comes from an important subgroup in our society: the dissident young. I say "important" because there are more of them than ever before, because they are noisier than ever before, because they have more power than ever before, because they will be here, and some of them may be running things, when you and I are gone. And they have risen up in their uninformed wisdom and pronounced us a collective loss.

Before Traffic Club, Pittsburgh, Jan. 22/ Vital Speeches, 3–15:343.

John W. Gardner
Chairman, National Urban Coalition

. . . it is a curious thing that all great leaders historically have had as one of their functions the function of calling people to their duty. When Winston Churchill talked about blood, sweat and tears, he was talking in the classic role of the leader, saying it was going to be difficult. There are hard tasks ahead, tasks that demand sacrifice of you. This function of leadership is very much neglected today. It's a very hard role for a politician to take; but the future of this nation depends upon it. Somebody has to say to the American people: "We have the toughest kind of tasks ahead. They're going to require me to give up something, you to give up something, corporate chairmen to give up something, unions, government workers and so on."

Interview, Washington/The Christian Science Monitor, 6–8:10.

Charles E. Goodell
United States Senator, R-N.Y.

The young cannot forgive those who clothe the evils in our nation as though they were virtues. They cannot excuse politicians who talk of law and order as a mask for repression. They cannot forgive leaders who dress up a war to save a corrupt dictatorship as a defense of "self-determination." They cannot forgive parents who espouse Christian charity on Sundays and then speak of black people on Mondays with anger and hate. And it is the young . . . who have been forced to die in a war they know to be senseless and wrong. It is they whose lives are ruled by a draft law that no one thinks is any good. It is they who are harassed by Draconian drug laws that treat marijuana as if it were heroin . . . It is they who are pent up in huge, impersonal education factories that waste their time in irrelevant and deadening routines.

San Francisco, April 26 / San Francisco
Examiner & Chronicle (This World), 5–3:6.

I love that flag. I like to see it waving. I don't like to see it waving to cover up our sins so we don't talk about them. I don't like to see it waving to divide us rather than unite us. That flag belongs to all of us, every one of us. And it doesn't do much good for (Vice President) Agnew . . . or anyone else to tell a housewife in Brooklyn or Buffalo who's been mugged last night to go home and wave that flag, our country is strong. It is strong, with all its weaknesses that we can correct.

Television address, New York, Oct. 25 /
The Washington Post, 10–30:A24.

Billy Graham
Evangelist

We are not only here today to honor America, but we have come as citizens to renew our dedication and allegiance to the principles and institutions that made her great. Lately, our institutions have been under attack: the Supreme Court, the Congress, the Presidency, the flag, the home, the educational system and even the church. But we are here today to say with loud voices that, in spite of their faults and failures, we believe in these institutions! . . . Pursue the vision, reach toward the goal, fulfill the dream. And

as you move to do it, never give in! Never give in! Never! Never! Never! Never!

At Honor America Day observance, Washington,
July 4 / The Washington Post, 7–5:A1.

Mark O. Hatfield
United States Senator, R-Ore.

The strength of our democracy rests not in uniformity of thought or conformity of attitudes. Those are the principles which control totalitarian societies. Rather, in our land, it is the diversity of opinion that gives us our true strength. We believe that the freedom of thought and expression—in peaceful means, protected by our law—is the great and distinctive quality of our society. It is freedom that we all cherish and this freedom which we all want to preserve. But in any pluralistic society, where we believe in the right of all men to live in freedom, we must also be undergirded by understanding, respect and love. There is no hope for freedom to survive without a framework of reconciliation. To listen, to understand, to respect the opinions of others and to build bonds of communication—all of us, whether young or old, must learn to practice these qualities if we are to protect our freedom. To exercise authority in the framework of love is the task for all of us—whether it be in our individual families or in our nation. We know that there will be no peace and no harmony among us if we believe that authority precludes love or that love denies authority. In this troubled age—as divisiveness and polarization threaten the strength of our land—I hope we can all choose the path of reconciliation. Our society needs to be brought together; we need to be healed. But this is more than can ever be accomplished by any act of Congress or by any expenditure of Federal money. It must begin within our own hearts and our own families and our own local communities.

Before Oregon Fire Chiefs Association /
Congressional Record, 7–15:S11353.

Theodore M. Hesburgh
President, University of Notre Dame

Patriotism has often been identified ex-

(THEODORE M. HESBURGH)

clusively with serving in the armed forces or participating in a war. It would seem to me that patriotism, as a virtue, is much broader than this—otherwise it would be a virtue largely limited to men. Patriotism is doing anything to serve one's country in whatever way it needs most to be served at a given point in history . . . Anyone who does anything good or productive for his or her country is a patriot, and no country could long survive or prosper without a very large percentage of citizens being true patriots.

Interview/Parade, 7–5:5.

Stephen Hess
National Chairman, 1970 White House Conference on Children and Youth

We have a huge number of young people in this country. We have prolonged their period of formal education as we never did before, as no other culture prolongs it or ever did prolong it. We keep our young people in a state of financial, emotional and social dependency until they are long past physical maturity. They are caught in the crunch between dependency and a natural drive for independence. Something's got to give here. And what is giving is the respect the kids used to have for authority, for traditional values and attitudes. They feel frustrated by their society, and so they turn on it. The United States has lived by the Protestant ethic for a long time. It may well be that we are entering a period of the protest ethic. But both words come from the same Latin roots. They mean "to bear public witness."

Before Pennsylvania Society of Newspaper Editors, Harrisburg/The Wall Street Journal, 4–14:14.

Eric Hoffer
Author, Philosopher

We (Americans) have become a nation of cowards. We used to be a country with courage. I am worried about a country in which

people will not speak out for what they believe.

San Francisco, Feb. 20/
Los Angeles Herald-Examiner, 2–22:A2.

Ernest F. Hollings
United States Senator, D-S.C.

. . . somehow it strikes me that we have had enough rips and roars in our society today, and that what is needed most is a talking of sense to our people. For, truly, America is fed up; America is in turmoil. Everyone is shouting and no one is listening. And rather than bring us together, the mood at this moment is "leave us alone." Gone is the old sense of community that united us for the challenges of the past. We don't face problems together anymore. We meet them as blocs and organizations. We identify not as Americans, but as hard-hats or students or militants or women liberators or as members of the silent majority. As little groups and cliques, we shout our non-negotiable demands, attempting to drown out all differing points of view. We fight for a spot in front of the television camera in the street, on the misguided assumption that emotional outbursts will somehow bring needed change. Our own group is always right. Our own group, if given its way, could usher in the millennium. The radical demands thorough change by sun-up tomorrow. "I have seen the vision," he says. "Follow me to Utopia." The arch-conservative sits, stubborn as a mule, refusing to concede that any change is desirable. Each group must have things its own way. Each would construct an America in its own straight-jacket image. And the creed is, "Do things my way, or get out." "America, love it or leave it"—but always with the stipulation that "I will decide what America means." The hard-hat wants no dialogue with the student; he wants the student to shut up. The student seeks no compromise with the hard-hat; he hopes for an America without hard-hats. The clamor of rhetoric increases, decibel by decibel, until the voices of reason are now effectively silenced. Meanwhile, everyone is in flight, fleeing from government—and, more important, fleeing from responsibility to one another. A country once excited by the challenge of change is now beset by fear. And so, the challenge tonight is the same as 100 years ago: "Shall we meanly lose or nobly save the last best hope on earth."

At Blue Key Service Fraternity, University of Georgia, Sept. 21/Vital Speeches, 11–1:37.

Hubert H. Humphrey
Former Vice President of the United States

In ways few of us would have predicted as recently as a decade ago, the basic assumptions of our society are being challenged. Today, young American and old attack the idea of affluence itself. Our national propensity for materialism is being questioned by serious adults as well as concerned young people. In the wake of this questioning, we must ask if we can once again invest our democratic enterprise with the moral purpose and the sense of values which have been our pride and our heritage.

Before Broadcast Advertising Club, Chicago, April 3/Variety, 4–8:38.

Hal Kanter
Television writer and producer

It is a particular quirk of American character that you can call an American almost any name you like and you will get either a mild rebuttal or some protestation. But if you tell somebody he has no sense of humor, he's really going to hit you in the mouth.

Panel discussion, Los Angeles/ Entertainment World, 2–27:14.

Edward M. Kennedy
United States Senator, D-Mass.

It is as bad to use the flag to beat a demonstrator for peace as it is to tear the flag to demonstrate for peace. It is not enough simply to paste the flag on our car windows and confess "my country right or wrong" any more than it is enough to fly the flag upside down to protest a national policy.

On Honor America Day, Wakefield, Mass., July 4/The Washington Post, 7–5:A21.

Perhaps never before in the history of the world has there been an emblem so full of the great aspirations of all men everywhere as the flag of the United States. Countless generations of immigrants have sought a new life and (a) new world in America, drawn by the stars and stripes and the promise of liberty and freedom. The flag our fathers received at their citizenship ceremony initiated them into the life of love and freedom. Our common aspirations today are as boundless as the mind of man. They surpass all contemporary debate. They exceed even the deepest divisions of our time, because they reflect the timeless quest of men to be free, to live in a society that is open, where the principles of freedom and justice and equality prevail. It is for this reason that patriotism and the flag can never be the special preserve of any particular party or any particular political philosophy. I love the flag no less because I believe America has lost its way in Vietnam. I love the flag no less because I want America to move ahead to right the wrongs we see in our society at home. Those of us who push America on do so out of love and hope for the America that can be. We are full of the awareness of how much is right with America, how much we have done in years gone by to fulfill the promise of democracy for all our people. We are not summer soldiers or sunshine patriots. We are patriots for all seasons, holding up to all Americans the mirror of the flag and the ideals it represents. If the lights begin to go out in America because men can no longer think what they feel or say what they think, the lights will begin to go out again all over the world, and the great experiment of 1776 will fail.

On Honor America Day, Wakefield, Mass., July 4/The Wall Street Journal, 8–7:6.

Louis L'Amour
Author

Every American has a right to be proud of his heritage. I don't mean we should turn into flagwavers: There are lots of things in our country that are far from perfect—but so

(LOUIS L'AMOUR)

is man. But the frontier people *were* larger than life. They rose to the occasion, built roads and towns and mines, educated their children, farmed Godforsaken land, kept the peace. I hope the millions who read my books have this feeling for our country and will stop shedding silly tears and go about doing today's jobs as well as they can.

Interview, Los Angeles/
Los Angeles Times, 7–12:G14.

John V. Lindsay
Mayor of New York

The revolutionary defiles the flag and the reactionary deifies it. Both offend reason and common sense.

At Williams College, Williamstown, Mass./
Quote, 7–19:49.

The flag that should unite us is now a symbol of defiant division . . . Sadly, we see the flag as a symbol of partisan political argument. If you wear a flag on your shirt, you're a "dove." If you wear a flag in your lapel, you're a "hawk." You can buy flags to plaster on cars or hats. There are flags to help sell gasoline, flags with the peace symbol instead of stars, flags appropriated for a candidate's name and party slogans. These days, whether two Americans talk to one another at all may well depend on where each wears his flag.

Before National Guard Association
of the United States, New York, Sept. 14/
The New York Times, 9–15:41.

Clare Boothe Luce
Playwright; Former diplomat

Could it be what is wrong in America is that we are hungry to communicate in terms of art, music, song and dance—communicate our common humanity, the great therapy of group art? Isn't it possible that we all, rich and poor alike, need a vision of beauty without which—even if we do not perish—we will not be remembered in history? . . . We need sing-outs, play-outs, dance-outs—not to solve problems, but to let off steam and pull us together.

Los Angeles/Los Angeles Times, 4–13:(4)12.

Louis B. Lundborg
Chairman, Bank of America

Let me leave no doubt about it: There are some real hard-core radicals bent on the destruction of what they call "the system." I know, because I have talked to a few of them. At the other end of the spectrum, there is another group—and I have no way of knowing how many there are in either group— that is as committed to this system as anyone in this audience. But in between is the great, great majority of students and other young people—troubled, disturbed, questioning, but uncommitted . . . We have two choices as to which way we can go. We can divide into camps and shoot it out; or we can try to find common ground so that we can grow together again. One course is easy, but is blind; the other course is hard and slow, but is the path of wisdom. One course leaves all the thinking to someone else; the other requires deep, painful thought in a never-ending search for answers. One course will bring bloodshed, destruction and ultimate crushing of freedom—the crushing of the human spirit; the other course can bring peace, and with it a hope for the rekindling of the American dream. The hour is late; there isn't much time. But the choice is still ours.

Before Rotary Club, Seattle, June 17/
Los Angeles Times, 6–21:F7.

There is a new value system emerging in this country. For generations, we have been mouthing the cliche, "You can't stand in the way of progress." Now there is a new generation that is saying, "The hell you can't." That generation—and an increasing number of its elders—are saying, "Prove to us that it really is progress." In a sense, that is the essence of everything that is stirring and boiling and seething. Thoughtful people in increasing numbers are asking about one thing after another, "Is it really progress—progress for the human condition?" What they say they want doesn't sound so different, you know, from what our founding fathers said they wanted. They said they wanted the freedom to be their own men, the freedom for self-realization. We have lost sight of that a bit in this century. But the young people are prodding us and saying, "Look, Dad—this is what it's all about."

San Francisco/Time, 9–7:10.

William J. McGill
Chancellor, University of California at San Diego; President-designate, Columbia University

We must begin to make the humane social order we believe in a reality instead of a platitude. We must demand high standards of honesty and integrity from our public officials. We must begin to mute politics and work cooperatively for racial harmony and human betterment. We must put an end to an ill-considered policy in which we draw boundaries around the expansion of Communist China by becoming the police agency of the entire Southeast Asian subcontinent. When all these things are done . . . we shall begin to see the natural death of the strange radicalism which has afflicted our youth. It will disappear when those purely American evils which generated it have disappeared.

Interview, San Diego/ The Christian Science Monitor, 6–6:8.

Rod McKuen
Poet, Songwriter

I've been all over the world, except for maybe two or three places. I want to live here. I'm so pro-American it's disgusting.

Interview, Los Angeles/Los Angeles Herald-Examiner, 8–2:F6.

Newton N. Minow
Former Chairman, Federal Communications Commission

We do not seem to trust each other as we used to. Laughter and joy are with us less often. What has happened to America? What has happened to us all?

San Francisco Examiner & Chronicle (This World), 6–21:2.

Thomas H. Moorer
Admiral, United States Navy; Chief of Naval Operations

The citizen in me directs concerned attention to our nation in a state of self-flagellation—to what might be called an ever-expanding condition of self-condemnation—to what seemingly is a national pastime of accepting unwarranted focus on the bizarre and the bad. Looking back over the past year or so—what is America to an Arab? A Spaniard? A Japanese? Or even a Washingtonian? While the image assessments may vary somewhat, are we not in the main a society beset by crime and characterized by revolution, social militancy, dissidence and drug addiction? Lost in the shuffle somehow, in my opinion, are such ennobling factors as: the will to work; the will to serve; the will to sacrifice for just cause. So seldom is focus placed on these attributes these days that they are all but forgotten, and those who abide by them are, in effect, second class citizens.

Before American Legion Security Commission, Washington, March 4/Vital Speeches, 4–15:392.

Hans J. Morgenthau
Professor of Political Science, University of Chicago

Revolution in this country is an utter impossibility . . . We are in a society at present which perhaps is not different from the society of the Roman emperors. (It is enormously stable, but) a decaying society, a society which is decaying exactly because it is so stable and cannot allow that stability to be challenged from within.

Before National Student Association, St. Paul, Minn., Aug. 18/Washington Star, 8–19:A2.

Edmund S. Muskie
United States Senator, D-Maine

How do we make America what its found-

(EDMUND S. MUSKIE)

ers set out to make it? How do we get to that goal in a country which has lost its direction, in a country which fancies itself as the policeman of the globe? Building this kind of America is the most exciting challenge I can remember in my lifetime. I see no reason for pessimism, no reason for doubt, no reason for suspicion and distrust and hatred.

The Washington Post, 10–19:A5.

Richard M. Nixon
President of the United States

I see an America in which we have abolished hunger, provided the means for every family in the nation to obtain a minimum income, made enormous progress in providing better housing, faster transportation, improved health and superior education. I see an America in which we have checked inflation and waged a winning war against crime. I see an America in which we have made great strides in stopping the pollution of our air, cleaning up our water, opening up new parks and continuing to explore space. Most important, I see an America at peace with all the nations of the world.

State of the Union address, Washington, Jan. 22/The Washington Post, 1–23:A15.

We can be the best-clothed, best-fed, best-housed people in the world, enjoying clean air, clean water and beautiful parks, but we could still be the unhappiest people in the world without that indefinable spirit—the lift of a driving dream which has made America from its beginning the hope of the world.

State of the Union address, Washington, Jan. 22/Los Angeles Times, 1–23:(1)20.

The decade of the sixties was . . . a period of great growth, economically. But in that same 10-year period we witnessed the greatest growth of crime, the greatest increase in inflation and the greatest social unrest in America in 100 years. Never has a nation seemed to have had more and enjoyed it less.

State of the Union address, Washington, Jan. 22/Los Angeles Times, 1–23:(1)20.

Let us tell young Americans—all Americans—that we should love America. But let us love her not because she is rich and not because she is strong, but because America is a good country and we are going to make her better.

Before United States Jaycees, St. Louis, June 25/U.S. News & World Report, 7–6:45.

A President always thinks about the legacy that he would like to leave the country from his years in office. I think often about that in terms of what I can leave for America's children. And I know that the first thing I would like to do for them is to bring peace. I speak not just of ending the war (in Vietnam), but of ending it in a way that will contribute to a lasting peace—so that theirs at last can be what we have not yet had in this century: a generation of peace. And I speak not only of the absence of war, but also of a peace in which we can have an open world—in which all the peoples of the world will have a chance to know one another, to communicate with one another, to respect one another. The second thing that, as President, I would like to leave for America's children is a strong, productive, creative economy—one that can provide every family with children a floor under its income higher than what now is the ceiling for most of the world's peoples. I want to leave them an economy that provides for jobs for all, with equal and full opportunity, producing not for war but for peace. Beyond this, I want America's children in the last generation of this century to have the best education, the best health, the best housing that any children have ever had anywhere, anytime. I want them to enjoy clean air and clean water and open spaces, and to restore the heritage of nature that is rightfully theirs. Although we will always have differences here in America, I hope the government can help achieve a better understanding among the generations, the races, the religions, and among those with different values and different life-styles. I would like to do all this, and to do it in a climate of freedom.

At opening of White House Conference on Children, Washington, Dec. 13/ National Observer, 12–21:12.

Tricia Nixon
Daughter of the President of the United States

The generation gap and all the other gaps are overplayed. It's only a minority who says there is a gap. Most young people aren't interested in rebellion. Throughout history, young people have always been more idealistic, until they reluctantly give up this idealism when they see the realities of the world.

San Francisco Examiner & Chronicle (This World), 2–8:2.

J. Milton Patrick
National Commander, American Legion

The gap that threatens our society does not involve generations or government credibility. It is the gap between the principle of protest, which we all uphold, and its abuse and misuse by those who have forgotten or ignored the sources of America's greatness.

Los Angeles, pub. May.

John J. Powers, Jr.
Chairman, Chas. Pfizer & Company, Inc.

. . . the generation gap is not new. It is and always has been part of the living process. It is not just youthful insights—which are sometimes very right—against adult judgments—which are sometimes very wrong. It is not just the physical prime of youth and the great need to be active against the slowly ebbing tide of adult years that makes of midnight an end, not a beginning. These are obvious and understandable and accepted. But consider when youthful curiosity has finally seen too much with the passing years, and novelty has lost its charm; when youthful imagination has been bent heavily under the adult load of routine and repeated tasks; when youthful daring has finally yielded to a great yearning to be secure and unchanged. These, indeed, are great and often disturbing

differences. And today, every facet of these differences has been magnified to startling proportions by the great conflicts, the fundamental changes, the swift flow of events of our times. Yes, and by the great dissatisfaction in our times, as men continuously and rightfully seek to improve their condition. Indeed, more than in any other age, there is real hope of what heretofore seemed only distant goals or glorious slogans. It has taken 200 years for Egalite, Fraternite and Liberte suddenly to seem visible of achievement. It is this, I venture to say, that has whetted the appetite of the new generation, which has caught the sense of justice and adventure of *our* youth in these tumultuous times, and made their voices louder and more demanding. But it is of some importance to recall that we provided the opportunity which they now grope to seize, which soon they must fully exploit, as they begin to take over our role and assume the responsibilities of their times.

At Poor Richard Club, Philadelphia, Jan. 17/Congressional Record, 2–9:E756.

Ronald Reagan
Governor of California

The world they (the younger generation) will take over is less than perfect. Poverty has not been eliminated, bigotry and injustice still exist in too many hearts, and man's greatest stupidity—war—still takes place. But it is a better world than we inherited, which in turn was better than our fathers took over, and so it will be, hopefully, for some generations to come. As for our generation, I have no intention of apologizing. No people in all history paid a higher price for freedom. And no people have done as much to advance the dignity of man.

Before California Chamber of Commerce, Sacramento, Sept. 4/Los Angeles Times, 9–5:(2)1.

Edwin O. Reischauer
Former United States Ambassador to Japan

Japan is built on the effective use of space, America on the effective use of time.

TV documentary on Japan/ National Observer, 6–1:16.

Abraham A. Ribicoff
United States Senator, D-Conn.

Let us be candid with one another. What is the condition prevailing in the United States today? The South hates the North; the North hates the South. What is their motive? The blacks hate the whites; the whites hate the blacks. What is their motive? The poor hate the rich; the rich hate the poor. What is their motive? The intellectuals hate the silent majority; the silent majority hates the intellectuals. What is their motive? Now we have reached the tragic circumstances where children hate one another. And what is their motive—what is the motive of children in our schools hating one another?

Before the Senate, Washington/
The Washington Post, 2–20:A6.

Elliot L. Richardson
Under Secretary of State of the United States

A society which allows its young to be spiritually cut adrift is a society which cuts itself off from its own future. The complex and difficult tasks of today and tomorrow demand patience and persistence and unity of effort, and of none is this more true than the slow labor of building a more secure peace, stone by careful stone. We need the understanding and help of the young, as you need ours. The work, in any case, cannot long continue without your help, for it will soon be yours to do if it is to be done at all.

At Lowell Technological Institute
commencement, Lowell, Mass.,
June 7/Vital Speeches, 7–15:585.

H. I. Romnes
Chairman, American Telephone &
Telegraph Company

There are a good many aspects of the current scene that I confess I do not understand. I do not understand, for example, how it can be believed that—in whatever cause they're used—shouted obscenities and mindless vandalism bring anything but discredit to that cause. I do not understand how understanding is served by burning books or banks—or

by flaunting the Viet Cong flag while desecrating our own. And I do not understand what it is that our society has done to some of its sons and daughters—very few, I am sure, but so often described as among the gentlest and brightest of your generation—that drives them to seek peace with the tactics of terror. And at the same time, I must tell you that I do not understand the members of my own generation who characterize —indeed stigmatize—yours on the basis of the actions of a tiny minority among you. Nor do I understand those of my contemporaries who appear to equate dissent with disloyalty, while at the same time they claim exclusive title to the badge of patriotism for themselves. Finally, I do not understand those— whatever banner they march under—who use it as an excuse to vent their spite against ideas not their own, people unlike themselves. What I *do* understand, however, is what every American must understand by now—and that is that we are a deeply troubled and divided country and that we had better begin to ask ourselves what is happening to our country before it is too late.

At St. Louis University commencement/
The Wall Street Journal, 7–3:4.

Vermont Royster
Editor, "The Wall Street Journal"

We're obviously in a very troubled time, in a period of social upheaval—touching race, family, church, universities. Whenever you get in a time like this—sort of like the Reformation—it's hard to know how it's going to come out . . . It's been enough to change the character of the country, and most of our problems today grow out of this change. I don't know whether it is for better or for worse, because I don't know how the story will end. Being middle-aged, I have at least a nostalgic regret that it has changed in this way. But regardless of whether it's good or bad—hell, it's inevitable. And when something is inevitable, you might just as well adjust yourself to it. I'm always pessimistic about the immediate present, but I'm always optimistic in the long run—however long that is. After all, the Dark Ages only lasted 500 years.

Interview, New York, Dec. 17/
The New York Times, 12–18:41.

Adela Rogers St. Johns
Author

The single greatest power the world has ever known is American women. And what are they doing? Going to psychiatrists with their nasty little problems, sipping martinis. We could do with a bit less deodorant and a little more honest sweat . . . I know what women can do, once they get off their duffs.

Interview, Los Angeles/
Los Angeles Times, 1–4:(I)16.

Francis W. Sargent
Governor of Massachusetts

We have a bad habit in America. A crisis becomes a fad and then a cliche without being solved. It works this way: We spot a problem, talk about it, focus the media on it, make it famous; we form committees; we spend money; the problem sweeps the country; it becomes a vogue, an "in thing" to worry about, a fad. But it is born to lose in the sweepstakes of public interest, born to short life in the intense competition for public attention.

Before Northern California Chapter,
American Institute of Architects, San
Francisco, Dec. 11/
San Francisco Examiner, 12–12:3.

Glenn T. Seaborg
Chairman, Atomic Energy Commission of the United States

Patriotism is a love of and a loyalty to one's land, its people and their highest ideals. But it is not a blind worship of any of these. It involves a love that recognizes weaknesses and a loyalty that is tolerant of imperfections, while it strives to overcome both and make its land and people an example for all mankind.

Interview/Parade, 7–5:4.

Jean-Jacques Servan-Schreiber
Journalist; Member, French National Assembly

The passion with which Americans are debating their problems . . . will not break the United States. On the contrary, it is healthier than the veil of silence which covers such debates in so-called closed societies.

Interview/The Dallas Times Herald, 8–10:A2.

Robert Shelton
Imperial Wizard of the Ku Klux Klan

If you are the loyal American you profess to be, any time you see one of those hipnick beatnicks pulling the American flag down . . . whale the living tar out of them.

Benson, La./The Dallas Times Herald,
8–10:A15.

Otis A. Singletary
President, University of Kentucky

. . . I believe this nation has a future. For all its problems, I believe this to be the most lovely and livable of all nations; and for all our faults, I believe that the record will show that Americans are basically a kind and generous and decent people. My basic claim here is that, despite all the clamor and confusion and criticism, we must be doing some things right. More is being done about schools and slums and farms than at any other time in our past. The much-maligned "over 30" generation is made up of men and women who survived a grinding depression, fought and bled to destroy Nazi militarism and supported the concept and the reality of a United Nations organization. That generation bailed Europe out of its postwar crisis, financed social and economic improvement in much of the underdeveloped world, began a determined assault on poverty at home, moved the nation more swiftly in the direction of racial equality and led the way into the new age of space and computer technology—a development that has only recently witnessed the remarkable sight of earthlings walking on the surface of the moon. Amidst all the soul-searching and blame-fixing and recriminations of our time,

(OTIS A. SINGLETARY)

I would remind you that we, as a people, have never been more prosperous, or for that matter more generous with our prosperity; we have never been more concerned than we are today about education or social justice or civil rights; we have never been more engaged in trying to bring some kind of decency and order into a world desperately in need of decency and order. We are, in short, trying more—and I would argue achieving more—but sometimes failing. And we seem to have developed—almost as a national characteristic—a tendency to concentrate on what is wrong to the exclusion of what is right.

At faculty dinner, University of Kentucky/
Los Angeles Herald-Examiner, 8–30:A4.

Margaret Chase Smith
United States Senator, R-Maine

In these troubled times, when the old saying, "see no evil, hear no evil, speak no evil," seems to have been replaced with a new creed of "see no good, hear no good, speak no good," let us recognize that no people in the history of the world have enjoyed as much freedom, liberty and unabridged right of dissent as today's Americans.

At Adelphi University commencement/
Life, 6–19:27.

True patriotism is not static. True patriotism is dynamic because its concept and application are not always the same with every person under every condition and at every time. It is an attitude or state of mind that must be carefully viewed before determining its credibility. For example, beware of the super-patriots. Are they really putting their country ahead of themselves? In their flamboyance, are they helping their country or are they hurting it? . . . Simply put, a patriot is not only one who loves his country, but one who will defend liberty. Perhaps the acid test of patriotism is just how much is a person willing to sacrifice for his country—whether that sacrifice be his life or his reputation or merely his convenience.

Interview/Parade, 7–5:4.

Many years ago, the word "square" was one of the most honored words in our vocabulary. The "square deal" was an honest deal. A "square meal" was a full and good meal. It was the "square shooter" rather than the sharpshooter who was admired. What is a "square" today? He's the fellow who never learned to get away with it; who gets choked up when the flag unfurls. There has been too much glorification of the angle-players, the corner-cutters and the goof-offs. One of America's greatest needs is for more people who are "square."

Quote, 12–6:545.

John J. Sparkman
United States Senator, D-Ala.

Patriotism is that quality of national pride which moves a citizen to see his country's welfare as foremost—even ahead of personal consideration. It is his willingness and sense of obligation to take up the defense of his country's vital interests with weapons as well as words when the need arises.

Interview/Parade, 7–5:5.

James Stewart
Actor

I wish today's kids would laugh a little more. I wish they wouldn't take themselves as seriously as they do. The young people I've worked with just don't seem to have fun in their craft. So many of them are completely undisciplined and selfish. They seem to be almost self-conscious in scenes. Oh, I wish there was more humor. When I got started, right in the heart of the Depression, the theatre was a bright, gay, lively, enthusiastic place, and the young people had *fun.* There was tremendous activity all up and down Broadway. The Group Theatre, the Theatre Guild, one playwright after another. The musicals—those wonderful Bert Lahr shows and wonderful comedians and wonderful Gershwin music—all in the middle of the blackest part of the Depression.

Interview, New York/
The New York Times, 2–22:(2)5.

David Susskind
Motion picture-stage-television producer

I've got a houseful of daughters. They do a lot of dating, and both the daughters and their dates have unanimous things in common. They're full of compassion and emotion and rhetoric. They have good instincts, bombast and all that sort of thing. But it all comes out in monosyllables . . . a kind of guttural "ya know, man . . . it's like aaaaa . . . it's heavy, ya know . . . it's like heavy, ya know, ya know, ya know?" I tell you, having an intellectual evening with a pair of them will put you in a strait jacket. Now, their hearts are in the right place, but there's no sequential logic to their argumentation, and there's no vocabulary to enforce their argumentation, and there's no vocabulary to reinforce their arguments. Shouldn't we be teaching them to speak better, to think straighter . . . how to make their points with the appropriate English language? The fact that some Senators and Congressmen are equally deficient isn't a terribly impressive argument.

Panel discussion, University of Utah/
National Observer, 12–14:14.

Pierre Elliott Trudeau
Prime Minister of Canada

The United States is a pretty tough, resilient society, and it's come through a lot of crises in its day. If, perchance, the present disturbances were to destroy that society in any lasting sense, I think it would be a great tragedy for the world. Because there's no doubt that, with all their evils and fallacies and weaknesses, the American people are a great people dedicated to freedom and dedicated to progress.

San Francisco Examiner, 11–2:40.

John V. Tunney
United States Representative, D-Calif.

Patriotism is never the special preserve of any particular party or political philosophy. We are all Americans, all sharing a common heritage and moving toward a common destiny. If the day ever comes when men's motives are impugned because of what they think and feel and say, then the lights will have gone out here in America, and they will soon thereafter go out all over the world.

Before San Francisco Junior Chamber of
Commerce, Sept. 25/
San Francisco Examiner, 9–26:5.

Peter Ustinov
Actor

Sometimes it strikes me that American democracy could be described as the inalienable right of the American to sit in his pajamas on his front porch with a can of beer, shouting, "Where else is this possible?"

Quote, 3–29:290.

Edward Bennett Williams
Lawyer

. . . there has been a tremendous breakdown of this country's religious tradition. If you don't have that tradition, you have to have something in lieu of it. That something, I would say, might have been a deep sense of vocation on the part of people, a willingness to try to be the best they could be at whatever they did—whether they were carpenters, shoemakers, baseball players, lawyers or doctors. But that sense of vocation and desire for excellence has . . . faded dramatically in my lifetime. In short, I don't think the kids care any more about attaining excellence in anything. They don't care about being the best they can be in light of their talents, because they're getting a free ride. They know that if they don't work, their parents aren't going to let them go hungry. They can live on a beach and throw rocks at the system—and know that we're going to take care of them.

Interview, Washington/
U.S. News & World Report, 9–21:98.

WHAT THEY SAID IN 1970

(EDWARD BENNETT WILLIAMS)

Our times are like the times Dickens described at the beginning of his most famous novel—"the best of times and the worst of times." It is the worst of times because never before has our society been so challenged in preserving order while retaining its liberty. It is the best of times because to our generation of Americans, more than to any other, has been given the opportunity of showing to the world that liberty and order are compatible concepts even during a period of social revolution. We are faced with a series of great opportunities wearing the disguise of insoluble problems.

Before State Bar of California, Los Angeles/
Los Angeles Times, 9–27:G1.

Raymond A. Withey
President, Green Mountain College

The complexity of the modern world forces upon us patterns of both patience and impatience. A businessman may rush to California in five hours, and yet wait patiently for a delayed jet take-off. A scientist may bolt instant coffee at a hurried breakfast, and then spend a day of slow, painstaking research in his laboratory. Americans love speed and power on the highway, but they are the most disciplined drivers in the world . . . Although we may endure bad service, rudeness and incompetent help with remarkable stoicism, we are impatient with life itself. In a complex, modern society characterized by our growing interdependence upon each other and a growing reliance on impersonal machines, we have had to learn a measure of patience. We are impatient with the social ills of the day, but in working out

solutions to them we have to be patient, recognizing that there are no easy, instant solutions. But we should not be so patient that we become overly cautious, thus losing sight of our goals and ultimate objectives. This is no time for hot heads and cold feet.

At Green Mountain College, Poultney,
Vt./National Observer, 9–21:15

Stephen M. Young
United States Senator, D-Ohio

. . . America's restless youth—the most aware, aroused generation in our history—needs a set of blueprints if they are to reform the ills of our society. Fiercely idealistic, some of our young people seem to believe we can end the war (in Vietnam) and eliminate social problems with talk of love; but many escape by copping out, taking drugs and living in a psychedelic dreamworld. All our young people would do well to follow the example of Mormon teenagers in Salt Lake City who recently mowed lawns, washed cars and did other chores to raise more than $35,000 to help build a Negro church. This college generation should understand there are no simple solutions and that tearing down our society—as urged by a minority—without any idea of how to reconstruct it, would bring anarchy and chaos. Adults should advise our youth to exchange rhetoric for practical solutions. Why not roll up their sleeves, pitch in and do something worthwhile? . . . Our youth should know they cannot expect to enjoy the blessings of our republic without active involvement and serious efforts to substitute deeds for dreams and words.

Before the Senate, Washington, July 15/
Congressional Record, 7–15:S11329.

Civil Rights

Ralph D. Abernathy
President, Southern Christian Leadership Conference

President Nixon has tried to turn back the clock of history . . . People are not going to sit idly by and allow this to happen . . . I will never lead any program of violence in this country, but honesty will cause me to admit that I don't know if people will continue to listen to the nonviolent voice.

Interview/Face the Nation, Columbia Broadcasting System, New York, 3–29.

Freedom of speech, freedom of the press, freedom of assembly and the right to protest for rights, spelled out in the Constitution of our nation, has always, at best, been limited for citizens living here in the Southern states. And the South has traditionally been a center of militarism and the police-state mentality, which is now increasingly becoming the lifestyle of government in the country as a whole . . . We have lived with this in one form or another since the founding of the republic . . . What is new is that, over the past 15 years, there has grown to maturity a movement here in the South, with national and international support, that is determined to establish freedom and representative government and an end to the tyranny of racism and war. And we are determined to do it in this decade of the seventies.

At Morehouse College, Atlanta, May 23/ The New York Times, 5–24:(1)1.

The black people will go back to Africa when the Germans go back to Germany, when the British go back to Britain, when the Frenchmen go back to France, when the Jews go back to Israel, when the Arabs go back to Jordan—when America returns the land to the people who were here first: the American Indian.

At California State College at Hayward, Nov. 9/San Francisco Examiner, 11–10:32.

Spiro T. Agnew
Vice President of the United States

. . . one thing our critics tend to forget is that 18 or 19 out of every 20 black men are not poor and jobless. They get up every morning and put in a full day's work, just as the majority of white Americans. They face the same problems, bear the same burdens and share the same hopes as white Americans. While there remains a clear discrepancy in both rewards and opportunities, the gaps are closing with each year, not widening. In bemoaning the fact that we have miles to go, it is time we recognized how far we have come. Where on earth has any great minority come so far, so fast, as our 22 million black Americans—out of slavery and through segregation to their current station in American society—in the course of a single century? This is a record that should inspire optimism and hope in America—not pessimism and despair.

St. Louis, Feb. 10/Human Events, 10–31:13.

I confirm that there is a conscious and determined effort on the part of the Nixon Administration to see that the South is treated in an even-handed manner with the rest of the nation . . . in the matter of school desegregation, in the matter of voting rights, in the matter of Supreme Court appointments and in any other matter of national interest. But I deny that it is a strategy of calculated planning. It is simply a matter of dispensing justice to a region of the country long deprived of it. And it's time our friends

51

in the North ripped off their masks of hypocrisy and faced that fact with us.

Edgefield, S.C., April 25/
San Francisco Examiner & Chronicle, 4–26:A2.

We must set aside the evils of sectionalism once and for all. Just as the South cannot afford to discriminate against any of its own people, the rest of the nation cannot afford to discriminate against the South.

Stone Mountain, Ga., May 9/
The Washington Post, 5–10:A30.

One of the things we're trying to do is to show the people of the United States that the blacks are not the only minority in this country. We're a nation made up of minorities. There are other people with causes; and nobody seems to be paying a great amount of attention to them. It would be a good idea to have a little paid to the Indians, who have a very just cause. And as for the Spanish-speaking people, the same thing. They've got a rate of educational achievement far below the blacks. They have unique problems of language and communication. And when we're talking about social improvement in the country, why should it go all one way?

Interview, Washington/
U.S. News & World Report, 8–24:36.

John Joseph Akar
Ambassador to the United States from
Sierra Leone

The system of racism in this country is the most irrational system on earth. I cannot accept it. I don't consider myself inferior or superior. In this country, what passes for intelligence is opportunity, and if the same opportunity were extended to everyone, then everyone would be intelligent. But things in this country will get worse before they get better. It's a great pity, but it's an indictment of the American white society. It's their fault for setting the climate that would make it possible for a Rap Brown to rap or a Stokely

Carmichael to stoke before blacks were given the rights they deserved.

Interview, Washington/
The Washington Post, 8–2:E10.

Clifford Alexander
Former Chairman, Equal Employment
Opportunity Commission of the
United States

We should describe this Administration for what it is. We should describe Spiro Agnew as a racist, because that is what he is . . . This Administration is not afraid of (former Alabama Governor) George Wallace—they're in alliance with George Wallace.

Before Democratic Policy Council's committee
on national priorities, Washington, Feb. 24/
The Washington Post, 2–25:A6.

Saul Alinsky
Sociologist

Civil rights is a movement, and a movement without organization is nothing more than a bowel movement.

Time, 3–2:57.

Sure, the blacks' demand for separatism is wrong. It's one of the irrationalities you have to accept, part of life, part of growing up. After all, we've made black the color of everything ugly and shameful. Nobody's ever pinkmailed, he's blackmailed. Nobody is ever kicked out of a club on a blue list, it's a blacklist. We use black for mourning, for funerals. We've made it the color of tragedy, of evil. We talk about black days of infamy. So it's natural for them to react by saying black is beautiful. In the end, they'll see that black is beautiful and ugly. White is beautiful and ugly. Every color is beautiful and ugly.

Interview/The Wall Street Journal, 4–8:14.

I like the (Black) Panthers. I really do. They're nuts, of course; but they're really a fantasy of that senile political paranoiac in Washington, (FBI Director) J. Edgar Hoover. They 1   en't got the numbers, and they know nothing about revolutionary tactics. What kind of a revolutionary is it who shouts that all power comes out of the muzzle of a gun when he knows damn well the other side's got all the guns?

San Francisco Examiner & Chronicle
(This World), 9–20:2.

Joseph L. Alioto
Mayor of San Francisco

I believe there are less-disruptive and less-confusing ways of achieving integration. So far as I'm concerned and most San Franciscans are concerned, they don't want busing. The blacks don't want it. The Chinese don't want it. The whites don't want it. And I don't think that busing is educationally desirable.

News conference, San Francisco/
San Francisco Examiner & Chronicle
(This World), 2–8:5.

James B. Allen
United States Senator, D-Ala.

Here we are with a crash program to end segregation in the South. We are busing thousands of students hundreds of miles to achieve racial balance. We are closing schools to put children from one school into schools that are already overcrowded. That is what we are doing in the South and what is being done to us. But in New York, between 1967 and 1968, the number of pupils attending mostly black schools rose dramatically. Not only are they not ending segregation in New York—they are becoming more segregated; whereas in the South, we are willing and we are offering to throw the doors of our school buildings open to any children to come in and go to school and have the opportunity of getting a quality education. We want to see our educators return to educating our children, not just busing our children all over the place.

Before the Senate, Washington, Feb. 9/
Congressional Record, 2–9:S1458.

Edwin C. Berry
Executive director, Chicago Urban League

The battle lines have been drawn. The enemy is not the vulgar bigot. Instead, it is the gentle white person who speaks the rhetoric of equality but has not the slightest idea what the words mean. The problem standing in the way of white understanding is that the story of black America has been told upside down. We talk in terms of our problems and not in terms of our achievements. The important thing is that, despite subjugating, the great percentage of Negro adults are making it without resorting to illegal acts.

Before Joint Negro Appeal of Chicago/
The Wall Street Journal, 1–7:12.

Andrew F. Brimmer
Member, Federal Reserve Board

While not meaning to deny or demean the recent impressive economic gains by Negroes, we must be careful that no one is lulled into believing, falsely, that the economic problems of Negroes have been solved. It would be a serious mistake to conclude that the black community has been so blessed with the benefits of economic advancement that public policy—which played such a vital role in the 1960s—need no longer treat poverty and deprivation among such a large segment of society as a matter of national concern.

At Tuskegee Institute, March 21/
San Francisco Examiner & Chronicle, 3–22:A23.

I am told that black students apparently do not see the relevancy of economics to the kind of issues which concern them most, such as racism and the celebration of black culture. In the absence of this appreciation, one can easily find himself adrift in a flood of glamorous, but ill-conceived, schemes advanced with a hopeful promise of improvement in the black community. Rather than accepting such schemes at face value, Negroes should insist that they be tested in the crucible of rigorous economic reasoning.

At Atlanta University, Oct. 16/
The New York Times, 10–17:32.

Harry F. Byrd, Jr.
United States Senator, D-Va.

The courts have accepted an unsound and

(HARRY F. BYRD, JR.)

legalistic theory which maintains that Southern segregation is somehow different from Northern segregation.

The Dallas Times Herald, 2–17:A2.

Robert C. Byrd
United States Senator, D-W. Va.

During the past two or three years, we have witnessed the open violation of the 1964 Civil Rights Act on the part of Federal authorities. Students have been assigned by race in order to overcome racial imbalance. Students have been transported from one school to another or from one school district to another in order to overcome racial imbalance. Where is the equal protection of the law as between those, both black and white, who are compelled to move or be bused away from their own neighborhood schools, and those, black and white, who are not compelled to move? Where is the equal protection of the law as between children who are provided free bus service if they choose to go in a direction that will achieve racial balance and those children who choose to go in any other direction? Here is, indeed, an incredible spectacle. Despite the Congress of the United States having enacted a statute requiring that " 'desegregation' shall not mean the assignment of students to public schools in order to overcome racial imbalance," a department of the U.S. government proceeds to spend vast sums of tax money collected from American citizens, as a means of inveigling school administrators to join with it—the Federal Department of Health, Education and Welfare—in violating the express will of Congress. The fund amounts, however, to hundreds of millions of dollars, and, with a temptation so great, many succumb. As Huck Finn observed, "The money fetches 'em."

Before the Senate, Washington, Feb. 9/
Congressional Record, 2–9:S1494.

No integration will ever be meaningful or lasting unless it is purely voluntary. If integration results from the free and voluntary choice of individuals, there can be no quarrel with it from a legal standpoint. But there is and should be quarrel with those who declare that our Constitution orders and compels forced integration. To force integration in the name of the Constitution and against the will of children and their parents, black and white, is an unforgivable subversion of the document.

Before the Senate, Washington, Feb. 9/
Congressional Record, 2–9:S1494.

Al Capp
Cartoonist

. . . I'm convinced the Ku Klux Klan invented the (Black) Panthers, who have created more hatred against the blacks in five years than the Klan managed in a hundred.

Newsweek, 6–22:79.

Louis Cassels
Senior editor, United Press International

With very few exceptions, Negroes of all income levels, all degrees of militance and all regions of the country are convinced that Mr. Nixon is deliberately selling their interests down the river in order to solidify his hold on the votes of the up-tight middle-class whites—not just in the South, but even more importantly in the North.

Before UPI publishers and editors/Plainview
(Tex.) Daily Herald, 5–7:10.

James E. Cheek
President, Howard University

I do not think the Administration is consciously anti-Negro. But whether it is *unconsciously* anti-Negro remains to be seen.

Interview/Face the Nation, Columbia
Broadcasting System, 8–2.

Shirley Chisholm
United States Representative, D-N.Y.

(During World War II) it was not the Italians and Germans who were rounded up, but the Japanese-Americans who were easily identifiable because of their skin. Today, it is not the Ku Klux Klan or the syndicate whose doors are being kicked in; it is the Black Panthers. Skin, skin, skin color, gentlemen; that is the criteria. It makes us special targets.

Before House Committee on Internal Security,
Washington, March 17/
The New York Times, 3–18:16.

Like black people, women have had it with this bias. We are no longer content to trade off our minds and abilities in exchange for having doors opened for us by gallant men. While most men will laugh jeeringly at the fledgling women's liberation groups springing up across the nation, they should know that countless women—including their cohorts, their wives and especially their daughters—silently applaud such groups' existence.

The Christian Science Monitor, 4–24:14.

Ramsey Clark
Former Attorney General of the
United States

There is probably only one place on earth that it can be shown that black and white and brown and yellow can live together with dignity and respect and love. It is here in America. We have no greater challenge.

Before Senate Equal Educational Opportunity
Committee, Washington, July 7/
The New York Times, 7–8:28.

William L. Clay
United States Representative, D-Mo.

The Nixon posture on civil rights and the conscious, well-publicized effort on the part of this Administration to retreat from pursuit of freedoms for black citizens have been at issue since Mr. Nixon assumed office. The alienation between the black populace and this President is severe. It is as deep as it is dangerous. The President's position on the Voting Rights Act extension, his position on school desegregation, his Supreme Court nominations of two Southern racists, his veto of Federal education funds and his refusal to place a priority on the domestic concerns (of) hunger, housing, poverty and employment

testify to his apathy not only toward black people, but toward all poor Americans who, since January, 1969, have truly known what it means to be "forgotten."

Before the House, Washington, May 18/
Los Angeles Times, 5–19:(1)22.

James S. Coleman
Professor of Sociology,
Johns Hopkins University

School integration is vital not merely for some vague, generalized social purposes, but because it is the most consistent mechanism for improving the quality of education of disadvantaged children . . . If we abandon integration, we strongly risk creating all over the country the same kind of apartheid that has existed in the South since Reconstruction.

Interview, Washington, March 8/
The New York Times, 3–9:1.

. . . there is no distinction between "de jure" and "de facto" segregation . . . The effect of segregation on children is quite independent of its origin.

Before Senate Select Committee on Equal
Educational Opportunity, Washington, April
21/The Washington Post, 4–22:A2.

John Conyers, Jr.
United States Representative, D-Mich.

. . . there's no question that Nixon's attitude toward black people in America is almost unbelievable . . . There are certain forces that, as the President, even Nixon can't change . . . He has a tremendous opportunity to unite the nation . . . and he's completely blowing it—doing just the opposite.

Interview, Washington/
The Christian Science Monitor, 4–23:2.

Miles Davis
Jazz musician

It's a white man's world. The record companies make idols out of white artists. They don't sell black artists like that. Why do movies always show only white sex? Man, you know whites are going to hold onto the

(MILES DAVIS)

power and the money. The white man leaning back smoking his cigar, he's not going to move. He wants everything just the same. He won't do anything he isn't forced to. That's what makes our music different. It comes from a people who have had to learn how to make the white man move.

Interview/Newsweek, 3–23:100.

James O. Eastland
United States Senator, D-Miss.

I am incensed and insulted at the attitude taken by certain liberal editorial writers and others who condemn the white parents and students for not accepting conditions which are completely unacceptable to more than 98 per cent of the white parents and students in the United States. The truth and the fact is that almost no white parent wants his child to attend a school where Negro students are in the vast majority. In cities such as Washington, D.C., such parents flee to the "safe" suburbs of Maryland and Virginia. I do not condemn them for this; in my judgment, they have every right to act in the best interests of their children.

Before the Senate, Washington, Feb. 9/
Congressional Record, 2–9:S1454.

Helen G. Edmonds
United States delegate to the United
Nations; Dean, Graduate School,
North Carolina Central University

It can be easy to attach too much importance to their (radical groups) impractical and genocidal solutions for hastening the day of total elimination of discrimination, or their equally fanatical plans and activities of sporadic bombings designed to overthrow the government. These obsessions may be held by small, articulate racial groups. But the majority—rank and file—of racial minorities do not subscribe to these fanatical programs. It would be a tragedy of supreme proportions for any nation to overemphasize the antics of "playing revolution," to mislead the facts of our times, and say the

United States has not moved forward in the area of eliminating racial discrimination.

At United Nations, N.Y., Oct. 27/
The New York Times, 10–28:8.

John D. Ehrlichman
Assistant to the President of the
United States for Domestic Affairs

. . . the interests of the country as a whole cannot necessarily be defined in terms of the interests of a racial minority. The experience of the last six or seven years is that we can overemphasize the problems of a minority. This leads to an overescalation of promises and expectations. I see this Administration engaged in a strategy aimed at solving frustrations, but at the same time mindful of a danger of overpromising, a strategy embodied in a series of measures aimed at improving income and providing jobs that are not racially labeled but which can reasonably be expected to benefit minorities more than anyone else.

Interview/The New York Times Magazine,
4–12:62.

Osborn Elliott
Editor-in-chief, "Newsweek" magazine

One of the biggest myths, in my view, is the concept of the "melting pot." The fact is that the melting pot has never really operated as advertised. As Jesse Jackson, Chicago's black preacher, has pointed out, our society is more like a pot of vegetable soup than a melting pot. Americans tend to retain their ethnic identities far longer than commonly assumed. Once we have accepted this as the reality, I think we are in a far better position to understand the conflicting demands and needs and perceptions of the various groups, and to begin to reconcile them.

At University of California at Riverside/
National Observer, 7–13:14.

Sam J. Ervin, Jr.
United States Senator, D-N.C.

During the past week, a Federal district court sitting in Charlotte, N.C., has entered an order requiring the busing of 5,000 little black children away from their neighborhood schools to other schools in remote areas of the city and county, and the busing of 5,000 little white children from their neighborhood schools into what are, to them, remote areas of the city and the county—all for the purpose of integrating their bodies rather than enlightening their minds. To my mind, it is unspeakable tyranny in any government which undertakes to make such helpless and hapless pawns of little children . . . I wish some human being could tell me how tyranny of that sort contributes toward education. I wish someone would tell me how tyranny of that sort contributes to respect for the Federal courts of this country. I wish someone would tell me why such tyranny as that should be tolerated in a land which boasts that it is the land of the free.

Before the Senate, Washington, Feb. 10/
Congressional Record, 2–10:S1583.

Charles Evers
Mayor, Fayette, Miss.

I'm not bragging, believe me, when I say I have been a success. Maybe I'm a little different than some other people. I have worked hard. I'm strict. I don't believe, never have, in going around yelling, "Kill honkies . . . burn down the town!" I believe in getting along, opening up lines of communication, talking to people, making an occasional compromise, if necessary. I believe mostly in helping my people, getting them jobs, educating them, lifting their morale, encouraging them. You don't do that by messing around, yelling, "Honky!"

Interview, Fayette/Los Angeles Times,
1–22:(1)5.

The white folks were mean to us; they kept us poor and ignorant and they kept us from registering (to vote). But now we have peeped his trump cards. Now we see that the white man's trump cards are economics and the vote, and now we are beginning to use the same trump cards . . . Well, white folks, we are not going to hate you. We're just going to keep on winning elections, keep

on praying for you and keep on watching you, too—to make sure we don't go back where we came from.

Celebrating his first year in office, Fayette/
The New York Times, 8–30:(1)66.

Earl Faircloth
Attorney General of Florida

Even though you (school officials) and I and the Governor, as well as the parents of school children in this state, violently oppose busing students to achieve integration, and even though we believe some of the orders are totally irresponsible, irrational and unrealistic, still we are bound to obey and not to defy. The principle was written in blood at Appomattox a little over a century ago.

Feb. 2/San Francisco Examiner & Chronicle
(This World), 2–8:11.

James Farmer
Assistant Secretary for Administration, Department of Health, Education and Welfare of the United States

I have sought quietly, inside, to pursue the illusive objectives of lasting change for my people . . . The achievements are not sufficient, or fast enough, to satisfy my appetite for progress . . . I must confess that I chafe in the ponderous bureaucracy, and long—especially now—for my old role as advocate, critic, activist.

News conference announcing his resignation,
Washington, Dec. 7/
The Dallas Times Herald, 12–8:A2, A15.

Frankie M. Freeman
Commissioner, United States Commission on Civil Rights

A new type of (civil rights) movement is developing that, even more than the old, reaches out to involve all segments of the community. This type of constituency gives the new movement more power than the old civil rights movement, which was basically middle-class oriented and middle-class developed and so limited in concept and effectiveness.

At NAACP Freedom Fund Dinner/
Quote, 5–31:519.

(FRANKIE M. FREEMAN)

Rather than face up to the bitter truth that the system has not responded to the need for change, a large number of whites believes that if only enough repressive pressure is applied, if only attention can be diverted from the racial problems, then this nation can return to the past and the headache she now experiences will go away. It is difficult to imagine a more dangerous game than this, for all it accomplishes is to under-evaluate the seriousness of the problem and to over-evaluate the ability of force and repression to stifle ideas.

At NAACP Freedom Fund dinner/
Quote, 8–30:196.

Betty Friedan
Founder, National Organization for
Women

I palpably feel that women's consciousness is changing, and it's irrelevant to me whether 500 or 5,000 women turn out (for women's liberation demonstrations). This (demonstration) is already a huge success, because the women's movement is going to be the biggest movement for social and political change in the 1970s.

Interview, Washington, March 8/
The New York Times, 3–9:1.

Eli Ginzberg
Professor of Economics, Columbia
University

There is absolutely no doubt in my mind that the Negro middle class is growing—and changing—rapidly. This represents our major hope for a resolution of racial conflict in this country.

U.S. News & World Report, 6–1:19.

Barry M. Goldwater
United States Senator, R-Ariz.

(HEW Secretary Robert H.) Finch goes all over the place on civil rights. And I have to say this: The President sort of jumps all over hell and back on civil rights. He's here today and there tomorrow and back here the next day, and I imagine Finch has pretty hard time knowing what to do. Nix on's always been that way, but he's a helluv lot better than he was.

Interview, Washington
The Dallas Times Herald, 3–11:AA

Martha W. Griffiths
United States Representative, D-Mich.

The Constitution, written in the time of sailing ships and horse-drawn carriages, has been quite adequate to cover the problem of automobiles, submarines, jet take-off and trips to the moon. Yet it took a constitutional amendment to change a woman, who was admittedly a citizen, into a voter.

Washington, Aug. 10/Milwaukee Journal
8–11:

Gus Hall
General secretary, Communist Party of the
United States

We, like many other Americans, are against racism. Many see the moral unjustness of racist practices. We welcome this—is helpful, but it is not enough. From time before the Bible, people have spoken about the brotherhood of man—as a moral precept It obviously has not been enough. Marxism Leninism exposes the root of racism. It does not accept the concept that racism, chauvinism, is an inherent, inborn, hapless characteristic of sections of human society. It exposes its class roots—that it is an instrument of exploitation—a system for extra profits.

Before Young Workers Liberation League
Chicago, Feb. 8/Daily World, 2–28:M

Margaret M. Heckler
United States Representative, R-Mass.

Women are the one minority group that is still considered fashionable to discrimi nate against.

Quote, 2–8:12

Theodore M. Hesburgh
President, University of Notre Dame; Chai

an, United States Commission on Civil
ights

Unless we get serious about this (civil
ghts), the country is . . . on a collision
ourse with everything the opposite of what
ie Constitution stands for . . . But people
en't lying awake nights worrying about it.
think the American people today need a
rrible shaking in this area . . . I think
ie American people today are very con-
rned about civil rights as long as it doesn't
ost them anything.

News conference, Washington, Oct. 12/
Los Angeles Herald-Examiner, 10–12:A3.

alter E. Hoffman
nited States District Judge for the Eastern
istrict of Virginia

We are forcing integration. That's what
ie NAACP wants; that is what the Justice
epartment wants; and that's what the
ourth Circuit Court of Appeals wants. It's
n objective that I think is ridiculous, but
bviously I've been declared wrong. There-
ore, let's get on with it. I want to get what-
ver maximum busing facilities are avail-
ble. Everyone is going to scream when
-and-7-year-olds are put on buses and
erded out to another school when there is
school right across the street.

U.S. News & World Report, 8–24:11.

en Holman
irector, Community Relations Service, De-
artment of Justice of the United States

I started out at 14 picketing for integra-
on, but it's just not going to work. We've
ot to admit publicly that we've failed, so
e can stop pursuing this phantom and con-
entrate instead on gilding the ghetto . . .

Newsweek, 2–23:108.

inwood Holton
overnor of Virginia

Let our goal in Virginia be an aristocracy
f ability, regardless of race, color or creed
. . No more must the slogan, "states
ghts," sound a recalcitrant and defensive

note for the people of the South. For the era
of defiance is behind us.

San Francisco Examiner & Chronicle
(This World), 1–25:2.

Sarah Hughes
United States District Judge for the North-
ern District of Texas

I nearly always got what I wanted, but,
then, I went after it. That is the whole key
to the women's rights movement. Women
are going to have to ask for what they want.
The Equal Rights Amendment will change
a few laws and remove *legal* discrimination
against women, but it won't make bank presidents or Cabinet officers out of them. They
will have to do that for themselves.

Interview/Life, 9–4:20.

Roy Innis
Director, Congress of Racial Equality

I say that integration should not be an end
in itself. It should be a means to an end—
toward true equality and justice. But if it's
obvious that integration is not achieving
those ends, then you seek other means. I
blame the Easterners and the Northerners
for this emphasis on integration. They
steam-rollered the whole country into feeling that there was something synonymous
between integration as a means and integration as an end . . . When you say "civil
rights leaders," you are talking about the
Eastern-Northern civil rights aristocracy
and their Utopian friends. To be very frank
with you, I'm going to ignore those guys.
They can roll along with me, or we'll roll on
by them.

Interview, Washington/
U.S. News & World Report, 3–2:31.

You can force integration if you want to,
but the whites will go to private schools or
leave the area. Where does it end? How
much of our dignity should we drag in the
dirt chasing whites around the country?

Before Congress of African Peoples, Atlanta/
The Christian Science Monitor, 9–14:13.

WHAT THEY SAID IN 1970

Jesse L. Jackson
Director, Operation Breadbasket, Southern Christian Leadership Conference

We must not forget that the black community is separate from the white community. But blacks did not do the separating and do not have the power to do the integrating. The white community is separate and independent. The black community is also separate, but dependent. Whites control themselves, but they also control us.

*Interview, Chicago/
The Christian Science Monitor, 3–5:2.*

Integration is not the opposite of segregation. The mixing of races is not a political process, but a biological process that was done by the racist rapist. The time for integration is past.

*Before Congress of African People, Atlanta/
U.S. News & World Report, 9–21:83.*

Jacob K. Javits
United States Senator, R-N.Y.

There is indeed separation of the races in too many of the schools of the North, but its cause, quality and remedy differ markedly from the segregation in a state like Mississippi. And, even to this day, the extent of segregation is much more widespread and resistance to desegregation much greater and more strongly entrenched—premised as it is in a "social order"—in the South than in the North.

*Before the Senate, Washington, Feb. 17/
Daily World, 2–18:4.*

Coretta Scott King
Widow of Dr. Martin Luther King, Jr.

Sometimes the issues dramatized by "women's lib" are not really basic to freeing women. With all the injustice a black woman lives with, she is not concerned about getting into a man's bar.

Newsweek, 8–31:47.

Jerris Leonard
Assistant Attorney General, Civil Rights Division, Department of Justice of the United States

Each and every school district in South Carolina must be absolutely in compliance with the (desegregation) law no later than September. Not negotiating, not thinking of drawing up a plan—the plan must be completely implemented before the opening of school in September . . . Freedom of choice is no longer a viable, acceptable method of desegregation. Freedom of choice just will not be accepted by the courts. For all practical purposes, freedom of choice is dead.

Columbia, S.C./National Observer, 5–4:6.

Ronald O. Lippitt
Professor of Psychology and Sociology, University of Michigan

I think we can predict that, in another 10 years, the intensity of the conflict on many dimensions between the males and females in our society is going to be where the conflict is today between teen-agers and parents and between blacks and whites. We're just beginning to see the revolt of women.

Plainview (Tex.) Daily Herald, 8–28:6.

Lester B. Maddox
Governor of Georgia

I am a segregationist. By that, I mean a person who has enough racial pride and wants to preserve it. A racist is one who doesn't care . . .

*Television interview/The Dick Cavett Show,
American Broadcasting Company, Dec. 18.*

Carl McIntire
Evangelist

All the decrees in the world can't make a white man love a black man or a black man love a white man. Only God can do that.

Interview/The Washington Post, 10–2:A22.

Margaret Mead
Anthropologist

It's (women's rights) not a question of legislation or prejudice. It's a question of the

60

way our society is organized. We have nominally given women freedom, but have not given it to them in fact. We have created a life-style that penalizes women's intellect and even denigrates (those) who gladly spend time at homemaking.

Before New York City Commission on Human Rights, Sept. 22 / The New York Times, 9–23:55.

George Meany
President, American Federation of Labor-Congress of Industrial Organizations

On the civil-rights business, I think he (President Nixon) is very, very bad because he is obviously attempting to carry water on both shoulders . . . He wants to do, on the record, what the civil-rights people expect —especially in regard to integration of the schools in the South—and at the same time he wants to keep (Senator) Strom Thurmond happy. Now, he just can't do both. . . .

News conference, Aug. 31 / U.S. News & World Report, 9–7:61.

James A. Michener
Author

I am not for Negro rights because I love the Negro, but because I love all citizens. I love the grand possibilities of this nation and do not wish to see them diminish because we fail to utilize one of our greatest resources, the abilities of our 25 million black people.

San Francisco Examiner & Chronicle (This World), 4–5:2.

John N. Mitchell
Attorney General of the United States

In the field of civil rights, we think that our record here in the (Justice) Department —across the board, from school desegregation through public accommodation and the fair employment practices—we think it will stand alongside anybody's.

Interview, Washington / San Francisco Examiner & Chronicle, 1–25:A13.

The Black Panthers were in existence long before we came into office, and I would guess there are probably fewer Black Panthers now than there were then. I also find in talking to some of these people that they don't understand the system, and least of all they don't understand this Administration, because they've been led by siren leaders who don't want them to understand.

The Washington Post, 4–19:A20.

Walter F. Mondale
United States Senator, D-Minn.

We should describe (Vice President) Spiro Agnew as a racist, because that is what he is.

Before Democratic Policy Council Committee on National Priorities, Washington, Feb. 24 / Lubbock (Tex.) Avalanche Journal, 2–25:A5.

John Morsell
Assistant executive director, National Association for the Advancement of Colored People

This is the first Administration (Nixon's) which has made it a matter of calculated policy to work against the needs and aspirations of its largest minority . . . the first Administration in 50 years that can properly be characterized as anti-Negro.

San Francisco / San Francisco Examiner & Chronicle (This World), 3–15:10.

Daniel P. Moynihan
Counsellor to the President of the United States

Five years ago, we had passed major laws broadening Negro rights in the South. There was evidence of progress and a general state of optimism among our leaders that the spirit of the (1963) March on Washington really lived and that we could translate those hopes into reality. But there was another reality, barely sensed—the reality of an extraordinarily tough lower-class problem in the Northern slums . . . pretty soon, in Watts, we learned how homicidal and hurt they (the urban blacks) really were. Since then, not surprisingly, the image of the Negro has changed—from the image of the March on Washington to the image of the

(DANIEL P. MOYNIHAN)

Black Panther. This image is the worst possible case for integration. Just as I had tried to tell (President Lyndon B.) Johnson that the image of the Southern Negro was not the only reality in 1965, so it seemed to me necessary to tell Nixon that the image of the Panther was not the only reality now.

Interview/The New York Times, 3–15:(4)2.

The idea has grown that whether you're white or black is the most important thing in the world . . . As this preoccupation with race increases, we tend to get ourselves into that old Southern model of race relations where there are just two characters, "Whitey" and "Blackie," and they live in one permanent state of estrangement, hostility and fear of one another. I happen to think that most of our social problems commonly associated with race are, in fact, not associated with race at all, but with social class. So if you solve the social-class problems, most race problems would disappear . . . All I'm saying is that we need a period in which Negro progress continues and racial rhetoric fades. I think that less public preoccupation with race would be a good thing. We should follow the precepts of the Civil Rights Act, and act as though race didn't exist. I've spent a lot of my life writing about ethnic history in this country, and I have argued, as a matter of fact, that ethnic groups do have a meaning. They have value and they are things that people preserve as a form of identity. But it's one thing to preserve an identity. It's another thing to translate it into an obsession. And that is what I mean.

Interview, Washington/
U.S. News & World Report, 6–15:67.

Gunnar Myrdal
Swedish sociologist

I am firmly convinced that a majority of the white people (in America) will not be able to use state power to organize segregation. They will never be able to organize a

Fascist state. The white man can frustrat the Negro, starve him, beat him and some times kill him, but he does not have th moral stamina to make Negro subjugatio legal and approved by society.

Accepting honorary doctor of laws degree
Atlanta University/Los Angeles Time.
11–9:(1)3(

Huey P. Newton
Minister of defense, Black Panther Party

We will change this society. It is up to th oppressor to decide whether this will be peaceful change. We will use whateve means is necessary. We will have our man hood even if we have to level the earth.

At Revolutionary Peoples Constitutiona
Convention, Philadelphia
The New York Times, 9–13:(4)!

Richard M. Nixon
President of the United States

. . . if everybody in Washington in gov ernment service who belongs—has belonge(or does belong—to a restricted golf club wer to leave government service, this (city would have the highest rate of unemploy ment of any . . . city in the country.

News conference, Washington, Jan. 30
The New York Times, 1–31:1(

I think the problem we (this Administra tion) confronted when we came in was a per formance gap with regard to black people i America—big promises and little action— and, as a result, immense frustration whic(flared into violence. Now I know all th words, I know all the gimmicks and th phrases that would win the applause o black audiences and professional civil right leaders. I'm not going to use them. I'm inter ested in deeds. I'm interested in closing th performance gap. And if we can get our we(fare reform, if we can stop the rise of crim which terrorizes those who live in our cen tral cities, if we can move on the program that I mention with regard to rural Americ —where 52 per cent of the black people liv —if we can provide the job opportunity an(

e opportunity for business enterprise for
ack people and other minority groups that
is Administration stands for, then, when I
ish office, I would rather be measured by
y deeds than all the fancy speeches I may
ve made. And I think then the black peo-
e may approve of what we did. I don't
ink I'm going to win them with words.

News conference, Washington, Jan. 30/
The New York Times, 1–31:14.

I was talking to a very distinguished Ne-
educator from Columbia University, Dr.
arles Hamilton, recently. He pointed out
at in the last 10 years the number of Ne-
oes who had moved above the poverty line
s 35 per cent—a greater percentage than
ites who moved above the poverty line in
at same period. He pointed out another
toric fact: the fact that in America today
ere are more Negro Americans in college
an there are Englishmen in college in Eng-
d or Frenchmen in college in France.
d we have, of course, reduced the legal
rriers for voting rights, for jobs and op-
rtunities in housing. All of these things
ve occurred. What I am saying simply is
s: We have come a long way, but we have
ong way to go.

Before United States Jaycees, St. Louis, June
25/U.S. News & World Report, 7–6:45.

The first Americans—the Indians—are the
st isolated minority group in our nation.
om the time of their first contact with
ropean settlers, the American Indians
ve been oppressed and brutalized, de-
ved of their ancestral lands and denied
opportunity to control their own des-
y.

Washington/Newsweek, 7–20:18.

Let me be very direct and very candid
th regard to where we stand on the prob-
n of school desegregation. The highest
urt of the land has spoken. The unitary
ool system must replace the dual school
tem throughout the United States. The
v having been determined, it is the respon-
ility of those in the Federal government

—and particularly the responsibility of the
President of the United States—to uphold
the law. And I shall meet that responsibility.
However, in upholding the law—a law which
requires a very significant social change, one
that has enormous ramifications as it affects
the communities, the schools, the homes of
so many people in the Southern states involved—there are different approaches. One
approach is simply to sit back and wait for
school to open and for trouble to start. And
then, if trouble begins, to order in the Federal enforcers to see that the law is complied
with. I rejected that approach from the beginning. Normally, that is enough. When
the Congress passes a law or when the Supreme Court decides or interprets a law in a
certain way, it is only the responsibility of
the President, the Attorney General and
others to enforce the law. But in this
instance, in the event that the law is not
complied with, in the event that there are
difficulties, as has been predicted in many
quarters, those who will suffer will not simply be this generation; it will be primarily
the next generation, the students, the children in the school districts involved. They
will pay the price for the failure, a failure of
leadership, and it is here that I point out
that leadership, strong leadership, is not
limited simply to enforcing the law when
the law is broken. We believe, all of us, in
law and order and justice. We believe in
enforcing the law. But I also believe that
leadership in an instance like this requires
some preventive action. We are trying to
take some preventive action, and we are getting magnificent cooperation from dedicated people in the seven states involved.

News conference, New Orleans, Aug. 14/
Los Angeles Times, 8–16:A5.

We do not believe the constitutional mandate that schools be desegregated requires
compulsory busing for the sole purpose of
achieving an arbitrary racial balance. We
oppose such compulsory busing, and we
favor the neighborhood-school concept.

Asheville, N.C., Oct. 20/
The New York Times, 10–21:54.

WHAT THEY SAID IN 1970

(RICHARD M. NIXON)

. . . I can assure that it is not the policy of this government to use the power of the Federal government or Federal funds . . . in ways not required by the law, for forced integration of the suburbs. I believe that forced integration in the suburbs is not in the national interest.

*News conference, Washington, Dec. 10/
The New York Times, 12–11:32.*

Max Rafferty
California State Superintendent of Public Instruction

Group-ism is not what our racial minorities need. They've had too much of that already. When you react to stimuli only as a member of a group; when you find your self-respect and self-fulfillment only as a member of a group; when you vote only as a member of a group—then you are just asking to be treated according to the lowest common denominator of that same group, whatever it is.

*At Troy (Ala.) State University, Aug. 14/
Vital Speeches, 10–1:754.*

John R. Rarick
United States Representative, D-La.

This Saturday will mark the second anniversary of the death of Martin Luther King, called by (FBI Director) J. Edgar Hoover the country's biggest liar. The slavemasters of conspiracy who created and used him during his life are still trying to get profit from their investment. They will not let their creation rest in peace, and they are now exploiting his family for their own purposes. We should note for the record that this man during his lifetime served his masters faithfully. When it served their purpose for him to break the law, he broke the law cheerfully. When it served their purpose to produce a riot, he piously produced a "non-violent riot" . . . When it served their purpose for him to lie, he lied with gusto . . . The untimely death of this Communist puppet occurred at the very time he had ceased to be

valuable alive. Now, watching the tremendous effort to canonize him, it makes one wonder whether the attempt to manufacture this saint would have been possible if he . . . had gotten drunk and drowned in his private heated swimming pool, as did his brother. One must conclude that he even died on cue. Do not the responsible government officials who have in their possession the full and documented story, with all of the evidence, have an obligation to tell the American people the truth about this man?

*Before the House, Washington, April 2/
Congressional Record, 4–2:H2637.*

Abraham A. Ribicoff
United States Senator, D-Conn.

The North is guilty of monumental hypocrisy in its treatment of the black man. Without question, Northern communities have been as systematic and as consistent as Southern communities in denying the black man and his children the opportunities that exist for white people. The plain fact is that racism is rampant throughout the country. It knows no geographical boundary and has known none since the great migration of rural blacks after World War II.

*Before the Senate, Washington, Feb. 9/
U.S. News & World Report, 2–23:32.*

. . . basically, the problem of schools being segregated is due to the fact that we have a segregated society, and that we are not going to solve the problem of the schools by busing. Who are we, whose faces are white, to think that the blacks ought to be bused? Who are we, whose faces are white, who send our children to white schools or private schools, to think that because a person is poor or because a person lives in the ghetto he wants his black child carted 20 miles away? Who are we to think that we can play with the lives of children? I do not think that busing will solve our problems. We are talking about busing children five or ten miles away, taking them outside the ghetto. You are doing more harm and hurt to a child than would be done by letting him remain in a black school with decent teachers and a good curriculum.

Before the Senate, Washington, Feb. 9/
Congressional Record, 2–9:S1474.

This nation is on the road to apartheid. It's being driven there by a President trying to develop a Southern accent, a Congress suffering political paralysis and many of us here in this room.

Before American Society of Newspaper Editors,
San Francisco, May 13/
Los Angeles Herald-Examiner, 5–13:A4.

Distrust, hostility and bitterness are increasing among minority-group citizens of this country, especially in the major population centers, North and South, where whites continue to flee the inner city. Unless we take action soon to correct this volatile situation, the breach between the races will pass the point of no return. One hundred years ago, Abraham Lincoln warned that this nation could not survive half slave and half free. Nor will we endure if we permit the formation of separate black and white societies that communicate with each other by sending ambassadors across boundaries of hate and fear.

Before the Senate, Washington, Nov. 30/
The New York Times, 11–29:(1)42.

George W. Romney

Secretary of Housing and Urban Development of the United States

I am convinced that busing is not the basis for overcoming the vital problems resulting from the separation of our people in most communities. It's a superficial compromise . . . Shuttling black children back and forth to schools in white neighborhoods, and white children back and forth to schools in black neighborhoods, makes no more sense than shuttling suburban workers back and forth to jobs in the central city, and inner-city workers back and forth to jobs in the suburban areas. Long distance busing of school children and long distance busing of workers is equally absurd.

Topeka, Kan./
San Francisco Examiner & Chronicle
(Real Estate), 2–8:A.

There's been a lot of loose talk about a HUD policy of "forced integration" of the suburbs. There is no such policy. The Department does encourage integration through voluntary action. And we have a statutory mandate to enforce a national policy of fair housing. But our role is not to prescribe quotas of numerical standards which a community must meet . . . For any community to receive our HUD grants, they must take affirmative action to prevent discrimination in the choice of a house or a community in which to live.

Before suburban mayors, Warren, Mich., July
27/U.S. News & World Report, 8–10:23.

Bayard Rustin

Executive director, A. Philip Randolph Institute

If the black people have endured the Ku Klux Klan and (former Alabama Governor) George Wallace and their ilk for 300 years, white people can endure a few blacks like Rap Brown and Stokely (Carmichael) for a while . . .

Before AFL-CIO Committee on Political
Education/Memphis Commercial Appeal,
8–12:15.

All the talk about "soul food," "soul studies" and the concentration on minor economic activities that the ghetto makes possible are not strategies for the seventies. Little going on has any effect on improving the ghetto. It cannot be improved. It must be abolished.

New York, Dec. 14/The New York Times,
12–15:40.

The only power blacks have is when they share and join that power with whites.

San Francisco Examiner & Chronicle
(This World), 12–20:2.

Bernard G. Segal
President, American Bar Association

We must avoid, at all costs, falling victim to the dangerous logic that equates the quelling of racial disturbances by some with the taking away or slowing up of further civil rights of all.

San Francisco Examiner & Chronicle
(This World), 5–10:2.

Samuel J. Simmons
Assistant Secretary for Equal Opportunity, Department of Housing and Urban Development of the United States

It is true that more blacks and other minority people live in the suburbs than did 10 years ago. But the movement of whites to the suburbs has risen far more rapidly, and we are even more suspicious of what is meant by black movement to the suburbs. We suspect that most of those black Americans are moving into new minority enclaves in suburban areas or that existing ghettos have flowed over existing city boundaries.

Los Angeles Times, 12–10:(1A)13.

Victor Solomon
Associate director, Congress of Racial Equality

The thing black people have always been fighting for is equality, not integration. Integration was just a means. The goodies were in the white schools. The black schools were starved. Integration was a way for blacks to hitch a ride.

The Washington Post, 2–5:A4.

Stephen G. Spottswood
Chairman, National Association for the Advancement of Colored People

We ask again, why is it that white people always manage to find some issue other than race to which they give their priority attention, the latest of which is pollution and the ecology? If racial justice and civil rights had commanded just 10 per cent of the attention that white liberals have given to the Vietnam war, we would not be in the position

we are today—and it is unlikely that we would have Nixon in the White House, either.

At NAACP convention, Cincinnati, June 29/
The New York Times, 6–30:25.

We have worked too long and too hard, made too many sacrifices, spent too much money, shed too much blood, lost too many lives fighting to vindicate our manhood as full participants in the American system to allow our victories to be nullified by phony liberals, die-hard racists, discouraged and demoralized Negroes and power-seeking politicians.

At NAACP convention, Cincinnati, June 29/
The New York Times, 6–30:25.

For the first time since Woodrow Wilson, we have a national Administration that can be rightly characterized as anti-Negro. This is the first time since 1920 that the national Administration has made it a matter of calculated policy to work against the needs and aspirations of the largest minority of its citizens.

At NAACP convention, Cincinnati, June 29/
The New York Times, 6–30:25.

John Stennis
United States Senator, D-Miss.

I tell you right now that the black children in the South are getting along all right. I do not claim any credit for anything, but they know that. They know that I have been interested in them since way back when I was a young man and a young lawyer. Let me qualify that to say that I know something about these people, and they are coming along all right. They are mighty happy.

Before the Senate, Washington, Feb. 5/
Congressional Record, 2–5:S1296.

I am not one to make threats, but there are some who take this matter (busing for school integration) lightly. I say they are going to hear from "mama" and "papa." They will hear from "mama" especially. They will not permit their children to be boxed up and crated around all over the city like common animals, if they can help it. They will not allow it. If anyone does not believe the growing sentiment in his part of the country against all this busing and invading homes and violating the rights of the people, he had better put his ear a little closer to the ground. I say that as a friend.

Before the Senate, Washington, Feb. 5/
Congressional Record, 2–5:S1301.

Herman E. Talmadge
United States Senator, D-Ga.

Well, we have eliminated all segregation, North and South, first by the Brown decision in 1954 and also by the Civil Rights Act of 1964. But when you eliminate segregation, then where are you? Are you going to run out and run down people and drag them into schools where they don't want to attend, and do the same for teachers? And if you are going to adopt that policy, are you going to make it universal about neighborhoods, working conditions and otherwise? I don't think you can have a police state, and that is what would be required to achieve it.

Interview/Meet the Press, National
Broadcasting Company, 3–1.

Daniel C. Thompson
Professor of Sociology, Dillard University

You have a "silent majority" among blacks just as you do among whites—people working hard to own their homes and get their kids the best possible education. But they're also concerned about gaining acceptance for blacks as a race, not just for themselves as individuals. Out of these people, I think, is coming a leadership that will be much wider in its knowledge, able to live both as blacks and as members of the whole community.

U.S. News & World Report, 6–1:21.

Strom Thurmond
United States Senator, R-S.C.

. . . I condemn these actions (Justice Department's pursuing forced school integration); I strongly condemn them; without end I condemn them. They are wrong as social policy, and they are wrong as law . . . I am warning the Nixon Administration—I repeat, I am warning the Nixon Administration today—that the people of the South and the people of the nation will not support such unreasonable policies. I remind the Chief Executive that the Presidency is an elective office, and that what the people give the people also can take away.

Before the Senate, Washington, July 17/
The Washington Post, 7–18:E12.

The Northern press in the past has accused me of being a racist, and I just can't imagine what they mean if they know the true facts. I have always stated equal opportunity for all people. I've always stated equal opportunity for school children, and I want to see all of them have equal opportunities. But because I have not favored special privileges for any one group, I think some have felt that I was a racist; or because I have opposed the busing of children to bring about racial integration—even though there is no law that requires that.

Interview/The Washington Post, 10–30:A7.

Lionel Tiger
Author; Social anthropologist

My whole argument about the feminist movement is that the women start from exactly the wrong point of view. Rather than starting from the notion that males and females are the same, they should start from the notion that they are different and that they have different life experiences. Then you might actually get somewhere. This would mean that you have a career structure for women that is different from the one for males, and thus women would be discriminated *for*. I'm all in favor of discriminating *for* females.

Interview/Time, 8–31:21.

Kenneth Tollett
Dean,
Texas Southern University Law School

Of the many lessons learned in the civil

(KENNETH TOLLETT)

rights movement, none is more potent than that nobody is listened to in this country unless he shouts, or responded to unless he raises hell.

Los Angeles, April 25/Los Angeles Times,
4–27:(2)2.

Joe D. Waggonner, Jr.
United States Representative, D-La.

Even the extreme left *New York Times* admits that forced mixing of the races (in schools) has not worked; that student absences now run from 40 to 50 per cent; that racial violence is the common denominator in schools from coast to coast. In those cases where actual violence has not flared, it seethes beneath the surface. Teaching and learning are sidelines; the major interest is survival. This is the condition which has been brought about by sociological meddling. That this era is dying is occasion for rejoicing. It should never have been born, and only the militant whites and blacks who make their sorry living promoting racial strife and hatred will mourn its passing.

Before the House, Washington, March 2/
Congressional Record, 3–2:H1388.

George C. Wallace
Former Governor of Alabama

I believe in the American dream of a better life for everyone, regardless of race, color or creed. It has been the liberal establishment that has forced upon average citizens the fears of race that have brought about the breakdown of race relations in such citadels of liberalism as New York. In the capital of the Confederacy, there is racial peace and tranquility. It's a sad day that we have allowed the destruction of race relations by liberals in many sections of the country. I think it was a preconceived plan and a conspiracy.

Interview, Montgomery, Ala./
The Christian Science Monitor, 1–5:9.

Earl Warren
Former Chief Justice of the United States

The one thing that has the badge of insolubility on it is the problem of how we are to live together in harmony and mutual respect. We have boasted for almost 200 years that we are a plural society, wherein we achieve unity through diversity and accommodate diversity through unity. But the sins of former years are upon us, and it is my belief that the question of whether we can permanently have such a society is the greatest problem before the American people today . . . It . . . seems clear to me that, if we are ever to have a placid nation again, at least during the lifetime of our children and their children, it will be necessary for us to set aside our prejudices on account of race or color, and be willing to live in a plural society where American citizenship means, in fact as well as in precept, that all men are created equal, and as such are entitled to life, liberty and the pursuit of happiness. There is only one other alternative—chaos.

Before American Academy of Arts and Sciences,
Cambridge, Mass./The New York Times,
10–31:29.

Roy Wilkins
Executive director, National Association
for the Advancement of Colored People

It does not matter whether it (racial separatism) comes out of a white mouth, as with the 1930 Communists, out of a black, as in the case of Marcus Garvey, whether it is published with government funds, as with the American Colonization Society, or whether it is yelled in cadence by the young black separatists of 1970—it is the tranquilizer that precedes the suicide of a people.

At NAACP convention, Cincinnati, June 30/
The New York Times, 7–1:33.

They (black separatists) talk a complete apartheid, except on one point: They want white money. They preach black manhood—established with white financing. The news for them is that manhood purchased on that basis is worthless in the marketplace of self-respect in which every man—white, black, yellow or brown—must face himself before his secret mirror.

At NAACP convention, Cincinnati, June 30/
U.S. News & World Report, 7–13:73.

Hosea Williams
Vice president,
Southern Christian Leadership Conference

I am black and I am proud. I am black and I know that I am beautiful. Me being black and beautiful does not make white folks ugly just because they are white. Now, there are some ugly white folks. I think (Georgia Governor) Lester Maddox is a very ugly man. I think the United States Attorney General Mitchell is a very ugly man. And, in fact, (President) Richard Nixon is ugly, too.

Barnesville, Ga., May 22/
The New York Times, 5–24:(1)38.

Black power has nothing to do with violence. Black power is when black people respect themselves. Black power is when black men stop allowing themselves to be duped into filling the jailhouses while white men fill the colleges . . . Black power is when we refuse to fight thousands of miles away from home for freedoms over there that we cannot enjoy here.

Barnesville, Ga., May 22/
The New York Times, 5–24:(1)38.

I . . . envision a shift of the main battleground of civil rights from the North back to the South. I never did buy the Northern move. I was the only executive on Dr. (Martin Luther) King's staff that he never did get up North; and I say, today, the only chance that the young Northerners have, both black and white, lies in what happens in the South.

Interview/Time, 6–1:11.

John Bell Williams
Governor of Mississippi

. . . Mississippi has been used as a proving ground for every kind of radical so-called "civil rights" experiment that could be dreamed up by the witch hunters of the pseudo-liberal left and their fellow revolutionaries. These elements have had the full support of fawning Federal Administrations fearing the power of their strategically-located and rigidly-controlled bloc votes. Even Presidents of the United States, dreading the wrath of their vengeance, have cravenly yielded to their demands, however unreasonable or unconstitutional. They have furnished them troops, money and legal aid, and they have placed entire departments of the Federal government at their disposal. Even before Lyndon Johnson led the cheers for these radicals by chanting their theme song, "We Shall Overcome," to a joint session of the United States Congress, the Southern States—and Mississippi in particular—have been open, defenseless, marked and singular targets for all the vitriolic hate and abuse that could be heaped upon us by anyone with a politically-motivated cause.

Radio-TV address, Jackson, Miss., Jan. 3/
Vital Speeches, 3–1:306.

Samuel W. Yorty
Mayor of Los Angeles

The idea that our neighborhood schools should be destroyed and that students, particularly those in the lower grade levels, should be involuntarily forced to go long distances to accomplish a social purpose without maintaining the consent of the people is a very dangerous thing . . . Many people throughout the United States are watching the agony of the South experiencing this problem; but these same people have little idea that the problem may be coming their way very soon.

Los Angeles, Feb. 12/
Los Angeles Herald-Examiner, 2–13:A3.

Whitney M. Young, Jr.
Executive director, National Urban League

Work must be done in the next few years to project the strengths of black people. We are seen always as a problem and a burden, never as an asset. I don't know of any other

(WHITNEY M. YOUNG, JR.)

group of people who could have survived and grown if they hadn't had some hidden assets like resilience and patience and soul, or whatever it is. We need to let white America know that we're talking not about cultural absorption but about cultural exchange. We don't know how to make napalm; they're smarter than we are on that. We don't know how to do price fixing. We don't know how to manipulate the stock market. But that apparently has not led to a very happy America, even at the very highest levels. When they begin to see that we bring something to the New Order, then this old condescending feeling of always giving and never taking will change.

Interview/Time, 4–6:27.

Critical as I have been of (Nixon) Administration actions, I do admit that there are some signs that elements of this Administration are moving forward to bring about change . . . All these may be but straws in the wind, but it would be a mistake for us to fail to recognize that within every Administration there are contending forces. To cease to fight for our victories and to fail to negotiate with those in power is to leave the field to the political Neanderthals that so far seem to have dominated decision-making in the past four years.

At 60th anniversary meeting of National Urban League, New York, July 19/ The New York Times Magazine, 9–20:76.

White Americans who engage in wishful thinking that we (black Americans) are going to take them off the hook and solve their problems by all of us collectively moving to separate states or leaving en masse for Africa should be told loudly and clearly, "Forget it." We are here to stay, and in the process we are going to make this country live up to its Judeo-Christian ethics and its democratic promise, or see it go down the drain of history as immoral and hypocritical, deserving of its fate.

Before International Congress of African People, Atlanta, Sept. 5/ The New York Times, 9–6:(1)40.

I can't afford the luxury of a completely dogmatic position that says, "I won't make any compromises," because I'm dealing with the real world. People tell me, "Whitney, under no circumstances should you accept a position with the Nixon Administration. You'll be helping Republicans." This cannot be my overriding consideration. That must be whether what I do will help the masses of black people. I can leave the Urban League tomorrow at double or triple my salary in private industry, but the masses can't. I could take a very strong, idealistic position and not be hurt personally by it. But somebody's got to deal in a very practical way with the issues that are before them, and there's nobody else who's got the entree with the decision makers.

Interview, New Rochelle, N.Y./ The New York Times Magazine, 9–20:32.

Commerce · Industry · Finance

George W. Andrews
United States Representative, D-Ark.

The growing problem of cheap textile imports flooding this country, principally from Japan, reached the critical stage some time ago. It is time for the President to stop talking and act—act to place limitations on total textile imports, and act now. To do less would be to kill this valuable industry and throw millions of Americans out of work. Minimum wage earners cannot compete with coolie labor, nor should they be expected to.

Before the House, Washington, Jan. 26/
Congressional Record, 1–26:E298.

William M. Batten
Chairman, J. C. Penney Company

There is a common misconception about business and businessmen. We are often looked upon as the Establishment—whatever that is—dedicated to the preservation of the status quo. In fact, we are revolutionists. Business is in revolution. The concept of free enterprise is itself a very revolutionary idea. It is still not an accepted thought in most countries. It is not designed to preserve the status quo. It is designed for change. Successful corporate management concerns itself with the forces of change. It creates, directs and manages change.

Quote, 7–26:75.

Werner A. Baum
President, University of Rhode Island

It somehow amazes me that the American businessman, who has at his disposal all the resources, techniques and knowledge for selling his product, still hasn't done a good job selling himself to the younger generation.

Nation's Business, May:58.

Helen Delich Bentley
Chairman, Federal Maritime Commission

If we don't match foreign shipping, we are going to be in trouble. In Europe, they're realistic. The more difficult we make it to trade with the U.S. because of labor costs, ocean-carrying costs, regulations and paperwork, the more the whole of the U.S. is going to suffer. The world's a big place. Other people don't have to buy from us any more if they don't want to.

News conference, Los Angeles, May 20/
Los Angeles Herald-Examiner, 5–21:A16.

William Bernbach
Chairman, Doyle-Dane-Bernbach

The big thing is recognizing that honesty sells. There is no reason why honesty cannot be combined with the skills of persuasion. People are shouted at by so many manufacturers today that they don't know what to believe.

Time, 2–16:86.

Alan Bible
United States Senator, D-Nev.

Many students of business size have a tendency to emphasize the advantages of big business over small business; but that is a mistake. Those who are close to the small businesses of America know very well that they are truly the foundation of the American economy . . . its true wellspring, if you please.

Quote, 11–29:506.

Edwin S. Bingham
President,
California Mortgage Bankers Association

We've submitted a proposed constitutional amendment to the (California) Legislature. The amendment would remove the

(EDWIN S. BINGHAM)

10% usury ceiling on loans to corporations or partnerships . . . I'm not quarreling with the usury ceilings on loans to consumers. Certainly you have to have some protection for the individual. But when you prevent development companies from tapping a source —even a high-cost source—of mortgage financing money, you're doing a disservice to everyone. If the apartment units aren't built, homes will be even more scarce and rents will continue going up. Besides, protecting a corporation or real estate partnership from paying usurious interest is like protecting J. P. Morgan from being swindled in the stock market.

Before California Mortgage Bankers Association, Palm Springs, Calif./ Los Angeles Times, 4–27:(3)12.

Edward L. Bond, Jr.
Chairman, Young & Rubicam, Inc.

Unfortunately, business is today's whipping boy. And because advertising is the part of business that has the greatest visibility, we have become a prime target for these attacks. Business, including advertising, is "it" today. Corporate performance is anybody's target. We are being blamed for the air we breathe, the water we drink, the superabundance of choice in the marketplace, the conditions of our ghetto and the outflow of gold. You name the crime, we're guilty of it.

Before National Industrial Conference Board Marketing Conference, New York, Oct. 15/ Vital Speeches, 12–1:125.

L. E. J. Brouwer
Senior managing director, Royal Dutch/Shell

Oil is seldom found where it is most needed, and seldom most needed where it is found.

Time, 5–4:91.

Max E. Brunk
Professor of Marketing, Cornell University

I reject the contention that the consumer is ignorant, stupid or uninformed merely because her actions are not consistent with either my beliefs or the beliefs of any professional consumerist. In my opinion, consumers with dollars in their pockets are not, by any stretch of the imagination, weak. To the contrary, they are the most merciless, meanest, toughest market disciplinarians I know.

Before National Broiler Council, Atlanta/ Washington Star, 10–22:A9

Hamer H. Budge
Chairman, Securities and Exchange Commission of the United States

We very much want the public to participate in the equity market on the exchanges, and if the industry can't stay in business handling public orders, the public won't have access to the markets. Personally, I think it would be a real tragedy if the grandfather can't buy 10 shares of AT&T for the grandchild.

Interview, Washington/ The Christian Science Monitor, 4–10:B8.

I'm sure no one would appreciate my saying that a sharp drop in stock prices is a good thing—least of all, those who have lost money. But I think it is important that for the first time a great many people in this country have learned that free markets go down as well as up. That is one of the great things about markets in the United States: There are no artificial stimuli to make them rise or fall. We should be grateful that they are unmanaged—that they move up and down freely.

Interview, Washington/ U.S. News & World Report, 9–7:52.

Should the American people ever reach the conclusion that they are not getting a fair shake in the (securities) market, we will see an end to the type of markets we have known. That would be a tragedy for the United States, because it is through the open market that we raise money for corporate endeavors. We have prided ourselves for years on having the best and freest markets in the world. I'm satisfied that we still have them—that a person can be confident when he buys securities that he is getting an honest product at an honest price. But if the public ever should get the opposite impression, we would have cataclysmic days ahead.

Interview, Washington/
U.S. News & World Report, 9-7:56.

Arthur F. Burns
Chairman, Federal Reserve Board

It would be a disastrous mistake to use Federal monies to keep unsound firms from failing, or to substitute public for private tests of creditworthiness, or to convey the impression that the Federal government will bail out loosely-managed or speculative enterprises. But there may be a role for Federal guarantees in helping basically sound firms that experience temporary financial distress to find access to funds where the alternative might be a degree of financial dislocation inimical to the national interest.

Before Joint Congressional Economic
Committee, Washington, July 23/
U.S. News & World Report, 8-3:55.

Merger activity has slowed materially since mid-1969. To some degree, this is a response to the growing concern in government circles over the dangers that may inhere in large concentrations of economic power. But it stems mainly from the fact that businessmen are recognizing that time and energy can usually be spent more productively in searching for ways to increase the economic efficiency of their firm than in a scramble for corporate acquisitions.

At Pepperdine College "Great Issues Series"
lectures, Los Angeles, Dec. 7/
The New York Times, 12-8:34.

J. Phil Campbell
Under Secretary of Agriculture
of the United States

Our urban friends in the nonfarming part of American society seem to think that agriculture is a completely subsidized, noncompetitive industry—that every farmer has

a guaranteed income—and that farmers are in effect wards of the government. Nothing could be farther from the truth. The plain fact is that there is still more competition and more risk in agriculture than industry ever thought of. There are literally hundreds of thousands of farmers all producing the same products. Show me an industry—any industry—with that kind of competition.

Before Independent Bankers Association of
America, Honolulu, March 17/
Vital Speeches, 5-1:432.

Leo Cherne
Executive director,
Research Institute of America

A revolution in advertising is already in motion. Consumer cynicism has already forced the advertiser toward humor, toward the underclaim or no claim at all. But this in turn will be replaced by a growing demand for concrete, believable and accurate information.

Before Business Publications Audit Meeting,
Chicago, Feb. 18/Vital Speeches, 4-15:411.

There is not an appetite or need, human desire or human satisfaction which is not at the core of the energy we call business. Without need, we in business are nothing. With it, we have helped shape the human experience into a most magnificent experiment. Chance, it is said, is the hand of God intervening in human history. But I'm sure He won't mind if we help a bit.

Before Business Publications Audit meeting,
Chicago, Feb. 18/Vital Speeches, 4-15:411.

A. W. Clausen
President, Bank of America

Commercial banks have historically been forced to bear the lion's share of the burdens of Federal monetary policy. In the process, their ability to accomplish what is expected of them in serving the public and the needs of public policy has been seriously hampered. The function of the banking system in the implementation of monetary policy has been vastly misunderstood by the American public and, indeed, by some of our law-

(A. W. CLAUSEN)

makers in Washington. The result has been that the banks—bearing the brunt of Federal monetary policies—have received an undeserved and unfavorable public image, while their less-regulated brethren, unfettered and, in some cases, subsidized, have emerged from the difficult tight money conditions of the past few years with their public image untarnished. On the simple basis of equity and effectiveness, I think it is time that the more onerous burdens of Federal financial control be spread more evenly throughout the financial system.

Before Economic Club, New York, April 2 /
Vital Speeches, 5–1:430.

If the American people fail to achieve the political and social goals they choose for themselves for the remainder of this century, it'll be in large part because they have failed to strengthen and preserve the open market financial system which permits their implementation.

Before Economic Club, New York, April 2 /
Quote 6–7:530.

In reality, there is probably no major industrial nation that does not stand to lose by rampant restrictionism, and none that does not stand to gain by dynamic trade flows. The whole trend of world economic development . . . has been founded on the realization—as a matter of enlightened self-interest —that the individual growth and social welfare of every nation are inexorably tied to the collaborative growth and welfare of all. Multinationalism, not go-it-alone nationalism, is today's constructive, expanding reality—and tomorrow's. The economic and social progress of large as well as small nations depends on it. The editors of *Fortune* magazine put the case as succinctly as anyone in their last issue. Any battle for a return to protectionism is, in the magazine's phrase, "the wrong war—in the wrong world."

Before Japan-America Society and American
Chamber of Commerce in Japan, Tokyo,
Sept. 8 / Vital Speeches, 10–1:748.

It may sound heretical . . . to say that business enterprise is not an absolute necessity to a human culture. But it happens to be a fact, documented by history and anthropology. The culture of ancient Egypt lasted more than three thousand years—six times as long as our own so far, if we date the beginning of modern commercial society with the discovery of America. And ancient Egypt functioned—more than three thousand years —without anything resembling what we today understand by the terms "corporate enterprise" or even "money." I don't recommend that culture as a way of life we would want to emulate. It was a slave economy; the fruits of labor were for a very small elite— and the great mass of the people subsisted in the most hideous misery and want. But the culture could and did survive without "business." Within our own span of years, we have witnessed the rise of the Soviet socialist empire. It survives without anything you or I would call a private corporation and little that approaches our own monetary mechanism. It survives and is far stronger than anyone might have expected, watching its turbulent beginnings in 1917. Again, I do not commend this system to anyone. The prospect for the individual in Soviet Russia is stark, grim and hollow in terms of personal freedom of choice and personal opportunity. But the culture can and does exist without business. I mention these two examples from history—and there are others—because it is easy to mislead ourselves into thinking there is something preordained about our profit-motivated, free-market, private-enterprise system—that is, as they used to say of gold, universal and immutable. I personally believe it is the system which offers the human individual the greatest hope in the world we're entering. But its status in that world is not guaranteed. It must be earned. And it can be earned and enhanced only if it recognizes and uses its own greatest strengths: its innate adaptability and its capacity to manage change to provide services which society as a whole needs or desires—and cannot achieve as well through other means.

*At Los Angeles Chamber of Commerce
Business Outlook Conference/
The Wall Street Journal, 12–24:4.*

Edward N. Cole
President, General Motors Corporation

The fact is that much of the so-called youth advertising is not even understood by the youths themselves . . . Most of the young people and virtually all of the older ones won't have any idea what you are talking about. The average youth of today is sophisticated, better educated than ever before in our history. They've learned to develop and enjoy diversity. There are times for swinging and times for serious planning of their lives and their careers. And yet advertising too often makes the mistake of assuming that a swinger is a swinger—and nothing else at any time. In my opinion, such an attitude is an insult to the intelligence of the young adult.

Changing Times, May:44.

John B. Connally
Former Governor of Texas

. . . we should recognize that the fundamental prosperity of this nation has been built upon the concept of being a free trader, of exporting what we build, what we make; of exporting our education, our ideas, our brains, our capital and our commodities to nations throughout this world; and we have been highly successful at it . . . We live in a world of trade.

*Before Investment Bankers Association, Boca
Raton, Fla., Dec. 2/
The Washington Post, 12–20:E1.*

James C. Corman
United States Representative, D-Calif.

In this deadly game of protectionism, there can be no winners—only embittered losers. For if our generation should have learned anything from two costly world wars, it should be that nations that can't trade with each other in peace achieve their social contacts under more violent and unproductive circumstances.

Washington/Los Angeles Times, 11–20:(1)12.

Bernard Cornfeld
Chairman, Investors Overseas Services, Ltd.

If the course of economic decision-making does not change, and if the American securities industry continues to be attacked and weakened and made unprofitable by a regulatory body that simply doesn't understand it, there will be less opportunity to make money in the American stock market and less money will be coming here.

New York, Feb. 4/The New York Times, 2–5:51.

(Commenting on IOS's financial problems): I set out to build up a business in the mutual-fund field, and I think I succeeded. But I like to live well, I like the good life and —let's face it—I'm a lousy administrator.

Time, 5–25:90.

Kenneth N. Davis, Jr.
*Assistant Secretary of Commerce for
Domestic and International Business
of the United States*

For a business to be strong today, it is no longer enough just to be able to compete effectively with other American companies here at home. The world has suddenly become a global marketplace! We must now compete more effectively in this new global environment if we are to stay strong as industries and as a nation . . . No longer can we treat inflation, consumerism and antitrust matters from a strictly domestic viewpoint.

*Before Electronics Industries Association,
Washington, March 9/Vital Speeches, 4–15:390.*

The old protectionism-versus-free-trade argument has become a very sterile issue, I believe. Instead, we should all recognize that there are strong competitors all around the world today—in Europe, the Far East and elsewhere. After World War II, the United States set out to build up industrial strength in all parts of the world to meet the needs of

(KENNETH N. DAVIS, JR.)

all people. An expansionist trade policy was a key part of the program. Now that we have been successful in creating worthy competitors, and with the onward thrust of modern transportation and communications technology, we should not turn back toward protectionism! Rather, we must keep moving ahead toward trade expansion. But now we must insist more firmly on receiving fair competitive treatment—treatment which just isn't being given to us by many of our trading partners.

Before Electronics Industries Association,
Washington, March 9/Vital Speeches, 4–15:391.

Referring . . . to Europe and Japan, it is urgent that these nations re-examine their current trade attitudes toward the United States, the world's biggest market. The benefits of continued trade expansion for all the world are inestimable. The losses from a turn toward world protectionism or to policies of national or regional special advantage would be irretrievable. For the benefit of all the world's trade, it is time for Japan and Europe to respond more fairly than heretofore to the 20 years of U.S. leadership in expansionist world trade policy.

Before Electronics Industries Association,
Washington, March 9/Vital Speeches, 4–15:392.

B. R. Dorsey
President, Gulf Oil Corporation

Over the next ten years, the public will demand justification for just about everything American industry is doing. If we have a point to make, and I am sure we do, then we had better start finding ways to make it.

Time, 5–11:96.

Eric Drake
Chairman, British Petroleum
Company, Ltd.

. . . I've always admired tremendously the accessibility of American business executives. No matter how important they are—with a carpet on the floor and a great title on the door—Americans have always made a point of having an open door. I don't think it's quite so open as some of them would pretend; otherwise they'd have no time to get on with the job. But I think one's always got to be prepared to talk to anybody who really wants to talk, and that isn't only with your own people. I think one's always got to be prepared to discuss the company's views on any subject.

Interview, London/Nation's Business, July:66.

Philip Elman
Commissioner, Federal Trade Commission

The public suffers from too much of the wrong kind of regulation. Broadly speaking, government regulation is necessary and justified only when it serves the public interest, not the special interests of private groups or industries . . . So-called "infant" industries may perhaps need a helping hand from government for a short time; but we should not go on sheltering and subsidizing them forever in the guise of protective regulation.

Before Antitrust Section, American Bar
Association, St. Louis, Aug. 11/
The Wall Street Journal, 8–12:8.

John S. Fielden
Dean, Boston University College of
Business Administration

I think that for extremely complex causes we're entering into a period of increased corporate democracy with all that will be good and bad about it. But it will be coming. For example, I think you'll find salary ranges shrinking, that in this corporate democracy it'll be much more difficult to justify the president of a company's receiving a salary infinitely greater than that received by the President of the United States. I think that you'll find more meaningful boards of directors being truly responsive not only to the wishes of the stockholders, but to the needs of the employes. I think that you will see super-remunerative stock options disappearing, or at least being made available to more than just a favored few. I think that you will see corporations, if they are to survive, made dramatically more responsive to the needs of society. Just as universities, corporations will be forced to examine more closely their relationships with the military and with political groups. I think you will find corporate presidents facing, head-on, the question of whether their corporations can afford a social conscience, whether maximum returns to stockholders is the ultimate goal.

Before Advertising Club of Boston/
The Wall Street Journal, 2–4:12.

Henry Ford II
Chairman, Ford Motor Company

. . . the most effective way to encourage business to serve new public needs is to rely, when possible, on market incentives. When the marketplace does not automatically translate a public need into a market demand, then government action may be required to change market conditions . . . When the need for abatement of air pollution was recognized, the government established realistic emission standards. By doing so, the government created a market and the auto industry has moved quickly to supply it.

At Harvard Business School Public Affairs
Forum/The Wall Street Journal, 2–17:12.

On non-military goods, I see no reason why we should not trade with the U.S.S.R. The United States needs to trade and the U.S.S.R. needs to trade. I am a free trader.

News conference, Moscow/
The Christian Science Monitor, 4–23:3.

Milton Friedman
Professor of Economics,
University of Chicago

There is only one "social responsibility" of business: to use its resources and engage in activities designed to increase its profits, so long as it stays within the rules of the game—which is to say, engages in open and free competition, without deception or fraud.

Before Mont Pelerin Society of International
Economists, Munich/Human Events, 9–19:17.

John Kenneth Galbraith
Professor of Economics, Harvard University

I am persuaded there are substantial areas of modern business enterprise—notably the railroads and the weapons firms, as well as sectors of the housing industry—which do not function effectively or efficiently under private ownership. What we have had in the past 25 years is a kind of disguised form of socialism, in which we closed our eyes to the fact that these industries are very largely under public sponsorship, through subsidies and regulations. In the case of the munitions industries, for example, it's been a device for paying larger salaries and getting some degree of private support for the Pentagon from what amounts to a public bureaucracy. My own feeling is that as long as liberals in the United States are elaborately explaining they are not socialists, as they have in the past, they won't take hold of these industries and have pride in some areas of public activity, notably the Tennessee Valley Authority.

Interview, Los Angeles Times, 10–4:G1.

Frank C. Graham, Jr.
Chairman, American Stock Exchange

This industry basically is restructuring itself without any direction. It's going helter-skelter all over the place. What we need is leadership.

The New York Times, 2–22:(3)1.

Bess Myerson Grant
Commissioner for Consumer Affairs
of New York City

The consumer movement is at a critical point in its history, and we face a critical danger—the danger that we will be fooled by fake reform. Deceptive packaging and mislabeling are as insidious on the Congressional calendar as they are on the supermarket shelf.

Before Consumer Federation of America,
Washington, Jan. 15/
San Francisco Examiner & Chronicle
(This World), 1–25:11.

Robert W. Haack
President, New York Stock Exchange

I am afraid we too often take for granted the benefits of a sophisticated, efficient central securities market. Without the New York Stock Exchange, our present standard of living would never have been reached. Our economy would function at a much lower level of activity, with capital in reduced supply and less impelled to seek out opportunities for growth. In a world which often sneers at the profit incentive, we may lose sight of the fact that we can afford to focus on improving the quality of life today precisely because our national affluence has made this possible. I take pride in the role our Exchange has played in the development of our economy . . . without the New York Stock Exchange, and the efficient allocation of resources it promotes, all the laudable efforts now going forward to reduce poverty, to restore better health to our central cities, to eradicate pollution and to improve the quality of life, would be impossible.

*Before Economic Club, New York, Nov. 17 /
Vital Speeches, 12–15:140.*

Bluntly stated, the securities industry, more than any other industry in America, engages in mazes of blatant gimmickry . . . Deals are frequently involved, complicated and bizarre, and do no credit to the donor or beneficiary of the reciprocation. I have no legitimate quarrel with any competitive success which is properly achieved by a regional stock exchange; and some of them have been innovative in a credible manner. In the main, however, their success has been predicated on their willingness to adopt less-rigid rules concerning institutional membership and/or to engage in reciprocity. As a result, these marketplaces, with little or no depth or liquidity, have become nothing more than rebate mechanisms to get commissions to those who do not qualify or to return them to institutions.

*Before Economic Club, New York, Nov. 17 /
Vital Speeches, 12–15:141.*

Floyd D. Hall
Chairman, Eastern Air Lines

. . . if we can't derive a considerably stronger resulting company in a merger than two lines had been independently, I do not see any real reason for trying to merge. Where you would get a merged company whose financial basis was stronger than either of two individual companies—and this can be done—then I think you would have a good, logical reason for pursuing a merger.

*Interview, New York /
The New York Times, 3–15:(3)8.*

Orval Hansen
United States Representative, R-Ida.

I am a firm believer in reciprocal trade, but a $7 billion balance-of-payments deficit last year and a continuing flood of cheaply-produced foreign imports that are disrupting U.S. industry and displacing U.S. workers is not what I would call reciprocal. As we pursue this liberal foreign-trade policy, our negotiators would do well to consider some of the facts of life, or at least the facts of hard-nosed bargaining, with some traders who are expert in this sort of thing.

*Before the House, Washington, March 2 /
Congressional Record, 3–2:S2721.*

Howard C. Harder
Chairman, CPC International, Inc.

The safety of the consumer is an imperative. There can be no justification—economic or moral—to take chances that an informed consumer would not take. The consuming public has responsibilities as well. It has an obligation to be informed, to maintain its sense of proportion. The consuming public should recognize that industry is a part of society, and not separate. It should appreciate that we are trying with all our strength to be responsive, and that we are not driven by economic motivations alone, but that if sometimes this appears to be the case, it is because ours is the difficult role of converting ideas and wishes into practical applications. The consuming public should not make reckless accusations or prejudge us, impugning the integrity of an entire industry. The public might even have a little empathy for the position we are in —trying to reconcile a contradictory array of public priorities and objectives in order to guide our actions.

At CPC annual meeting/
The Wall Street Journal, 9–1:10.

Bryce N. Harlow
Assistant to the President of the United States

President Nixon profoundly respects the critical contribution made by industry to the vitality and strength of the American economy. But if this respect were to over-influence his actions, I am certain that the fall of 1972 would bring a new team, and a hostile team, to the White House.

Before Government Affairs Conference,
American Advertising Federation, Washington,
Feb. 2/The New York Times, 2–3:67.

Jacob K. Javits
United States Senator, R-N.Y.

We are a preponderant economic power. Everything we do has such impact that we cannot indulge ourselves in trade quotas. The standard for us cannot be the standard of "do unto others." As a preponderant power, we must accept temporary inequities. If we fight back with quotas, it would lead to a world eruption . . . It also would have implications for our peace and security. A breakdown in trade relations is bound to have a spillover prejudicial to our many multilateral relations.

Interview, Washington/
The New York Times, 10–18:(3)2.

Henry Kearns
Chairman,
Export-Import Bank of the United States

Only by expansion of exports can we achieve the necessary positive goal in our balance of payments. (However), an expansion of exports requires a relatively open in-

ternational trade policy . . . Among the most apparent of the dark clouds threatening the economic horizon of the 1970s are those purveyors of doubt who would ask us to restrict our external trade. If they should succeed in leading us to take such a backward step, we shall surely witness—indeed, participate in—the degradation of the most productive economy in the history of mankind.

Before Foreign Trade Association of Southern
California, Los Angeles, May 21/
Los Angeles Times, 5–22:(3)19.

Kirk Kerkorian
Financier

If economists were any good at business, they would be rich men instead of advisers to rich men.

Time, 7–27:65.

Andrew Kershaw
President, Ogilvy & Mather

A good advertising man who is also a good businessman has an interesting edge over everyone. He works for a lot of clients, knows a little about a lot, and agile minds can transfer ideas from industry to industry like a bee hopping from plant to plant. Businessmen don't have a window on the world. I wish they'd use their agencies to provide that window.

Interview, New York/
The New York Times, 1–4:(3)14.

Miles W. Kirkpatrick
Chairman, Federal Trade Commission

You don't give out traffic tickets when the bank is being robbed down the street. I hope that we (FTC) can get the big cases—those that are really important. We will get some of the "traffic violators," but I don't think we should waste our substance on too many of them . . . Major industries touch more consumers than minor industries do, that's for sure . . . The more consumers that are ultimately touched by the cases that we bring, the more we will be enforcing the law.

Interview, Washington/
The Washington Post, 10–25:G1.

79

Virginia H. Knauer
Adviser to the President of the
United States for Consumer Affairs

The responsiveness of a firm to the consumer is directly proportionate to the distance on the organization chart from the consumer to the chairman of the board.

Before Federal Bar Association, Washington,
Sept. 17 / The Dallas Times Herald, 9–17:A2.

Russell B. Long
United States Senator, D-La.

The Department of Commerce statistics give a false impression that this country enjoys a highly-favorable balance of trade, when, in fact, if our trade balance was actually tabulated, it would show an unfavorable balance of trade. Our own negotiators use misleading trade statistics—misleading Congress, misleading the American public, misleading the world, and defeating our own objectives in representing American interests.

Quote, 11–29:521.

Louis B. Lundborg
Chairman, Bank of America

So often, young people have a tendency to assume there is no conscience at all in corporate leadership, that there is no sense of responsibility, that we are either blind or callous to the problems. I have a very deep conviction that there is more real responsibility in business leadership today than ever in the whole history of this country or the world. In all my contacts with business leaders, I know there is no condoning of corporate immorality of any kind. There is a real recognition that the corporation has a kind of public responsibility. I think that banking and other business cannot be divorced from the ultimate best interests of the people. We cannot exist in a kind of vacuum or detachment from the well-being of the people.

Interview, San Francisco /
The Dallas Times Herald, 10–26:A21.

Warren G. Magnuson
United States Senator, D-Wash.

The essence of the consumer movement is not that business will be saddled with burdensome restrictions, reporting requirements and regulation. It is, rather, new and altered relationships in the marketplace; new factors to be considered in design, production and distribution; and new responsibility for social consequences hitherto taken for granted. It means that business as an institution will have to accomodate itself to newly emerging forces and demands.

Before the Senate, Washington, Feb. 5 /
Congressional Record, 2–5:S1264.

Franco Maria Malfatti
President,
European Common Market Commission

It is no secret that there are dangerous protectionist tendencies in the U.S.—which are in direct conflict with U.S. policy since the end of World War II. We sincerely hope they will be reversed . . . Some adjustments are painful. But a country as rich and powerful as the U.S.—the mecca of competitive free enterprise—certainly has the means to adjust and adapt itself with a minimum of pain. A powerful European Common Market is in the interests of the U.S. Look at what happened to transatlantic trade since the Common Market began. It has tripled.

Interview, Rome / Newsweek, 8–17:51.

Joseph Martin, Jr.
General counsel, Federal Trade Commission

The growth of modern advertising has been, at best, a mixed blessing. (Advertising) can and does serve some very useful purposes, but too often it appeals to the wrong emotions. The average person lives surrounded by insistent attempts to capture his attention, to excite his fear or envy, to arouse his desire, or to tap his pocketbook . . . The old standards of what can be appropriately said in advertising is rapidly losing its acceptability. Unsubstantiated claims will have to be replaced by statements of tested facts. And affirmative disclosure of provable product characteristics will be required. The businessman should ride herd on his advertising manager or agency, as the case may be. When they pass from legitimate vaunting of the true performance merits of a product to the cruder forms of attracting attention—such as games of chance and appeals to personal insecurity—the prudent businessman should put his foot down.

Before Furniture Club, Chicago/
Variety, 10–14:40.

C. Peter McColough
President, Xerox Corporation

There's been a lot of debate recently . . . about economic dangers that result when large companies acquire other companies in unrelated industries. To me, however, the real danger—and the danger in any corporation whose top management is remote and must impose consistent business practices on the local resources it controls—is not economic. It's the danger of becoming faceless and compassionless—of being too removed to act and too isolated to understand.

At Fairfield University, Conn./
The Wall Street Journal, 1–12:10.

There's no doubt in my mind that the effectiveness—both economic and social—of corporations in the 1970s will be directly related to how much freedom of decision they allow their own people at the point which most intimately feels the impact of that decision.

Quote, 2–8:126.

William M. McCulloch
United States Representative, R-Ohio

There is some convincing evidence that some of the conglomerate mergers have been motivated not by the desire to provide the consumer with a better product at a lower price, but by a greed for gold embodied in financial machinations which have proved detrimental to the shareholders of the companies involved, as well as the public at large.

Before House antitrust subcommittee,
Washington, Jan. 28/Los Angeles Times,
1–29:(3)10.

Neil H. McElroy
Chairman, Procter & Gamble Company

There is no question that government has to be a factor in our economy. Those who believe in the free enterprise system hope that government participation can be kept at a minimum so that a maximum of independent decisions can be made by the business community . . . On the other hand, I do feel this country has made an incredible prosperity for its people by leaving the maximum number of decisions not just to management of companies, but to individuals as individuals. And the further you restrict this, the more you change the entire character of our society.

Interview, Cincinnati/Nation's Business,
Aug.:62

Richard W. McLaren
Assistant Attorney General, Antitrust
Division, Department of Justice of the
United States

We have never been trying to close off mergers completely. One of the incentives for a fellow to go out and build his own corporation and make a contribution, innovate, be a competitor, is the prospect of selling out some day. If you close off mergers entirely, you close off the possibility of selling out. To the extent that mergers involve smaller companies, I don't think this is a threat to the economy.

Interview, Washington/
The Christian Science Monitor, 1–29:10.

This is a no-win job. It is certainly not the place to make friends and influence people.

Interview, Washington/
The Christian Science Monitor, 1–29:10.

Charles W. V. Meares
Chairman,
New York Life Insurance Company

In the challenging days of tomorrow, businessmen will continue to be architects of change and improvement in our society. Their skill and experience as problem-solvers will more and more be brought to bear on our social, as well as our economic, dilemmas. Business achievement will come to be measured by the new criterion of how effectively it solves the multiple problems of an expanding and complex civilization. But if business and its leaders are to be successful in this new endeavor, they will depend, to an enormous degree, upon attracting to their ranks the most talented of our concerned young men and women. The rub, of course, is that these bright young people are apt to disturb us the most, because they vigorously challenge the status quo. Nevertheless, they are precisely the ones that we in business must enlist in our cause, for they possess that flexibility of mind which, particularly in the young, produces challenging and disturbing, but often worthwhile, new thoughts and new programs.

At President's Council, White Sulphur Springs,
W. Va./The Wall Street Journal, 12–3:14.

John N. Mitchell
Attorney General of the United States

There seems to be a long-standing tradition in Washington that says that the securities markets are not a proper subject for discussion. One reason for this tradition is this: Wall Street was once the habitat of men in silk hats and diamond stickpins, and no self-respecting political figure could afford to be associated with them. Another reason is this: Communist propaganda for a century has been depicting Wall Street as the nerve center for all warmongering ... With 28 million American stockholders affected by the market, a government that is compassionate about unemployment must also be concerned about "uninvestment." And with peace the most bullish element in the market of our times, the myth of the Wall Street

warmonger has been exploded forever. Wi[th]
no disrespect intended to the symbol of t[he]
Soviets, war is obviously bearish.

Cleveland, Miss., May 1
U.S. News & World Report, 6–1:.

Ralph Nader
Lawyer; Consumer rights advocate

The government is basically controlled [by]
the industries which it purports to regulate[.]

News conference, Dallas, Jan. 3
The Dallas Times Herald, 1–30:A

For generations, the Interstate Commer[ce]
Commission has operated as a shield pr[o]
tecting and preserving economic grou[ps]
from the discipline of the marketplace.

The Dallas Times Herald, 3–16:A

Nothing short of a Federal investigatio[n]
can begin to disclose the abuses which hav[e]
woven a fine web of mutually implicating r[e]
lationships between businessmen and go[v]
ernment officials.

The Dallas Times Herald, 8–10:A

Big business almost systematically refus[es]
to document its wide-ranging claims. Hu[n]
dreds of millions of dollars are used, not t[o]
inform the consumer, but to deceive ...
undermines the cornerstone of the marke[t]
which is intelligent consumer-buying, so th[e]
consumer can reward quality and reject th[e]
shoddy.

News conference, Washington, Dec. 1[1]
Los Angeles Times, 12–12(1)2

John E. O'Toole
President, Foote, Cone & Belding

(Advertising) agencies have, more ofte[n]
than not, allowed the personality of th[e]
brand to derive not from the distilled essenc[e]
of what the brand is, but from the person[al]
life-style of the copywriter or the last mov[ie]
the art director saw—or sometimes from th[e]
image the agency itself wants to project fo[r]
new business purposes. Or sometimes fro[m]
nothing at all except a demented compu[ter]

on to be "with it"—which inevitably in-
olves expressionless teenyboppers wriggling
o expressionless music. The same teenybop-
ers, I swear, in everybody's commercials.
There's the unique personality?

*Before American Association of Advertising
Agencies, White Sulphur Springs, W. Va./
Los Angeles Times, 4–27:(3)10.*

Wright Patman
United States Representative, D-Tex.

It is as clear today as it was in the wake of
the great depression that the business of
anking should be exclusively banking. It
could be firmly separated from non-banking
enterprises. The banks have a lucr ve fran-
hise in their loan-making powers, and these
owers should be used to promote competi-
ve enterprise and not to stifle it. Surely, no
ne denies that the banks have tremendous
ower and influence. What public good is
rved by allowing the one-bank holding
ompany devices to extend this power into
very corner of American business? What
ublic good is served by expanding the
ower of Chase Manhattan . . . the Bank of
merica, the Continental Illinois National
ank, or any of the other banking giants?
What public good is served by extending the
ower and the influence of a David Rocke-
ller (chairman of Chase Manhattan) over
merican life?

*Before directors, National Association of
Insurance Agents, Dallas, April 28/
Vital Speeches, 6–15:525.*

Peter G. Peterson
Chairman, Bell & Howell Company

It seems to me that one of the most con-
picuous trends in our society today is the
desire and demand for openness, particular-
' by the young. All institutions—political,
ducational and business—are facing an in-
reasing credibility gap and are under pres-
ure to communicate with their publics more
penly, more simply and more humanely. I
hink the demand for candor is, on the
hole, a good, if occasionally a painful,
hing for a company. Candor forces the com-

pany to define its problems more precisely,
since it can't hide behind a lot of self-
defensive euphemisms that you know at least
as well as I—like "increased start-up costs"
instead of poor forecasting, "new product investments" instead of product mistakes and
losses, etc. Having defined its problems, the
company is more likely to attack them rationally and solve them. I feel this kind of
corporate honesty will pay off, both for the
individual company and for business as a
whole.

*At Bell & Howell annual meeting/
The Wall Street Journal, 7–3:4.*

Ronald Reagan
Governor of California

. . . in my country some 25 years ago, you
could make a long distance call on a privately owned telephone system from San Francisco to New York for $28. For that same
amount of money, you could send 1,376 letters. Today, you could make the same telephone call for two dollars and a half and for
that amount you can only send 41 letters. So
the government is investigating the Bell
System!

London/The Wall Street Journal, 2–19:16.

Donald T. Regan
*President,
Merrill Lynch, Pierce, Fenner & Smith*

It (Wall Street) is not just simply a place
where rich people trade pieces of paper for
fun and profit . . . Wall Street is the nation's
financial capital. The most significant thing
that happens there is that money in huge
amounts flows in, is reorganized, and flows
out again, redirected by investment bankers
to where it will do the most good . . . This
year, Wall Street will raise for American
corporations 25 billion dollars in capital by
the issuance of corporate bonds. State, city
and local governments will raise another 16
billion dollars for such things as sewers and
schools and roads. Government agencies will
go to the well for about 9.5 billion dollars.
And perhaps another 6 billion will be raised
by issuing common stock. So, through the

(DONALD T. REGAN)

Wall Street mechanism, in one way or another, some 57 billion dollars will be raised this year.

At National Press Club, Washington, Sept. 15/
U.S. News & World Report, 9–28:61.

Wall Street is hiding behind a protective pricing system, while it preaches free competition and free markets. That is like catching Carrie Nation tippling in the basement. We say that competition is good for everybody. We base our investment advice on the competitive stance of the company we are analyzing. The price of a stock is set by the forces operative in the marketplace. Yet we live as exceptions to our own rules.

Before Rotary Club, Dallas, Dec. 2/
The New York Times, 12–3:73.

James M. Roche
Chairman, General Motors Corporation

There is more to productivity than just quantity—quality is involved. Improved productivity is needed more than ever if America's automobile manufacturers are to meet the unprecedented new competition from overseas. Management continues willing to live up to its part of the improvement-factor clause. The vital question is: Are the unions and the individual employes willing to live up to their end? We must restore the balance that has been lost between wages and productivity. We must receive the fair day's work for which we pay the fair day's wage. Nothing less than the American future—the kind of country we will pass on to our children—is at stake.

St. Louis/National Observer, 3–2:8.

I suggest that the critics of our society consider for a moment that a worker in the U.S.S.R. must labor for approximately 40 months to earn the price of a typical Russian car, while here in the United States the average worker needs to work less than six months for a good U.S. automobile. Facts such as these are hard to refute. So, instead, our critics say that they are meaningless—

another mark of the decadence of our materialistic society. They say we attach a dollar sign to too many values, that we sacrifice cultural and spiritual values for material comforts and possessions. Industry is said to be engaged in a single-minded pursuit of profit, without due regard for social progress. I submit that profit and social progress go together and in our free economy are inseparable. The job of business is to provide the consumer with goods and services, with the most satisfaction at the lowest economic cost. To do this, business must innovate; it must grow, create more jobs, more opportunities. One overriding task of our times is to inculcate our young people with a firm belief in our free-enterprise system. We can hardly expect our system to survive for another generation if the coming generation does not believe in it. There is ample evidence that this is so. Doubt, disbelief, pessimism, skepticism and a cynical distrust are the intellectual fashions of the day. It is essential that we who believe in free enterprise advocate it to our young people. If our system is to survive, we desperately need their understanding, their belief, their support.

At 150th anniversary celebration of Oakland
County, Mich./The Wall Street Journal, 8–24:8.

David Rockefeller
President,
Chase Manhattan Bank, New York

In this decade of the seventies, corporations must bear the cost of social responsibility or the consequences of evading it.

Human Events, 5–2:11.

Nat S. Rogers
President, American Bankers Association

Banks are in the business of extending credit. To believe that any bank would jeopardize broad market areas in order to favor a subsidiary is to misconceive the nature of the banking business. Simply because a bank is part of a company which also has a leasing subsidiary or a data processing subsidiary, does not mean it would risk losing valuable customer relationships with independent firms by acts of favoritism or coercion, even if such were legally possible . . . I suggest that so long as we maintain a competitive financial system in which banks are full participants, the marketplace itself is a ruthless but fair preventive for the kinds of problems which are thrown up by the proponents of banking legislation.

Before Senate Banking Committee, Washington,
May 25 / The New York Times, 5–26:53.

John P. Saylor
United States Representative, R-Pa.

Of all the world's nations, Japan is the most active and aggressive exporter and the most carefully protective importer. At the same time she floods American markets with her goods, she has the most restrictive trade regulations to protect her own markets. Japan's restrictions on U.S. goods are tighter than on the goods from any other nation or group of nations in the world. In 1969, we received $540 million worth of textiles from Japan, while we sold only $15 million to her. By comparison, Japan bought far more from the less-developed countries, the European Economic Community and the European Free Trade Association than from the United States. The major reason why import competition from Japan is so damaging to the American economic system is the drastic wage gap between U.S. and Japanese wages. The typical American textile worker earns $2.43 an hour; his counterpart in Japan gets 53¢ per hour; and in Korea and Taiwan, the figure is 11¢ per hour . . . After all is said and done, what we are facing is competition from the sweat-shops of the Far East. I will not advocate that the American textile worker lower his standard of living to keep his job—but that is exactly what the free-traders are advocating.

Before the House, Washington, July 14 /
Congressional Record, 7–14:H6713.

Jean-Jacques Servan-Schreiber
Journalist;
Member, French National Assembly

From the radicalism of the young stems a deeply-felt conviction that a system which allows the excesses of economic competition to ride herd over social life is basically immoral. Herein lie the roots of rebellion, roots which cannot be eradicated by the elders in a fit of blind rage. Those who run the great multi-national corporations know the sincerity of their children's concern. They get it at the breakfast table every morning.

Before Senate Subcommittee on Foreign
Economic Policy, Washington /
The Christian Science Monitor, 8–7:2.

The ferociousness of competition among business enterprises is a locomotive of innovational development and enrichment. It must be given full play . . . The modern market economy, with its freedom of private initiative and the bracing energy of competition, is a powerful tool for material progress . . . but the main goal of politics is to prevent this ferociousness from hurting man himself.

Before Senate Subcommittee on Foreign
Economic Policy, Washington /
The Christian Science Monitor, 8–7:2.

Dan Seymour
President, J. Walter Thompson Company

Beyond the growth, the tremendous appeal of international business is in its day-to-day excitement. But beyond even that is a bigger lure: its possibilities as an area in which we can seriously contribute to a true and strong international unity . . . Let us make no mistake about it: It will be business that feeds the world, and de-pollutes the world, and works out the systems that will support life somehow among the fearsome mistakes the politicians make in each generation. It has to be business, because we all know governments really can't do much about anything.

Before International Advertising Association,
New York, June 9 / Vital Speeches, 9–1:680.

Edgar B. Speer
President, United States Steel Corporation

What we aren't doing is to make our

(EDGAR B. SPEER)

young people realize that the sale of a product does not just end with the sale of a physical item; rather, it fulfills a human need ... Unless we make our youth cognizant of the role of business in society, we have lost our youth. And when you lose your youth, you lose your future.

Houston/Quote, 6–28:617.

Howard Stein
President, Dreyfus Fund

The big issue is whether the financial community in general, and the stock exchanges in particular, are going to remain "clubs." We have to open them up, encourage new blood and turn them into institutions that respond to public needs.

Interview, New York/Time, 8-24:55.

Peter Tennant
Director general,
British National Export Council

World trade is indivisible, and whoever the (proposed American protectionist trade) bill may be designed not to hit, there is no doubt that it will hit us all. This bill invites retaliation the moment it has the Presidential assent, and retaliation in a form which many Congressmen and a great many American industrialists will regret ... At a time when America is trying to increase her surplus on visible trade to relieve pressure on the dollar, it seems crazy to pass protectionist legislation which will invite those hit by the curbs to retaliate. Europe is far less dependent on imports of food, oil or raw materials from the United States than she used to be. She could manage without importing many of the manufactured goods she currently buys from the United States.

Before American Chamber of Commerce,
London, Nov. 19/The New York Times,
11–20:26.

Sam Thurm
Vice president for advertising, Lever
Brothers Company; Chairman, American
Advertising Federation

As their assumptions reveal, the critics advertising think the consumer is an idi They think we think so, too. And th visualize us as itinerant merchants wi pushcarts, or proprietors of elaborate me cine shows taking the rubes for as mu money as we can get, and moving on, nev to be seen again. On the contrary, we rely the consumer's intelligence to listen, to co pare, to be convinced by our best argumen We rely on his or her interest in new pr ducts, new benefits, new ways of puttir goods to use, to profit and to enjoyment.

Washington, Feb. 2/The New York Tim
2–4:

Robert C. Townsend
Former president, Avis Rent-a-Car

I hate conglomerates. Excellence and s are fundamentally incompatible.

Interview/Newsweek, 3–2:

Jane Trahey
President, Trahey-Wolff Advertising;
Advertising Woman of the Year

Nudity in advertising? What's that? We still retouching belly buttons for *The Ne York Times* and *The New Yorker*.

Interview, Los Angeles/Los Angeles Tim
2–25:(4

Caspar W. Weinberger
Chairman, Federal Trade Commission

... I think the best consumer protectic of all would be done by self-policing, se regulated programs that would elimina the need for any government action, becau they would be based on a recognition business of the desirability and improv profits available in products that did not quire any recalls or produce demands f increased government regulation.

Interview, Washingto
Nation's Business, April:

Some are telling us at the Federal Trade Commission that it is anti-business for us to push consumer protection and quality control. My feeling is that this program will help business on the basis of that old copybook maxim, "Honesty is the best policy."

Before Mass Retailing Institute, Washington, May 13 / The New York Times, 5–14:57.

Walter H. Wheeler

Chairman, executive committee, Pitney-Bowes, Inc.

The really top business executive is a totally different breed of cat inside than a lot of junior executives, boys down the line, and the general public think he is. He is often a quiet-spoken fellow, an unassuming kind of fellow. I've gotten a good deal of help, I think, from some talks I had years ago with Walter Gifford, who was president of AT&T. I remember he told me that one of the hardest jobs he had—any top executive had—was to find men with a good balance of mind and morals. The experts are a dime a dozen. But to get a well-balanced human being who has imagination, but a lot of human common sense with it, who doesn't kid himself, put on a lot of airs or go off half-cocked and is persevering, is very difficult.

Interview / Nation's Business, Feb.:78.

Harold M. Williams

Chairman, Norton Simon, Inc.

Too often, business has appeared inani-

mate; it's appeared to be above being human. Instead of obfuscating its problems, American business should be willing to show its human strengths and weaknesses . . . My thesis is that the choice being faced by business is not to do or not to do, but to do or have done to it.

Interview, Los Angeles / Los Angeles Times, 5–24:I1.

Woodrow Wirsig

President, Better Business Bureau of Metropolitan New York

An atmosphere of suspicion and hostility toward business has been fostered without establishing any sound reason. (It is a false assumption that) consumers are helpless, ignorant, constantly in need of protection they don't have. It is a false assumption that the consumer has the unquestioned, unqualified right to instant perfection in the market place.

At "Consumerism and Its Impact on Corporate Profits" conference, New York, Feb. 17 / The Washington Post, 2–19:C5.

If we had tried to get to the moon with as little scientific method as we presently apply to consumer affairs in this country, we would still be sputtering on the ground.

Before Better Business Bureau of Scranton, Pa. / The Dallas Times Herald, 9–16:A2.

Crime

Spiro T. Agnew
Vice President of the United States

The working people of this country are outraged about crime and violence in their streets and parks. President Nixon has sent to Congress 13 pieces of legislation to deal with the crime crisis, and Congress has not sent back a single one. If the President doesn't get his legislation, then the people ought to get themselves a new Congress.

Lincoln Day address, St. Louis, Feb. 10/
Human Events, 3–7:19.

Whenever the President or I raise the anticrime issue, the chorus comes back from Capitol Hill: "The Nixon Administration wants repression." Well, that's either slander or stupidity. No citizen who respects the law need fear anything from this government. No Administration is more committed to the civil rights of every American. But the President's definition of civil rights encompasses the right of black Americans to be secure in the central city, the right of small businessmen to be free of violence at the hands of drug addicts and the right of women to be free to walk the streets and parks without being attacked or molested by hoodlums and thugs. Clearly, those civil rights are not going to be restored until we get a new Congress that cares about law and order.

Time, 9–21:15.

Myrl E. Alexander
Former Director,
United States Bureau of Prisons

Revamping the (prison) system is going to cost a lot of money. But the people we're turning out of prisons are costing us a lot more.

Time, 3–2:66.

Saul Alinsky
Sociologist

What I think we're going to see, finally, is black (police) officers in the ghettos; and it will happen, because white officers no longer want to go there. Know what I think will happen then? The black officers will get shot, too. The killing will go on until the large elements of the black community have had it, as far as crime among themselves is concerned.

Interview, Chicago/
San Francisco Examiner & Chronicle, 9–13:B12.

Raymond Aron
Professor of Faculty Letters,
Paris University

You (the United States) are a violent country with an extraordinary attachment to legal niceties. In most of the detective novels of America that I have read, the police know who the criminal is but can't do anything about locking him up. We don't understand how your criminals can go in and out of prison so many times. I am bewildered that you can identify every member of the Mafia, and they still continue to go about their business. It is well and good to have a system that protects the innocent, but surely there must be something wrong with a system that also protects the criminal.

Interview, Paris/
The New York Times Magazine, 4–19:97.

Julian Bond
Georgia State Legislator

If the provisions of the inane Washington, D.C., "no-knock law" are any indication of what is in store for us in the future, and if the gate-mouthed Maryland farmer who presides over the Senate (Vice President Agnew) is to continue his rantings in concert with the little tyrant who runs the FBI (J. Edgar Hoover), then we must prepare for a time of trouble.

Before Philadelphia Bar Association, Atlantic City, N.J., Sept. 11 | The New York Times, 9–12:3.

Paul L. Briand, Jr.
Professor of English, State University of New York at Oswego

America was born in violence, she lives in violence, and—unless she heeds the problems which beset her at home—she will die in violence. Crimes of violence in America will double in 1972—the rate is nine times faster than the growth of population. More crime is committed in New York City than in England, Wales and Scotland combined. In 1968, serious crimes in America totalled 9,-000,000. America loves violence. It *is* as American as apple pie and the corner drugstore. The cult of the gun, epitomized in our mythic hero, the western cowboy, and in his city cousin, the private eye, best explains, perhaps, our firm and ingrained belief in violence as the quickest and easiest way to solve our problems.

At S.U.N.Y. convocation, July 8 | Quote, 12–27:613.

Warren E. Burger
Chief Justice of the United States

Do you know, or can you conceive, of an industrial enterprise involving 200,000 employees which turns out a critical product, which would use 50 to 150-year-old plants, equipment and techniques, no research, low pay and little or no training for its production workers, no long-range planning, no concern for its output or quality control? These questions answer themselves. Yet, with notable exceptions in a few of the states and the Federal system, this is a description of the process we use to deal with . . . 200,-000 prisoners. Is it any wonder that we find a grim and distressing "recall" of 65% of the human output of these prisons "back to the factory"? This is a true pollution of society, and it manifests itself in the highest crime

rate in our 200 years of existence, with most crimes being committed by "graduates" from these penal institutions.

Before Association of the Bar of the City of New York, Feb. 17 | Vital Speeches, 3–15:324.

We take on a burden when we put a man behind walls, and that burden is to give him a chance to change. If we deny him that, we deny his status as a human being, and to deny that is to diminish our humanity and plant the seeds of future anguish for ourselves . . . When a sheriff or a marshal takes a man from a courthouse in a prison van and transports him to confinement for two or three or ten years, this is our act. We have tolled the bell for him. And whether we like it or not, we have made him our collective responsibility. We are free to do something about him; he's not.

Before Association of the Bar of the City of New York, Feb. 17 | The New York Times, 2–18:16.

To put a person behind (prison) walls and not change him is to win a battle and lose a war.

Before Association of the Bar of the City of New York, Feb. 17 | Quote, 5–3:412.

A visit to most prisons will make one a zealot for reform.

San Francisco Examiner & Chronicle (This World), 4–19:3.

. . . the correctional system at the third stage of justice is at least as important as the police at the first stage and the courts at the center.

At National Governors Conference, Lake of the Ozarks, Mo., Aug. 12 | Chicago Daily News, 8–12:19.

Robert C. Byrd
United States Senator, D-W. Va.

Washington, D. C., has become the mecca of the rapist, the mugger, the robber and the

(ROBERT C. BYRD)

thief—a veritable jungle of fear and crime and violence.

U. S. News & World Report, 8–3:59.

Bill Chappell, Jr.
United States Representative, D-Fla.

Many shirk their responsibility for the crime rise by "scapegoating" the police and other law enforcement officers. But I believe all responsible will agree that the accusing finger has been pointed at our nation's law enforcement officers too long. It is the local law enforcement officer who stands between the law-abiding citizen and the criminal, between the looter and the shopkeeper, between the child and the molester, between the Students for a Democratic Society and the targets of their storm-trooper tactics, between anarchy and violence and the peace and security of the United States. And too often he has stood alone.

Before Kiwanis and Rotary Clubs, Ocala, Fla.,
March 30/Vital Speeches, 5–1:425.

Too often . . . we find people looking to the Federal government as a cure-all for their problems. Even now, there are those who are suggesting a Federal law enforcement system. We hope no American really wants this, for only local law enforcement can be both creative and flexible enough to respond to the particular needs of a community. None of us want a Federal police.

Before Kiwanis and Rotary Clubs, Ocala, Fla.,
March 30/Vital Speeches, 5–1:425.

Ramsey Clark
Former Attorney General of the United States

If an investigator has to be anything, he has to be a disenthralled observer, a hard, hard pursuer of facts. He cannot be ideological. For reasons that are unfortunate, in my judgment, the FBI became ideological some time back. This has put scales over its eyes.

New York, Nov. 17/The Washington Post,
11–18:A3.

Tom Clark
Former Associate Justice, Supreme Court of the United States

(There must be) more than just a get tough policy (to deal with crime). We have tried increasing penalties—take narcotics and prohibition—and found it didn't deter any. Crime has to do with the economy and the community in which a person is reared . . . Before we cut crime, we're going to have to start changing the atmosphere that produces it.

Interview, Washington/
The Dallas Times Herald, 7–31:A

William Clifford
Special adviser to the United Nations on social problems

You can almost tell how highly-developed a country is by looking at its crime rate. It a very new idea—that, as we develop economically, we are creating our crime, rather in the same way we create air and water pollution.

At United Nations Congress on Prevention of
Crime and Treatment of Offenders, Kyoto,
Japan/Milwaukee Journal, 8–24:1

Lloyd N. Cutler
Executive director, National Commission on Violence

Police, courts and corrections, and the various professional personnel associated with these agencies, all cope with crime largely in isolation from one another and from radically different perspectives. Not only are the several components of the criminal-justice process often ineffective and poorly administered, but the whole process, for lack of appropriate coordinating structures and procedures, is less than the sum of its parts.

New York/The Christian Science Monitor,
5–8:1

Roger O. Egeberg
Assistant Secretary for Health and Scientific Affairs, Department of Health, Education and Welfare of the United States

We must take into account in legislation

easures the critical distinction between the ldict who sells drugs for support of his abit and the calculating exploiter who is in e illicit drug business for its immense rofits.

Washington, March 2/
Los Angeles Herald-Examiner, 3–3:A5.

m J. Ervin, Jr.
nited States Senator, D-N.C.

Preventive-detention legislation convicts dividuals of "probable" guilt and "danerousness," and sentences them to 60 days' nprisonment without trial and conviction. ich flagrant violation of due process smacks a police state rather than a democracy nder law.

Before Senate Subcommittee on
Constitutional Rights, Washington/
National Observer, 6–1:2.

I hear the siren voice of that old devil, olitical expediency, whisper in my ear, You better vote for the D.C. (crime) bill ecause it's a law-and-order bill. It's not potically sagacious, not politically wise, to te against a law-and-order bill."

San Francisco Examiner & Chronicle
(This World), 8–2:8.

American patriots died in the flames for e privilege of having their homes regarded their castles. They died in the flames of e Revolution to secure the right which e prophet Micah called the right to sit nder their own fig trees, where none could ake them afraid. Yet, we see their descenants asking that we legitimize something hich was so bad in the eyes of our ancestors at they rebelled against the mother coun-y and obtained their freedom in order to cape from such tyranny. Now, we have the resident of the United States and the Deartment of Justice urging that this tyranny e given the sanction of Congress, in the rm of the District of Columbia crime bill.

Before the Senate, Washington/
The New York Times Magazine, 11–15:107.

Stanford Felder
City editor, Washington "Daily News"

Crime is the obsession of this city. It can control where people live, where they shop, how late they stay out, what friends they visit, what restaurants they frequent.

Newsweek, 1–12:19.

John Heffernan
Vice president, International Conference of Police Associations

There are cobwebs on the electric chair because judges and juries are listening to bleeding hearts. There's too much due process of law.

Daily World, 7–24:7.

J. Edgar Hoover
Director, Federal Bureau of Investigation

I still believe that punishment is a deterrent. Where a serious crime has been committed, a substantial sentence should be imposed.

Interview, Nov. 16/
The Washington Post, 11–17:A1.

I have been accused of opposing parole and probation. I'm heartily in favor of them. But I am vigorously opposed to the abuse of parole and probation. The bleeding hearts on parole boards ought to be a little tougher.

Interview/Time, 12–14:16.

Leon Jaworski
Lawyer; Former head, Committee on Crime Prevention and Control, American Bar Association

The one condition that needs remedying more than any other is the congestion that now prevails in so many courts. I believe there is no deterrent to crime more effective than speedy trial and sentencing. Now, I'm not for a moment suggesting that there be any rights denied to the accused. I strongly insist that all constitutional rights be strictly observed. But when you find a person arrested and then waiting perhaps a year or two, as is often the case, before he's brought

(LEON JAWORSKI)

to trial, you have these results: If he's innocent, you have subjected an accused who couldn't get out on bail to languishing in jail all that time. The chances are that he will not be as good a citizen when he gets out. If he was guilty, again having to languish that long, the chances for his rehabilitation are less. Most jails do not have a rehabilitation program. Then, the very fact that he has been kept in jail that long awaiting trial causes a very definite deterrent insofar as effective prosecution is concerned. Often, the witnesses and some of the evidence are no longer available. Another factor: When those who are inclined toward crime realize that they are going to be faced with speedy trials and with speedy justice, they will not be as likely to yield to the temptation of crime. We should learn from the experience of England, where the interval between arrest and trial is short and the crime rate low compared with ours.

Interview/U.S. News & World Report, 7-20:41.

Richard G. Kleindienst
Deputy Attorney General of the United States

The crime rate will be reduced when the offenders who are apprehended are processed without delay. When nine to twelve months elapse between arrest and trial because of choked and crowded courts, swift, sure justice is an idle pipedream. Crime will not be deterred by protracted proceedings; it will not be deterred by backlogs and delays.

Before American Trial Lawyers Association, Freeport, Bahamas, Jan. 30/ Vital Speeches, 4-1:355.

John V. Lindsay
Mayor of New York

Reliance on terror is one kind of dangerous response to a troubled time. There is another kind of response—equally false, but more dangerous. And that is the turn toward

repression, toward repudiation of our rights and liberties—a turn supported by some in the highest levels of power. Either out of ignorance or out of calculated political cynicism, our citizens are being told that crime will stop if we erase the Bill of Rights . . .

San Francisco Examiner & Chronicle (This World), 4-12:2.

While Houston can talk to the moon, police stations often cannot talk to a patrolman a few blocks away. A missile can span continents in 30 minutes, but it takes St. Louis days to trace a fingerprint from Chicago. We have developed sophisticated and expensive equipment to sense an enemy in an Asian swamp, but a housing policeman in Newark lacks even a simple television monitor to check the hallways he must walk alone. The real victims of all this are the men and women and children who have placed their trust in someone else to enforce the law. That trust is precious. We are on the verge of losing it. And the real villain is our nation's priorities. $80 billion are spent for defense and war abroad, but less than $500 million are earmarked for safety in our streets at home.

Before American Bar Association, St. Louis, Aug. 12/Milwaukee Journal, 8-13:16.

Law-and-order works when you open a new narcotics center in New York City; when you hire more policemen in Los Angeles; when you computerize court calendars in Pittsburgh. It's not as dramatic as talking tough. It may not be good political gamesmanship. But tedious, systematic, nuts-and-bolts work is the only way to re-build criminal justice.

Before American Bar Association, St. Louis, Aug. 12/Time, 8-24:29.

The criminal offender usually does his time in a prison that is a school for crime. He is finally released with nothing more than a free bus ride back to the slum he came from.

It is almost assured that he will return to a life against the law.

*Before American Bar Association, St. Louis,
Aug. 12/The Washington Post, 8–18:A16.*

Oliver Lofton
*Associate Director, Community Relations
Service, Department of Justice of the United
States*

. . . I . . . wish there was a way, a panacea for eliminating the spectre of organized crime from our nation. There is a way, but I am not so sure it could be called a panacea. It might start in the courtroom with judges who would have become so sensitive to the dispensing of justice that when the known generals or lieutenants of organized crime are convicted for tax evasion, instead of receiving the minimum sentence, they receive a sentence that would more realistically reflect society's abhorrence with the enormity of their participation in the pollution of our American way of life. For mark me well— unless we begin to show some measurable successes in relieving the stranglehold of organized crime in our ghettos, 10 years from now we may well find that the prediction of organized crime—that it will one day put a man in the White House—has indeed come true.

*Before Organized Crime Training Conference,
University of Oklahoma Center for Continuing
Education, March 5/Congressional Record,
5–4:H3847.*

Allard K. Lowenstein
United States Representative, D-N.Y.

There is a difference between ordinary citizens violating the law and law-enforcement officials violating the law. What ends constitutional government and jeopardizes freedom most is when agencies charged with upholding the law break it.

Look, 8–25:38.

Crawford Martin
Attorney General of Texas

Our laws are really not written to combat an organized criminal underworld. Our whole philosophy of law, of constitutional safeguards for the defendant, is designed for the individual criminal and not designed to cope with the existence of an underworld set up on a corporate basis. It's like trying to get at the corporation president by arresting the janitor.

*Austin, Nov. 9/
The Dallas Times Herald, 11–10:A8.*

William H. McGlothlin
*Department of Psychology, University of
California at Los Angeles*

If marijuana were to suddenly replace alcohol as the socially-approved intoxicant, I would predict, with a high degree of confidence, that crimes of violence would be significantly reduced.

Los Angeles Times, 2–5:(2)7.

John Misterly
Sheriff, Sacramento County, Calif.

I have been responsible for eliminating the Hell's Angels, the Mafia, organized prostitution, organized gambling, topless and bottomless joints and pornography stores. I have controlled the hippies and have waged constant war on narcotic use and juvenile delinquency. Sacramento County is one of the cleanest counties, as far as crime is concerned, that we have. And one of the reasons is . . . that we keep the pressure on.

Sacramento/Los Angeles Times, 2–20:(1)7.

John N. Mitchell
Attorney General of the United States

Public officials at every level—and the public itself—must be prepared to expend large sums if they really are serious about controlling crime. There can be no real progress in any important area of our national life—no progress for anybody—if crime continues to grow unchecked.

*Washington, Jan. 18/Los Angeles Times,
1–19:(1)5.*

. . . I believe that there has been a steady, if all too slow, progress and understanding among the police forces of this country as to

(JOHN N. MITCHELL)

the problems of the minority groups, and there have been at least attempted better police relations. And this is something that I strongly advocate, so that when the policeman goes into a minority-group area with his cruiser, it is not an invading army; it is somebody that has some rapport, and is in there to carry out his proper functions.

Interview, Washington/
Los Angeles Herald-Examiner, 1–25:A14.

A direct grant program to the cities would make Washington a dictator over every anti-crime project in the country. It would also, by necessity, spawn an enormous Federal bueaucracy to evaluate these programs and would undermine the whole concept of a Federal-state cooperative partnership which this Administration is attempting to establish in the anticrime area and in other areas of social progress.

Before National League of Cities, Washington,
March 9/The New York Times, 3–10:21.

The Attorney General must personally approve each wiretap or bugging order issued by the Federal government. If whoever sits in this chair exercises that power with restraint, I don't feel we are going to invade the privacy of anybody whose privacy shouldn't be invaded . . . From what I see, not using it is like fighting with one hand tied behind your back. Organized crime is big business. They are very resourceful people. It is awfully hard to get informants within their setups. They are clever in the cover-ups of their activities. But they have to use telephones.

Interview, Washington/
Nation's Business, June:37.

Unfortunately, the serious and critical subject of wiretapping is charged with emotion and prejudice. The term "wiretap" triggers in many people all manner of bogeys —flagrant invasion of privacy, thought control and, to use a word you and I have heard

lately, repression. Well, in reviewing our u of wiretapping in the last year-and-a-half, think you'll agree that the only repressic that has resulted is the repression of crime.

Before International Association
Chiefs of Police, Atlantic City, N.
Oct. 5/Vital Speeches, 11–1:3

Robert M. Morgenthau
Former United States Attorney for the
Southern District of New York

It would be unfortunate indeed if the A ministration's war on crime were ever to l viewed as solely a war on the crimes of tl poor and underprivileged. We cannot expe the millions of these honest Americans . . to pay taxes without question if their gover ment is willing to overlook the fraud of the wealthy and powerful citizens who disco ered in foreign bank secrecy an almost total secure means by which to evade taxes.

Before House Banking and Curren
Committee, Washingto
The Wall Street Journal, 2–17:1

Daniel P. Moynihan
Counsellor to the
President of the United States

If you want to get rid of crime, get rid poverty and racial isolation. And don't k yourself—the correlation is absolute.

U.S. News & World Report, 3–16:1

Patrick V. Murphy
Police Commissioner, City of New York

As we motorized our policeman during tl past quarter of a century, we gave him m bility and the possibility to respond rapid to the call for help. However, we have i personalized police service as a result. ! many citizens see the policeman as a fellc riding by quickly in the car. We must c more about getting that man—who needs tl car and the radio—in closer contact with tl citizens.

Interview/Man in Office, WNBC-T
New York, 11–

We (the police) have nothing to do wi the conviction and sentencing of those :

sted and placed on trial. If we were totally
icient in solving all cases and brought in
ch perfect cases that there was a 100% con-
ction rate, we still wouldn't be solving the
oblem. Ninety-nine out of 100 who go to
ison come out. And if they haven't been
formed, then we are up against the wall.

Interview, New York/
Los Angeles Times, 12–2:(6)13.

In the span of history, it was only yester-
y that shotguns rode the horse-drawn
hicles and every householder was armed.
ne stagecoach has disappeared, but the
adly firearm is still with us, with an esti-
ated hundred million guns in the hands of
ivate citizens ... Under the deceptive guise
freedom and the belief that citizens must
armed to resist tyranny, the American
ople tolerate and abet assault, robbery,
urder and street crimes at gunpoint. If this
freedom in its finest form, it is also free-
m in its final hour.

Before National Association of Citizens
Crime Commissions, Washington/
National Observer, 12–14:14.

chard M. Nixon
esident of the United States

We have heard a great deal of overblown
etoric during the sixties in which the word
var" has perhaps too often been used—the
r on poverty, the war on misery, the war
disease, the war on hunger. If there is one
ea where the word "war" is appropriate, it
in the fight against crime. We must declare
d win the war against the criminal ele-
ents which increasingly threaten our cities,
r homes and our lives.

State of the Union address, Washington,
Jan. 22/Los Angeles Times, 1–23:(1)20.

The major failure of this Congress has
en its failure to act on any of these (anti-
me) bills. Partisanship is no excuse ...
ime, respect for law, dealing with crime—
ese are issues that are above partisan poli-
s, and I think it is time for Congress to get

off the dead center on which it presently has
been operating, to get these bills out of committee, to give the members of the House
and Senate a chance to operate and get them
down here on the President's desk for signature.

Washington, June 11/
Los Angeles Times, 6–12:(1)10.

Here they are (the police), underpaid, in a
dangerous job, protecting us; and instead of
calling them pigs and spitting on them and
shouting profane slogans at them as they go
about their jobs, let's give them respect. We
may not be able to pay our police as much
as their hazardous duty requires; but we can
all give them (the) respect and backing that
they should have, the backing for justice, for
fairness and for the hard work that all of
them are engaged in in our behalf.

Kansas City, Oct. 20/
The Washington Post, 10–21:A1.

William H. Rehnquist
Assistant Attorney General
of the United States

(Former Attorney General) Ramsey Clark
was an outspoken advocate of the civil liberties of the individual, and the rights of the
criminal defendant. Many agreed with him;
many disagreed with him. John Mitchell,
from his position as (current) Attorney General, chooses to place more emphasis on the
right of society to apprehend and punish
those guilty of crime. Many agree with him,
and many disagree with him. These points
of view are, basically, two sides of the same
coin; and just as Ramsey Clark would not
have advocated the wholesale freeing of
criminal defendants on technicalities, neither would John Mitchell advocate the
wholesale incarceration of criminal defendants regardless of violations of their constitutional rights. The matter is one of emphasis and degree, not of black and white.

At University of Arizona/
Los Angeles Times, 5–3:F3.

William B. Saxbe
United States Senator, R-Ohio

The only way to prevent this kind of blackmail (political kidnaping) is to make it a Federal offense for anyone (in government) to accede to this kind of thing. For example, if I am picked up—and I certainly haven't been threatened—and they write in and tell some government official, "If you don't release so-and-so we're going to kill Saxbe," I think if that official turns that criminal loose, he ought to be prosecuted.

Interview/The Dallas Times Herald,
10–15:A1.

Danny Thomas
Actor

Always in my heart and mind has been what can I do for that public servant (the police officer) who stands so defenseless, who, on a simple misdemeanor, gives his life to some idiot, some nut . . . who hates the country, hates the flag . . . It wouldn't have happened in my day. We were brought up by men, not imitations of men. The law enforcement officer is a human being. He's not a member of some subversive organization. He's not a member of the Gestapo.

Los Angeles, May 15/
Los Angeles Herald-Examiner, 5–15:A2.

Earl Warren
Former Chief Justice of the United States

In searching for means to reduce crime, the full responsibility should not be put upon any one or all of the law-enforcement agencies. The police, the prosecutors, the lawyers and the courts have great burdens to carry in this field, but they cannot be justly charged with all the conditions that bring crime to such gigantic proportions. They are not responsible for the ignorance, the poverty, the disease, the degradation or the racial tensions which exist in the ghettos, nor the millions of drunks and alcoholics who contribute so much to crime. Certainly, they cannot be faulted for the debasement of the stage and screen nor the appetite of the public for the pornography and sadism which is so pervasive in both forms of entertainment. Neither can they be held responsible for the aura of violence which has been fed by war through the past quarter of a century. They cannot be accountable for the failure of citizens to report crime or to give testimony concerning it. These are things that society in general has responsibility for. We hear much these days about the necessity for cooling off the economy to stop inflation. It is about time that we take steps to cool off society if the law-enforcement officers of the nation are to be expected to stop the inflation of crime.

At Milton S. Eisenhower Symposium,
Baltimore, Nov. 13/The Washington Post,
11–19:A18.

It is my firm belief that organized crime can never exist to any marked degree in any large community unless one or more of the law-enforcement agencies have been corrupted. This is a harsh statement; but I know that close scrutiny of conditions wherever such crime exists will show that it is protected.

At Johns Hopkins University, Nov. 13/
The New York Times, 11–15:(1)28.

Edward Bennett Williams
Lawyer

. . . there is a lot of talk that the decisions out of the old Warren Court were too liberal, were too soft on the criminal; but I think that this is really not addressing one's attention to the real problem. Because I could take you tonight to the precinct stations in the inner city and we could sit there all evening. We could sit there for weeks. And of all the kids who are brought in off the street under arrest for doing their mischief, you wouldn't find one kid who ever heard of the Mallory case or the Mapp case or the Escobedo case or the Miranda case. You wouldn't find one kid who gave one fleeting thought to his constitutional rights or criminal procedures before he went out in the streets to do his crime. They go out on the premise that they aren't going to be caught, and the record shows that they're pretty much right. The odds are overwhelmingly with them that they aren't going to be caught.

*Television interview, Washington, Feb. 15/
U.S. News & World Report, 3–16:20.*

The greatest deterrent to crime in the street is a visible policeman.

*Television interview, Washington, Feb. 15/
U.S. News & World Report, 3–16:20.*

We don't have enough police. We don't pay them enough. We expect so much of them now. We expect our policemen to be professionals—we should treat them like professionals. We expect them to know the law. We expect them to know first aid. We expect them to be family counselors. We expect them to be sociologists. We expect them to have the wisdom of Job—the wisdom of Solomon and the patience of Job—the agility of a Jim Brown, and we give them $150 a week and a gun.

*Television interview, Washington, Feb. 15/
U.S. News & World Report, 3–16:21.*

Wiretapping isn't going to solve many robberies, burglaries and larcenies. The "no-knock" procedure recently approved by Congress for Washington, D.C., would permit law-enforcement officers to break into premises without notice for certain reasons—but this isn't going to solve the crime problem. And "preventive detention," which denies bail to "dangerous" persons accused of crime, is not going to stop crime.

*Interview, Washington/
U.S. News & World Report, 9–21:96.*

To advocate the overturning of Supreme Court decisions and to seek adoption of wiretapping and eavesdropping legislation, "no-knock" entries by the police, preventive detention and other infringements on traditional civil liberties as a means of stemming the rising crime rate is like prescribing Bayer aspirin for a brain tumor.

*Before State Bar of California, Los Angeles/
Los Angeles Times, 9–27:G2.*

Will R. Wilson
*Assistant Attorney General,
Criminal Division, Department of
Justice of the United States*

If we are able to keep the public support and the budgetary support that we now have, and if we don't have some national emergency to divert attention, we can break the rackets—and we will break them.

Plainview (Tex.) Daily Herald, 2–25:6.

Stephen M. Young
United States Senator, D-Ohio

I disagree with the Administration over why the crime rate is coming down in Washington, D.C. People are locking themselves up at night. There's not as many muggees to be mugged.

*Interview, Washington/
Los Angeles Times, 8–13:(1A)4.*

Education

Ruth M. Adams
President, Wellesley College

. . . the woman's college will have instability in maintaining identity, but it will survive. The instability in the woman's college is largely due to the fact that the high school junior or senior indicates that she's interested first in a coeducational institution. My opinion is that there are still many young women who still appreciate the unique factors of self-realization that may be found in a woman's college. I sense a loss when I see a range of college choices for students diminished. Students aren't all alike; so the institutions shouldn't be, either.

Interview, Dallas /
The Dallas Times Herald, 10–20:B1.

Mortimer Adler
Author, Educator

The aim of schooling should be to make children learners. But our schools are trying to make children "learned"—to teach them facts—rather than learners, people who can continue to absorb information . . . The inertia of the school system is something it would take 10 Niagara Falls to move.

Los Angeles / Los Angeles Times, 12–15:(4)3.

Spiro T. Agnew
Vice President of the United States

For those who think that there should be ethnic quotas, or race quotas, or socio-economic class quotas in the admissions to colleges and universities, I would address this question: When next you are sick, do you wish to be attended by a physician who entered medical school to fill a quota or because of his medical aptitude? When next you travel by jet airplane, do you want to go in a plane designed by engineers selected to

fill a quota or by aptitude? When next you build a house, do you want an architect selected for architectural school by aptitude or by quota?

Lincoln Day address, Chicago, Feb. 12 /
Human Events, 3–7:18.

Let us support those courageous administrators, professors and students who are standing up for the traditional rights of the academic community. Can it be that within the faculty lounges there is also a Great Silent Majority?

Fort Lauderdale, Fla., April 28 /
Time, 5–11:20.

I do not feel that our traditional four-year institutions should lower their sights or their standards for the sole purpose of opening their doors wider . . . For each youth unprepared for a college curriculum who is brought in under a quota system, some better-prepared student is denied entrance. Admitting the obligation to compensate for past deprivation and discrimination, it just does not make sense to atone by discriminating against and depriving someone else. . .

Des Moines, April 13 /
U.S. News & World Report, 6–8:39.

James E. Allen, Jr.
Commissioner of Education
of the United States

Effective educational reform and renewal can hardly be expected in an educational enterprise that devotes less than one-half of one per cent of its annual budget to research and development . . . Education is no longer a nine-to-three operation or a college-campus operation. It is the entire environment . . . We need to seek a broader interpretation of education that discards rigid structuring for a free adaptation to differing needs, timing and goals—an interpretation that encompasses the total life and environment of the young.

Before American Association of School Administrators, Atlantic City, N.J., Feb. 14/ The Dallas Times Herald, 2–15:A4.

Of all the failures of our educational system, none is more indefensible than the failure to teach every child to read.

Before American Association of Colleges for Teacher Education, Chicago, Feb. 26/ The New York Times, 2–28:12.

When I ask people what they're *really* concerned about in education—whether I'm talking to a cab driver or a Senator—they invariably say it's reading, writing and arithmetic. With its innate wisdom, the American public understands that the first of the three Rs is basic.

Interview, Washington/Family Weekly, 3–15:6.

. . . the fact of inflation and tight fiscal policies cannot deny or mitigate the present urgent needs of education . . . Children cannot be placed in deep freeze to await more favorable educational or economic conditions. For them the time is now.

Before National Committee for Support of the Public Schools, Washington, March 24/ The Washington Post, 3–25:A2.

The public school system, by and large, has been geared to preparing people for college or general education. Those who are not going to college—and that is at least half of our high school graduates—are neglected in many school systems. Consequently, parents, the community, the school, all look upon vocational education as a lower-status kind of education. This needs to be corrected—by the educator's making it clear that he considers vocational education just as important as advanced liberal arts education. And we need to change Federal policy so that it places vocational education in the schools on a par with training for those who are unemployed or are dropouts . . . An investment in vocational education would yield a large return to society.

Interview, Washington/ Nation's Business, June:71.

James E. Allen, Jr.
Former Commissioner of Education of the United States

I am more than ever convinced that education should not be coupled with any other department of government and that it must have the separate status that allows for sharp and undivided focus on its policies and support. The new structure could be a separate Federal Department of Education, with a Cabinet-level officer as its head, or perhaps a Federal department headed by a National Board of Education responsible for policy development and for the appointment of the chief administrative officer. (The objective) should be to minimize partisan political considerations and the influence of vested interests and to provide for the continuing implementation of plans and programs that will reduce the disruptions caused by changes in administration.

Before Education Commission of the States, Denver, July 11/ The New York Times, 7–12:(1)24.

Unfortunately, the President has done very little about the pressing needs of education today. But even more tragic, it is difficult to find any indication that he even cares about what is happening to American schools . . . All across the nation, schools and colleges are facing the tremendous financial burden which many of them just won't be able to carry without more support from the Federal government. But the President is ignoring that need, and is placing his priorities, instead, in other areas, such as defense . . . I tried time after time to get through to the President and others in the White House the fact that education is such an important part of American society that it cannot be

(JAMES E. ALLEN, JR.)

ignored by the Federal government. But I usually found it impossible to get a fair hearing for my concerns.

Interview, Dayton, Ohio/
The Dallas Times Herald, 11–13:A3.

Dwight W. Allen
Dean, School of Education,
University of Massachusetts

Money isn't the reason schools are as bad as they are. Right now, it's difficult to see the quality difference between a school spending $500 per pupil and asking $600 to do needed experimentation, and a suburban school spending $2,000 per pupil and arguing it can't really do the job unless it gets $2,200 per child.

At White House Conference on
Children, Washington/
The Christian Science Monitor, 12–18:3.

William A. Arrowsmith
Professor of Classics, University of Texas

Only when the liberal arts colleges renounce their professionalism and devote themselves seriously with all their resources to the education of teachers will public education ever become the instrument of a great democratic culture.

At Dartmouth College commencement/
The Dallas Times Herald, 6–15:A2.

William S. Banowsky
Chancellor, Pepperdine College at Malibu

The challenge of our time is to educate hearts as well as minds. Education cannot be dispensed like aspirin or cough medicine; nor can college students be vaccinated with the facts. Students are wary of teachings which put a price on everything and values on nothing.

Los Angeles, April 20/
Los Angeles Herald-Examiner, 4–21:A7.

Reinhard Bendix
Professor of Sociology, University of

California at Berkeley; President,
American Sociological Association

Increasingly, politicians, administrators, the general public and not a few scientists who should know better have called upon the universities to help solve the race problem, the urban crisis, generational conflict, pollution, the arms race . . . In their relations with the young generations, the universities cannot resolve issues like the Vietnam war, race relations or the uses of technology which the political leadership has so far failed to resolve. The universities should not be asked to make the attempt . . . Political problems are for politicians to solve.

Before American Sociological Association,
Washington, Aug. 31/
The New York Times, 9–1:20.

Louis T. Benezet
President, Claremont University Center

The (college) president has been too lax, he has been too firm and unyielding; he has not listened to his faculty, he has indulged his faculty or his students; he has acted too fast, he has waited too long to act; he has called in the police, he hasn't called in the police. Whatever it is he should have done, he didn't do; whatever he shouldn't have done, he foolishly did do.

U.S. News & World Report, 8–3:32.

George C. S. Benson
Director, ROTC Affairs, Department of
Defense of the United States

It seems to me that an education is not really liberal unless the educators feel some sense of responsibility to help the student think his way towards a better world. This better world need not be strictly a "do-gooder" paradise. It may be the spiritual world of the trained theological thinker. It may be some kind of scientific Utopia. To me, it is the shaping of institutions which gives every individual a real chance to make something of himself. All I am saying is that I would not wish to keep on a liberal arts faculty a person who had no ambition for better things to come.

At Woodstock (Md.) Conference, March 7/
Vital Speeches, 6–15:543.

Edward J. Bloustein
President, Bennington College

We seem to have turned higher education into preparatory schools for the professions. But the only reason for going to college is to become a better person—to understand what human values are, to make choices in light of cultural heritages.

Interview, New York/
Los Angeles Times, 1–11:A23.

Administering a college today is like playing chess on the open deck of the sinking *Titanic*. To make matters worse, the chess rules seem to be changing as the game proceeds.

Before Association of American
Colleges, Houston, Jan. 12/
The New York Times, 1–13:18.

Julian Bond
Georgia State Legislator

The idea that black universities like Lincoln are quiet places where little happens is a terrible lie. Martin Luther King didn't graduate from Harvard, and the first black Supreme Court Justice, Thurgood Marshall, a graduate of Lincoln, class of 1930, didn't go to Yale.

At Lincoln University (Pa.) commencement/
The New York Times, 6–9:24.

Daniel J. Boorstin
Director, National Museum of History
and Technology, Washington

The tendency of teachers to give in to the demands for "relevance" is . . . a kind of surrender of academic ideals. A professor could very well tell his students: "I don't care if you are interested in ancient history or not. I think ancient history is an important thing to know about, and I'm going to teach ancient history. If you don't want to come to my classes, you can go and study

something else." Instead of that, many professors adapt their subjects into voguish topics like "black studies" and other kinds of racist trash. Thereby, they deprive the student of his opportunity to learn; because what the teacher ought to be teaching is what the student doesn't know—and doesn't even know that he doesn't know.

Interview, Washington/
U.S. News & World Report, 10–19:66.

I think we have always attached more importance to our institutions of higher learning than is justified. It is easy for people to believe that if the colleges and universities are falling apart, American life also is falling apart. I would insist that our colleges and universities—more so, perhaps, than in any other country—are only a small part of our organs of intellectual inquiry.

Interview, Washington/
U.S. News & World Report, 10–19:66.

Kingman Brewster, Jr.
President, Yale University

The great majority of students (do not) want to spend very much of their time or energy in the guidance and governance of their university. In the longer, duller life between crises, it is even more demonstrable that to the average student the purpose of university life is learning and living, not governing. Most students would rather have the policies of the university directed by the faculty and administration than by their classmates.

Newsweek, 6–15:70.

. . . any system in which some of the brightest and most talented people are bored or frustrated is obviously in need of reform. I think it's not unfair to say that some of the brightest and most talented students in high school or prep school are bored with it in their last year of enrollment; and certainly some of the brightest and most highly motivated college students are bored in the last year of their college careers; and certainly a lot of the brightest and most highly moti-

(KINGMAN BREWSTER, JR.)

vated graduate and professional students are bored in the last couple of years of professional or graduate school. Well, that's at least —if that's true—a sign that we are in need of a basic educational reappraisal and overhaul...

At panel discussion, New York/
The New York Times, 7–13:24.

McGeorge Bundy
President, Ford Foundation

The university is for learning—not for politics, not for growing up, not even for virtue, except as these things cut in and out of learning and except also as they are necessary elements of all good human activity.

San Francisco Examiner & Chronicle
(This World), 7–12:2.

If learning is what a man learns for his own purposes, then open learning requires equal respect for differing and even conflicting purposes. Such equal respect forbids institutional partisanship on the divisive issues of the day ... The university's existential commitment to freedom of learning demands its political neutrality. In most times in this country, this proposition needs to be heard by the angry apostles of things-as-they-are. Today it needs to be heard by the angry apostles of change. But it does not rest on political considerations. It rests on the requirements of learning itself.

Before American Management Association
conference on education and training, New
York/The Christian Science Monitor, 8–5:12.

John H. Bunzel
President, San Jose State College

The university cannot permit questions of scholarship or aesthetic taste to be resolved by popular vote. I have heard it said that if students in English voted to remove Shakespeare from the curriculum because he is no longer relevant, the faculty should go along. There are a lot of things wrong with that sentiment. Putting Shakespeare to a vote in-

dicates confusion not only about democracy but the ballot box. Asking students to vote on something they have not thought very long or hard about is to put ignorance on a par with knowledge and the inexperience of youthful judgment against the experience of professional and cultivated taste. Furthermore, the principle, once legitimatized, will not stop with Shakespeare.

Before San Jose State College faculty/
The Wall Street Journal, 10–8:10.

The classroom should not be a place where we simply discuss the student's inner life or what he may feel are his immediate needs. This is not to suggest that emotional responses to experience are unimportant. It is simply to say that group therapy or encounter sessions are not a substitute for rigorous and rational thought. Education must be something more than a "happening."

Before San Jose State College faculty/
The Wall Street Journal, 10–8:10.

Hugh Calkins
Chairman, National Advisory Council
on Vocational Education

The relationship between education and income is beyond question. The only thing that is remarkable is that for so long we have taxed income without allocating a specific part of an increased tax to that national service which most contributes to the development of the income.

Quote, 5–10:433.

Glenn Campbell
Director, Hoover Institution,
Stanford University

The frequent depiction of the university as crushed between the extremes of the right and the left is a lot of bunk. It is crystal clear that the politicizing of our universities is coming from the left and that it is coming from inside the academy, not from the outside.

Plainview (Tex.) Daily Herald, 12–3:8.

Al Capp
Cartoonist

One of the immutable laws of Nature is that the college student is inferior to every other class. The instant he registers as one, he confesses to the world that he needs four more years of its indulgence and charity before he can contribute anything to it. It is a shameful and pitiful state, and it would seem prudent for anyone in it not to attract attention to himself.

At Princeton University/Newsweek, 7–6:4.

E. Laurence Chalmers, Jr.
Chancellor, University of Kansas

. . . I believe that many students—perhaps most—believe, either correctly or incorrectly, that they are regarded primarily by the community as consumers, and not as fellow citizens. The analogy that students have made in recent years is that if they're serving in the military at age 18, they're men; but if they're enrolled at a college or university, they're in some ambivalent position halfway between childhood and manhood. On the other side of the coin, there is no question in my mind that many citizens of the community view the university as an institution that draws its sustenance from the community, but doesn't replace it with anything. It's these two rather massive sets of attitudes that, whatever their basis or lack of basis in fact, need to be resolved if there is to be a much better bridge between the community and the campus.

Interview/U.S. News & World Report, 9–7:22.

James E. Cheek
President, Howard University

I think it's going to be exceedingly difficult to attract able men (to college presidencies) because a great deal of joy has gone out of the job. There is not the same personal satisfaction. Too much of the time is spent refereeing disputes—putting out fires.

Newsweek, 8–31:69.

Leo Cherne
Executive director, Research Institute of America

The colleges of the country will be the new high schools, finishing the work undone in the earlier years. And for those really requiring higher education, smaller elite colleges and graduate schools will educate the professional increasingly needed. And of those professions, management will be the most necessary, the most highly paid and much the most difficult.

At Business Publications Audit meeting, Chicago, Feb. 18/Vital Speeches, 4–15:411.

Charles R. DeCarlo
President, Sarah Lawrence College

I think we're honestly not looking at the fact that there's just an awful lot of hogwash in the educational system that's being taught. And that's from the primary school to the professional school.

At panel discussion, New York/ The New York Times, 7–13:24.

Thomas J. Dodd
United States Senator, D-Conn.

Harassed by parents, teachers, students and outsiders, the school principal—and indeed the entire school system in many cases —has reduced teaching to the level of keeping discipline.

U.S. News & World Report, 1–26:9.

Glenn S. Dumke
Chancellor, California State College System

Many excellent faculty members who are good citizens in every sense of the word will on occasions follow the lead of the radicals in issues pertaining to academic freedom because they feel the principle is too valuable to be eroded. They will defend a broad interpretation of it which incorporates some misuse rather than suffer any diminution of its fundamental meaning.

Before Comstock Club, Sacramento/ Los Angeles Times, 4–27:(1)24.

(GLENN S. DUMKE)

The scholar can be nothing but a scholar. The moment he becomes a partisan, he loses his objectivity and no longer can study the problems before him with the sole purpose of arriving at truth. Society is willing to insulate him from all kinds of pressures if he sticks to his main job. If he ceases that job, then the insulation will be removed and academic freedom will disappear. Consequently, we will no longer have institutions of education in the sense we have had them in the past . . . The student or professor who unwisely says we must become "involved" is saying, in effect, that we must destroy education and replace it with politics.

At Town Hall, Long Beach, Calif., Sept. 17/
Los Angeles Herald-Examiner, 9–18:A7.

James O. Eastland
United States Senator, D-Miss.

. . . the Federal courts and HEW, in their blind zeal to bring about instant total integration and revolutionize the social and economic structure of the South, have taken actions which have caused many public school buildings and facilities in my state to be abandoned. These school buildings and facilities are sitting unused. Like all vacant property, these buildings and facilities are deteriorating in value. Why should not the Federal government pay from its Treasury a fair and just amount of money to compensate for this terrible loss to the school systems?

Before the Senate, Washington, Jan. 26/
Congressional Record, 1–26:S549.

Robert H. Finch
Secretary of Health, Education and Welfare of the United States

Those who are most eager to force the billion dollars plus upon HEW have made it perfectly clear that education is like motherhood, and you can't go wrong when you vote more money for it. But *we* have a slogan, too, which we're going to frame and put on the wall, paraphrasing a distinguished

Senator: "Inflation, even in the pursuit of education, is a vice; but education without inflation is a virtue."

Los Angeles Times, 1–26:(2)7.

Robben W. Fleming
President, University of Michigan

I cannot imagine anyone who is a (college) president saying he is really enjoying himself. My regret is about how much time I spend on often unconstructive things instead of on ways to improve the entire educational process. You're just trying to preserve some semblance of stability.

Newsweek, 8–31:68.

Charles Frankel
Professor of Philosophy,
Columbia University

At the heart of a university is a fundamental assumption. It is that *ideas* should triumph within them, not people's interests or demands, and that ideas triumph by meeting independent standards of logic and evidence, and not by political maneuvers, opinion-management, or the pressure of the mass will. This is an ethical principle, and an extremely difficult one to implement. People in universities often fail to live up to it. But they cannot abandon commitment to it without declaring that the university is not committed to science, to learning and to the independent criticism of society.

Los Angeles Times, 3–6:(2)7.

Roger A. Freeman
Special Assistant to the President of the United States; Senior fellow, Hoover Institution, Stanford University

You can't just buy education. Nor can education be given on a silver spoon. The price of education is hard work, for which there is no substitute in this world. What determines the quality of education is the capacity of the child. All these billions we have spent for compensatory education have been, in my opinion, about as effective as the incantations of an African witch doctor.

Interview/U.S. News & World Report, 1–26:46.

Roger A. Freeman
Senior fellow, Hoover Institution, Stanford University; Former Special Assistant to the President of the United States

We are in danger of producing an educated proletariat. That's dynamite! We have to be selective on who we allow to go through (higher education). If not, we will have a large number of highly-trained and unemployed people. That's what happened in Germany; I saw it happen.

San Francisco Examiner & Chronicle (This World), 11–8:2.

John W. Gardner
Chairman, National Urban Coalition

If we profess to care about education but won't tax ourselves or vote the school bonds to finance it, then we don't deserve to be free citizens . . . I'm sick of citizens who act as though the schools can survive without money.

Before National Committee for Support of the Public Schools, Washington, March 23 / The Washington Post, 3–24:A2.

Robert F. Goheen
President, Princeton University

Clearly, if the university is to become more politicized, there's going to be great damage to the notion of academic freedom within the institution—the ability of the faculty and the students to think as their own best judgment and learning leads them to think, rather than be guided by democratic votes on policy within the institution. And if the institution becomes politicized, it seems to me there's going to be great damage in terms of our external relationships and the willingness of other elements of the society to support the institution.

At panel discussion, New York / The New York Times, 7–13:24.

Paul Goodman
Author

In my opinion, most high schools should simply be abolished. My argument is that the way you learn to live in the world is to live in the world, the way you learn to swim. The point of elementary education is to see that they have grown up a little bit so that they can be thrown into the water. The need for schooling is a hoax which has been sold by educational imperialists.

Before House Subcommittee on Education, Washington / Los Angeles Herald-Examiner, 3–29:A5.

Lincoln Gordon
President, Johns Hopkins University

For the high-school graduate who has his heart set on a medical career and is eager to plunge into premedical preparation, by all means let him enter college at once and even accelerate his program, consistent with his abilities and the necessities of sound scientific and professional training. For another without such clear-cut vocational motivation, but with a strong taste for general book learning, let him enter at once a liberal-arts course and gradually find his life goals as his formal education proceeds. But for many, the sense of purpose and the urge for higher education will form more slowly, and they should enter college only when they want it and feel ready for it. Or if they enter and become disaffected, they should be able to drop out without shame until they find themselves truly ready. Some will never reach that stage, but a great many will do so in the fullness of time.

At inauguration of Harlan Cleveland as president of University of Hawaii, Honolulu / National Observer, 10–12:9.

We must, in all candor, admit that much of the working time of many students, even in our most prestigious universities, is spent in grubbing for credits and grades, getting required courses out of the way, or simply passing time for the necessary two or four or more years until the appropriate diploma is conferred. Some will reply that this is no cause for concern. The United States is a wealthy country, they say, which can afford this kind of luxury; and anyway, these stu-

(LINCOLN GORDON)

dents meet other youngsters, enjoy extracurricular activities, or cut their teeth in politics in their search for student power. If little happens to their minds, at least their emotional and gregarious impulses have an outlet. That might be termed the "summer resort" theory of college attendance. But it would be more effective and less costly to design institutions directly for such purposes, and not to confuse them with truly educational institutions.

At inauguration of Harlan Cleveland as president of University of Hawaii, Honolulu/ National Observer, 10–12:9.

Samuel B. Gould
Chancellor, State University of New York

Instantaneous communication through the mass media and through newly developed electronic means has cut very deeply into the university's earlier monopoly on learning. Students come to the university campus with a greatly conditioned vision of life and the world around them. They quickly begin to look upon the university, as any bold adventurer might, as the unnecessarily fussy but well meaning aunt or uncle who keeps warning about wearing one's galoshes to prevent the common cold, when he is already busy putting on his space suit.

U.S. News & World Report, 1–12:29.

Faculties are very liberal about causes that don't touch them personally and very conservative about anything that does touch them personally. At least, this has been my general experience. You can get some of them to run to the barricades on almost any issue in which they do not have a truly personal stake. But when it comes to matters of their departmental affairs, their courses of study, their salaries, their fringe benefits—all the things that relate to their own particular bailiwick—they are usually very conservative. The same could probably be said about many administrators.

Interview/U.S. News & World Report, 6–8:80.

. . . I would at least guess that the university of the future will be a far more flexible kind of institution than we ever suspected it might be. I think it will be an institution that will draw together all the different educational and cultural forces that surround it —the forces of the community—and will use all those forces as part of a person's education. This means that a student will be able to move freely in and out of campuses and many other agencies that can contribute to his learning. He will get some of his education in a museum. He will get some of it listening to symphonies. He will get some of it from working in libraries. He will get some of it from being in business and industry or government, where certain training processes can go forward. I think every single educational and training entity that exists in a community will become part of this total process—and a university will be nothing more than a loose federation of all these entities.

Interview/U.S. News & World Report, 6–8:82.

Samuel B. Gould
Former chancellor, State University of New York

There seem to be only four kinds of (university) presidents left: those in transition, those in flight, those in desperation and those who are newly annointed.

The Washington Post, 10–18:A2.

(What he "misses" about higher education): The glow of physical well-being that comes from leaping back and forth across the generation gap. The surge of creativity felt each day as one prepares tomorrow's statement expressing firmness in the face of every student threat and, at the same time, the most stalwart defense of academic freedom and supreme faith in youth. The eye-watering happiness that comes of walking through the haze settling over the student lounges where hospitality is king and the pot is always simmering. The brilliant prose styles of student newspaper columnists and editorial writers as they skillfully improvise on four-letter words, making every verb irregular, every tense imperfect, every noun peculiarly singular and possessive, and always arriving at amazingly erotic and unlikely conjunctions. The wonderful pause in the day's occupation, otherwise known as the children's hour, when the legal injunction has just been served and the offices are once more quiet, with only the debris left by passionate environmentalists to mark what has happened.

Before American Council on Education/
The New York Times, 10–28:43.

W. Harold Grant
Professor of Administration and Higher Education, Michigan State University

At any one stage in history, one social institution seems to be the integrating force, demanding the service of all the rest. Early in history it was the military. Then the church came to dominate. At present, the economic system seems to dominate. Now, a new institution is coming to the foreground—education. Tremendous numbers of people are going to school. Instead of the college being a separate institution, the community is becoming part of the college.

U.S. News & World Report, 1–12:31.

George Gumeson
Cabrillo College, Aptos, Calif.

Only in jail and in school does one need a pass to go to the bathroom or to go to another room to get a book. Too many schools are repressive places, where teachers are asked to endure the unenforceable or to be censors of student attitudes and expressions instead of being free to practice their professions.

San Francisco, July 4/
San Francisco Examiner & Chronicle, 7–5:A3.

Norman Hackerman
President, Rice University

The "half life" of a university president has fallen from a decade or so to about two years. After that, people on campus are only half as willing to accept his authority as before. But if no one at all has the authority to act on a decision, there can be no debate, only shouting of slogans; no negotiation, only demands.

Newsweek, 8–31:70.

Fred Harvey Harrington
President, University of Wisconsin

We in public higher education rest upon the democratic principle that while learning helps the individual, it is mostly for the benefit of our society, economy, government, culture. Thus, society should bear most of the cost of this education. If we abandon this principle, if we require the student to shoulder the full cost, we bring the end of public higher education in the American tradition.

U.S. News & World Report, 2–9:33.

Richard A. Harvill
President, University of Arizona

There's no question of a growing public feeling that if colleges can't govern themselves, they will be governed by others.

The Wall Street Journal, 9–4:1.

S. I. Hayakawa
President, San Francisco State College

To dedicate oneself to the defense of academic freedom is perhaps the most important thing an educator can do.

San Francisco/The Christian Science Monitor,
1–16:2.

There are an awful lot of professors who feel what they do in their departments is their own damn business and not the taxpayers'. The taxpayers will never take that. The professoriat ought to have a deeper sense of their own responsibility to our society as a whole.

Interview, San Francisco/
Los Angeles Herald-Examiner, 2–22:A20.

Student deferments for the draft have been a disaster, producing in effect a privileged elite who must remain in college to protect their privileged status. Even more

WHAT THEY SAID IN 1970

seriously, there is the prevailing upper-middle-class expectation that everyone should go to college—preferably a "good" college . . . What we need for young men and women in America now are two things. First, all who want higher education and cannot get it should be given a chance to get it. Secondly—and this applies especially to the upper-middle-class—all who don't want higher education, or are not sure they want it, should have the freedom to postpone college or not go to college at all—a freedom which is now felt not to exist at all because of the draft.

Before President's Commission on
Student Unrest/
The Wall Street Journal, 8–3:8.

As an educator, I cannot emphasize strongly enough the importance of a two or three-year or longer interval of work experience between high school and college. People who return to colleges after a few years in the world are likely to have a clear-cut purpose in mind. With a background of experience against which to make their judgments, with adolescent identity problems out of the way, students over 22, over 32, over 52 are almost always our best students. Perhaps higher education at the college and university level is too precious to be wasted on the immature.

Before President's Commission on
Student Unrest/
The Wall Street Journal, 8–3:8.

. . . the college-educated classes have been moving farther and farther away from the middle and lower-middle classes. Their professors teach them to look down on the American Legion, Lions Club and the Rotary—all the popular manifestations of everyday culture. The problem is how to produce an educated class that stays in touch with middle America; and I don't know how we can do that.

The Dallas Times Herald, 10–23:A10.

Theodore M. Hesburgh
President, University of Notre Dame

The way things are going, no intelligent guy in his right mind would want to be a university administrator.

Parade, 10–4:4.

In the 25 years that I have been associated with the university . . . I can think of no period more difficult than the present. Never before has the university taken on more tasks, and been asked to undertake many more, while the sources of support, both public and private, both moral and financial, seem to be drying up.

The New York Times, 10–25:(4)11.

Roger W. Heyns
Chancellor, University of California at Berkeley

The biggest asset he (his successor) will have is his word. He must tell the same thing to everyone—not tell the students what *they* want to hear and the faculty what *it* wants and the Regents what *they* want. If you're honest, you'll find yourself telling people what they don't want to hear.

Announcing his resignation, Berkeley, Nov. 13/
The New York Times, 11–15:(1)64.

Charles J. Hitch
President, University of California

The university must always maintain its institutional integrity. If it yields wholly to external pressures, it cannot long remain a great university. However, we need the public to understand us—for we are dependent upon public funds.

Interview, Berkeley, Calif./
The Christian Science Monitor, 3–25:3.

Orvel E. Hooker
Assistant Professor of Speech,
Millsaps College

Let students work through a level of achievement. If a student can advance through Speech 101 in five weeks, let him do so. If it takes him a year, that is his business. Make education an achievement, not a reward for sitting through a prescribed number of classroom hours and emerging victorious.

Jackson, Miss., Feb. 26/
Vital Speeches, 5–1:441.

John A. Howard
President, Rockford College

. . . we in the liberal arts colleges face a double challenge: first, to steep ourselves in the wisdom of the ages at a time when innovation and "nowness" have upstaged wisdom—and we must, I think, be wary of the product or project sold on the basis of its innovativeness; and second, to diminish the hurly-burly of the campus scene so that our primary attentions can be directed to learning and contemplation, rather than dissipated in the constant warring of power politics . . . Higher education has become sort of a perpetual rush-hour. Perhaps we need to acknowledge that circumstance and try to develop an educational vehicle that will shut out some of the noise and distraction on all sides, a vehicle which is not sold because of its innovation and gimmickry but which will be intentionally designed for the slow pace of learning, which wisdom requires.

Opening convocation address, Rockford
College, Sept. 9/Vital Speeches, 10–1:746.

It is both the task and the opportunity of the liberal arts to engage in a profound scrutiny of the nature of man and to discover what has given purpose and meaning to man's life in the past and what are accepted standards and limits which have made living together in a society bearable or even enjoyable. We must, I believe, eradicate the foolish bias which assumes that that which has been said and thought and done in the past is irrelevant and recognize that, on the contrary, it is only by familiarizing ourselves with the experience of an ancient China or recent England or classical Greece and Rome that we can better interpret what is happening now and more clearly perceive the options which are open to us.

Opening convocation address, Rockford
College, Sept. 9/Vital Speeches, 10–1:746.

Samuel P. Huntington
Professor of Government,
Harvard University

These days, faculty members cannot help but be somewhat wary of students, and it is not just because we think they may disrupt our classes or burn our files. The cause is something much more fundamental. It is because students and faculty increasingly tend to worship at different altars and judge by different codes.

Los Angeles Times, 1–5:(1)10.

Joseph Kaplan
Professor of Physics, University
of California at Los Angeles

There are purists who think athletics don't belong in the university. But we have to recognize sports as part of a man's training, or forget the whole damned thing.

Interview/Los Angeles Times, 3–26:(7)1.

Barnaby C. Keeney
Chairman, National Endowment
for the Humanities

There is a great imbalance in education, at every level from school through graduate school, in favor of the sciences. It is obvious from even the most casual inspection of any university campus, where most of the new buildings are for scientific uses. I support and have supported government sponsorship of scientific research and teaching, but the imbalance is now so serious that it is seriously threatening the education of our next generation.

Before Senate-House subcommittee hearing
on the Arts and Humanities Act of 1965,
Washington, Jan. 26/The New York Times,
1–27:31.

Virginia H. Knauer
Adviser to the President of the
United States for Consumer Affairs

For our educational institutions to be totally responsive, they must teach students not only how to exist but how to live.

The Dallas Times Herald, 11–9:A2.

Philip B. Kurland
Professor of Law, University of Chicago

One part of the dogma of the "new university" is its concept of egalitarianism . . . Thus, students must be admitted without regard to their demonstrated intellectual capacities. Students must not be graded, because this results in invidious comparisons between those who have performed well and those who have not. Faculty members must be hired or retained not because they have shown capacities for research and teaching in a given area, but because we must assign appropriate egalitarian quotas by sex, by race, by political persuasions and—in remembrance of things past—by religion. Moreover, the judgment about faculty capacity is not to be made by those knowledgeable in the field, but by students, in terms of how they "relate" to the faculty member—him or her or it, as the case may be. It is this egalitarianism that bottoms the claim of students to participate in the governance of the university. The fact that they indicate no knowledge of the function of university governance is irrelevant. It is argued that when they are admitted to the university community as students, they have been judged competent to share in university administration. They are indeed right, if their concept of a university as an egalitarian political institution is accurate. Only if the old-fashioned notion were to prevail, that a university is a place exclusively for the discovery and communication of knowledge by those best qualified to perform those tasks, should the student claim for a share in university government be rejected.

Before Chicago Bar Association, Jan. 22/
Vital Speeches, 3–1:316.

Whether the "new university"—with its preference for instinctual forces over reason, with its preference for egalitarianism over individuality, excellence and professionalism, with its preference for political rather than intellectual objectives—whether the new university will prevail over the old is not yet fully determined. But the odds are in

its favor. For there are too few to stand up and fight against the perversions that are promised—too few students, too few faculty, too few university administrators. Those among them who do not endorse the new university prefer to compromise with it. Once again, the price of peace in our time may prove exhorbitant.

Before Chicago Bar Association, Jan. 22/
Congressional Record, 2–9:S1420.

Richard W. Lyman
Acting president, Stanford University

I believe with every fiber of my being that the university cannot remain the true home of free inquiry—questioning, if you like—if it is subordinated to political purposes. A great university does not exist to make people happy by confirming their prejudices. It exists to keep alive the impossible but essential human quest for answers to the ultimate question, "What is Truth?", and to all the lesser questions that flow therefrom. To convert it into the ally or pawn of the New Left, Old Right, or, for that matter, the Middle-Aged Center, is to betray that purpose. Defenses against that betrayal were never more needed than they are today.

At Stanford Men's Club, San Francisco,
Aug. 12/Los Angeles Times, 10–4:G3.

If universities allow themselves to become instruments of general political movements, they will be up for grabs, so to speak. They may start out on what the majority considers the side of the angels. But the day will come when they are captured by what may be the non-angels.

Interview/San Francisco Examiner & Chronicle,
8–16:A5.

Richard W. Lyman
President, Stanford University

The university, if anything at all, should be a free marketplace of ideas, and it would be undesirable to try to screen out the undesirable people or people who are likely to provoke difficulties. That's not on the list of possible actions. Attempts to allow only

"safe" speakers on campus would themselves become volatile issues immediately—and rightfully so.
Interview, Stanford University/
The Christian Science Monitor, 12–2:10.

A "comfortable university" is virtually a contradiction in terms. We exist to disturb and activate the minds of men and women.
Los Angeles Herald-Examiner, 12–30:C2.

Mike Mansfield
United States Senator, D-Mont.

It is so easy to vote millions for ABMs and SSTs and then to reject money for the ABCs.
Washington, Aug. 18/
Los Angeles Herald-Examiner, 8–19:A2.

Lewis B. Mayhew
Professor of Higher Education,
Stanford University

Academic freedom is a concept developed to protect the professor in his role as rational enquirer. Some professors are making use of the techniques of the demagogue or politician—and still claiming academic freedom. But once you move into the political arena, you open yourself to the same consequences befalling political figures. Furthermore, too many faculty members have insisted on their own academic freedom but have been careless about the students' rights to question, criticize or dissent. Unless the professoriate begins to monitor itself, it will be getting monitoring from the outside—and that will mean a loss of academic freedom.
U.S. News & World Report, 6–15:38.

William J. McGill
Chancellor, University of California
at San Diego; President-designate,
Columbia University

I have a serious concern that universities might have overextended themselves and there might be a need for retrenchment. For instance, there is a basic question whether we are producing too many Ph.D.'s.
Interview, La Jolla, Calif., Feb. 3/
The New York Times, 2–4:44.

Colleges and universities are being increasingly used as storage areas for bored young people who have no idea where they are going.
Cleveland Plain Dealer, 8–14:A12.

It seems to me that a university community is the most politically conscious and one of the most politically inept groups in society. The reason is that the political arts are not known on campus. The primary political arts are persuasion and compromise, and these matters never really develop to any degree on a university campus. We're political amateurs, and the enthusiasm of political movements is likely to manifest itself in ways that are rather more dangerous to the university's status as a special place where no real political commitments are made. It's not likely to result in violence. It's likely to result in major embarrassments.
Interview, San Diego/
The New York Times Magazine, 8–23:77.

William J. McGill
President, Columbia University

Believe me, we in higher education are very nervous, and thus (this) decade is likely to produce reorganization, curriculum reform, redefinition of professional life and a variety of other innovations unlike anything seen in the last 50 years. Our survival depends on it.
At Columbia University Charter Day
dinner, New York, Dec. 11/
The New York Times, 12–12:36.

William G. Milliken
Governor of Michigan

Education is in deep trouble in my state and in the country. Many people have little faith in the job our schools are doing and many students have little faith that they are being taught anything of value and usefulness . . . We cannot create . . . confidence by reciting a litany of accomplishments—all the money we are spending, all of the schools we are building, all of the new programs we have initiated. We can only create or re-

(WILLIAM G. MILLIKEN)

create this confidence by eliminating our failures so that people will no longer be able to ask us why Johnny can't read or why Johnny insists on breaking all of the windows in his school.

Before Education Commission of the States, Denver, July 9/The New York Times, 7–10:21.

Robert W. Morse
President, Case Western Reserve University

It is not the task of universities to pacify youth any more than it is to indulge their fantasies. Our task is to educate them . . . If universities are ever free of controversy or project a feeling of comfort and security to all, then that is when we should worry most about them.

Plainview (Tex.) Daily Herald, 7–28:4.

For too long now, too many have stood by as the office of president in one university after another has been attacked. Those who toy with that office tamper with the integrity of the university itself. If universities are to survive, then we must restore confidence in the office of the president.

At St. Louis University, Oct. 18/ The Washington Post, 10–18:A2.

Emil M. Mrak
Chancellor Emeritus, University of California at Davis

What we need most . . . is the public realization that not every youngster wants to go to college, that a college degree is not a guarantee of a good life, that a person with a skill or a trade can be as financially successful as a person with a Ph.D., and that society needs skilled persons as well as intellectuals.

San Francisco Examiner & Chronicle (This World), 9–20:31.

A. M. Nicholi II
Psychiatrist, Harvard University Medical School

If year after year he (the college president)

marches to the tune of external sources—especially to the tune of his wealthy, more conservative alumni—he will be out of step with his internal constituency, his faculty and students. On the other hand, when he becomes involved with students, he tends to alienate many of his wealthiest alumni. He cannot continue to serve two masters.

San Francisco Examiner & Chronicle (This World), 5–31:2.

Richard M. Nixon
President of the United States

If most or all private schools were to close or turn public, the added burden on public funds by the end of the 1970s would exceed 4 billion dollars per year in operations and with an estimated 5 billion more needed for facilities. There is an equally important consideration: These schools—nonsectarian, Catholic, Jewish, Protestant and other—often add a dimension of spiritual value to education, affirming in children a moral code by which to live. No government can be indifferent to the potential collapse of such schools.

April 21/U.S. News & World Report, 5–4:36.

Charles E. Odegaard
President, University of Washington

The university is founded on the proposition that some people know more than others. To convert it into an egalitarian democracy, with all votes equal, would be to repudiate the qualitative pursuit of learning.

Newsweek, 6–15:70.

Robert Olds
Director, Center for Communications Studies, Santa Barbara, Calif.

Higher education is still trying to use an ancient management framework developed for a little handpicked cluster of professors and students to run a massive, diverse, comprehensive institution with a student body of 10 to 40 thousand.

Before American Association of School Administrators, Atlantic City, N.J., Feb. 16/ The Dallas Times Herald, 2–17:A5.

Wright Patman
United States Representative, D-Tex.

It is most unfortunate that the Administration should demand a cutback in appropriations for Federal education programs, particularly at a time when hundreds of school districts face critical fiscal problems in their efforts to expand and improve education . . . To default on this obligation is not only to dishonor the government's commitment to education, but is false economy since, in the long run, we can only lose by short-changing the education of our children.

Before the House, Washington, Jan. 26/
Congressional Record, 1–26:305.

Nathan M. Pusey
President, Harvard University

Add the uncertainties occasioned by the general state of the economy, the declining Vietnam war, by impending legislation, the market, the enormous and increasing needs of many other competing good causes, public and private worry, and it appears almost certain that the years immediately ahead will be more difficult financially for higher education in this country than any we have experienced for a long time.

Cambridge, Mass., Jan. 18/
The New York Times, 1–19:23.

Max Rafferty
California State Superintendent
of Public Instruction

Once the Federal government begins direct financing of schools you're going to see the end of local control. I don't think it's necessary. If the Federal government would return to the states the tax sources it has been taking away from them, every state would easily meet its school costs.

The New York Times, 5–24:(1)48.

One college undergraduate wrote me recently as follows: "I'm photographed, inoculated, taped, carded and filed. I have a parking pass and a library pass and a lab pass. I sit in a lecture class with 600 others, and I'm number 327. The professor's lecture is piped in electronically; I never see him. The multiple-choice tests I take are graded automatically. I engage in group activities, group health services and group recreation. But I came to college to find *myself*—to learn how to become a *person*. Instead, I've become a *number*" . . . No wonder our colleges are turning into huge factories. When people are conditioned from early childhood to believe that adjustment to one's environment is the supreme goal of life; when they are taught day after day that acceptance by the group is more important than the development of the individual's own abilities; when they are grouped by social age down in the grades and always passed through the school with their peers, regardless of whether or not they are able to meet any standards of performance . . . how else can you expect our colleges and universities to deal with products of such a system of education? They have been conditioned to conform. They have been trained to cooperate. They have been educated to adjust.

At Troy (Ala.) State University, Aug. 14/
Vital Speeches, 10–1:753.

Education cannot . . . make people want to do what's obviously good for them. (The role of education is to) give Americans the facts . . . teach them how to organize those facts . . . even build up certain desirable work habits and patterns of stimulus-response. But it cannot—by merely holding up the good, the beautiful and the true to its captive audience—make that audience hanker after these fine old attributes.

Before Women's Christian Temperance
Union, Los Angeles, Sept. 6/
Los Angeles Herald-Examiner, 9–7:A3.

Ronald Reagan
Governor of California

Young men and women go to college to find themselves as individuals. They see the names of distinguished scholars in the catalogue and sign up for courses with the belief that they will learn and grow and be

(RONALD REAGAN)

stimulated by contact with these men. All too often they are herded into gigantic classes taught by teaching assistants hardly older than themselves. The feeling comes that they're nameless, faceless numbers on an assembly line—green cap at one end, cap and gown and an automated diploma at the other.

The New York Times Magazine, 1–11:85.

Bevington Reed
Texas Commissioner of Higher Education

At the beginning of the decade of the 1970s, higher education in this state and nation stands on a true watershed. Behind us lie the traditions of a quiet university campus dominated by scholarly presidents, where students were seeking knowledge and not asking embarrassing questions about the relevancy of our preachings to our own actions, where faculty grew old in quiet abstract discussions far removed and truly isolated from the social and political activism of the day . . . We stand on the very cutting edge of the old and the new. Old solutions, old ways of administration and old ways of teaching must yield to new concepts.

Abilene, Tex., Feb. 21 /
Fort Worth Star-Telegram, 2–22:A1.

David Reuben
Psychiatrist, Author

I'm for sex education for parents. It's *their* job. Sex education is not basket weaving—it is teaching facts and human values without moralizing. Delegating the responsibility to some old maid who is not equipped to teach it may cut down on parental guilt—but it doesn't help the child. Many sex education classes in school are like dog food: Made with wonderful odor and color to please the master, but the dog couldn't care less.

Interview / Los Angeles Times, 1–25:D1.

The best sex education is from parent to child. It is the most intimate, most personal, most important subject human beings can

talk about. If given in love and understanding, it is the foundation for a child's life of happiness. But . . . most people cannot tell their children about sex, because their parents didn't tell them . . . and *their* parents didn't tell *them*. So the school has to take over. Then it is usually a gym teacher picked to teach sex education classes.

Los Angeles / Los Angeles Herald-Examiner, 9–17:B4.

Terry Sanford
President, Duke University

Teaching reason is the mission upon which universities today are based. We don't believe in fighting fire with fire. We fight fire with water and force with reason.

Before Duke alumni, New York, Nov. 5 /
The Dallas Times Herald, 11–8:A50.

Harvey B. Scribner
Chancellor, New York City School System

For every youngster who gains intellectually and psychologically as he passes through our schools, there is another who is pushed out, turned off or scarred as a result of his school experience. For a whole variety of reasons and for a variety of people, our schools are unequal and unfair. And nowhere is this more true than in the schools of our biggest cities . . .

Before Public Education Association /
Daily World, 10–14:7.

In the schools, we tend to emphasize schooling instead of learning, buildings instead of space, the passing of tests instead of the acquisition of an education. We squabble in the name of reform; instead of cooperating on common goals for the sake of reform . . . In short, we ought to ask questions about the needs of kids and not the needs of schools.

At metropolitan conference of B'nai B'rith, New York, Nov. 15 / The New York Times, 11–16:27.

Thomas A. Shaheen
Superintendent of Schools of San Francisco

Our schools are organized on a semi-prison

proach, on crime and punishment, and ops and robbers techniques. We have lack trust: sign-in and sign-out slips, detention stems, wardens and jailors, fear of escape, gimentation, limited opportunities for oice, barricaded or locked toilet rooms, ll-like classrooms. Why are we surprised at some youngsters rebel? Is it not surprising that more of them do not?

Before American Jewish Congress,
San Francisco, Sept. 22/
San Francisco Chronicle, 9–24:8.

Charles Silberman
Editor, "Fortune" magazine

It is not possible to spend any prolonged period visiting public school classrooms without being appalled by the mutilation visible everywhere. There is mutilation of spontaneity, of joy in learning, of pleasure in creating, of a sense of self. Because we all like the schools so much for granted, we fail to appreciate what grim, joyless places most American schools are, how oppressive and petty are the rules by which they are governed, how intellectually sterile and esthetically barren the atmosphere, what an appalling lack of civility obtains on the part of teachers and principals and what contempt they unconsciously display for children as children.

Before National Education Association, San
Francisco/San Francisco Examiner & Chronicle
(This World), 7–12:17.

Benjamin Spock
Physician, Author

Schools and colleges are all imbued with the idea that it's the man's world that should be studied. They study the great men of history—of economics, military affairs and politics. I think we should say more about the role women play in the world. We should go over every course of study. In history, we should emphasize Napoleon's mother as well as Napoleon, and in English make sure to include women novelists and poetesses.

Interview, New York/
The New York Times, 1–28:42.

Joseph Tussman
Professor of Philosophy, University
of California at Berkeley

The educational system is a farce, but to let students tell you how to remake it is equivalent to letting the sickest patients take over the practice of medicine because doctors often make mistakes.

Interview/
The New York Times Magazine, 1–11:28.

Robert C. Tyson
Chairman, Finance Committee,
United States Steel Corporation

The independence of private institutions . . . helps keep the state-supported institutions of higher learning on their toes, in terms of vying for students and faculty—in quality if not in quantity . . . Government-supported schools, in turn, if only by their sheer magnitude, help keep the private institutions on their toes. Thus, higher education is furthered by the quality of the system.

Before Independent College Funds of
America, Palm Springs, Calif., March 9/
Los Angeles Herald-Examiner, 3–4:A13.

Eric A. Walker
President, Pennsylvania State University

There are too many people today who want the university to devote its entire time and resources to following one path or another—to ending poverty, fighting racism, stopping crime in the streets, ending the war in Vietnam. Everyone seems to want the university to do everything—and all at once. But the question is, should universities stand at the beck and call of every politician or special interest group? Should the universities become action outfits? Should they become forums for various political movements? It seems to me that for universities to go out and attempt to change the world is to make it very difficult for them to serve as repositories of knowledge and as unbiased critics of the passing scene. An actor is not in a position to critically analyze the play in which he is engaged. And no man should be

115

(ERIC A. WALKER)

able to serve in the dual capacity as judge and jury. It is my feeling that many colleges and universities are now devoting so much time to trying to change the world that they have forgotten not only their research functions, but their teaching functions, also. And as they fail in their primary function, it is inevitable that eventually a reassessment will come and people will ask why do they exist at all.

Before All-Pennsylvania College Alumni Association, Washington, Feb. 7 / Vital Speeches, 4–1:362.

George C. Wallace
Former Governor of Alabama

The President had better heed this warning . . . The average citizen in my part of the country knows that the Nixon Administration is destroying the public schools, and a President who destroys the public schools is going to end up being a one-term President.

Interview, New York / Face the Nation, Columbia Broadcasting System, 9–18.

Ernest L. Wilkinson
President, Brigham Young University

Our attitude of insisting on moral and spiritual as well as intellectual standards is admittedly contrary to the prevailing trend in a great many universities and colleges which have abandoned any attempt to supervise the moral life of their students. We feel, however, that to indulge irresponsible student conduct is to abdicate our role as educators.

At Brigham Young University / Los Angeles Times, 3–23:(1)23.

Eugene S. Wilson
Director of admissions, Amherst College

Most college freshmen have the intellectual ability to handle their academic programs. What they lack is the ability to make wise choices when the colleges suddenly grant them almost complete freedom from the restraints and direction they have been accustomed to at home and at school.

San Francisco Examiner & Chronicle, 8–30:2.

William R. Wood
President, University of Alaska

In some instances, the groves of academe are almost indistinguishable from the asphalt jungle . . . Upon occasion, the campus should be drenched with the sounds of music, morning chimes, evening chimes, skating music, serenades, band or guitar—at other times, silence to the point of stillness.

Before International College and University Conference and Exposition, Atlantic City, N.J., March 17 / The New York Times, 3–18:53.

John Cardinal Wright
Prefect, Congregation of the Clergy, Roman Curia, the Vatican

. . . for a long time we lived in a liberal-arts civilization. The great universities of England, the United States, Germany, France were liberal-arts universities. They've been replaced, in the main, by technological institutes, by technology—which is to say that the sense of "know why" has yielded to the sense of "know how."

Interview, Vatican City / U.S. News & World Report, 8–31:56.

Howard J. Zitko
Chairman, World University

. . . the true purpose of the university is to universalize, to broaden horizons, to eliminate boundaries, to abolish restrictions, to expand consciousness—express it however you will. Education should be an adventure in the ever-widening comprehension of truth. And truth is universal—infinite in scope and limitless in application. More often than not, education is an arbitrary brake on the learning process, whereby knowledge must be made to fit certain preconceived conditions and circumstances that have had their origins far back in the night of time. I think I know what is plaguing our students. The university, as it is presently constituted, has become so impersonal in its methods and policies, so departmentalized in its functions and controls, so degree-conscious, so fearful of contradicting the wrongs of society, so dependent on political patronage and outside economic pressure, that it has taken sanctuary in the "merchandising" of knowledge and has forgotten how to stimulate the art of caring. This is the vital flaw in academic practice. A student who may become an intellectual giant under university tutelage, but who has cultivated no ability to love his own kind, much less his enemies, is a shell, living in a social vacuum and displaying all the qualities of a spiritual primitive.

At International Conference of World University, Washington, Aug. 1 / Vital Speeches, 9–1:693.

STUDENT DISSENT

Gardner Ackley
Professor of Economics,
University of Michigan

Last Wednesday, I watched the faculty of my own department, assembled in the chairman's office, discuss a demand that all classes in our building be shut down, OR ELSE. We discussed this while the entrances to the building were sealed, and while the halls outside the rooms in which we were meeting were patrolled by men carrying pipes and clubs. We sought guidance from the college and were told: "Do what you think best. You will have no protection." And so we cravenly capitulated, in fear—if not for our own safety—for that of our students and employes. That day, the truth lay in those clubs.

Seattle Times, 6–21:A12.

Ruth M. Adams
President, Wellesley College

I feel the consumer has a right to say if the product is good or bad, even in the schools. Where student concerns about areas that are appropriate matters of concern are given and where protest has led to progress and reform, I feel a great deal has been accomplished. But where students have engaged in the wrong topics and have used violent measures, they have been throwing a great shadow over the good that might be done.

Interview, Dallas/
The Dallas Times Herald, 10–20:B1.

Spiro T. Agnew
Vice President of the United States

I'd love to be able to go onto some of the embattled college campuses and speak to an audience that came to listen and absorb what I had to say. Unfortunately, today this is not possible. Because of the dissidents, the dissenters—those who rally favor for their point of view not by dialogue and discussion, not by moving closer together through an eventual accommodation of viewpoints of disparity—these will not allow the free interchange of information and will bus their supporters for the purpose of disruption from one college to another. It only takes a small group to make it impossible for anyone to be heard. And I believe it's one of the tragedies of our times that many fine students—the preponderant majority of students who would like a chance to hear principals in public life give vent to their opinions and possibly to engage in dialogue and discussion—are prohibited from doing this by those who characterize themselves as intellectuals but remain the most visceral people in the world.

Lincoln Day address, Chicago, Feb. 12
Human Events, 3–7:18

It is late in the day—but it is not too late to save the colleges and universities of this country from the future anarchic dreamer have in store. It will take courage, and it will probably involve the kind of confrontations understandably distasteful to men of thought . . . Campus anarchy that might have been nipped in the bud at Berkeley with a single act of administrative decisiveness and faculty courage can now be obtained only at considerable cost. But the sooner the price of saving the universities is paid, the better.

April 28/National Review, 5–19:496

Let us not be naive enough to believe that there are no seeds of revolution in the rebellion that radical young people describe as 'the movement." Let us be candid enough to face the fact that the spawning ground and sanctuary of the movement is the American university. Few institutions are more vital to a free society; none is so susceptible to capture and destruction by the radical or criminal left. Small wonder, then, that each year a new group of impressionable consumers falls victim to the totalitarian ptomaine dispensed by those who disparage our system . . . The real pity is that many of the students of our universities really feel that the theatrical radicals are the architects of a brave, new, compassionate world, spiced with rock music, "acid" and pot.

Fort Lauderdale, Fla., April 28/Time, 5–11:20.

When peace comes through appeasement and capitulation—that sellout is intellectual treason. A concise and clear set of rules for campus conduct should be established, transmitted to incoming freshmen and enforced —with immediate expulsion the penalty for serious violations. The rule of reason is the guiding principle in an academic community, and those who apply the rule of force have no business being there.

Fort Lauderdale, Fla., April 28/Time, 5–11:20.

Long before I became a household word, violence was rampant in this country. The Berkeley campuses exploded when I was still back in county government. Columbia University was turned topsy-turvey long before President Nixon was even inaugurated. And yet you (students) say my rhetoric has caused the violence. Let me point out something else: Student violence is a way of life in Germany, in Japan, in England, in many other countries where the effect of my rhetoric is virtually nonexistent. Now, to use me as some convenient *bête noire* for the violence that's existed in this country because of the disgusting permissive attitudes of the people in command of the college campuses is one of the most ridiculous charges I've ever heard.

TV panel discussion/The David Frost Show, Westinghouse Broadcasting Company, 9–25.

The university disruptions of the last half-decade are blamed on everybody and everything in this society, when the blame belongs squarely on the disrupters themselves and on their apologists in the larger community. The primary responsibility for maintaining academic freedom within a campus community does not belong on the steps of the White House. It belongs on the steps of the university administration building and at the door of the faculty lounge . . . The President cannot replace the campus cop.

At Republican luncheon, Sioux Falls, S.D., Sept. 29/National Observer, 10–5:3.

To lay the responsibility for ending student disruption at the doorstep of the President (Nixon)—in office 20 months—is scapegoating of the most irresponsible sort. The suggestion that vigorous public condemnation of antisocial conduct is somehow, *ex post facto,* a cause of that conduct is more of the same remorseless nonsense that we have been hearing for years.

At Republican luncheon, Sioux Falls, S.D., Sept. 29/Newsweek, 10–12:36.

Gordon Allott
United States Senator, R-Colo.

This Commission (President's Commission on Campus Unrest) has already done damage simply by failing to be manfully indignant when radical witnesses have suggested that riots are justifiable until the government does what radicals demand. A report that fails to express vigorous indignation about coercion from the left will amount to a stab in the back to the moderates and the majority. If the Commission does administer this stab in the back, then we will be faced with a grim irony: The Commission established to investigate disorder will have become a cause of disorder.

Chicago/Human Events, 9–12:4.

Robert H. Atwell
Vice chancellor, University of Wisconsin; President-designate, Pitzer College

One need not defend the stupid, vicious

119

(ROBERT H. ATWELL)

and destructive acts of a few young people in order to be critical of the absence of any serious administration or regent tactic other than massive police action . . . Those who share power in the university are remote, aloof and defensive. They have accommodated to the forces of . . . reaction to the point where I believe that they have lost the confidence of a majority of . . . actively concerned students of all political persuasions.

Madison, Wis., Aug. 21/
The Washington Post, 8–22:A13.

Stephen K. Bailey
Chairman, Policy Institute, Syracuse
University Research Corporation; Member,
New York State Board of Regents

Under duress, we are beginning to change. It seems too bad that we have to wait until deans are carried down the stairs or principals are locked in the *john* before we can reshape our thinking and procedures.

Before conference of school superintendents,
Columbia University/
The New York Times, 7–12:(1)45.

When the Abbe Sieyes, vicar general of the diocese of Chartres, was asked what he did during the French Revolution, he replied, "I survived." As I watch the melancholy list grow of friends who have resigned —voluntarily or under duress—from college presidencies and school superintendencies during the past few years—or, more tragically, have dropped dead of heart attacks or committed suicide—I begin to wonder how many contemporary educational leaders will survive the current educational revolution. Revolutions are insatiable maws—with a cavernous appetite for men's lives and fortunes. The most civilized are a peculiar delicacy of the revolutionary appetite, for, unconsumed, they stand in the way of the necessary over-simplifications of the revolutionary mind. And they are readily betrayed into revolutionary hands by the old guard, who

always find perceptive consciences a threat and an embarrassment to the status quo.

The Wall Street Journal, 9–3:8.

Jaime Benitez
President, University of Puerto Rico

Our experience served to demonstrate what is now becoming obvious throughout the United States—that the basic role of a university is to educate. Endeavoring to change it into a political arena is bad for the university and harmful to the community. It generally generates a reaction in the community which affects the whole nature of the university . . . The sad experience people at the university must take into account is that when you start pushing you might get pushed back, because politics is a two-way street.

The Washington Post, 2–7:A14.

Winton M. Blount
Postmaster General of the United States

Today, the idiocy of university students, who are frequently unqualified even to attend a university, distasting the courses they will take, the system under which they will be graded and the people they will study under, is matched only by the absurdity of those administrators who tolerate this idiocy.

Plainview (Tex.) Daily Herald, 5–21:8.

Daniel J. Boorstin
Director, National Museum of History and
Technology, Washington

There are many wonderful things about being young; but there are also many lesswonderful things. Yet, every time another college building is burned down, or more rocks are thrown, some public figure feels it necessary to tell us how wonderful "young people" are.

Interview, Washington/
U.S. News & World Report, 10–19:66.

Julian P. Boyd
Historian

Our colleges and universities have become enclaves of irrationality. Many therein, even those who have dedicated their lives to learning, have deliberately rejected the ideal of dispassionate objectivity. Others, no less consciously, have trampled on the rights of their fellows, have employed force to achieve their ends, have destroyed files representing the life work of scholars, have actually engaged in the burning of books, have denied the right to others to be heard and, in a time of tolerance so limitless as to permit an unprecedented freedom of expression, have declared that the society of which they are a part is oppressive, tyrannical and decadent. Instead of that climate of comity, tolerance and respect, wherein all questions may be freely asked and no answers forbidden, there exists a climate of conformity that is suffocating to the spirit of rationality.

At Trenton (N.J.) State College/
The Wall Street Journal, 10–21:14.

Kingman Brewster, Jr.
President, Yale University

Most students are smart enough to know there are no easy answers. But they would like their elders to admit that the questions are real.

Before American Newspaper Publishers
Association, New York/Time, 5–4:60.

Jacob Bronowski
Deputy director, Salk Institute

The campuses are full of young men and women in open mutiny. Why? Because they are 18, 19 and 20 in birth age, and we treat them as if they were still the students of 50 years ago. But the fact is that they are all 20, 21 and 22 in true biological age. They are grown men and women who should have started their college careers two years earlier. Biological age has shifted during the past 50 years by at least 18 months in men and 15 months in women. These great hairy creatures going about in beards and sandals are the natural outcome of being treated as children, people whose age on the birth certificate bears no relation to what their true age is.

Interview/San Francisco Examiner & Chronicle
(California Living), 3–1:25.

Joel T. Broyhill
United States Representative, R-Va.

Enough is enough and we're all fed up. What should be done is to kick them (college protestors) the hell out of college . . . Many of these young people are looking for any excuse they can find to burn, smash and go down to the reflecting pool and swim naked . . . If they'd (the news media) stop running a camera every time one of these punks demonstrates, 95 per cent of these demonstrations would dry up . . . Some of the blood caused by the demonstrators is on the hands of the press.

Washington, May 14/
The Dallas Times Herald, 5–15:A5.

James M. Buchanan
Professor of Economics, Virginia Polytechnic Institute

How can we ask the taxpayer to support the education of students who occupy buildings, block major traffic arteries and disrupt normal educational processes? The answer is that we cannot. To do so would clearly be fraudulent. Yet most academic personnel would be aghast at my statements here. They feel, for some strange reason, that the academicians are God's chosen people in the modern world, and that the taxpayer should continue to throw his money over the ivy wall, so to speak; that it is boorish of him to so much as inquire as to what goes on behind these walls. The modern academician seems in this respect, as in others, to have lost elementary common sense.

Before Phi Kappa Phi, Virginia Polytechnic
Institute/The Wall Street Journal, 7–31:6.

William R. Butler
Professor of Education, University of Miami

I have long been concerned that, if the professionally-oriented, hard-working moderate student tends to lose sight of the politi-

(WILLIAM R. BUTLER)

cal threat on his campus, and if the moderate and conservative viewpoint is not expressed today, then this critical student input on campus will be missing. We must realize that a major portion of the extra-curricular life on many campuses may soon become controlled by the radical student element— for example, the student government, the student publications, the student radio stations and, most vitally, the management of student fees used to support activities on campus. The radical segment of our student bodies in recent years has become quite politically adept.

Before Institute of Engineering Deans,
University of Miami, May 4/
Vital Speeches, 7–1:568.

Robert C. Byrd
United States Senator, D-W. Va.

I have only contempt for school administrators who would try to contend that a riot on a college campus is somehow different from a riot elsewhere.

Plainview (Tex.) Daily Herald, 12–27:A6.

Al Capp
Cartoonist

I've had people tell me they agree with me fully, but they wonder if I'm not coming down too hard on the kids. But the kids— bless them—keep outdoing themselves to earn every charge I make against them.

Human Events, 4–25:18.

David F. Cargo
Governor of New Mexico

I am setting up a council of all student-body presidents in the state. I'm trying to open lines of communication with the students, but it is difficult. For example, you hold a meeting with students and all of a sudden a nice-looking girl pops up and uses language at you that would curl a sailor's hair.

Washington/U.S. News & World Report,
5–25:25.

W. Eugene Clingan
Assistant vice chancellor for student affairs
University of Wisconsin

Universities are going to start making demands of their students. The freewheeling days of last May's student strikes cannot be allowed to stand as precedents. We are insisting this year that *everyone* has rights, not just the radicals. We cannot play games any more.

Time, 9–21:6

Wayne A. Danielson
Dean, School of Communication,
University of Texas at Austin

It will be years before we, in the slow pace of scholarly thought, get around to making an accurate assessment of what the (1970 graduates) did to or for American higher education. My personal feeling, however, is that when the last shot dies away and the last can of tear gas is thrown away, we will find that this generation of students left more than they took, added more than they subtracted.

At commencement, University of Texas
Austin School of Communication
Quote, 9–20:27

Harris L. Dante
Chairman, Faculty Senate,
Kent State University

Universities are not very popular across our nation today. Fears generated by the tactics of a small minority are both understandable and justifiable. However, there real danger that education itself, and the universities as institutions, are coming be regarded as a conspiratorial cause for the ills of our society.

At commencement, Kent State University
June 13/The New York Times, 6–14:(1)

Robert J. Dole
United States Senator, R-Kan.

When students attack members of the National Guard, they are not attacking the establishment; they are attacking, for the most part, young men—men of their own generation

tion, some of whom also go to college or work and have wives and babies—young men serving out their obligations to their country or who feel a duty to serve their country. I urge the young people on our campuses to take a second look at those they vent their protests on. They are black; they are white or brown. They have every degree of intelligence and education. The only thing separating them from their counterparts on campus is a uniform and the fact that they are present, not to create violence, but to prevent it if possible . . .

Before the Senate, Washington, May 5 / U.S. News & World Report, 5-18:92.

Robert H. Finch
Secretary of Health, Education and Welfare of the United States

It is perfectly true that students have no monopoly on wisdom. They did not suddenly "discover" war or hunger or poverty or discrimination. But, as it always has been through history, they are the least able to compromise with injustice. They have no tolerance for race hatreds. They have no patience with the deferral of burning problems . . . We should take students seriously, not because they are future voters or because they pose a threat to democratic process—but because they help voice the nation's conscience. It slanders an entire generation to confuse a militant fringe with the vast preponderance of deeply-concerned, genuinely motivated young citizens—and it throws them into the extremists' arms.

At Arizona State University commencement, June 2 / The Washington Post, 6-7:B6.

Robben W. Fleming
President, University of Michigan

It is sad to see the Vice President of the United States launch superficial attacks on universities for their failure to curb turbulence and for eroding standards by admitting black students. Every study of campus turbulence shows that it is directly related to national policies which are largely beyond the control of universities, but which

are unpopular with the youth of the country.

At University of Michigan commencement, May 2 / San Francisco Examiner & Chronicle, 5-3:A25.

Roger A. Freeman
Special Assistant to the President of the United States; Senior fellow, Hoover Institution, Stanford University

Mass riots, violence and wanton destruction . . . have taken place on about 500 campuses over the past six years . . . There are laws against such acts on the books of every state, imposing long prison sentences. Are the criminals who committed these acts now serving time in penitentiaries? How many of the faculty and students who participated have been expelled? Blackmail and violence have often been rewarded by college administrators with concessions and surrender. Most of the time, little effort was exerted to apprehend offenders, and, if identified, they were usually granted amnesty. Small wonder that a reign of terror continues on campuses. Nor will it end until either the presidents and trustees of colleges and universities live up to their responsibilities—or somebody else does the job for them, which would, of course, be far less desirable.

Before Washington State Research Council, Washington, June 19 / Vital Speeches, 7-15:596.

. . . a university which takes a stand on a political issue—and a violent stand at that—destroys its value and forfeits its claim to be a center for impartial study and teaching. It transgresses upon the rights of the members of the academic community with different views. It is too often forgotten that most parents send their children to college to learn, not to decide public policy. If students were mature enough to exercise such judgments, they would not need to go to college.

Before Washington State Research Council, Washington, June 19 / Vital Speeches, 7-15:597.

John W. Gardner
Chairman, National Urban Coalition

. . . the tragic thing is that the small num-

(JOHN W. GARDNER)

ber of extremists, with their resort to absolutely inexcusable acts, have confused and masked very important peaceful protest on the part of large numbers of students. And it's terribly important to distinguish between those two. The American who looks out and sees only the violence and coercion, the rock-throwing and window-breaking and arson, and doesn't see the peaceful dissent of large numbers of students who are perfectly decent Americans trying to say something about our society, worried about things in our society, the American who doesn't see this is making a grave mistake.

Interview, Washington /
The Christian Science Monitor, 6–8:10.

Samuel B. Gould
Chancellor, State University of New York

Some students are more interested in things that are emotional and instinctive than they are in things that you figure out intellectually. They have said that—as they look at what's happened in this world—when they see the kind of world we have created by the use of reason, this is sufficient to warrant doing away with reason as the way in which we run the world for the future. Now, this may sound like a completely wild statement on their part, but this is the way they feel. And this is why you see the beginning of a retreat from reason taking place on the campus.

Interview/U.S. News & World Report, 6–8:79.

We have a small group of students who are dedicated to the proposition that they want to tear down whatever exists at present as a system in this country, whether it be a university or a financial system or a judicial system or whatever. They are not of a mind to sit around with us and discuss what would be a better way. They do not talk about improving what presently exists. They really want chaos—and they say so openly. Now, there's no way you can reason with or bar-

gain with a group of that sort. You simpl have to recognize their goals and try to de fend yourself against them. This has bee one of our most difficult and perplexin problems.

Interview/U.S. News & World Report, 6–8:8.

Philip Handler
President, National Academy of Sciences

My recent experiences with universit groups have generally not been happy o pleasant. I have tried talking to them abou the benefits and possibilities of science re search in helping solve our problems. The will boo and hiss, or get up and walk out. am persuaded that the faculty members wh encourage and support them in such action are not actually stupid on this point. Bu they are running scared. The students ma not be running the universities, but ther appear to be student groups that don't in tend to let anyone else run them. Terrorisr has always worked that way. It's a very in sidious thing . . .

Interview, Washington
The Christian Science Monitor, 9–4:?

S. I. Hayakawa
President, San Francisco State College

Protest leaders, at least on the San Fran cisco State College campus, eventually re vealed themselves to be striving for the im position of their brand of authoritarian con trol. In other words, they were not intereste in justice and improvement, merely a chang in command from the freedom establishe by the State of California to the revolutior ary leadership of the masses from whom without prior consultation, they presume to speak.

Before Association of American College
Houston, Jan. 12
Los Angeles Herald-Examiner, 1–12:A.

What we are really dealing with (in stu dent violence) is Nazi-type techniques. I ar not going to take it; I am not going to stan for it . . . When you've got a problem with swine, you've got to call in the "pigs."

Before Association of American Colleges, Houston, Jan. 12/The New York Times, 1–13:18.

If the majority of students at Stanford vote for the continuance of ROTC, the elitists will say they'll shut it down anyhow. "What the hell does the majority know?" they ask.

Before American Newspaper Publishers Association, New York/Time, 5–4:60.

Campuses should always be in a state of unrest. There should be constant exchanges, arguments, disputations going on, or otherwise there is no intellectual life. Unrest is one thing; destruction is another.

Before Commonwealth Club, San Francisco, Sept. 25/San Francisco Examiner, 9–26:3.

Alexander Heard
Chancellor, Vanderbilt University

Campuses have been faced in these last few years by conditions that they did not have to contend with before, and I think these instances of not just violence, but other forms of protest, have exposed how fragile a university is; how fragile a college is; and they have exposed the fact that often authority and responsibility are not commensurate. University presidents are often held responsible for things over which (they have) no authority.

Interview/Meet the Press, National Broadcasting Company, Washington, 8–30.

Theodore M. Hesburgh
President, University of Notre Dame

It is . . . an historic fact that any group, and particularly a university community, does not understand not being understood. What is more serious, young people in the university do not realize how much the university depends upon the support of the larger surrounding society. Even less do they understand that when their frustrations about the problems of the larger community lead them to act in anger and, at times, with violence, there is only one normal response from that larger community, namely, counterviolence and repressive action . . . The fact is that almost every state in the Union has considered in its legislature some punitive legislation against faculty and students—about half of which has been enacted into law. Trustees and Governors have practically forced the resignation of a number of (university) presidents, for instance in Texas, Oklahoma and California. Feeling is running high against many highly visible universities, and the witch hunters are out and at work. Both Federal and state programs of support for higher education have been reduced or tied to impossible conditions. Many private universities find themselves hard put to hold fast to the support they now have, much less to augment it. Disaffection with universities, their presidents, their faculties and their students is simply a growing fact of life that will probably get worse.

Before University of Notre Dame faculty/ The New York Times, 10–17:29.

Stephen Hess
National Chairman, 1970 White House Conference on Children and Youth

Certainly, this generation is much more aware—more activist—than those of the past. I've been reading the proceedings of the 1960 White House Conference on Children and Youth. Speaker after speaker arose to bemoan the apathy of youth and to wonder how we might strike some sparks among them. Clearly, that is not our problem today.

Interview, Washington/ U.S. News & World Report, 2–16:56.

Very often campus confrontations never get to the point of assessing political or economic realities. Long before that can occur, a process of obfuscation has usually set in. When students want the university to help sponsor low-cost housing in the surrounding community, the demand somehow becomes a call for cessation of "urban imperialism." When minority groups seek more representation in admissions, the issue too often be-

(STEPHEN HESS)

comes "the racists versus the people." And university administrators are quite adept at this technique also. Reasonable requests for university action are changed in administration statements into "unreasonable demands that threaten the very life of the institution." Even more distasteful is the tendency for some students, professors, administrators and trustees to attempt to use campus unrest for their own selfish purposes. Those who make statements whose sole purpose is to be quoted in *The New York Times* serve only to further weaken the university and make a mockery of both movements for reform and attempts to preserve the university.

Before American Association of Student Governments/The Wall Street Journal, 11–9:12.

James M. Hester
President, New York University

If there is a deepening of the apprehension about the (Vietnam) war . . . and if there is a growing frustration with (students') attempts to communicate with the political process . . . the position of the . . . super-radical leaders—claiming to be the authentic spokesmen for peace—will become stronger. If we allow this serious problem among our students to deteriorate, we are opening up the conditions in which those who are really bent on revolution will have every opportunity to advance their cause.

Television interview, May 31 / Los Angeles Herald-Examiner, 6–1:A12.

Walter J. Hickel
Secretary of the Interior of the United States

Today's college students, with a few exceptions, do not want to be pushed into the corner of violence. Peace is more than their motto; it is their instinct, and will remain so unless they are radicalized by isolation and hostility.

San Francisco Examiner & Chronicle (This World), 5–31:2.

Of course rioting and violence are nega-

tive. So is the rhetoric of polarization. As hard as we may try, we cannot "tear the nation together" . . . (But) I refuse to agree with those who settle for the cheap answers. They want the government to deal with consequences, not causes. These are the people who demand law and order, but refuse to concern themselves with why there is hatred, frustration and violence in the land. They want a crackdown on drug traffic, but they don't address themselves to why there is the boredom and emptiness which craves escape. I, for one, find the student mood and movement at a most helpful stage. There is a depth of maturity entering into it, a bigness of understanding which puts to shame some of the thinking I hear coming from other quarters. When change is found difficult, the immature turn to violence or they drop out; the mature dig in.

Before American Association of Student Governments, Washington, Sept. 25 / San Francisco Chronicle, 9–26:

Charles J. Hitch
President, University of California

Classrooms are disrupted in the name of education; speakers are shouted down in the name of free speech; job recruiters are driven from the campus in the name of morality and demands for total conformity to a particular line of thought are made in the name of nonconformity and dissent . . . The crowd that turns into a mob is an insult to the principles of democratic society, and it is a moral insult to the fundamentals of a university . . . Perhaps it is my own nature, but I am nauseated by the support that some of my academic colleagues give to this sick, ignorant, indulgent irrationalism.

Before UC Board of Regents / Los Angeles Times, 3–23:(I)

Ernest F. Hollings
United States Senator, D-S.C.

Impatience is the mark of the student. Born and bred on instant food, raised and schooled on instant credit, they expect ant government. The student movement at followed Gene McCarthy was motivated the hope for peace and new leadership. he students made their mark in over a zen primaries. But when they failed in icago (at the Democratic convention), ey immediately cried fraud, and quit. *Our neration would have savored the progress ade, come back and tried again. But not day's generation; they fail to appreciate at America and the road to freedom is not e 100-yard-dash, but the endurance con- t.*

At Blue Key Service Fraternity, University of Georgia, Sept. 21/Vital Speeches, 11–1:38.

ney Hook
*ofessor of Philosophy,
w York University*

Some faculty apologists for the student els have sought to play down the enor- ty of the offenses against intellectual and demic freedom by dismissing them as onsequential. "Just a few buildings rned," they say. This is as if one were to enuate the corruption of justice by the mbers of magistrates not bribed, or lynch- s by their infrequency. The sober fact is t violence has reached such proportions the campuses today that the whole atmo- ere of American—and many European Japanese—universities has been trans- med. The appeal to reason is no longer icient to resolve problems or even to keep peace. In order to make itself heard in e of our most prestigious institutions, appeal to reason must appeal to the ice.

*At Stanford University/
The Washington Post, 5–17:B4.*

ntellectual unrest is not a problem but a ue, and no university can have too much t if it is engaged in genuine educational s. The problem and threat is *not* aca- ic unrest but academic *disruption* and *ence* which flow from substituting for academic goals of learning the political s of action. Some administrators who

have abetted the erosion of the academic ideal are seeking to muddy the waters by pretending that the public is getting fed up with controversy, and that the chief threat to academic freedom today comes from with- out and not from within. This is noisome hogwash. The objection is not to contro- versy, for intellectual controversy is the life of mind. The public objection is to *how* controversy is carried on . . .

Before President's Commission on Campus Disorders/Los Angeles Times, 8–30:F7.

J. Edgar Hoover
Director, Federal Bureau of Investigation

A lot has been said in the press about the FBI swarming onto the campuses. The FBI is not on any campus. A Princeton professor blamed me for having agents on the campus, and he even called me a bastard. I wrote him that the FBI never goes on a campus except to investigate bombings of federally-funded buildings; and while I do not indulge in vul- garity, I called him a liar. It's an absolute lie. Of course, most students think we shouldn't go unless they invite us. They can have as many demonstrations, sit-ins, lay-ins as they want, and we will never look into it. I think students have a perfect right to dis- sent and to express their views through proper channels. But they ought not to re- solve their differences by throwing bricks and bottles on the streets.

Interview/Time, 12–14:17.

Bob Jones, Jr.
*President, Bob Jones University,
Greenville, S.C.*

I'm all for the police shooting to kill when anyone is in mob violence attempting to destroy property and attack law enforcement officers. More power to them. While I grieve for their families, I say those young people (killed at Kent State University) got exactly what they were entitled to, and what they should have expected . . .

*Greenville, S.C., May 7/
Los Angeles Times, 5–9:(1)12.*

127

Kenneth Keniston
Member of faculty, Yale
University Medical School

If we are to stop the killing on campus, we must take the murderous weapons out of the hands of civil authorities who have so far done the killing.

Before President's Commission on
Campus Unrest, Washington, July 24 /
The Washington Post, 7–25:A4.

Edward M. Kennedy
United States Senator, D-Mass.

The stage is set for a new political activism in America . . . For the undergraduates of Boston University and a large part of the generation of college students graduating this year around America, it is fair to say that final examinations were held in Washington, D.C., last weekend (at an antiwar rally), instead of on the campuses of their universities . . . For many, one week on Capitol Hill was worth four years of political science in college.

At Boston University, May 17 /
Los Angeles Times, 5–18:(1)6.

Turmoil on the campus lends itself to the wildest and basest forms of political rhetoric. The kind of demagoguery we hear from our Vice President (Spiro Agnew) provides a thick smoke screen behind which some elements in our society can hide what they themselves are really doing to this nation. For those who pander to public emotion and perplexity at events on campus are also those who allow the war (in Vietnam) to continue, and who disorder our national priorities so that we invest in SSTs and ABMs instead of teachers and health care for our sick. And so, in large part because mainstream America is preoccupied with concern about the campus, we all suffer.

At Boston University, Sept. 13 /
The Dallas Times Herald, 9–14:A8.

Those who seek change by the threat of use of force must be identified and isolated, and subjected to the sanctions of criminal law. They are the hijackers of the university . . . and, like hijackers, they must be deterred and repudiated . . . Any person who lends them aid and comfort, any person who grants them sympathy and support, must share the burden of guilt.

San Francisco Examiner & Chronicle
(This World), 10–18:2

Today, sadly, neither the President nor any of the highest officials of his Administration can travel freely to the campuses of our country. Of all the deep concerns that plague the nation today, perhaps the deepest is the isolation of our leaders from our youth, the alienation of our present from our future. The scream of the young girl kneeling beside her dead friend on the grass at Kent State (University) is the scream of America. That terrible scene—and the photograph of the National Guard firing wildly into the Kent students, and the bullet-riddled Jackson (State University) dormitor —have become symbols of the tortured spirit of America, just as Picasso's "Guernica" and Goya's painting of the firing squad in Madrid transformed lonely killings in the past into timeless symbols of man's brutality to man.

Before President's Commission on
Campus Unrest, Washington, July 15 /
Congressional Record, 7–15:S11349

Clark Kerr
Chairman, Carnegie Commission on Higher
Education; Former president,
University of California

The three greatest issues facing the United States today are, in my opinion: 1. The contribution we can make to the peace of the world, particularly in Southeast Asia; 2. Full equality for all our citizens; 3. The preservation of our environment. Campus unrest reflects these issues. If we try to put down campus unrest without doing something about peace, equality and environment, we will end up with repression. Students are like the rest of us. They react to the same issues, only they do so ahead of the adult society

This has been the historical pattern in this country . . . What's happening to the students is what's happening all over the United States, only in a more exaggerated way. This unrest occurs because there are unsolved problems.

News conference/
The Wall Street Journal, 7-23:10.

William M. Kunstler
Civil rights lawyer

Another form resistance could take would be the burning down of a particular college building at a safe time—that is, when no one is in it, when no danger to human life is involved . . . if a point has been reached in a given situation where the mechanisms of society are not responding to serious grievances . . . You must remember that Hiroshima was a pretty good example of arson, and that was an act of the United States government.

Interview/Newsweek, 9-21:57.

Philip B. Kurland
Professor of Law, University of Chicago

We are told that this—*i.e.,* the current student generation—is the best-informed group of students that we have ever known. It's a generation with lots of new scientific data and almost no knowledge of history. It is an amnesic generation. And, to the extent that they are better informed, it is through information provided them by their predecessors. As has been noted before, even a pygmy can see further than a giant, if he is standing on the giant's shoulders. It is said that this is the student generation whose morality is somehow higher than those who preceded it, because it is a sincere group. Indeed, sincerity is suggested to be adequate excuse for any misconduct they may indulge. But there are precedents here, too. Theirs is the morality and sincerity that have typified all the zealots that have come before them. Theirs is the morality, for example, of the Spanish Inquisition that sincerely sought to save the souls of men, even if it had to send them to hell by fire in the course of making the ef-

fort toward reform. It is a morality that justifies its admittedly miserable means by its allegedly enlightened goals. The fact is that this student generation is not a righteous group—only a self-righteous one.

Before Chicago Bar Association, Jan. 22/
Vital Speeches, 3-1:315.

. . . the myth has it that the recalcitrants among the students are only a small number of the student population. And this . . . is true, if the only ones to be counted are those active in using force to impose their wills. But if one looks to the numbers who are either sympathetic to or apathetic about such behavior, the proportion is very high indeed. One looks in vain for student opposition to the destructive activities of their colleagues. For the fact is that a very large number of students are in sympathy with the goals of the so-called "student movement."

Before Chicago Bar Association, Jan. 22/
Vital Speeches, 3-1:315.

Those university presidents who are enjoying . . . the peace that has descended on campuses during this academic year might recognize that it has been bought at the price of surrender.

Quote, 3-1:193.

Clifford L. Lord
President, Hofstra University

Two months ago I was in Madison, Wisconsin, visiting friends. One professor, a former assistant president, now a departmental chairman, said sadly, "Cliff, this university is being destroyed before our eyes, and there seems to be nothing anyone can do about it." You and I are not going to sit by and do nothing if anyone starts the process which could lead to the destruction of this university. We are educators, not skull crackers. We believe in reason and the rational process. But the true revolutionary does not. And if the rational process should fail, I do not for a minute believe that we are obligated to preside at our own demolition. As Jefferson put it, "Error may be tolerated

(CLIFFORD L. LORD)

where reason is free to combat it." But force, coercion, violence, the threat of violence, extortion under such threats, are something far different and will not be tolerated.

Before Hofstra University faculty/
The Wall Street Journal, 10–6:18.

Allard K. Lowenstein
United States Representative, D-N.Y.

Some . . . people who favor violence are cowards. Any time they get counter-violence, they scream and howl they're being repressed. Beating up professors in the name of social justice is something I don't buy.

Look, 8–25:38.

Richard W. Lyman
Acting president, Stanford University

The penalties (for campus disorders) often have been almost ludicrously lenient. I don't believe expulsion will take us back to the 1950s, as some believe.

Interview/San Francisco Examiner & Chronicle,
8–16:A5.

Richard W. Lyman
President, Stanford University

The relationship between terrorism and anything a university president might do is certainly less than the relationship was a year or so ago with the more massive movements of campus protest. Terrorists operate in secret, in small groups, and necessarily with some tight discipline. If a student is resorting to that, the chances are he is beyond the reach of anything that can be called communication.

Interview/Los Angeles Herald-Examiner,
10–13:A10.

Archibald MacLeish
Poet, Playwright

(Conflicts at the nation's universities) are not disciplinary troubles, whatever the generation now in middle age may say about them. They are not, as the more romantic of the young believe, "revolutionary," meaning political, troubles. They are troubles at the heart of human life; troubles in the culture itself, in the civilization; troubles that cannot be cured by ranting at the government, however misguided or misdirected, or by sending in the National Guard, whatever the provocation; but only by restoring the culture to wholeness and to health, which means by restoring the precarious balance between society and the self.

At inauguration of Hampshire College,
Amherst, Mass./Time, 10–19:14.

William J. McGill
Chanceller, University of California at San Diego; President-designate, Columbia University

Just the other day, as I walked across my campus, a student looked at me very angrily and said, "There goes the pig-chancellor." With this kind of popularity on campus matching an equally low public standing in San Diego, I felt it was time to move. At Columbia, at least I can be pig-president.

Before American College Public Relations
Association/Los Angeles Times, 7–12:F1.

Violence on campuses at present is unrelated to student unrest. The violent elements on campus are very small militant groups. On this campus, as at Columbia, it's perfectly evident that we're seeing the development of small militant communities which thrive somewhere near a university and use the liberal climate of the university as a friendly environment. I know that's the case at Columbia. I know that many of the tough radicals who show up late at night on the Columbia campus have nothing to do with the student body.

Interview, San Diego/
The New York Times Magazine, 8–23:77.

James A. Michener
Author

You cannot even build a sewer without knowledgeable people. Those determined to close down the universities are my enemies.

Quote, 12–27:599.

John N. Mitchell
Attorney General of the United States

He's (President Nixon) probably the most informed President there's ever been. He reads everything and remembers it all. I really can't understand how people can call him isolated. He's aware of everything that's going on. I'll tell you who's not informed, though. It's these stupid kids. Why, they don't know the issues. They pick the rhetoric that they want to hear right off the top of an issue and never finish reading to the bottom. Why, I talked to the kids from Harvard Law School in my office, and I was flabbergasted at how uninformed they are about what's going on inside government. And the professors are just as bad if not worse. They don't know anything. Nor do these stupid bastards who are running our educational institutions. You know, we have the finest educational system in the world, and they're trying to destroy it. Well, I'll tell you what's going to happen. If they keep on, nobody is going to support any of these institutions any more, and we're going to lose our precious heritage: the higher educational institutions in this country.

Interview, Washington/
Los Angeles Times, 9–20:A1.

Grover E. Murray
President, Texas Technological University

There are those who are annoyed, repulsed, repelled or appalled by the frequent demonstrations and increasing violence. Many are bewildered or confused by the apparent ingratitude of the young for the society in which they are privileged to live. These responses show a lack of understanding for the feelings of the young. Whether one agrees with them on particular issues— and there are disagreements among the young—it must be acknowledged that the protests about the Indochina war, about the mutilation of our environment, about dis-

crimination and about practices in higher education stem basically from our republic's first principles and an intense concern for our nation's future . . . When the present unrest has subsided—which it will in time— it will not be "business as usual." The nation will come out of these wrenching years of turmoil a changed and improved society.

Interview, Lubbock, Tex./
Los Angeles Times, 12–6:G8.

Edmund S. Muskie
United States Senator, D-Maine

Student dissent has not been a disease of the body politic. It has instead been a welcome sign of health . . . It is a sign that millions of young people would rather improve America than escape or reject her . . . that they would rather have America united than fearful and insecure.

At University of New Hampshire
commencement/Quote, 7–5:1.

Richard M. Nixon
President of the United States

I wish to reaffirm a point I have often made—I do not approve of interference by the Federal government in the internal affairs of our colleges and universities. I am gravely concerned, of course, about the problem of student unrest. At the same time, I have recognized that enforcement of discipline and the maintenance of order in our schools is primarily the responsibility of the schools themselves. The Federal government is ill-fitted to play the role of policeman on our college and university campuses.

Washington/U.S. News & World Report, 1–12:6.

. . . you see these bums . . . blowing up the campuses. Listen, the boys on the college campuses today are the luckiest people in the world, going to the greatest universities, and here they are burning up the books. I mean, storming around about this issue (Vietnam) . . . Get rid of the war and there'll be another (issue).

Washington, May 1/Los Angeles Times,
5–2:(1)1.

(RICHARD M. NIXON)

I would certainly regret that my use of the word "bums" was interpreted to apply to those who dissent . . . I have for years defended the right of dissent. (But) I have always opposed the use of violence . . . When students on university campuses burn buildings, when they engage in violence, when they break up furniture, when they terrorize their fellow students and terrorize the faculty, then I think "bums" is perhaps too kind a word to apply to that kind of person.

News conference, Washington, May 8/
Los Angeles Herald-Examiner, 5–9:A2.

The problem of communicating with students and other groups is a perennial one. It existed in previous Administrations; it exists in this one. However, I would only say that in order to maintain balance we have to recognize that for university presidents and professors and other leaders to put the blame for the problems of the universities on the government primarily, I think, is very shortsighted. We're ending the war (in Vietnam); we will bring it to an end. We will bring the draft to an end and have a volunteer armed service. We're going to deal with the problems of the environment; we're going to clean up the air and the water. All of these things can be done and will be done by government. We're reforming government to make it more responsive to the people—more power to the people, rather than more power in Washington, D.C. But once all those things are done, still the emptiness and the shallowness, the superficiality that many college students find in college curricula will still be there. And still, when that is done, the problem that we have of dissent on campus—not remaining in peaceful challenge, which is perfectly appropriate and defensible, but dissent becoming sometimes violent, sometimes illegal, sometimes shouting obscenities when visiting speakers come to campus—this is a problem that is not a problem for government. We cannot solve it. It

is a problem which college administrators and college faculties must face up to.

News conference, Los Angeles, July 30/
U.S. News & World Report, 8–10:33.

. . . what corrodes a society even more deeply than violence itself is the acceptance of violence, the condoning of terror, the excusing of inhuman acts in a misguided effort to accommodate the community's standards to those of the violent few . . . Nowhere should the rule of reason be more respected or more jealously guarded than in the halls of our great universities. Yet, as we know, at some of our great universities small bands of destructionists have been allowed to impose their own rule of arbitrary force. Because of this, we face the greatest crisis in the history of American education today. In times past, we have faced shortages of classrooms, shortages of teachers, shortages that could always be made up by appropriations of money. These material shortages are nothing compared to the crisis of the spirit which rocks hundreds of campuses across the country today. And because of this, to put it bluntly, today higher education in America risks losing that essential support it has had since the beginning of this country: the support of the American people.

At Kansas State University, Sept. 16/
Los Angeles Times, 9–17:(1)16.

Law and order are not code words for racism and repression. Law and order are code words for freedom from fear. This new attitude means that parents must exercise their responsibility for moral guidance. It means that college administrators must stop caving in to the demands of the radical few. And it means that moderate students must take a position that says to the violent: "Hit the books or hit the road."

At Republican campaign rally, Phoenix,
Oct. 31/The New York Times, 11–1:(1)66.

Lawrence F. O'Brien
Chairman, Democratic National Committee
I do not prejudge the investigation of the

massacre that is now being conducted (at Kent State University) in Ohio, but I can only wonder . . . whether those (National Guard) triggers would have been pulled if the elected leaders in this country had acted differently. I can only speculate in sorrow whether those young people would have been killed were it not for the Nixon-Agnew-Mitchell inflammatory rhetoric—the rhetoric that appeals to the fears and prejudices and darker impulses that lurk within mankind.

Milwaukee, May 9/
U.S. News & World Report, 5–25:98.

Charles F. Palmer
President, National Student Association

As long as the war in Indochina continues with no end in sight . . . as long as there is poverty in this country . . . until these things are changed, we will continue to make life uncomfortable, and at times unlivable, for the men in positions of power and influence.

At hearings of the President's Commission on Campus Unrest, Washington/
The New York Times, 7–19:(4)1.

Claiborne Pell
United States Senator, D-R.I.

I do not agree that live ammunition should ever be issued for use against students. When troops are sent in to confront students, water cannon, tear gas and truncheons should be enough. This has been the experience of other governments. I would hope we had learned from that experience.

Before the Senate, Washington, May 5/
U.S. News & World Report, 5–18:94.

Georges Pompidou
President of France

The most dangerous thing about student riots is that adults take them seriously. Thus, they become a real problem. Otherwise, it would simply be a matter of letting the students grow older.

Interview, Paris/Life, 2–20:37.

Nathan M. Pusey
President, Harvard University

It is my conviction that deceitful talk and the tendencies toward coercive action (by student militants) could not have the inroads they have in academic communities in recent years had all of us to whom they are deeply repulsive been more ready to oppose them.

At Harvard University/
National Observer, 6–15:10.

One can read through all the leaflets circulated by these extremists who have dwelt among us in recent years—bent on slandering an institution it might have assumed they would love, or lovingly find fault with—without discovering a single effort to clarify, to analyze, to explain or honestly represent. Always they insinuate, distort, accuse—their aim being not to identify and correct real abuses, but always rather by crying alarm intentionally to arouse and inflame passions in order to build support for "non-negotiable demands," and by this means to enlarge their following and enhance their power.

At Harvard University commencement/
The Christian Science Monitor, 6–19:14.

Ronald Reagan
Governor of California

We have every legitimate channel—more than any other people have ever had—for registering dissent: by way of our elections, by way of our influence on legislators to get things done and changed. You have to come to the realization that some of the causes for which the students are rallying the most have evidently not met the democratic test of being a majority viewpoint. Therefore, when they suddenly say, "Well, it's hopeless, we've tried our disapproval and therefore we now are justified in violent action," what they are in effect saying is that, "We haven't been able to persuade the majority of our citizens to go along with us. Therefore, because we, the minority, can't have our way, we'll tear the place down."

Interview, Sacramento/
The Christian Science Monitor, 5–14:2.

Victor G. Rosenblum
President, Reed College

There is an inconsistency here between the claim that better education leads to a better world and the attempt to blame educators and students for student ferment. The innovator in education will be an agitator as well; and only if we fear change will we make scapegoats of those trying to make us aware of inadequacy and need.

*San Francisco Examiner & Chronicle
(This World), 8–9:2.*

Francis W. Sargent
Governor of Massachusetts

These kids who are protesting are not the lunatic fringe. They are normal people who are frustrated and worried. Of course, there are some on the far left, but they are not representative. The political impact of this unrest will be felt. The young people and others are going to support candidates who think their way. They already are working toward the next election.

*Washington/U.S. News & World Report,
5–25:24.*

William B. Saxbe
United States Senator, R-Ohio

Dr. (Benjamin) Spock said today—it just came over the wire—that this incident (Kent State University shootings) shows that our government would kill rather than allow dissent. This is exactly the way it came over—that this incident shows that our government would kill rather than permit dissent. If there is anything that is completely wrong, it is a statement like that; because here are National Guardsmen, scared to death, with no orders to shoot anybody—in fact, I know that they have been impressed at every step of the way, "This is never done except when you are in danger yourself." But suppose . . . that they are given no ammunition, and they are sent out there, and everyone knows they have no ammunition, and the next thing their helmet is knocked off, their gun is taken away from them, they are publicly humiliated and defenseless. I wish that we could send our policemen out without guns. I wish that we could send all our peace officers out without any means of violence, even a club. But this cannot happen, and today we have to be realistic.

*Before the Senate, Washington, May 5/
U.S. News & World Report, 5–18:94.*

William W. Scranton
Chairman, President's Commission on Campus Unrest

The Commission's report . . . does not point the finger of blame for the increase in campus disorders at anyone. We were not charged to find blame. Instead, the report lifted this issue above the level of accusation and blame and asked for leadership from all involved to bring us together, back from the brink of deep division and further alienation . . . If anybody says that is "pablum for permissiveness," I don't think they understood.

*News conference, Chicago, Dec. 13/
The Washington Post, 12–15:A9.*

Karl Shapiro
Professor of English, University of California at Davis

Who would have thought, at least since the defeat of Hitler, that American professors would begin to remove their notes and files from their offices and take them home; that they would begin to remove their best or their irreplaceable volumes; that libraries would begin the reduplication of indexes as a safety measure; that specifically-trained police and guards and firemen would replace the old innocuous campus cop? I apologize for evoking these commonplaces, and yet who—except Lewis Carroll perhaps—would have dreamed of students acquiring the power to fire faculties, presidents and chancellors, to determine curricula and, worst of all, to force personal political opinion and dogma upon the teaching community at large and upon society itself? All under the name of Idealism, of course.

*Before California Library Association,
San Francisco/Human Events, 7–11:9.*

William L. Shirer
Author

Today, you go around to Harvard, UCLA or any place and try to give these kids a lot of nonsense about violence, working within the system and all the freedoms we've enjoyed—all of which contain a grain of truth —and the chances are you won't be able to finish your speech. These kids are aroused and know something about politics, economics, social problems and racial tensions, and they're committed in the thing. I think it's probably the most exciting and intelligent college generation we've ever had, and yet there's an awful lot of old stick-in-the-mud fuddy-duds who think they've gone to hell.

Interview, Beverly Hills, Calif./
Los Angeles Times, 3–13:(2)8.

Margaret Chase Smith
United States Senator, R-Maine

The antidemocratic arrogance and nihilism from the political left is an extremism that has spawned a polarization of our people and increasingly forcing upon the people the narrow choice between anarchy and repression. And make no mistake about it: If that narrow choice has to be made, the American people, even if with reluctance and misgiving, will choose repression. An overwhelming majority of Americans believe that: Trespass is trespass—whether on the campus or off; violence is violence— whether on the campus or off; arson is arson —whether on the campus or off; killing is killing—whether on the campus or off: The campus cannot degenerate into a privileged sanctuary for obscenity, trespass, violence, arson and killing with special immunity for participants in such acts. Criminal acts, active or by negligence, cannot be condoned or excused because of panic, whether the offender be a policeman, a National Guardsman, a student, or one of us in this legislative body. Repression is preferable to anarchy to most Americans.

Before the Senate, Washington,
June 1/Time, 6–15:18.

Preston Smith
Governor of Texas

While I still have great confidence in the vast majority of our young people, the time has now come to put a stop to such foolishness (campus disruption). When a public official—myself or anyone else—cannot go on the campus of a state-supported university to deliver a speech without being subjected to the rantings of a handful of unwashed, intolerant, ill-informed students, the time has come to act. If the students cannot behave themselves and live under the rules of the institutions—just as private citizens are required to obey the law—then there is no place for them in our halls of learning. If college administrators cannot control this sorry spectacle, we must find ways to step in and straighten out these undisciplined young people—both student and non-student—who stir up this kind of disturbance.

Houston, Oct. 8/The Washington Post,
10–9:A2.

Ralph T. Smith
United States Senator, R-Ill.

We must start doing something about the stormtroopers in hippie beads. And I think the place to start is our homes. If I had a youngster like that in college, I would not continue to finance his negative attempt at education and his raids on the college administration building. I would rather send him a bar of soap and a copy of the Golden Rule. And then I would search my soul to see where I had failed with him—how I had permitted him to get so far off the track— and to see what I might do to straighten out his warped thinking. And if all else failed, I would be willing to buy him a ticket—a one-way ticket—to go live in some one of the totalitarian countries whose philosophy and tactics are so dear to the hearts of the destroyer.

Before Veterans of Foreign Wars/
The Wall Street Journal, 5–18:8.

Rhoten A. Smith
President, Northern Illinois University

We have . . . been dealing with a new phenomenon—a body of student opinion too wide and too serious to be dismissed as "a few radicals." Meeting student dissent with force is one way of coping. But . . . I hope we now realize that force of arms is the least satisfactory way imaginable of dealing with the genuine concern of students about the war (in Vietnam) and national conditions.

Before Illinois House of Representatives,
Springfield, May 25/
The New York Times, 5–26:26.

Arleigh B. Templeton
President,
University of Texas at San Antonio

The faculty has to keep in touch with the realism of their own discipline on campus. We shouldn't blame the kids for everything during campus unrest, and we should not be afraid to admit we are wrong on certain occasions.

Panel discussion at Texas Daily Newspaper
Association meeting, Longview, Tex., Aug. 18/
The Dallas Times Herald, 8–19:A6.

Oswald Tippo
Chancellor, University of Massachusetts

We will be subject to repressive legislation and serious budget cuts, even warnings of withdrawal of complete state support, if we have any more building takeovers, if we have any more interference with free speech and free movement including attendance at class, if we have continued defacing of buildings and damage to buildings, if we continue to have strikes and other interruptions of academic work, and if we do not keep the campus open for those who come here for the serious purpose of study and teaching. Certainly, you have to be a moron to think that the taxpayers of this state will continue to appropriate large sums of money—money which is desperately needed for other purposes—if the university does not stay open to provide the education for which the money is voted. It is my sober judgment that this university cannot long survive unless we take immediate steps to put our house in order.

At opening convocation, University of
Massachusetts/The Wall Street Journal,
10–6:18.

William P. Tolley
Chancellor emeritus, Syracuse University

One of the unhappy facts of the current student rebellion is that it is self-defeating. It sows the wind—and almost certainly will reap the whirlwind. This is already beginning to occur in Japan and France. We do not have a repressive society. We have a remarkably tolerant and permissive society. But if the disruptions continue, we may have a repressive society. What the student activists may succeed in doing is to pave the way for a police state. Already they have achieved a striking resemblance to the situation in Germany in the years just prior to Hitler. The greatest of blunders, of course, was the closing of universities. Professor Richard Piper said it all when he remarked, "When a worker goes out on strike, he lays down his tools. When a student goes out on strike, he lays down his brain." The strike against the freest of our institutions is an assault against reason.

At Elmira (N.Y.) College commencement/
The Wall Street Journal, 9–8:16.

Joseph Tussman
Professor of Philosophy,
University of California at Berkeley

Faculties everywhere are acquiescing in the idea that the university must be relevant, and relevant means being immediately active in a political sense. Is Harvard, Cornell or Berkeley the better for it? What has it done except to brutilize everything?

Interview/The New York Times Magazine,
1–11:60.

Frank E. Vandiver
Acting president, Rice University

Universities and colleges are places of

contemplation and reflection, not of confrontation and rebellion. They are being turned by present conflict into political instruments to be aimed at the so-called ills of society. This shift in direction denies the real purpose of the university—which is to discover and teach truth. When truth is distorted to fit the prejudice of the moment, when teaching becomes a form of propaganda, then learning lapses into a kind of darkness which will lead surely to a triumph of ignorance.

At College of the Mainland, Texas City, Tex., May 27 / The Dallas Times Herald, 5–28:A7.

The Environment

Joy Adamson
Author

When I first arrived in Kenya 34 years ago, the train to Nairobi passed through plains filled with running game. Today, you are lucky if you see a few ostriches and wildebeests on the trip . . . Wildlife is something that man cannot construct. Once it is gone, it is gone forever. Man can rebuild a pyramid, but he can't rebuild ecology, or a giraffe.

Interview, Lake Naivasha, Kenya/
The Christian Science Monitor, 8–31:7.

Wayne N. Aspinall
United States Representative, D-Colo.

. . . there is no monetary cost in saving ourselves the half-billion dollar annual cost of litter pollution. The answer, quite simply, is discipline. That is all it takes. Discipline—on the part of all of us. Overnight we could wipe out a $500 million annual debt. This is money that could be used for solving pollution problems that are not the result of simple carelessness, but the inevitable consequence of an expanding population.

Before the House, Washington, Jan. 26/
Congressional Record, 1–26:H247.

J. Paul Austin
President, Coca-Cola Company

Man is a doer. He's a road-builder, a house-builder, a tree-cutter—an industrious, hard-working chap whose very industry determines the size of his rewards. And, being rather selfish—or shall I say, operating in his own self-interest, anyway—this doer, this creature with the big brain, has chopped and hacked and paved and built . . . and polluted his way from one end of this once-virgin land of ours to the other. So why not? Isn't that the way things simply *are*? Nobody is known to have achieved commercial greatness in this society by whiling away his hours beside some pastoral pond, Thoreau to the contrary notwithstanding. Really . . . isn't that the popular, no-nonsense attitude . . . the industrialized heritage we've been taught since we were children? Yes, it is. Hard-driving free enterprise is a fine old tradition in this country. It's what's made this country what it is. So what is *wrong* with free-wheeling progress? Maybe nothing is wrong with it. But on the other hand, maybe the ecologists are trying to tell us something. They're telling us, in quite clear tones, that if we keep all this up, we're going to "advance" ourselves into oblivion—an oblivion comprised of undrinkable water and air that can't be breathed. Listen to what they're saying. Think about some of the mid-twentieth century realities they're pointing out to us as we plunge headlong in pursuit of "progress."

Before Georgia Bankers Association, Atlanta,
April 16/Vital Speeches, 5–15:471.

Larry Barnett
Sociologist,
California State College at Los Angeles

No one knows what the optimum (U.S. population) level is. If we're willing to give up our present way of life—our automobiles, our visits to natural parks, our system of public education, and forgo private homes for high-rise apartments—then we could afford, perhaps, another couple of hundred million people. It all depends on your values.

Newsweek, 3–30:87.

Thomas Hart Benton
Artist

We've gotten so damned serious with our technology. Americans used to *play* with their rivers—Mike Fink and the keelboatmen, that kind of thing. Joyful work it was.

If every American could run the Buffalo (River) just once, the way we did today, then I think our rivers would be beyond the reach of trouble.

At the Buffalo River, Arkansas/
Sports Illustrated, 8–10:34.

Phillip Berry
President, Sierra Club

The popularity of our cause (ecological conservation) has attracted some whose motives must be questioned . . . Politicians paying lip service, industrialists laying down public relations smokescreens and anarchists voicing legitimate concerns about the environment for the ulterior purpose of attacking democratic institutions, are all suspect.

The New York Times, 2–24:28.

George Brown
United States Representative, D-Calif.

The Establishment sees this (Earth Day) as a great big anti-litter campaign. Wait until they find out what it really means. Most Establishment people don't have any idea of what it would mean to their life-style to clean up our earth.

April 22/Newsweek, 5–4:27.

Zbigniew Brzezinski
Director, Research Institute of Communist Affairs, Columbia University

. . . man has lived in combat with nature. Man has won that war—and pollution is part of the carnage of his victory.

Interview, New York/
The New York Times, 8–12:30.

Donald C. Burnham
Chairman,
Westinghouse Electric Corporation

I consider our work in nuclear power to be of vital importance in the fight to protect the environment. The smokeless, odorless, clean and safe nuclear generating station has been developed at a critical moment in our history . . . perhaps the best single weapon in our fight against pollution.

Fort Collins, Colo./
The New York Times, 7–20:38.

George Bush
United States Representative, R-Tex.

On April 22, which is "Earth Day," many students' suggestions will be thoughtful and sincere and will warrant consideration. Yet, by its nature, the teach-in does not provide an outlet for much of the good, solid thinking of many students. Clearly, a one-day Earth Day to discuss the problems of two centuries of environment deterioration will not do. Simply to know what is wrong, to learn what has brought our environment to its present dismal state, to express dissatisfaction, is not enough. We need to encourage our bright students, who have the scholarship to offer constructive thought and who desperately desire to, to contribute organized thinking to solving the environmental problems of our society.

Human Events, 4-25:18.

Leo Cherne
Executive director,
Research Institute of America

At the very peak of our progress, the air is foul, the beaches are filthy, the lakes and rivers die, some plants wither, birds flee, the garbage piles up. Last year, America built a mountain of rubbish which includes 26 billion bottles and jars, 48 billion metal cans and 65 billion metal and plastic caps. The beer can, once made of cheap steel, has been largely replaced by the aluminum can which virtually defies the corrosion of air or the erosion of time. More than a score of different kinds of plastic are now virtually indestructible. To this add the human waste, the manufacturing wastes, the chemicals, acids, the algae-destroying insecticides, the whole range of biocidal materials which are already making visible inroads on photosynthesis— and without nature's photosynthesis, we are without oxygen. By the year 2000, millions of Americans may be wearing respiratory devices.

Before Business Publications Audit meeting,
Chicago, Feb. 18/Vital Speeches, 4–15:408.

Frederick J. Clarke
Lt. Gen. and Chief of Engineers,
United States Army

(Ecological reform) is not a proper subject for rabble-rousing techniques, for the angry retort, the sarcastic personal slur, the glib misuse of statements far detached from their context and too often from reality.

Human Events, 4–18:6.

We find people denouncing papermills while consuming ever-increasing quantities of paper; driving their cars all over the country to berate the petroleum industry; burning electricity at meetings to upbraid the power industry; getting up in the morning, drinking a glass of Florida orange juice and denouncing the conversion of swamplands into orchards. They keep demanding more and more uses of their natural resources while demanding that they be left untouched. And your political leaders and public agencies are put in the intolerable position of being asked to heed simultaneously the demands expressed by the public in meeting-halls and indignation-meetings on the one hand, and the largely contradictory demands made by that same public in the marketplace and the employment bureau and the obstetrical ward on the other hand—because too many people have not considered the full implications of the courses they endorse.

Before Rivers and Harbors Congress, Washington/The Wall Street Journal, 4–27:14.

LaMont Cole
Professor of Zoology, Cornell University

There has been so much progress (toward bettering the environment) in the past five years that if I'm not careful I'm liable to become a little optimistic.

Time, 2–2:62.

We could make the earth uninhabitable and not realize it for perhaps 25 to 30 years. It could already have happened.

San Francisco Examiner & Chronicle, 3–15:B5.

Donald C. Cook
President,
American Electric Power Company

It is one thing to say that a utility company must spend 100 million dollars on air-pollution-control equipment. It is another for the customers to realize that their electric bills must increase by 15 million dollars a year to make this expenditure possible.

U.S. News & World Report, 2–2:21.

Jacques Cousteau
Underwater explorer

Imagine how clever of mankind, when he has a big slick of poison on top of the water, to add something to it that will make it sink slowly and kill everything in its path, all the way to the bottom.

Sports Illustrated, 5–11:19.

Walter Cronkite
News commentator,
Columbia Broadcasting System

Though we are just six per cent of the world's population . . . we create just about one half of the world's pollution. In fact, America's very success has become a planetary menace, second only, perhaps, to nuclear war.

San Francisco Examiner & Chronicle, 3–15:B5.

John M. DeNoyer
Director, Earth Observation Programs,
National Aeronautics and Space
Administration of the United States

Perhaps the single most important event of the last decade which has made man aware of the urgent need to preserve his environment was his first view of his home from outer space. This view of earth made man intimately aware of this unique and limited environment in which life must be sustained.

The Christian Science Monitor, 12–23:9.

Lee A. DuBridge
Science Adviser to the
President of the United States

. . . many people say that it's only India

or China or Africa that should be worried about population increase. The fact of the matter is that population growth in this country is a far more serious problem than that in developing countries. Those countries do not use many resources. It is the relatively slow-growing populations of the advanced nations, producing wastes at a rapid rate, that are a greater threat to the earth's environment.

Interview, Washington/
U.S. News & World Report, 1–19:48.

Fertility has been the key to the survival of every species. And now, for the first time in earth's history, there has emerged one creature for which fertility is not a blessing but a curse. That creature is man . . .

The New York Times, 1–21:46.

Jacques Duhamel
Minister of Agriculture of France

Too often, nature conservationists have tended to mount purely defensive campaigns . . . The result has been a profound communications gap between those concerned with building, producing or equipping and those concerned with conservation. Today we must replace mere protest by a counterproject. Nature conservation policy must be dynamic and not static.

Before European Conservation Conference,
Strasbourg, France/
The Christian Science Monitor, 2–17:3.

Roger O. Egeberg
Assistant Secretary for Health and Scientific Affairs, Department of Health, Education and Welfare of the United States

At the present birth rate, we'll have to build a city for a quarter million people every 30 or 40 days till the year 2000, probably even faster than that. We might be able to build the cities, but what do we do with all the stuff thrown out on the land and into the air?

San Francisco Examiner & Chronicle
(This World), 5–3:2.

Paul R. Ehrlich
Professor of Biology, Stanford University

Some biologists feel that compulsory family regulation will be necessary to retard population growth. It is a dismal prospect—except when viewed as an alternative to Armageddon.

Quote, 1–11:25.

We are playing environmental roulette: overbreeding, putting crud in the atmosphere, poisoning our water, killing our fish, sloshing pesticides which kill the insects that kill the pests—sheer idiocy!—heading straight into the worst crisis mankind has ever seen.

Interview, Los Angeles/
Los Angeles Times, 2–13:(4)1.

His (President Nixon's) State of the Union message makes it abundantly clear that he can be counted on to do practically nothing (about the environment). He addressed himself to one tiny part of the problem—sewage disposal—and the $4 billion he allocated in Federal funds for use over the next five years is totally inadequate. To make matters worse, the type of sewage plants this money is going into are the type that foul up the water with phosphates and nitrates. And if we ever should get our country on the right road with the right leaders, we're still going to have to work doubly hard to see to it that their counterparts in the Soviet Union, China and so on are also removed from power and put out on the happy farm where they belong.

Interview/Look, 4–21:44.

(The U.S. Department of Agriculture is) a subsidiary of the petrochemical industry that produces DDT and the other insecticides. The Department has no ecological knowledge whatever and is strongly in league with the very elements it ought to be regulating. Letting Agriculture control registration of pesticides is like letting the fox guard the henhouse.

Interview/Look, 4–21:44.

(PAUL R. EHRLICH)

Even if we prevented all *unwanted* children—the goal of family planning—we would still have a severe population problem. People *want* too many children. Family planning is a disaster because it is giving people a false sense of security. No one should have more than two children; anything beyond that is irresponsible, suicidal.

Interview/Look, 4–21:44.

People must remember that if they're against birth control they're in favor of misery and death. The arithmetic is very simple: Either the birth rate has to come down or the death rate is going to go up. I think that people who say we have to have the maximum number of people, regardless of what kind of misery they live in, are ordinarily well-fed people. This idea that the supreme value for human beings is to reproduce huge numbers essentially devalues the human being to the level of, say, a fruit fly.

Interview/Quote, 6–22:579.

Rolf Eliassen
Professor of Civil Engineering,
Stanford University

One of the things we've got to watch out for is that technology has become the target of so many so-called ecological conservationists. Technology is being held responsible for the ecological crisis they say exists. Now, we technologists could avert the crisis if this country were to insist on using technology more extensively to control pollution and to create a better environment for man and his future generations.

San Francisco Examiner & Chronicle, 5–31:B7.

David Epel
Professor, Hopkins Marine Station
of Stanford University

What I am going to tell you today may seem difficult to believe. Indeed, being an optimist, I find it hard to believe myself. But, being a scientist, I have tried to objectively analyze the data and have come to the following two conclusions: The first is that the oceans are beginning to die from chemical pollution; the second, and even more disturbing, is that NOTHING is being done about it—very few people know about it; no one is watching the world . . . If left uncontrolled, it will result in the death of the oceans . . . the oceans are the toilets of the world and . . . it is very easy to pollute it. Freshwater lakes and streams replace their water every few months or every few years. However, there is no plug in the bottom of the sea.

Before Commonwealth Club of California,
March 13/Vital Speeches, 4–15:411.

Robert H. Finch
Secretary of Health, Education and
Welfare of the United States

Unless the American people are really prepared to pay pollution "taxes" and meet the cost of environmental restoration, no political authority can control the excesses of affluence or rampant technology—that is, no political authority that would be tolerable to our society . . . Other human civilizations disappeared because of overgrazing or deforestation altering the climate and poisoning the water. But they probably were not aware what was happening. We do know.

At "Environment: The Quest for Quality"
conference, Washington, Feb. 18/
The Christian Science Monitor, 2–24:11.

. . . the environment bag seems to be everybody's bag. And my only concern is that the "great awakening" of public interest in the environment might emerge and subside as just another passing fad.

Washington/The New York Times, 3–1:(4)7.

Henry Ford II
Chairman, Ford Motor Company

We have a strong vested interest in the survival of the internal combustion engine, but we have a far stronger vested interest in the survival of our company.

Quote, 5–17:457.

Milton Friedman
Professor of Economics,
University of Chicago

From a rational—or economic—point of view, the proper question to ask is, "What is the right amount of pollution?" Well, "no pollution" is *not* the right amount of pollution because, for example, one way to have no pollution is to make the automobile—and all internal combustion vehicles—illegal in the United States. If you did that, however, the people would be in an intolerable position. They would find themselves starving to death because then we would not be able to produce or transport food. The cost of eliminating pollution by that means would be greater than the gain you would get from it. People would rather suffer with the present amount of pollution with automobiles than have no automobiles. Perhaps there are less costly ways of eliminating pollution, and I hope there are. But you always have to ask yourself the question, "Is the cost that is required to get a certain reduction in pollution greater or less than the gain for reducing the pollution?"

Interview, Chicago/Human Events, 4–25:13.

. . . the real source of pollution is mostly the consumer. If you and I want to buy products which have to be produced by plants which pour out smoke, then the pollution comes from us. If utility plants use coal which produces smoke, then we, the people who insist on having electric power, are the ones who are the polluters. The corporations are only our agents and our intermediaries. They have no personal desire. If it's profitable for them not to pollute, they will not pollute. If it is profitable for them to pollute, they will pollute. They are transmitting our instructions.

Interview, Chicago/Human Events, 4–25:13.

Luther P. Gerlach
Anthropologist, University of Minnesota

People felt ecology would unite the country. It will be more divisive than black power, even more divisive than the war in Vietnam. The conflicts in ecology are latent. Ecology demands more fundamental changes than any other revolution.

Los Angeles Herald-Examiner, 5–10:A15.

Arthur Godfrey
Radio-television entertainer

As a young flyer I used to drink in the clean vistas, the commanding view of America from spacious skies. As the years passed, I began to observe I wasn't flying from town to town anymore. I was flying from smoky spot to smoky spot.

Interview, Los Angeles/
The Christian Science Monitor, 1–8:17.

Technology cannot make one square millimeter of soil, one drop of water, or one breath of air. But those same brains that are the vast organization that put men on the moon and, still more incredibly, brought safely back to earth a crippled spaceship, could, given the same priorities and support, clean up the pollution in a decade. We should rid the Army Engineers of their beaver complex and put their great organization to work building sewage-treatment facilities instead of dams. Let the aeronautical designers shelve the SST (supersonic transport) for awhile and put their brains to work on non-polluting ground transportation facilities.

At Bradley University, Peoria, Ill./
National Observer, 7–13:14.

J. J. Greene
Minister of Energy, Mines and
Resources of Canada

It is to be hoped that a great and powerful nation, which can afford to travel to the moon and to spend $50 billion a year for a war, will soon be able to afford to clean up its stinking and befouling tons of waste before dumping them in its neighbor's backyard.

Burlington, Ont., Nov. 20/
The New York Times, 11–22:(1)82.

WHAT THEY SAID IN 1970

Aire J. Haagen-Smit
Professor of Bio-organic Chemistry,
California Institute of Technology

We are now critically examining the dogmas of the past, and one of these is: Is growth the indication of prosperity; is it the ideal we should strive for? Are more people, more goods used or wasted, *progress?* Or do we have to improve the *quality* of our life? These questions were taboo only a few years ago. Nowadays we can raise them without being branded radicals.

Before American Society of Landscape
Architects, Williamsburg, Va., April 28 /
Vital Speeches, 7–1:575.

Philip Handler
President, National Academy of Sciences

There are many people today who naively think we can retreat from our technological civilization and get closer to nature and have less technology and so less pollutant . . . It's very easy to sell that on every university campus. But it is not a sensible approach to our problems . . . The answer, of course, is not to go back to the horse, but to develop automobile engines which don't pollute. I know no other way to do it. The way to keep water clean is more technology; to keep the air clean, is more technology . . .

Interview, Washington /
The Christian Science Monitor, 9–4:7.

C. Howard Hardesty, Jr.
Senior vice president,
Continental Oil Company

We can improve our environment; we can make it cleaner. But the price of caring for 200 million Americans, or 300 million in another 30 years, is simply this: We will have to tolerate *some* noise and *some* inconvenience. We are an imperfect society, and adding 100 million more people will not make it any more perfect.

Quote, 8–9:135.

J. George Harrar
President, Rockefeller Foundation

Morally, no society has the right to over-utilize the world's resources for its own contemporary and selfish interests. Man must understand biological systems and conduct his affairs in such ways as to improve the quality of life rather than degrade it through wanton experience . . . We, in the more advanced nations at least, should put considerably less emphasis on that form of economic growth that simply multiplies production and consumption of material goods. Our resources are not limitless, and when those that are non-renewable are consumed or transformed, they can never be replenished . . . More attention could and should be devoted to services and to those areas of life that enrich the quality of human existence: cultural activities, the arts, literature, intellectual and scientific pursuits, esthetic improvements and human relationships.

Before House Select Subcommittee on
Education, New York, April 11 /
The New York Times, 4–12:(1)40.

C. M. Heinen
Chief engineer, Materials Laboratories,
Chrysler Corporation

Somehow, the hysterical side-effects of air pollution concern have to stop. Air pollution control is not a circus. It is not a medium for a cynical pitchman to sell products and images. It must not be exploited by those whose only ability is grandstanding. It does not need heroes or villains or exaggerations or crises. The need for good, sound air pollution control does not require these type of people to sell air quality. My greatest fear, at this time, for the air pollution control effort is that the public will catch up to the exaggerations and scares. When this happens, an over-reaction will set in to the "great air pollution crisis," and it could join the midis, the hoola hoops and the flying saucers.

At Cleaner Air Week luncheon, Chicago /
The Wall Street Journal, 12–17:12.

Christian A. Herter, Jr.
Special assistant to the Secretary of State
of the United States

As the world's greatest and most prolific

polluter, as the earth's most technologically advanced nation, as the globe's most powerful despoiler and manipulator of nature, we bear an Altantean responsibility. We must lead the battle against man's wiliest, strongest and most terrible enemy—himself.

Before Los Angeles World Affairs Council,
Los Angeles, May 15 /
Los Angeles Herald-Examiner, 5–16:A4.

Walter J. Hickel
Secretary of the Interior of the United States

The polluters will have to pay. But it will be the cost of doing business.

Interview / Face the Nation, Columbia
Broadcasting System, 1–25.

We didn't see the environment issue coming this fast. But it's the biggest thing going. The Net Natural Environment is more important than the Gross National Product. We've got to think about God and not materialism.

Interview, Washington /
Los Angeles Times, 3–13:(2)7.

At the moment we are not suffering from overpopulation. In our national parks, like Yosemite, it is not too many people but too many cars. Get in an airplane, go up 30,000 feet and see America. Fly across it. There are clusters of people on the coasts, a few clusters here and there in the heartland. But there are thousands and thousands of square miles in which you see nothing. There is still an opportunity to challenge vacant space. That is what brought me to Alaska in 1940. We need a way to attract people to those places. Perhaps we need to give tax concessions to industry to locate in towns with a population of 10,000 or 15,000. In the future, population is going to have to be controlled on a world basis, by education or planning how to disperse it best.

Interview, April 22 / Sports Illustrated, 5–4:28.

Thomas S. Kleppe
United States Representative, R-N.D.

America's eyes have been on the "glamour sciences" in recent years—the wonders of medicine, of electronics and astronauts in outer space. And they *are* wonders. But down on earth, on thousands of fields of different kinds of soils, conservationists have been at work. What they have done to keep the soils from wearing out equals any moon landing man will ever make. Soil on earth lies as far as the eye can see. It covers millions upon millions of acres around the globe. Yet, it is a rare thing and cannot be replaced. This soil is a living thing, yet it can be destroyed. This soil is God's gift to mankind, given unto our stewardship. Yet it can be destroyed and wasted. This soil is fruitful; yet it can become sterile. This soil produces crops and grasses and trees. It cannot be duplicated by chemistry or physics. This soil is an intricate house of myriad elements. Yet it is so commonplace as to be known as "dirt." Soil fills the flowerpots in Baltimore, serves as a garden in Minnesota, produces an orchard in California and bears wheat in North Dakota. It is the source of our nourishment; it provides the means of our protection. God has willed we can live with it. We cannot live without it.

Before the House, Washington, May 4 /
Congressional Record, 5–4:E3859.

Wilson M. Laird
Director, Office of Oil and Gas, Department of the Interior of the United States

Somehow, Americans must be made aware that cleaning up our environment is a costly, slow, and difficult process, and that we'll never complete it within the lifetime of anyone in this room. They need to understand that it is not just a matter of signing petitions and passing laws and setting up commissions. It is also a matter of higher taxes, higher prices, of inconvenience, of changed modes of living and, above all, of forebearance and self-discipline on the part of each individual citizen. There is simply no place in the new scheme of things for the litterbug.

Before Institute on Petroleum Exploration
and Economics, Dallas, March 5 /
Vital Speeches, 4–15:399.

Scott Lang
President,
Harvard Environmental Law Society

People on the left are bored with demonstrations, people on the right are scared of them and people in the middle don't care. The issues in ecology are not that singular for mass marches yet.

Newsweek, 5–4:27.

Lester B. Lave
Economist,
Carnegie-Mellon University School of
Industrial Administration, Pittsburgh

For the average middle-class American family living in an urban area, abating air pollution is the single most important thing we could do to improve health. If we could reduce air pollution by 50%, it would save nearly as much in money and life as if we found a complete cure for cancer.

Milwaukee Journal, 8–24:9.

Chauncey D. Leake
Lecturer in medicine, University of
California Medical Center, San Francisco

When there isn't too much of anything, you don't get too bothered. A little DDT and a little smog never worried us until it became too much DDT and too much smog. The same thing can happen with noise.

Plainview (Tex.) Daily Herald, 7–17:6.

Anne Morrow Lindbergh
Author, Conservationist

The cherry tree myth, as it came to me as a child, had a moral which I took to be: "It's not so bad to cut down the cherry tree as long as you don't lie about it." I accepted it once, but I have begun to wonder. The cherry tree is gone, and too many of them have been cut down already. I'm for the cherry tree.

At Smith College, Northampton, Mass.,
Feb. 20/The New York Times, 2–21:12.

Charles A. Lindbergh
Aviator

After millions of years of successful evolution, human life is now deteriorating genetically and environmentally at an alarming and exponential rate. Basically, we seem to be retrograding rather than evolving. We have only to look about us to verify this fact: to see megalopolizing cities, the breakdown of nature, the pollution of air, water and earth; to see crime, vice and dissatisfaction webbing like a cancer across the surface of our world. We know that, tens of thousands of years ago, man departed from both the hazards and the security of instinct's natural selection, and that his intellectual reactions have become too powerful to permit him ever to return. That is why I have turned my attention from technological progress to life, from the civilized to the wild. In wildness there is a lens to the past, to the present and to the future, offered to us for the looking—a direction, a successful selection, an awareness of values that confronts us with the need for and the means of our salvation. Let us never forget that wildness has developed life, including the human species. By comparison, our own accomplishments are trivial.

Congressional Record, 3–9:E1768.

Jon Lindbergh
Chairman, Washington State
Oceanographic Commission

Pesticide residue in the oceans is similar to having arsenic in a well.

San Francisco Examiner, 12–29:26.

John V. Lindsay
Mayor of New York

Behind the complex predictions and obscure language, beyond words like ecology, environment and pollution, there is a simple question: Do we want to live or die?

New York, April 22/
The New York Times, 4–23:30.

We could divert $3 billion from the luxury pollutant called the SST to clean the air it is supposed to fly through. We could save the forests in America instead of defoliating forests in Asia. We could make the imple decision that it is wrong—wrong for ourselves, wrong for our children and wrong for the nation—to spend $80 billion for defense and war abroad, and less than 2% as much for survival in a decent environment here at home.

Before National Conference on Government, Portland, Ore./Los Angeles Times, 8–26:(1)17.

Louis B. Lundborg
Chairman, Bank of America

There is a new generation that is saying: "I have only one life to live on this earth. Will it be a better life for me if the stream where I used to fish is polluted by industrial wastes? Will it be a better life for me if the beach where I used to swim is polluted by sewage? Will it be a better life for me if my ears are shocked and my windows rattled every few minutes by sonic booms? Will it be a better life for me if I have no clean air to breathe?" They will ask, "Is this really progress? If it is, I don't need it." And we shouldn't have to wait for them to ask the question; because these should be our questions, too. This deterioration of the quality of life isn't something that just happens to other people; when it happens, it happens to us, too.

Before Rotary Club, Seattle, June 17/ Los Angeles Times, 6–21:F7.

Birny Mason, Jr.
Chairman, Union Carbide Corporation

I don't think anyone today would dispute the basic premise that, one way or the other, this country has been neglectful (about pollution) and the neglect is catching up with us very rapidly. However, as in so many of these things that have public interest, you get an emotional factor that can get out of balance. This is a danger. You very seldom get the right answers to problems through exercise of your emotions. This is to me a perfect illustration of the kind of problem that ought not to be made controversial, with conflicts between government, industry and the academic world. All of these elements should be able to work together to

come to a sound solution. So I would hope that realistic—not disruptive—programs are developed.

Interview, New York/ Nation's Business, Sept.:64.

Jean Mayer
Professor of Nutrition, Harvard University

Pesticides were at one time considered an unadulterated blessing. We have learned since that, while they are by no means an unmitigated disaster, they, too, exact a price; the nature of the pesticide, the mode of employ and ecological situation determine that price; and for some combinations the price is higher than what we are willing to pay . . . With all biological phenomena so closely interrelated, any action harsh enough to significantly alter one basic aspect of the environment may snowball and drastically change the whole ecology.

At Charles Allen Thomas Science Symposium, St. Louis, March 5/ Vital Speeches, 4–15:406.

Rich people occupy more space, consume more of each natural resource, disturb the ecology more and create more land, air, water, chemical and radioactive pollution than poor people. So it can be argued that, from many viewpoints, it is even more urgent to control the numbers of the rich than it is to control the numbers of the poor.

Los Angeles Herald-Examiner, 5–10:A16.

John T. Middleton
Commissioner, National Air Pollution Control Administration

Government and industry together are spending only millions annually to fight air pollution. When we consider the priceless benefits of clean air to our health, adequate control of pollution is a bargain.

U.S. News & World Report, 8–17:38.

Thomas J. McIntyre
United States Senator, D-N.H.

. . . at a time when the environmental crisis is on the minds of all Americans, there

(THOMAS J. MCINTYRE)

is a manifest need for deep thought about its implications and meaning in the everyday lives of our citizens. As has often happened, however, the sounds of crisis have not yet been followed by the comprehensive philosophical and moral commitments necessary to change the ways of the past. Business-as-usual will continue until certain basic recognitions are made. Our political system, which is basically sound and sufficiently adaptable to accommodate needed changes, must adjust to the new demands of ecosystematic realities. Scientific discoveries must be evaluated according to new considerations which weight the benefits to be derived against possible ecological side-effects. Most important, however, will be the readiness of the average citizen to participate fully in a re-evaluation of the ecological impact of his daily activities. This will be the most complex hurdle; for any proper adjustment will involve changing deeply-ingrained habits of consumption, basic desires and fundamental philosophical beliefs.

Before the Senate, Washington, July 14 / Congressional Record, 7–14:S11217.

Joseph M. Montoya
United States Senator, D-N.M.

When we fouled our waters with pesticides, human wastes, industrial filth and a dozen other forms of garbage, society looked the other way. As millions of autos spewed lead into the air over our cities, we put it off as a threat that would never materialize in full. As our own garbage piled up around us in mountains, we made jokes about how we could utilize it for recreation or for artificial reefs to encourage fishing. Now we face extermination and slow death by our own polluting hands because of what we have done to nature. Only swift realization and instant action will save us from the fruits of our own folly . . .

Before the Senate, Washington, April 7 / Congressional Record, 4–7:S5223.

Thomas H. Moorer
Admiral, United States Navy; Chief of Naval Operations

There is no question about the fact that we have big changes ahead in our future use of the oceans . . . The oceans offer a great potential for the acquisition of food and for the acquisition of all kinds of metals which exist on the bottom of the ocean. As the population expands and as the resources that are on the land decrease . . . the world is going to have to turn to the sea in order to support the world's future population.

Quote, 3–22:180.

Edward P. Morgan
News commentator, American Broadcasting Company

It's one thing to want to enrich the quality of American life. It's another to pause and realize how much our culture and our economy revolve around the motor car. With the car as our status symbol, we have allowed ourselves to become what might be called the Pollutocrats.

Radio broadcast / The Wall Street Journal, 2–2:10.

Robert Moses
Former New York City Parks Commissioner

I am worried when our country goes on an ideological spree, binge, rampage or crusade, whether for conservation or any other cause. It is bad for a wealthy nation to become selfish, slothful, wasteful and indifferent to its God-given resources and beauties. On the other hand, esthetics and industry are not irreconcilable. I fear the unkept promise more than the unlit lamp and the ungirt loin.

Before American Society of Civil Engineers, New York, Feb. 18 / The New York Times, 2–22:(1)63.

Daniel P. Moynihan
Counsellor to the President of the United States

There is no government in history that has ever had any effect whatever on population . . . One of the nice things about people is they don't pay too much attention to government ... particularly with respect to the number of children they have.

Interview/Face the Nation,
Columbia Broadcasting System, 1–25.

Is there an optimum population for the country? Who can say? It surely is not one million. But is it one billion? Or, to ask it another way, how long do we want to stand in line to go to a movie?

Interview, Washington, March 16/
The New York Times, 3–17:26.

Edmund S. Muskie
United States Senator, D-Maine

As recently as two or three years ago, if I had called a press conference on this subject (pollution), I could have used a much smaller room.

Before Senate Public Works Committee,
Washington, Jan. 23/
San Francisco Examiner & Chronicle
(This World), 2–1:6.

Fighting inflation is a battle of the highest priority; but the Administration has chosen to fight that battle at the expense of our air, our water, our land and our people. Do most Americans feel that the SST, space exploration, the ABM and atomic energy are more important than our air, our water, our land, our homes and our health? These are the kinds of decisions that the Administration has made. They are not decisions with which America can survive. It is a sham to say that we cannot afford the protection of our environment, the fight against hunger and poverty, or homes and medical care for our people. We can afford these domestic programs—and fight the battle of inflation—if we admit that we cannot afford other programs which are much less important. We need some things, and we do not need others. It is time we understood that difference and made our nation's budget reflect that understanding.

Feb. 3/Congressional Record, 2–9:S1433.

Maybe we ought to set some standards on the standard of living. You talk about the auto; that's only part of it. In a consumer-oriented society, everything we produce leads to waste. This is the problem we face in a consumer society that's also a free one. How far do we go?

Before Senate Subcommittee on Air and
Water Pollution, Washington, March 16/
Los Angeles Herald-Examiner, 3–17:A8.

I challenge the auto industry to provide clean (pollution free) cars by 1975. They say they can't do it; but industry said the same thing when President Roosevelt asked for 100,000 planes in World War II and when President Kennedy asked for a man on the moon by 1970.

The New York Times, 9–20:(4)6.

Ralph Nader
Lawyer; Consumer rights advocate

It is a crime for a man to relieve himself in the Detroit River, but not for an industry to relieve itself in the Detroit River. It costs $25 to drop a banana peel in Yosemite. But what fines have been levied for all the havoc (offshore oil drilling leaks) in Santa Barbara? We talk about the Chicago Seven. Who is prosecuting the Santa Barbara Six?

Los Angeles, May 25/
Los Angeles Times, 5–27:(4)1.

Anti-pollution bills have been on the books for a long time. Pollution is one of the worst forms of violence. Where have been the calls for "law and order"? Who has charged government with "coddling" corporations? Has anybody raised the question of "permissiveness"?

Los Angeles, May 25/
Los Angeles Times, 5–27:(4)8.

Gaylord Nelson
United States Senator, D-Wis.

America has bought environmental disaster on a national installment plan. Buy affluence now and let future generations pay the price.

Before the Senate, Washington, Jan. 20/
The Washington Post, 1–20:A2.

(GAYLORD NELSON)

Progress—American style—is adding up each year to 200 million tons of smoke and fumes, 7 million junked cars, 20 million tons of paper, 76 billion "disposable" containers and tens of millions of tons of sewage and industrial wastes. It is estimated that every man, woman and child in this country is now generating five pounds of refuse a day from household, commercial and industrial wastes. To quote balladeer Pete Seeger, Americans now find themselves "standing knee deep in garbage, throwing rockets at the moon."

Before the Senate, Washington, Feb. 19/
Vital Speeches, 3–15:326.

We don't really teach young people about the environment and what it means to the livability of the world if we continue to degrade the environment, whether from the standpoint of scenic beauty or throwing trash in the streets or putting pollutants in the rivers or the air. I think this is a great void in our school systems at all levels.

Interview/Quote, 3–22:269.

Earth Day may be a turning point in American history. It may be the birth date of a new American ethic that rejects the frontier philosophy that the continent was put here for our plunder, and accepts the idea that even urbanized, affluent, mobile societies are interdependent with the fragile, life-sustaining systems of the air, the water, the land.

Denver, April 22/Time, 5–4:16.

Destroy the richness of the sea and you eliminate one of the greatest resources for feeding an exploding world population. Even today, there are nations, such as Japan, that depend almost entirely on the sea for their food and for many other critical resources. Upset the intricate ecological systems of the oceans, and you run the grave risk of throwing all natural systems so seriously out of balance that the planet will no longer sustain any life. The evidence is pouring in that we are already well on the way to causing drastic and lasting damage to the ocean environment.

Quote, May: 398.

At the current rate of introduction of pollutants into the air, within 25 years there will not be a single metropolitan area in America where you'll be able to go outside for any period of time without a gas mask.

San Francisco Examiner, 8–6:30.

If we cannot protect the health of the nation (by controlling pollution) because it would require some tough decisions that interfere with the traditional right to do business as usual, then I suggest that both the system and the people are in jeopardy.

Quote, 9–6:217.

Richard M. Nixon
President of the United States

The 1970s absolutely must be the years when America pays its debt to the past by reclaiming the purity of its air, its waters and our living environment. It is literally now or never.

News conference, San Clemente, Calif., Jan. 1/
The New York Times, 1–2:1.

The great question of the seventies is shall we surrender to our surroundings, or shall we make our peace with nature and begin to make reparations for the damage we have done to our air, our land and our water? Restoring nature to its natural state is a cause beyond party and beyond factions. It has become a common cause for all the people of America. It is a cause of particular concern to young Americans—because they, more than we, will reap the grim consequences of our failure to act on programs which are needed now if we are to prevent disaster later.

State of the Union address, Washington,
Jan. 22/Los Angeles Times, 1-23:(1)20.

If we succeed in initiating a program that

effective in cleaning up our air and in cleaning up our water and in saving our recreation lands, there will be plenty of credit for everyone. If we don't succeed, who is to blame isn't going to matter.

Chicago, Feb. 6/The New York Times, 2–7:1.

The forces which shape the environment are just as subtle and difficult to master as those which shape the economy.

Quote, 3–22:265.

Prince Philip
Duke of Edinburgh

. . . conservation of the environment cannot be measured directly in economic terms. Indeed, whenever conservation gets into an economic argument, it is inevitably made to look as if it were opposed to all forms of economic development. When a national park stands in the way of the exploitation of a natural resource, such as potash for example, the national interest measured in the economic terms of exports and balance of payments wins every time. Economic advantage is easily measured in cash terms; social cost is just a figure of speech. The Gross National Product, which is rapidly assuming the religious significance of a graven image, can be worked out by any competent accountant. But exactly how do you arrive at a comparable figure for the quality of life? The trouble is that conservation is a cultural, moral, ethical or even a religious issue. It is to do with belief and conscience; it is to do with future generations and the fate of the world as the habitat for all forms of life as we know it. The fact is that the subject of conservation has become a large and extremely awkward spanner in our well-oiled, materialist economic system. We have got to the point where we believe that every problem is an economic problem, and, if something can't be measured directly in terms of money, it just doesn't exist. Because conservation is a new and awkward problem, I suspect many people fondly hope that, by ignoring it, the problem will go away.

The New York Times, 11–4:43.

Ronald Reagan
Governor of California

There is no subject more on our minds than the preservation of our environment and the absolute necessity of waging an all-out war against the debauching of that environment. A booming economy and the "good life" will be no good at all if our air is too dirty to breathe, our water too polluted to use, our surroundings too noisy and our land too cluttered and littered to allow us to live decently.

State of the State address, Sacramento,
Jan. 6/National Observer, 2–2:6.

Walter P. Reuther
President, United Auto Workers of America

We're going to say pollution is a matter for collective bargaining—because it is, if the auto industry continues its gross neglect as the world's biggest air polluter. If the industry does not accept responsibility for this, then society, as a matter of survival, will intervene, and our job security is involved.

At UAW convention, Atlantic City,
March 13/Daily World, 3–14:5.

Peter Ritchie-Calder
Professor, University of Edinburgh;
Member, British House of Lords

The spoil heaps of this civilization, if anyone discovered it from outer space, would be identified not by the shards of broken earthenware, but by plastic ice cream tubs. It would be a civilization that went not with a bang but a ripple.

Before House of Lords, London/
The New York Times, 3–15:(4)5.

I still believe we can husband the creatures of the sea as we have husbanded the creatures of the land. I still believe we can enhance the world's food supply from the ocean. But we are rapidly reducing our options if we tolerate the kind of irresponsible and avaricious ignorance which is threatening the living waters of the sea as it has destroyed so much of the living waters of the land.

Before Congress of Food Science and Technology, Washington, Aug. 10/ The Washington Post, 8–11:A9.

John D. Rockefeller III
Philanthropist; Chairman, Commission on Population Growth and the American Future

The population problem underlies and is basic to the solution of most of our other problems. The average citizen doesn't appreciate the social and economic implications of population growth and what it does to the quality of all our lives. Rather than think of population control as a negative thing, we should see that it can be enriching.

Newsweek, 3–30:87.

Nelson A. Rockefeller
Governor of New York

As long as consumers expect goods to be produced at the lowest possible cost, in the largest possible quantity, at the greatest possible convenience, without regard to environmental consequences, then all the nature-loving rhetoric on earth is not going to save the earth.

At dedication of Hudson Highlands State Park, Cold Spring, N.Y., May 23/ The New York Times, 5–24:(1)37.

Louis H. Roddis, Jr.
President, Consolidated Edison Company of New York

Many have donned concern for the environment like a hula hoop. Awareness threatens to become frenzy. Scarcely a public official lives who has not embraced it. But let us be sure it doesn't die in that embrace. Let us be on guard that when the media's attention flags, when dire warnings are repeated so often they echo revival tent descriptions of hell—with as little effect on life style— that, in short, we don't get bored.

Washington/The New York Times, 3–1:(4)7.

William D. Ruckelshaus
Administrator, Environmental Protection Agency of the United States

Under the statutes, as they are presently written, the states are the primary enforcement tool in both air and water (pollution). And the problem with the states as regulators of industry—and, for that matter, as regulators of their municipalities, but industry in particular—is that the states compete so fiercely for industry that they are not the best regulators in the world. And so, what we have to do, it seems to me, is to try to make the states better regulators by proving to them that, if they don't do the job, the Federal government will move in very quickly.

Interview, Washington/ National Observer, 12–21:7.

It's going to be said I'm acting politically (in policing polluters), that I'm acting arbitrarily and capriciously. I'm trying very scrupulously not to have that charge be accurate. But there is nothing I can do to keep it from being made, because it is going to be made . . . I'm sure there will be people requesting that I don't sue a particular polluter because of his friendship with somebody in the Administration. But I have been given the mandate by the Congress and by the President to enforce the laws, and to do so fairly. And that's what I intend to do.

Interview, Washington/ National Observer, 12–21:7.

Paul D. Saltman
Biochemist; Provost, Revelle College, University of California at San Diego

We are worried today about . . . population, famine, pollution of the atmosphere, the hydrosphere, ecosphere, even perhaps the psychosphere of man. All of these problems have their solution in science and technology—to be sure, in unity with man's values, his morality and his ethics. How are we to control population without the full cooperation of science and technology, medicine, philosophers, government, politics, sociology, religion? Can we pull them apart? Famine will not be stopped by people carrying placards in parades. Famine will be stopped by those men who can fix nitrogen cheaply at low temperature and low pressures and bring nitrogen fertilizers to the world, by the geneticists who will be able to breed plants with high lysine, tryptophane and methionine content in their protein. It will not be effected by slogans and bumper stickers.

Lecture/Los Angeles Times, 9–13:D2.

James H. Scheuer
United States Representative, D-N.Y.

I don't think it's fair to say that people concerned about ecology and environment want us to go back to the cracker barrel. We're trying to change things, but we're not trying to turn the clock back on disposables. If we can design a metal skin to encircle the globe in which three guys can travel to the moon and withstand these incredible variations of heat and cold and God knows what, scientists and economists can design a beer, or your liquid detergent, container that won't present such an environmental problem.

Interview/Quote, 5–31:509.

Wally Schirra
Former astronaut

From earth to orbit, you've heard us astronauts say the view is fantastic. It's not the black in space we're talking about. It's earth we're talking about. If we can help get earth back on an even keel, fine. I don't mean reform earth. I just mean give it a chance to live, to breathe. The moon is not hospitable. Venus is not hospitable. Mars is not hospitable. We'd better do what we can to clean up earth, because this is where we're going to be.

Nation's Business, April:82.

Glenn T. Seaborg
Chairman, Atomic Energy Commission of the United States

What we are seeking today in the anguish

over environmental feedback and the piling of crisis upon crisis is not a forecast of doom. It is the birth pangs of a new world—the period of struggle in which we are making the physical transition from man to mankind. This organic mankind must learn to exist as an integral and contributing part of the earth, that up to now supported it unquestioningly.

San Francisco Examiner & Chronicle (This World), 5–10:2.

Pete Seeger
Folksinger

We have the know-how to end pollution. But where's the money coming from? This is the 1971 Federal budget for water treatment—one-half of one per cent of the total Federal budget. That is what is known as the "all-out" war on pollution.

Washington, April 23/ The Washington Post, 4–24:B10.

Frederick E. Smith
Professor, Harvard University Graduate School of Design

If man is doomed, he is doomed to live. The ocean is not going to die; the biosphere is not going to become extinct; and man is not going to become extinct (in the foreseeable future). Some of my associates think I am a Pollyanna because I fail to predict the end of the earth.

Boston, Oct. 22/Los Angeles, 10–23:(1)12.

Frederik Smith
Associate, Rockefeller Family and Associates

The environmental job that looms up before us is a massive one, but it has to be done. It will take the ablest planning we have seen in this country since the space effort was organized. It will require very large chunks of money. It will show on the Bottom Line of the Annual Report. It will make a serious dent in our Gross National Product, at least temporarily, although curing some of the expensive side effects of some of our problems —of which environmental pollution is one— may in the end improve the GNP. The clean-

(FREDERIK SMITH)

up job has to be done—make no mistake about that. The economic system in all its ramifications must be harnessed and put unequivocally in the service of the people and their priority needs, rather than vice versa—make no mistake about that, either.

Before Missouri Valley Electric Association Engineering Conference, Kansas City, April 15/Vital Speeches, 5–1:428.

George A. Spater
President, American Airlines

Nature has a self-cleaning mechanism capable of handling a large amount of pollution, including that made by man. But no one knows how close we are to overloading the mechanism. Every thinking person is concerned by the possibility that we may be dangerously close to that point—and perhaps in some areas may already have exceeded nature's ability to cleanse.

Panel discussion before American Management Association/ The Wall Street Journal. 8–18:10.

William B. Spong, Jr.
United States Senator, D-Va.

The development of our ocean resources is one of the urgent tasks facing this nation in the decade ahead. For thousands of years, men have harvested the fruits of the sea. But only in the last decades have they come to appreciate the full potential of its vast resources and to develop the scientific knowledge and technology necessary to explore it. The time is at hand when those resources will be in critical demand. Thirty years from now, world population will have doubled, bringing with it a desperate search for new sources of food. Industry, with its heavy call on raw materials of all kinds, should expand at even greater rates. This growth will be beyond anything our land resources alone can support. A turn to the oceans is inevitable . . .

Before Kiwanis Capital District Training Conference, Norfolk, Va., Jan. 24/ Vital Speeches, 2–15:261.

William L. Springer
United States Representative, R-Ill.

As concerned as we are about the air we breathe and its effect on public health, we stand a good chance of being engulfed by a tidal wave of trash before air pollution gets to us. Our way of life has brought about a flood of convenient packages which can neither be consumed or successfully disposed of . . . we are presently in the predicament of the Australian who went crazy trying to throw away his old boomerang.

Before the House, Washington, The Wall Street Journal, 6–29:10

Elvis J. Stahr, Jr.
President, National Audubon Society

This question of ecological survival isn't just a matter of what people would like. Nature doesn't care what people would like. She's going to exact a price for all the damage we do to her—and that price may be far higher than some of the sacrifices man now seems to be willing to make.

New York/Los Angeles Times, 6–21:A2

Maurice H. Stans
Secretary of Commerce of the United States

By the year 2000, eighty-five per cent of our population of 300,000,000 will be urban. Picture, if you will, four gigantic clusters of metropolitan areas in the nation—what the urban scholar Jean Gottmann so aptly called megalopolis. There's Bos-Wash, an unbroken stretch of people, homes, factories, highways, railroads and power lines from Boston to Washington. There's Chi-Pitts, a solid belt of heavy industry from Chicago to Pittsburgh. There's San-San, from San Francisco to San Diego. And there's Ja-Mi, the fourth megalopolis along Florida's east coast from Jacksonville to Miami. Each will constitute a new phenomenon on this earth—a human agglomeration of size, density and complexity never before known. And in combination, these vast megalopoli will have the potential of posing megaton problems that will make solving our present difficulties look like child's play. It is not very pleasant o contemplate what such an anthill society would mean to this nation.

At American University, Washington/
National Observer, 3–16:15.

John E. Swearingen
Chairman,
Standard Oil Company of Indiana

A society capable of interplanetary travel can surely devise the technology to control its own wastes. But broad public support of the necessary steps and a willingness to share in the costs are indispensable. This is one more counter where no free lunch is available, and the sooner the public faces up to that fact the sooner we will be on our way. Public enthusiasm for pollution control is matched by a reluctance to pay even a modest share of the costs. All members of society have created the problem and all will have to be party to the solution.

The Wall Street Journal, 1–8:6.

Gardiner Symonds
Chairman, Tenneco, Inc.

I am sure that all of us are in favor of good environment as much as anyone . . . Industry has been working at the problem. I'd be the first to say that much, much more needs to be done . . . But it takes hard, unglamorous, sustained, day-to-day work in the laboratories and the factories to get the job done— not a headline-grabbing show aimed at a convenient target . . . My point is that it is not just a business or industry problem, with industry operating in some manner against the public interest. Better environment is a problem for our entire society. It will take work by all of us, not just lashing out at some easy target—as long as it is the other fellow.

Before American Petroleum Institute,
Los Angeles, May 14/Vital Speeches,
7–1:557, 558.

U Thant
Secretary-General of the United Nations

Plunder, befouling and destruction of our native earth have already gone too far for us to rely any more on pious hopes, belated promises and tardy efforts at self-discipline.

If effective measures are to be taken in time, we need something new, and we need it speedily—a global authority with the support and agreement of governments and of other powerful interests, which can pull together all the piecemeal efforts now being made and which fill the gaps where something needs to be done.

At University of Texas at Austin, May 14/
Los Angeles Times, 5–15:(1)7.

As we watch the sun go down evening after evening through the smog across the poisoned waters of our native earth, we must ask ourselves seriously whether we really wish some future universal historian on another planet to say, "With all their genius and their skill, they ran out of foresight and air and food and water and ideas."

At United Nations, N.Y., Oct. 24/
The New York Times, 10–25:(1)1.

Myron Tribus
Assistant Secretary of Commerce of the
United States for Science and Technology

On the early frontier, it was possible for the settler to dump his garbage out his window, or at least in the nearest dry wash, without disturbing anyone, not even the coyotes. For some reason, it has been impossible for the average American to get used to the idea that he no longer lives under these conditions, that the land and the air and the water are not unlimited resources for private exploitation. We have trouble realizing that the day when our nearest neighbor was ten miles away is gone, that it will never come again for probably 90 per cent of us. Still, we think in the manner of the frontier, and we yearn for that idyllic time which most of us never knew and most of us could not tolerate if we were suddenly transported back. This individualistic fetish has been a large factor, along with plain carelessness, for producing the imbalances we now see and fear in our ecology.

At National Bureau of Standards Summer
Student Seminar, Gaithersburg, Md.,
Aug. 19/Vital Speeches, 9–15:718.

WHAT THEY SAID IN 1970

Morris K. Udall
United States Representative, D-Ariz.

The price of a decent environment may be cars with 60-horsepower engines instead of 360, and fewer gadgets and higher taxes. But there will be more fishing streams. We might have fewer supersonic transports, but nicer beaches and forests.

Newsweek, 1–26:40.

Stewart L. Udall
Former Secretary of the Interior of the United States

I came in (as Interior Secretary) as a classic conservationist—you know, preservation of nature and seashores, of birdlife and wildlife, of endangered species. Then, gradually, it came over me that man himself was an endangered species, that we were part of the same chain of life as the birds. Only in the last three years I was in office did I see it as a whole piece. We'd erred in thinking environment was simply a matter of managing natural resources. What had to be managed was man himself.

Life, 6–26:38.

John A. Volpe
Secretary of Transportation of the United States

The President was dead serious when he talked about protecting our environment. And so am I. I can tell any city or state official looking for funds from us that no road or airport or transit system is going to be built that doesn't take the environment into consideration. I'm not one of those who believe we have raped the country by building roads. That just isn't so. But we can pay more attention to trying to save this grove of trees or this parkland.

Nation's Business, April:41.

J. Wreford Watson
Professor of Geography, University of Edinburgh, Scotland

The geography of newness has become an essential part of America. Newness is adopted almost for its own sake. The passion for newness dominates the American view. Innovations and discards, expressways and scrapheaps go side by side. There is an annual change to new cars matched by an almost annual widening and regrading of roads. The constant building of new offices vies with the modernization of factories. An explosion of new houses has taken place round every city. So little of old America has been left that a concerted effort has had to be made to reconstruct the lost landscapes of the past. Little is made to stand or to last; that is why so much of it ends up on the rubbish dump. Every year, over a ton of rubbish for each person in America is thrown out on city streets or city parks. This amounts to one billion pounds of waste each day, costing America $4.5 billion to clean up. New York generates three times as much waste per capita as London. Americans are "the wastemakers." In addition, the landscape is littered with the relics of outdated roads and bridges, with torn-up railways, with abandoned farms, with dying villages and with ghost towns—with all, in fact, that has been superseded by the new and the better. Last century, virgin land typified the American myth; devirginated America is today's symbol. The decay and sterilization of farm land in prospect of redevelopment for urban purposes goes on everywhere, even before development takes place. Great tracts around American cities look like deserts of weed and scrub, as speculators have bought out farms in the hope of selling at a profit to new housing, new highways and new shopping centers. This landscape of newness has been won only by a constant attack upon nature, which, in a curious way, has brought man back to nature. Although the American has plundered nature with a zeal that is almost savage, he has, at the same time, turned to and longed to be one with nature. He has developed a strange love-hate relationship that is seen everywhere in the land.

Before British Association for the Advancement of Science/ The New York Times, 12–23:27.

Kenneth E. Watt
Professor of Zoology,
University of California at Davis

The history of movements like this (ecology) is not very promising. We had great movements on civil rights and the Vietnamese war. The problems are still with us, but the movements have died away . . . But about five years from now, it will become increasingly clear . . . that what we ecologists are saying now is true, and then the political pressure for change will become inexorable.

At Swarthmore College/
National Observer, 4–27:2.

Edgar Wayburn
President, Sierra Club

As we dump our garbage into our oceans, let us be aware that we are not disposing of it, merely relocating it.

Quote, 1–11:32.

John Cardinal Wright
Prefect, Congregation of the Clergy,
Roman Curia, the Vatican

The Church's main complaint at the moment about this "exploding population" argument, and the related arguments, is that there isn't any serious effort being made . . . to teach family planning consistent with human dignity and moral standards. Quite the contrary: There is an obvious, open conspiracy at politically-controlled family limitation. We Americans even seek to link family limitation to our foreign aid. We have population experts with consular offices all over the world, especially in Latin America. We have Senators now proposing that precisely the poor—for whom they are supposed to be, or pretend to be, speaking—are going to be taxed if they have more than two children. This whole campaign, from beginning to end, adds up to something which a recent magazine article has called "the nonsense explosion." It's the making of a tyranny the likes of which we have never seen—the tyranny that will make it necessary to get a license to have a baby, or to get permission from public authority to remain fertile and capable of having children. It is this that the Church is fighting.

Interview, Vatican City/
U.S. News & World Report, 8–31:57.

Charles W. Yost
United States Ambassador
to the United Nations

With a human population of three and a half billion today, and the prospect of seven billion by the year 2000, our first priority is not to create an earthly paradise but to maintain a habitable world. We need a balance between economic growth and the health of our global ecology. Such a balance does not exist in public policy today in any nation, let alone in the international community. The immediate and often short-sighted demands of production and consumption still have almost exclusive priority. We have only begun to combat, or even to comprehend, the devastating impact of these activities on the living environment of air, water, earth and forms of life on which man, because of his biological inheritance, absolutely depends for survival and well-being.

Before Economic and Social Council,
Geneva, Switzerland, July 14/
Vital Speeches, 8–15:651.

Foreign Affairs

Dean Acheson
*Former Secretary of State
of the United States*

We must remind ourselves and the world that we have force and are prepared to employ it wisely . . . Force is a factor that should not be wrongly employed; it cannot be rashly overused or apparently discarded.

*Interview, Sandy Spring, Md./
The New York Times, 9–20:(4)16.*

The "Nixon Doctrine" is not a great contribution to the enlightenment of the world. It was a polite way of saying, "Some of my predecessors made stupid mistakes, and I am trying to right them."

*News conference, Washington, Dec. 9/
The Washington Post, 12–10:A8.*

Spiro T. Agnew
Vice President of the United States

Some people back home are so anxious to make friends of our enemies, they even seem ready to make enemies of our friends.

*Bangkok, Thailand/
Los Angeles Herald-Examiner, 1–9:A10.*

We are attempting to de-emphasize paternalism and to emphasize partnership. We do not expect everyone in the world to adopt the American system. All we expect is that free men, wherever they are, will have the ability to choose, in a representative way, what system of government they live under.

*Auckland, New Zealand, Jan. 16/
Los Angeles Times, 1–17:(1)13.*

It's hard to talk about "doctrines" without sounding doctrinaire. But let me try. The Monroe Doctrine said to Europe, "Stay out of this hemisphere." The Truman Doctrine said to the Soviet Union, "Stay out of countries that want to remain non-Communist." The Nixon Doctrine says, "We'll help our friends who are willing to help themselves." Each of these doctrines was enunciated at a critical turning-point in our history. The first two were right for their time. The Nixon Doctrine is right for our time.

*Before California Newspaper Publishers
Association, Los Angeles, Feb. 5/
Congressional Record, 2–5:S1290.*

In certain intellectual and political circles, there is an opinion that America should isolate herself from world affairs. To my mind, this is another sign of illness: It demands that a vigorous, powerful nation withdraw from the world scene and commit its full resources in solving our internal problems. We should—according to this point of view—not get involved abroad. But this misses what is the most elementary and most obvious fact of our times: We are involved.

*Before Drugs, Chemicals and Allied
Trades Association, New York, March 5/
Los Angeles Herald-Examiner, 3–6:A4.*

As one looks back over the diplomatic disasters that have befallen the West and the friends of the West over three decades—at Teheran, Yalta, Cairo, in every great diplomatic conference that turned out to be a loss for the West and freedom—one can find the unmistakeable footprints of W. Averell Harriman.

*Cleveland, June 20/The New York Times,
6–21:(1)39.*

One thing is becoming clearer to me every day, and that is that the mood of the people is heavily protective of the President's function in foreign affairs. There is great resentment across this country of the attitudes of ome of the critics who wish to strip the 'resident of his constitutional powers. I ave heard many people who, of their own nitiative, bring up this question: "What in he world is the Senate of the United States rying to do—divide the country in the eyes f our enemies by constantly carping and riticizing our foreign policy?"

Interview, Washington/
U.S. News & World Report, 8–24:36.

. . . however they are judged by friend or e, Americans are known as men who keep heir promises and who regard their commitents as binding.

Seoul, South Korea, Aug. 24 /
The New York Times, 8–25:3.

George D. Aiken
United States Senator, R-Vt.

Somewhere in between the notion that we an tell everybody how to run their country nd fight their wars and the ostrich-like at-tude of Fortress America, we have to de-elop a foreign policy for the future. Maybe we promise less, we will achieve more . . . faybe if we walk a little more humbly and lk a little more softly, we will approach le day when we will not have to carry quite big a stick.

Montpelier, Vt., Feb. 14 /
San Francisco Examiner & Chronicle
(This World), 2–22:2.

No President in these times can ever hope fashion foreign policy in the inner sanc-im of the White House without risking rave repercussions at home and abroad.

Daily World, 11–25:2.

Raymond Aron
Professor of Faculty Letters,
Paris University

Certainly the CIA has become a sort of nythical monster. When something hap-ens, like the fall of (Norodom) Sihanouk Cambodia, the first reaction is to blame le CIA. And it is true that the United States as gone to the extreme of playing a domi-

nating role almost everywhere in the world. People react to this role in different degrees —doubt, repulsion, hate, admiration, a mix-ture of all sorts of feelings. The CIA is the dark side of the American imperium. The American technology is the half-bright side, and the completely bright side is difficult to find. It is against human nature to like the most powerful nation or the most powerful man.

Interview, New York /
The Christian Science Monitor, 5–22:7.

Eugene Carson Blake
General secretary,
World Council of Churches

Too much of American foreign policy is made in the Kremlin. What they in the Kremlin are for, we are against. Unless we find an answer to this shallow anti-Commu-nism, the cold war will be perpetuated.

San Francisco Examiner & Chronicle
(This World), 1–25:2.

William G. Bray
United States Representative, R-Ind.

Four times in this century American youth have gone abroad to fight for the freedom of other peoples. Each time, our goal was al-truistic. We assisted friends and enemies alike, and we have never asked for or re-ceived anything in return. We may have been in error, at times, in helping others so freely; we may have trusted those who were untrustworthy; but our errors have been on the part of trust, love and altruism, instead of hate and selfishness. Why should the New Left attack America? The answer is simple: The United States is the last great and powerful bastion of freedom capable of stop-ping an aggressor from riding over the world.

Indianapolis, May /
Congressional Record, 7–14:S6671.

Frank Church
United States Senator, D-Idaho

When we pour our money into budgetary support for a notoriously authoritarian gov-ernment, when we supply it with riot guns,

(FRANK CHURCH)

tear gas and Mace, intelligent young Americans who still want to believe in our professed ideals begin to ask elemental questions ... A crisis of spirit arises when our foreign policy comes unhinged from the historic values we hold dear as a people; and when the role of the United States in the world becomes inexplicable to its own young citizens. This is happening to us. Its occurrence is of more fundamental importance than any question of economic theory, investment policy or diplomatic tactics.

Before the Senate, Washington, April 10/
The New York Times, 4–11:3.

The greatest danger to our democracy, I dare say, is not that the Communists will destroy it, but that we will betray it by the very means chosen to defend it. Foreign policy is not and cannot be permitted to become an end in itself. It is, rather, a means toward an end, which in our case is not only safety of the U.S., but the preservation of her democratic values.

Quote, 5–24:485.

Cyrus S. Eaton
Chairman, Chesapeake & Ohio Railway

The great threat to capitalism is our vast expenditures abroad. It is crippling us financially. When I was in Laos and Cambodia, I was shocked at the spending of U.S. dollars there. Here we would call it bribery. Over there they call it "efforts in behalf of democracy." We are just buying people by the thousands to get people to adhere to democracy.

Before Joint Congressional Economic
Committee, Washington, July 13/
Los Angeles Herald-Examiner, 7–13:B4.

Gerald R. Ford
United States Representative, R-Mich.

The actions of five Presidents have been aimed at keeping us as a global power. That's our fate—whether we like it or not.

Interview, Alexandria, Va./
The Washington Post, 7–5:G13.

J. William Fulbright
United States Senator, D-Ark.

We are getting to the point that we no longer have an American foreign policy; we have only a collection of foreign policies. I mean that every foreign country has its own special pleaders in the United States, and its special interests. And in all these cases, where is the interest of the United States? Is the American interest just Korea; is it Taiwan; is it Israel? Are we active only in the interest of X, Y and Z? Does anybody talk of the interest of the United States? Does it really make any sense that we specify amounts of aid for X, Y and Z? I do not think it does. This is why I object to specifying funds ... for any country. A precedent is set. And if Senator X gets his pet project for his country, then Senator Y is bound to have to do the same thing. We end up with a situation in which nobody is particularly concerned about the United States and *its* budget problems.

Before the Senate, Washington, Jan. 28/
Congressional Record, 1–28:S767.

It takes more than Realpolitik to explain ... gratuitous friendliness toward rightwing dictators ... I suspect that the explanation lies in that attitude of crusading anti-Communism which has colored so much of American foreign policy over the years. The charm of the rightwing dictators has been their staunch anti-Communism, and that appears to have been enough to compensate for such trivial defects as their despotism and corruption.

Before the Senate, Washington, April 2/
Congressional Record, 4–2:S4935.

"Isolationist" is merely a perjorative term that people use, hopefully to discredit you ... I don't know of anybody who is an isolationist in the sense that they want to come home and have nothing to do with the world ... Our role in the world should be a modest one; we have, as they say, so much to be modest about. It's a big country, but it has big problems; and I don't think it has the back ground, experience or the capacity to organize everybody else's business. I certainly don't subscribe to the view that we should respond to every country's request.

Interview, Washington/
San Francisco Examiner & Chronicle, 4–19:B8.

Wherever American tax dollars for waging a war go, the American flag inevitably follows.

Washington, Aug. 21/
Memphis Commercial Appeal, 8–22:1.

It is a tragedy that the confidence in the UN has eroded to the point where it is. We ourselves, the United States, have almost ignored it. I remember when the trouble started in Vietnam, and Senator (Wayne) Morse said, "Why didn't you take this to the Security Council?" Well, it just seemed it never did occur to the American government to do it. After he said it, they made sort of motions to do it. It just didn't occur to them. It was like when we moved into the Dominican Republic, someone said, "Why didn't you take it to the OAS?" Well, as an afterthought they thought of it. But we have, ourselves, almost completely ignored the international organizations to which we have really devoted our word through treaties. But I think it is time we revive it, because, in the long run, this is about the only real hope for any progress out of the law of the jungle in which we live.

Interview/Meet the Press,
National Broadcasting Company, 8–23.

Barry M. Goldwater
United States Senator, R-Ariz.

The concerted, many-faceted campaign to slash defense funds coincided precisely with a period of massive armaments buildup in the Soviet Union. While we are being urged to slash overall defense funds and eliminate many types of weapons systems, the Russians have been rapidly stockpiling more and more intercontinental ballistic missiles, deploying an ABM system, building new fighter planes and developing a wartime navy

capable of dominating every major waterway in the world. Now, we have a drive to prohibit the United States from even developing two prototype SSTs, while three other nations, including the Soviet Union, are already testing aircraft of this type. These moves aimed at our defense capabilities and our transportation potential appear for all the world like unrelated developments. I hope this is the case. But I do not like the overall picture, which shows a determined group of Americans working night and day to reduce our capability in areas of direct and strategic competition with other nations. I repeat, regardless of the motivation, the result, if all these drives are successful, will be to end this country's leadership of the free world and reduce us to the status of a second-or third-class power. This result, strangely enough, comes at a time when liberals in this country are making full use of the nation's weariness and frustration over Vietnam to develop a new brand of isolationism for this country. If we are second best in the air and second or third best in military capability and isolationist in our foreign affairs, America's time of greatness and promise will be forever ended.

Before the Senate, Washington, Oct. 2/
Vital Speeches, 11–1:43.

John A. Gronouski
Former United States Ambassador to Poland

I think it's incumbent upon the most powerful nation in the world (the United States) on the one hand and the most populous nation (Communist China) on the other hand to have some sort of communication . . . We can't ignore three quarters of a billion people, and they can't ignore a trillion GNP in power.

Interview/National Observer, 1–19:24.

H. R. Gross
United States Representative, R-Iowa

A few days ago it was announced in far-off New Delhi that the United States . . . made another big loan to India—$80 million—to be repaid in 40 years (if ever) at "2 to 3 per

(H. R. GROSS)

cent interest." May the good Lord have mercy on us, for apparently no one else does.

Human Events, 4–18:11.

Gus Hall
General secretary,
Communist Party of the United States

(The) erosion in the position of U.S. capitalism does not stop at the water's edge. There has been a further deterioration in the U.S. world position. Nixon's political barnstorming jaunts to Italy, Spain, Ireland and Yugoslavia have not reversed this process. Most of the capitalist countries, to one extent or another, are taking steps of accommodation reflecting the new world reality. They are forced to bend because of the growing power of the world revolutionary processes. More and more, U.S. imperialism is becoming the lone exception to this trend. Each step of adjusting to new world realities by the other capitalist countries is a step that further isolates U.S. imperialism. Each step is a rejection of the policies of military aggression pursued by U.S. imperialism. The erosion of the U.S. world position is involved in the agreements being worked out between the Soviet Union and the Federal Republic of Germany (West Germany). It is a factor in the negotiations and the agreements between the Bonn government and Poland. It is a factor in the progress toward a European security treaty. It is involved in the talks between the two Germanys. It is involved in the new level of trade between the capitalist countries of Europe and the lands of socialism. The erosion of U.S. imperialism's world position and its further isolation in the world is clear in the recognition of the People's Republic of China (Communist China) by Canada and Italy, as well as in the majority vote in the UN to drop the Chiang Kai-shek regime and give People's China its rightful seat. Because of this trend, the isolator is becoming isolated.

Before national committee, Communist Party
of the United States/Daily World, 12–5:M2.

W. Averell Harriman
Former United States Ambassador-at-Large

We ought to recognize that our attitude in the world is best exemplified when we show interest and concern for the welfare of other people—not how we can lord it over other people. And we've got to quit thinking that we, a very small percentage of the world's population, can tell everybody where to get off and what they can do. I resent the people who do that. I think the American people have got the good traditional insight that started with our missionaries—to be good neighbors everywhere in the world.

Interview, Washington/
The Christian Science Monitor, 12–30:5.

Stephen Hess
National Chairman, 1970 White House
Conference on Children and Youth

Youth not only has no first-hand knowledge of the Cold War, but also it is a generation that tends to disbelieve anything it cannot feel, hear or see. To some young people, what is past is not so much prolog as nonexistent. Therefore, any foreign policy based solely on containment is viewed, at least among student activists, as unreal. The real reasons (they believe), therefore, must be economic gain, imperialistic design or pride, all of which are unacceptable.

Before Los Angeles World Affairs Council/
Los Angeles Times, 11–11:(4)13.

Bruce K. Holloway
General, United States Air Force;
Commander-in-Chief,
Strategic Air Command

We are called "imperialists." But where is the empire? Where is the territory? Where are the slaves? Where is the booty? Everyone knows that the treasures of empire simply do not exist for us. In the years of our great power, we have given, not gotten. We have voluntarily relinquished the stuff of past empires. We have departed great world war holdings in the Pacific, Africa and Europe. We have granted a promised independence to the Philippine Islands. We have granted the equality of statehood to Hawaii and Alaska. And we have provided brains, brawn and billions to help peoples all over the world. Our compassionate use of great power is unique in the experience of man. Historians will find it to have been a startling departure. But I submit . . . that it has been predictable, because it is in great part a reflection of our belief in the very values we prize so greatly.

At Texas A & M University, Jan. 17/
Vital Speeches, 2–15:263.

Hubert H. Humphrey
Former Vice President of the United States

History will show that my generation came out of World War II with two convictions: no more isolationism, and the need for collective security. Well, it's lost in the emotionalism over Vietnam. But these ideas worked in our relationship to Europe, and our intentions were good when we undertook a middle course in Vietnam. We just don't know enough about that part of the world. We've learned a lesson. It's difficult to get students to see that. They just don't have a concept of history. I talk about Franklin Roosevelt and then they think of Teddy Roosevelt. I asked some graduate students to name six accomplishments of the New Deal, and they couldn't do it.

Interview, Minneapolis/
Memphis Commercial Appeal, 8–19:7.

We are entering a new epoch in foreign policy, with a transition like that after World War II. I don't want Democrats to go berserk, to cop out, to go crypto-isolationist. We can't withdraw from the world order.

News conference, Washington/
The Christian Science Monitor, 12–15:7.

Roy Jenkins
Deputy leader, British Labor Party

(The United States now is) almost engulfed by her appalling domestic problems,

some of them caused and exacerbated by her involvement elsewhere in the world . . . I hope and believe she will not become isolationist; but her energies for a long time to come are bound to be greatly absorbed by her domestic schisms . . . There have been times in the life of most of us when great rays of hope have come from America . . . But I could not say that today.

Before Labor Committee for Europe,
Blackpool, England, Sept. 28/
The New York Times, 9–29:2.

Franklyn A. Johnson
President, William H. Donner Foundation;
Visiting Professor of Government,
John Jay College, New York

We are limited in power and, of course, must select points of vital interest. But if we accept the dogma of "no more Vietnams," will we *really* adhere to it if enemies of the free western world should attack the British Isles, or Israel, or Canada, or Mexico, or Panama, or Colombia, or Nicaragua, or the Philippines, or Australia, or Ethiopia, or Iceland, or Greenland, or Western Europe as a whole? Or even independent Communist Yugoslavia? Or suppose that China, for the second time in a decade, launched an assault against her neighbor, India, and threatened to harness those hundreds of millions in slave labor for her own possible expanding aggressive plans, nuclear and otherwise. Would we *really* continue to mouth, "No more Vietnams," as an updated equivalent of "America first" and "Why die for Danzig?" and "Forward to Munich" of the 1930s appeasers? I hope to God not! . . . As for policing the world: Nations need some form of policeman, or potential policeman, as much as do individuals . . . Looking backward, can anyone *really* believe this earth would not be very different—and far more disadvantageous to the free world—if since 1945 the U.S. had *not* exercised such direct policeman functions as the Greek-Turk aid program, forming NATO, the Korean action, resisting the Berlin blockade, forcing missiles out of Cuba, and backing South

(FRANKLYN A. JOHNSON)

Vietnam and other neighboring governments in Laos, Cambodia and Thailand?

At Rutgers University, Feb. 4 /
Vital Speeches, 4–1:374.

David M. Kennedy
Secretary of the Treasury
of the United States

To be effective abroad, we must be effective at home. We must continue our efforts to control inflation. We must not slacken now that the goal of an uninflated economy growing at a considerable rate is in sight. We must mind our business in such a way, paying for our demands as we go, that we will continue to be the inspiration for those who need development assistance.

Before Cincinnati Council of World Affairs /
The Dallas Times Herald, 2–27:A15.

Henry A. Kissinger
Assistant to the President of the United
States for National Security Affairs

I consider him (President Nixon) extremely well prepared in foreign affairs. He is very systematic and thoughtful. When you talk to him about a country, you don't have to explain where it is or who its leaders are and its problems. He knows it. He's probably been there. He has a feeling about it. And then he chews the problem over and over. He is easy to work for. He is thoughtful, very polite, but aloof. He is sensitive, and his antennae are remarkable for other people's moods . . . He goes at foreign policy in the most analytical way. In terms of my function, I feel intellectually comfortable.

Interview, Washington /
San Francisco Examiner & Chronicle, 8–23:A21.

Melvin R. Laird
Secretary of Defense of the United States

. . . the Nixon Doctrine assures our allies throughout the world that we will continue to meet our treaty obligations to them, but that we may meet them on a somewhat differ-

ent basis. We will meet them as necessary through increased military assistance and through air and sea support. But as for meeting our obligations with large ground forces, that is most unlikely.

Interview, Washington /
U.S. News & World Report, 5–11:72.

Our national security strategy for the 1970s is founded on three pillars: partnership, strength and a willingness to negotiate. This is how we intend to fulfill our new peacekeeping role. As is true for all broad concepts, the term "peace keeping" can be and has been misunderstood. In restoring and maintaining peace, we are determined to avoid isolationism and yet to shun, also, the role of world policeman.

At United States Air Force Academy
commencement / Life, 6–19:27.

Alfred M. Landon
Former Governor of Kansas

When you put it all together, it (President Nixon's foreign policy) means a gradual disengagement from the containment-of-communism policies of Truman, Eisenhower, Kennedy and Johnson, without returning to the smug isolationism of Coolidge, Hoover and Franklin Roosevelt in the 1920s and 1930s.

National Observer, 8–24:2.

. . . I said during World War II that our greatest weakness internationally is in emotionalism. Reform the world in mass in our own image! I think there's been too much of that in our foreign aid program, for instance —trying to establish in tribal Africa, for instance, or in Asia, the American form of government. They don't know anything about democratic processes. Where should we draw the line? We should draw it in keeping with a pragmatic, realistic international policy which does not involve us in trying to police the whole world.

Interview, Topeka, Kan. /
Congressional Record, 2–20:S2080.

Lyman L. Lemnitzer
General, United States Army (Ret.); Former Supreme Allied Commander-Europe

For my part, I can detect no softening in the Communists' tone, no change in their objectives and no relaxation of their stand. However, there does seem to be a new note of conviction among those who claim to see not only detente between East and West, but even rapprochement. On several important issues there seems to be a growing readiness in the West to volunteer specific and substantial concessions. To the extent that this attitude is genuine on *both* sides, it is without question a great step forward. But it would be dangerous if wishful thinking were to cloud realities. And it seems to me that some of our Allies—and some Americans— are tending to be willing to relax our collective guard and reduce our collective effort on the basis of assumptions which have not yet been proved to be justified. Certainly, at a time when the role of Allies is increasingly important for united effectiveness, this tendency I have mentioned is a complicating factor.

At U.S. Army War College commencement,
Carlisle Barracks, Pa., June 15/
Vital Speeches, 8–15:670.

. . . our relations throughout the world are becoming increasingly complex. In a number of cases, nations with which we wish to maintain harmonious relations are antagonistic to each other. There are also many cases where we can cooperate with a nation on one level but must compete on another. There is the continuing need for accurate international communication. There are nations whose internal policies we cannot approve, but whose strategic importance compels our support . . . There must . . . be an understanding of the psychological, technological and political outlook and capabilities of the people with whom we want to work. This includes an ability to recognize and comprehend *their* objectives, *their* aspirations and the political and economic and psychological constraints under which *they* must operate.

At U.S. Army War College commencement,
Carlisle Barracks, Pa., June 15/
Vital Speeches, 8–15:671.

Charles McC. Mathias, Jr.
United States Senator, R-Md.

If the United States is to develop foreign policies suitable for the Seventies, worthy of the support of those who have been estranged from our policies in the Sixties, we must clear away the legislative and conceptual debris of the Fifties. And if this process of modernizing our policies is to be durable and democratic, immune to sudden reversal in a crisis under the pressure of an aroused and uninformed public opinion, the Congress must play a key role in preparing itself and its constituencies. Congress must share with the President the educational leadership burdens in foreign affairs.

Before the Senate, Washington, Feb. 5/
Congressional Record, 2–5:S1272.

As we go through the next few months and years—and I think it is going to be clear that the first line of defense of America is in America—that we will recognize that the children we are educating today and the sick we are healing today and the jobs we are creating and training people for today are all the real strength, the real future and the real hope of America. And so I think that in a very real sense we will be turning inward. It's a curious thing about American history that we have had the greatest influence in the world when we have been performing well as a nation, not as the world policeman, not as a world evangelist, but as an example —showing what a free society, a dynamic society and a pluralistic society can do. And I think that in this sense we can look forward to a renaissance of enormous prestige and influence in the world by improving the conditions within our own borders which are so desperately out of kilter right now.

Interview, Washington/
The Christian Science Monitor, 3–2:3.

165

George S. McGovern
United States Senator, D-S.D.

Mr. Nixon has really devoted his public career for the last quarter of a century to fighting Communism. He thinks that almost any kind of a government, no matter how tyrannical, would be better than a Communist government—even one, I suspect, that had the support of their own people.

Washington, July 12/Daily World, 7–14:11.

Daniel P. Moynihan
*Counsellor to the President
of the United States*

. . . so much of what university intellectuals detest about American foreign policy is so indisputably the product of American intellectuals.

*Before American Council on Education,
St. Louis/The New York Times, 11–6:39.*

Edmund S. Muskie
United States Senator, D-Maine

We have seen that foreign assistance raises complex and difficult issues. Without it, however, the prospects for the economic and social progress of the underdeveloped are at best gloomy and uncertain. No long-term prospects for mankind are more frightening than that of the world becoming divided into two camps, of which one is non-black, non-young and non-poor.

*At International Development Conference,
Washington, Feb. 25/The New York Times,
2–26:12.*

Richard M. Nixon
President of the United States

The nations of each part of the world should assume the responsibility for their own well-being; and they themselves should determine the terms of that well-being. We shall be faithful to our treaty commitments, but we shall reduce our involvement and our presence in other nations' affairs. To insist that other nations play a role is not a retreat from responsibility, but a sharing of responsibility.

*State of the Union address, Washington,
Jan. 22/Los Angeles Times, 1–23:(1)20.*

We have a greater destiny than to conquer the world. We can give more to the world than other nations have given—spiritual leadership and idealism. That is something material strength or military power cannot provide.

*At Presidential Prayer Breakfast, Washington,
Feb. 5/Los Angeles Herald-Examiner, 2–5:A3.*

Small nations all over the world find themselves under attack from within and from without. If, when the chips are down, the world's most powerful nation—the United States of America—acts like a pitiful, helpless giant, the forces of totalitarianism and anarchy will threaten free nations and free institutions throughout the world. It is not our power but our will and character that are being tested . . .

*Radio-TV address, Washington, April 30/
The New York Times, 5–4:2.*

The whole thrust, the whole purpose, of this Administration's foreign policy—whether in Vietnam or the Middle East, or in Europe, or in relations with the developing countries or the Communist powers—is to meet our responsibilities in such a way that at last we can have what we have not had in this century: a full generation of peace.

*At Kansas State University, Sept. 16/
Los Angeles Times, 9–17:(1)17.*

We have great power. We have great responsibilities that go with that power. If we do not meet these responsibilities, the chances for people who do not have power throughout the world to grow up in independence and freedom will be completely wiped out on this earth. And so the people of the United States will meet their responsibilities—responsibilities that they did not ask for but that we have to defend not only for ourselves but also when asked to do so and when it seems to be in their interests and ours.

*Timahoe, Ireland, Oct. 5/
Los Angeles Herald-Examiner, 10–5:A2.*

In my talks with leaders all over the world, I find that there are those who may not agree with all of our policies. But no world leader to whom I have talked fears that the United States will use its power to dominate another country or destroy its independence. We can be proud that this is the cornerstone of America's foreign policy.

Radio-TV address, Washington, Oct. 7/
Los Angeles Times, 10–8:(1)27.

We all must recognize that the United States and the Soviet Union have very profound and fundamental differences. It would not be realistic, therefore, to suggest that our differences can be eliminated merely by better personal relationships between the heads of our governments. Such a view would slight the seriousness of our disagreements. Genuine progress in our relations calls for specifics, not merely atmospherics. A true detente is built by a series of actions, not by a superficial shift in the apparent mood. It would not be realistic to suggest that all we need to improve our relations is "better mutual understanding." Understanding is necessary. But we do understand one another well enough to know that our differences are real, and that in many respects we will continue to be competitors. Our task is to keep that competition peaceful and to make it creative. Neither would it be realistic to deny that power has a role in our relations. Power is a fact of international life. Our mutual obligation is to discipline that power, and to seek, together with other nations, to ensure that it is used to maintain the peace rather than to threaten the peace.

At 25th anniversary session of United Nations
General Assembly, New York, Oct. 23/
U.S. News & World Report, 11–2:70.

. . . United States-Soviet relations are going to continue to be difficult. But the significant thing is that we are negotiating and not confronting. We're talking at SALT. We're very far apart because our vital interests are involved, but we are talking . . . And so it is with Berlin, and so it is with the Mid-

east. I'm not suggesting that we're going to find easy agreement, because we are too great powers that are going to continue to be competitive for our lifetime. But I believe that we must continue on the path of negotiation.

News conference, Washington, Dec. 10/
The New York Times, 12–11:32.

David Packard
Deputy Secretary of Defense
of the United States

I believe that the best hope of reducing our overseas involvements and expenditures lies in getting allied and friendly nations to do even more than they are now doing in their own defense. To realize that hope, however, requires that we must continue, if requested, to give or sell them the tools they need for this bigger load we are urging them to assume.

Before House Foreign Affairs Committee,
Washington, Feb. 5/The Washington Post,
2–6:A4.

Olof Palme
Prime Minister of Sweden

. . . the relations between the American and the Swedish people are characterized by a long traditional friendship, of personal ties, of a wide exchange in the economic and cultural fields, of a common heritage in the development of a free and open society. Yet sometimes I have seen Sweden characterized as anti-American because we have at times been critical toward American policies. We in Sweden have not for a moment seen things this way. One would rather put the question in the following way: What kind of friends do we want? Do we want to stand up and be counted, or do we want them to stand up for their honest opinions, also, when they do not coincide with ours? For our part, we will not give up the long-standing tradition of genuine friendship with the American people.

Before National Press Club, Washington,
June 5/Vital Speeches, 7–15:579.

Claiborne Pell
United States Senator, D-R.I.

Our history has shown that we are better off—and certainly our taxpayers are better off—with countries neutral, or even opposed, to us, rather than with vulnerable, mushy allies unable to survive without American assistance.

Before the Senate, Washington, June 29/
The Washington Post, 6-29:A2.

Thomas M. Pelly
United States Representative, R-Wash.

The closure of the U.S. consulate in Salisbury, Rhodesia, by our Department of State is another sorry example of our government's placing improper priorities in foreign policy. While this move was made for the stated purpose of opposing the internal policies of the Ian Smith government, it is well known that it was actually an act of appeasement to gain the bloc of African votes in the United States and to support the British government. However, the inconsistency in this thinking is appalling. Rhodesia has historically been a friend of the United States. She has never lifted a finger to harm our country or her citizens. Yet, we turn our backs on the facts with regard to the lack of support we received from England over Cuba and the tragedy of British-flag vessels that have for years carried arms and ammunition into North Vietnam to be used against our fighting men; there were 74 such arrivals in 1969. The State Department's withdrawal of our consulate in Rhodesia marked another sorry day in our foreign policy, and it forces me to say, as I have for many years, that it is time for a thorough change of personnel in all the policy-making positions in the Department of State. It is time to put America first!

Human Events, 3-21:23.

Georges Pompidou
President of France

I cannot speak for others, but it seems to me that the present trend in America—which is probably not to try to assume all the responsibilities in the world at all times—is a trend which is fairly natural. But that is not isolationism. I cannot believe in American isolationism.

Interview, Paris/
U.S. News & World Report, 3-2:45.

Elliot L. Richardson
Under Secretary of State of the United States

. . . if the emerging generation has been conditioned by the events of its own era to accept a new and entirely different set of foreign policy assumptions, it does not automatically follow that the latter are all correct, or, conversely, that the axioms of the previous generation—many of which continue to guide our foreign policy—are all wrong. It would be folly to allow the "lessons of involvement" to stampede us into the abandonment of all the earlier and bitter "lessons of isolationism." The simplistic slogan, "No More Vietnams," will be clearly no more infallable as a guide to foreign policy in the complex and shifting world of the 1970s than "No More Munichs" was adequate for the jungles and rice paddies of Southeast Asia in the 1960s.

At Lowell Technological Institute
commencement, Lowell, Mass., June 7/
Vital Speeches, 7-15:584.

William P. Rogers
Secretary of State of the United States

I am the *adviser* to the President on foreign policy. Let there be no mistake about it! *He* is the man who *makes* foreign policy.

The Washington Post, 1-19:A8.

It is true we have taken some action to reduce our military expenditures, to reduce the number of men in our armed forces and to reduce our presence in certain countries. But that is not to suggest that we are going to withdraw from the world, that we are going to take any precipitate action to reduce our presence or that a policy of "neoisolation" is a possibility in the future.

Interview, Washington/
U.S. News & World Report, 1-26:29.

When you are as strong as the U.S. is, you don't have to shout it from the rooftops. The Russians know very well how strong we are; and if we tell them something quietly, I think it does the job. Make the other side appreciate your strength—but don't be offensive about it.

Time, 8–10:23.

Eugene V. Rostow
Professor of Law, Yale University; Former Under Secretary for Political Affairs, Department of State of the United States

Our safety as a nation has always depended—and this was perceived early in the history of the Republic—on there being a balance of power in Asia, so that no hegemonic power, no one power, would acquire so much strength in either place that it would be free of all restraints from rivals at home, and thus be able to become a threat to the United States . . . Many people say this policy is globalism, or it's an anti-Communist crusade. It's neither one . . . The United States never dreamed of attacking the Soviet Union or of delivering an ultimatum to the Soviet Union at a time when we had the nuclear monopoly. Nor, indeed, did we undertake to change the arrangements which emerged in Eastern Europe . . .

Interview/The Wall Street Journal, 7–14:12.

Walt W. Rostow
Professor of History, University of Texas; Former Foreign Affairs Adviser to the President of the United States

. . . history is ruthless with those who build their policies on illusion. And I believe it is an illusion to hold that America, at this time in history, can safely walk away from its commitments and interests in Asia, or in Europe, or the Middle East. I see no other viable course—in an age of nuclear weapons and instant communications, where the global community is being pulled closer together every day—than to play a responsible role on the world scene; to move patiently and cautiously toward a world of partnership and fair shares, while continuing to grapple at home with the long agenda of unfinished business in this rich, but troubled, society of ours.

At Naval War College, Newport, R.I., June 19/Vital Speeches, 9–1:687.

Dean Rusk
Former Secretary of State of the United States

It is simply too late in history to pursue a policy of total hostility for any nation or any people. We must set aside our glandular reactions and try to find agreement, even with those that consider themselves our personal adversaries.

Quote, 2–15:145.

Jean-Jacques Servan-Schreiber
Journalist; Member, French National Assembly

The power of the United States is virtually unchecked today. The President can make a military decision to invade Cambodia after talking to a handful of people, and it affects the entire world. It is our task in Europe to form a power that will counterbalance the United States, and force it to negotiate and take into account the ideas and needs of others. The Soviet Union is preoccupied with its own problems and not able to act as a constructive check on the United States.

Washington/The Christian Science Monitor, 8–7:2.

John J. Sparkman
United States Senator, D-Ala.

Current social and economic pressures which tend to turn our thinking inward and to place greater emphasis on our domestic problems can work against an orderly re-examination of the requirements of our defense posture. The pendulum can swing too far, forcing us into the kind of isolation that has brought the world so much grief in the past and would surely bring even greater grief in the future.

At National War College, Washington, Sept. 21/ Los Angeles Herald-Examiner, 9–21:A8.

Howard Stein
President, Dreyfus Fund

What is happening on Wall Street is what is happening in the world. We are overextended morally, economically and politically, and we are about to get our first margin call as a national power.

Time, 5–18:80.

Strom Thurmond
United States Senator, R-S.C.

What this country needs is more Caesars and fewer Chamberlains.

At "Salute to Mendel Rivers"
luncheon, Washington, Aug. 12/
The Washington Post, 8–18:A16.

Stephen M. Young
United States Senator, D-Ohio

One wonders how many millions of dollars for military and economic aid he (Vice President Agnew) will offer Thailand (on his current trip) . . . Americans should say, "Spiro, please come home. Spiro, preside over the Senate. We Americans have been giving billions of dollars of taxpayers' money in recent years, so, Spiro Agnew, please don't do this to us. Please come home."

Before the Senate, Washington, Aug. 27/
Cleveland Plain Dealer, 8–28:A9.

Ronald L. Ziegler
Press Secretary to the President
of the United States

The bearer of a United States passport carries with him prima facie evidence of United States citizenship, and the holding of a U.S. citizen as hostage is, of course, totally unacceptable to the United States government. I think it goes without saying that we deplore and denounce the holding of hostages by any nation.

Washington, Sept. 14/
Los Angeles Times, 9–15:(1)1.

Spiro T. Agnew
Vice President of the United States

We cannot govern with the consent of the governed unless we respect the right of dissent of the governed.

*Detroit, June 15 / The New York Times,
6–16:26.*

If a man is old enough to serve his nation at arms at 18, is he not old enough to vote? If a woman is considered mature enough to enter a lifetime contract of marriage at 18, is she not mature enough to vote? . . . Once our young people are permitted the privilege of sounding off at the polls, there will be less need to sound off in the streets. They'll have the chance to be counted where it counts.

*Before International Telephone and
Telegraph Corporation executives,
Washington, June 17 /
The New York Times, 6–18:38.*

If you have a government that's dominated by one party, you have tranquility politically. But tranquility doesn't mean that people are totally aware of what's going on in government. It generally means just the opposite. It means that too many things are happening behind the scenes in closed decisions without the knowledge of the media or the people of the state. When you have an adversary political climate, even though it may be slow (in) the implementation of reform and programs, it does assure that they receive the fullest debate and consideration, and it does assure that the poor parts of those programs will be opened to the public scrutiny before they are enacted into law.

*Dallas, Oct. 13 /
The Washington Post, 10–14:A6.*

We neglected to transmit something important during the time we were succeeding in offering our fellow Americans and our children new hope and new freedom. That something important was this: a respect for the system itself that has produced this enormous change for the better. Only with renewed respect for the American system itself can all of us gain the perspective that shows the system in its true light: changing, improving, succeeding. We will never gain that perspective, that necessary respect for the American system, from the lunatic fringe who only want to tear the system down so they can erect nothing in its place.

*Amarillo, Tex. / The Dallas Times Herald,
10–19:A24.*

If anyone wants to paint a picture of Congress this year, I'm pretty sure it would have to be a still-life.

Plainview (Tex.) Daily Herald, 11–12:12.

Gordon Allott
United States Senator, R-Colo.

It seems to be that the only thing that has exceeded the excessive accumulation of power in the Presidency is the outlandish expectations people have come to have of particular Presidents.

Quote, 11–8:446.

Birch Bayh
United States Senator, D-Ind.

I am confident that when the question of electoral reform is analyzed on its merits, direct popular election (of the President) will be found far and away the most necessary, the most desirable, the most effective reform.

*Before the Senate, Washington, Aug. 14 /
The New York Times, 8–15:11.*

Wallace F. Bennett
United States Senator, R-Utah

When people created government as a de-

(WALLACE F. BENNETT)

vice to solve their common problems, they had to endow it with power to act and to agree to be bound by its action. Power thus became the vital living force in government; and, in this sense, it may be likened to a huge magnifying glass capable of focusing the united personal powers of a whole people on their common problems. But magnifying glasses can become burning glasses if the power is carelessly concentrated. Similarly, governments too powerful can become destructive even of those who created them. Indeed, one might say that governments may be said to resemble the creature made out of human parts by Dr. Frankenstein and that for us, as for the good doctor in the story, the ultimate risk is that government may turn on its creators and destroy their happiness rather than promote it. The key to good government, then, is good people—both in and out of it. And by "good" we should mean spiritually strong.

At Senate Prayer Breakfast, Jan. 28/
Congressional Record, 2–10:S1620.

Winton M. Blount
Postmaster General of the United States

The present postal system is outdated by at least a century. It runs an annual deficit of over a billion dollars. It has an employe turnover rate of over 20 per cent a year. It functions constantly on the rim of disaster, and the only thing that keeps it from sliding over the edge is the dedication of the postal employes . . . along with a bit of luck, I think.

Before Menswear Retailers of America, Dallas,
Feb. 9/The Dallas Times Herald, 2–9:A1.

In my opinion, the Post Office business— and it *is* a business—is very similar to a nationwide utility. It's a materials-handling business in a logistical time frame. And I think that techniques and methods and management ideas that are successful in the business world are completely applicable to the Post Office Department, if we can just strip away the restrictions that have been placed

on it for all these years. And that's what we're trying to do.

Interview, Washington/
U.S. News & World Report, 5–4:46.

Kingman Brewster, Jr.
President, Yale University

Truly independent courts, universities, newspapers are, of course, a continuous irritation and frequently real trouble-makers for any government. It is the unique Anglo-American heritage, however, to have preserved and protected these critics as needling monitors of official accountability—accountability to law, accountability to professional criticism and accountability to public opinion.

Before American Newspaper Publishers
Association Bureau of Advertising,
New York/Los Angeles Times, 4–26:G3.

David Brinkley
News commentator, National
Broadcasting Company

In 25 years of working in Washington and watching government at close range, I have concluded that it does not do its job. The only departments that do a decent job are the fish and wildlife, forestry and park services and the space agency. You'll notice that these agencies deal with fish, forests, flowers and the moon—not the ordinary affairs of people.

St. Louis/Daily World, 11-21:11.

Edward W. Brooke
United States Senator, R-Mass.

If we (in the Senate) stop calling each other "distinguished," we might save 10 working days.

Dec. 31/Los Angeles Times, 1–1(1971):(1)13.

Arthur F. Burns
Chairman-designate, Federal Reserve Board

I think that the Federal Reserve Board must work closely with the Executive in the sense that it must be fully aware of the financial policies that are being pursued by the Treasury and elsewhere within the Executive, so that the Federal Reserve actions can be co-ordinated so far as it is reasonable with the actions taken by the Executive. However, the Federal Reserve Board has a very special status. Under legislation, it must exercise its own judgment always; it cannot be guided by the Executive authority.

At his confirmation hearing, Washington/
The Washington Post, 2–8:F1.

Robert C. Byrd
United States Senator, D-W.Va.

I pride myself on being the general flunky of the Senate.

Before the Senate, Washington, Feb. 27/
Congressional Record, 2–27:S2529.

William T. Cahill
Governor of New Jersey

Our nation must turn its energies and resources to the serious problems at home. The new proposed federalism must be made to work. The states can no longer supply on their own the needs of their people. The Federal government must accept the burden or share the dollars.

Inaugural address, Trenton, Jan. 20/
The New York Times, 1–21:33.

Emanuel Celler
United States Representative, D-N.Y.

I'll fight it (lowering the voting age to 18), come hell or high water . . . When we consider how easily the adolescent is inflamed, how easy for him at that age to see in patterns of black and white, without shadings, we can readily understand why the demagogue, the dictator and the hypnotic orator have been able, historically, to capture the youth of the land.

Washington/The Dallas Times Herald, 3–14:A8.

Ramsey Clark
Former Attorney General
of the United States

We subject 10 to 12 million young citizens between 17 and 21 years of age to taxation

without representation. This is four times the population of the Colonies the night the tea was dumped in Boston Harbor.

Before Senate subcommittee on lowering
the voting age, Washington, Feb. 17/
The New York Times, 2–18:20.

We need to recognize that dissent is the voice of powerless people; and the task of government is to provide ways to communicate effectively with these people.

Washington, March 14/
The New York Times, 3–15:(1)33.

Robert J. Dole
United States Senator, R-Kan.

Congress does have the constitutional power to declare war. We also have the power with reference to military appropriations. But there's a corresponding power . . . the President has, as the Commander-in-Chief, to make war, to make policy. And he has the inferred power as the Chief Executive to carry it out to the best of his responsibility, to carry out the laws and to make foreign policy. I think it's a shared responsibility. I don't agree with those in Congress who say it should be all our way, and I don't agree with those in the Executive who say it should be all the President's way. I think we have a shared responsibility.

Interview, Washington/
The Christian Science Monitor, 5–22:2.

John D. Ehrlichman
Assistant to the President of the
United States for Domestic Affairs

I am certainly not a conservative, not a Goldwater. My affinity for Richard Nixon stems in part from the fact that he is not rigid in his attitudes toward the use of Federal Power. I think that there are some problems in which the Federal government is bound to be less effective than some other governmental entity, and that is why we are pushing for some kind of revenue sharing. But it (the Federal government) can be a mighty engine for good, and I would not be slow to use it for proper ends if I were convinced

(JOHN D. EHRLICHMAN)

that it was constitutional and consistent with sound practices.

Interview/The New York Times Magazine, 4–12:62.

There are a lot of bright people in the government with bright ideas, and it's my responsibility to make sure the President sees them. But the point is they've got to reach him in an orderly way. Some Presidents may thrive on confusion. Not this one (Nixon). It's not his style. He wants the options, sure, but he wants them packaged in the best possible form.

Interview/The New York Times Magazine, 4–12:74.

Sam J. Ervin, Jr.
United States Senator, D-N.C.

Direct popular elections would necessitate uniform Federal voting requirements and centralized administration of Presidential election machinery . . . The power of this centralized administration over the Presidential election would, of necessity, be quite considerable. The danger of its misuse is both obvious and frightening.

U.S. News & World Report, 5–11:26.

. . . the new technology has been quietly, but steadily, endowing officials with the unprecedented political power which accompanies computers and data banks and scientific techniques of managing information. It has given government the power to take note of anything, whether it be right or wrong, relevant to any purpose or not, and to retain it forever. Unfortunately, this revolution is coming about under outdated laws and Executive orders governing the record-keeping and the concepts of privacy and confidentiality relevant to an earlier time. These developments are particularly significant in their effect on the First Amendment to our Constitution. No longer can a man march with a sign down Pennsylvania Avenue and then return to his hometown, his identity forgotten, if not his cause. No longer does the memory of the authorship of a political article fade as the pages of his rhetoric yellow and crumble with time. No longer are the flamboyant words exchanged in debate allowed to echo into the past and lose their relevance with the issue of the moment which prompted them. No longer can a man be assured of his enjoyment of the harvest of wisdom and maturity which comes with age, when the indiscretions of youth, if noticed at all, are spread about in forgotten file cabinets in basement archives. Instead, today, his activities are recorded in computers or data banks, or if not, they may well be a part of a great investigative index.

Before the Senate, Washington/ The Wall Street Journal, 9–14:12.

Our system cannot survive if citizen participation is limited merely to registering disagreement with official policy. The policies, themselves, must be the product of the people's views. The protection and encouragement of such participation is a principle purpose of the First Amendment.

November/The New York Times, 12–27:(1)44.

Reuven Frank
President, National Broadcasting Company News

The Constitution is a very simple document. It is clearer in its aims than in its instructions. That is why the Constitution has changed so little while the United States has changed so much. It might be worth considering that perhaps all those changes would have taken place under a different Constitution. But that would have meant changing the Constitution itself each time, and some of those times might have caused violence. As it is, this simple document has allowed for 200 years of rapid, revolutionary and often unexpected changes within American society. As it stands, the document does for Americans of the late twentieth century world what it did for Americans of the late

eighteenth century world, by allowing
change, but not changing.

> *At Yale University, Feb. 17/*
> *Vital Speeches, 3–15:333.*

John W. Gardner
Chairman, National Urban Coalition

Few institutions in our national life are
as gravely in need of renewal as the Congress of the United States.

> *Newsweek, 2–2:20.*

Our political and governmental processes
have grown so unresponsive, so ill-designed
for contemporary purposes, that they waste
the taxpayers' money, mangle good programs and smother every good man who gets
into the system.

> *Washington, July 30/*
> *The New York Times, 7–31:1.*

People are bored with their state legislatures, they are bored with their city councils
and they pay little attention to the Congress
of the United States.

> *Television interview/*
> *Los Angeles Times, 9–20:A13.*

John W. Gardner
*Chairman, Common Cause; Former
chairman, National Urban Coalition*

It may be true to a few individuals that
they have done everything possible to work
within the system—but it isn't true of Americans generally. Well-motivated Americans
have barely begun to do the things they
ought to be doing. They have shamefully
neglected their political and governmental
institutions. They have allowed the public
process to decay . . . As a result, self-government is in a mess.

> *Before United Press International
> conference of editors and publishers,
> Williamsburg, Va./*
> *The Dallas Times Herald, 10–20:A16.*

Congress is creaky, cranky and obsolescent,
and the best men in it can't make it work.

> *News conference, Washington, Oct. 28/*
> *The Washington Post, 10–29:A2.*

Arthur J. Goldberg
*Former Associate Justice, Supreme Court
of the United States; Candidate for
Democratic Party nomination for
Governor of New York*

There are eleven . . . words which should
characterize the process of government:
open, participatory, just, responsive, nonviolent, democratic, imaginative, effective,
accountable, committed, foresighted . . . I
want to end government by crisis and substitute government which anticipates crisis
and averts it. I want to end government by
the few for the few and substitute government which is truly of, by and for the people. I want to end government by promise
and press release and substitute government
by performance. I want to end the divisions
which are tearing at us and substitute government which actively seeks to bring people together and reconcile their differences.

> *News conference, New York, June 20/*
> *The New York Times, 6–21:(1)68.*

Barry M. Goldwater
United States Senator, R-Ariz.

Some more idealism will do us all good. It
will help remove the crusty, shop-worn reasons why the policies and goals which are
promised to voters don't ever seem to get accomplished. It will make us find the positive
answers that will put us on the right track.
Instead of explaining why this law or that
program can't benefit the public the way we
thought it would when it was passed, idealism will send us searching for innovations
and new departures that will get the job
done. Whether we are speaking of world
peace, cleaning the air and water, stopping
crime in the streets, eliminating smut in the
mails, or any other important goal, the energies and enthusiasm and urgings of young
Americans will help us do our best.

> *The Wall Street Journal, 3–20:10.*

To me, one thing is clear: The idea (voting at age 18) has found its time. This is the
year to act. The proposal for giving full citi-

zenship to young Americans is right—I know it in my heart.

Quote, 4–5:313.

. . . the bureaucracy which the Federal government maintains today has actually become a problem of man's ability to govern himself in time of massive technological change and population growth. It is so massive that it literally feeds on itself. It is so large that no one in or out of government can accurately define its power and scope. It is so intricate that it lends itself to a large range of abuses—some criminal and deliberate, others unwitting and inept. The government is so large that institutions doing business with it, or attempting to do business with it, are forced to hire trained experts just to show them around through the labyrinthine maze made up of hundreds of departments, bureaus, commissions, offices and agencies . . . the size of the Federal bureaucracy—which just keeps "growing like topsy" year after year after year despite the unfair and growing burden which it places on the taxpayer—is compounding the difficulty and confusion which the average American encounters as he attempts to function in today's society. If this continues, the day will come when not only business will choke to death on government red tape, but the average American wage-earner and property-holder will suffocate as well.

Before the Senate, Washington, July 14/
Vital Speeches, 8–15:642.

. . . any man who finds himself running for the top office in this nation on a major party ticket is forced to give some thought and some study to the whole question of how to go about staffing the national government. This whole problem is so vast that no man with even an outside chance of becoming President can do any less than to devote long hours of very concentrated study to the structuring and functioning of the Federal government. When you come up against

such a possibility, you begin to understand that just the problem of finding qualified people to man the very highest echelon of government requires much searching and much investigating. I doubt if the average American has any idea what a tremendous undertaking this becomes.

Before the Senate, Washington, July 14/
Vital Speeches, 8–15:645.

Lincoln Gordon
President, Johns Hopkins University

To be sure, constitutional democracy is often slow and frustrating in its workings. It is most frustrating to minorities who have not yet been able to persuade majorities to their cause, or which are unwilling to conciliate their views sufficiently with others to form working majorities. It is also frustrating to those so certain that they alone know what is right and moral that they forget that tolerance of other views is also a virtue. But it is not an unresponsive system, given time and persistence, and it is open to your active participation. So I hope the recent fervor for political action by your generation will not prove a passing fad. I hope many of you will go actively into public life. I hope you will not give up if all the results you want don't come forth this year, or in 1972, or in 1984, or even in the year 2000, when most of you will still be younger than I am now. When constitutional democracy is once abandoned, history suggests that it is a long time before the postman knocks again.

At Johns Hopkins University commencement/
The Wall Street Journal, 6–29:10.

Philip C. Habib
Diplomat

Each day of my 21 years of foreign service has started with the feeling there were things worth doing. I have never been bored, my time is not wasted and there is a constant, gratifying theme in service to the nation. Federal service is not a preserve of mediocrity.

Interview/Nation's Business, Sept.:37.

H. R. Haldeman
*Assistant to the President
of the United States*

I agree that the place (the White House) could entrap a President. That's why President Nixon physically leaves the place and goes to Camp David or Key Biscayne. (John F.) Kennedy said that one good thing about the White House is that it was a short walk to the office—but that cuts both ways.

Time, 6–8:20.

Bryce N. Harlow
*Counsellor to the President
of the United States*

The first six months of any new Administration, especially when there's a change of party, is like walking through a vat of acid. The politicians literally mob you en masse. Their hunger for jobs is insatiable, frightening really. There are 20 applicants for every vacancy, and they can't understand why you don't throw out thousands of the infidels overnight to make room for the faithful.

The New York Times Magazine, 2–1:46.

People who hold staff jobs are truly public servants. I prefer to remain in a collaborative relationship with those who are elected. You forfeit some standing in your own right as a career assistant to the great, but you don't lose all originality and become a cipher. If you do the job long enough and well enough, you get some recognition in your own right.

Los Angeles Times, 3–15:A20.

S. I. Hayakawa
President, San Francisco State College

My argument for the lowered voting age is that modern men and women are arriving at biological maturity earlier than ever, but are kept in social immaturity longer than ever—by compulsory schooling, by the demand that they go to college, by exclusionary practices of both employers and unions. By the age of 18, a young man or woman is ready and eager to be involved in adult concerns. The vote will be an adult concern that will make at least one change in the young person's life.

Quote, 5–10:449.

Richard Hofstadter
*Professor of American History,
Columbia University*

One of America's outstanding characteristics is that for a society that is in so much trouble and has so many reasons for agitation on war and racial justice, it has remarkably little repressive apparatus and is remarkably open to peaceful dissent. Those who tell you about repression and try to tell us that America is really Fascist simply have no idea of what they are talking about . . . This society has had less repression in recent years than at most times in its past, and less repression than all but a handful of other societies on the surface of the globe. "Repression" is one of those imbecile catchwords of our era—like "genocide" and "imperialism"—that have had all the meaning washed out of them.

Interview/Newsweek, 7–6:23.

Frank Horton
United States Representative, R-N.Y.

No matter which party controls the Executive Branch, the hot voice of humanity is often unheard in the chilly corridors of power.

*At Computer Audit Systems, Concord, N.H.,
Sept. 15/Vital Speeches, 11–1:46.*

Roman L. Hruska
United States Senator, R-Neb.

With reference to statistics such as those . . . that 18-year-olds are old enough to fight, pay taxes, work, drive cars—I think that is all true; I accept it . . . However, I do not like to place my brief for the conclusion they should vote on the ground of being old enough to fight. I would prefer to put it on the basis on which President Nixon put it. He recited all of these things and then said these are not the reasons he favors lowering the voting age. The reason he favors lower-

(ROMAN L. HRUSKA)

ing the voting age is the 18-year-olds are *smart* enough to vote.

Before the Senate, Washington, March 11 /
Congressional Record, 3–11:S3500.

Hubert H. Humphrey
Former Vice President of the United States

. . . I have mixed emotions about the Nixon Administration. It gives attention to what I call management details, but is lacking in that certain something, that intangible, that charismatic quality which I believe is so essential in a time of strife and turmoil and change and difficulty. You have to give people more than just a good ledger sheet. You have to give them inspiration and uplift and hope.

Interview, Washington /
The Christian Science Monitor, 1–12:1.

. . . I happen to believe that the major conflict in American life today is not between liberals and conservatives. I think it's between those who wish to destroy the system on the one hand and those who wish to change it and make it work a little better, or considerably better. For those of us who want to preserve the system and alter it to make it work better rather than to destroy it, you need a clear, unmistakable call of the bugle. If the trumpet is uncertain, or even if it's muted, it does not rally the forces.

Interview, Washington /
The Christian Science Monitor, 1–12:3.

As Vice President, you have immense responsibility—that is, you are supposed to—but no authority. As a Senator, you have great authority, and the question of how much responsibility you exercise depends upon your own self-discipline. You see, the Senate offers you the chance to be the tribune of the people. You can't always do all you'd like to have done, but at least you can alert people to what needs to be done. And you can help mobilize public opinion. The Senate is where you can do a lot of little things that add up to a rather big total.

Interview, Waverly, Minn. /
The Washington Post, 6–14:H2.

Leon Jaworksi
President-elect, American Bar Association

In this republic, there are available ample processes to register grievances, to protest and seek changes, prescribed and fully protected by Article I of the Bill of Rights. Open to all of us are processes of a democracy: the use of the petition and the ballot box and the abiding-by-majority rule. Since the founding of our nation, groups who felt oppressed have resorted to these democratic channels. Some have succeeded, some have failed. Revolutionary change overnight is not to be expected in a democracy—where change is slow and often long-considered. But when change does come, it comes without an overthrow of government and with the retention of freedoms more precious than the redresses for which even the best-intentioned of revolutionaries are reaching.

Before Christian Life Commission,
Baptist General Convention of Texas /
The Dallas Times Herald, 10–15:A28.

Nicholas Johnson
Commissioner, Federal Communications Commission

President Nixon has demonstrated perhaps the most extreme case of "government by television" we have seen since the little screen exploded in our midst as a political phenomenon.

London, Dec. 14 /
San Francisco Examiner, 12–14:33.

Walter H. Judd
Lecturer, Physician

It is commonly said that, in a democracy, decisions are made by a majority of the people. Of course, that is not true. Decisions are made by the majority of those who make themselves heard—a very different thing.

Quote, 11–8:438.

Edward M. Kennedy
United States Senator, D-Mass.

I feel the Senate is where the action is, where the great issues of war and peace, human rights and the problems of poverty are being debated. And, with certain exceptions, you really *can* get a vote there on important matters. I would say the Senate is the greatest forum for change in our country and the system.

Interview, Boston/
The New York Times Magazine, 5–24:80.

Our leaders have taken an oath to preserve, protect and defend the Constitution and, by implication, the goals and ideals for which it stands. It appears that the Constitution is being compromised at every opportunity—in civil rights, in civil liberties, in the assumption of war-making powers, in attempting to constrict the power of advice and consent and, more broadly, by encouraging a divisiveness and combativeness among our people that is tearing the nation apart. We were told we would be brought together, but, at the point of contact, we have found fists and gas and bullets.

At Manhattanville College commencement,
Purchase, N.Y., May 30/The New York Times,
6–1:13.

We will have a different country tomorrow when 18-year-olds begin to vote, because they will not be dropouts from the political process.

December/The New York Times, 12–27:(4)2.

Joseph M. Kennick
California State Senator

Some legislators labor under the impression (that) the more bills you introduce, the more effective you are. They use them to impress constituents. They might send out a newsletter saying they introduced 87 bills. But what they don't say is that 86 of them were laughed out of existence.

Los Angeles Times, 2–19:(1)31.

Henry A. Kissinger
Assistant to the President of the United States for National Security Affairs

One of the worst misconceptions is the idea that a Presidential assistant exercises some Svengali influence over the President . . . It would be preposterous to pretend I don't have *any* influence. I do. But my position is something like this: I say to the President, "You've got this problem and you have three or four different ways of going at it and here are the different points of view." When he asks what I think, I tell him. But a President is never dependent on one man. He can't afford to be.

Interview, Washington/
San Francisco Examiner & Chronicle,
8–23:A21.

Josef Krips
Orchestra conductor

I would . . . not like to be President of the United States, even if they doubled my income. Do you think anyone in the world is great enough to be President of this? This is not a nation—this is Mankind!

Interview, Los Angeles/
San Francisco Examiner & Chronicle
(California Living), 8–30:20.

William M. Kunstler
Civil rights lawyer

The silent majority is not a bunch of evil people. They think the college kids are going crazy. They worry about their homes, their jobs and their investments. They don't want to upset the boat in any way. They want to believe in this country. They want to believe in it so badly, they become ugly. We have an Administration right now that wants to take away the rights guaranteed by the Constitution. The darndest thing is that 90% of (the) American people are ready to let them do it—just for the sake of keeping things quiet.

Interview/Los Angeles Times, 8–9:F3.

Alfred M. Landon
Former Governor of Kansas

. . . if I had been elected President, there would have been more antitrust suits filed; I can tell you that. But who can say whether things would have been better if one could go back and change this isolated fact of history or that? History is made up of interrelated parts and has to be viewed whole. Commenting on it is far less hazardous than making it. I can tell you this, though. We have developed in this country today a sounder political life than ever before.

Interview, Topeka, Kan./
Los Angeles Times, 5–24:A10.

Harold LeVander
Governor of Minnesota

The damned-if-you-do and damned-if-you-don't-nature of the governor's job can make you a cynic.

The Dallas Times Herald, 1–27:A2.

Allard K. Lowenstein
United States Representative, D-N.Y.

If you think life in the university is irrelevant, you should try sitting in the House of Representatives. The way we choose our leadership in the House is through this process we call "galloping geriatrics." Whoever lasts the longest ends up in positions of authority.

At Tufts University commencement/
Life, 6–19:26.

You get used to seeing things happen in the House that you don't believe . . . To what degree is it useful to participate in the charades accepted here? On anything significant, they rarely give you a recorded vote. The procedures lack any fundamentally democratic quality. The average age of the committee chairmen is three years beyond the compulsory retirement age of most companies.

Look, 8–25:38.

Clark MacGregor
United States Representative, R-Minn.

I know Wally Hickel (recently fired Secretary of the Interior) said, "I had to do it my way." And that explains the difficulty. Because when you're appointed by the President, you have to do it *his* way.

Dec. 1/The New York Times, 12–2:31.

Mike Mansfield
United States Senator, D-Mont.

Government spending, to put it bluntly, is seriously out of date. It is not how much is being spent. It is *how* it is being spent. Priorities are still determined largely by yesterday's fears and fallacies. They scarcely meet today's urgencies. They only begin to perceive tomorrow's needs.

Radio-TV address, Washington, June 24/
U.S. News & World Report, 7–6:69.

Eugene J. McCarthy
United States Senator, D-Minn . . .

You kind of hate to give up the Senate. It's a good address.

Interview, Washington/
Los Angeles Times, 5–24:F2.

John W. McCormack
United States Representative, D-Mass.;
Speaker of the House

I think it is correct to say that the Speaker of the House does occupy the second most powerful position in our government. In theory, the Vice President is second to the President; but in actual terms of power and influence in our government, the Speaker ranks second. I don't say that to downgrade in any way the office of the Vice President. That is just the way it is.

Interview, Washington/
U.S. News & World Report, 7–27:61.

George S. McGovern
United States Senator, D-S.D.

Come home, America—from Vietnam and Laos and Cambodia—where we are wasting young blood in support of a political regime that does not have the respect of its own citizens. Come home, America—from the bitterness and evil of racism to the dignity of brotherhood. Come home, America—from the politics of manipulation and division to the politics of hope and reconciliation. Come home, America—from boasts of a silent majority to the higher ground of conscience and responsibility. Come home, America—from the intimidation of the free press to the guarantee of the Bill of Rights. Come home, America—from the hunger of little children, from the loneliness of the aging poor, from the despair of the homeless, the jobless, the uncared-for sick, to a society that cherishes the human spirit.

> *At Trinity College commencement/*
> *Life, 6–19:27.*

All my life I have heard Republicans and conservative Democrats complaining about the growth of centralized power in the Federal Executive. Vietnam and Cambodia have convinced me that you conservatives were right. We have permitted the war power—which the authors of the Constitution wisely gave to us (Senators) as the people's representatives—to slip out of our hands until it now resides behind closed doors at the State Department, the CIA, the Pentagon and the basement of the White House.

> *San Francisco Examiner & Chronicle*
> *(This World), 9–6:2.*

W. Walter Menninger
Psychiatrist; Member, National Commission on the Causes and Prevention of Violence

Giving the 18-to-21-year-olds the voting privilege is one step toward building more responsible citizens—but only one step. There are other important steps, not the least of which is giving youth the opportunity also to be a part of government at *all* levels. At the national level and in those cities and counties with representative government as well, youth should be present and meaningfully engaged. Not only can they profit from the participation as a means of learning, but they can also contribute a per-

spective, a vigor, an idealism which are all too often lacking.

> *Before Senate subcommittee on*
> *Constitutional Amendments, Washington,*
> *Feb. 16/Congressional Record, 3–6:S3130.*

Abner J. Mikva
United States Representative, D-Ill.

What have we done for the people? What has Congress really done about the real problems? What have we done about teenage gangs? What have we done about unemployment? About the racial situation? About the schools? The quality of life—is it any better for Congress having met these two years? Nothing came out of this Congress for *people*—nothing like social security, nothing like Medicare. Well, yes, the 18-year-old vote, that was something specific, something good and concrete. But . . .

> *Interview, Washington/*
> *Los Angeles Times, 11–22:A7.*

John N. Mitchell
Attorney General of the United States

When I first came to Washington, there were those who said: "What does a Wall Street lawyer know about being Attorney General?" And when I discuss the economy today, I am sure there will be some who will say: "What does an Attorney General know about Wall Street?"

> *Cleveland, Miss., May 19/*
> *U.S. News & World Report, 6–1:39.*

This Administration has a strategy. Let me make it plain that it is a national strategy, a strategy of reform of national affairs to bring about a new steadiness of progress. We are convinced that this strategy will work. We have some evidence that it is beginning to work already—especially in the economic field. We intend to persevere, and . . . businessmen would do well to make . . . plans and investments on the basis of the elements of certainty provided by a government that already has a record of doing what it said it would do. Our strategy is fallible, but it is not frantic. It is sounder, we believe, than

(JOHN N. MITCHELL)

any other strategy we have heard—and has certainly been better than the makeshift policy of the past. Nobody can assure you that this strategy is perfect, but let me assure you here and now that it will be followed. We will be sensitive to trends and will adapt our tactics, but there will be no flip-flops in the basic design. The people put a man in the Oval Office to take the long view and to act in the best interests of all the people. That is what he is doing now. I am confident that it will become increasingly apparent that—in our time and with this President— it is not a good idea to sell this country short.

Cleveland, Miss., May 19/
U.S. News & World Report, 6–1:41.

If there is any greater proof that the First Amendment is alive and well and that it is working in today's society, we need only look at the recent growth and vitality of citizen-action programs—most of them depending upon young people for their strongest support. What this proves beyond a reasonable doubt is that there is more freedom of speech and more freedom of assembly today than at any time in our nation's history. And so long as I am Attorney General, I will do everything within my power to see that these rights continue to flourish.

Before State Bar Association of Texas/
Los Angeles Times, 7–12:F2.

Thomas H. Moorer
Admiral, United States Navy; Chairman, Joint Chiefs of Staff

You must keep in mind that our nation's leadership must operate in the hard, cruel and demanding world and not in the dream world of opinion . . . Their decisions must be made in the world as it exists today and not as we would hope it to be.

San Francisco Examiner & Chronicle
(This World), 11–1:2.

Frank E. Moss
United States Senator, D-Utah

Opponents of lowering the voting age . . . hold that despite the other rights and duties given to young people, they are still too immature to vote. Young people are said to be too rebellious and militant. But such beliefs have no basis in fact. Of the millions of college students, studies show that less than one-half of 1% were engaged in any kind of disruptions that involved violence. This image of immaturity and rebelliousness no doubt comes from watching the television news. But those older people sincerely concerned about maturity should remember that there are over 11 million young people in this age group and only a tiny minority of them ever get on television. Opponents of the 18-year-old vote should look around at their own children or grandchildren before concluding that all young people riot. This country should stop penalizing the great majority of young people for the transgressions of a few. It is time to make young people full participants in the democratic process instead of preaching to them how good our democracy is. We can give 18-to-21-year-olds the vote now, this session of Congress. We need not wait for the drawn-out process of a constitutional amendment.

Before the Senate, Washington, March 11/
Congressional Record, 3–11:S3510.

Daniel P. Moynihan
Counsellor to the President of the United States

It (government) cannot provide values to persons who have none, or who have lost those they had. It cannot provide a meaning to life. It cannot provide inner peace. It can provide outlets for moral energies, but it cannot create those energies.

Los Angeles Times, 2–15:G3.

The Federal bureaucracy is an unknown quantity. It doesn't go to dinner in Georgetown; it doesn't publish journals; it doesn't testify before congressional committees; it has no spokesmen. The great achievement s to read it right. It gets less readable all the time.

Life, 12–18:2.

Richard M. Nixon
President of the United States

It is time to quit putting good money into bad programs. Otherwise, we will end up with bad money as well as bad programs.

State of the Union address, Washington, Jan. 22/Los Angeles Times, 1–23:(1)20.

Washington must lead and Washington must supply assistance for all the programs. But I want members of our Cabinet to know what the people out in the heartland think. I want them to know what their needs are, what they think we ought to do. That is why we are here.

Indianapolis, Feb. 5/ The New York Times, 2–6:12.

I am a political man. I know how popular it is to be for big spending programs in an election year. But I also know that big spenders are only popular as long as they are picking up the check. When somebody else picks up the check, they become very unpopular. And when the American people learn that the big spenders in Congress are primarily responsible for higher prices, and eventually even higher taxes, I think that the American people will turn on the big spenders politically.

News Conference, Washington, July 20/ The New York Times, 7–21:16.

I think that sometimes the Senate would do better to do what the House does, to get out throughout the country and see what the country is thinking . . . There is sort of an intellectual incest (in Washington) which really reduces the level of the dialogue, and you have to go to the country now and then to get a real feeling of what people are thinking.

The New York Times, 7–26:(4)1.

Remember the old quiz programs with the isolation booth? That's what we are like in Washington. We can hear the questions, but we can't hear what the folks outside are saying.

News conference/Newsweek, 7–27:13B.

Here in Washington, in government, we have a tendency to think about things in a mass—about cities of more than a million, or people over 65 or under 21, or about whole school systems or health-delivery systems. Just yesterday, I spent most of the day working on next year's budget—on the billions for this and the billions for that, and how, perhaps, a hundred million could be saved here in order to be used there, trying to balance the needs and hopes of dozens of government departments and agencies that operate thousands of programs involving millions of people. Sometimes, after doing that, I find myself reflecting on both the necessity and the impersonality of it all. Budgets have to be made and they have to be followed, because this is the way the real world operates; and governments have to deal with great masses of people, because this is the way governments operate. But how far removed this can get us from the perspective of the individual person! How great a tendency there is in government to lose track of people as people—to get so wrapped up in charts and projections and columns of numbers that we lose sight of what ultimately it is all about!

At opening of White House Conference on Children, Washington, Dec. 13/ National Observer, 12–21:12.

Richard L. Ottinger
United States Representative, D-N.Y.

I don't buy big government. You can never find the person who's responsible.

Interview/The New York Times, 3–15:(1)49.

Robert W. Packwood
United States Senator, R-Ore.

The seniority system, as we presently use it, has caused the Congress to be a laughing stock among the public. Even the law of the

(ROBERT W. PACKWOOD)

jungle operates on the survival of the fittest. Congress operates only on the principle of "survival."

The Dallas Times Herald, 8–25:A2.

William Proxmire
United States Senator, D-Wis.

The American public is convinced that Congress is spending money like a drunken sailor and that only the President can hold back the dam.

Cleveland Plain Dealer, 8–12:B2.

Ronald Reagan
Governor of California

If we give the vote to 18-year-olds, the next President of the United States will have three things to worry about: Vietnam, inflation and acne.

*At annual Host Breakfast, Sacramento/
Los Angeles Herald-Examiner, 9–5:A5.*

George E. Reedy
Former Press Secretary to the President of the United States

It's very hard for a President to find a place after he leaves office. After all, he can't run for Pope.

*Before National Press Club, Washington,
April 21/The Dallas Times Herald, 4–22:A9.*

William H. Rehnquist
*Assistant Attorney General
of the United States*

The government as an employer has a legitimate and constitutionally recognized interest in limiting public criticism on the part of its employes, even though that same government as a sovereign has no similar constitutionally valid claim to limit dissent on the part of its citizens.

*Before Federal Bar Association, Washington,
Sept. 18/Los Angeles Times, 9–19:(1)6.*

Abraham A. Ribicoff
United States Senator, D-Conn.

I don't think these college kids are sick at all. There are too many of us in Congress who are too goddamn old. The problems of society are not going to be solved by a bunch of 70-year-olds. We sit smugly here in Congress and the Executive Branch and we think we have all the answers. We should spend time with high school and college students.

*News conference, Washington, May 18/
San Francisco Examiner & Chronicle
(This World), 5–24:2.*

Vernon B. Romney
Attorney General of Utah

We're getting very, very weary of the Federal government taking over all the powers of the States. If this trend keeps up, we'll find we are just 50 colonies.

Quote, 9–20:265.

William B. Saxbe
United States Senator, R-Ohio

I've had the feeling for some time that the Senate is the biggest time-waster I've been in . . . The Senators get up and talk, and there may be one or two members on the floor. Most of it is for local consumption. There is little debate. Then we have a quorum call to delay and let the next guy know it's time for him to come over and talk. I recognize they have to campaign, but I just don't understand why the leadership of both sides doesn't crack the whip . . . This fiddling-while-Rome-burns attitude is something that seems to pervade the whole country.

*Interview, Washington, Sept. 2/
Los Angeles Times, 9–3:(1)28.*

Today, instead of being a group of men who get together on the floor to debate issues, the Senate is a place where men stand up and read long statements—page after page of boilerplate written by somebody else—just to "get it in the *Record*." A Senator often is just a conduit between some ghost writer and the *Congressional Record*.

*Interview, Washington/
San Francisco Examiner, 11–16:12.*

Hugh Scott
United States Senator, R-Pa.

We must retreat from demagoguery in all its oratorical fulmination . . . Let government inject some youthful idealism. Let us not resign government to the apathetic, cynical or the coldly pragmatic.

At hearings of President's Commission on Campus Unrest, Washington/Quote, 8–9:121.

Frank Shakespeare
Director, United States Information Agency

I have found that, frequently, the press of the U.S. has been immensely suspicious of some of the things we do at the USIA, because they read into the fact that, if you're a conservative—which I am—you are doing these things for some very particular conservative reasons. What I have tried to do about that, and propose to keep doing, is to keep this agency a glass house. Any newsman who wants to can come in and see everything; he can see our programs, he can listen to the *Voice of America,* he can check our people in the field, he can go visit our libraries. We don't have anything that is not fully exposed to everybody, because we're an informational medium. And I'm content to make explanations to anyone who first does his homework. I emphasize—*does his homework.*

Interview, Washington/TV Guide, 12–5:12.

William L. Shirer
Author, Journalist

. . . if our affluent society turned into one of hardship, I think you'd get by the consent of the people a very right-wing society and government in which freedom would be greatly restricted. The people would be calm and you wouldn't have to have a dictator in the goading sense that Hitler or Mussolini—or on the Communist side, Stalin —were dictators. It would be a sort of dictatorship by approval.

Interview, Beverly Hills, Calif./ Los Angeles Times, 3–13:(2)1.

John Virgil Singleton, Jr.
United States District Judge, Southern District of Texas

I do not know what is going on in the world today. I do not know what is going on in the minds of young people. I cannot understand how an intelligent young man could, in his mind, living in this country, accepting the benefits of this free society, have the idea that he can substitute his opinion and his judgment for that made by the leadership of this country, and thereby act according to his own judgment and opinions in matters regarding national policy . . . The President of the United States, whoever he may be, has an awesome responsibility in the area of foreign affairs. He has the responsibility—and not another living soul—to determine what is the best interest of this country; wherein does this country have to demonstrate its strength, and when and why. And when he makes that determination as the Commander-in-Chief under our Constitution, and young people are called upon to respond, they must respond. That is what it is all about. That is what life is all about. There are no free rides. For some reason, young people today seem to think that they are supposed to have a free ride—someone else is supposed to take care of them. That just is not right. Society is not built on that premise.

May 7/U.S. News & World Report, 6–8:27.

Albert Szent-Gyorgyi
Biologist

The only way we can survive is to make a new beginning. There is one factor that makes a new beginning very difficult—that the human brain freezes up for new ideas at a certain age, around 40. And our whole government is over this age.

Interview, Woods Hole, Mass./ The New York Times, 2–20:49.

Pierre Elliott Trudeau
Prime Minister of Canada

The art of government is to do as much as

(PIERRE ELLIOTT TRUDEAU)

you can for all sectors, but to order your priorities in such a way that you are doing most for the most needy first. You also have to make the other people understand that yes, they have a good cause, but since we can't do everything for everybody all the time, we have to choose.

Interview/Time, 4–27:44.

Joseph D. Tydings
United States Senator, D-Md.

Institutions of government are only as good as the people who serve them. These people must be above reproach. This requirement is absolute. For the strength of our democratic government rests on the public respect and confidence which the citizens of the United States have in their leaders. This respect and confidence applies equally to all branches of government. Positions of power within the Judicial, Legislative and Executive branches are a public trust. A breach of this trust is an abuse of power. It will destroy the respect and confidence upon which free government rests. Ultimately and inevitably, it will destroy free government itself. Impropriety, or even the appearance of impropriety, has no place in the government of the United States of America.

*Before the Senate, Washington, March 9/
Washington Star, 8–24:A7.*

Gore Vidal
Author

I see a most repressive time building up. I think the "rule of the colonels" is coming. I regard the Attorney General (Mitchell) as a colonel. I regard (Vice President) Agnew as a colonel. I regard (President) Nixon as a possible colonel. I'm not saying they're going to arrange a *putsch* like that in Greece, because in the United States we do things a bit differently, and at the moment they don't have to; they *have* the country. Nor do I see them immediately suspending elections. But I *can* see them abrogating the First Amendment.

Interview, Rome/TV Guide, 3–21:28.

John J. Williams
United States Senator, R-Del.

Youth are idealistic, and when they see evidence of corruption in high office, they hastily blame it on the "system." It is our duty to make them see that a few bad apples don't make the system bad. But we should show them that we will do something about the corruption, even though these men may be our own buddies. People will only respect (elected officials) if we respect ourselves. And if we have any self-respect at all, we will expose the corruption and get rid of the unprincipled men among us.

Interview/Human Events, 11–28:13.

. . . when I first came to the Senate, I looked around and wondered how in the world I ever got elected to a body of such able and wise men. Now, I look around and wonder how the devil some of these men ever got here.

Interview/Human Events, 11–28:13

Gardner Ackley
*Former Chairman, Council of Economic
Advisors to President Lyndon B. Johnson*

Inflation is not going to be halted . . . unless we succeed in deflating a bit . . . the air of righteous indignation which powerful and already affluent unions are allowed by the rest of us to assume in their wage negotiations, and with which they rally their troops; unless we succeed in diluting the public sympathy and support which unions of the high-paid receive when they try to better their relative incomes, and the public acclaim and admiration which accrues for their great achievements on behalf of their poor and downtrodden members.

*Ann Arbor, Mich./
The Washington Post, 11–26:A18.*

Spiro T. Agnew
Vice President of the United States

To hear the (Democratic) Party—that piled up 58 billion dollars of deficits and created the worst inflation this country ever had—complaining about the purchasing power of the dollar just tugged at my heartstrings.

February 9/U.S. News & World Report, 6–8:39.

To the able-bodied person who says, "The world owes me a living," we say: "Mister, you're wrong." But to the person willing to work who says, "This nation owes me a chance," we say: "Friend, you're right." That's the work ethic that guides the leaders of this country today. It does not make government the "employer of last resort," providing meaningless make-work jobs; it does make government responsible for enforcing equal opportunity, for ending discrimination based on race or sex or any other unfair

basis and for managing our economic affairs in a way that permits solid growth without inflation.

*Before Order of American Hellenic Educational
Progressive Association, Washington, March 9/
U.S. News & World Report, 3–23:85.*

The inflated prices you now have to pay in your supermarket can be directly traced to the huge budget deficits incurred before President Nixon took office in 1969. You are paying more for your food and clothing because fiscally myopic and politically irresponsible men were unwilling to live within the limits of Federal income during a time of furious economic activity. The party and the men who fed that inflation have made careers of professing their heartfelt concern for the very poor and the elderly in our society. I know of nothing more cynical, more cruel, in American politics. It is always the poor and the elderly who suffer the most in the kind of inflation generated in the past.

Time, 9–21:15.

Carl Albert
United States Representative, D-Okla.

This Administration has, by its misguided economic policies, achieved a truly remarkable economic paradox—at one and the same time, almost unprecedented inflation coupled with an economic turndown.

The New York Times, 1–25:(4)1.

It is past time for the President and his economic advisers to recognize the effect of their failing policies on the lives of millions of Americans. The unemployed, now reaching almost 4 million, are real people—not just cold statistics. The millions more who have had work-weeks and incomes reduced are real American working men and women,

(CARL ALBERT)

who daily face the growing difficulties of maintaining a decent living standard as accelerated inflation robs them of their purchasing power for the necessities of life. It is time that they recognize that the elderly on fixed incomes are robbed by the continuing inflation. About the only discourse we hear from the White House and the Administration economists is an effort to shift blame for present economic woes to past Administrations. I must remind them that President Richard Nixon has been President of the United States now for almost 14 months, and in that period we have seen a rapid acceleration of inflation, a deepening recession and policies favoring the vested interests and monied sources. The working men, the poor, the elderly, the small businessman and the minorities are being made to pay for the Nixon inflation and the Nixon recession. I call on the President to utilize the anti-inflation and anti-recession tools which Congress has provided and to join concerned legislators in providing an economic climate that will right the deteriorating economic conditions. I call on the Republican economists to consider the human toll that their "favor the rich" policies are exacting on the working people, the housewives, the elderly and the small businessmen. We no longer need to debate economic terminology. We are in a recession, and the Administration must recognize the conditions and display leadership and concern to correct misguided policies.

Before the House, Washington, March 9/
Congressional Record, 3–9:H1587.

The moral authority of the most powerful office in the world (President of the United States) remains one of the strongest unused influences in maintaining some semblance of control (over inflation). Wage and price guidelines, or jawboning—by whatever name —must be effected to exert the full influence

and impact of the Administration in dampening costs and expanding the economy.

News conference, Washington, Dec. 3/
The New York Times, 12–4:26.

Joseph L. Alioto
Mayor of San Francisco

The property-taxpayer has had it. You can't get blood out of a turnip.

San Francisco/
Los Angeles Herald-Examiner, 3–14:A2.

Howard H. Baker
United States Senator, R-Tenn.

However legitimate his demands, I do not believe that any government employe has the right to strike against his government that hired him. The postal strike was against the law and it was wrong. To pursue a strike by employes against the government to its extreme would amount to insurrection.

Human Events, 4–18:14.

Birch Bayh
United States Senator, D-Ind.

President Nixon has made it possible for every American to live in a more expensive neighborhood without even having to move.

Before American Federation of State, County and Municipal Employes/Daily World, 6–13:7.

Joseph A. Beirne
President, Communications Workers of America

Many people these days want someone else to decide difficult issues for them. But passing a law for compulsory arbitration of (labor) disputes is the first step toward the corporate state where some officials will tell everyone how to run his business and his life.

Miami Beach/
U.S. News & World Report, 2–23:87.

Winton M. Blount
Postmaster General of the United States

Tax reductions sound very attractive to the voting public. That's what makes the fight against inflation both difficult and thankless. It is a matter where political exediency and fiscal responsibility are completely at odds with each other.

Before Menswear Retailers of America, Dallas,
Feb. 9/The Dallas Times Herald, 2-9:A14.

Lemuel R. Boulware
Former vice president,
General Electric Company

Inflation is a consumer tax. It is the most deceitful, the most brutal and the most debilitating of all taxes. It cannot be escaped by consumers; employers cannot protect their employes against it. Inflation is not caused by war or by business greed. Inflation comes only from government manufacturing money—and credit—faster than we manufacture goods. It purposely taxes citizens in a way most will not suspect and for uses they would not permit if they knew *they* were footing the bill.

Before National Investor Relations Institute,
Washington, Nov. 7/Vital Speeches, 12-15:156.

W. A. (Tony) Boyle
President, United Mine Workers of America

People say I have a corrupt union. I took over what John L. Lewis built up, and it's no better or no worse than it was then.

Radio interview/
The Washington Post, 1-8:A10.

Arthur F. Burns
Chairman, Federal Reserve Board

. . . we should not close our minds—*we should not close our minds*—to the possibility that an incomes policy, provided it stopped well short of direct price and wage controls and was used merely as a supplement to over-all fiscal and monetary measures, might speed us through this transitional period of cost-push inflation. I recognize that an incomes policy may not have a lasting effect on the structure of costs and prices if its use is restricted to a transitional period of cost-push inflation. Moreover, it seems clear to me that an incomes policy applied over a long period would be completely impractical. Even with these reservations, however, there may be a useful—albeit a very modest—role for an incomes policy to play in shortening the period between suppression

of excess demand and restoration of reasonable price stability.

Before American Bankers Association,
Hot Springs, Va., May 18/
U.S. News & World Report, 6-1:41.

I fully understand the frustration of workers who have seen inflation erode the real value of past wage increases. But it is clearly in the interest of labor to recognize that economic recovery, as well as the battle against inflation, will be impeded by wage settlements that greatly exceed probable productivity gains. In a society such as ours, which rightly values full employment, monetary and fiscal tools are inadequate for dealing with sources of price inflation such as are plaguing us now—that is, pressures on costs arising from excessive wage increases.

At Pepperdine College "Great Issues Series"
lectures, Los Angeles, Dec. 7/
The New York Times, 12-8:34.

John W. Byrnes
United States Representative, R-Wis.

The first path to wisdom is to recognize that all levels of government are squeezing blood from the same turnip—the American taxpayer—and that no gimmick, such as revenue sharing, to disguise which level is putting on the pressure, is going to make it any easier for him . . . The crucial error in revenue sharing is that it encourages irresponsible spending. It does so by removing from one set of legislators the onus of levying taxes to pay for the spending they authorize, thus eliminating the best restraint we have against unjustifiable spending. It's great for state and local legislators. It's bad for the people they represent . . .

Before City Council, Appleton, Wis., Aug. 27/
Los Angeles Herald-Examiner, 8-28:A5.

George Champion
Former chairman, Chase Manhattan Bank

When people expect inflation, they do their best to hedge against it. In so doing, they often overreact. They build inventories too high, expand capacity too fast, grant

(GEORGE CHAMPION)

larger-than-justified wage increases and speculate wildly in land, commodities and securities. In short, they do all the things that fuel a boom-and-bust cycle.

U.S. News & World Report, 2-2:21.

Sheldon S. Cohen
Former Commissioner, Internal Revenue Service of the United States

Nobody likes to pay taxes, but we can't stop pollution, rebuild our cities and reduce poverty without the needed funds. We've got to pay the price. You've got to look at it two ways. As Sheldon Cohen, I'm happy to have a few more bucks in my pocket; but when I look at the United States as a whole, I see many things that ought to be done.

News conference, Los Angeles, Jan. 20/
Los Angeles Times, 1-21:(3)16.

Edward N. Cole
President, General Motors Corporation

Neither the business enterprise nor the public welfare can long endure the staggering economic losses, social frustrations, personal hardships and health hazards which result from unnecessary strikes—in both private and public fields.

U.S. News & World Report, 4-27:82.

James M. Collins
United States Representative, R-Tex.

The year 1970 is a political year. Political demagogs are having a field day on how they are going to cut the interest rates. The same big spenders are the ones who toss their head to the sky and moan like a coyote in the wilderness. Then they vote to spend money on foreign aid, poverty programs that end up increasing the number of poor, more supergrade Federal bureaucrats, and double spending on an extravagant concert hall.

Before the House, Washington, Feb. 9/
Congressional Record, 2-9:H698.

John B. Connally
Former Governor of Texas

I don't think we need any more "Republican prosperity." I've got all the Republican prosperity I want. I've got all the 9 and 10 per cent interest I want. I've got all the unemployment I want. Thank you just the same.

Plano, Tex., Oct. 9/
The Washington Post, 12-25:A1

Inflation is an enemy of all the people of this nation . . . we cannot endure it unchecked for an extended period of time; and they (Nixon Administration) have undertaken to do what they could about it—short of such drastic action as wage and price controls. The Administration should be commended and not condemned for recognizing the problem and having the courage to do something about it. They have not been entirely successful, not at all. With the weapons that they have, I do not think they can wholly accomplish the purpose short of wage and price controls, something they don't want to ask for and which the American people don't want imposed. Nevertheless, they have undertaken steps to alleviate the problem, but frankly without much thanks—it appeared on Election Day—from the American people . . .

Before Investment Bankers Association,
Boca Raton, Fla., Dec. 2,
The Washington Post, 12-20:E1

Howard Frazier
President, Consumer Federation of America

If Robert Louis Stevenson had lived long enough to witness the introduction of credit buying, I don't think he would have so blithely jingled that, "The world is so full of a number of things, we really should all be as happy as kings." To buy those number of things, Americans are paying a king's ransom in interest rates. We are a nation of royalty in hock. It has been said that the reason the majority of American families don't own an elephant is because they have never been

ffered an elephant for a dollar down and
asy weekly payments.

Before Sunday Evening Forum, Tucson/
Quote, 4–12:341.

aylord A. Freeman, Jr.
hairman, First National Bank of Chicago

For a long time after World War II, we
ere telling the rest of the world how to be-
ave financially. We told other countries to
ncourage savings, to discourage imports, to
alance their budgets and bring spending
nder control. Now those comments are
oming back to haunt us. If you are a com-
ercial banker from the United States trav-
ling abroad—as I have been doing in the
ast couple of months—you would know be-
ore you went in to see the governor of the
entral bank of any particular country just
hat he was going to tell you. He would sug-
est that the U.S. needs to get a grip on in-
ation, to maintain a balanced budget and
improve its foreign-trade balance.

Interview/U.S. News & World Report, 6–29:40.

Our people want employment up. They
ant wages up. They want profits up. They
ant the stock market up. If prices go up,
o, well, they'll take care of themselves by
eping in debt and paying off with con-
nually cheaper dollars.

Nov. 24/U.S. News & World Report, 12–7:16.

oger A. Freeman
*ecial Assistant to the President of the
nited States; Senior fellow, Hoover
stitution, Stanford University*

It is a natural and understandable ten-
ncy for people to try to offset the impact
higher prices by boosting their income
d, grudgingly, spending more money inead of reducing their demands. It is as if
a football game we were not seeing well
ough over the heads of the people in front
us and decided to stand up. We'll see
tter—temporarily. But when the other peo-
e also stand up, we and everybody else will
e no better than we did before. More likely,

we'll see less. And if we sit down, we'll see
nothing.

Los Angeles Times, 6–14:G7.

We have been complaining about inflation, pointing fingers in several directions,
demanding that government discipline
unions and management by guideposts, jawboning, fines or controls. But only government, itself, can and does create inflation,
largely through budget deficits, easy money
and lopsided labor policies; and only government can stop inflation—by exercising self-
discipline, which so far it has shown no inclination of doing.

*Before Government Research Association,
Chicago, Sept. 1/Vital Speeches, 10–15:22.*

Milton Friedman
*Professor of Economics,
University of Chicago*

For 2000 years, going back to the Roman
Empire, there has never in history been a
period in which wage and price controls
have stopped inflation. They attack the
symptoms of inflation and not the cause of
inflation.

San Francisco Examiner & Chronicle, 1–25:A12.

Inflation is made in Washington—nowhere else.

Interview, Chicago/Chicago Daily News, 7–29:3.

Any industry or labor group that holds
down its prices or wages "in the social interest" is not contributing to stopping inflation.
All it's doing is pinching a big balloon in one
corner. It's just driving the air somewhere
else.

Interview, Chicago/Chicago Daily News, 7–29:4.

In order to stop inflation, there has to be
pressure on producers and employes. We
have to make it more difficult for producers
to sell their products and for employes to
get jobs.

Cleveland Plain Dealer, 8–22:A8.

When people speak of the "recession of
1970," it's a triumph of rhetoric over reality.

191

WHAT THEY SAID IN 1970

(MILTON FRIEDMAN)

If you listen to newspaper and TV commentators, you'd think we're going through a major crisis. From the tone of voice, you'd think we're repeating something like 1929 to '32 or '37 and '38. In fact, we're going through a very mild recession, in which output has stayed constant or declined negligibly, and in which unemployment—though it has risen to a level of 5.6%—is very much lower than the peak reached in '60 and '61, which in itself was mild. This recession is a consequence of meeting the inflationary surge which preceded it.

Interview/Los Angeles Times, 12–20:H2.

Martin R. Gainsbrugh
Senior vice president and chief economist, National Industrial Conference Board

We can have a recession if we want it—but who needs it?

Before Texas Bankers Association, Fort Worth, Feb. 21/Fort Worth Star Telegram, 2–22:1.

John Kenneth Galbraith
Professor of Economics, Harvard University

If at any time in the last 20 or 30 years we had had a Harvard graduate student up for his Ph.D. and he had been asked if it would be possible to have rapidly growing unemployment, rapidly increasing prices, a vast stock market collapse, almost a total housing depression—all in the middle of a war—and this fellow had said yes, we would have flunked him. Yet, this is something the (Nixon) Administration has managed to bring off.

News conference, Milwaukee, Aug. 11/ Milwaukee Journal, 8–11:3.

The archbishops of our economic faith . . . still hold that St. Peter asks applicants only what they've done to increase the gross national product. But the consequences are no longer theoretical. We can now see what a single-minded preoccupation with growth does to the environment. And expanding consumption isn't the guarantee of utter happiness that my friendly critics once held it to be. A new generation . . . realizes that a great many people consume what they are persuaded to consume . . . In a rational life style, some people could find contentment (in) working, drawing, painting, scribbling or making love in a suitably discreet way. None of these requires an expanding economy.

Interview/Los Angeles Times, 12–20:H4

Nathaniel Goldfinger
Economist, American Federation of Labor-Congress of Industrial Organizations

The recession that the American economy has unfortunately gone through over the past year was man-made. It was engineered by the United States government; it was engineered by the (Nixon) Administration in the guise of an anti-inflation policy.

Radio interview/ The Dallas Times Herald, 9–30:A2

Barry M. Goldwater
United States Senator, R-Ariz.

The day of reckoning is at hand, and I don't believe that we are going to attack the root causes of this debilitating and discouraging price inflation until Congress develops some guts. Not until Congress takes action to cut down on the powers, the liberties, the immunities and the privileges of our large labor unions will we make the kind of progress which is needed.

Before Industrial College of the Armed Forces, Washington, Jan. 13/ Los Angeles Herald-Examiner, 1–15:A4

. . . We're going to have massive unemployment if this inflation doesn't stop. I was the happiest man in the world back in the '30s when Congress passed the Wagner Act. Labor was weak then. Now labor sits on the other side of the table with all the muscle. I don't know what changes there should be and I don't want to see labor's right to strike ever denied, or compulsory arbitration. But we are at the point where we must level their power to that of this equation.

Waco (Tex.) News-Tribune, 1–27:A

Kermit Gordon
President, Brookings Institution

I hope this never happens, but the time may come when the (new gross-national-product "clock" in the Commerce Department building) may have to run backwards for a time. Is the mechanism reversible? With hundreds of tourists streaming through the lobby every day, will any Administration be willing to show them a clock running backwards?

The Washington Post, 12–27:C1.

Fred R. Harris
United States Senator, D-Okla.

(The Nixon Administration) is deliberately raising interest rates and deliberately trying to put hundreds of thousands out of work (to control inflation). I say this is a wretched and heartless policy.

Oklahoma City, Feb. 20/
The Washington Post, 2–21:A2.

Fred L. Hartley
President,
Union Oil Company of California

The time may be close at hand for the federal government to impose price, wage and credit controls before a shattering of the economic system occurs. It is not possible for American industry to keep up with excessive wage demands or higher interest rates by innovating productivity increases. Current theories of economic restraints to control inflation have already proven that they are completely inadequate to counter this kind of inflationary pressure.

Jan. 5/The New York Times, 1–6:53.

Walter W. Heller
Former Chairman, Council of
Economic Advisers to the
President of the United States

Let's face it—we now live in an inflation-prone economy. (In a country aiming for full employment) the toughest economic-policy nut to crack, bar none, is inflation. No free economy yet has cracked it.

Newsweek, 1–12:58.

I think the country is going to be willing to settle for about 3 per cent inflation. It wouldn't like it, but it would accept it. 3 per cent would still be better than the average of the world that we compete with.

News conference, Washington, Jan. 26/
The Washington Post, 1–27:D7.

The missing link in the Nixon (job training and welfare reform) program is a government guarantee of a job, either through government employment of last resort or temporarily subsidized private employment. Job training and income maintenance and unemployment compensation are all well and good, but there must be a job at the end of the line.

Before House Banking Subcommittee,
Washington, March 10/
The New York Times, 3–11:18.

(Much of the inflationary trouble today) stems from the surprisingly dogmatic, almost theological, Nixonian adherence to a hands-off policy in the wage-price-field—a policy that delights labor, pleases business, puzzles the financial community both here and abroad—and shortchanges the public.

Before Joint Congressional Economic
Committee, Washington, July 16/
The Washington Post, 7–17:A8.

The President has to talk tough to big business and big labor. He has to tell them that those who are using their market power to gouge the public through unwarranted wage and price boosts have got to stop. He has to let the nation have some idea of what "unwarranted" means. Unless he defines sin and identifies the sinners, how can he mobilize public opinion against the decisions that keep the price-wage spiral turning?

Time, 12–14:90.

James D. Hodgson
Under Secretary of Labor
of the United States

We in the Labor Department have a responsibility for protecting and preserving

193

(JAMES D. HODGSON)

the institution (collective bargaining) . . . Basically, the parties themselves . . . have the most to gain or lose by making the bargaining process succeed. So we put the responsibility for doing just that on the parties. No cheap cop-out exists through government intervention. President Nixon congratulates the parties to a settlement after the settlement has been reached, rather than boxing their ears in advance to see that it is reached.

Jan. 26/U.S. News & World Report, 6–22:86.

Sidney Homer
Investment banker

Under (President Lyndon) Johnson, the policy of "no recession ever" became explicit and was widely accepted by economists, both of the left and of the right, and by a large preponderance of businessmen. This naturally touched off a capital-goods boom. Prices and costs started to rise after years of stability . . . Finally, in recent years, civil disorders and social-reform proposals have seemed to provide an even more positive assurance that recessions will be politically unacceptable at any time ever and at any cost . . . Such an assured point of view is entirely novel, and I believe it is the basis for the expectations of unending inflationary prosperity which have developed over the last three years. These expectations are basically responsible for our high rate of inflation and our capital market distortions.

The New York Times Magazine, 2–22:52.

Max Ilke
Former Under Secretary of Finance of Switzerland

President Nixon's Administration has been moving in the right direction—toward greater monetary and fiscal restraint. These policies should not be relaxed before there are definite signs that the wage-and-price spiral will be checked, and should even then be eased only cautiously to make sure that inflationary expectations will not flare up again. The most important thing in our time is the fight against inflation. The U.S. must take the lead in this struggle. The world needs a healthy and stable dollar.

Interview/U.S. News & World Report, 4–13:70.

David M. Kennedy
Secretary of the Treasury of the United States

I know there are those who doubt the determination of our anti-inflation effort, who believe that prices will continue to rise and who are making their borrowing, lending, spending and other decisions accordingly. I want to say, as strongly as I can, that they are badly mistaken. We will continue our policies of restraint until we have restored basic health and stability to the economy. To do less—to back off once the going gets a little rough and unpopular—might please some people, but would be a disservice to all.

New York, Feb. 3/ Los Angeles Herald-Examiner, 2–4:B1.

We have rejected government controls over free markets and our free society and have relied instead on policies more appropriate to a nation of free citizens, policies of economic restraint. Instead of trying to control the actions and choices of American workers and American business and industry, we have restrained government expenditures and held down the growth of the money supply. In the process, we have maintained traditional freedoms, while controlling and reducing the forces that were primarily responsible for the start and build-up of the present inflation. By this time, there should be little doubt that our policies of fiscal and monetary restraint are succeeding.

At Sponsors' Day Dinner of University of Virginia's Graduate School of Business Administration, Charlottesville, Oct. 23/ The Washington Post, 10–24:E5.

Lane Kirkland
Secretary-treasurer, American Federation of Labor–Congress of Industrial Organizations

There has been a steady and consistent reduction in the commitment of men to work as a way of life. That movement has accelerated in recent times. The expansion of paid leisure time will continue, and there may well be a greater tendency to choose leisure over additions to income where that choice can be made.

Time, 3–23:77.

R. Heath Larry
Vice chairman,
United States Steel Corporation

Conventional wisdom says there are only two solutions (to inflation): direct wage and price controls, which are no answer at all; or a restrictive monetary and fiscal policy which strengthens employer resistance by eroding profits—and reduces the value of the strike weapon by reducing alternate employment opportunities. There must be a third—and free labor and free management must try to find it, if that's what they want to remain.

At collective bargaining forum, New York/
U.S. News & World Report, 6–1:61.

George H. Mahon
United States Representative, D-Tex.

. . . everybody is talking about big spending, but nobody is talking in a very loud voice about attractive new tax programs which will raise massive sums of additional revenue to pay for the spending programs. Unless some way can be found to rectify this situation, we are, in my judgment, headed toward fiscal and economic chaos. If there is to be a hero in the 1970s, he may be the man who entices the people to vote upon themselves the taxes required to pay for all our programs to clean up the environment, stamp out disease, eliminate poverty and educate everybody. Everybody can dramatize the need for spending. Why cannot somebody dramatize the need to collect the revenue? Is it not true that, if we finance these programs by deficit spending, the money will not buy much and our efforts will fail?

Before the House, Washington, Feb. 10/
Congressional Record, 2–10:E817.

Mike Mansfield
United States Senator, D-Mont.

Three words say a great deal about the nation's economy: inflation, unemployment and war. Whether the term is used or not, these words spell recession. That is today's fact. It is not a political fact; it is an economic fact. References to the mistakes of the past cannot paper over it. The rhetoric of a radiant tomorrow does not alter it.

Radio-TV address, Washington, June 24/
U.S. News & World Report, 7–6:68.

Charles McC. Mathias, Jr.
United States Senator, R-Md.

In political terms, wage and price controls would be an easy remedy to adopt (to fight inflation). Every Gallup and Harris poll on the subject indicates that the people favor this approach. Yet, this enthusiasm is likely to decline abruptly when the real consequences become clear: severe distortions in the economy, black marketeering, huge and intrusive bureaucracy and, in the end, a real contraction in our economic freedom and growth. It is possible that we will ultimately be driven to this route. But we should regard it as the very last resort and should not entertain illusions about its effects.

At Montgomery County (Md.)
Sentinel luncheon, Jan. 16/
Congressional Record, 1–28:S759.

Paul W. McCracken
Chairman, Council of Economic Advisers to the President of the United States

There is a moral dimension to controls, too. People who know how to work the angles do all right. The honest man doesn't do as well. That's inherent in a system of controls. They foster black markets, gray markets, influence-peddling. Moreover, once you go in for controls you find it hard to get away from them. The idea of effective controls for only a short period simply ignores history. Any rational economist will tell you that rent controls, for example, seriously limit the supply of housing. Yet here we are, 25 years after World War II, and we still

(PAUL W. MCCRACKEN)

have rent ceilings in some cities. These are the places where people experience the ultimate in housing distress—serious difficulties in finding apartments. One prediction is pretty safe: The popularity of this approach would fade fast if we were to go that route.

Interview, Washington/
U.S. News & World Report, 1–12:55.

The golden rule of economic policy is that the right time to change will seem to be premature at the time.

Washington, March 17/
Los Angeles Times, 3–18:(1)5.

I don't see much evidence in our own experience or in international experience that wage and price controls have much relevance to our kinds of problems. There's no sense in posting a speed limit unless you're prepared to post the traffic cop there to enforce it. If you are going to have wage and price controls, you are going to have to have the bureaucracy to enforce them. The World War II experience with wage-price ceilings enforcement suggests that to do relatively the same thing today we would have to spend close to a billion dollars a year.

Interview, Washington/
Los Angeles Times, 4–20:(3)12.

. . . the United States has been far more effective in stemming inflation than most Western societies, such as West Germany, the United Kingdom and others. The export-import balance is one of the measures. And it is quite clear that the demand for American goods and capital overseas remains very strong, perhaps inflationary—but because of *their* inflation, not ours . . . I think it may be essential for Americans to understand that their economic problems are vastly less critical—and less repressive in any long term —than the problems of our neighbor nations.

Interview, Los Angeles/
Los Angeles Herald-Examiner, 8–27:D4.

Robert E. McNair
Governor of South Carolina

Not too many people care whether they call it a slowdown, or a cutback, or a recession, or a depression, or whatever. All they know is that the prices keep getting higher, the jobs keep getting scarcer and the promises keep getting louder.

San Francisco Examiner & Chronicle
(This World), 8–30:2.

George Meany
President, American Federation of Labor–
Congress of Industrial Organizations

Employees of the government have exactly the same desires and aspirations as do employees in the private sector. They have the same need for self-expression and self-determination—and the process of collective negotiation of the conditions under which they will labor is just as valid in public employment as it is elsewhere in labor-management relations. We in the AFL-CIO quite candidly see these negotiations as setting the stage for the future. We believe that collective bargaining can be—and should be —extended to all workers in the Federal government.

News conference, Washington, April 16/
The New York Times, 4–17:18.

Production is falling; jobs are vanishing; soaring prices are pushing the cost of living to record heights; the workers' buying power is dropping steadily. The results for America's wage-earners, pensioners, the poor and small businessmen have been anything but bright. For them, the Administration's medicine has meant higher prices for everything they buy, layoffs or shortened paychecks, exhorbitant interest for the money they must borrow and, for many, the end to the dream of a family home or education for their children.

News conference, Aug. 31/
The New York Times, 9–6:(4)10.

Our members are basically Americans. They basically believe in the American sysem, and maybe they have a greater stake in he system now than they had 15 or 20 years go; because under the system and under our rade-union policy they have become middle lass, if you want to say it. They have a reater stake. You can be quite radical if you vere involved in a labor dispute where eople are getting 30 cents an hour, because f you pull an honest strike all you lose is 30 ents an hour. But you have people who are naking $8,000 or $9,000 a year, paying off nortgages, with kids going to college; you aave an entirely different situation when ou think about calling them on strike. They aave got obligations that are quite costly— nsurance payments and all that sort of thing. o this makes the strike much less desirable s a weapon. Naturally, we wouldn't want o give it up as a weapon, but I can say ... quite frankly that more and more people in he trade-union movement—I mean at the ighest levels—are thinking of other ways to dvance without the use of the strike weap-n ... What it adds up to is that while strikes aave their part and all that—and we certain-y have advocated for years that you have got o have the right to strike—we find more and nore that strikes really don't settle a thing.

News conference, Aug. 31/
U.S. News & World Report, 9–7:59.

Raymond W. Miller
President, World Trade Relations, Inc.

Academicians, teachers and members of he clergy, in particular, are hard hit by in-lation, because their retirement incomes are ixed by dollars with no escalation clauses. This is one of the basic reasons why such eople today are questioning their loyalty o the nation. They are the real molders of pinion in America and are the ones who aave, in decades past, been most universally oatriotic. History teaches, however, as in the ase of China, that the greatest single cause or disloyalty to government is the loss of aith in the coin of the realm.

Before Transportation Association of America,
Ponte Verde, Fla./Quote, 2–1:106.

John N. Mitchell
Attorney General of the United States

At a time last year when "inflation psy-chology" was rampant, the President made clear that he intended to help cool the over-heated economy. At the time, not everyone believed it would actually happen. But now —to put it mildly—there seems to be univer-sal agreement that the economy is no longer racing at an unsustainable pace. We have done what we said we had to do.

At Delta State College, Cleveland, Miss.,
May 19/U.S. News & World Report, 6–1:40.

... wage and price controls, with the ra-tioning, black marketeering and govern-ment domination that follow in their wake, are not now and never have been a part of our economic strategy. Forget about them.

At Delta State College, Cleveland, Miss.,
May 19/U.S. News & World Report, 6–1:40.

Frank E. Moss
United States Senator, D-Utah

If unemployment were our only problem, I would not be so apprehensive. But ... our rising rate of unemployment is coupled with high interest rates and rising prices—gallop-ing inflation. Prices are rising at the annual rate of 6.6 per cent—a faster rate of increase than the rate which skyrocketed prices in 1969. Interest rates continue at or near rec-ord highs. We now have the worst of both worlds; we have double economic jeopardy; inflation and unemployment ... The Ad-ministration says that it has been trying to cure inflation and that unemployment is one of the side effects—undesirable, but neces-sary. There is an old saying about curing the disease but killing the patient. Our present economic policies seem to be killing the pa-tient without even curing the disease.

Before the Senate, Washington, May 14/
Congressional Record, 5–14:S7167.

George Murphy
United States Senator, R-Calif.

When I first came to the Senate, the (la-bor) union people said to me, "We can count on your vote, can't we?" And I said, "When

(GEORGE MURPHY)

you are right." They didn't like that—they want it whole hog.

Interview, Washington/
Los Angeles Times, 12–27:H1.

Richard M. Nixon
President of the United States

Millions of Americans are forced to go into debt today because the Federal government decided to go into debt yesterday. We must balance our Federal budget so that American families will have a better chance to balance their family budgets. Only with the cooperation of the Congress can we meet this highest priority objective of responsible government.

State of the Union address, Washington,
Jan. 22/Los Angeles Times, 1–23:(1)20.

We spend more for health and education than any nation in the world. We're able to do this—and I hope we can continue to do so in the future—because we have the great good fortune to be the richest nation by far in the whole history of the world. But we can spend ourselves poor. That is why, no matter how popular a spending program is, if I determine that its enactment will have the effect of raising your prices or raising your taxes, I will not approve that program.

Television address, Washington, Jan. 26/
The New York Times/1–27:24.

I respect his (Arthur F. Burns) independence. However, I hope that independently he will conclude that my views are the ones that should be followed.

At Burns' swearing in as Federal Reserve
Board Chairman, Washington, Jan. 31/
The Washington Post, 2–1:A1.

. . . many people wonder why we are easing some of the restraints on the economy before we've seen dramatic results in slowing down the rise in the cost of living. Why, they ask, don't we keep on with all of our measures to hold down the economy until price

rises stop completely. Let me put it this way: It's a little like trying to bring a boat into a dock. You turn down the power well before you get to the dock and let the boat coast in. Now, if you waited until you reached the dock to turn down the power, you'd soon have to buy a new dock or a new boat. In the same way, we're heading for the dock of price stability. We have to ease up on the power of our restraint and let our momentum carry us safely into port. That's why our independent central banking system has seen fit to ease up in the money supply. That is why I relaxed the cutback on Federal-assisted construction projects and why I have not asked for a new surtax. These actions are not a signal that we are giving up our fight against inflation. On the contrary, they mean that there was already enough power applied to reach the dock, and now we'd better make sure that we don't damage the boat.

Radio-TV address, Washington, June 17/
The New York Times, 6–18:24.

I will not take this nation down the road of wage and price controls, however politically expedient that may seem. Controls and rationing may seem like an easy way out, but they are really an easy way in—to more trouble, to the explosion that follows when you try to clamp a lid on a rising head of steam without turning down the fire under the pot. Wage and price controls only postpone a day of reckoning. And, in so doing, they rob every American of a very important part of his freedom.

Radio-TV address, Washington, June 17/
The New York Times, 6–18:24.

Seventeen months ago, when this Administration took office, we stood at a crossroads of economic policy. There were actually four roads open to us. One was the road of runaway inflation—to do nothing about government spending and rising prices, to let the boom go on booming until the bubble burst. That was the road the nation was taken on in the sixties . . . The road headed in the opposite direction from that one was a possible choice as well. Let the economy go through the wringer, as some suggested, and bring on a major recession. Well, that would stop inflation abruptly—but at a cost in human terms of broken careers and broken lives that this nation must never again have to pay. A third choice was the route of wage and price controls—which would lead to rationing, black marketing, total Federal bureaucratic domination. And it would never get at the real causes of inflation. That left a fourth choice: to cut down the sharp rise in Federal spending and to restrain the economy firmly and steadily. And that way, prices would slow their rise without too great a hardship on the working man, the businessman and the investor. That was the road of responsibility. That was the road we chose. And that is the road we are continuing on today.

Radio-TV address, Washington, June 17/
The New York Times, 6–18:24.

As we look at the economy of this country, we see troubles. And as we look at the causes of those troubles, one of them primarily is that we are having the difficult transition which must always take place when you move from a wartime to a peacetime economy. Seven hundred thousand men who are in the armed services or in defense plants have now had to find civilian employment. This has meant more unemployment than we would want. It has meant some dislocations in the economy. But it is a cost that is worthwhile, because I say to you: This economy is strong; this economy is sound; and it is time—and I believe this is the time—when America can demonstrate that we can have prosperity without war, prosperity with peace in the United States of America.

Before United States Jaycees, St. Louis, June 25/
U.S. News & World Report, 7–6:45.

I realize that an election year is a tempting time for people in politics to say "yes" to every spending bill. But if I were to sign these bills (education and independent of-

fice appropriations) that spend nearly $1 billion more than we can now afford, I would be saying "yes" to higher interest rates, "yes" to higher taxes. When it comes to spending the people's money, the Congress understandably is sometimes affected by proposals that would benefit some of the people. The responsibility of the President is to weigh the interests of *all* the people. By the action I am taking today (vetoing the bills), I am saying "no" to bigger spending and "no" to higher prices in the interests of all the American people.

News conference, Washington, Aug. 11/
The New York Times, 8–12:1.

If Congress believes that price and wage controls are needed in today's economy—despite all the evident disadvantages and against my strong recommendations—it should face up to its responsibilities and make such controls mandatory.

Washington, Aug. 17/
Los Angeles Times, 8–18:(1)4.

Government has done its part to hold the line. This is the critical moment, then, for business and labor to make a special effort to exercise more restraint in price and wage decisions. This is the moment for labor and management to stop freezing into wage settlement and price actions any expectation that inflation will continue in the future at its peak rate of the past. Any wage or price decision that makes the flat and irreversible assumption of a high rate of inflation ahead is against the public interest and against the real interest of the working man.

Before National Association of Manufacturers,
New York, Dec. 4/
Los Angeles Herald-Examiner, 12–4:A1.

Too many people make the mistake of thinking that because government is the distributor of so much wealth, government must be the source of that wealth. Nothing could be farther from the truth. You cannot pass a law raising a nation's standard of living. You cannot legislate into being the resources

(RICHARD M. NIXON)

to solve our problems. On the contrary, the only place you can turn to for the ability to help other people is that place that is so often denounced as the citadel of self-interest—the private-enterprise system. The next time you hear someone running that system down, the next time you hear the product of that system derided as "material" or unworthy of man's highest ideals, remember this: A nation with the greatest social goals, with the most perfect political system, but without a strong and free economy, is like a magnificent automobile without an engine. We in America have that engine; it is something to be proud of, not ashamed of; it gives power to our purpose.

Before National Association of Manufacturers,
New York, Dec. 4 /
The New York Times, 12–5:18.

Lawrence F. O'Brien
Chairman, Democratic National Committee

"Nixonomics" means that all the things that should go up—the stock market, corporate profits, real spendable income, productivity—go down, and all the things that should go down—unemployment, prices, interest rates—go up.

Before Women's National Democratic Club,
May 21 / The Washington Post, 5–22:A1.

I submit . . . that few Presidents ever had the fortune of inheriting such a healthy economy (as President Nixon did), and even fewer Administrations made such a mess of what they inherited.

Platte County, Mo., Sept. 9 /
The Dallas Times Herald, 9–10:A19.

Arthur M. Okun
Former Chairman, Council of Economic
Advisers to the President of the
United States

When markets are exceedingly weak, no businessman will dare raise his prices for fear of losing his markets; and no workers—organized or unorganized—will demand significant wage increases for fear of losing

their jobs. The problem of curing inflation is difficult and demanding only because we will not take this decapitation cure for the headache of rising prices.

The New York Times Magazine, 2–22:25.

A Democratic Senator told me that while economists keep advocating incomes policy, they are just asking a crow to make music. This President (Nixon) can't sing.

Time, 12–14:90.

Leif H. Olsen
Senior vice president and economist,
First National City Bank, New York

Everybody thinks that profits are just a problem for management and that no one else has to worry. But profits determine the level of employment, plant and equipment spending and government revenues. You cannot have a turn-around in the economy until you have a turn-around in profits.

Time, 5–4:90.

I find it rather curious that even as inflation begins to lessen, imaginative lawmakers and economists become very busy designing direct controls and structural changes to try to protect housing and other sectors from the pressures of anti-inflationary policies. It would make more sense to try to avoid the causes of inflation rather than build into our economy accommodations to inflation. We may very well have future periods of inflation. But if we understand that excessively expansive monetary and fiscal policies cause the inflation in the first instance, shouldn't we make a strong effort to avoid these policies?

The Wall Street Journal, 9–4:6

Wright Patman
United States Representative, D-Tex.

Fighting inflation with high interest i just as illogical as fighting a fire with gaso line instead of water. It just makes the situa tion worse.

Before the House, Washington, March 9
Congressional Record, 3–9:H1597

Unfortunately, we have some people in this country who do not care deeply for the American way of life. These people quite readily accept a shift from a competitive, free enterprise system to a tightly controlled and concentrated economy. Happily, the great majority of the American people believe in our system and are adamantly opposed to a concentration of economic power in the hands of a few ... Concentration of economic power—economic fascism—threatens every free democratic institution in America. And for the consumer, a concentration of economic power would invariably mean higher prices, poorer products and services, fewer choices—not to mention a general loss of freedom for the entire nation.

Before directors, National Association of
Insurance Agents, Dallas, April 28/
Vital Speeches, 6–15:524.

Georges Pompidou
President of France

It's certain that the role of the American economy in the Western world's economy is such that an American recession would bring, necessarily, serious consequences for other countries, and consequently for France ... I hope, for my part, that the American economy maintains a reasonable rate of expansion, but I also hope for the elimination of the inflation that you have at the present time in the U.S., because it affects the whole world ... You export inflation. You also export recession. And it would be the worst thing of all if you exported both at the same time.

Interview, Paris/
U.S. News & World Report, 3–2:46.

Ronald Reagan
Governor of California

In private industry, the strike is a legitimate tool which can be used to close down a business until agreement has been reached through negotiations. In government, we cannot shut down the assembly line. Government is constitutionally and morally bound to provide certain basic services. Govern-

ment has no choice but to continue operations any way it can. A strike against the government is a strike against the people, and the people are the ultimate source of government's authority. Final decisions must rest with elected officials.

Los Angeles Times, 4–20:(1)1.

Walter P. Reuther
President, United Auto Workers of America

In 1970, we are bargaining for the future—and the economic climate now will have nothing to do with what we do about the future. We have to let these corporations know that they will not be able to hide behind Nixon's recession.

Newsweek, 4–6:77.

I see where George Meany, at the AFL-CIO Executive Council meeting in Miami Beach, agreed to ending votes by union members on union contracts. As long as I have a voice, the rank and file will vote on these contracts. And if Congress tries to enforce any idea of stopping the rank and file from voting on contracts, the UAW will march on Washington and do a most effective job of stopping them.

At UAW convention, Atlantic City, N.J.,
April 20/Daily World, 4–21:5.

Pierre Rinfret
Economist

You cannot stop inflation—period. All you can hope to do is minimize it.

At the Yale Club, New York, Jan. 12/
Los Angeles Herald-Examiner, 1–12:B6.

James M. Roche
Chairman, General Motors Corporation

We must all—management, employes, union leaders—decide now if we are to counter or to surrender to the pressures of cost and inflation. Whether we can meet the crisis of cost will have the most far-reaching consequences. Our nation can no longer afford the erosion of confidence that comes with inflation: Its cruel inequities—the loss of pur-

(JAMES M. ROCHE)

chasing power to (the) pensioned and to others on fixed incomes, and the extra-harsh toll it exacts from the poor; the diversion of capital and manpower from production to speculation, which inflation encourages; to price American products out of the markets of the world and to risk a further weakening of the dollar as an international reserve currency.

Before Chamber of Commerce,
St. Louis, Feb. 20/
The Dallas Times Herald, 2–22:A32.

Bayard Rustin
Executive director,
A. Philip Randolph Institute

Mr. Nixon has dared to say the only way to deal with inflation is through unemployment—that your children will go without milk to deal with the problem of inflation.

San Francisco Examiner & Chronicle
(This World), 6–21:2.

Paul A. Samuelson
Professor of Economics,
Massachusetts Institute of Technology

If there were good economic policies coming out of Washington, you shouldn't have to ask why a man lost his job; you should only have to ask why he can't get a new one.

Radio interview, Boston, Oct. 25/
Los Angeles Times, 10–27:(1)8.

William F. Schmick, Jr.
President, American Newspaper
Publishers Association

Inability of management to control labor's insatiable demands is a root cause of the inflationary spiral we are trapped in today, and it is time the government recognized it. It is axiomatic that higher wages cause higher prices. It is likewise clear that as a consequence of overly protective labor laws, the pendulum has swung too far to the side of unionism.

Before American Newspaper Publishers
Association, New York, April 21/
The Dallas Times Herald, 4–22:A9.

Pierre-Paul Schweitzer
Managing director,
International Monetary Fund

No country intent on restoring or maintaining financial stability can afford to dispense with any instrument which can properly service this end. In this context, I wouldn't exclude incomes policy.

May 19/U.S. News & World Report, 6–1:37.

F. Ritter Shumway
President, Chamber of Commerce
of the United States

I think the time has come when there should be a greater balancing of the scales between labor and management. Until the Wagner Act was passed, there certainly was an imbalance in favor of management. Over the years, the balance has changed, and it is now heavily weighted in favor of labor. And management stands helpless before the demands of labor, as witnessed by the settlements that have been made recently.

Interview, Rochester, N.Y./
Nation's Business, May:52.

William H. Smith
Deputy Commissioner,
Internal Revenue Service

We are fond of saying that the American tax system is a self-assessment tax system, and so it is. But we do not really know why people comply, nor, indeed, do we know as much about the revenue gap as we would like—by that I mean the amount of revenue that should be raised by the tax statutes but that is escaping collection. I suspect we get good compliance in this country for a variety of reasons . . . patriotism, good citizenship, common honesty—call it what you will—undoubtedly play a large part. Another element is the psychology of efficiency that the Internal Revenue Service has built up over the years. This is a subtle thing that grows gradually and, like most intangibles, takes a long time to achieve but can be lost much more quickly.

Before University of Miami Tax Conference,
May 12/Vital Speeches, 8–15:660.

Some citizens who disagree with certain of the Federal government's programs have tried to withhold that part of their taxes they ascribe to such programs. And we have seen increasingly sophisticated techniques of harassment designed to throw monkey wrenches into the machinery of tax administration . . . Cicero said that taxes are the sinews of the state—and those who would seek to embarrass or even destroy the state seem to know this.

Before University of Miami Tax Conference,
May 12/Vital Speeches, 8–15:664.

Maurice H. Stans
Secretary of Commerce
of the United States

Isn't it about time that someone came up with a more rational way to settle disputes than through strikes and lockouts? Such head-knocking methods may have been the only recourse to the two parties in the brutal beginnings of the industrial revolution . . . but must we suffer through more of the same for the next 20 years?

Before Economic Club of New York/
The Christian Science Monitor, 3–7:14.

Herbert Stein
Member, Council of Economic Advisers to
the President of the United States

By now, the performance of the economy has been precisely located on the political map. The performance has not been as good as we said it would be, but much better than we said it would have been if the Democrats were in office. The performance has been better than the Democrats said we would do, but not as good as they said they would have done if they had been in office.

London/The Dallas Times Herald, 10–28:A20.

Franklin Stockbridge
Executive vice president, Security Pacific
National Bank, Los Angeles

I can't remember a time when professional economists so strongly disagreed about the fundamental facts of the economy. One will look at a set of data and say flatly the reces-

sion is getting worse, while another, looking at exactly the same material, will announce the economy has turned around and we're starting off a period of vigorous expansion.

U.S. News & World Report, 5–18:22.

Carl B. Stokes
Mayor of Cleveland

Any time a man says this nation can exist with a seven per cent unemployment rate, he is either out of his mind or displaying a callous disregard for human need.

Quote, 7–19:49.

Joseph D. Tydings
United States Senator, D-Md.

(President Nixon) has refused to meet the problem of inflation head on . . . Instead of acting like a President, he appoints a committee. You can't substitute a committee for a President.

Washington, Aug. 10/
The Washington Post, 8–11:C2.

Charles E. Walker
President, Union Barge Line

Why is the wonderful technology of our time unable to produce the additional leisure all of us were told would develop? The answer is that in our economy the emphasis is shifting from the production of goods to the production of service. There are more professional people, more maintainers of broken-down equipment, more managers and, above all, more people in local, state and Federal government in proportion to the rest of the workers in the society than ever before. Productivity increases in service-type jobs have been either nil or not more than 1% per year. My point is that if you come out of school looking for a three-day week you are going to be disappointed.

At Point Park College, Pittsburgh/
The Wall Street Journal, 5–1:10.

Charls E. Walker
Under Secretary of the Treasury
of the United States

This hiatus in economic growth, which

(CHARLS E. WALKER)

should continue well into 1970, is not to be decried. It can be "the economic pause that refreshes." It will set the stage for healthy and balanced growth in the years ahead. It is the uncomfortable but necessary transition from overheating and demand-pull inflation to stable wage and price patterns.

Before National Industrial Conference Board,
New York, Feb. 27 /
Los Angeles Herald-Examiner, 2–27:C6.

The (Nixon) Administration is concerned about unemployment and will not deem its policies to be fully successful until all of those who are able, willing and seeking to work can find useful employment opportunities. But to have attempted to maintain jobs through inflation would have ultimately been self-defeating; sooner or later, a reaction would set in that could shoot unemployment back to the high levels of the early 1960s, or even higher.

News conference, Los Angeles, Oct. 22 /
Los Angeles Times, 10–23:(3)13.

A badly overheated economy has been cooled, inflation is being brought under control, financial markets are operating efficiently, a housing boom is in prospect and the road back to full employment is clearly charted.

At bankers meeting, Georgetown University /
San Francisco Examiner, 10–31:2.

George C. Wallace
Former Governor of Alabama

It (inflation) is a very serious situation. Certainly, I don't want to see unemployment continue to go up. I oppose the high interest rates that are hurting every one of us. I have no use for wage-price controls, but if inflation continues and controls become necessary, then they should be on everything and not just on wages and prices.

Interview, Montgomery, Ala. /
The Christian Science Monitor, 1–5:9.

One of the great issues today is the matter of taxation. The American people are not as interested in tax reform, per se, as in tax relief. Tax relief for the mass of the lower-income people and the middle class is something that must come about. The income tax has got to the point where it is almost confiscatory. Even the middle class cannot meet the payments on the necessities of life. They are tired of seeing their money go down the drain to countries that won't aid us in the war in Vietnam and as welfare payments to people who aren't willing to work.

Interview / Montgomery, Ala. /
The Christian Science Monitor, 1–5:9.

Murray L. Weidenbaum
Assistant Secretary for Economic Policy,
Department of the Treasury of the
United States

Even in an economy as rich and productive as ours, resources are limited. Claims on output must be balanced against the economy's capacity to produce. As always, priorities will be established—either by design or by default—to permit the satisfaction of some demands over others. But any enlightened attempt to reorder and establish priorities cannot take place until we possess a clear understanding both of the existing general ordering of priorities and the nature of the possible choices to be made.

Los Angeles Times, 7–5:A18.

In earlier periods when wages went up far less rapidly, the real living standard of the average worker rose steadily. But, since wage rates have escalated, the average worker's real living standard has tended to stagnate. Literally, "The faster we go, the behinder we get."

U.S. News & World Report, 12–7:16.

Charles Winick
Professor of Sociology,
City College of New York

The vast increase in the number of temporary employes in this country may be contributing to the development of a large number of workers who do not possess traditional feelings of loyalty to and indentification with the company which employs them. For such workers, alienation and a cynical attitude toward the job are more likely than is the case with salaried regular employes. If the employes feel keenly enough about seeking some form of collective action in order to seek redress for their grievances, a new kind of labor union may emerge. The membership of such a union of temporary employes has the potential for crippling a huge segment of our economy by a strike.

The New York Times, 1–4:(3)26.

Leonard Woodcock
President,
United Auto Workers of America

We are determined to win contracts that will provide equity for the workers and of which Walter Reuther (late UAW president) would be proud. It is defense spending, not the workers, which is responsible for fueling the fires of inflation, and in 1970 we will not be denied our equity.

Detroit, May 22/
The Washington Post, 5–23:A4.

. . . the pricing policies of the General Motors Corporation are set—figuring their costs, operating 180 days a year—to give them a rate of return on their net investment, after payment of taxes, of 20 per cent. It is an outrageously high profit formula. That's the inflationary factor in the automobile industry —not the wages of the automobile workers, which are very low, very low.

Interview/Meet the Press, National
Broadcasting Company, Washington, 9–6.

Jerry Wurf
President, American Federation of State,
County and Municipal Employees

Government workers have proved that when they are not dealt with justly, they will defy the law. And they have proved that, in such situations, government is powerless.

Newsweek, 5–4:78A.

Ralph W. Yarborough
United States Senator, D-Tex.

The cost of living has gone up like a rocket, and the Administration's so-called methods of fighting inflation have been like a booster to the inflation rocket ship, sending it higher and higher.

Before Texas Council of Machinists and
Aerospace Workers, San Antonio, Feb. 28/
The Dallas Times Herald, 3–1:A36.

Whitney M. Young, Jr.
Director, National Urban League

When it's a recession for white people, it's a serious depression for black people.

News conference, New York, July 21/
The Dallas Times Herald, 7–22:A17.

Law • The Judiciary

Spiro T. Agnew
Vice President of the United States

The trial of the Chicago Seven, or Eight, was a stormy footnote to the 1968 Democratic Convention. It could have been a test of the constitutionality of the Civil Rights Act. (Instead) the script was written for drama, not for justice, and the outrageous courtroom conduct totally obfuscated the constitutional question . . . The courts need lawyers who are not self-proclaimed disciples of a new cult, and reporters who do not predetermine the guilt or innocence of the defendant.

Phoenix, Feb. 27 /
The Dallas Times Herald, 3–1:A5.

That crowd in the Senate, which talks so much about ending discrimination, committed an act of discrimination—against the South. They went over to the Supreme Court and nailed a shingle to the door that reads, "No Southerners Need Apply."

Memphis, Sept. 22 /
Los Angeles Times, 9–23:(1)10.

. . . Richard Nixon remains determined to achieve a better ideological and geographical balance on the Supreme Court. His resolution to achieve that balance will never waver, despite those radical-liberals who still control the Senate.

Greenville, S.C., Oct. 26 /
Los Angeles Herald-Examiner, 10–26:A3.

James B. Allen
United States Senator, D-Ala.

May the day never come when a line will be drawn across a map of the United States and the statement made that no person south of that line can aspire to serve on the Su-

preme Court. It is my hope that this is not the attitude of the United States Senate, and for that reason I deplore the statement of the President (Nixon) that for his next appointment to the Supreme Court he intends to look to sections other than the South for his nominee.

Before the Senate, Washington, April 10 /
Los Angeles Times, 4–11:A1.

F. Lee Bailey
Lawyer

On the outside, we pull a jury from the streets and put them back there after the trial. In the case of military justice, the commander who orders the trial—a guy who is himself convinced that there are good grounds for conviction—selects the jury. And if the case is a heavy one, the officer in the jury sits there and reflects on his career in the military. He says, "If I do justice, my conscience will feel better for a couple of days, but that son of a gun, the presiding officer, is going to remember me for years" . . . The only time you can count on a military defense lawyer to whale the hell out of the military—and that's a defense lawyer's job—is when the lawyer is getting out of the service very soon and he doesn't give a damn what his superior officers put in his fitness report.

Newsweek, 8–31:22.

Those who think the information brought out at a criminal trial is the truth, the whole truth and nothing but the truth, are fools. Prosecuting or defending a case is nothing more than getting to those people who will talk for your side, who will say what you want said. That guy who said I pick apart the law isn't totally wrong. I use the law to frustrate the law. But I didn't set up the ground rules. I'm only a player in the game.

*Interview, Detroit/
The New York Times Magazine, 9–20:44.*

I would rather see the law moving toward the day when we could scientifically determine innocence or guilt, instead of having to play the theatre that is the trial to see if innocence or guilt can be proved by the cunning of prosecution or defense.

*Interview, Marshfield, Mass./
The New York Times Magazine, 9–20:57.*

Joseph A. Ball
*Former president,
American College of Trial Lawyers*

Most of the clients that I represent in a criminal case I detest. But I get them a good trial, and I try to win for them because I'm a professional in the courtroom. I try to use my experience and what talents I have . . . I don't have to love him to do a good job. As a matter of fact, I find that the more I become involved emotionally in my client's cause, the less able I am to make the most for him.

*Before Young Lawyers Section of American
Bar Association, St. Louis/
Los Angeles Herald-Examiner, 8–23:A16.*

Birch Bayh
United States Senator, D-Ind.

There are a number of very eminent legal minds in the South. To suggest to those who live in the South that Judge G. Harrold Carswell is the best they could find (for the Supreme Court) should be an insult.

The Dallas Times Herald, 4–10:A2.

Melvin Belli
Lawyer

. . . we are coming into the Golden Age of Law. We've really gotten meaningful in our relationship to the guy in the bucket. It is the new breed of lawyers, the young kids fresh out of law school, who are bringing this refreshing change. In the old days, it was the thing to join the "respected" Establishment

law firm. Security personified. Today, the reverse is true. The young attorney won't join anything unless he knows his prospective employer is involved in cost-free, diligent community and minority group activity. These kids are imbued with the idea—and rightly so—that the law isn't just for Wall Street or the New England Protestant, but (for) the guy below, who can utilize the very laws that used to keep him in line.

*Interview, San Francisco/
San Francisco Examiner & Chronicle
(Sunday Women), 10–4:1.*

Hugo L. Black
*Associate Justice,
Supreme Court of the United States*

It is essential to the proper administration of criminal justice that dignity, order and decorum be the hallmarks of all court proceedings in our country . . . The flagrant disregard in the courtroom of elementary standards of proper conduct should not and cannot be tolerated. We believe trial judges confronted with disruptive, contumacious, stubbornly defiant defendants must be given sufficient discretion to meet the circumstances in each case.

*Washington, March 31/
The New York Times, 4–1:1.*

I believe the Court has no power to add to or subtract from the procedures set forth by the Founders (of the Constitution) . . . I shall not at any time surrender my belief that that document itself should be our guide—not our own concept of what is fair, decent and right.

The New York Times Magazine, 5–24:84.

Harry A. Blackmun
*Judge, Eighth Circuit Court of Appeals;
Nominee for United States Supreme
Court Justice*

Law is, in part, social. Man is a social being. I can't get alarmed when they (the Supreme Court) overrule a prior decision, especially if it is 5-4. Who is to say that five men

(HARRY A. BLACKMUN)

10 years ago were right whereas five men looking the other direction today are wrong?

Interview, Rochester, Minn./
Los Angeles Herald-Examiner, 4–20:A13.

What comes through to me most clearly is the utter respect which the little person has for the Supreme Court . . . and I think that the little person feels this is the real bastion of freedom and protection of strength in this nation.

Before Senate Judiciary Committee/
U.S. News & World Report, 5–18:48.

Kingman Brewster, Jr.
President, Yale University

Things have come to such a pass that I am skeptical of the ability of black revolutionaries to achieve a fair trial anywhere in the U.S.

New Haven, Conn./Time, 5–4:59.

Edward W. Brooke
United States Senator, R-Mass.

I think in the future the President can no longer rely on the Attorney General and the Justice Department. He must take more personal participation in the selection of Supreme Court Justices.

The Dallas Times Herald, 4–13:A2.

Warren E. Burger
Chief Justice of the United States

I see two basic purposes of any system of justice: the first, to protect society; the second, to correct the wrongdoer. If I am right on this point, we should stop thinking of it as something which begins with an arrest and ends with a final judgment of guilt. We must see it as embracing the entire spectrum, including that crucial period which begins when the litigation is over (and) the sentence is being carried out. It is here that the success or failure of our society will make itself known.

Before Association of the Bar of the
City of New York, Feb. 17/
Vital Speeches, 3–15:323.

That courtrooms or trials are disrupted or sought to be used as stages for demonstrations or a forum for propaganda is not entirely a "new thing," but has been uncommon because Americans in the long run have trusted the legal system, the bar and the courts. Like generals who have no wars for a generation and are out of practice, we judges have perhaps been sluggish in responding to the new ways of trying legal and factual issues. But in time we do respond . . . It would be foolhardy not to be concerned about the turmoil and strife and violence we witness, much of it mindless and devoid of constructive ends. But concern must not give way to panic.

At American Law Institute, Washington,
May 19/National Observer, 5–25:6.

Of immediate relevance to us as lawyers is that gnawing doubt whether our system of justice, especially criminal justice, is sturdy enough to withstand the assaults which are leveled at it. Some say we must "crack down," that we must "smash" the challengers and restore tight discipline. In periods of stress there are always some voices raised urging that we suspend fundamental guarantees and take short cuts as a matter of self-protection. But this is not our way of doing things, short of a great national emergency. If we have the long view, we see that we have never been a tightly disciplined people and, reflecting this, our legal structure has been more relaxed than that of many other societies. If this has negative aspects, it also gives us a resiliency to tide us over and enable us to meet any crisis as it arises. We will respond slowly, but that is the nature of a democratic society. In those few periods of our history when we suspended basic guarantees of the individual in times of great national emergency, we often found, in retrospect, that we had overreacted.

At American Law Institute, Washington,
May 19/Time, 6–1:9.

. . . judges have been too timid and the bar

has been too apathetic to make clear to the public and the Congress the needs of the courts . . . In the supermarket age, we are like a merchant trying to operate a cracker-barrel corner grocery store with the methods and equipment of 1900.

State of the Judiciary address, St. Louis, Aug. 10/Washington Star, 8-10:A21.

(American) social and economic upheavals tend to wind up on the doorsteps of the court . . . The Federal court system is for a limited purpose, and lawyers, the Congress and the public must examine carefully each demand they make on that system. People speak glibly of putting all the problems of pollution, of crowded cities, of consumer class actions and others in the Federal courts. We should look more to state courts familiar with local conditions and local problems.

State of the Judiciary address, St. Louis, Aug. 10/Los Angeles Times, 8-11:(1)7.

A sense of confidence in the courts is essential to maintain the fabric of ordered liberty for a free people. Three things could destroy that confidence and do incalculable damage to society. One is that people come to believe that inefficiency and delay will drain even a just judgment of its value. One is that people who have long been exploited come to believe that courts cannot vindicate their legal rights from fraud and over-reaching in the smaller transactions of daily life. One is that people come to believe that the law—in the larger sense—cannot fulfill its primary function to protect them and their families in their homes and on the public streets. I have great confidence in our basic system and its foundations, in the dedicated judges and others in the judicial system, and in the lawyers of America. Continuity with change is the genius of the American system, and both are essential to fulfill the promise of equal justice under law.

State of the Judiciary address, St. Louis, Aug. 10/Los Angeles Times, 8-16:G2.

There is a growing of thought in the pro-

fession and among judges that, with the vast expansion of courts and growth of judicial power, some kind of accommodation must be made between the imperatives of judicial independence and the public interest.

At dinner honoring John C. Bell, Jr., Chief Justice, Pennsylvania Supreme Court, Philadelphia, Nov. 14/ The Washington Post, 11-15:A1.

The most severe criticism of courts in general and the jury system in particular has come in recent years from laymen who have served on juries. They're called; they must be there, let us say, at 9 o'clock; and then they spend two-thirds of their time for several weeks sitting around waiting for something to do. The machinery for handling jurors is not good; but a large part of this is inherent in the jury system. All litigation is inherently a clumsy, time-consuming business.

Interview/ U.S. News & World Report, 12-14:40.

G. Harrold Carswell
United States Supreme Court nominee

I've read a summary of what is attributed to me as a young candidate some 22 years ago. Specifically and categorically, I denounce and reject the words themselves and the ideas they represent. They're obnoxious and abhorrent to my personal philosophy. There is nothing in my private life, nor is there anything in my public record of some 17 years, which could possibly indicate that I harbor racist sentiments or the insulting suggestion of racial superiority. I do not so do, and my record so shows. Incidentally, I lost that election because I was considered too liberal.

Television interview, Irwinton, Ga., Jan. 21/ The New York Times, 1-23:16.

G. Harrold Carswell
Unsuccessful United States Supreme Court nominee

From all the morass of written legal expression, much of it conflicting, meaningless

WHAT THEY SAID IN 1970

(G. HARROLD CARSWELL)

or plain useless, one may be forgiven his yearning for a clearer light on the pathway to the household of that elusive lady, Justice —lest one be accused of mediocrity.

At Mercer University (Georgia)/
Newsweek, 5–11:65.

Bill Chappell, Jr.
United States Representative, D-Fla.

Many in this country have come to regard the Supreme Court with such reverence that it can do no wrong—even when it hands down irresponsible decisions that cripple the police in their efforts to prevent crime, detect criminals and prosecute them. Its rulings on mob marches, riots, pornography and subversive activity are all contributing to the crime wave.

Before Kiwanis and Rotary Clubs, Ocala, Fla.,
March 30/Vital Speeches, 5–1:423.

Walter Cronkite
News commentator,
Columbia Broadcasting System

The advantage (in TV coverage of trials), it seems to me, is clear to the defendant in assuring that some small knot of people are not going to pass judgment upon him and that he's going to get everything he's entitled to in the sense of a fair, judicious proceeding.

Television discussion/The Advocates,
National Educational Television, 3–22.

Thomas J. Dodd
United States Senator, D-Conn.

It is highly improbable that the no-knock provision, once it is part of the Federal law on narcotics, will be abused for all sorts of fanciful reasons. If I thought for a minute that this provision would result in the smashing in of the doors or windows of my house, or anyone else's, I would not be here defending it. And I think that interpretation is stretching the situation beyond all reality.

Before the Senate, Washington, Jan. 26/
Congressional Record, 1–26:S589.

William O. Douglas
Associate Justice,
Supreme Court of the United States

(If his book, *Points of Rebellion,* advo cates rebellion), I'll eat it—without mayo naise or anything.

Quote, 5–31:52

Jack Edwards
United States Senator, R-Ala.

My only hope is that during the next thre years President Nixon will be able to a point several more men who will seek to r turn the (Supreme) Court to its proper pos tion in our governmental process. More me like Chief Justice Burger and Judge (G. Ha rold) Carswell should be sitting on the benc of the highest judicial authority of this cou try. If those disruptive justices now holdin rein on that Court are permitted to continu their wanton destruction of our gover mental process through their usurpation the legislative authority invested in Co gress, this country truly will be ready fo revolution. I may well be leading the va guard.

*Before the House, Washington, Feb. *
Congressional Record, 2–5:H63

Sam J. Ervin, Jr.
United States Senator, D-N.C.

If we are to have law-enforcement in th country, we must have respect for our law and we must have respect for the manner i which those charged with enforcing thos laws act. It would do nothing to promote th cause of law enforcement in the narcotic field or the marijuana field or the field c dangerous substances for the Congress of th United States to authorize law enforcemen officers to emulate and follow the exampl set by burglars who break into people houses without notice and without inform ing them of their purpose.

Before the Senate, Washington, Jan. 26
Congressional Record, 1–26:S58

. . . some people think that usurpation c power by a court is sacrosanct. But if ther

a usurpation of power that is more repre-
ensible than any other usurpation of
ower, it is usurpation of power by judges
ho hold office for life and are beyond the
each of the people of this nation.

Before the Senate, Washington, Feb. 5 /
Congressional Record, 2–5:S1310.

I have said that the controlling element
n the Supreme Court in recent years has
een composed of judicial activists—and
idicial activists are men of good intentions.
'hey think that they can impove on the
onstitution that we have, and so they exer-
se their power and undertake to change the
ieaning of the Constitution to reflect their
ersonal views while they are professing to
interpret" the Constitution. I think every
iformed lawyer in the United States will
dmit that to be true privately, and I think
iat most intellectually honest lawyers will
dmit it publicly.

Before the Senate, Washington, Feb. 10 /
Congressional Record, 2–10:S1603.

When you take men who have served long
erms as Federal judges and appoint *them*
xclusively to the Supreme Court, you get
ien who see from one viewpoint—the Fed-
ral viewpoint. They do not see the value of
ie states.

Radio interview, WPTF, Raleigh, N.C.,
Oct. 27 / The Washington Post, 10–29:A4.

With due deference to all other men in all
enerations, I confess my belief that the
rorld has never known any other group as
rell-qualified as the Founding Fathers to
rrite organic law for a people dedicated to
he freedom of the individual. They were
ersed in the heartbreak history of man's
ght for freedom, and knew that a nation
rhich ignores the lessons taught by such his-
ory is doomed to repeat the mistakes of the
iast.

The New York Times Magazine, 11–15:127.

ierald R. Ford
Inited States Representative, R-Mich.

I concede that William O. Douglas has a

right to write and publish what he pleases.
But I suggest that for Associate Justice Douglas to put his name to such an inflammatory
volume as *Points of Rebellion,* at a critical
time in our history when peace and order is
what we need, is less than judicial good behavior . . . Public confidence in the United
States Supreme Court diminishes every day
that Mr. Douglas remains on it . . . He is unfit and should be removed. I would vote to
impeach him right now.

Before the House, Washington, April 15 /
The Washington Post, 4–16:4;
Human Events, 4–25:4.

Philip A. Hart
United States Senator, D-Mich.

It's the first time I've ever heard that argument, and I hope it's the last—that we
should look for mediocrity when we staff the
Supreme Court of the United States. We
should look for the best, the very best. Even
those who advance his (G. Harrold Carswell's) cause have implied that he is something less than that.

San Francisco Examiner & Chronicle
(This World), 3–22:11.

Clement F. Haynsworth
Unsuccessful U.S. Supreme Court nominee

I was sitting at home one night when the
Senate was debating my nomination to the
Supreme Court, and I was reading articles
about myself in *The New York Times* and
Washington Post. I put down my paper and
said to my wife, "You know, dear, this man
will never do. He's just awful. We've got to
get ourselves another nominee."

National Observer, 3–30:2.

Theodore M. Hesburgh
President, University of Notre Dame

Those who look to the law as an important
arbiter of right and wrong and find that
some laws are implemented while others are
not, despair of the fairness of the system.
This cannot be allowed to happen.

The New York Times, 10–18:(4)3.

Kenneth J. Hodgson
Major General and Judge Advocate
General, United States Army

It's become very popular to be critical of anything military—whether it's military music, military strategy or military justice. Military justice is as good or better than the justice in 48 out of the 50 states. We have a very good system that I'm very proud of. What we have is the *appearance* of evil. And, as Marshall McLuhan would say, that's what we have to deal with.

Interview/Newsweek, 8–31:22.

E. Adamson Hoebel
Professor of Anthropology,
University of Minnesota

If we are to survive, it will be through continued use and strengthening of that major tool of social control developed and used by the 30,000 generations of men who have preceded us—law. I believe that the basic postulates of our law system are good: humanitarian, equalitarian and pragmatic. Although many changes are clearly needed in our legal procedures to apply the law justly, I believe these changes are coming. If the rational militants would apply their energies to the vast educational job needed, and to winning allies in translating our unmet goals into reality, our timetable could be speeded up. If they persist in present tactics, strong repressive measures are inevitable —with far less "liberty and justice for all."

At United Press International Editors and Publishers Conference, Williamsburg, Va./ Los Angeles Times, 10–25:H3.

Julius J. Hoffman
Judge, United States District Court for the Northern District of Illinois

(If crime is increasing nationally), it is due in large part to the fact that waiting in the wings are lawyers willing to go beyond their professional responsibility, professional rights and professional duty.

At contempt sentencing of attorney William M. Kunstler at "Chicago conspiracy trial," Feb. 15/Los Angeles Times, 2–16:(1)1.

Roman L. Hruska
United States Senator, R-Neb.

If the Senate is to look at the *qualities* of a (Supreme Court nominee), we are engaging in the business of "appointing." That's for the President to decide. He is the appointing authority. We should look at a man's personal integrity, demeanor, capacity to be a judge, and then decide.

Before the Senate, Washington, March 16/ The New York Times, 3–17:21.

Even if he (G. Harrold Carswell) were mediocre, there are a lot of mediocre judges and people and lawyers, and they are entitled to a little representation (on the U.S. Supreme Court), aren't they? We can't have all Brandeises, Frankfurters and Cardozos and stuff like that there.

Interview, Washington, March 16/ The New York Times, 3–17:21.

Hubert H. Humphrey
Former Vice President of the United States

I don't think you should hold a man accountable for a speech that he made 20 or 25 years ago under entirely different circumstances. If (Supreme Court nominee G. Harrold Carswell's) record shows a sense of balance and a sense of openness, then he should be confirmed.

Interview/Issues and Answers, American Broadcasting Company, 1–25.

Daniel K. Inouye
United States Senator, D-Hawaii

The only good thing I've heard about Judge (G. Harrold) Carswell is that the next nominee (for the Supreme Court) will be worse.

San Francisco Examiner & Chronicle (This World), 3–22:10.

Jacob K. Javits
United States Senator, D-N.Y.

The high responsibility of bench and bar is to hold fast to the Bill of Rights when the strong winds of public opinion may cause even the Congress to sway.

Before Association of the Bar of the City of New York, Feb. 9/ The New York Times, 2–10:15.

Irving R. Kaufman
Judge, United States Court of Appeals for the Second Circuit

These defendants (who disrupt the courtroom) claim to have lost faith in the judicial process. They view their day in court as a performance, an opportunity to make a spectacular appeal to the press and public by showing their disrespect for our system of law, rather than a reasoned appeal to the judge and jury. Before other defendants respond to the siren call—believing that absence of manners and disruptive conduct are effective trial tactics—it is important to make them aware that these superficially-appealing stratagems are self-defeating . . . Have defendants who place the *trial* on trial forgotten the lessons of history? What would they substitute for our public trial, conducted by adversaries and circumscribed by rules of evidence, rules of orderliness, courtesy and dignity? Would they honestly prefer the violence of an ordeal by combat or the spectacle of a Roman circus?

Before Fordham Law Alumni Association, New York, March 7/ The New York Times, 3–8:(1)88.

William M. Kunstler
Civil rights lawyer

I am trembling because I am so outraged. I haven't been able to get this out before, and I am saying it now, and then I want you to put me in jail if you want to. I have sat here for four and a half months and watched the objections denied and sustained by Your Honor (Judge Julius Hoffman), and I know that this is not a fair trial. I know it in my heart. I am going to turn back to my seat with the realization that everything I have learned throughout my life has come to naught, that there is no meaning in this court, that there is no law in this court and

these men are going to jail by virtue of a legal lynching and that Your Honor is wholly responsible for that; and if this is what your career is going to end on, if this is what your pride is going to be built on, I can only say to Your Honor, "Good luck to you."

At the "Chicago conspiracy trial," Feb. 2/ The New York Times, 2–3:12.

I have tried with all of my heart faithfully to represent my clients in the face of what I considered and still consider repressive and unjust conduct toward them. If I have to pay with my liberty for such representation, then that is the price of my beliefs and sensibilities. I can only hope that my fate does not deter other lawyers throughout the country who, in the difficult days that lie ahead, will be asked to defend clients against a steadily increasing governmental encroachment upon their most fundamental liberties . . . I may not be the greatest lawyer in the world, but I think I am, at this moment . . . the most privileged—being punished for what I believe in.

At his sentencing for contempt at the "Chicago conspiracy trial," Feb. 15/ The New York Times, 2–16:22.

I only defend those whose goals I share. I'm not a lawyer for hire. I only defend those I love.

Time, 6–29:40.

The American Bar Association formula of a lawyer for hire specifically excludes those who most need legal help—the vast army of the poor.

Quote, 8–2:97.

I can see nothing wrong whatsoever in confining yourself—except in rare situations where there is no lawyer available for certain defendants—to those (defendants) whose goals you generally share. I think to share those goals is an important aspect of a lawyer's task. He's not a eunuch to be gravitating as some sort of intercessor between

(WILLIAM M. KUNSTLER)

the court and the client. He's the client's man. That's why I don't like to consider myself an officer of any court. I am the client's man—solely and exclusively.

*Before Young Lawyers Section of
American Bar Association, St. Louis/
Los Angeles Herald-Examiner, 8–23:A16.*

John V. Lindsay
Mayor of New York

When you try political activists under a conspiracy charge—long considered to be the most dubious kind of criminal charge, difficult to define or to limit—and when a trial becomes fundamentally an examination of political acts and beliefs, then guilt or innocence becomes almost irrelevant.

*At centennial of Association of the Bar
of the City of New York, Feb. 17/
The New York Times, 2–21:50.*

The courts are institutional cripples, stumbling along in the pattern of an outworn tradition, compiling a record of incredible inefficiency.

*Before American Bar Association,
St. Louis, Aug. 12/
The New York Times, 8–22:22.*

John L. McClellan
United States Senator, D-Ark.

To hold the allegiance of the now-lawabiding, society must show each man that no man is above the law.

*Before the Senate, Washington/
U.S. News & World Report, 2–2:12.*

Instead of helping stem the tide of permissiveness, civil disobedience and lawlessness . . . our Supreme Court has chosen this era of turmoil and turbulence to reinterpret and give new construction and meaning to many parts of the Constitution . . . We are now having changes on the Court. I hope these changes are for the better and that we have already reached the high-water mark

of activism and false liberalism which ha too often prevailed in recent years.

*At FBI National Academy, Washingto
May 27/The Washington Post, 5–28:A*

George S. McGovern
United States Senator, D-S.D.

Back in 1968 he (President Nixon) said h would give us (Supreme Court) justices the caliber of Brandeis, Holmes and Ca dozo; but he gave us Burger, Haynswort and Carswell. That's really a credibility ga

The Dallas Times Herald, 2–12:A

Clarence Mitchell
*Washington Bureau director, National
Association for the Advancement
of Colored People*

No platitudes and no excuses offered f the nominee can ever erase the fact that o this day an advocate of white supremacy (S preme Court nominee G. Harrold Carswel . . . got the support of an official body of th United States Senate (the Judiciary Con mittee). This is moral bankruptcy at i worst.

Los Angeles Times, 2–22:G

John N. Mitchell
Attorney General of the United States

. . . if we would have nominated a thir (Southern judge for the Supreme Court), would be the same old round again, only th time not (because of) "mediocrity." They' (the liberals) really attacking our Souther nominees for their philosophy. And whe *The Washington Post* and *The New Yor Times* hammer away 30 days in a row, ther is an effect on the Senate. Those 13 Senato who voted against (G. Harrold) Carswe voted their consciences, but they were al affected by the press coverage.

*Interview, Washington
Los Angeles Times, 4–27:(2)*

Richard M. Nixon
President of the United States

Judges Carswell and Haynsworth (unsu

ssful nominees to the U.S. Supreme Court) ve endured with admirable dignity vicious saults on their intelligence, their honesty d their character. They have been falsely arged with being racist. But when all pocrisy is stripped away, the real issue was eir philosophy of strict construction of the nstitution—a philosophy that I share— d the fact that they had the misfortune of ing born in the South . . .

April 8/The Dallas Times Herald, 4–12:A30.

What is centrally at issue in this nomina- n (of G. Harrold Carswell to the Supreme urt) is the constitutional responsibility of e President to appoint members of the urt—and whether this responsibility can frustrated by those who wish to substitute eir own philosophy or their own subjec- e judgment for that of the one person en- sted by the Constitution with the power appointment.

San Francisco Examiner & Chronicle (This World), 4–12:2.

Let us understand, all judges are not roes; all policemen are not heroes; and all ose charged with crime are not guilty. But us well understand, too, that the system, e system in which we protect the rights of e innocent, in which the guilty man re- ives a fair trial and gets the best possible fense, that system must be preserved. And less we stand up for the system, unless we e that order in the courtroom is respected, less we quit glorifying those who deliber- ely disrupt, and unless we begin to recog- ze that when a judge necessarily—after in- nse provocation—must hold individuals in ntempt of court, that that judge is justi- d, that he is acting in our behalf, then the stem will break down . . . In the final anal- is, unless the American people have within eir hearts a respect for the system—the sys- m of law and order and justice which we ve inherited from over hundreds of years hen anything we do at the governmental vel will not be successful. It is that system

that is now under attack in so many areas.

News conference, Denver, Aug. 3/ U.S. News & World Report, 8–17:70.

Charles A. O'Brien
Deputy Attorney General of California

(Police) too often . . . are asked to enforce unwise laws and, occasionally, unjust laws . . . Self-appointed spokesmen for law and order do not help the police by passing laws which are virtually impossible to enforce.

Los Angeles, March 25/ Los Angeles Times, 3–26:(2)2.

J. Milton Patrick
National Commander, American Legion

A former Justice of the United States Su- preme Court said recently, "History shows that the first evidence of each society's decay appeared in the toleration of disobedience of its laws." Thoughtful Americans wonder if the decade now ending has brought so- ciety to the brink of decay.

Los Angeles, Jan. 5/Vital Speeches, 3–15:341.

Francis T. P. Plimpton
President, Association of the Bar of the City of New York

This association traditionally does not comment on nominations for the bench out- side of our area . . . but I cannot help express- ing the wish that the President of the United States' second and third nominees to the Supreme Court (Clement F. Haynsworth and G. Harrold Carswell) could have ap- proached in stature, experience, attitudes and integrity his first nominee (Warren E. Burger).

Before Association of the Bar of the City of New York, Feb. 17/ The New York Times, 2–18:16.

Ronald Reagan
Governor of California

Why does a criminal defendant with a clever lawyer seem able to run circles around some of our finest prosecutors with a seem- ingly bottomless barrel of time-consuming tricks? The public is frustrated and fed up

(RONALD REAGAN)

with the sort of behavior that some defendants—and, indeed, some of their lawyers—are seemingly able to get away with in courtrooms; behavior that would not be tolerated in any kindergarten.

Before California State Bar Association,
Los Angeles/ Los Angeles Times, 9–21:(2)6.

Simon H. Rifkind
Former Judge, United States District Court
for the Southern District of New York

Disruption in the courtroom on my table of the Ten Commandments is treason. A lawyer who engages in the deliberate destruction of a judicial proceeding—no matter what the provocation—is like a priest who defiles the altar of his church.

Panel discussion, St. Louis, Aug. 7 /
Los Angeles Times, 8–8:(1)11.

J. L. Robertson
Vice Chairman, Federal Reserve Board

One of the remarkable achievements of any civilization, including our own, is the establishment of the rule of law. This involves securing the consent of something like 99% of the population that they will abide by certain rules. I do not know exactly what the percentage is, but it has to be pretty close to unanimous consent for the system to work. If any substantial percentage of the population refuses to observe the agreed rules—the law—then the whole system breaks down. We do not have enough policemen and prisons to make the system work if a substantial portion of the population is determined to ignore or defy the law.

Before directors of Federal Reserve Bank
of San Francisco, Phoenix, May 14 /
Vital Speeches, 6–15:521.

William J. Scherle
United States Representative, R-Iowa

Supreme Court Justice William O. Douglas, self-appointed messiah of the hippies and yippies, is at it again. This time, the aging Lothario practically invites his long-haired mental midgets to thumb their noses at the law-enforcement agencies of this country and obey only the laws which agree with their naive philosophy. In his soon-to-be-published book, *Points of Rebellion,* the 71-year-old swinger, with a penchant for wives a half-century younger than he, endlessly tirades against the FBI, CIA, local police officials, educators and every other organization or person with a semblance of dignified authority. He heaps praise upon the degenerate disciples of disorder while strongly hinting that the philosophy of citizens concerned about rampant crime and riotous behavior parallels that of Adolf Hitler. The Justice—an obvious student of the extracurricular activities of Henry VIII—attempts to draw the ridiculous comparison between George II and what he describes as today's "Establishment." If Justice Douglas, whom the taxpayers are subsidizing at $60,000 a year for life, really believes his own drivel, he should resign from the Court and spend his time hiking down the pointless paths tread by the rest of the anarchists.

Before the House, Washington, Feb. 5 /
Congressional Record, 2–5:E707.

Hugh Scott
United States Senator, R-Pa.

I point out that the very knee-jerk type of liberal who objects to (Supreme Court nominee) Judge (G. Harrold) Carswell is very often the same person who found no objection to supporting Senator Kefauver, from Tennessee, for the Vice Presidency, or Senator Sparkman, from Alabama, for the Vice Presidency . . . And these are mostly men who were able to support the Democratic ticket without a qualm and had nothing whatever to say about Southern segregationists or strict constructionists or anything else.

Interview, Washington, March 8 /
Los Angeles Times, 3–9:(1)2.

Raymond P. Shafer
Governor of Pennsylvania

I think that the most important issue, whether you call it political or anything else, facing our society today, our free society today, is that of being an orderly society . . . all of our institutions are being tested, and unless we can abide by our own rules—and, after all, that is all law is, our own rules so we will get along together just a little bit better—then we as a civilization will soon disintegrate. That is why it is very important that we do have an updating of our laws to protect society, as well as abide by our basic constitutional rights for the individual man.

Interview/Meet the Press,
National Broadcasting Company, Denver, 8–9.

Michael I. Sovern
Dean, Columbia University Law School

The idea that we should spend all our time in law school teaching people how to win instead of how to settle is very damaging in this day and age.

Time, 4–20:45.

Roger J. Traynor
Former Chief Justice, Supreme Court of California

What a judge does with his time while he is not on the bench is of great interest to the public. It is absolutely necessary that the clear light of day should illuminate any off-the-bench activity by a judge—and particularly any money he makes off of it.

Before Conference of Chief Justices, St. Louis,
Aug. 6/The New York Times, 8–9:(4)12.

Earl Warren
Former Chief Justice of the United States

The greatest weakness of our judicial system is that it has become clogged and does not function in a fluent fashion resulting in prompt determination of the guilt or innocence of those charged with crime. Today, in many communities in the United States, it takes from three to four years to have a jury trial in a civil case, and in many of those same jurisdictions it will take a year or even more to have a jury trial in a criminal case.

At Johns Hopkins University, Nov. 14/
San Francisco Examiner & Chronicle,
11–15:A10.

It cost $328 million to build our last modern cruiser for the Navy. Last year, it cost $128 million to operate our whole Federal judicial system. This is six-hundredths of one per cent of our national budget—a small amount, indeed, to spend on it toward the internal security of our nation.

At Johns Hopkins University, Nov. 14/
San Francisco Examiner & Chronicle,
11–15:A10.

Edward Bennett Williams
Lawyer

. . . in England I spent a whole summer watching the British (legal) system work several years ago. If a man is convicted in Old Bailey today, (by a) jury of his peers, three weeks later he's in the British Court of Criminal Appeal, and a decision comes down that very day. Now the punishments that are administered in the British system are less severe than those administered here in the United States; but they are administered swiftly, and there is a respect for the court that I think is ebbing away here in the United States.

Television interview, Washington, Feb. 15/
U.S. News & World Report, 3–16:21.

The last bastion of respect for government is in the judiciary. People don't respect the legislative branch anymore, and are highly critical of the executive. If respect for courts erodes, this country is in deep trouble.

Interview/Los Angeles Times, 3–19:(2)7.

Perhaps the worst fault of our judicial system is the outrageous delay after a "guilty" verdict—the time it takes to exhaust the defendant's rights of appeal. It is very difficult to explain to an intelligent layman why, when a jury of 12 persons finds a man guilty beyond reasonable doubt of committing armed robbery, he and his lawyers can tinker with the appellate process for two years before he faces the day of reckoning. This situation boggles the mind of all concerned intelligent people. They can't understand why the judicial system is so unresponsive to the

(EDWARD BENNETT WILLIAMS)

needs of society, and they find no satisfactory answer to the mystery.

Interview, Washington/
U.S. News & World Report, 9–21:95.

I think the method of selecting jurors in many states is one of the most archaic things about our system of criminal justice at the trial level . . . You don't need six weeks to get a jury. You can get a jury to try fairly any case that you can conceive of in one day or less. I've tried some cases that have gotten a lot of attention in the press, and never have I taken more than a day to get a jury. You know, Clarence Darrow—after trying some of the most newsworthy cases in American history—said that, on reflection, he thought that he would have been as well off had he taken the first 12 people who went into the jury box.

Interview, Washington/
U.S. News & World Report, 9–21:95.

The legal system isn't working. It is like a scarecrow in the field that doesn't scare the crows any more because it is too beaten and tattered—and the crows are sitting on the arms and cawing their contemptuous defiance.

Interview, Washington/
U.S. News & World Report, 9–21:96.

I have participated in a large number of Senate hearings which were televised, and I am impressed with how much they differ from nontelevised hearings. Everybody has a little "ham" in him, and unfortunately television elicits it. Too often the participants get concerned with their histrionic performances and forget their real roles. I'm afraid that televising trials would inhibit to a large degree the search for truth in the courtroom.

Interview, Washington/
U.S. News & World Report, 9–21:98.

Leon Wolfstone
President, American Trial Lawyers
Association

If you made every moment of a day that a defendant is in contempt a separate offense, you could give him a sentence that would last until his reincarnation.

Newsweek, 3–2:25.

piro T. Agnew
ice President of the United States

The threat of violent revolution (is a) lear and present danger . . . (The greatest threat to the nation is) not the war in Vietam, nor inflation, nor the environment . . . is: Will the government of this country emain in the hands of its elected officials or ill it descend to the streets?

Before National Governors Conference, Washington, Feb. 26/ The Dallas Times Herald, 2–27:A5.

The liberal media have been calling on ne to lower my voice and seek accord with ll citizens. Nothing would please me more han to see . . . us return to discussion and ebate within our institutions, to see dissatis- ed citizens return to the elective process to hange government, to see an end to the vil- ification, the obscenity, vandalism and the iolence that become the standard tactics of hose who claim to act in the interest of eace and freedom. But I want you to know will not make a unilateral withdrawal and hereby abridge the confidence of the silent najority.

Atlanta/National Observer, 3–2:10.

Confronted with a choice, the American eople would choose the policeman's trun- heon over the anarchist's bomb.

Before American Legion, Portland, Ore., Sept. 2/Los Angeles Herald-Examiner, 9–2:A2.

Sen Barnes
Lieutenant-Governor of Texas

Violence as a means of resolving specific problems such as Indochina, race relations, young and old, rich and poor, the economy nd safeguarding our constitutional free- loms is self-defeating. In fact, it almost al- ways assures the contrary result. For those who desire change within the system, vio- lence is tactfully stupid . . . All people in this . . . country must dramatize the issues in every peaceful, legitimate, law-abiding ave- nue that is open to you. It's a cold, practical political fact (that) change is accomplished by power. This power in our system is in the ballot box.

Before Fort Worth Chamber of Commerce, June 30/The Dallas Times Herald, 7–1:A5.

Winton M. Blount
Postmaster General of the United States

(Radicals) offer destruction, but no solu- tion. Perhaps the exalting of ignorance is ex- cusable to a point. But, finally, the combina- tion of ignorance and rebellion is too ex- plosive to tolerate. Our history shows all too clearly in which direction the middle class moves when it is frightened, angry or threat- ened. It goes to the right, not to the left. The more frightened it becomes, the angrier it gets, the more extreme its action. And Amer- ica has the largest middle class in the world. We must get away from the notion that the democratic process is designed to be perfec- tion. It is designed to permit improvement.

Before Omicron Delta Kappa fraternity/ Time, 5–4:14.

Paul L. Briand, Jr.
Professor of English, State University of New York at Oswego

America was born in violence, she lives in violence and—unless she heeds the problems which beset her at home—she will die in vio- lence.

Convocation address at summer session, College of Arts and Sciences, S.U.N.Y. at Oswego, July 8/Quote, 10–18:374.

(PAUL L. BRIAND, JR.)

The behavior of the young should be testimony enough that the portrayal of crime, sex, and violence in our mass media results from observation and imitation in criminal, sexual and violent behavior. It is the young who are hurling excrement and destroying property in their confrontations with the establishment; it is the young for whom the sexy and violent movies are made—they are the modern day movie audience—and for whom the sexual revolution is taking place; it is the young who are committing crimes in America—50 per cent of them by youngsters under 18 years of age; and it is the young who get into more automobile accidents than anybody else. As the older generation has sown, so now must it reap. It had better start pointing its index finger of blame and accusation at itself.

At S.U.N.Y. convocation, July 8/
Quote, 12–27:613.

George Brown
United States Representative, D-Calif.

Those who commit violence in the street as a protest are idiots who have destroyed the beauty of American dissent.

At Long Beach (Calif.) State College, Feb. 27/
Los Angeles Herald-Examiner, 2–27:A4.

Zbigniew Brzezinski
Director, Research Institute on Communist Affairs, Columbia University

The short-range effect of violence could be to push the country toward the Right and to produce a far greater preoccupation with what can be called "law and order" and that in effect can become repression. It seems to me that anyone who is interested in preserving liberal, democratic order in the United States ought to be particularly insistent right now on combining social change with orderly procedure. Unless we combine both, we will have, initially, some change and vio-

lence and, later on, no change accompanied by repression.

Interview, New York/
The Christian Science Monitor, 3–31:2.

Warren E. Burger
Chief Justice of the United States

It would be foolhardy not to be concerned about the turmoil and strife and violence we witness, much of it mindless and devoid of constructive ends. But concern must not give way to panic . . . our institutions are durable enough to surmount any attack.

At American Law Institute, Washington,
May 19/San Francisco Examiner & Chronicle,
5–24:B2.

Al Capp
Cartoonist

If burning down a building is protesting for peace, then armed robbery is private enterprise and rape is cultural exchange.

Los Angeles Herald-Examiner, 5–13:A12.

Bill Chappell, Jr.
United States Representative, D-Fla.

The Constitution guarantees to every American the right to lawfully dissent, to speak his piece, but not to do as he pleases. Our forefathers gave us one of the most powerful methods of dissent that any country has ever known—the ballot box, a free press, the right to lawfully assemble. But when the courts ruled that certain disruptive marches were in order because of their own sense of social reform, the destruction and riots that followed must be laid at the judicial doorstep.

Before Kiwanis and Rotary Clubs, Ocala, Fla.,
March 30/Vital Speeches, 5–1:424.

Ramsey Clark
Former Attorney General
of the United States

I think turbulence and instability and the anonymity of the individual in America all tend to cause us to seek violence as a problem-solver, because we do not see any other way to solve our problems. In the American tradition, we have glorified the power of violence and ignored its pity. I think it is possible, within one generation, to condition the propensity for violence out of the American society. We have no greater challenge. Violence is no longer tolerable as an interpersonal or an international problem solver.

Interview/The Wall Street Journal, 7–13:8.

If you think mere force can control our teeming millions, then the turbulence we've seen is only prologue.

At American University, Washington/
The Dallas Times Herald, 10–16:A26.

J.V. Clyne
Former Justice, Supreme Court of British Columbia, Canada

Challenges to the law today take the beguilingly innocent form of a defense of conscience. Now, conscience is an admirable thing and men who are ruled by their consciences are universally respected. This innocent word, however, has been put to a more sinister use by our new breed of revolutionary. We are told that the truly free man can be bound by no laws except those which his conscience tells him to obey. He need accept no obligations except those which depend on individual consent. This is a doctrine that has widespread appeal because it sounds so very moral, yet it is used to give the appearance of high principle to lawlessness. One may say he refuses to pay taxes because, deep in his conscience, he disapproves of the way they are spent. One may even justify theft on the grounds that he doesn't hold with notions of private property. There is no idea more dangerous to the existence of an orderly human community than the doctrine that among the duties that are placed upon him the citizen is free to pick and choose those that he will perform.

At Town Hall, Los Angeles/
National Observer, 3–16:15.

Edward M. Davis
Chief of Police of Los Angeles

The revolutionaries are running loose on the streets with all of their freedom, and the people are locked up in their homes and locked up in their public buildings . . . There are two specters that worry the chief of police in this area: One is that if the police are sufficiently consumed in guarding police buildings and public buildings and taking care of rampant crime, then the revolutionaries could well take over the city. And you will probably see that, unless something is done about it in this decade . . . The other specter is the silent majority, most of whom have guns in their homes. There are many more guns than policemen; there are more guns than people. If you ever get the people of this country taking the law into their own hands, then we will have a state of chaos that would be extremely difficult to recover from. The frustrated people of this country—of all races, black and white and of whatever ethnic derivation—are all afraid and are all waiting and are all ready, and we are scared to death of all those guns in all those homes. And they are there, believe me, in great, great numbers . . .

Before Senate Judiciary Subcommittee on
Internal Security, Washington/
U.S. News & World Report, 10–26:86.

James O. Eastland
United States Senator, D-Miss.

We need to attempt to devise a legislative program which will support the effort of state and local government to stop the killing and wounding of police officers . . . These vicious attacks on officers, the murder and maiming of lawmen, are assaults of the most dangerous nature on the structure of law and order which supports civilized society. This is a war against the police. These deliberate attacks are too widespread to suggest separate and isolated acts of violence. These attacks are tied together and connected in various ways. These instances of deadly violence, fitting into an ominous pattern, are part of a wave of guerrilla warfare which threatens to undermine a pillar of law

(JAMES O. EASTLAND)

and order from one end of this nation to the other . . .

Before Senate Judiciary Subcommittee on Internal Security, Washington/ U.S. News & World Report, 10–26:82.

Fred W. Friendly
Professor of Journalism, Columbia University; Former president, Columbia Broadcasting System News

There must be something between anarchy and authoritarianism. The gutless ones are those who throw rocks or stand idly by.

The New York Times, 5–24:(1)68.

Clifford P. Hansen
United States Senator, R-Wyo.

I think a part of the problem we are witnessing today results from the fact that this age of ours, this generation of ours, has been entirely too permissive in what it has done. We failed as parents to draw proper guidelines for our young people before they reached their teens. We failed to draw proper guidelines for our young people when they entered their teens. As a consequence, being typically human, a few are testing the reins to see how far they can go. I really believe what they want older people to say is, "Stop here." I deplore the loss of life that occurred on the campus of Kent State University. But I think it is important, and it is important now, that everyone in America realize that the laws of this land must be obeyed. We are going to have to learn that if we are to have society at all, if those who wish to dissent want to be heard, if we are going to bring about changes in order to make this society more responsive to the needs of this generation and still keep the kind of government we have, we must recognize that, after hearing everybody, the majority in this country still write the laws and what they believe must still be the law of the land . . .

Before the Senate, Washington, May 5/ U.S. News & World Report, 5–18:94.

John J. Harrington
President, Fraternal Order of Police

There is a thin line between civilizatio and the jungle. The line is law and order.

Cleveland Plain Dealer, 8–12:B.

Joseph Heller
Author

I find it hard to believe that incitement t riot, incitement to violence, is a crime. If i were, Spiro Agnew would be in jail today and Richard Nixon would be in jail wit him.

At North Texas State University, May 7 The Dallas Times Herald, 5–8:C2

Lewis B. Hershey
Former Director, Selective Service System

A person can protest until he's black i the face; but when he violates the law, he' a criminal.

San Francisco Examiner & Chronicl (This World), 2–22:

Theodore M. Hesburgh
President, University of Notre Dame

The fact is, we simply can't go on like thi in this country. We're way over the line. I relations between humans, guns and knive symbolize an underlying reliance on vic lence. It has become almost a rule of life i this country for a person to say, "I'll kil you," and mean it.

Los Angeles Times, 3–16:(2)8

Eric Hoffer
Author, Philosopher

You need order in order to have a civilizec society. Fear and freedom are mutually ex clusive. Right now, you are not living in a free society. The choice we have is betwee two non-free societies. One, the society w have now, with all the constitutional guaran tees of individual freedom and all thes things, and yet we cannot control these wil ful savages, these beasts masquerading a men, who mug us, rob us, who do anything they want with us. This is one kind of non free society. The other is a dictatorship, where you have no freedom to say what you want, but the streets are safe all the time. And I'll bet you 80 per cent of the people, if they could choose, would vote for a dictatorship.

Interview, Berkeley, Calif./
The Dallas Times Herald, 10–22:A16.

Sidney Hook
Professor of Philosophy, New York University

Violence in the academy is an outgrowth of violence in the streets and cities of the country. That is where the gravest current danger lies. Were violence confined to the universities alone, its evils could not long continue if only because the state and society, on whose support the universities ultimately depend, would restrict and perhaps cancel their precarious autonomy. In the democratic community at large, the resort to violence attacks that community at its foundations—and this, regardless of the merit of the cause or the sincerity and self-righteousness of the "engagers" and the "engagees" . . . In the end, then, the great paradox and the great truth is that, in a democratic society, freedom, which is often invoked to justify violence, is itself imperiled by the exercise of violence. The ideologists of violence in a democracy are the sappers and miners of the forces of despotism—the gravediggers, willing or unwilling, of the precious heritage of freedom.

At Stanford University/
The Washington Post, 5–17:B4.

Hubert H. Humphrey
Former Vice President of the United States

Black militants, burning and shooting, may well have set back the course of civil rights for a decade. White radicals rampaging on campuses may have spawned an anti-university backlash that could set back the cause of higher education by a decade. Draft resisters who take the law into their own hands serve neither the cause of peace nor of

draft reform . . . and that is not "well-meaning" in my book.

Before American Bar Association, St. Louis/
Newsweek, 8–24:25.

I am a liberal and proud of it. I also believe in law and order. There is nothing inconsistent in that.

The New York Times, 9–13:(1)1.

David Ifshin
President-elect, National Student Association

I have never been involved in violence myself, and I hope I never will be. But I don't condemn violence; I don't deplore it. I understand why it is happening, and I'm very sympathetic to that. But I don't endorse it.

St. Paul, Aug. 19/
The Washington Post, 8–20:A4.

Jacob K. Javits
United States Senator, R-N.Y.

There is no reason for giving up the law-and-order issue to the conservatives. There is no reason why liberals cannot be just as firm and even more effective in crime control. There is no Republican or Democratic way to patrol a beat.

Houston, Dec. 5/
The New York Times, 12–6:(1)46.

Leon Jaworski
Lawyer; Former head, American Bar Association's Committee on Crime Prevention and Control

I believe that our young people today must realize that, if there are grievances that are just, there are ways of resolving those grievances without having to resort to violence. It may take longer, it may mean that the efforts will have to be more extensive than they had hoped would be the case; but if they feel that they must resort to violence and to disorder and to disruptions, then they are tearing down the very processes that are so important to them and to their future happiness. They must learn that once we

(LEON JAWORSKI)

lose respect for law, loss of our freedoms will be next.

Interview/U.S. News & World Report,
7-20:42.

Edward M. Kennedy
United States Senator, D-Mass.

I'm an authority on violence, and there's no place for it in our society.

At Yale University, April 22 / Time, 5-4:59.

Richard G. Kleindienst
Deputy Attorney General of the United States

The best thing that happened to violent revolutionaries and radical militants is free speech. Be sure that they speak and everybody hears them. Young people who hear them a few times realize that what they are saying is poppycock.

Before Illinois law enforcement officers,
Washington, Aug. 12 /
Chicago Daily News, 8-12:18.

William F. Knowland
Editor and publisher, "Oakland Tribune";
Former United States Senator, R-Calif.

If brute power, the torch and the gun in the hands of the mob—black or white—is to overcome or seriously challenge our process of law, then, indeed, our nation is facing the greatest crisis since the Civil War.

Before California Press Association,
San Francisco / The Washington Post, 12-6:K2.

William M. Kunstler
Civil rights lawyer

People are no longer going to content themselves with a picket line around a building. People are going to occupy the building. People are going to take over the building. And I rather imagine, unless government listens, people are going to burn down the building.

At University of Notre Dame /
The New York Times Magazine, 4-19:91.

You must resist, and resistance means everything short of revolution—and if resistance doesn't work, revolt.

At anti-war rally, New York /
Human Events, 4-25:2.

Even though I don't like it (violence), I think it is sometimes entirely necessary for the attainment of certain social ends. When do I think it's necessary? I think it, or the fear of it, the threat of violence, is necessary when people come to the conclusion—the reasoned conclusion—that all non-violent methods have failed or will be useless.

Interview/Los Angeles Times, 8-9:F3.

Klaus Liepmann
Chairman, Music Department, Massachusetts Institute of Technology

This is the only time I have spoken in a faculty meeting during my 23 years at MIT. However, there are times when "business as usual" becomes a crime. All this reminds me sadly of the Hitler years in Germany . . . when citizens were turned against each other, one side calling the other "Communists, traitors, bums," when atrocities were committed in the name of law and order . . . In Germany, great masses of people, notably the intellectuals, remained passive —they called it "nonpolitical" . . . I feel it is our duty as intellectuals and artists to speak up now and to act now

At Massachusetts Institute of Technology /
Newsweek, 5-18:30.

John V. Lindsay
Mayor of New York

The blunt, hard fact is that we in this nation appear headed for a new period of repression—more dangerous than at any time in years. The frenzy, the bitterness, the tumult of the last few years have led many people—including many in positions of power—to expect peace and order to come by whittling away at the Bill of Rights of our Constitution.

*At centennial of Association of the Bar
of the City of New York, Feb. 17/
The New York Times, 2–21:50.*

Reliance on terror is one kind of dangerous response to a troubled time. There is another kind of response—equally false, but even more dangerous. And that is the turn toward repression, toward repudiation of our rights and liberties—a turn supported by some in the highest levels of power. Either out of ignorance or out of calculated political cynicism, our citizens are being told that crime will stop if we erase the Bill of Rights; that unity will come if we repress dissent; that racial conflict will end if we ignore racial justice; and that protest will cease if we intimidate the people who report it.

*At University of California at Berkeley,
April 2/Los Angeles Times, 4–3:(1)31.*

Louis B. Lundborg
Chairman, Bank of America

I am not afraid the left-wing radicals will win. I am only afraid of how they will be defeated. The natural sequel to left-wing radical rebellion is right-wing reaction and repression. History shows only too plainly that repression doesn't repress only the bad guys; it ends up by controlling and repressing everyone—particularly everyone who disagrees with the party in power. It won't be easy to cool the current unrest because we've already begun to choose up sides in ways that typically lead to trouble. We can see the polarizing taking shape with people on both sides tending to lump whole segments of the population together as "we" and "they." It is dangerous enough to pin labels on people at any time, but this is being done in an atmosphere of name-calling that does nothing to cool off the temperature.

*Before Rotary Club, Seattle, June 17/
Los Angeles Times, 6–21:F7.*

We all lose by violence, whether we be young, old, liberal, conservative, hippie or square. As a nation, we are wounded by such acts, whenever they occur; and, as individuals, we lose one of the foundation stones of all our freedom to live our lives.

San Francisco/Time, 9–7:10.

Archibald MacLeish
Poet, Playwright

I don't see how there could be two opinions about the use of violence. Our forefathers were very clear on the fundamental right of revolution, and I suppose the right of revolution involves the use of violence. But violence today is not really used for revolution, but just to make life so miserable for everybody that you will hope something will happen. This is a form of cheating. I don't see how you justify it.

*Interview, Philadelphia/
Los Angeles Times, 11–20:(1)7.*

Lester G. Maddox
Governor of Georgia

These people (rioters) ought to be shot down when they get involved in running into stores, looting and rioting. When people are shooting at policemen, they have forfeited their right to a trial.

*News conference, Atlanta, Sept. 2/
Washington Star, 9–3:B6.*

Charles McC. Mathias, Jr.
United States Senator, R-Md.

It is dangerous for citizens to prance on the borders of anarchy, and equally dangerous for high officials to play brinksmanship on the edge of repression. We must avoid making martyrs out of our nuisances.

*Washington, May 1/
The Washington Post, 5–2:A2.*

John N. Mitchell
Attorney General of the United States

There can be no greater evidence of disorder in society than the sound of gunfire on a college campus. From Kent State to Jackson State, we have seen the citadels of reason turn into fortresses of force; and, as a result,

(JOHN N. MITCHELL)

the nation has witnessed the saddest semester in the history of American education. I will not offer judgments now on matters under urgent investigation, but I will say this: This is a nation determined to live within the law. Neither violent demonstrations nor unrestrained reactions are part of that law. There are 200 million innocent bystanders in America who must be protected, and the first duty of the peacekeeping forces is to protect the innocent. The hope for order in our society goes far beyond the intelligent use of restraint in keeping the peace. It draws upon the natural revulsion to violence on the part of the American people, which is making itself felt now within every group and each generation.

At Delta State College, Cleveland, Miss.,
May 19/U.S. News & World Report, 6–1:41.

I would remind all law-enforcement agencies—whether they be local police, state police or National Guardsmen—that the first requirement of professional law-enforcement officers is the protection of the public. One can recognize the provocations which often accompany civil disorders, but trained law-enforcement personnel have a responsibility to keep their cool and to utilize only such minimum force as is required to protect the safety of the general public, the bystanders and themselves.

Los Angeles Times, 5–24:G2.

Given our times, we cannot expect political demonstrations to be conducted like prayer meetings. We must expect language which may incite hostility or may be obscene. This is because the First Amendment protects all of us, including men and women who choose to be unruly, unreasonable and impolite.

Before Texas bar associations, San Antonio,
July 2/The Washington Post, 7–4:A1.

Edmund S. Muskie
United States Senator, D-Maine

All of us in public office must exercise restraint—from the President and Vice President to members of Congress, to governors and state legislators, to mayors, to National Guardsmen and police. We cannot expect those who disagree with national policies to be restrained if those in power do not set an example of self-control. We cannot expect those who want change to work within our political system if those who represent the system label all those seeking change as "traitors." We cannot expect those who are disaffected to be nonviolent if those charged with public safety rely on violence to keep order. All those who want their rights respected and their views heard must respect the rights of other. Nothing we do can restore the lives of the students slain at Kent State. But we can act, and act now, to prevent a similar occurrence.

Before the Senate, Washington, May 5/
U.S. News & World Report, 5–18:95.

For four years, a conservative Republican has been Governor of California, yet there is no more law and order in California today than when he took office. (Although) a Democratic Congress has passed sweeping legislation . . . America is no more orderly or lawful, nor its streets more safe, than was the case two years ago, or four or six. We must deal with symptoms, strive to prevent crime, halt violence and punish the wrongdoer. But we must also look for the deeper causes, in the structure of our society. If one of your loved ones is sick, you do not think it is soft or undisciplined of a doctor to try and discover the agents of illness. But you would soon discard a doctor who thought it enough to stand by the bed and righteously curse the disease.

Television address, Nov. 2/
Los Angeles Times, 11–3:(1)5.

Richard M. Nixon
President of the United States

You hear them night after night on television—people shouting obscenities about America and what we stand for. You hear those who shout against the speakers and shout them down, who will not listen. And then you hear those who engage in violence. You hear those, and see them, who, without reason, kill policemen and injure them, and the rest. And you wonder: Is that the voice of America? I say to you it is not. It is a loud voice, but, my friends, there is a way to answer. Don't answer with violence. Don't answer by shouting the same senseless words that they use. Answer in the powerful way that Americans have always answered. Let the majority of Americans speak up . . . speak up with your votes. That is the way to answer.

> *Republican campaign speech,*
> *Burlington, Vt., Oct. 17 /*
> *The New York Times, 10–18:(1)1.*

Some say that the violent dissent is caused by the war in Vietnam. It is about time we branded this line of thinking, this alibi for violence, for what it is: pure nonsense. There is no greater hypocrisy than a man carrying a banner that says "peace" in one hand while hurling a rock or a bomb with the other hand. The war is ending and the violence is increasing, sure signs that the alibis are worthless. Violence in America today is not caused by the war, not caused by repression. There is no romantic ideal involved. Let's recognize them for what they are: not romantic revolutionaries, but the same thugs and hoodlums that have always plagued a good people.

> *At Republican campaign rally, Phoenix,*
> *Oct. 31 / The Dallas Times Herald, 11–1:A5.*

One approach holds that violence will end as we end the (Vietnam) war; that violence will end as we give more power to those who demand more power; that violence will end as we end hunger and poverty in America. The people who believe in this approach are sincere Americans . . . But I believe that their approach has led us down a path of appeasement that has resulted in the very thing that these people abhor most: the increase in violence and the limiting of personal freedoms . . . For a decade, their approach dominated America. It has obviously failed.

> *At Republican campaign rally,*
> *Phoenix, Oct. 31 /*
> *Los Angeles Times, 11–3:(1)10.*

John O. Pastore
United States Senator, D-R.I.

If we're going to call out the National Guard and say to that young man in a soldier's uniform, "You carry a gun but you can't have a bullet in it," I say don't give him a gun at all . . . If the National Guard is going to be called out to stop anarchy, to suppress riots, you've got to treat them as soldiers.

> *Washington, Aug. 19 /*
> *Memphis Commercial Appeal, 8–20:5.*

J. Milton Patrick
National Commander, American Legion

If it becomes necessary to call out the National Guard, for God's sake let's keep bullets in their rifles.

> *Portland, Ore./Daily World, 8–29:5.*

Ronald Reagan
Governor of California

They (militants) want disruption. Their goal is to prove this system of ours, faced with crisis, will not work. If it takes a blood bath, let's get it over with. No more appeasement.

> *Plainview (Tex.) Daily Herald, 5–8:6.*

All these fiendish tactics—the bombings, the hijackings and the kidnapings—have one thing in common: They ruin the lives of helpless, innocent people who want nothing more than to live in harmony with their fellow men. It's truly a shame that in this society of hard-working progressive people, there are a few who lurk in the shadows waiting for a chance to return us to the jungle.

> *At Republican luncheon, Palo Alto, Calif.,*
> *Oct. 22 / Los Angeles Times, 10–23:(1)20.*

227

J.L. Robertson
Vice Chairman, Federal Reserve Board

If a society permits its young people to be taught, by one means or another, that it is exciting to rob banks and noble to blow them up, no one should be surprised if some of those young people decide to engage in those activities . . . There are some very respectable people, including some eminent jurists, who contend that a truly free society must permit the advocacy of anything and everything, no matter how repugnant it may be. (It is) an incredible theory, unsanctioned by history, untenable in logic and repudiated by experience, (that) freedom of speech is indeed an absolute, which should under no circumstances be subjected to any restraint.

Before National Association of Bank Women, Washington, Sept. 21/Washington Star, 9–22:B7.

Benjamin Spock
Physician, Author

Our country is already a police state. But the only people who realize this as yet are the groups that happen to have had personal experience in being repressed—black militants, anti-war demonstrators, student dissenters.

San Francisco Examiner & Chronicle (This World), 2–1:2.

Strom Thurmond
United States Senator, R-S.C.

Nothing encourages a riot mood more than the belief that authorities are powerless or too weak-willed to enforce order. Will we learn from the riots? Will we learn from Vietnam? Or will the war against the would-be American guerrillas also be a "no-win war"?

San Francisco Examiner & Chronicle (This World), 9–20:2.

George C. Wallace
Former Governor of Alabama

I think the police and National Guard ought to be used where acts of dissent get out of bounds and endanger the security of people on the street and endanger property. I know that some acts of dissent are only annoying and I don't think you should stop anyone from dissenting just because what they do or how they look annoys you. I think dissent should be stopped only when it turns to violence—and particularly when it endangers the internal security of our country . . . I think the average citizen, and particularly the middle class, are sick and tired of this. Unless some of our politicians catch on, some of them are going to be out of office.

Interview, Montgomery, Ala./ The Christian Science Monitor, 1–5:9.

Lynn White
Professor of History, University of California at Los Angeles

We live in a violent world. Violence fluctuates. I think it's fluctuating up at the present time, and I don't think this ought to be obscured. That would be folly. But taking the whole of history since antiquity, when we begin to know how people lived in some detail, I would say there is less violence today than in most past periods.

Interview, Los Angeles/ Los Angeles Times, 2–24:(1)17.

Edward Bennett Williams
Lawyer

I hate crime and violence of any kind. I love peace, order and law in that order. And I believe that peace is the tranquility of order, and without law there can be no order.

Before State Bar of California, Los Angeles/ Los Angeles Times, 9–27:G1.

Will R. Wilson
Assistant Attorney General, Criminal Division, Department of Justice of the United States

The use of terror as a political tactic is foreign to the American political tradition . . . We wish to emphasize that the suppression of terroristic tactics is not a repression of free speech or the right to dissent or the right to protest, but is punishment for crime; and that the prevention of crime through firm and decisive action followed by appropriate punishment is, has been and should continue to be the traditional response of the American political system to those who persist in violating the law.

Human Events, 10–10:14.

Robert P. Wolff
Professor of Law, Columbia University

No one, not even a citizen of a true democracy, has an obligation to obey the law.

New York, April 30/
The New York Times, 5–1:37.

Whitney M. Young, Jr.
Executive director, National Urban League

While acts of violence produce temporary fright and fear, and even some minimal programs, the over-all result has been far much more death and destruction for the victims of oppression, the mobilization of more effective means to suppress and the rise of a public attitude that develops and condones further vindictive, if not unconstitutional, measures of surveillance, apprehension and incarceration. A society which will kill its own, as we saw at Kent State (University), will not hesitate to kill those it regards as alien.

Before International Congress of African People, Atlanta, Sept. 5/The New York Times, 9–6:(1)40.

National Defense · The Military

Spiro T. Agnew
Vice President of the United States

A year ago last summer, in the midst of the debate about the ABM, the charge you kept hearing on television and seeing in headlines was this: "ABM will doom the SALT talks and ruin the chances for arms control." Well, now we have an ABM. And, largely because we do, the SALT talks show some specific progress toward arms control. Do you suppose you will hear one cheer from the professional pessimists? Not a chance. They will say—with a perfectly straight face —that as long as one bow and arrow exist in the world, we will have failed.

San Diego, Calif., Sept. 11/
Human Events, 10–31:12.

Carl Albert
United States Representative, D-Okla.

I think we're (Democrats) equally concerned, with the Republicans, that the United States never become a second-rate defense power. In the world in which we live, we can never downgrade the basic priority of our strength as against the top Communist powers. We all agree on this. That's hardly a party issue.

Interview, Washington/
U.S. News & World Report, 8–24:59.

Robert Anderson
President,
North American Rockwell Corporation

. . . despite the high priority we all place on national survival, the defense industry today is being subjected to incredible denunciation. The attack has a violence unparalleled in American history . . . so vehement have been the attacks, that many sincere people are troubled when they read of excessive profits, cost overruns, lack of government control over expenditures and so on . . . (But) can you imagine an automobile manufacturer contracting at a fixed price to deliver a model 1977 automobile six years from now? And an automobile, let me add, is infinitely less complicated than a modern weapons system . . . What is never captured in the blazing headlines of cost overruns is the reality of endless changes, of inflation, of the costly impact of solving problems which could not be foreseen. These are the realities which accompany the advancement of technological frontiers.

Before Commonwealth Club, San Francisco,
July 10/Vital Speeches, 8–15:655.

This country is in second place behind the Soviet Union in the development of new weapons systems. Let me repeat, *we are behind* the Russians at this moment . . . Continuation of that downward trend . . . is a direct threat to America's long-time confidence that it can meet any challenge in defense, in atomic energy or in space. What adds to the seriousness of this lagging research and development effort is the certainty that never again will we have the luxury of time to catch up if an enemy attacks. Never again will we have the nearly two years between the invasion of Belgium and the sinking of the *Lusitania*. Never again will we have a year and more between the Battle of Britain and the disaster of Pearl Harbor.

Before Commonwealth Club, San Francisco,
July 10/Vital Speeches, 8–15:656.

George C. S. Benson
Director, ROTC Affairs, Department of
Defense of the United States

I suppose some people, assuming that our military started the Vietnam war, have worked up their emotional objections to the Vietnam war to the point where they view our American military services as "destructive." It is a fair guess that the same people did not have the same reactions to our military services during World War II, and would not have similar reactions to some other conflicts in the future. I, personally, found the American Army to be a highly responsible instrument of national democratic desires in World War II. I have not seen any real evidence that the Vietnam war was a mistake forced on us by the military. It seems to me important that we judge our country's institutions on the basis of some mild degree of perspective, and not on the basis of our reaction to one war.

At Woodstock (Md.) Conference, March 7/
Vital Speeches, 6–15:544.

Omar N. Bradley
General, United States Army (Ret.)

I believe our greatest danger is still imperialist Communism and those Communist countries which wish to spread their domination throughout the world under the guise of Communist Utopia.

Before National Press Club, Washington/
Plainview (Tex.) Daily Herald, 3–15:10A.

William G. Bray
United States Representative, R-Ind.

We do not need to go back 20 centuries to realize the danger and evil that can result from allowing blind trust, stupidity and selfishness to wreck a civilization. It was less than 40 years ago that (Neville) Chamberlain tucked his umbrella under his arm and went to Munich to appease Hitler and give him what Chamberlain did not have to give: the freedom of Czechoslovakia. Many of us still remember the wild cheering that followed Chamberlain's proud announcement: "We have attained peace in our time" . . . Now, as then, we have the doom-shouters, who, at the top of their lungs, scream that we are drifting into a militaristic society and shriek incessantly of what this is doing to us

as individuals and to us as a nation . . . These shouters, like Chamberlain, seem to have forgotten that freedom and liberty are expensive luxuries; but their alternative—slavery—can be even more expensive.

Indianapolis, May/
Congressional Record, 7–14:E6669.

McGeorge Bundy
President, Ford Foundation; Former
Assistant to the President of the United
States for National Security Affairs

I believe there will not be much progress (at the SALT talks) until the United States is prepared to make a specific proposal. I think the odds are heavy that it will prove wise and right for us to move first . . . Soviet wariness is at least equal to our own. Our experience, understanding and present strength make it right for us to take the initiative.

The Christian Science Monitor, 4–16:1.

Vannevar Bush
Scientist; Honorary chairman,
Massachusetts Institute of Technology

I don't think this ABM thing makes sense, because I don't think the damned thing will work. We are on the verge of coming to an understanding with the Russians to tone down the whole thing, and I think they are ready to agree. So we ought to tone down our emphasis on anything of that sort.

Interview, Belmont, Mass., March 11/
The New York Times, 3–12:25.

James F. Calvert
Rear Admiral, United States Navy;
Superintendent, U.S. Naval Academy

If you allow military training to get downtrodden and produce only intellectuals, you have officers who can't work with enlisted men. But if you emphasize the production of officers to the exclusion of everything else, you'll end up with fine-looking, dedicated people who are a little vacant.

Time, 5–11:50.

Clifford P. Case
United States Senator, R-N.J.

Honest differences still exist even among the experts concerning the practicality and effect of a volunteer army. Not the least of these is the possible development of an officer military elite relatively isolated from the mainstream of American life, and enlisted ranks manned even more than they are now by the poor and underprivileged of America.

*Before the Senate, Washington, Aug. 25 /
The Dallas Times Herald, 8–25 :A6.*

John H. Chafee
Secretary of the Navy of the United States

. . . the abuse being given the serviceman today is undeserved and unfair and he should not be called upon to tolerate it. In fact, he won't and isn't. He's getting out of the armed services of his country in large numbers—to their great detriment.

*Before World Affairs Council, Los Angeles,
March 4 / Los Angeles Times, 3–5 :(1)3.*

Leonard F. Chapman, Jr.
Commandant, United States Marine Corps

If we are to eliminate the draft, cut defense spending and still hope to meet the increasing demands of the security of this country, then every American who wears a uniform must count full measure. Each individual must offer quality services, professional ability—and most of all, dedication.

*Before National Press Club, Washington /
Quote, 9–20 :266.*

Shirley Chisholm
United States Representative, D-N.Y.

Men are oppressed by requirements of the Selective Service Act . . . Each sex, I believe, should be liable when necessary to serve and defend this country.

*Before the House, Washington /
U.S. News & World Report, 8–24 :30.*

Barber B. Conable, Jr.
United States Representative, R-N.Y.

One of the stickiest problems with which Defense has to grapple is the problem of what to do with a "not-very-satisfactory" or "overly-expensive" end product of a five-or-six-year procurement contract. Do you chuck the whole thing, write it all off as a mistake, put the company—which probably is working on several other vital defense contracts—into bankruptcy by refusing to pay, and start the whole five-or-six-year process again from scratch, even though you need the weapons now, not five or six years from now? Or do you make the best of a bad deal someone else made five or six years ago, thus inviting the scorn of a vigilant press and the outrage of the taxpayers? If you have the answer to that one, please let Secretary (of Defense) Laird know. I am sure he will be grateful.

*Before the House, Washington /
Human Events, 9–12 :23.*

Robert J. Dole
United States Senator, R-Kan.

The time has come again when the Senate of the United States either gives the President the tools to bring peace and security, or denies them . . . If, as has been suggested by some, we cancel, delay or put in "escrow" funds for further ABM deployment in the hope that this will facilitate negotiations, (at SALT talks) we would be guilty of the sheerest folly. *Safeguard* (ABM) in escrow is the same as national security in escrow.

*Before the Senate, Washington, Aug. 10 /
Los Angeles Times, 8–10 :(1)7.*

Gilbert M. Fitzhugh
*Chairman, Metropolitan Life Insurance
Company; Chairman, Presidential
commission studying the Defense
Department*

It's (the Pentagon) just an amorphous lump, with nobody in charge of anything. There is nobody you can point your finger at if anything goes wrong, and there is nobody you can pin a medal on if it goes right, because everything is everybody's business. What is everybody's business is nobody's business.

*News conference, Washington, July 28 /
Time / 8–10 :8.*

John S. Foster, Jr.
Director, Defense Research and
Engineering, Department of Defense
of the United States

. . . surprising as it may seem to Americans—who are used to our technological superiority in defense—the U.S. will lose technological superiority to the Soviets in the next several years, if present trends continue. It's a struggle that largely goes on in secret, but already we can see some of the things to come in new top-quality Soviet weapons. Further, if this loss of leadership occurs in three to four years, we will face certainly an extremely expensive, perhaps an impossible, task if we choose to attempt to regain our leadership even by 1985 . . . We are used to being the nation that makes the leaps ahead in defense technology. In the future, the big surprises may well come from the other side.

Interview, Washington /
U.S. News & World Report, 11–30:24.

Roger A. Freeman
Senior fellow, Hoover Institution, Stanford
University; Former Special Assistant to the
President of the United States

The only meaningful way to measure our national defense is by the potential of the countries against which we may have to defend ourselves someday. By that yardstick, we fall woefully short . . . It is not widely known that much of the Vietnam operation was carried on by depleting the rest of our defense establishment of its best men and equipment. We are now left with a Swiss cheese defense . . .

At Hoover Institution seminar, Pasadena,
Calif., Nov. 8 / Los Angeles Times, 11–9:(2)1.

Our national priorities must be reordered in the decade ahead if the United States is to survive as a nation. The trend of shifting huge resources into so-called social welfare programs, at the expense of our military preparedness, which prevailed during the 1952-1971 period, must be reversed. We must review hundreds of domestic programs, com-

pare their output with their input, measure in each case the tangible return which our taxpayers receive on their huge investment and weed out or revise those with little or no return. We will inevitably make some mistakes, but such mistakes can be corrected —in domestic programs. We may have no chance for a second guess, get no opportunity for a second try, in national defense. If we miss the first time, if we are not adequately prepared against our opponents to begin with, we may never get a second chance. The two oceans which shielded us 'till World War II have long since been made ineffective by technological progress. If at first we don't succeed—we are through. Time is running out. If we do not act decisively now and in the decade ahead, we may be known in future history books as the generation that inherited America from its fathers and lost it because we were too shortsighted to preserve it for our children, too occupied with trivial day-to-day conveniences to assure the survival of free government in this world.

Los Angeles Times, 11–29:F7.

J. William Fulbright
United States Senator, D-Ark.

(Referring to Pentagon reports of a Russian submarine base under construction in Cuba): It happens every year at appropriations time. Last year it was the (Russian) SS-9 missiles. Now it's a submarine base. They (the Pentagon) are hoodwinking the American people, and they are using the press to do it.

Interview, Washington /
The Dallas Times Herald, 10–5:A1.

The military establishment runs the whole country.

Interview / Face the Nation,
Columbia Broadcasting System, Nov. 29.

Barry M. Goldwater
United States Senator, R-Ariz.

The committees headed by Senators (William) Proxmire and (J. William) Fulbright that continually complain about the cost of

(BARRY M. GOLDWATER)

staying even with our adversaries in the business of defense never get around to complaining about wastage of the tax payers' money in programs which bear the labels "health, education and welfare." It almost seems that to these groups the words "defense" or "military" are synonymous with evil and are legitimate prey for any kind of legislative reform or financial pruning, but that programs having a high-sounding purpose and listed under words like "welfare" or "education" or "anti-poverty" or "housing" are automatically so noble in their intent that they are above scrutiny by the searchers for waste and certainly above suspicion in the whole field of overfunding.

Waco (Tex.) News-Tribune, 1–27:A4.

I wish it were possible for me to join those members of Congress who want to cut the military budget to nothing because in their vague minds they see no threat from the Soviets or China. But I am old enough to have lived through this same thing before . . . We have an understandable desire—many Americans have an understandable desire—to be at peace. Lord knows, I do not want another war. One is enough. I do not want my grandchildren to have to suffer war, but neither do I want my children or grandchildren or the children of any American to be subjected to the dangerous, serious threat that our country was faced with in the late 1930s, when we knew we were going to have to go to war and we knew that we were not equipped. Thank God that in those days our weapons systems were such that the oceans that separated us allowed us time to build up an overwhelming Air Force, to build up an overwhelming Navy, to build and equip the best Army in the world, to build and equip the best Marines and Coast Guard that we have ever had . . . it is a different situation in the 1970s. We punch a button and in 15 minutes one of the largest countries in the world disappears. They punch a button and in 15 minutes the United States of America

is practically destroyed. What is going to prevent this from happening? I hate to say this because I know it shakes people, it hurts people, it makes them mad. They call me a "hawk" and warmonger and all that. But I suggest that we have not had a nuclear war because of the threat of the massive deterrent ability that we have maintained throughout the years, which the Soviet Union is now in the process of exceeding.

Before the Senate, Washington/
Los Angeles Times, 8–30:F7.

Charles E. Goodell
United States Senator, R-N.Y.

Expressions of personal political beliefs are clearly beyond the proper reach of military discipline. Political freedoms do not end when a person dons a uniform.

Washington/The Dallas Times Herald,
8–10:A5.

George A. Goodling
United States Representative, R-Pa.

It should be recognized that the ABM system is not offensive, but defensive, in nature. It is not devised to generate an arms race, but, instead, to prevent one. In effect, it is an insurance policy guarding against hazard, and, like an individual's insurance policy, one is not happy about meeting the premium payments, but he is pleased to have the policy if he is confronted by a hazard. Put another way, if we fund an ABM system and we find we do not need it, we will lose some money. However, if we do not fund such a system and we find we need it, we will lose a country . . .

Human Events, 11–28:23.

Robert P. Griffin
United States Senator, R-Mich.

It is inconceivable to me how any Senator would now vote to weaken our position at the SALT talks by indicating a lack of confidence in our most important bargaining point (*Safeguard* ABM), especially since that bargaining point is stronger now than it was a year ago. I do not know how the SALT talks will ultimately come out. Perhaps the talks will fail. I do know one thing: If this amendment (Cooper-Hart amendment limiting *Safeguard* deployment) should carry, and if the SALT talks should thereafter collapse, I would not want to be in the position of those who will vote today against the President of the United States.

Nashville Tennessean, 8–23:A6.

W. Averell Harriman
Former United States Ambassador-at-Large

The question is no longer between guns and butter. The question today is between bigger guns and the internal health of our country.

Plainview (Tex.) Daily Herald, 2–25:6.

Philip A. Hart
United States Senator, D-Mich.

History does not indicate that the policy of "arming to disarm" holds much promise. To the contrary, the arms limitation agreements we have reached with the Soviet Union have been preceded by the absence of such a policy . . . (In the Cooper-Hart amendment) we leave the President with a formidable bargaining chip he says he needs—the (ABM) sites at Grand Forks and Malmstrom —but we make clear to the world that we are not anxious to escalate the arms race . . . To those who fear that an expression of a desire to end the arms race might be interpreted as a sign of weakness, I say that Moscow knows the big bargaining chip is not found in partial deployment of (an ABM) system of doubtful reliability, but is found in the uncontested authorization request for research and development on a more effective defensive system and in the awareness that if SALT fails, such a system will undoubtedly be installed. Those who contend that deployment of *Safeguard* (ABM) as proposed by the Senate Armed Services Committee is not provocative cannot have it both ways. Either *Safeguard* is provocative and a bargaining chip, or it is not pro-

vocative and is not a bargaining chip. If *Safeguard* is not provocative, even supporters of phase II of *Safeguard* must admit that the argument that phase II is needed as a bargaining chip does not hold water. If *Safeguard* is provocative, then supporters of phase II must admit deployment threatens to escalate the arms race, and must weigh that danger against what history tells about the value of arming to disarm.

Before the Senate, Washington/ The Washington Post, 8–12:A14.

Mark O. Hatfield
United States Senator, R-Ore.

It is ironic that so unjust and inequitable an institution as peacetime conscription, with all of its inefficiencies, should be maintained by unproven assumptions, groundless fears and the mere momentum of the past 20 years . . . In June of 1971, the Selective Service Act will expire. If we act now and begin the process of building a voluntary military force, it will not be necessary to perpetuate conscription beyond that time.

Washington, July 7/ Los Angeles Times, 7–8:(1)6.

Warren E. Hearnes
Governor of Missouri

Our fellow citizens still believe in using a draft system to raise manpower for national defense. They still believe we must oppose Communism in Asia and elsewhere. No longer, however, do they believe we should have a draft that is full of loopholes. No longer do they believe our soldiers should be asked to fight a war where there is no permission for victory and no hope for negotiation. This is not a minority struggle, nor the private fight of one generation. This is a growing awareness among all Americans that our past mistakes must be corrected, not continued. If the leaders who can change these policies do not do so, then the people will change the leaders.

At William Jewell College, Liberty, Mo., Feb. 19/Vital Speeches, 3–15:338.

Henry M. Jackson
United States Senator, D-Wash.

As I see it, a convincing active defense of our deterrent says this to the Soviets: "We intend to keep our second-strike capability; we do not intend to allow you to acquire a first-strike capability. If you want to keep on building SS-9s, that's your business. But for every additional SS-9 that you buy, we are prepared to offset it." *Safeguard* (ABM), as a responsive and dynamic program, can say precisely that to Moscow.

Before the Senate, Washington/
Human Events, 8–15:3.

Donald E. Johnson
Administrator of Veterans Affairs, Veterans Administration of the United States

I have no basis on which to challenge the motives of these (Senators)—the Hatfields, the Goodells, the McGoverns, the Muskies, the Fulbrights and others—but I do challenge their reasoning . . . it is no longer enough to debate the merits of this great issue (the Hatfield-McGovern amendment) on the floor of the Senate. Now the Hatfields and the McGoverns and 22 of their fellow "doves" have become salesmen of surrender, selling the "sell-out" like some sell used cars or potato chips . . . But let me warn you, win or lose, Hatfield and McGovern and their allies will not stop with merely seeking surrender in Vietnam. They are already working diligently to make the United States incapable of defending its allies or itself.

Before Disabled American Veterans,
Los Angeles, July 28/
Los Angeles Herald-Examiner, 7–28:A2.

Edward M. Kennedy
United States Senator, D-Mass.

By insisting on immediate deployment of *Safeguard* (ABM) and MIRV, the administration is undermining the SALT talks. The United States has an obligation to follow a reasonable arms policy, whether SALT succeeds or not. The ABM is an unnecessary and unworkable system no matter what happens in Vienna. And MIRV is equally un-

necessary until we see that the Soviet Union has in fact embarked on a full scale ABM program.

At Massachusetts Institute of Technology,
May 15/The Washington Post, 5–16:A21.

We are in no danger of becoming a second-rank nuclear power. So we should not be panicked into accepting *Safeguard* (ABM).

Before the Senate, Washington, July 30/
Memphis Commercial Appeal, 7–31:9.

. . . given present technology, there can be no ABM defense to a Soviet missile attack which is successful in the long run. If the radar works and the missiles fire and the warheads destroy the incoming missiles high above the atmosphere—all highly questionable suppositions—the radioactivity released will kill a large portion of our population within a generation.

Before the Senate, Washington, July 30/
The Dallas Times Herald, 7–31:A10.

The United States already has ample bargaining chips (for the SALT talks) in unquestioned capacity to continue and even accelerate the arms race. It's this capacity which the Russians are concerned with, not an unbuilt ABM system of dubious efficacy.

Nashville Tennessean, 8–23:A6.

(Arguing against an all-volunteer Army): It is unwise to insulate from the horrors of war middle- and upper-class Americans who might lead the protest against senseless foreign adventures . . . I frankly might question, for example, whether the current pressures for de-escalation of the Indochina war would be as great if young men from every social background were not threatened with service in that war.

Washington, Aug. 25/
The Dallas Times Herald, 8–26:A14.

Robert Kilmarx
Member, senior staff, Center for Strategic & International Studies, Georgetown University

An address on the need for antiballistic

missiles and multiple independently targetable re-entry vehicles on ICBMs these days is often an invitation to risk the charge of socio-political irrelevance and insensitivity to higher imperatives. Advocates of new weapons systems are often assumed to be cursed by parochial concerns about the "quality of death," technological arrogance and strategic myopia. Seldom has the wrong debate on the wrong issues been held so long, as in this case. It has a life of its own—impervious to reason. It is perhaps a symbol of some form of leadership decay. For this is the age of the facile solution as well as Aquarius.

At Georgetown University Alumni Seminar,
Washington, June 12/
Vital Speeches, 7–15:602.

Foy D. Kohler
Former United States Ambassador
to the Soviet Union

I personally want to stress, as a result of my long experience in dealing with the Russians, my opinion that—far from deterring the SALT talks—our American decision to go ahead with the *Safeguard* (ABM) system will enhance the prospects for a meaningful agreement. We saw striking evidence of this last fall, when Moscow agreed to initiation of the SALT talks in Helsinki only after Congress approved the first phase of the President's *Safeguard* proposals.

Washington, June 24.

Melvin R. Laird
Secretary of Defense of the United States

We are moving toward smaller and more efficient military forces. Assisted both by the diminution of our role in Vietnam and by management reforms, we can provide the security which the nation requires with a trimmer defense establishment.

The New York Times, 2–4:14.

It is clear that the Soviet Union is embarked on an ambitious program to achieve a global military capability. The Soviets are continuing the rapid deployment of major strategic offensive weapons systems at a rate that could, by the mid 1970s, place us in a second-rate strategic position with regard to the future security of the free world.

Before joint session of Senate Armed
Services and Appropriations Committees,
Washington, Feb. 20/
Los Angeles Herald-Examiner, 2–20:A1.

We know that the (Communist) Chinese have the capability of testing an ICBM in the immediate future and that they are likely to have an operational capability in the next several years. A measured and orderly deployment of *Safeguard* ABM, taking only the minimum steps necessary to preserve our ability to meet the threat as it evolves, is both the most prudent and most economical course we can pursue.

The Christian Science Monitor, 2–25:5.

I read sometimes that I have created this sort of thing (Soviet threat) in order to have smoother sailing (on appropriations for *Safeguard* ABM) in Congress. This is something the Soviet Union has created. I haven't created it. I have been at the lower side of the estimates all the way through this business.

Washington, March 19/
The Washington Post, 3–20:A8.

It is the momentum of their (the Russians' military) program that concerns me, because if they keep this momentum going, they will be in a position where they will have a superior force and we will have a second-rate force. This concerns me because a decision to build new strategic weapons takes from five to seven years to implement . . . We have been delaying some tough, hard decisions on whether to go ahead with new strategic offensive systems because of the strategic arms limitation talks between the Russians and us. If we do not meet with some success in SALT, and if the Soviet Union keeps its momentum going, we are going to have to face up to going forward with new systems, new strategic weaponry. I would say

(MELVIN R. LAIRD)

we have, perhaps, from 12 to 18 months at the outside to begin the major offsetting actions that would be required in the face of that solution.

Interview, Washington/
U.S. News & World Report, 5–11:68.

There are a lot of people, I think, who are sincerely convinced that the only way to succeed in negotiations with the Soviet Union is for the United States to take unilateral action and halt the programs that are going forward at the present time. I am not convinced that this is the way to succeed. I think that any actions we take should be taken around the negotiating table and not on a unilateral basis. I think history has shown that, as far as negotiating with the Soviet Union is concerned, it is not the best course for us to negotiate from a position where they have all the cards in front of them and our negotiators are sitting in front of a bare table.

Interview, Washington/
U.S. News & World Report, 5–11:71.

Contrary to what some people may think in this country—and I'm afraid we haven't gotten the story across as well as we should—the United States is not and has not been escalating the arms race. Since 1965, in every major decision that has been made in this area, no one can accuse the United States of escalating the arms race. In fact, this Administration has tried to de-escalate. We've made our position clear that we're going to give every opportunity for the Vienna (arms limitation) talks to be successful. The time schedule is being established not by the United States but by the Soviet Union. And time is running out.

Interview, Washington/
U.S. News & World Report, 5–11:71.

Ralph E. Lapp
Physicist

We always react to a new threat in a stupid, panicky way. Look at that crazy radar system the Russians erected around Moscow. It was an easy target for us, almost like hitting the Houston Astrodome on a clear day. You could knock it out with one Hiroshima bomb a mile away. And yet, in response to that, we put multiple warheads on our *Minuteman* and *Poseidon* missiles, and the result is that we now have 6,500 warheads when all we needed was one.

Interview, Washington/
Los Angeles Herald-Examiner, 8–16:C3.

Lyman L. Lemnitzer
General, United States Army (Ret.); Former Supreme Allied Commander-Europe

These days it seems that no one has anything but bad to say about the military services. Moreover, resources allocated to military security are cut beyond what many objective, knowledgeable and thoughtful men believe prudent. Proposals for maintaining military effectiveness are too often opposed—not on logical grounds concerning whether or not they are needed, but emotionally, as a reflex action stemming from an unreasoning dislike of anything military just because it *is* military.

At U.S. Army War College commencement,
Carlisle Barracks, Pa., June 15/
Vital Speeches, 8–15:670.

Louis B. Lundborg
Chairman, Bank of America

Because many who have condemned our involvement in Vietnam have also wanted to abolish such things as ROTC, and because, consequently, many people have come to equate anti-Vietnam with military weakness, let me say that it is precisely because I want us to be strong—militarily as well as economically, politically, diplomatically—that I do not want to see us dissipate and squander that strength in such misguided ventures as this Vietnam war. I want us to have military strength. I just don't want the use of it to be dictated entirely by the military. The revulsion against our posture in Vietnam has been so strong that it has colored and distorted the attitude of our people, and particularly of our young people, toward military service of any kind. It is easy—too easy—to dismiss that as an indictment of our young people—as an evidence of the "weakness of their moral fiber." It is sufficiently more complex than that, that I would not want to be equally guilty of over-simplifying in the opposite direction. But certainly the disillusionment of our young over our whole Vietnam experience *has* weakened their willingness to follow adult leadership in *anything*. I shudder to think of our being confronted by a real military threat—a direct and immediate one—to our own national security while our youth are in this mood.

Before Senate Foreign Relations Committee, Washington/The Wall Street Journal, 4–24:12.

Mike Mansfield
United States Senator, D-Mont.

We are not going to achieve the kind of security that many people think we have just by spending billions and billions of dollars in stationing troops overseas, or in building missiles, if, at the same time, we allow our domestic difficulties to go to pot. It is not a case of priorities, one over the other. It is a case of balance between the security of this nation on the one hand, and the security of its people, internally and domestically, on the other.

Before the Senate, Washington, Feb. 20/ Congressional Record, 2–20:S2060.

I'm not keen on U.S. troops being stationed anywhere outside the United States.

Washington, Aug. 27/ Los Angeles Times, 8–28:(1)7.

John S. McCain, Jr.
Admiral, United States Navy; Commander-in-Chief, Pacific Command

Three times we have not only sheathed but thrown away our sword when the fighting stopped. We did this after World War I; we did it again after World War II; and to a large extent after the Korean War. Each time we were called upon to rearm under crisis conditions because we had let slip through our fingers the great deterrent force of "presence." I trust that we have learned our lesson.

Interview/Congressional Record, 2–5:E710.

John W. McCormack
United States Representative, D-Mass.

If there's one real message I'd like to leave it is about national defense. After Pearl Harbor, we could recover and build up our industrial, manpower and military resources after the fact. We no longer can do that now. We've got to be prepared before the fact. As of this time, I believe we are still prepared. If I were going to err in judgment where national defense is involved, I prefer to err on the side of strength rather than weakness. International Communism is still bent on world domination.

Interview, Washington/ Los Angeles Times, 11–16:(1)6.

George S. McGovern
United States Senator, D-S.D.

What are we to say of the priorities of the Nixon Administration when this week it tells us that it will veto the education bill because it is inflationary, but it warns Congress to hurry up and expand the ABM because, presumably, that is *not* inflationary. This is not only economic nonsense, it is a twisted sense of priorities.

Before Democratic Advisory Council Committee on National Priorities, Washington, Feb. 25/ The New York Times, 2–26:14.

Dean E. McHenry
Chancellor, University of California at Santa Cruz

The draft has become an abomination. For 30 years it has rested like a yoke on the necks of generations of young men. Sometimes it seems to me a grotesque credit card, to which diplomatic failures and military ventures may be charged. And the bill is paid by our able-bodied male youth aged 18 to 26.

Plainview (Tex.) Daily Herald, 6–29:4.

Gerald E. Mille
Rear Admiral, United States Navy;
Assistant Deputy Chief of
Naval Operations-Air

To control the oceans of the world, you have to cover them with air power. To do that, you've got to have aircraft carriers. Because we haven't been challenged on the seas for so many years, people have forgotten why we built aircraft carriers in the first place. We built them to sink other ships. Now there's another navy on the waters again (Soviet Navy). You can't handle them with land-based aircraft alone; you can't reach out far enough. The aircraft carrier is the one thing we've got that gives us the edge.

Interview/The New York Times, 8–22:4.

Thomas H. Moorer
Admiral, United States Navy;
Chairman-designate, Joint Chiefs of Staff

I don't think you will find a total atheist who has reached the peak of leadership in the armed forces.

Time, 5–11:49.

Under the U.S. Constitution we have civilian control of our military forces, and, consequently, decisions are made by the civilian leaders in the Executive and Legislative branches of our government. Speaking for myself and the other members of the Joint Chiefs of Staff, we fully support this concept which is inherent in a democracy. We wouldn't have it any other way.

Interview/Family Weekly, 7–26:5.

Richard M. Nixon
President of the United States

Those who would ask us to declare a unilateral moratorium on MIRV and ABM would concede to the Soviets the position of supremacy in military power on the globe . . . If present trends continue, the United States a very few years hence will find itself clearly in second position—with the Soviet Union indisputably the greatest military power on earth . . . The minute the word goes out . . . that the Soviet Union is the first power in the world, the eyes of Europe and Asia will no longer look to the United States but to Moscow. The American position in Europe and the Far East will crumble overnight.

Washington, April 23/
Los Angeles Times, 4–28:(2)7.

We have certainly no intention of disarming. What we are talking about in the SALT negotiations is not disarmament, but a limitation of arms—where we limit what we do and they limit what they do . . . Now, we can either continue this race, in which they continue their offensive missiles and we go forward with our defensive missiles, or we can reach an agreement. That is why, at this point, we have hopes of attempting to find—either on a comprehensive basis or, lacking a comprehensive basis, a selective basis—the first steps toward which the superpowers will limit the development of, and particularly the deployment of, more instruments of destruction when both have enough to destroy each other many times over.

News conference, Los Angeles, July 30/
U.S. News & World Report, 8–10:33.

David Packard
Deputy Secretary of Defense
of the United States

It is obviously necessary for our nation to have a strong defense industrial base. There has been a lot of talk about the "military-industrial complex" and a lot of criticism of it. I think we ought to remind ourselves that it wasn't too long ago that this industry was considered the "arsenal of democracy." Certainly we cannot have a strong defense capability without the support of a strong industry.

Interview, Washington/
U.S. News & World Report, 8–3:47.

We should buy only what we need—not systems you or anyone else thinks they can develop to do something that doesn't need to be done. The Defense Department has been led down the garden path for years on sophisticated systems that you promised would do all kinds of things for some optimistic cost. Too frequently we have been wrong in listening to you, and more frequently you have been unable to deliver on either of these promises—what it would do or what it would cost . . . We share the blame together. But the mistakes of the past cannot be repeated if we are to provide for the nation's defenses in today's climate of a critical public and a critical Congress. We are going to buy only things that we need, and we are going to make sure they work before we buy.

Before aerospace executives,
Los Angeles, Aug. 20/
The Washington Post, 8–21:A8.

William Proxmire
United States Senator, D-Wis.

We and the Soviet Union have enough to blow up the world many times over. Why do we need more (arms) to match each other in un-needed and excess capacity? We must re-order our priorities and reduce the excessive claims of our military . . .

Before the Senate, Washington, July 24/
The Dallas Times Herald, 7–25:A1.

If the initial planning estimate (for new weapons systems) is indeed nothing more than a guess, then I am happy to know this fact . . . It is incredible, and I can think of nothing more simplistic, for the United States Senate to accept guesswork when it comes to the cost implications of new weapons systems. That is the way we have been authorizing new weapons systems, and, once we authorize several million dollars, we are told that we do not want to waste that and that we had better authorize more or everything we have already spent will be gone. Perhaps, in the future, all planning estimates of the Department of Defense should be clearly labeled as "guesses." The difficulty, of course, with the guesswork thesis is that initial planning estimates are very often

presented . . . to get a program started with public funds, and frequently this means underestimating its future costs.

Before the Senate, Washington/
Washington Star, 8–8:A5.

(Regarding the Defense Department sharing with Lockheed Aircraft Corp. the loss on the C5 transport plane): Deputy Secretary of Defense David Packard has the dubious distinction of being midwife to one of the strangest offspring yet to be seen in the military industrial complex: the loss-plus contract . . . (The) only justification I can see for letting Lockheed off the hook on the C5, as well as the other contracts in dispute, is the determination that the military contract system has completely collapsed.

Washington, Dec. 31/
Los Angeles Herald-Examiner, 12–31:C6.

Hyman G. Rickover
Vice Admiral, United States Navy; Director,
Division of Naval Reactors, Atomic Energy
Commission of the United States

The Soviets are capable of starting tomorrow one of the biggest wars there has ever been—and I am frankly not confident the outcome would be in our favor.

Before Joint Congressional Committee
on Atomic Energy, March/
Los Angeles Times, 7–27:(1)6.

Classify the Pentagon people A, B and C. A does the work. B and C are given offices without secretaries, messengers, desks, rugs, telephones, typewriters or water pitchers. They do get scratch pads on which to write letters to each other in longhand. The letters would be dropped in dummy mail boxes and there would be no collection. The only writing instrument they could use would be crayons—if they had a sharp object, they might harm themselves. They could show up for work and leave any time they desired. Vacations would be unlimited. Their checks would be mailed to their homes. Why do you think this is so funny? You have all kinds of people in the Defense Department who are making work for the very few who are engaged in and capable of doing work.

Before House Appropriations Subcommittee,
Washington, May 13 /
The Dallas Times Herald, 8–16:A7.

If history teaches anything it is surely that weakness invites attack. This nation has no future if it allows itself to be outmatched militarily.

Charleston, W.Va./Human Events, 5–23:7.

Last year, I told this Committee that the Soviets would be up to us in nuclear submarines by the end of 1970. On the basis of what they are doing today, I was probably conservative . . . If we knew the precise status of all their submarines, we might find that they are ahead of us right now . . . They now have the largest and most modern submarine yards in the world . . . The lead in nuclear submarines we have so long enjoyed has just about disappeared.

Before Joint Congressional Committee
on Atomic Energy, Washington /
U.S. News & World Report, 8–17:21.

If we are weak and have inferior weapons, we will have war. But if we are strong, there will be no war.

San Francisco Examiner, 11–26:82.

L. Mendel Rivers
United States Representative, D-S.C.

The idea of preparing ourselves to defend against any military threat has acheived a state of incredible unpopularity. I expect that unpopularity to continue into the 1970s and the constant attack on military budget and organization to continue.

At Claremont (Calif.) Men's College,
April 23 / Los Angeles Times, 4–24:(2)8.

Never before in the 30 years of my membership in this body have I stepped into the well of this house with greater concern for the future of this nation. My critics, who are legion, will attempt to dismiss what I say today by categorizing them as the shrill cries of a hawk who is suffering the agonies of reduced defense expenditures . . . We seem to be hell-bent on national suicide. While we debate the question of maintaining our military capability, the Soviet Union quietly but openly forges ahead . . . (The Soviet Union) is inexorably pushing us out of the Mediterranean, is firmly entrenched in the Indian Ocean and is now established in the Caribbean.

Before the House, Washington, Sept. 28 /
The New York Times, 9–29:3.

Richard B. Russell
United States Senator, D-Ga.

If we continue this unilateral disarmament, Russia will not give us an agreement that will protect our vital interests. We must negotiate from strength to permit us to disarm with safety.

Washington, Feb. 3 /
Los Angeles Herald-Examiner, 2–3:A4.

Hugh Scott
United States Senator, R-Pa.

Congress has a unique opportunity to demonstrate its sensitivity to one of the greatest, most legitimate gripes of our young. The draft is antiquated, unacceptable, inequitable and basically unworkable, no matter how streamlined a lottery system we develop.

Before the Senate, Washington, July 24 /
Los Angeles Times, 7–25:(1)3.

Robert C. Seamans, Jr.
Secretary of the Air Force
of the United States

Our armed forces will be what our people want them to be. We need military men who are both effective in battle and good managers in time of peace. They must have a clear understanding of public policy and be wise in the handling of human problems. If we are going to continue to find military men of this caliber, we are going to have to show that we really want them . . . The men we need are some of the best young men in our society, men who could choose other fine, rewarding careers in civilian life. And since they—like their countrymen past and present—find no pleasure in warfare, there must be other compelling reasons for them to spend their lives in the armed forces of their country. Of course, they have the knowledge that, by preparing for defense, they are making war less likely; but this will mean something only if the public also appreciates the importance of that task and takes pains to show its appreciation.

Before World Affairs Council of
Orange County, Los Angeles, Nov. 20/
Vital Speeches, 12–15:135.

Howard K. Smith
News commentator,
American Broadcasting Company

Some (newsmen) have gone overboard in a wish to believe that our opponent (the Soviet Union) has exclusively peaceful aims and that there is no need for armaments and national security. The danger of Russian aggression is unreal to many of them, although some have begun to rethink since the invasion of Czechoslovakia. But there is a kind of basic bias in the left wing soul that gives the Russians the benefit of the doubt.

Interview, Washington/TV Guide, 2–28:10.

Theodore C. Sorensen
Former Special Counsel to the
President of the United States

If taxation without representation was tyranny, then conscription without representation is slavery.

At Senate hearing on lowering voting
age to 18, Washington/
Plainview (Tex.) Daily Herald, 3–6:6.

James Stewart
Actor

The whole attitude toward the military concerns me very much. There are forces today—and where they come from I don't know, probably both from within and without—that are trying to soil the image of the military. This is a very dangerous thing. I spent 27 years in the military and it meant a great deal to me in life. I know the principles and standards I learned made me a better civilian. It's disturbing to see these forces try to discredit the military and send it back into isolation like it was after World War I. I think the structure and base of the military contains some of the finest people in the country today—our professional military men.

Interview, New York/
The New York Times, 2–22:(2)5.

Carl B. Stokes
Mayor of Cleveland

The best source to look for the money so badly needed by the cities is this unjustifiable defense spending. These are tax dollars of the American people being spent without rationale, without consent of Congress and contrary to any sense of morality.

News conference, Denver, June 13/
San Francisco Examiner & Chronicle,
6–14:A18.

Stuart Symington
United States Senator, D-Mo.

With respect to sea power . . . either the Soviet Union is making a serious mistake with its plans (by concentrating on building nuclear submarines), or we are making a comparable mistake in ours (by concentrating on nuclear aircraft carriers). If the Soviets are right, we have made another multibillion-dollar mistake in weaponry; and in this case one which could have an important bearing on our future.

Before Junior Chamber of Commerce,
Florrisant, Mo., July 4/
The Washington Post, 7–5:A18.

Curtis W. Tarr
Director, Selective Service System
of the United States

Implicit in the President's executive order ending job and dependent deferments is the understanding that, from now on, we are not going to channel people into these things; and that, if they go, it is from their own free

(CURTIS W. TARR)

choice. This is an important change in the policy of Selective Service. And I subscribe to it entirely.

Interview, Washington/
U.S. News & World Report, 7–6:49.

We hope that Selective Service can operate so closely in conjunction with the armed-forces recruiters that we will both move toward the same goal: a volunteer force. Obviously, if recruitment goes up, draft calls go down—and everyone is happier. As far as my own future is concerned, I wouldn't be the least bit upset about working myself out of a job or reducing the size of Selective Service.

Interview, Washington/
U.S. News & World Report, 7–6:51.

I have always said that I would rather send a volunteer than a conscriptee (into war zones). But I believe we never will be able to fight a war with an all-volunteer force, and we in the Selective Service are making all our plans on the basis of a stand-by draft.

Saigon, South Vietnam, Dec. 12/
Los Angeles Times, 12–12:(1)23.

Edward Teller
Physicist

The Russians are superior to us today in nuclear weapons and are moving ahead of us. We can do nothing to stop them because our assembly lines for nuclear weapons and the appropriate means of delivering them are not working.

Quote, 3–15:241.

John G. Tower
United States Senator, R-Tex.

If America becomes second-rate militarily, we shall become second-rate economically . . . I have been called a "hawk," "saber rattler" and everything possible by *The New York Times* and other Eastern newspapers, but I know and you know that diplomacy alone never moved the Russians out of any place . . . National security is the top priority now; because, without it, we cannot enjoy the good life we all seek with any security.

At Republican fund-raising dinner,
Beaumont, Tex., Sept. 29/
The Dallas Times Herald, 9–30:A8.

We seek a generation of peace. But a generation of peace, if it comes, will come on (Russia's) terms if we don't look to the maintenance of a military posture superior, or at least at a parity, with the Soviet Union.

Before Retired Officers Association,
San Antonio, Nov. 19/
The Dallas Times Herald, 11–20:A14.

Joe D. Waggonner, Jr.
United States Representative, D-La.

The final measure of our ability to survive in a hostile world will not be based on how well we managed our domestic resources or how lavishly we have engineered programs of social reform, but how resolutely we have met and neutralized the threat of the Communist world. If we fail here, all else is meaningless. If we do not maintain a level of military capability that cannot be misread by the Kremlin, if our intent to survive and see that other free nations of the world survive is not above question, we will have created an atmosphere in which the Soviet Union will be tempted into action which could result in a nuclear holocaust. The issue before us is not involving the relative allocation of priorities in spending between defense and domestic programs. The issue is the fundamental question of our national survival. My convictions dictate to me that the first law of nature is survival, not social reform.

Human Events, 11–7:15.

Thomas J. Watson, Jr.
Chairman, International Business Machines

. . . our call to stop Communism anywhere —despite the price—drifted us into an unattainable goal in Vietnam . . . we pursued the Vietnam goal to a costly point. The lives of 40,000 of our men have been lost, vast resources have been wasted and the morale of our youth is eroded. Are we still aiming at eliminating Communism? Well, we'd better think again. It's a comfortable thought to believe that we can indeed make ourselves relatively safe and the Soviet Union unsafe with anti-missile missiles and so forth . . . Our efforts might leave 50 million survivors here at home instead of 25 when the holocaust is over, while we kill two-thirds of the Russians instead of only one-half . . . If we set our national goals on this basis, we'll be following an impossible path . . . one goal we should have in our minds for the 1970s is a more relaxed attitude, a detente . . . The most important national priority is first reaching some kind of arrangement with the Soviets. A lot is riding on those negotiations that began in Helsinki. If they fail, the 1970s will tend to be a replay of the '60s, with defense absorbing a goodly share of the new resources we generate.

Before Bond Club, New York/
Daily World, 3–17:6.

William C. Westmoreland
General and Chief of Staff,
United States Army

. . . the dissent that focuses on the military and its most visible presence on campus—ROTC—particularly disturbs me. Those who would separate the military from the educational institution cry that the study of war is the antithesis of all that the university stands for. Yet a tragic fact of life is that war is the paramount social problem of mankind. Accordingly, the study of conflict belongs on the campus—for we look to the academic community for unemotional, logical argument . . . for rational solutions to all societal problems. And yet I never cease to be amazed by those who all too often in discussions concerning the military become emotionally overwhelmed, and logic becomes illogic; rationality, irrationality . . . and argument, bombast. ROTC must continue on campus. Just as any organization seeks the college graduate, so also does the military . . . Our overriding concern should

be that our soldiers must be led by the very best. And if we cannot obtain the best from the campuses of America, where do we as a nation turn for quality leadership in the quantity we require in our armed forces?

At Lincoln Academy of Illinois,
Springfield, Jan. 31/Vital Speeches, 3–1:300.

The young men who are and will become our soldiers and junior officers have attitudes that differ from those of our older group of officers and noncommissioned officers. To ignore the social mores of this younger group is to blind ourselves to reality. Their values and attitudes need not necessarily be endorsed by Army leadership . . . yet we must recognize that they do exist. We must make service life better understood by those who fill our ranks. We will leave no stone unturned. We are willing to part from past practices where such practices no longer serve a productive and useful end. We are reviewing all our policies and administrative procedures . . . Nothing is considered sacrosanct, except where military order and discipline . . . the soul of the Army that insures success on the battlefield . . . are jeopardized. In this, we cannot and will not yield.

Before Association of the United States Army,
Washington, Oct. 30/Vital Speeches, 12–1:100.

I have committed the Army to an all-out effort in working toward a zero draft, volunteer force. We in the Army appreciate that movement toward this goal will take time. We believe that continuation of Selective Service beyond its expiration date of June 30, 1971, is essential to guarantee that our nation's defenses are not jeopardized. And most important, even though we reach a zero draft, Selective Service legislation should remain in force as national insurance.

At Veterans Day dinner,
Indianapolis, Nov. 10/
The New York Times, 11–12:31.

If attacks against the ROTC continue on campuses across the nation, if military service is increasingly looked on with disdain, if

(WILLIAM C. WESTMORELAND)

confidence in the armed forces wanes . . . in such an atmosphere, a voluntary military force is inconceivable.

At Veterans Day dinner,
Indianapolis, Nov. 10 / Daily World, 11–13:4.

G. H. Weyerhaeuser
President, Weyerhaeuser Company

The role of the military in contemporary society has often been misunderstood or misinterpreted. It is not, as the New Left would have it, a sort of Mafioso bodyguard, established to protect American economic interests abroad. Nor is it, as some of the Far Right would picture it, a sort of old-style western sheriff, which should be intent upon imposing the proper American life-styles or economic systems upon an errant world. Someone in Parliament recently summed up the Western military role in Europe pretty well. He said, in effect, that NATO never had as its intent the creation of Heaven on earth. Its role, he said, was instead the preventing of the occurrence of the opposite condition—an earthly hell.

Before Association of the United States
Army, Fort Lewis, Wash., Jan. 29 /
Vital Speeches, 3–1:312.

Earle G. Wheeler
General, United States Army;
Chairman, Joint Chiefs of Staff

. . . this hostility toward the American military—toward the so-called military-industrial complex—has reached such a stage that military people are debarred from going on some campuses for the purpose of recruiting young men for military service. We find that some colleges are refusing to engage in defense-research projects. This is to the detriment, I believe, not only of the scientific community, but certainly to the detriment of the security of the United States. This hostile atmosphere, which I fervently hope is a passing phase, causes young men to be reluctant to engage in military careers. I do not think this is good for the United States. I know it's not good for the American military.

Interview, Washington /
U.S. News & World Report, 4–20:34.

. . . I personally have yet to be convinced that you can stop the advance of science. In other words, what you're really talking about when you say, "We'll ban MIRV," is trying to ban scientific advance. It can't be done. Ever since the first prehistoric scientist devised the bow and arrow, military men have been trying to cope with the things the scientific community has come up with.

Interview, Washington /
U.S. News & World Report, 4–20:37.

Stephen M. Young
United States Senator, D-Ohio

The facts are, the past decade of armament development consumed more money and came up with fewer effective weapons than in any time in our nation's history.

Quote, 11–22:486.

Politics

Spiro T. Agnew
Vice President of the United States

Already they (Democrats) are carping that the mess (in the U.S.) hasn't been cleared up in a year. It's pretty hard to clean the floor when muddy-footed opposition congressmen keep tracking through the kitchen, looking for the cookie jar.

Lincoln, Neb., Feb. 9 /
The Dallas Times Herald, 2–10:A3.

For sheer political hypocrisy, rarely in our lifetime has there been a performance to match the anguished outrage and the howls of indignation emanating from Northern Democrats and the Eastern media as they watch Republican fortunes rise in the Southern states. The same Democrats who for decades scarcely glanced at the old Dixie girlfriend are suddenly shocked and appalled that the Republican Party is successfully courting that disillusioned lady. The same fellows who threw their hats in the air when Adlai Stevenson carried Arkansas, Georgia, Alabama and Mississippi now hint darkly that it was morally wrong for Richard Nixon to win the Carolinas, Florida, Virginia and Tennessee.

Lincoln Day address, St. Louis, Feb. 10 /
Human Events, 3–7:18.

. . . the Muskies and McGoverns contend that their support is slipping and ours growing because Republicans have adopted a cynical "Southern strategy" which "writes off the Northeast" and kowtows to biases and prejudices against black Americans. The charge is composed of 50 per cent politics and 50 per cent sour grapes. You cannot build an enduring political majority in this country by appealing to passions and prejudices that contradict the best and most basic ideals of its people. And the Republican Party of Richard Nixon does not intend to try.

Lincoln Day address, St. Louis, Feb. 10 /
Human Events, 3–7:18.

For all our Republican attacks on Roosevelt, Truman, Acheson, Kennedy and Johnson, they were assuredly a more impressive and formidable array of political adversaries than the present crop of complainers. The old lions and wolves of the Democratic party are gone or in retirement; and in their place we find only tabby cats and lap dogs.

Lincoln Day address, St. Louis, Feb. 10 /
Human Events, 3–7:18.

The rank-and-file Democrat in this country does not share the philosophy of permissiveness expressed by the best-publicized moral and intellectual leaders of our society; he reads with disgust all the rave reviews the press gives to the latest dirty movie or dirty book; he is starting to resent the use of his children as guinea pigs in the latest social experiment of some way-out educator who sends his own children to distant private schools; he wants to hear no more from the bleeding hearts who tell him to feel sorry for the criminals who have made his city unfit and unsafe for his family; he has had a bellyful of politicians who fawn over young radicals who have no manners and less sense; he is fed up with the "limousine liberals" running his party; he is fed up with the whole gang. And to those Democrats who have had enough of this kind of leadership, I say come on over to our side; there's lots of room in the inn . . .

Lincoln Day address, St. Louis, Feb. 10 /
Human Events, 3–7:19.

Senator (J. William) Fulbright said some months ago that if the Vietnam war went on

(SPIRO T. AGNEW)

much longer, the "best of our young people" would be in Canada. Let Senator Fulbright go prospecting for his future party leaders in the deserters' dens of Canada and Sweden; we Republicans shall look elsewhere. Indeed, as for those deserters, malcontents, radicals, incendiaries, the civil and uncivil disobedients among our young—SDS, PLP, Weathermen I and Weathermen II, the Revolutionary Action Movement, the Black United Front, Yippies, hippies, yahoos, Black Panthers, lions and tigers alike—I would swap the whole damn zoo for a single platoon of the kind of young Americans I saw in Vietnam.

Lincoln Day address, St. Louis, Feb. 10/
Human Events, 3–7:19.

It is not unusual, nor should it be distressing, that individuals of monumental ego among the failures of our society should attack everything fundamental to our free culture . . . We should not seem surprised that the neophyte politically ambitious loudly champion all causes of the least affluent. That works beautifully until they get elected and have to represent all the people. (The danger is) not in a fear of the kooks or demagogues themselves, but in their current respectability. Never in our history have we paid so much attention to so many odd characters. Twenty-five years ago, the tragi-comic antics of such societal misfits would have brought the establishment running after them with butterfly nets rather than television cameras.

At National Governors Conference, Washington,
Feb. 26/Los Angeles Herald-Examiner, 2–27:A6.

I've always considered myself a moderate —if you want to use the word moderate—in the sense that a moderate is generally a person who shares views with those considered liberal or conservative. For example, I might be considered very liberal in some way in domestic matters. I think I'm conservative in the sense that I want to see the United

States continue to play a world power's lead in world affairs, because I think it's necessary to our security and stability. I'm a conservative on matters of national defense. I guess I'm quite conservative in certain areas of economic policy. But as far as the development of the domestic priorities—the idea of the reconstitution of our urban areas, our cities, urban renewal . . . I have some very advanced or liberal attitudes in domestic matters. So I couldn't characterize myself as on either side of the spectrum.

Interview, Washington/
The Christian Science Monitor, 3–12:3.

From the moment I was chosen (for the Vice Presidency), it became—in the stark and breathless accounts of the media—a suddenly discovered plot hatched by Strom Thurmond and others to capture the South for Richard Nixon. As punishment for daring to be a Southern Vice Presidential candidate, I was ridiculed and derided. Like (Judge Clement F.) Haynsworth, my integrity was questioned; like (Judge G. Harrold) Carswell, my stature and credentials for high office were attacked. I am here because the people of the United States cannot be bullied the way some Senators can.

Edgefield, S.C., April 25/
San Francisco Examiner & Chronicle, 4–26:A2.

I'm not a bit interested in an Agnew Presidency. And as a matter of fact, I haven't even given thought to a continued Agnew Vice Presidency.

Television interview, Washington, May 17/
Los Angeles Times, 5–18:(1)7.

I have sworn to uphold the Constitution against all enemies, foreign and domestic. Those who tear our country apart or try to bring down its government are enemies, whether here or abroad, whether destroying libraries and classrooms on a college campus or firing at American troops from a rice paddy in Southeast Asia. I have an obligation to all of the people of the United States to call things as I see them, and I have an obligation to the President to support his actions in the best manner that I can. I choose my own words, and I set the tone of my speeches. As he said at his recent press conference, I am responsible for what I say. And I intend to be heard above the din, even if it means raising my voice. Nothing would be more pleasing to some of the editors and columnists I have quoted tonight than to have me simply shut up and disappear.

At Republican fund-raising dinner, Houston, May 22/The Washington Post, 5–23:A14.

(Representative) Mendel Rivers has worked tirelessly since coming to Congress in 1940 to make the world a more peaceful place. For example, he has supported every effort to get Communism out of Southeast Asia, to get Russia out of the Middle East and to get Senator J. William Fulbright out of Washington.

At "Salute to Mendel Rivers" luncheon, Washington, Aug. 12/ Los Angeles Herald-Examiner, 8–20:A10.

If we took into the hands of the Federal government all of the money that the Democrats would need for the programs that they propose, wo would no longer have a free economy. We would have socialism.

At Republican fund-raising dinner, Beverly Hills, Calif., Aug. 20/ The Dallas Times Herald, 8–21:A19.

I don't think it (the 18-year-old vote) will have any effect at all on the balance of political power. I've always said there is no constituency in this country known as "the young," devoted to one particular attitude. That just doesn't exist. And young people, for the most part, make their independent opinions. They are affected by their parents; they are affected by their employers; and there will be a fairly good cross-section of opinion to come out of the 18-year-old vote, in my judgment.

Interview, Washington/ U.S. News & World Report, 8–24:34.

. . . Democrats in Congress are guilty of a wimpering isolationism in foreign policy, a mulish obstructionism in domestic policy and a pusillanimous pussyfooting on the critical issue of law and order . . . Your country just cannot afford any more ultra-liberals in the United States Senate. Today's breed of radical-liberals posturing about the Senate is about as closely related to a Harry Truman as a chihuahua is to a timber wolf.

Springfield, Ill., Sept. 10/ Los Angeles Herald-Examiner, 9–14:A12.

My far-left friends in Congress never weary of telling me they are the good Samaritans; that they are more sensitive to the needs of the impoverished. Well, *we* believe in representing the poor, too; and we do. But the time has come for someone also to represent the workingmen of this country—the Forgotten Man of American politics. The President and I are applying for that job.

Springfield, Ill., Sept. 10/Time, 9–21:15.

(The "radical-liberal"): He is the kind who delays, or weakens or opposes every anti-crime bill the President sends up—at least until public pressure becomes irresistible. He supports every effort to undercut the President's authority in foreign policy. When the President asks for the money and weapons needed to maintain America's strength and commitments abroad, he will hint darkly that the President has been taken over by the "military-industrial complex." When the President uses force—as in Cambodia—to protect American lives, the radical-liberal gets almost hysterical. He excuses campus violence as the inevitable and justified response of the alienated, but he luridly denounces the reaction of workers and the peacekeeping efforts of the police as harbingers of fascism. He will bemoan the rise in prices—but vote for every spending bill that comes down the pike. In the Senate, he wants America to welch on all her commitments to the peoples of Asia, but he acts the jingo in the Middle East—blind to the truth that America's credibility is not something

WHAT THEY SAID IN 1970

(SPIRO T. AGNEW)

that can be destroyed in one corner of Asia and survive anywhere else in the world; either our word is good or it is not—and when we give our word, then it sticks through the tough times as well as the good times. The radical-liberal will not get exercised over the presence of hard-core pornography at the corner drug store—but don't let him catch your son praying in the public schools. The radical-liberal will not hesitate to demand the immediate use of the 82nd Airborne to integrate the schools of a Southern state—but he will buy his house so far out in the suburbs that you have to take the Metroliner to get there. The radical-liberal will want your child bused clear across town to meet someone's notion of proper racial balance—but his own kids will be off to Pennsy Prep. Such, my friends, are the "radical-liberals" in the Congress of the United States.

Albuquerque, Sept. 15 / Human Events, 9–26:5.

All I'm trying to do is the best job of being the Vice President that I can do—and that means supporting the President. We intend to re-elect President Nixon; whether I'm part of that or not is initially unimportant because the President is the important office. And if it's not advantageous for President Nixon to encourage me to run again with him, it wouldn't disturb me in the slightest, as long as he would be re-elected.

Interview, Memphis, Sept. 23 /
The New York Times, 9–24:8.

My rhetoric is no different than the rhetoric that has been turned upon me; and there is no way to say that this kind of hard political adversary language hasn't been used . . . I remind you of President Franklin Roosevelt with his ridicule of Martin, Barton and Fish, and some of the things he said about them. Harry Truman called his opponents "snollygosters," whatever that was; Teddy Roosevelt called them "pusillanimous pussy-

footers." The rhetoric hasn't changed. stole it from Teddy Roosevelt.

TV panel discussion / The David Frost Sho
Westinghouse Broadcasting Company, 9–2

. . . my mission (in traveling across th country) is to awaken Americans to the nee for sensible authority, to jolt good minds ou of the lethargy of habitual acquiescence, t mobilize a silent majority that cherishes th right values but has been bulldozed for yea into thinking those values are emba rassingly out of style . . . Of *course* I seek t make my views heard. A call to intellectu combat cannot be issued by a flute; it nee a trumpet.

Milwaukee, Sept. 2
Los Angeles Herald-Examiner, 9–27:A

Our party (Republican) was long ag known as the party of big business in th North and West. It is that no longer. Th working man is the forgotten man of Ame ican politics. But he is not forgotten by th President of the United States. Rejected an written off by the old elite, the workingma has become (the) cornerstone of the new ma jority.

At Republican campaign rally, Erie, Pa
Oct. 24 / The Washington Post, 10–25:A2

Life is a question of emphasis, really. haven't changed one view since the time was thought to be a liberal. If the issues un der debate today were housing, water pollu tion and tax reform, I would come out wit high liberal marks. If the issues yesterda had been violence and disruption and des crating of the flag, I would have had hig conservative marks. When I was Govern (of Maryland), I strongly supported Lyndo Johnson when there was a gubernatorial e fort to rally support against the war (in Vie nam). It is a matter of where the emph sis is.

Interview, Washington / Time, 10–26:2

1—Do you walk around with an expressio on your face that seems to say that the who

orld smells a little bit funny? 2—Do you
ish those great masses of people would stop
questioning your right to determine public
orals and public policy? 3—Do you think
at a college education makes you not only
tellectually superior, but morally superior
, well, to those who did not have your op-
ortunity? 4—Do you think that blue-collar
ork—like fixing an automobile or driving a
uck—is not nearly as dignified or significant
pushing a pencil at a tax-exempt founda-
on? 5—Does the very thought of a "silent
ajority" fill you with revulsion, while a
hrase like "power to the people" appears to
u as the essence of the revealed wisdom? 6
Does it make you feel warm and snugly
rotected to read *The New York Review of
ooks*? 7—Do you think it is awkward and
emeaning for United States Senators to
ave to submit themselves for re-election to
group you call "the great unwashed"? 8—
o you tune in a Presidential speech at the
d, just to get your opinions from the in-
ant analysis? 9—Did you ever go to sleep
d dream of J. William Fulbright becom-
g Secretary of State—without waking up
reaming? 10—Do you support a Constitu-
onal amendment to abolish the office of
ice President of the United States? My
iends, if your answer to even two or three
f these questions is "Yes," you may regard
urself as a full-fledged elitist, and you can
eat yourself to two seats on the aisle for *Oh!
alcutta!* But if your answer to each of these
uestions is a ringing, indignant "No"—then
elcome to the silent majority.
At Republican campaign dinner, Wilmington,
Del./The Wall Street Journal, 10–27:16.

On November 3, we Republicans made
olitical water run straight uphill . . . I see
at various pursed-lip pundits with 20-20
indsight have heartburn over this campaign
not simply over my part in it, but the Pres-
dent's part as well. In the heat of the cam-
aign, a whole bevy of Democrats—who
ent the last three years cozying up to rad-
al dissenters—turned tale and ran, un-
enching their fists in their frantic rush to

middle ground. No matter, though, say our
critics, that this climactic victory for reason
and order in America was forced by the Republican Party. No, the Republicans were
crude and inconsiderate to press the point,
and our adversaries were admirably clever to
change their spots so swiftly, so convincingly.
Well, my friends, for all that I have just one
word: hogwash.
At Republican fund-raising dinner, Washington,
Nov. 12/San Francisco Examiner, 11–13:2.

In the 92nd Congress, President Nixon
will fare better on foreign policy, better on
national defense, better on crime and law-
and-order, and at least some better on fiscal
responsibility. That's the nub of Election
1970. No thinking Republican should let
professional detractors in or out of office
brainwash him into thinking otherwise.
At Republican fund-raising dinner, Washington,
Nov. 12/San Francisco Examiner, 11–13:2.

During Campaign '70, we divided along
traditional adversary lines; and that's our
free system. You know, nothing was more
unreasonable to me than the cries of "Mr.
Vice President, you're dividing the country." What is an election if it's not an attempt to divide the voters of the country
between two or three candidates who may be
seeking an office? Heavens! If they don't divide, we may never have a result. After all,
that's our free system.
At Republican Governors Conference,
Sun Valley, Idaho, Dec. 15/
Los Angeles Herald-Examiner, 12–16:A3.

All through my political career, I was told,
"If you don't simplify your language, if you
don't stop using unusual words and phrase-
ology, you will never be able to be elected to
any office, because the people will think
you're trying to create a superiority image."
I rejected that. I think that the people really
understand a great deal more about the English language than most of us in public life
or in the journalistic profession give them

credit for. And I think they enjoy reading something that's a little bit different.

Interview/The New York Times Magazine,
12–27:29.

Carl Albert
United States Representative, D-Okla.

. . . this has been a reform-minded Congress. We've reformed the postal service, we've passed a tax-reform act and we're reforming the machinery of Congress. In the reform area the House has passed many bills —draft reform, which needs more work, 18-year-old vote, welfare reform, electoral-college reform and women's rights. This also is a priorities-minded Congress. I don't think any Congress has ever devoted as much time and attention to trying to evaluate the various programs with which we must be concerned and to assign priorities to them. This Congress is also to be commended in that it is an up-to-date Congress. Speaking as a Democrat, we are trying to meet our responsibilities. I think we, more than the Republicans, are interested in education, in health, in housing, in anti-pollution measures, in public works, in the problems of minority groups, in the lot of the average farmer; and we're more interested in the average working-person. Our record reflects our interest in human beings.

Interview, Washington/
U.S. News & World Report, 8–24:38.

Samuel Archibald
Executive director, Fair Campaign
Practices Committee

The old style of dirty politics is still with us . . . The problem of dirty politics is getting more subtle, so much more difficult to put your finger on that it's hard to handle or even hard to file a complaint . . . Beware the bewitching hour. If a new and sensational charge is brought up the weekend before election, it's almost certain to be an unfair charge, a false charge. If it were fair, it would

have been brought up earlier . . . early enough to be answered.

Washington, Oct. 29/
San Francisco Examiner, 10–30:11.

Birch Bayh
United States Senator, D-Ind.

Just being right on the issues is not enough today. We need a President who can strike a chord, who can make people put aside some of their pettiness, their devisiveness. There are some things only the President can provide; and if the time comes when I decide I can provide them, then hang on to your hats.

News conference, Washington, Dec. 4/
The New York Times, 12–5:16.

Julian Bond
Georgia State Legislator

Among young people, politics is becoming increasingly a despised profession, with fewer and fewer of them getting involved. It may end up completely in the hands of the TV technicians. But if all the young, from center to left, got into it—as they did for (Eugene J.) McCarthy and (Robert F.) Kennedy, they could clean house.

Look, 12–15:70.

Art Buchwald
Newspaper columnist

There was one main difference during the (1968 Presidential) campaign. Nixon looked like a guy you wouldn't buy a used car from. Humphrey looked like a guy who bought one. And Wallace looked like a guy who would steal one.

Before Menswear Retailers Association, Dallas,
Feb. 11/The Dallas Times Herald, 2–12:A22.

James L. Buckley
Conservative Party candidate for
United States Senator from New York

There was a time when it was the conservatives who were utterly predictable. Now the old fogies are the liberals, who have lived too long with their verities.

Time, 8–24:12.

William L. Buckley, Jr.
Newspaper columnist; Editor,
"National Review"

I think the idea of the Conservative Party as pariah is simply terminated. With the election of Jim Buckley to the (U.S.) Senate, people will no longer think—as they have been trained to think—of Conservatives as a batch of Birchers and a congeries of crackpots.

New York, Nov. 4 |
The New York Times, 11–5:31.

Mary Lou Burg
Vice chairman, Democratic
National Committee

It isn't enough to speak in high, pious tones about bringing us together and then send the Vice President (Agnew) out to polarize us as he runs amuck through an unabridged dictionary.

Before Women's National Democratic Club,
Washington | The Dallas Times Herald, 10–6:A2.

James MacGregor Burns
Professor of Government, Williams College

I have never favored a bi-partisan Presidency. It is well known that I lean toward strong Presidents; and I find that (Franklin D.) Roosevelt was quite partisan some of the time. (Lyndon B.) Johnson was, too, in that he stressed the Democratic platform all the way through. I feel the great Presidents have been partisan. I get the feeling that Mr. Nixon is tending toward the non-partisan, for instance with his appointment of (John B.) Connally as Secretary of the Treasury.

Interview, Washington |
The Washington Post, 11–27:G19.

Al Capp
Cartoonist

Herblock and (Art) Buchwald—and, yes, me too—we all grew up laughing at the right. In fact, it was in response to lunacy on the far right that we became humorists. Believe me, it was a wrenching experience for me suddenly to realize that the main source of

lunacy in our society had moved over to the far left.

Human Events, 4–25:18.

I'm a registered independent. I worked for Jack Kennedy and Adlai Stevenson and Lyndon Johnson. But I've always preferred to remain independent and attack any side that's gone crazy.

San Francisco Examiner & Chronicle, 8–23:A6.

G. Harrold Carswell
Unsuccessful United States Supreme Court nominee; Candidate for Republican U.S. Senate nomination in Florida

A fellow told me the other day that I was beginning to sound just like (Vice President) Spiro Agnew. I said, "Thank you! Thank you! Thank you!"

Campaign speech | The Dallas Times Herald,
7–23:A2.

What is so remarkable to me about this particular group of people ("Yankee liberals") . . . is that they have not come up with a single solution to the problem of crime. They've got the worst record with respect to narcotics; they've got the worst record with respect to race relations; they haven't solved a single ghetto problem; their schools are in terrible condition. And yet, they have the audacity, if you please—and I might even suggest the hypocrisy—to try to export their brand of government all over this nation. This is really an absurdity. Now, when those boys begin to find the answers to some of these great problems that they're so hand-wringingly concerned about, when they can tell us how to do it, when they can show us where they have done it, when they can give us a bill of accomplishment, then indeed I will say, "Let's rise to this and *hail* them as our leaders. Hosanna, come lead us!" But until they do, I think it ill behooves them to use the South as a whipping boy.

Campaign speech, St. Petersburg, Fla. |
The Wall Street Journal, 7–30:1.

253

John Chancellor
News commentator, National Broadcasting Company

Some citizens groups and public officials now feel that almost any rich man can hire himself a TV packager and make a very creditable run for a nomination, without making public appearances, holding press conferences or kissing babies . . . The Constitution sets the standards and qualifications for candidates, but it doesn't say anything about a million dollars. Yet in some states, a million dollars has become a qualification for office, and everyone agrees that's wrong.

Radio commentary/
National Broadcasting Company, 10–13.

Shirley Chisholm
United States Representative, D-N.Y.

The business of a national (political) convention is not to have fun—it is to nominate a President of the United States . . . Anyone who does not want to approach it in that spirit had better stay home—or tell his wife a lie so he can get away for the weekend to Miami or Atlantic City and get it out of his system.

Before National Democratic Rules Commission, New York, Aug. 14/
The New York Times, 8–15:23.

John Sherman Cooper
United States Senator, R-Ky.

The demands for money to pay television costs (in political campaigns) cannot be met unless a candidate is rich, or unless he accepts large contributions from labor unions or other private interests. The acceptance of such funds means that a candidate is placed in the position of being in the pocket of such contributors, or assumed to be by the contributor and by the public.

Before the Senate, Washington, Nov. 23/
The Washington Post, 11–26:A19.

Robert J. Dole
United States Senator, R-Kan.

Vice President Agnew is now a household word in Kansas. There is a feeling he has per-

formed a service for the Administration an⟩ the people. This is said to me sometimes b⟩ folks who would like to get a look at leade⟩ in Washington: "If you can't get Agnew, se⟩ if you can get Nixon."

U.S. News & World Report, 2–9:2⟩

The expense of running for public offic⟩ has reached scandalous levels. Sums whic⟩ once were registered as totals for Presidentia⟩ campaigns are now being run up in races fo⟩ Governor and Senator.

Before the Senate, Washington, Nov. 23⟩
The Washington Post, 11–26:A19⟩

Roger Fisher
Professor of Law, Harvard University

The silent majority are people who ca⟩ have an enormous impact on keeping Ame⟩ ica drifting. A lot of the silent majority wi⟩ make themselves felt by sitting in their arm⟩ chairs and stating their case to the pollster⟩ They don't think they know enough abou⟩ public affairs to do anything active, so the⟩ just cling to their chairs and turn off—whic⟩ is why they're called "silent," I suppose. Thi⟩ is a period of change, whether we like it o⟩ not, and change requires activism. If yo⟩ want things to be better—or if you wan⟩ things to be worse at a slower rate—it take⟩ getting into the act and speaking out.

Los Angeles Herald-Examiner, 1–14:D⟩

Gerald R. Ford
United States Representative, R-Mich.

(Vice President Agnew) has many thing⟩ in common with the miniskirt: Sometime⟩ he shocks; sometimes he entertains; some⟩ times he enlightens; but one way or anothe⟩ he's always in the public eye.

The New York Times, 9–20:(4)⟩

J. William Fulbright
United States Senator, D-Ark.

He's (Vice President Agnew) kind of ⟩ smart aleck, isn't he? He's feeling his oat⟩ and he's getting himself and others in trou⟩ ble in the process. He's making promises h⟩

n't fulfill . . . I think he has a bad case of
ie big head.

Interview, Washington, Jan. 13/
Los Angeles Times, 1–14:(1)15.

ohn W. Gardner
hairman, Common Cause

. . . one thing I think it would be very
ise for a President to do . . . is to an-
ounce that he was going to run for one
rm only. I think we're in for a series of
ie-term Presidents, anyway. I think that,
iless the Democratic Party splits wide open,
esident Nixon will prove to be a one-term
esident. I think he would have made more
story had he announced that at the be-
nning. Now, I know there are political ob-
rvers who say that it weakens a President
everyone knows his term is ending. But I
lieve that in these times, when the credi-
lity of public institutions is so damaged,
President is weakened even more by the
litical maneuvering he undertakes to in-
re his re-election.

Interview/WETA-TV, Washington, 12–17.

arry M. Goldwater
nited States Senator, R-Ariz.

If we do our job, we'll have two terms of
ixon and two terms of Agnew, and by that
ne (New York Mayor John) Lindsay will
: up around 70. He still might be good-
oking but would be kind of old for that
ack.

San Francisco Examiner & Chronicle
(This World), 3–1:2.

Very frankly, I believe that the (Nixon)
lministration is asking for trouble every
iy that it retains Republican appointees
io disagree fundamentally with the Presi-
:nt and his programs.

Before the Senate, Washington, July 14/
Vital Speeches, 8–15:645.

iarles E. Goodell
nited States Senator, R-N.Y.

The greatest abuse can be that of stultifi-
tion—of reducing a political contest to the

level of a sales pitch for a new type of ply-
wood . . . A candidate with slight qualifications but a large budget can too easily
succumb to the temptation of TV sloganeer-
ing—of skirting the issues and selling himself
in catchy 30-second spots that conceal more
than they reveal. The real victim of this tactic is the public—which finds itself voting for
an ad agency's skill, not a candidate's qualifications.

Before the Senate, Washington, Aug. 6/
The New York Times, 8–7:34.

W. Averell Harriman
Former United States Ambassador-at-Large

I'm an old man, and I don't want to die
with Richard Nixon in the White House.

Washington, January/Newsweek, 10–5:27.

Fred R. Harris
United States Senator, D-Okla.

The most dangerous but the most common
thing I have found is that people do not
basically believe politicians are going to do
anything for them.

Quote, Dec. 27:599.

Walter J. Hickel
Secretary of the Interior of the United States

I've always believed that if you do a good
job for all the people in the country, then
you do a good job for the President. And I
think that was what I was supposed to do.
And so I'll say that I'm going to do the best I
can. But if I go away, I'm going away with
an arrow in my heart, not a bullet in my
back.

Television interview/60 Minutes,
Columbia Broadcasting System, 11–24.

Walter J. Hickel
Former Secretary of the Interior
of the United States

I believe we are entering a new age. It is
going to demand a new breed of national
leader. It is going to require a new philosophy of government . . . We must inject in our
national leaders of all political parties a
quality of statesmanship which acts for the

WHAT THEY SAID IN 1970

good of the next generation and not for the next election.

Seattle, Dec. 17 / The Washington Post, 12–18:A7.

Ernest F. Hollings
United States Senator, D-S.C.

(Voters are) looking for performance, and when you bring a fellow (Vice President Spiro Agnew) out on a track that racks them and rapes them and rips them and rants them . . . that kind of politics is gone in America today . . . I don't think you're going to find President Nixon running Spiro all over the country in the fashion we saw the last two months in this country. If he does, he's a goner. I can tell you that.

Interview / Profile, Metromedia Radio, 11–15.

John A. Howard
President, Rockford College

Of all the terms in current usage, one of the most devastating, belittling, demeaning, stop-in-the-tracksing epithets that can be applied is "reactionary." It is a red-flag word, and the mere pronouncement of it tends to conjure up a vision of a dangerous, unthinking, unyielding type. And that is a paradox; for if the word does produce that result, it is an unthinking, unyielding reaction. The word "reactionary," used in a political or social context, properly describes one who favors a return to former political or social policies. Surely, thinking man does not want to rule out the possibility of reinstituting policies that have proven workable in the past when successor policies have proven ineffective. Thinking man doesn't; but contemporary man, blinded by the supposed virtue of innovation, seems to.

Opening convocation address, Rockford College, Sept. 9 / Vital Speeches, 10–1:744.

Harold E. Hughes
United States Senator, D-Iowa

If it is necessary to use character assassination to win political campaigns any more,

then the victory is not worth winning. 1970 will go down in American political history as the year of the badmouth. Worst of all, it is the nation and our entire system that is the greatest loser.

At Democratic fund-raising dinner, Sioux Falls, S.D., Oct. 12 / The Washington Post, 10–13:A6.

Hubert H. Humphrey
Former Vice President of the United States

People come to me and say, "Well, if it hadn't been for the Chicago convention, you would have won (the Presidency in 1968)." Somebody else says to me, "If you had money sooner, you would have won." Somebody else says to me, "Well, if (Sen. Eugene) McCarthy had come out and supported you sooner, you would have won." There are a lot of reasons. I tell you, if I had had a few more votes I'd have won.

Interview, Washington / The Christian Science Monitor, 1–10:7.

. . . as yet, I don't get the melody of the (Nixon) Administration. If there's music in this Administration—and I use that term for an editorial emphasis—I can't get the tune. I hear the lyrics, but I don't get the music. And I'm not sure the lyrics fit in with what is supposedly the score of the music of this Administration.

Interview, Washington / The Christian Science Monitor, 1–12:3

. . . I do believe that national conventions have an important—indeed, an essential—role in our political system, and should remain part of it.

Minneapolis, Jan. 15 / The New York Times, 1–16:10.

Mr. Nixon and company are putting band-aids on . . . wounds but not getting at the source of the trouble. They are mechanics, account executives. They are not artists of politics . . . They know how to manage, but they have no creativity. In other words, they know how to lay bricks but have no vision of a cathedral.

Los Angeles Herald-Examiner, 1–17:A10.

Once you run for President, every other office loses its luster—especially if you've also been Vice President. I did want to be President. I had great dreams for this country. I'm heartsick that I wasn't able to fulfill them from the White House. I have no forum now, but if I regain my forum in the Senate, I'll try to carry out my dreams from a legislative station.

Interview/Los Angeles Times, 7–1:(1)14.

What liberals must face up to is an ironical imperative: They must show the courage to take a "popular" position when the cause is right.

Before American Bar Association, St. Louis/
The Dallas Times Herald, 8–17:A20.

Chet Huntley

News commentator, National
Broadcasting Company

I've been with (President) Nixon socially; I've traveled with him in his private plane; I've seen him under many conditions. The shallowness of the man overwhelms me. The fact that he is President frightens me.

Interview/Life, 7-17:36.

Edward M. Kennedy

United States Senator, D-Mass.

A silent majority is unacceptable. In these times, to do nothing, to be silent, not to inquire, not to challenge, is to abdicate citizen responsibility. It is no excuse for an informed and literate citizen to claim that leaders have better or secret information, and thus forgo the right to hold a different opinion. In the first place, it is just not so; on most issues, all the relevant information is public. In the second place, the issues today really are issues of values, standards and ideals.

At Mount Holyoke College commencement/
Life, 6–19:26.

We simply cannot allow a love affair with campus youth on the issue of war (in Vietnam) to weaken or obscure the close tie the (Democratic) Party has always had with the labor movement and the working man. The umbrella of the Democratic Party is broad enough to cover every type of young American: the young hard-hat as well as the young dove, the worker as well as the student. We are the party of the poor, the black, the young and the college; but that is not all we are or ought to be. We must reach out to the un-poor, the un-black, the un-young and the un-college. We must be a party for all seasons, capable of adapting to all the constructive tensions in our society, capable of building the newer world we seek for all our citizens.

Before Youth Participation Subcommittee,
McGovern Commisson/The Wall Street Journal,
8–18:10.

Herbert G. Klein

Director of Communications for the
President of the United States

When there is a difference between the President and a Cabinet officer, the President will stay.

Before Gas Men's Roundtable/
The Dallas Times Herald, 12–2:A2.

John F. Kraft

Public-opinion analyst

Probably the most important lesson to be learned from recent elections—and it's even clearer now because of the degree of ticket-splitting that we just saw—is that voters are becoming more sophisticated and more able to decide for themselves how they want to vote, rather than have the party or the union or the local manufacturers' association tell them how they should vote. Another thing: More and more people are resenting being put in a slot as a Democrat or Republican, and they are finding it more comfortable to split their tickets. It's a matter of record.

Interview, Washington/
U.S. News & World Report, 11–23:29.

Alfred M. Landon

Former Governor of Kansas

Politics has always been an avocation with me, never a vocation. I never worried about

257

(ALFRED M. LANDON)

my political future. You can have a good time in politics if you have that attitude.

Interview, Topeka, Kan./
Los Angeles Times, 5–24:A11.

John V. Lindsay
Mayor of New York

This (the 1970 election campaign) is one of the few campaigns in memory in which men apparently are seeking not merely to defeat their opponents, but literally to eliminate them from public life. If they succeed, we will have taken a first dangerous step toward the construction of a single-minded state. When the President and his lieutenants tell us to be afraid, when they pretend that respected candidates condone violence—as though the "Weathermen" were running in this election—then they are deserting the essential principles of both parties. Some politicians think this strategy will win votes—and it may; but it is not America. It does not inform. It does not educate. It does not set a tone equal to America's beginnings.

At Family of Man dinner, New York, Oct. 26/
Los Angeles Herald-Examiner, 10–27:A6.

Our heritage calls for responsible men to fight hard for public office. It also expects candidates to conduct the contest in a rational atmosphere, to provide a setting in which the voters can reckon and choose. And always we ask political men, under the pressure of winning or losing, to campaign with grace and dignity—to set an example for people who must then live together no matter how they voted.

At Family of Man dinner, New York, Oct. 26/
The New York Times, 10–27:36.

Richard W. Lyman
President, Stanford Universty

To the extent that politics is a dirty business—and, like any business, it can be so, of course—it is not likely to get less so because people are apathetic about it.

Plainview (Tex.) Daily Herald, 10–20:8.

Lester G. Maddox
Governor of Georgia

All we've gotten out of the White House is double-talk. I say phooey. Phooey on all that double-talk.

News conference, Atlanta/
The Christian Science Monitor, 3–10:17.

Norman Mailer
Author

Left-wingers are incapable of conspiring because they're all egomaniacs.

At "Chicago conspiracy trial," Jan. 27/
The New York Times, 1–28:27.

Eugene J. McCarthy
United States Senator, D-Minn.

There are no set standards for judging the conduct of a Vice President; and as long as the Vice President's activities seemed not to be endorsed by the President of the United States and appear to be serving principally as a means of raising money for the Republican Party . . . there seemed little cause for concern. But within the last week, the President of the United States—moved perhaps by his observing that the Agnew method seemed too effective, or because he was moved in the heat of the campaign to return to the same methods he used somewhat successfully along the way in his own political career—has chosen to take up the same disturbing, and in some cases deceptive, political tactics that have marked the career of the Vice President during the last 12 months . . . The truth, which should be honored and guarded, is being redesigned and abused. Doubt, which should be isolated and eliminated if possible, is being expanded. (And) patriotism, which should be a badge and a shield of honor, is being forged into a weapon against all with whom one might disagree.

Democratic campaign speech, Boston, Oct. 29/
The Washington Post, 10–30/A4.

John W. McCormack
United States Representative, D-Mass.

Politics is the art and science of government. To be a successful politician, therefore, one must be close to those governed and must understand their needs and desires. I believe the best way to gain this knowledge of what the people want is to remain close to them, to mingle with them and to keep in touch with them. Politics, when properly practiced, is an honorable profession, one which should attract the best men and women.

Interview, Washington/
San Francisco Examiner, 12–23:10.

George S. McGovern
United States Senator, D-S.D.

I regard the Vice President's (Agnew) conduct ever since he has been in office as disgraceful. I think he has done more to divide and weaken the country, perhaps, than our enemies in Hanoi have done. He is undercutting the whole possibility for a unified American people. He is a divisive, damaging influence on the people of this country.

Television interview, June 21/
Los Angeles Herald-Examiner, 6–22:A4.

(The Nixon Administration) recklessly exploits disruption and division for its own political gain . . . The Vice President (Agnew) is able to practice deception with false innuendo and name-calling that lumps together critics of the Administration and the excesses of radicalism. And the President can continue to walk the high road of the rhetoric of conciliation while his Administration exploits the divisions and hatred in the land . . . This is the supreme irony of our time: the unholy alliance of undisciplined radicalism and the politics of manipulation.

Omaha, Sept. 19/
San Francisco Examiner & Chronicle, 9–20:A2.

I believe in the politics of reconciliation and of hope. We must persuade the angriest of students and the hardest-swinging hardhats that they are brothers and that we must heal the divisions in our land. Instead of the Republican strategy of division, we can build a bridge over troubled waters.

At Democratic campaign dinner, Bennington, Vt./The Washington Post, 10–18:A12.

In (Vice President) Agnew's recent political venture into my state of South Dakota, he, of course, reserved some of his harshest epithets for me. I always consider it a small badge of honor to be attacked by this impossible demagog. If he ever said anything good about me, I would know I was off the track.

Quote, 11–22:482.

John J. McKeithen
Governor of Louisiana

We (in the South) are being used as political pawns by that bunch of hypocrites up there (in the North) in two ways: one, with what they call school desegregation, and the second is (the charge of) Mafia influence in (Southern) state government . . . Why, everyone knows that the best way to get votes in the (Northeast) is by jumping on the South.

News conference, Baton Rouge, La., Aug. 20/
Washington Star, 8–21:A5.

George Meany
President, American Federation of Labor-Congress of Industrial Organizations

I think it (the union members' political thinking) is changing to some extent. Not so much that our people are looking to the Republicans, but they are looking less to the Democrats because, actually, the Democratic Party has disintegrated—it is not the so-called liberal party that is was a few years ago. It almost has got to be the party of the extremists insofar as these so-called liberals or new lefts, or whatever you want to call them, have taken over the Democratic Party. As they take it over, and as they move more and more to the left—and I mean way over to the left— I think more and more (they) are going to lose the support of our members.

News conference, Aug. 31/
U.S. News & World Report, 9–7:60.

John N. Mitchell
Attorney General of the United States

No question about it. I'm the liberal of the Nixon Administration.

Interview / The Washington Post, 1–19:A8.

Given our times, we cannot expect political demonstrations to be conducted like prayer meetings. We must expect language which may incite hostility or may be obscene. This is because the First Amendment protects all of us, including men and women who choose to be unruly, unreasonable and impolite.

*Before Texas bar associations, July 2 /
Los Angeles Times, 7–4:(1)2.*

There is no such thing as the "New Left." This country is going so far right, you are not even going to recognize it.

*Interview, Washington /
Los Angeles Times, 9–20:(1)9.*

Walter F. Mondale
United States Senator, D-Minn.

The politics of violence, the politics of intolerant confrontation are kicking back, providing an opportunity to be elected not on a program, but just by being against such tactics. We have tried the violent-confrontation politics the last few years, and we have earned Ronald Reagan, Richard Nixon, Attorney General John N. Mitchell and a whole host of cheap politicians. . .

*At Massachusetts Institute of Technology,
Aug. 7 / Washington Star, 8–8:A2.*

Charles Morgan, Jr.
*Southern director,
American Civil Liberties Union*

President (Nixon) may not know it, but his Southern strategy won't work. The only way to outflank (former Alabama Governor) George Wallace is to go into the Gulf of Mexico.

Atlanta / The New York Times, 2–15:(1)25.

Daniel P. Moynihan
*Counsellor to the President
of the United States*

(Today's liberal is) a well-educated middle-class person with an immense feeling of security and status and an almost impervious conditioning. This has led to an extraordinary decline in the sensitivity of liberal political thinking. Liberals have come to view the working-class experience as somehow debasing—and that amounts to a debasement of the only experience most people have. I have a feeling that behind a great deal of liberal posturing is nothing more than a Tory will to power.

Time, 3–16:26.

Time and again, (President Nixon) has said things of startling insight, taken positions of great political courage and intellectual daring, only to be greeted with silence or incomprehension in our own ranks. The prime consequence of this is that the people in the nation who take these matters seriously have never been required to take *us* seriously.

*Before government and Cabinet
officials, Washington, Dec. 21 /
The New York Times, 12–23:54.*

Edmund S. Muskie
United States Senator, D-Maine

All he's (Vice President Agnew) proven since 1968 is that he's discovered the dictionary. Ask this Administration the most straightforward questions and someone will run for the nearest dictionary—not for an answer, but for the most tongue-tying words he can find to avoid an answer. This Administration just does not use or understand plain talk.

Newsweek, 10–5:28.

. . . we need simple communication about the serious problems that are tearing our society apart. Instead, he (Vice President Agnew) gives tongue-twisting, dazzling rhetoric from some dictionary. What does "nattering nabobs of nepotism" mean? Tell me what it means.

At Democratic fund-raising party, Lincoln, Maine/The Washington Post, 10–19:A5.

. . . there are those who seek to turn our common distress to partisan advantages, not by offering better solutions, but with empty threat and malicious slander. They imply that Democratic candidates for high office in Texas and California, in Illinois and Tennessee, in Utah and Maryland, and among my New England neighbors from Vermont and Connecticut, men who have courageously pursued their convictions in the service of the republic in war and peace—that these men actually favor violence and champion the wrongdoer. That is a lie, and the American people know it is a lie. And what are we to think when men in positions of public trust openly declare: that the party of Franklin Roosevelt and Harry Truman, which led us out of depression and to victory over international barbarism; the party of John Kennedy, who was slain in the service of the country he inspired; the party of Lyndon Johnson, who withstood the fury of countless demonstrations in order to pursue a course he believed in; the party of Robert Kennedy, murdered on the eve of his greatest triumphs; how dare they tell us that this party is less devoted or less courageous in maintaining American principles and values than are they themselves. This is nonsense, and we all know it is nonsense.

Television address, Nov. 2/ The New York Times, 11–3:40.

Richard M. Nixon
President of the United States

There were those who said when I chose him (Vice President Agnew), "Well, that proves the new President doesn't know how to choose men." Well, if that is the kind of mistakes I've made, I'm proud of this one, believe me.

Washington, March 11/ San Francisco Examiner & Chronicle (This World), 3–22:2.

There is an old and cynical adage that says in an election year the smart politician is one who votes for all bills to spend money and votes against all bills to raise taxes. But in this election year of 1970, that old adage cannot apply. The American people will see through any attempt by anyone to play politics with their cost of living. And whenever a member of Congress displays the imagination to introduce a bill that calls for more spending, let him display the courage to introduce a bill to raise the taxes to pay for that new program. Long before the art of economics had a name, it was called political arithmetic. The American people expect their elected officials to do their political arithmetic honestly.

Radio-TV address, Washington, June 17/ The New York Times, 6–18:24.

One vote is worth a hundred obscene slogans.

Teterboro, N.J., Oct. 17/ The New York Times, 10–18:(1)1.

As is usually the case in an off-year election, I note that both parties are making claims of victory. (Democratic) chairman (Lawrence) O'Brien, with justification, points to the fact that in the state races his party picked up several Governorships. On the other hand, we are very happy to see that, in the two biggest states, California and New York, Governor (Ronald) Reagan and Governor (Nelson) Rockefeller won overwhelming victories. In the national races . . . I think the best analysis of that can be given by quoting what Walter Lippmann had to say after the election—in which the results were somewhat parallel to this—in 1962. He said then that, according to the rules of the political game as it has been played in this country for the last 50 years, when the party in power loses little, if anything, in an off-year election, it has to be called a victory. Consequently, I would call this a victory by that standard.

News conference, San Clemente, Calif., Nov. 4/U.S. News & World Report, 11–16:31.

WHAT THEY SAID IN 1970

(RICHARD M. NIXON)

There are only two issues in the country: peace and the pocketbook. We had peace in this (1970) election, but we couldn't run the country properly and still have the pocketbook issue on our side. Next time, we're going to have both peace and the pocketbook, and we're going to win.

Newsweek, 11–30:15.

. . . I feel that it is my responsibility as President to do everything that I can to work for the election of men who will help support me in keeping the pledges that I made to the American people when I ran for President. I did everything that I could in 1970, to the best of my ability, to meet that responsibility. And, after the election, I commented upon the election and gave my views on it . . . views which differed from some of those here in this room. Having done that, however, it is now my responsibility, now that the people have spoken, to work with those men and those women elected by the people in 1970. And I can only hope that, in the year 1971, Democrats and Republicans will work with the President . . .

News conference, Washington, Dec. 10/
The New York Times, 12–11:32.

Lawrence F. O'Brien
Chairman, Democratic National Committee

The costs of campaigning, primarily television costs, have escalated campaign procedures in this country to a point where there's a serious question in my mind about the retention of the two-party system. In my judgment, you cannot continue this process under these circumstances. There must be some kind of provision made to ensure equity and equality . . . the presentation of views and candidates of the two major parties. And, in all candor, the Democratic Party cannot cope with the Republican Party in this private financing area.

Interview/Meet the Press,
National Broadcasting Company, 3–15.

The old days of patronage and power brokers are gone. The name of the game these days in American politics is image and issues. And money, of course—lots of money.

Newsweek, 4–13:100.

Projecting . . . into 1972 and the Presidential election, I think that the overriding problem is apparent, that is that there is a political revolution ongoing. The two-party concept is being challenged; the traditional strength of the Democratic Party can no longer be taken for granted. We must prove our case to the new generation and others, and the party label is no longer as strong a force as it has been in the past. I do believe the two-party system will survive, but there are times when I wonder if I'm not being overly optimistic.

Interview, Washington/
The Dallas Times Herald, 4–22:A35.

One of the issues foremost in the minds of our disenchanted youth is the political party that conducted the 1968 Democratic National Convention. On this subject, their memories are long, their charity short. The scenes within and beyond that turbulent convention hall have been played and replayed, scrutinized, analyzed and widely condemned. It happened; our party was a part of it; and the question that should command our attention is : "What will we do in the future?"

Before "youth participation subcommittee"
of McGovern Commission, Washington,
July 29/Washington Star, 7–29:A6.

There is a void between Nixon, his Cabinet and Congress. Nixon's Administration has done practically nothing constructive, yet takes all credit for initiating legislation actually proposed by the Democrats. The Administration lacks recognition of people. It is only concerned with charts and statistics.

News conference, Cleveland, July 30/
Cleveland Plain Dealer, 7–31:A8.

The Nixon Administration silently and grudgingly grinds out a few programs for blacks, while winking at those it seeks to woo by its "Southern strategy."

Canton, Ohio, July 30/
Cleveland Plain Dealer, 7–31:A8.

Through television and radio, the (political) party in power will be able to exert tremendous influence and control over public opinion in this country, with the opposition left almost helpless to communicate . . . I do not exaggerate when I say the unrestrained power of television and radio could sound the death-knell for the two-party system—and that may not be too distant.

News conference, Washington, Aug. 20/
Cleveland Plain Dealer, 8–21:A11.

. . . on the basis of his total failure to execute the official duties of his office, one is tempted to describe Mr. (Spiro) Agnew as the first Vice President in American history to go A.W.O.L.

Indianapolis, Sept. 11/
The New York Times, 9–12:8.

The Vice President's (Agnew) intent, as he thumbs his way through the unabridged dictionary, is to blame Democrats for everything . . . even the corn leaf blight.

Minneapolis, Sept. 24/
Los Angeles Times, 9–25:(1)6.

(President) Nixon and his rejected retinue of Republican retreads should be desperate, because the American voters understand that words cannot permanently take the place of deeds.

Springfield, Pa., Oct. 15/
The Washington Post, 10–17:A3.

The Nixon Administration lacks initiative, it lacks imagination, it lacks compassion for human needs. It has established no rapport, no communication, with the people. It has given the nation no clear vision of a direction for the future.

Washington, Dec. 27/
The Washington Post, 12–28:A14.

James G. O'Hara
United States Representative, D-Mich.

Those of us who have felt that the Nixon Administration is devoid of a sense of humor may have been proven wrong. At least, I hope so. A careful examination of the proposed new ceremonial uniform for the White House Hussars, and of the nationwide editorial response, would tend to indicate that the entire proposition was a put-on from the start. Only a President with a deep and incredibly subtle sense of the ridiculous could have so unerringly hit the national funny-bone. In a time when the news is so somber, in a time when the President sorrowfully but unmovingly decides that we cannot afford to educate our children and must reduce our efforts to wipe out disease, in a time when the national budget seeks to portray a nation which is simply fiscally unable to cope with problems affecting its very survival, it is, I suppose, heartening to have leadership that can give us, if not bread, at least comic opera.

Before the House, Washington, Feb. 5/
Congressional Record, 2–5:E698.

Thomas P. O'Neill, Jr.
United States Representative, D-Mass.

The last three Presidents of the United States all served in this body—Mr. Nixon, Mr. Johnson and Mr. Kennedy. And if someone were writing the memoirs of any of them on the important issues of the time in which they served . . . one would have to surmise or guess how they stood on the vital questions of the day, because there would be no record . . .

Before the House/Newsweek, 8–10:18.

Richard L. Ottinger
United States Representative, D-N.Y.

You can't "buy" an election. You can't win if you don't stand for something.

Interview, New York/
The New York Times, 5–21:37.

WHAT THEY SAID IN 1970

Ronald Reagan
Governor of California

(The 1970 election) was the greatest proof of the swing to the right. We have pushed the opposition party in our direction. How many Democrats had the courage to run on a liberal philosophy? There were Democratic candidates saying things in this election that they crucified (Senator Barry) Goldwater for saying six years ago.

Interview/Human Events, 12–12:9

Walter P. Reuther
President,
United Auto Workers of America

The ultra-left extremists, with their revolutionary slogans and their reckless behavior, can sow the seeds of fascism. These young people who, in their revolutionary zeal, are afflicted with what Lenin called "infantile leftism," do not understand the essential dynamics of social change . . . They think what they need to do is bring society down in total ruins and then out of the ashes of the old they will build the new . . . When you are in favor of destroying the system, the worst enemy is anyone who is trying to make the system work and make it responsive to human needs.

News conference, Atlantic City, N.J., April 22/
The Washington Post, 4–23:A2.

Frank Reynolds
News commentator,
American Broadcasting Company

Let the candidates appear on news programs or debates, but deny them the right to buy time on the people's airwaves in order to let their image-makers mislead the people—or trick them, or overwhelm them . . . The problem is not just the quantity of campaign commercials, it is their quality—or a better word would be their honesty—that needs to be examined. The 10-second or 60-second commercial is made to order for trickery, innuendo, implications of treason, smear or irrelevance. In Illinois, a candidate for the Senate seems to be running against, or maybe with, Jerry Rubin. In Indiana, a candidate for the Senate is portrayed as an enemy of American soldiers in Vietnam. In Tennessee, an incumbent Senator is said to be finding his most powerful commercial to be one in which he plays checkers with an old gaffer and loses . . . thereby establishing his folksiness. Well, there is a way to eliminate such nonsense—not from campaigns, but from our home screens. And that is to simply declare television and radio off-limits—not to candidates, but to the political commercial . . . There is a precedent for such strong action. Cigarette commercials will be banned from the air after the first of the year for the very good reason that cigarette smoking is injurious to public health. The slick political commercials now polluting the air are no less injurious to our political health.

Television commentary, American
Broadcasting Company Evening News, 10–13.

Donald Rumsfeld
Assistant to the President of the United States; Director, Office of Economic Opportunity

. . . my code says: "By golly, I'm part of this Administration; and if I don't want to be part of this Administration, I can leave it." One man got elected President of the United States; and while he's there, you support the dickens out of him.

Interview/The New York Times Magazine,
12–13:25.

Richard M. Scammon
Political analyst

Some groups in American life vote monolithically. Young people don't. The Mississippi farm boy and the black militant in Chicago and the Scarsdale kid who goes to Harvard have little in common with each other—except that they're all young, and they all have just one vote.

The New York Times, 12–22:16.

Hugh Scott
United States Senator, R-Pa.

The mood of the Congress is urgently and recklessly spendthrift, as it always is in an election year. July money is being used to buy November votes.
Washington, July 29 /
The Washington Post, 7–30:A2.

Eric Sevareid
News commentator,
Columbia Broadcasting System

I don't think there's a deep polarization in the country as a whole; no, I don't. Everybody said that in 1968—that we were coming apart, that there would be a whole new politics. Then you had the election, which is the only kind of test we get on a national basis, and this really didn't show up. You see, I don't believe fundamentally that most Americans are alienated from their country or its system or their generation. There's an awful lot of irritation with a lot of things. But how deep it goes is very questionable.
Interview / TV Guide, 3–14:6.

R. Sargent Shriver
Former United States
Ambassador to France

He (Vice President Agnew) calls names that hurt as much as "pig," "nigger" or "pollack." He calls his fellow Americans "fat Japs," "effete snobs," "rotten apples," "traitors." What kind of public official is that? Will you be the next one on his list? In these days, we need men who multiply compassion, understanding, respect for one another. We are all Americans. We should be treated like Americans—at least by the highest officials of the land. Compare these deaf officials to Abraham Lincoln. Even in the midst of a bloody civil war, he never called Southerners nasty names. He never called Jefferson Davis a snob, or General Lee a bum, or Stonewall Jackson a traitor, or the young people of the South rotten apples. They were still Americans to him. The moment the war was over, Lincoln said, "with malice toward none, with charity for all" . . . That's

the way an American President and Vice President should speak.
Before Polish American Congress, Chicago,
Aug. 14 / Milwaukee Journal, 8–15:7.

There are those who say the way to win an election is to appeal to the majority, to indulge your prejudices if you want. If you don't like Negroes, go ahead, express it; they're never going to be a majority of Americans. If you don't like the poor, go ahead, say it; they're only a small percentage. If you don't like students or the young or long hair, go ahead, let them have it. Sure, you might win an election. But at the same (time), you're going to tear this country apart and cause America to lose her soul.
Democratic campaign speech, Boston /
The Washington Post, 10–30:A8.

Howard K. Smith
News Commentator,
American Broadcasting Company

The negative attitude (by the press) which destroyed Lyndon Johnson is now waiting to be applied to Richard Nixon. Johnson was actually politically assassinated; and some are trying to assassinate Nixon politically. They hate Richard Nixon irrationally.
Interview, Washington / TV Guide, 2–28:8.

Once it was hard to be a liberal. Today it's "in." The ex-underdogs, the ex-outcasts, the ex-rebels are satisfied bourgeois today, who pay $150 a plate at Americans for Democratic Action dinners . . . They want to cling to the thrill of the old days, of triumph and hard fighting. So they cling to the label "liberal," and they cling to those who seem strong—namely, the New Left. The New Left shouts tirades, rather than offering reasoned arguments. People bow down to them, so they have come to *seem* strong, to *seem* sure of themselves. As a result, there's a gravitation to them by the liberals who are *not* sure of themselves. This has given the New Left grave power over the old left.
Interview, Washington / TV Guide, 2–28:11.

(HOWARD K. SMITH)

Men who were utterly unknown when this year began have leapt suddenly to fame and the right to govern us solely by pouring fabulous fortunes into the media. They tell you you can't change the system. Dean Burch of the FCC is one who says that. That is nonsense. The British did. There, men with modest means are on the same footing as wealthy candidates. If we don't get a grip on things soon, we are going to suffer something much worse than pollution or crime—and that is the evaporation of American democracy.

Daily Variety, 10–28:10.

Jack Steele
Managing editor, Scripps-Howard
Newspaper Alliance

In his first year in the White House, he (President Nixon) has been surprised to find that things are just as bad as he said they were before he got there.

Before Gridiron Club, Washington, March 14/
The Dallas Times Herald, 3–15:A15.

Adlai Stevenson III
Democratic candidate for United States
Senator from Illinois

Candidates always promise change. It is easy, for it signifies to every listener what he wishes to believe. They leave to the future the meaning of change—and then the promises go unredeemed.

San Francisco Examiner & Chronicle, 9–20:A30.

Strom Thurmond
United States Senator, R-S.C.

Maturity in politics demands a pragmatic acceptance of the practical methods of getting one's principles put into practice . . . Any man who wants to serve his constituents well eventually finds he must adapt to the system.

Human Events, 6–20:4.

I have been watching the (Nixon) Administration since it came into power a year and a half ago. I have noticed that, since the President has been in office, he has become surrounded by liberal and ultra-liberal advisers. The advice that these people give is not in the best interest of either President Nixon or the country. The philosophy which these people espouse and which they give to the President is a sectional philosophy—the philosophy of the Northeast. It is not the philosophy of the South or of the West or of the Midwest. Those who support the philosophy of the Northeast did not support the President in 1968, and they will not support him in 1972. If President Nixon is to be successful in 1972, he must listen to the voice of the great majority. He must take the pulse of America's great heartland. He must keep faith with those who put their trust in him.

Before the Senate, Washington, July 17/
The Washington Post, 7–18:E12.

John G. Tower
United States Senator, R-Tex.

The radical right is the symptom of the disease we call extremism. The radical left is the disease itself.

The New York Times Magazine, 4–26:114.

Joseph D. Tydings
United States Senator, D-Md.

. . . it's all part of a dream that (Vice President) Spiro Agnew is having this fall; a dream about the United States Senate, suddenly docile and submissive, populated by little mechanical puppets who are called Republican Senators, Class of '71, programmed by the Republican National Committee to march in lock-step to the commands of the White House. These are magical little men, these puppets of the Agnew dream. They are faceless, colorless and spineless. They speak only by order, and then quite softly. They never question the Administration's judgment in foreign affairs, even when the lives of American boys are at stake. They accept without a peep, indeed, they even praise the Administration for its Republican high interest rates, what the Administration calls "acceptable unemployment" and decisions of the Republican Administration which mean layoffs from thousands of jobs for workers . . . Gone from the Senate of Spiro Agnew's dream are seasoned and sensitive men who understand and care deeply about the subjects of their concerns: about justice, about poverty, about violence, about the environment, about war and peace . . . No voices of concern stir this dream of Spiro Agnew's. No intolerable conditions cry for solution. What matter that 200,000 American boys may still be in the swamps of Indochina 10 years from now? What matter that millions of Americans still go to bed hungry every night in this country? What matter that, on the eve of our 200th anniversary as a nation, millions of Americans still await fulfillment of the sacred promises of the Declaration of Independence? In the comfortable Senate of the Agnew dream, a little rhetoric, a few speeches, a few convenient scapegoats make all of the problems drift away.

Washington, Oct. 21 /
The Washington Post, 10–22:A15.

Jess Unruh
California State Assemblyman

To continue the aura of the amateur in politics is the height of hypocrisy.

The Washington Post, 3–11:A2.

Gore Vidal
Author

What has Ted (Senator Edward M.) Kennedy ever done that makes him Presidential? He's a Kennedy, but that should not be a reason. It is not, I hope, a hereditary post. The sooner he withdraws from public life the better.

Interview, Rome / TV Guide, 3–21:28.

George Wald
Professor of Biology, Harvard University

Where is the man who embodies all the things we hope for and need, and has charisma besides? The point is, we don't find him any more. But perhaps this is a good thing. Perhaps the time has come for Amer-

ican politics to grow up past father figures and deal with issues.

At New York University commencement,
June 9 / The New York Times, 6–10:30.

George C. Wallace
Former Governor of Alabama

I think I represent the majority viewpoint in this country; and if I don't now, I will by 1972.

San Francisco Examiner & Chronicle
(This World), 1–11:2.

(Vice President) Agnew talks right, and he sounds right, and I'm glad he talks the way he does. But I want some action instead of talk.

San Francisco Examiner & Chronicle, 3–15:A24.

Robert Welch
President, John Birch Society

I don't think the Communists now number more than 2% of the population. But if they get up to about 3%, they can take over everything.

News conference, Akron, Ohio, Aug. 14 /
Cleveland Plain Dealer, 8–15:A10.

John J. Williams
United States Senator, R-Del.

I've never seen such a confused state of affairs (in the Senate). There are so many filibusters running around that, unless we put white hats on one group and dark hats on the other, I do not know who is threatening to filibuster and who is not . . . one wonders whether the filibusters are not filibustering the filibusters.

Washington / The New York Times, 12–20:(4)2.

Sheldon Wolin
Professor of Political Science,
University of California at Berkeley

The political life of this country is exhibiting unmistakable signs of derangement and systemic disorder. I would submit that the present crisis is the most profound one in our entire national history—more profound than

267

(SHELDON WOLIN)

either World War I or II, more profound than even the Civil War, and more profound than the struggle for national independence in the 18th century. In contrast to previous crises, the present one finds the country not only divided, confused, embittered, frustrated and enraged, but lacking the one vital element of self-confidence.

Before American Psychiatric Association,
San Francisco/Time, 5–25:14.

John Cardinal Wright
Prefect, Congregation of the Clergy,
Roman Curia, the Vatican

I do not know what the word "conservative" means any more. I know what it used to mean. It used to mean those who wanted to conserve certain values. I don't know what the word "liberal" means now . . . So I tend to avoid these two words . . . I favor what Arthur Schlesinger, Sr., at Harvard used to call "the vital center"—the place where people meet to find out how much is true in each position and how the common good of the person will be served by both, not by either alone.

Interview, Vatican City/
U.S. News & World Report/8–31:61.

Stephen M. Young
United States Senator, D-Ohio

(Vice President Spiro T. Agnew) is a very able lawyer. He manifests leadership qualities. He is far more personable than Richard Nixon. I'm not going to say anything derogatory about him—but I disagree with everything he says.

Interview, Washington/
The Dallas Times Herald, 8–19:AAA2.

It's a sad thing . . . only the wealthy men can become (political) candidates. It's very frightening, but now more money must be spent by a candidate for the Senate than the total of the salary of that office for six years.

Interview, Washington/
The Dallas Times Herald, 8–19:AAA2.

Whitney M. Young, Jr.
Executive director, National Urban League

(The Nixon Administration's record) has been consistent for its inconsistency . . . It's been marked by great unevenness, by a sort of indecisive flabbiness. It's sort of like Jell-O; you can't really get hold of it, you know. It's what I call "white magic"; you know—now you see it, now you don't.

News conference, New York, Aug. 19/
The New York Times, 8–20:1.

Ralph D. Abernathy
*Chairman, Southern Christian
Leadership Conference*

(The United States has committed) many, many crimes . . . against the vast majority of the population (during the past 200 years). The United States shot down and killed Medgar Evers, Jimmy Jackson, Malcolm X, Martin Luther King, John F. Kennedy, Bobby Kennedy, and every day she is killing our girls and boys through starvation and malnutrition.

*Before Southern Christian Leadership
Conference, Atlanta/
The Washington Post, 8–15:A6.*

Morris B. Abram
Former president, Brandeis University

The Gross National Product of the United States is now approximately $1 trillion and will soon zoom to $1 trillion $300 billion before we celebrate our 200th birthday. Yet, this is not a happy country. Leaving aside all efforts at public psycho-analysis, there is one economic circumstance which is partly responsible for this public unhappiness. A higher percentage of the Gross National Product of this country is absorbed by the private sector than in any other advanced Western state. The public sector of our country is simply starved. The percentage of our production spent in the public sector vacillates between 28% and 29%, compared with 38%, which is not unusual, in the advanced Western Europe society. It is no wonder, then, that our public transportation is so chaotic and decrepit, our schools so ill-functioning, our infant mortality rate so high, and that eyesores and irritants affront us whenever we look carefully at the environment in which we live. And even within this grossly distorted division of the national income, we suffer from the misordering of priorities so that, for example, though we are all terrorized by the crime rate, we continue to spend less on all forms of public law enforcement, including judicial administration and correction, than we spend on crop subsidies. At some point, responsible people, including the politicians in the formal power structure, many of whom already know what is required, and businessmen in the formal power structure, who may not have considered the question, must face and resolve the contradiction between private affluence and public squalor . . .

*At program sponsored by Fry Consultants, Inc./
The Wall Street Journal, 10–28:18.*

Spiro T. Agnew
Vice President of the United States

The way our welfare system encourages idleness is a scandal. The way our welfare system actually breaks up families is a scandal. The way our welfare system robs human beings of their dignity—binding succeeding generations in a lifetime of despair—is the worst scandal of all.

*Before Order of American Hellenic Educational
Progressive Association, Washington, March 9/
U.S. News & World Report, 3–23:84.*

When a man who has nothing gets something, his natural impulse is not to be humbly thankful, but to want more. That's human nature. And that drive to get more is the power behind the American economic system. Certainly, that progress shakes up the status quo. Certainly, it creates new strains in the social fabric when the old rigid lines between social classes become blurred. When the percentage of people who are poor is cut almost in half in less than a generation, there is bound to be unrest—but it is the kind of unrest that is a sign of progress.

Amarillo, Tex./
The Dallas Times Herald, 10–19:A24.

George W. Albee
President, American Psychological Association

Neither our President nor Vice President gives any clear sign of compassion or concern for the poor, the weak, the sick, the unemployed, the helpless, nor willingness to tackle seriously the urgent problems in our increasingly polluted, over-crowded, ghettoized society. Instead, they give all sorts of signals to the prejudiced, the affluent, the hard hats and the vigilantes.

Milwaukee, June 18/
The Washington Post, 6–19:A3.

Saul Alinsky
Sociologist

Student radicals accuse me of organizing the poor for decadent, degenerate, bourgeois, bankrupt, immoral values. But do you know what the poor want? They want a bigger slice of those decadent, degenerate, bourgeois, bankrupt, immoral values.

Time, 3–2:57.

Here (in the U.S.), the poor are the minority. Here, most of the people are dieting, while the have-nots are dying. The power lies in the vast middle-class mass. It is here where the die will be cast.

At Smithsonian Institution symposium,
Washington, Nov. 19/
The New York Times, 11–20:44.

Alden G. Barber
Chief executive, Boy Scouts of America

Our main job is to serve youth, and if that means less emphasis on some of the traditional Scouting themes, such as hiking and camping, and more emphasis on the themes

relevant to what's going on today, such as helping the nation's poor and disadvantaged, then that's the direction we must take. If we don't stay flexible, we'll fall behind and eventually cease to function.

The New York Times, 2–6:14.

David L. Bazelon
Judge, United States Court of Appeals, District of Columbia Circuit

First the Kerner Report and now the Eisenhower Report have told us there is no pill, no Yellow Brick Road, no easy solution. We have to change our way of life if we're going to do something about ghetto life. But we don't like that answer—so we're still holding meetings, looking for the experts who will play the role of the Wizard of Oz and save us all from having to deal with the real underlying problems.

San Francisco Examiner & Chronicle
(This World), 3–29:2.

Robert L. Bernstein
President, Random House

Even a casual look at our Federal budget will show that a lot of money is being spent on outer space. I would propose that our government spend some money on inner space as well . . . I suggest that space agency officials go into the ghettoes and then ask themselves a few questions. Is there enough space there for the adults of the future to build their minds so that they will be able to deal with the problems they are going to have to face? Is there enough space for them to do their homework? Is there enough space for them to read, to understand the ideas that will influence their adult thinking? Is there enough space for them to realize that a lot has been accomplished in this country—and that they are better off building it than destroying it? Should the space agency answer "no" to even one of these questions, then I suggest that it divert some of the money now assigned to outer space and spend it on inner space.

Interview, Wall Street Journal, 8–21:8.

Julian Bond
Georgia State Legislator

In a country where more money is spent on pet food than on food stamps, and legislation for the poor is laughed out of Congress, you may be the generation of reporters to write the obituary for all of us.

Before minority-group graduates of Columbia University School of Journalism summer program, New York, Aug. 28/ The New York Times, 8–29:11.

Charles Bowser
Executive director, Philadelphia Urban Coalition

When a man thinks there is no hope, that there is nothing he can aspire to, he becomes deadly. The President (Nixon) makes a serious error when he says he's not going to (be judged by promises). President Kennedy hardly accomplished anything, when you look back on it; but he talked about things the way it is and we could have faith in him. You go into any house in the ghetto and there's a greasy picture of him tacked up on the wall.

San Francisco Examiner & Chronicle (This World), 5–31:21.

James L. Buckley
United States Senator-elect, C-N.Y.

The one thing I want to prove in six years (in the Senate) is that a man can call himself a conservative and care about people in the ghetto.

Interview, New York, Dec. 15/ Los Angeles Herald-Examiner, 12–16:A9.

C. W. Cook
Chairman, General Foods Corporation

You have to measure "affluence" against your own national needs. The gigantic task confronting us—better education facilities, improving the lot of disadvantaged blacks, low-cost housing, cleaning up the pollution menace, fixing up our transportation facilities—the cost that lies ahead exceeds our immediate resources, even if the Vietnam war were to end today. We are better off than

some other countries, but this can be misleading. The test of "affluence" for a society is how much that society still has to do. And we've got a lot to do.

Interview/The New York Times, 9–20:(2)23.

Alan Cranston
United States Senator, D-Calif.

I believe we will meet our domestic needs only if they are shown to be complementary to our defense and space efforts, not contradictory or competitive to them. We will succeed in meeting and mastering these domestic needs only if we muster the will to meet them. When we realize that building a sound and solid society at home is just as important to our national security and survival as our military strength abroad, we will be on our way.

Before Western Electronics Manufacturers Association, Palo Alto, Calif., Jan. 15/ Congressional Record, 2–10:S1559.

Roger A. Freeman
Senior fellow, Hoover Institution, Stanford University; Former Special Assistant to the President of the United States

Twenty-two years ago, we started an urban renewal program which, at a huge expense, has since destroyed three times as many dwellings as it has completed, and has built mostly apartments which the former residents of the area cannot afford. It has been called a slum removal program because it has mainly shifted slums from one part of the city to another, sometimes spawned "instant slums" to replace the old ones. The true welfare-state enthusiasts blind themselves to the fact that slums are not decaying buildings, but people.

Before Government Research Corporation, Chicago, Sept. 1/Vital Speeches, 10–15:22.

Kenneth E. Frick
Administrator, Agricultural Stabilization and Conservation Service of the United States

I don't like welfare programs. I am getting damn tired of farmers crawling into Wash-

(KENNETH E. FRICK)

ington on their hands and knees asking for handouts.

The Washington Post, 3–6:D15.

Jack Geiger
*Chairman, Department of Community
Health and Social Medicine,
Tufts University Medical School*

We have sat here in our institutions and said, "Okay, if you're sick, come in; we'll lay on hands; we'll treat you; we'll fix you up; and then we will send you happily back out to a social or biological or physical environment that overwhelmingly determines that you're going to get sick again." There is just no point in treating rat bites and ignoring the rats.

*Interview, Boston /
The Dallas Times Herald, 8–9:A34.*

For many people in poverty, particularly rural poverty, the recent national focus on the environment must seem a bitter irony. For us, the issue is not pollution but survival —and it always has been. The rural poor have been drinking dirty water, fighting the elements, living amid society's garbage long before the nation became concerned about smog on Park Avenue, industrial pollution on Lake Erie or the exhaust fumes from automobiles on the Los Angeles freeways. I am not, of course, opposing that national concern; I am asking you to look at some of the environmental pictures (of poverty) we have provided you and consider whether we are entitled to cynicism, if you neglect the human environmental needs of the poor—literally matters of life and death—in favor of a focus on environmental quality for the affluent.

*Before Senate Committee on Nutrition and
Human Needs, Washington /
The Washington Post, 9–29:A18.*

Eugene A. Gulledge
*Commissioner, Federal Housing
Administration*

This country has roughly 65 million living units. Perhaps 90 per cent of those living units are fairly decent houses in fairly decent locations. About 10 per cent of them are something less than adequate housing. Therefore, I translate it into a proposition that 90 per cent of the people are comfortable and 10 per cent uncomfortable, and it's hard to get the 90 per cent to do something about the 10 per cent.

*Interview, Washington, Sept. 27 /
The Washington Post, 9–28:D11.*

Clifford M. Hardin
Secretary of Agriculture of the United States

We are going to succeed with President Nixon's program to eradicate hunger in this country . . . By the end of the year there should not be any hungry at all, or just a few who don't know about it (the program). When we say eradication, we're hoping for 90-some-odd per cent.

*News conference, Los Angeles, Sept. 24 /
Los Angeles Times, 9–25:(1)3.*

Fred R. Harris
United States Senator, D-Okla.

The present welfare system is designed to save money instead of people and, tragically, ends up doing neither.

*Before Americans for Democratic Action,
Pittsburgh, Feb. 11 /
The Dallas Times Herald, 2–12:A7.*

Programs that retrain people for jobs that don't exist can only add to . . . frustration. If we really want to put people to work, we must provide them more than training. There must be jobs.

*Before the Senate, Washington, Aug. 20 /
The New York Times, 8–21:20.*

Vance O. Hartke
United States Senator, D-Ind.

The choice is not between children receiving milk and children receiving lunches. The choice is between milk for children and huge sums of money for supersonic transports, foreign aid give-aways and Pentagon gadgetry.

Quote, 10–4:313.

Theodore M. Hesburgh
President, University of Notre Dame;
Chairman, United States Commission
on Civil Rights

If this country really believes what it says about the Declaration of Independence, the Constitution and the Bill of Rights, then we'd make sure every public dollar spent in this country is spent with regard to human needs.

Quote, 9–20:265.

Ernest F. Hollings
United States Senator, D-S.C.

From 10 to 15 million Americans are hungry—constantly and chronically. This is hunger all the more cruel because it is not necessary. Without harvesting a single additional bushel of wheat, another ear of corn or another pound of potatoes, this country could provide each of its inhabitants with a decent diet. It's not a question of whether we *can* do it, but whether we *will* do it.

Washington/Los Angeles Times, 11–29:A2.

John V. Lindsay
Mayor of New York

Passage of reform legislation by Congress will not by itself break the vicious cycle of poverty, particularly in our nation's impacted urban areas. Permanent change in the lives of the nation's poor requires a national policy which, at a minimum, provides five things: guaranteed employment for everyone willing or able to work; Social Security coverage for the aged, blind and disabled now supported by insufficient welfare benefits; a full negative income tax or child allowance program; a new assistance program for all citizens in need of temporary financial aid; expanded Federal support for a broad range of rehabilitative services for welfare recipients, including day care, manpower training, consumer and homemaking councils, and health services. Without a na-

tional commitment to these broader goals, conditions in our nation's cities cannot significantly improve or change.

Washington/
The Christian Science Monitor, 3–9:5.

Edward J. Logue
President, New York State
Urban Development Corporation

What is needed is very simple. We need a serious national commitment to the goal of providing decent housing for everyone who needs it. Private enterprise can't do the job alone; the cities and the states can't do the job alone. Probably the best thing to do is scrap our present approach to the problem and start all over again. But, so far, neither the President nor the Congress has made a commitment to housing. They are not interested; it is just not very high on their priority list.

Interview, New York/
The New York Times Magazine, 3–1:39.

Robert S. McNamara
President, International Bank for
Reconstruction and Development

The poor in America are like the poor everywhere. Statistically, their economic condition is improving; but the progress is so slow in relation to the more advantaged groups in society that they are actually growing poorer relative to the rich. The point is illustrative of a phenomenon common throughout the world. Though men have inhabited the same planet for more than a million years, they coexist today in communities that range in the extremes—from stone-age simplicity to space-age sophistication.

At Columbia University Conference on
International Economic Development, New
York, Feb. 20/Vital Speeches, 3–15:339.

Walter F. Mondale
United States Senator, D-Minn.

A migrant camp is a microcosm of nearly every social ill . . . every injustice . . . and everything shameful in our society: poverty almost beyond belief, rampant disease and

(WALTER F. MONDALE)

malnutrition, racism, filth and squalor, pitiful children drained of pride and hope, exploitation and powerlessness, and the inability or the unwillingness of public and private institutions at all levels to erase this terrible blight on our country.

Daily World, 7–25:7.

Daniel P. Moynihan
Counsellor to the President of the United States

The great problem of the welfare system is that it has made assistance contingent on a person's being dependent—down and out—saying, in effect: "I'm helpless and you've got to help me." And you can make people helpless if you treat them as if they're helpless.

Interview, Washington/
U.S. News & World Report, 6–15:65.

Gaylord Nelson
United States Senator, D-Wis.

Ecology is concerned with all the relationships of all living things with the environment and with each other. Our goal is not just a clean environment while leaving Appalachia and the ghettos. Our goal is an environment of decency and equality and respect for all creatures, without ghettos, discrimination, poverty, hunger and war.

At University of Michigan, Ann Arbor,
March 12/The New York Times, 3–13:2.2

Richard M. Nixon
President of the United States

For the Senate to adjourn without enacting this measure (Family Assistance Plan) would be a tragedy of missed opportunity . . . In terms of its consequences for children, I think it can fairly be said to be the most important piece of social legislation in our nation's history.

At opening of White House Conference on
Children, Washington, Dec. 13/
San Francisco Examiner, 12–14:2.

WPA-type jobs are not the answer for the men and women who have them, for government which is less efficient as a result, or for the taxpayers who must foot the bill. Such a program represents a reversion to the remedies that were tried 35 years ago. Surely, it is an inappropriate and ineffective response to the problems of the '70s.

Washington, December/
Human Events, 1–2(1971):3.

In the last 10 years alone, the number of children on welfare has nearly tripled, to more than six million. Six million. Six million children caught up in an unfair and tragic system that rewards people for not working, instead of providing the incentives for self-support and independence; that drives families apart, instead of holding them together; that brings welfare snoopers into their homes; that robs them of pride and destroys dignity. I want to change all that. The welfare system has become a consuming, monstrous, inhuman outrage against the community, against the family, against the individual . . . and, most of all, against the very children whom it was meant to help. We have taken long strides toward ending racial segregation; but welfare segregation can be almost as insidious.

At opening of White House Conference on
Children, Washington, Dec. 13/
National Observer, 12–21:12.

Jeno Paulucci
Chairman, J.F.P. Enterprises;
Founder, Chun King Corporation

Once, I stood in a long, slow-moving relief line to get a handout. I couldn't stomach it, so I just stepped out of line and never returned. Today, I'm still adamantly against any type of dole or relief except for the helpless indigent. The able-bodied man, or even boy, can always find a way to earn a living. Who can deny that the Federal government has become too powerful and too paternalistic? These days, a person can live well without working one day in his life. All he needs is a lazy disposition and a conniving mind. This is wrong as sin, and, if allowed to con-

tinue, could destroy the America we know.
Interview, Duluth, Minn./
Nation's Business, March:64.

Ronald Reagan
Governor of California

At the beginning of the last decade, a young leader stood on the steps of the nation's capital and exhorted America: "Ask not what your country can do for you; ask what you can do for your country." His challenge struck a chord in our hearts. Now, on the threshold of a new decade, we might well add: Ask what we can do for ourselves. Ask what we can do to solve the problems of human misery without waiting for yet another government program.
State of the State address, Sacramento, Jan. 6/
The New York Times, 1–7:24.

Welfare's purpose should be to eliminate, as far as possible, the need for its own existence.
State of the State address, Sacramento, Jan. 6/
Los Angeles Times, 1–7:(1)29.

We don't have to make a field trip to a ghetto or sharecropper's farm to look upon poverty. We lived it, through the depths of a great depression. Perhaps this is why we have taxed ourselves at a rate higher than any society ever imposed on itself to provide for the less-fortunate. It is true (that) in this effort our hearts ran away with our heads, and our attempt at public welfare is a Frankenstein monster, a colossal failure.
Before Illinois Manufacturers Associations,
Chicago, Dec. 10/
San Francisco Examiner, 12–11:18.

George W. Romney
Secretary of Housing and Urban
Development of the United States

Meeting our housing needs can be the nation's greatest economic opportunity in the years ahead. This can be the principal stimulant of future sound, economic growth when inflation has been curbed. It can provide the new jobs needed when our involvement in Vietnam is over. We must expand the base of the housing industry. There is enough work to be done to keep all of us, and all of you, busy for years to come. For our biggest undeveloped domestic market is housing.
Before National Association of Home Builders,
Houston, Jan. 19/Vital Speeches, 3–1:312.

Donald Rumsfeld
Assistant to the President of the United
States; Director, Office of Economic
Opportunity

Confrontation politics doesn't help the poor, although it occasionally helps to promote some self-styled spokesmen for the poor . . . A great deal of money, time and energy has been wasted in the kinds of hostilities and fights that only produce polarization, withdrawal and separation of racial and economic groups.
Interview, Los Angeles, Aug. 27/
Los Angeles Times, 8–28:(3)23.

Carl B. Stokes
Mayor of Cleveland

As I look at the people who aren't being fed, who aren't being clothed, who aren't being housed, I ask how can you be more systematically eliminated than if you were put through a gas chamber.
Before Leadership Conference on Civil Rights,
Washington, March 9/
The New York Times, 3–10:24.

The overwhelming (majority of) people in this country want to work. They don't want handouts . . . People aren't born dregs. They develop that way.
Before Senate Finance Committee, Washington,
Sept. 1/Los Angeles Times, 9–2:(1)6.

Dale Tussing
Associate Professor of Economics,
Syracuse University

We underestimate the poverty of the American poor. It's better to be poor in a poor society than in a rich one.
Before American Council on Consumer
Interests, Columbia, Mo./
The Christian Science Monitor, 4–24:14.

Albert A. Walsh
*Housing and Development Administrator
of New York City*

We have not produced housing. We have produced paperwork, red tape, reams and reams of reports, endless lists of recommendations, hundreds and hundreds of amendments to laws. Our housing situation is no better off today than it was in 1930; I'd dare say we are worse off. Two-thirds of our nonwhite families in center cities are forced to call decayed, blighted and rat-infested pigsties their "home."

*At Apartment Builder and Developer
Conference, Miami Beach/
The New York Times, 4–19:(1)62.*

What is developing is a growing crisis among middle-income groups searching for housing. This will become a crisis, nationwide, when there is nothing on the market for the young family on their first job. Historically, this nation has not solved its problems until they become problems for the middle class. Housing is now becoming a problem for the middle class.

U.S. News & World Report, 6–15:76.

Whitney M. Young, Jr.
Executive director, National Urban League

Nothing is more irritating than to visit Western Germany, and other countries in Europe that have been aided by our tax dollars, and find no slums and no unemployment, then go to the Harlems of this country and see the widows of people who died in World War II and the mothers of sons who died in World War II living in hovels.

*News conference, New York, July 20/
Daily World, 7–23:7.*

Frank E. Barnett

Chairman, Union Pacific Railroad

The President talks of traveling to Mars when the commuter can't even get from New York to Washington on time.

The Dallas Times Herald, 3–11:A2.

Clarence J. Brown

United States Representative, R-Ohio

If the Joint Economic Committee (which is debating funding for the supersonic transport) had been advising Queen Isabella, we would still be in Barcelona waiting to prove the world round before daring the Atlantic.

Washington, Aug. 19/
The New York Times, 8–20:9.

Secor D. Browne

Chairman, Civil Aeronautics Board
of the United States

The trouble is that some carriers (airlines) haven't looked at their routes in years. They haven't asked themselves, "Why are we flying from East Elbow to West Loincloth?" (There are) too many routes, too many schedules, too many big planes. We have far more seats than bottoms to fill them. It's that simple . . . The worst thing we (CAB) could do now would be to roll over and play dead while fares were permitted to go up all over the place. The carriers having difficulties must come to grips with their own problems . . . There's nothing cataclysmic about a carrier failing. The government has no obligation to keep an airline in business.

Interview/Newsweek, 10–19:85.

Howard W. Cannon

United States Senator, D-Nev.

It is not uncommon for people who fly regularly to experience delays of hours to take off or land. The airlines and the FAA have recently estimated the direct operating cost to the scheduled airlines industries which are attributable to terminal delays. The rate of growth of this loss is alarming . . . One airline alone estimated that flight delays caused primarily by air traffic control or airport deficiencies were responsible for additional direct operating costs to it of at least $24 million in 1968. These numbers do not include costs incurred by the traveling public and special passenger services—such as hotel accommodations, meals, transportation and telephone calls. The loss of confidence in air travel resulting from the unreliable service has not been measured, but it must be quite significant. If the system is not fundamentally overhauled, the prospects for the next decade are very grim.

Before the Senate, Washington, Jan. 26/
Congressional Record, 1–26:S558.

Krafft A. Ehricke

Chief scientific advisor, advanced programs
of the Space and Science Division,
North American Rockwell Corporation

I see the rebirth of the zeppelin . . . and by the end of this decade. The SST will be flying too high and fast for local hops, and the jumbo jet will be limited by airport and passenger capacity. The zeppelin offers almost unlimited possibilities as far as comfort, safety, passenger and cargo capacity goes, with virtually no ground space required for landings and take-offs . . . Really, by the 1990s these giants could reach a mile long in length, carry up to 4,000 passengers and tons of cargo. They would really be the supertankers of today's travel scene.

Interview, Los Angeles/
Los Angeles Herald-Examiner, 1–4:D14.

Henry Ford II
Chairman, Ford Motor Company

I think the glamour of the automobile is decreasing. People are looking at it now as a machine to get from place to place to do something else.

Interview / Time, 2–23:80.

Automobiles, as long as I'm going to be a working man, are certainly going to be the basic means of transportation in this country and other parts of the world . . . Mass transportation in certain areas is certainly a necessity, but if you think mass transportation is going to replace the automobile, I think you're whistling Dixie or taking pot. It just isn't going to be—not in my lifetime, anyhow.

*Interview, Detroit /
The New York Times, 9–23:71.*

I think the real problem today is that our industry and our company has a credibility gap. We have a credibility gap everywhere. We have a credibility gap with the Federal government, with the Executive branch, with the Legislative branch. We've got a credibility gap with the state governments and with the public. And we just have to do something about it. If you ask me what we're going to do, I can't specifically tell you. But I can tell you this much: And that is, we're not as bad as we're made out to be.

*Interview, Detroit /
Los Angeles Herald-Examiner, 9–27:B5.*

I'm talking about those legislators who vote to ban the internal combustion engine before a usable substitute can be identified; about those governments that are suing to force us to recall all the cars built since 1953 and rebuild them to emission standards that did not exist until 1968; about those Federal safety emission control authorities who seem unwilling to acknowledge that inventions cannot always be scheduled, or that it does take a certain irreducible amount of time to make changes in the nation's largest industry and with complex consumer pro-

ducts; about critics who ignore our accomplishments, distort the past and impugn our motives. Nobody knows better than I do that the automobile industry has come to the end of an era. The American people demand safer, cleaner, more reliable cars and better service. Those are legitimate demands which must be met. We have made substantial progress toward meeting them, and we are going to make more. This will require major and rapid changes in how cars are designed, manufactured and serviced. Those changes cannot be completed overnight. And they will not come one moment sooner because of deadlines which demand the impossible.

*Las Vegas, Aug. 18 /
Cleveland Plain Dealer, 8–19:A11.*

Milton Friedman
*Professor of Economics,
University of Chicago*

If the SST is worth building, the market will make it in Boeing's interest to build without a subsidy. If a subsidy is needed, the SST should not be built.

Washington Star, 9–15:A4.

J. William Fulbright
United States Senator, D-Ark.

We're going to have the worst of both worlds if we're going to start bailing people out of mismanaged private enterprise. It is utterly inexcusable for the government to rescue private investors who took a risk in the first place. I think it's much better to nationalize the railroads than to subsidize them.

Daily World, 7–11:4.

Whitney Gillilland
*Vice Chairman, Civil Aeronautics Board
of the United States*

As for the environmental problems connected with the supersonic transport, there may be an answer. Perhaps we ought to abandon the designs now contemplated, and instead direct our efforts to a supersonic flying submarine. Then, we could build the airports under water. If not, then at least his generation has more hair to tear than any other in modern times.

The Wall Street Journal, 10–19:12.

Barry M. Goldwater
United States Senator, R-Ariz.

No matter what we do here, there is going to be supersonic transportation in the world, and on a globe-circling basis, in a very few years. That is as certain as the development of the automobile was in the early part of this century. The development of an SST program is a measure of transportation progress. It will come as quickly as it is feasible. In Europe, it is already feasible. Not only the Soviets, but the French and British, are busy testing SST prototypes which will shortly be moved into production and placed in operation on regularly-scheduled world airlines . . . I would remind the Members (of the Senate) that for many years our nation was able to overcome competition from foreign countries using cheap labor by the simple expedient of being able to build a "better mousetrap." And in the "mousetrap" business we were unchallenged. Whether the "mousetrap" involved tanks, guns or planes to defeat the Axis, or housing materials to overcome postwar shortage, or automobiles of a superior nature, we always came up with the better product. In space today, our "mousetrap" is one that was capable of landing men on the moon before any other nation or collection of nations. And, against this backdrop, we have Members of this body telling us that, in SST development, we not only cannot build a better mousetrap, we cannot even build one.

*Before the Senate, Washington, Oct. 2/
Vital Speeches, 11–1:40.*

Thomas M. Goodfellow
*President, Association of
American Railroads*

Railroads are needed. Railroads are in deep trouble. Railroads need help. Railroads must modernize and expand. That requires money. Railroads aren't earning or attracting money . . . Our immediate goal is keeping our heads above water—and barring the door against the bogyman of bankruptcy.

*Before Rotary Club, San Francisco, Sept. 22/
Vital Speeches, 11–1:56.*

There seems to be a lot of loose talk these days about nationalization, piece-meal or all at once, as a solution to railroad problems. I'm personally convinced . . . that nationalization is the worst possible solution . . . Whether railroads are privately owned and managed, or managed by government, the money they require will have to be found, because there is no better way to get done the transportation job that railroads do and can do. Nationalization would be costly— some $60 billion to start with, merely to effect a transfer of title, without even making a start on improving the present plant. Nationalization in other nations shows enormous losses, paid for by the taxpayers. Nationalization in our political system would be a long and painful process, disruptive in many ways, especially in terms of inefficient and deteriorating service.

*Before Rotary Club, San Francisco, Sept. 22/
Vital Speeches, 11–1:57.*

William Haddon, Jr.
*President, Insurance Institute
for Highway Safety*

The automobile purchaser today is paying twice for the privilege of owning a car whose front and rear ends are designed to look like French pastries in the ads and showrooms, and to act like antique porcelain or aluminum foil in minor collisions. First, he pays when he buys the car for the privilege of owning expensive-to-shape, ostensibly sales-promoting—and, incidentally, environmentally inappropriate—exterior designs, (in) whose rendering the stylist's hand rather than the engineer's is wastefully dominant. Next, when his vehicle experiences what is euphemistically called a "fender bender," he pays again—this time the many hundreds of dollars required as the cost of replacing such inappropriate parts to undo the damage caused or aggravated by the cosmetic design

(WILLIAM HADDON, JR.)

and manufacture of his vehicle's exterior in the first place.

Before Congressional subcommittee,
Washington/Quote, 8–9:123.

Najeeb E. Halaby
President, Pan American World Airways

The automobile and aviation industries are relatively new. Both have aimed at the mass market. Both have changed the quality of life, not by selling hardware but by merchandising mobility. In fact, we're really "merchants of mobility" by offering man more dominion over time and space; by translating the expression, "expanding his horizons," from poetry to hard fact; by holding out a whole new range of aspirations; and by adding a whole new dimension to man's life and outlook.

Before Economic Club of Detroit/
Congressional Record, 2–10:S1563.

The supersonics are coming—as surely as tomorrow. You will be flying one version or another by 1980 and be trying to remember what the great debate was all about.

Time, 6–1:64.

I think this industry is largely responsible for its own problems, particularly of competition. Top management has let the lawyers and marketers take over and use every pressure and propaganda to produce overcompetition. Right now, we are witnessing the worst of regulated enterprise and all the risk of competitiveness. You can't blame it all on Washington. *We've* got to work our way out of it.

The New York Times, 11–1:(3)2.

The SST is coming. The sole question is whether we (the U.S.) do it, or whether we let somebody else do it. If we do it, we will gain the benefits. If somebody else does it, we will lose world leadership in aviation as we have lost it in shipping. As we look around

the world and see what is happening in steel production, automobile production, textile production, is there not some basis for the conclusion that we had better hold tight to what production advantages we have?

News conference, New York, Dec. 7/
The New York Times, 12–8:20.

Ben Heineman
President, Northwest Industries, Inc.—
parent company of North Western Railroad

At present, the railroads have the worst of all possible worlds. The managements have the responsibility for running them, but government has all the authority. I used to say that, as chief executive of a railroad, I was able to make an important decision: I could decide whether to paint our freight cars red or green.

Time, 7–6:59.

William P. Lear
Industrialist

When I said I was through with the steam-auto idea, I really meant it. I said it looked so discouraging, so complicated, that it was very likely the gas turbine would be preferable. I still thought so up to three months ago. But it's a sorry man who can't change his mind when new facts become available. And the discovery of Learium was just such a fact. Now I'm just as convinced that it's not only possible but probable that steam automobiles are the wave of the future.

Los Angeles, Aug. 31/
Los Angeles Times, 9–1:(2)8.

Wassily Leontief
Professor of Economics, Harvard University

The development and construction of these super planes (SST) . . . will absorb many billion dollars of public and private—but mostly public—money, several hundred thousand years of skilled labor and huge amounts of other valuable economic resources. At a time when the shortage of such resources compels us to forego badly needed improvements in public health care, education, housing and mass transportation, to give priority to the SST is nothing short of frivolous.

Washington Star, 9–15:A4.

William Magruder
Director, Supersonic Transport Program,
Department of Transportation
of the United States

I've heard it all: The supersonic transport is going to modify the climate; it's going to bring on another ice age; or it's going to melt the icecaps. Lord, three major volcanic eruptions in the last 90 years ejected more gunk into the atmosphere than all of mankind's activities. This country needs the SST.

Interview, Washington/Newsweek, 8–17:66.

George Meany
President, American Federation of
Labor-Congress of Industrial Organizations

I would advocate that the government take over the railroads. Other governments do it. We're not doing very well now under private management . . . the way the railroads are being operated now, that might be an improvement.

Washington/San Francisco Examiner, 11–11:2.

James B. Pearson
United States Senator, R-Kan.

The real issue is whether supersonic aircraft will be a transportation advance and will meet transportation needs. The SST is glamorous, but there are unsolved problems in air transportation, in rail transportation and mass transit which must carry a high priority.

Washington, Aug. 27/
The New York Times, 8–28:51.

William Proxmire
United States Senator, D-Wis.

I urge the Civil Aeronautics Board move to revoke the permit of any foreign air carrier to land in the United States that continues to serve any country which accepts a hijacker or which harbors, finances, or in any way sanctions terrorists and saboteurs who murder and destroy civilian passengers, crews and planes.

Washington/
The Christian Science Monitor, 3–6:2.

If Congress succeeds in re-ordering its priorities this year, there is no doubt in my mind that the SST will wind up right at the bottom of the list—where it belongs.

Washington, Aug. 19/Washington Star, 8–19:A1.

We are being asked to spend $290 million this year for transportation (the SST) for one- half of 1 per cent of the people—the jet-setters—to fly overseas, and we are spending $204 million this year for urban mass transportation for millions of people to get to work. Does that make any sense?

Newsweek, 12–14:83.

Elwood Quesada
Member of the board, American Airlines;
Former Administrator, Federal
Aviation Administration

The feeling among airline executives is to wish that the SST would go away.

Before joint Congressional subcommittee on
the SST, Washington/Time, 6–1:64.

Henry S. Reuss
United States Representative, D-Wis.

The taxpayer's revolt continues. There is inflation at the rate of 7.2%. An extra million persons are unemployed. Interest rates are the highest in 100 years. Wall Street is a shambles. Yet the taxpayers are mocked by this flying dodo bird (the supersonic transport) that will add $290 million in taxes this year.

Before the House, Washington, May 27/
Los Angeles Times, 5–28:(1)4.

W. Thomas Rice
Chairman, Seaboard Coast Line
Railroad Company

I look at what the railroads are and the part they play in our American way of life. We cannot operate without the railroads, as

(W. THOMAS RICE)

we know America today. A realistic approach . . . on the part of the government is absolutely essential. If we can be made competitive, we can make it on our own, in my opinion. Our continued competition with other modes of transportation which are supported by vast sums of taxpayers' dollars puts us at a severe disadvantage . . . I believe, in the final analysis, that we will get some needed legislation, and we will get a new attitude by the regulatory bodies as to what the railroads really mean to America.

Interview, Richmond, Va./
Nation's Business, Nov.:66.

James M. Roche
Chairman, General Motors Corporation

Planned obsolescence, in my opinion, is another word for progress. Nobody in the industry coined that phrase. But if we had not had the annual model change, I don't think the auto industry would be in the position it's in today. I think all you'd have to do to prove that is to compare one of today's cars with one that was built four or five years ago.

Interview/Newsweek, 4–6:75.

The most promising (engine) continues to be the internal-combustion engine. We've tried steam, electric cars, turbines, even fuel cells. It's just not possible to provide the kind of system that the United States is accustomed to other than by internal combustion.

Interview/Newsweek, 4–6:75.

John H. Shaffer
Administrator, Federal Aviation Administration

The record clearly indicates that the airports of this country and the nation's air-navigation system are safer than those of any country in the world. I agree that our airports are inadequate and inefficient, but that doesn't mean they aren't safe.

Interview, Washington/
U.S. News & World Report, 8–10:38.

There is no question in my mind that there will be a demand for supersonic flight simply because we're able to do more work in the same unit of time. The SST, flying at three times the speed of the 747, although it will carry only two-thirds the load, will do twice as much work as the 747 in the same period of time, with the same size crew. That's real, measurable productivity. We are going to see a one-day world, in which one can go from any point on the globe to any other point in the same day.

Interview, Washington/
U.S. News & World Report, 8–10:40.

I do not believe that all railroads, bus companies, airline companies can operate profitably as long as they are as compartmentalized by mode as they currently are. I submit we will see total-transportation companies emerge to offer a passenger and shipper the best mode or combination of modes of travel between two points, whatever that might be—bus, train, plane, helicopter, ship, barge or combination thereof.

Interview, Washington/
U.S. News & World Report, 8–10:42.

The SST . . . is as natural in the evolution of aviation as running is after walking.

Before FAA employes/
Dallas Times Herald, 8–21:A2.

Charles C. Tillinghast, Jr.
Chairman, Trans World Airlines

I have to say, in all candor, that I think we are still a long way from developing in the international community the attitude that is necessary to put an end to virtually all hijacking of airline planes. What must be done is to get the nations of the world to refuse to tolerate aerial hijacking, just as centuries ago they finally got together and put an end to piracy on the seas. Until we achieve that attitude around the world, we in the airline business are going to have to be aggressive in the use of measures that will physically prevent hijacking: armed guards on planes, searches of passengers and their

ıggage, electronic devices to spot weapons.
hese measures are not going to be fool-
roof. We can't guarantee that some person
on't slip aboard and commandeer a flight.
ut these precautions will make hijacking a
retty sticky business instead of the virtual
o-risk adventure it has been until recently.

Interview, Washington/
U.S. News & World Report, 10–12:48.

Even if the U.S. doesn't build an SST, I
ıink there is no doubt that faster-than-
ound planes will be in airline service by
980. I am assuming that the British and
rench will carry through development of
ıe *Concorde* or some derivative of it. There
robably will be a Russian supersonic trans-
ort flying, too . . . I think there ought to be
n American SST because of a very simple
ıct—which is that the United States has a
ıost difficult and delicate balance-of-
ayments problem. Our balance-of-payments
ı propped up more than anything else—
ther than possibly agricultural exports—by
xport of aircraft and aircraft parts. The
ıinute we default the aircraft field to other
ountries and we, the airlines of the U.S., be-
ın spending dollars abroad to buy aircraft,
his balance-of-payments situation is going
o get far worse. I know there are some well-
nown economists saying that this isn't so. I
ave read what they say and, frankly, I think
t mostly sophistry.

Interview, Washington/
U.S. News & World Report, 10–12:50.

ﬕtuart G. Tipton
ᵖresident, Air Transport Association
ᵒf America

We of the airline industry may look back
on the past with pride. We may look at the
ᵖresent with satisfaction. But we regard the
uture as a challenge for accomplishment of
ı greater goal—to make air travel so totally
afe that it will quiet the cynics, appease the
ıoubters, reassure the fearful.

Nation's Business, March:76.

Douglas Toms
Director, National Highway Safety Bureau

There's no longer any question but that
we can build cars that are both beautiful and
in which it will be all but impossible to kill
yourself. We're heading in that direction
right now. Auto safety is becoming a very
sexy field.

Newsweek, 9–7:54.

B. J. Vierling
Acting director of supersonic transport
development, Federal Aviation
Administration

Most of the objections that have been
brought against the SST take what I feel is a
shortsighted view. They reflect a technological pessimism that is inconsistent with our
history and out of character with our national traditions . . . I don't believe that we
should reject out of hand what promises to
be better and faster just because we think
what we already have is good enough, fast
enough or can't be improved. I don't believe
it is logical to resist new developments in
transportation and new frontiers in speed
when the whole course of civilization is a
travelog of successively better forms of transportation and consecutively higher speeds.

Philadelphia/National Observer, 1–12:16.

John A. Volpe
Secretary of Transportation
of the United States

I am, very frankly, skeptical that we can
continue to plan around the automobile as
we have been doing . . . I believe that cities
cannot survive without alternative modes of
transportation—pollution-free buses, rapid
rail-cars, subways and other more exotic vehicles based on advances in aerospace technology.

Before National Research Council, Washington,
Jan. 14/Los Angeles Herald-Examiner, 1–15:A6.

Never mind the fact that an automobile is
some 20 feet long, weighs 2 tons and carries,
on the average, 1.6 people on each trip.

(JOHN A. VOLPE)

Never mind the fact that the internal-combustion engine—depending on whether you listen to its fans or its critics—generates from 50 to 80 per cent of all the air pollution we breathe every day. Never mind the fact that the automobile kills 55,000 people every year, over 150 every day. Never mind the fact that the leading cause of death among our young people, aged 16 to 25, is the highway crash. Never mind the fact that, in America today, we have one linear mile of highway for every square mile of land, and, with the automobile population growing by 10,000 vehicles every 24 hours, the demand for additional pavement is enormous. Over and above all these items, we must accept the fact that there are those in our economy for whom the automobile is far too expensive a purchase. We must accept the fact that all our proposed social remedies—such as model-cities projects, health centers, evening college classes, job centers, suburban employment opportunities and you-name-it—just aren't going to get full utilization if we make automobile ownership an unwritten prerequisite for participation. Because of these factors, we attach great importance to public transportation.

Before Chamber of Commerce, Worcester, Mass., Jan. 27/ Congressional Record, 1–28:E419.

It will not happen today, and not this year, but it is something we are working on—a trust fund that would incorporate all modes of transportation with designated accounts for highways, mass transit, railroad, aviation and other modes. We think this is the direction that the total transportation program must move.

News conference, New York, Jan. 28/ The New York Times, 1–29:62.

Intermodal transportation—that's the answer. Modes of transportation that are inter-dependent. A total balanced transportation system. You can't depend on the automobile alone any more. You've got to get rid of the imbalance.

Nation's Business, April:40.

We've got to double our transportation capacity in the next 20 years. Think of that. In 20 years we've got to match all of history. When I get through, I'd like to feel I have developed a balanced transportation system. America is going to grow; we know that. But the way it grows is what's important. And transportation will determine in a big way where we are at the end of the decade.

Nation's Business, April:43.

Henry C. Wallich
Professor of Economics, Yale University

If it were possible to outlaw supersonic transports—no matter what countries would build and operate them—a strong case could be made for pronouncing such a ban. The gains from faster and more frequent travel seem small relative to the injury from noise and possibly other environmental damage. Unfortunately, this decision is not in our hands. The (British-French) *Concorde* is being built and will fly whether or not the (United States) SST is built. If the *Concorde* proves to be commercially viable, the U.S. then had better proceed to capture such economic advantages as are to be had by building the plane. Failure to build would inflict lasting balance-of-payment damage with little compensating environmental gain.

The New York Times, 9–16:93.

Sidney R. Yates
United States Representative, D-Ill.

The SST, which looked like a supersonic marvel on paper, looks more and more like a supersonic white elephant as the time approaches to begin prototype construction.

U.S. News & World Report, 5–25:70.

William T. Cahill
Governor of New Jersey

The Federal government can no longer avoid its responsibility to the Newarks of this country. Housing, health, education and the myriad problems of urban America cannot wait much longer. Newark is a sign of the times—the end result of a series of mistakes throughout the years . . . Newark is a signal of the storms ahead—approaching urban storms that can bring our major cities and our sovereign states to financial destruction. Newark, and all the Newarks of this country, desperately need Federal funds to survive.

Trenton, N.J., Dec. 23 /
The New York Times, 12–24:41.

Jerome P. Cavanagh
Former Mayor of Detroit

I know it's trite to say money is the answer. I know that some academics now find it stylish to deny that there is an urban crisis at all, let alone one that money can solve. But once—just once—I'd like to try money.
The New York Times, 5–22:21.

Frederick J. Close
Chairman, Aluminum Company of America

Most of our difficulties stem from the fact that more and more Americans are living closer and closer together, clustered in our great urban complexes—their daily lives increasingly dependent on each other. So all of the problems and pressures of our society converge to hit and hurt us where we live: in our cities.

Before Association of Western Advertisers,
Los Angeles, March 19 /
Los Angeles Herald-Examiner, 3–20:A15.

Lawrence M. Cox
Assistant Secretary for Renewal and Housing Assistance, Department of Housing and Urban Development of the United States

It may be that in the 1950s we could afford to have a sort of never-ending slum-clearance program, where a city kept coming back for more and more. We weren't really spending money very fast then. There were only 100 to 200 cities in the program. Now, there are over 1,000—either in or seeking projects. The competition for money is stiff. It will get stiffer. We can't afford the luxury of things we could have had then. Now we are faced with reality.
U.S. News & World Report, 4–20:28.

John Kenneth Galbraith
Professor of Economics, Harvard University

I am persuaded on this point: that much of the urban problem in the United States is the result of trying to run cities on the cheap; trying to run cities without adequate funds for the police, without adequate funds for sanitation, without adequate funds for housing, without adequate funds for recreation, without adequate funds for hospitals, without adequate funds for welfare, without adequate funds for all the peculiar problems, the peculiarly expensive problems, of the modern metropolis. The one thing we have never understood was how expensive the very big city is . . .
Interview/Los Angeles Times, 10–4:G2.

Donald M. Graham
Chairman, Continental Illinois National Bank and Trust Company of Chicago

I see no reason for concluding that lack of private credit or investment has been a major contributing cause of urban decline.

(DONALD M. GRAHAM)

Credit is a tail of the dog; it is not the dog. We need to understand the underlying factors which, in fact, cause the existence of a "credit-deficient" environment. Underemployment, a consequent fluctuating income base, low-quality education and educational facilities, inadequate transportation, deteriorated housing, poor quality of public services, and a host of related market factors—these are the reasons why credit and investment capital have been slow to find their way into the ghetto. All these—which we see clearly as inequities and human lacks—are functions of the demand inadequacy of the inner-city credit and investment capital market. Inner-city ghettos simply have not had the essential market characteristics necessary to bid effectively for capital in the market as we know it. There is a direct relationship between the economic base of any given area and the allocation of credit and investment capital to it. Areas that have an adequate economic base can compete for credit and capital; those without such a base cannot compete.

At American Bar Association symposium /
The Wall Street Journal, 3–2:10.

Walter J. Hickel
Secretary of the Interior
of the United States

A man can live in a slum out in the open spaces and be happier than a man of means who lives in the city and can't get that "spiritual renewal." We've just made life miserable for ourselves in these urban areas.

Interview, Washington /
Los Angeles Times, 3–13:(2)7.

That's one of the problems in this country—the approach taken with the cities. We—both Republicans and Democrats—over the years have spent billions of dollars attempting to improve the physical surroundings of those in the cities. But it's the inner man in the inner city we should work with. Let's try to change his outlook. Bring him out here,

where he can rough it without toilets an running water, and he loves it. His who perspective—outlook on life—changes.

Moose, Wyo., July :
The Dallas Times Herald, 7–3:D

James J. Howard
United States Representative, D-N.J.

I feel it is long past due that we shoul consider the urban and suburban dweller This Congress has shown it is willing to she out about $290 million as a beginning fo the SST, which will provide for the je setters to get from New York to a cockta party in London in less time than many con muters can get from Asbury Park to Ne York City to work.

Quote, 11–29:50

Alex Inkeles
Professor of Sociology, Harvard University

We have found no evidence that more ex posure to modern influences means mor psychic stress. If a man in one of these de veloping countries shows signs of psych stress, it isn't the TV, it isn't the noise or th dirty air, it isn't the eight-hour shift in th factory, it isn't the crowded buses, it isn't be cause he's moved from somewhere else. In deed, exposure to modernization and rapi social change decreases the psychosomat symptoms. The more modern a man—th greater his sense of personal efficacy, th greater his interest and participation in pul lic affairs and his openness to new exper ence—the better his psychic health. In pe centage terms, the difference is small, but certainly leads us away from an indictmer of the city's "terrors."

Interview, Cambridge, Mass
The New York Times, 5–26:1

Harold LeVander
Governor of Minnesota

52% of the people in Minnesota live i seven counties in the metropolitan area The other 48% live in 80 counties. Th seven urban counties are growing. The othe

counties are declining. We are trying to
promote a "rural renaissance." It is this
heavy concentration of people in the metropolitan areas that has caused pollution,
crime and housing problems.

At National Governors Conference,
Lake of the Ozarks, Mo./
U.S. News & World Report, 8-24:14.

John V. Lindsay
Mayor of New York

The Congress must approve revenue-
sharing in 1971. And it must approve a
revenue-sharing plan that is worth more than
its name. If this country could afford to
spend $17 billion on the Marshall Plan for
the cities and states of Europe, if we could
afford $18 billion to defend the state of
South Korea, if we were willing to pour
$100 billion in the villages of Vietnam for a
war no general could win, then surely the
nation could afford to share $10 billion of
its revenues—now—to save our cities and suburbs and states.

Before National League of Cities, Atlanta,
Dec. 8/The New York Times, 12-9:55.

Hubert G. Locke
Professor of Human Relations,
Wayne State University

. . . our cities are simply too big for any of
us to entertain any reasonable hope of establishing a sense of community—either community identity, community involvement or
community responsibility. And without a
sense of community, our best efforts to make
cities livable will lead only to further frustration, decay and chaos . . . I propose, therefore, that we set ourselves to the urgent task
of breaking up our cities into more meaningful and manageable community units—
that we decentralize cities in such a way that
citizens can begin to regain a sense of confidence in the processes of the city, to feel that
their voices will be heard, their decisions
counted and their judgments taken seriously.

Interview/Daily World, 6-9:6.

Richard G. Lugar
Mayor of Indianapolis

The general problem that many cities
have is some type of reconciliation between
the inner-city and the outer-city—the core
area with high-cost citizens flowing in and
high-production citizens flowing out, the
black and white exodus of persons who are
able to afford a down payment on property
somewhere outside the central city. The
polarizations are obvious. People are spending a great deal of time and effort trying to
get away from each other.

Indianapolis/Los Angeles Times, 2-11:(1A)2.

Henry Maier
Mayor of Milwaukee

In the past 25 years, there has been a movement from countryside to city which may
well be the greatest migration in the history
of the world. At the same time there has
been a vast migration from the city to the
suburbs. Two caravans have passed on the
urban highway: the Cadillacs of the rich
heading for the green fields of suburbia; the
jalopies of the poor headed for the hand-me-
down housing of the inner city. These dual
migrations have now produced a nation in
which there are probably more slum dwellers
than there are farmers.

Quote, 2-15.

Emmett McGaughey
Vice president, Los Angeles
Board of Police Commissioners

Our cities are under attack and our peace
officers . . . are the only hope for preservation
of civilization. The strength and trust of our
urbanized nation must be in the cities. If
those cities are no longer safe places in which
to live, to work and to play, then we have no
country.

Los Angeles, April 8/
Los Angeles Herald-Examiner, 4-9:A10.

William S. Moorehead
United States Representative, D-Pa.

We in Pittsburgh are beginning to realize

(WILLIAM S. MOOREHEAD)

that people are more important than pavement, homes more important than highways.

Quote, 11–29:505.

Daniel P. Moynihan
Counsellor to the President
of the United States

The economics of new cities—or of "new towns," as they are sometimes called—are very elusive. As the President has said, we have to develop a national growth policy. But it seems likely that our big cities now will be our big cities a century from now. And as long as we have the great majority of our population living in cities, we can expect that city problems will persist.

Interview, Washington/
U.S. News & World Report, 6–15:64.

Arthur Naftalin
Former Mayor of Minneapolis

It's time that the central cities acknowledge defeat and that they move to claim the entitlement of any vanquished foe, which, in their case, is to be rescued and rehabilitated by their own adversaries: suburbs, state, the national government and their own constituencies.

Before National League of Cities, Atlanta,
Dec. 8/ The Dallas Times Herald, 12–8:A10.

Richard M. Nixon
President of the United States

What rural America most needs is a new kind of assistance. It needs to be dealt with, not as a separate nation, but as part of an overall growth policy for all America. We must create a new rural environment that will not only stem the migration to urban centers but reverse it.

San Francisco Examiner & Chronicle
(Real Estate), 1–25:A.

Wright Patman
United States Representative, D-Tex.

Over 50 per cent of the area of many of our major cities is now taken up by roadways

and parking lots. Let me stress this fact that over one-half of the land area of large cities of this country is unavailable for housing, parks, office buildings, centers for social and cultural activities and, most fundamentally, people.

Quote, 10–25:387.

Abraham A. Ribicoff
United States Senator, D-Conn.

We cannot solve our urban crisis unless we include the suburbs in the solution. We can talk all we want about rebuilding the "ghetto," better housing, tax incentives for job development and massive funds for education. Hopefully, we may even do this. But improving the "ghetto" is not enough . . . The suburbs are the new America. That is where the private economy is moving, that is where our growing population will be housed.

Before the Senate, Washington, Feb. 9/
U.S. News & World Report, 2–23:32.

George W. Romney
Secretary of Housing and Urban
Development of the United States

Cities should be designed by people for people. Most of our major cities today have been designed by the automobile for the automobile.

Quote, 6–21:577.

We cannot escape the fact that there is simply not enough land in our crowded cities to build the tremendous amount of housing that is going to be necessary in the next decade—especially housing for low and moderate-income people. We have no choice but to build outside the central cities. If the suburbanites refuse to see their obligations —their opportunity—it's possible the courts will see it for them.

U.S. News & World Report, 6–22:39.

Joseph L. Spengler
Professor of Economics, Duke University

Men are finding that the big city is unsuited to rational government and the good life, resembling as it does a zoo where crowded, anxiety-ridden animals fight their kind instead of getting along as they instinctively do in the forest.

At conference sponsored by Carolina Population Center of University of North Carolina, Chapel Hill/The New York Times, 10–25:(1)4.

Joseph D. Tydings
United States Senator, D-Md.

The decay of the central city is much more serious than most people realize. The average person does not comprehend the extent of family breakdowns, how impoverished the schools are, how bad the welfare system is in holding the family together, how bad transportation is. The cancer of the inner city is much worse than generally realized.

U.S. News & World Report, 3–16:16.

Wes Uhlman
Mayor of Seattle

Reapportionment has suburbanized the legislatures, and the suburbanites are as hostile to the city as the farmers ever were.

The New York Times, 6–24:(1)54.

John A. Volpe
Secretary of Transportation of the United States

I've learned this—as a businessman, a Governor and now as a Cabinet officer: A city which doesn't develop a means to move large numbers of people effectively and efficiently from where they are to where they want to go is a city of obsolescence.

Nation's Business, April:43.

Walter E. Washington
Mayor of Washington

There are no simple answers to the urban crisis. The problems of congestion, misery, tension and racial discrimination have been woven into our human fabric.

At Bishop College, Dallas/ The Dallas Times Herald, 1–28:A30.

PART TWO

International Affairs

Africa

Chinua Achebe
Nigerian writer and publisher

Biafra is just an idea now. It doesn't exist any more. It ceased to exist at the moment of surrender. But the memory of Biafra is a different thing. It can be just nostalgic; the government can make it meaningless if we find that, under them, we are happier than ever. But if people start to say, "It might have been better the other way," then the idea of Biafra would stay alive. The burden rests with those who fought for one Nigeria. The man who is defeated is entitled to sulk. Only the victor can afford to be magnanimous.

Interview, University of Nsukka, Nigeria/
The Washington Post, 12–6:C1.

Peter Afolabi
Consul-General of Nigeria in New York

We have always believed that private businessmen have a big role to play in the development of the Nigerian economy. There must be a strong private sector to absorb the shocks of nation-building, to provide employment and to help solve the problems of widespread poverty. Government cannot do everything; its budget is too small. But with strong private enterprise and the stability we want, people can work for development.

The New York Times, 2–8:(3)13.

Richard M. Akwei
Ambassador to the United Nations
from Ghana

Its (the United States) attitude toward the apartheid problem cannot be dissociated from its attitude to its own black American problem. Indeed, in the view of educated Africans, the African problem is only the black American problem writ large on an international canvas. The two problems are indissolubly linked in the minds of educated Africans. In the same way that there is no rational explanation for the continued discrimination and poverty of black Americans in the United States, there is no rational explanation for the present involvement of the United States in South Africa . . . If it (the United States) needs neither South African money nor South African military alliance, we are entitled to ask: Is the present United States policy on apartheid only an extension of the long and sinister arm of the Southern strategy to our oppressed continent?

Before United Nations Security Council,
New York/Daily World, 8–5:10.

Okoi Arikpo
Foreign Minister of Nigeria

Like all major powers, the Russians have tried, and they still try, to build up as much influence as possible in Nigeria. We are friendlier with the Russians than we were, and this is likely to continue. But they are careful not to try to impose their views on us. Our relations are business-like, because we paid for everything we got. They have asked for no bases and would get none if they did. So there is no reason to assume that they do not respect our sovereignty.

Interview, Lagos/
Chicago Daily News, 8–29:8.

Houari Boumedienne
President of Algeria

Some American circles say that Algeria is being re-colonized by the Russians. French circles claim that we are being re-colonized by the Americans. We are very jealous of our independence, but we have no complex about colonization.

Interview, Algiers/
The Washington Post, 12–16:A15.

(HOUARI BOUMEDIENNE)

Our people would not understand if our government closed its doors to the revolutionaries who come here from all over the world. The only thing we do is give them (the revolutionaries) freedom of expression . . . Our philosophy is very clear. We forbid them to act against their own countries . . . but Algeria has a tradition of asylum, and we cannot go against it.

Interview, Algiers/
The Washington Post, 12–18:A27.

Abdou Diouf
Prime Minister of Senegal

A technocrat is thought to be somebody who does not place enough value on the human and political aspects of life . . .I am often called that because I have arrived at this position after having proved myself as a civil servant, rather than in the party or in politics. But I reject that reasoning. I am not a technocrat because I believe in going toward the people, in using scientific methods but taking the human and political aspects into account as well.

Interview, Dakar/
The Washington Post, 8–17:A23.

Philip Effiong
Major General and acting Chief of State of Biafra

We are firm, we are loyal citizens of Nigeria, and we accept the authority of the Federal Military Government of Nigeria. The Republic of Biafra ceases to exist.

At surrender ceremonies, Lagos/Time, 1–26:18.

C. Clyde Ferguson
United States Ambassador to Uganda

One of the first things you find out, as a black American visiting Africa, is how American you are. An American black is not an African. His style of life is American. No American black can relate to a tribe, nor does he have any heritage of language, like the Italian-, Polish- or German-Americans. You have to learn as an outsider.

Kampala, Uganda/
Los Angeles Times, 12–10:(7)7.

Yakubu Gowon
Chief of State of Nigeria

The so-called rising sun of Biafra has set forever. Nigerians must pay homage to the fallen of both sides and build a newer and greater Nigeria as a monument to them . . . It would be a great disservice to Nigeria ever again to use the term "Biafra."

Lagos, Jan. 15/
Los Angeles Herald-Examiner, 1–16:A3.

The levelheaded economic policies which stood us well for the war (with Biafra) also offer a good ground for optimism as we harness them to the task of reconstruction. Reconstruction is not simply replacing damaged houses, roads and bridges, or doing the same old things in the same old way. Our objective is the rapid establishment of a virile, prosperous and progressive African society that is able to stand on its own feet.

Interview, Lagos/Time, 2–9:27.

Nigeria has no bitterness toward Tanzania, Gabon, Ivory Coast, Zambia and other countries that supported the (Biafran) rebellion. It is only regrettable that these nations could not see the continental and international damage that their misguided action could have caused if the secessionists had been successful. However, if even now these countries come forward and offer their right hand of friendship, Nigeria will be prepared to forgive and forget.

Interview, Lagos/Time, 2–9:28.

I am a great believer that the military is not meant to rule. Its function is to support the civilian government of the day. Stability in any country requires a military that is loyal to civilian government. The trouble with military rule is that every colonel or general is soon full of ambition. The navy

takes over today and the army tomorrow . . .
(As for Nigeria), we've got to return to civilian rule. (But) I will never hand the government over in chaos.

> *Interview, Lagos/*
> *Chicago Daily News, 8–29:8.*

de Villiers Graaff
Leader, United Party of South Africa

We will retain white leadership for all South Africa in our political life. It is not prejudice but the facts of history that make the white man the initiator of progress and the bearer of the culture that makes for higher civilization on the African continent.

> *Campaign speech/*
> *The Christian Science Monitor, 4–18:2.*

Edward Heath
Prime Minister of the United Kingdom

It is not our purpose to encourage the South African government in its apartheid policies, or to confer on South Africa a degree of international respectability which she would not otherwise enjoy . . . but abhorrence of apartheid is a moral attitude, not a policy, and it is certainly not a categorical imperative against any contact with the South Africans . . . We do ask our Commonwealth colleagues to accept that our right to (make) decisions in pursuance of British interest is not less than theirs to pursue the policies that serve their interests. If the Commonwealth is to maintain its value and meaning to us all, it must be an institution in which, without bringing into question the whole structure of the Commonwealth, genuine differences of approach and of interest can be clearly recognized, rationally discussed and, where necessary, accepted.

> *At Lord Mayor of London's banquet,*
> *London, Nov. 16/*
> *The Washington Post, 11–17:A14.*

Joseph Iyalla
Nigerian Ambassador to the United States

We want to do for ourselves, because this is the whole part of being independent. But we have no illusions that we can find the technology and the techniques that we need for reconstruction and to get development moving again. We welcome trade and investment, and we look to our friends to help . . . We look for a time of greater cooperation and work and to the success of our policies of forgetting the past. We are determined that there will be no second-class type of Nigerians; and we are doing this not to please others, but for our own interest, for our own country.

> *Before American-Nigerian Chamber of*
> *Commerce, New York, Feb. 11/*
> *The New York Times, 2–12:59.*

Leabua Jonathan
Prime Minister of Lesotho

I have seized power. I admit it, I am not ashamed of it and I know that in my country the majority of the people are behind me.

> *News conference, Maseru, Lesotho, Jan. 31/*
> *The Washington Post, 2–1:A20.*

Kenneth D. Kaunda
President of Zambia

. . . basically, Africa is interested in other people coming in to participate in our development effort with us, on the understanding that we don't mean to kick them out when the development is done—that the time will come when we would say that now we have plenty of money, we have plenty of know-how and now we are going to say to the white people, to the brown people, to the yellow people who have been here that they now have to get out. We do not expect that. We must emphasize that point . . . We do not want temporary passengers. Those must go. But those who are determined to share with us what we have—sorrows or joys—they are most welcome. And they will be with us until they die, shall we say.

> *Interview, Lusaka/*
> *U.S. News & World Report, 7–6:55.*

We are prepared to assist the Portuguese authorities in any efforts designed to prepare the people of Angola, Mozambique and Guinea-Bissau for self-determination and in-

(KENNETH D. KAUNDA)

dependence . . . The onus is on the Portuguese government. But if they continue with their inflexible policy, Africa has no choice but to continue supporting the freedomfighters in their struggle for freedom, peace and justice.

At United Nations, N.Y./
The Christian Science Monitor, 10–22:3.

Jomo Kenyatta
President of Kenya

We fought the colonialists in order to uplift the living standards of our people. We cannot do this if the economy of the country is not in the hands of the people . . . We fought for political independence and we must fight for economic independence.

At installation for second term as President,
Nairobi, Jan. 29/The New York Times, 1–30:3.

Eugene J. McCarthy
United States Senator, D-Minn.

The United States should have called for an arms embargo when the (Nigeria-Biafra) war began in 1967. We should have actively sought a truce. We should have used our good offices to promote negotiations for resolving the differences. We should have pressed for a de-escalation of great-power involvement. We should have sought to form a multinational effort to provide the logistic support required for an adequate relief effort. We should have accepted Biafra's right to a separate national existence and have looked to possible recognition of Biafra by the United Nations and other nations. We should have sought to disentangle the Nigerian-Biafran war from cold war considerations and from the politics of oil and trade. We missed the chance of using Nigeria as a testing ground for reducing tensions among the great powers—since their interests were less serious here than elsewhere—and missed a chance of proving to many African countries, already resentful of the involvements of the great powers in their lands, our

opposition to great-power competition in Africa. We did none of these things.

Before the Senate, Washington, Jan. 28/
Congressional Record, 1–28:S733.

Robert S. McNamara
President, International Bank for
Reconstruction and Development

Africa is the continent of the future. I am convinced that this is where many of the greatest development opportunities of the coming years are going to be found.

Dar es Salaam, Tanzania/
Los Angeles Times, 1–9:(3)16.

David D. Newsom
Assistant Secretary for African Affairs,
Department of State of the United States

No African problem has demanded and received greater attention from this Administration than the problem of southern Africa. Fundamental to our thinking about this area is our deep opposition to racial discrimination. We sympathize, everywhere, with aspirations for equality and dignity. We can readily understand how the policies of apartheid and colonialism generate demands for redress and change. How that change is to be effected, however, raises important questions, including our posture toward force and violence. Many Africans, faced with the continuation of systems which disregard the principle of human equality, see no alternative but violence. In the absence of change for the better in southern Africa, this feeling is likely to grow, despite the fact that most African leaders today earnestly hope for a more moderate solution. The United States has indicated its fundamental opposition to the system of apartheid and to minority rule. But we do not believe the use of force is the answer. We do not believe it is a feasible answer, given the strength of the white regimes in the area. We do not believe it is a just answer, because violence rarely brings justice to all. We do not believe it is a humane answer.

Before Chicago Committee, Chicago Club,
Sept. 17/Vital Speeches, 11–1:52.

Moto Nkama
*Minister of State for Foreign Affairs
of Zambia*

It (Rhodesia) has kicked out no fewer than 50 journalists in its attempt to suppress the freedom of the press. It has refused entry into Rhodesia to no fewer than 400 applicants every year. Religious missionaries have been no exception in this campaign. In short, it is a regime that has shown every intolerance to all those opposed to it.

*Before United Nations Security Council,
New York/
The Christian Science Monitor, 3–14:7.*

Julius Nyerere
President of Tanzania

We have always accepted that Moslems can have four wives and tribalists can have 10 or 20. But if I should take a second wife, I could be prosecuted. Yet the police constable who arrested me might be a polygamist. The prosecutor might be a polygamist, as well as the magistrate who sentenced me to four years at hard labor. This is ridiculous.

Time, 4–20:35.

Qabus bin Said
Sultan of Oman

I am a man with one foot in my country—backward as it is, with its tribal customs, its life dominated by Islam—and the other in the 20th century. I must be very careful to keep my balance . . . Most of the population that lives in the interior of the country still does not live with its time. What these people want, before anything else, is education and health . . . Most of the people do not even know what a vote is . . . In these conditions, to set up a parliament would be like building a huge dome without either walls or foundations: It might, perhaps, give a nice impression to the outside world, but it would be nothing but a big show.

Interview/The Washington Post, 12–27:D1

John R. Rarick
United States Representative, D-La.

The (Ian) Smith government has won the unquestioned loyalty of the great majority of Rhodesians of all races, and has maintained under difficult conditions a civilization which is the envy of much of the world. Like the United States, the Republic of Rhodesia represents the continuing growth and development of the English system of freedom under law which has made us the very model of freedom under law. There is no question about either its desire or its ability to fulfill its role as a civilized government of a civilized nation. Agreements made will be kept. Obligations incurred will be honored. American citizens traveling in Salisbury will be safer than in Washington. I know, for I have seen both.

*Before the House, Washington, March 12/
Vital Speeches, 5–1:434.*

In Africa, full diplomatic recognition, huge sums of American tax dollars and kowtowing and scraping are accorded the comic opera tribal states, totally incapable of anything but a tribal existence. Civilized nations —Christian, and the inheritors of Western culture and civilization—are held up to scorn and ridicule. If this were not serious it would be humorous. But it is deadly serious. The location of Southern Africa makes it one of the geographical keys to today's world. The mineral wealth of the continent makes it a key to the future of man . . . That our government is on a suicidal course is not an accident. That we alter that course is imperative. If our present leaders fail to do so, their successors will.

*Before the House, Washington, March 12/
Vital Speeches, 5–1:437.*

Abraham A. Ribicoff
United States Senator, D-Conn.

The French government's speed in seeking to replace us in Libya is truly amazing. They might not even have to cut the grass around the runways at Wheelus (Air Force Base) after we depart.

Before the Senate, Washington, Jan. 26/
Congressional Record, 1–26:S534.

William P. Rogers
Secretary of State of the United States

One cannot fail to be struck by the deeply-felt desire of leaders of independent African nations to assist other African populations who have not yet had an opportunity to express their own self-determination. This "unfinished business" of the emergence of Africa is something with which we are and will remain identified.

Kinshasa, The Congo, Feb. 18/
The New York Times, 2–19:10.

. . . we oppose the continuation in Africa of systems based on racial discrimination. We do this because of our own heritage and moral principles and our belief in the dignity of man. Their continuance is not in the interest of stability and development of the continent.

Kinshasa, The Congo, Feb. 18/
Los Angeles Times, 2–19:(1)17.

Carl T. Rowan
American journalist

Africans in South Africa are getting one of the rawest deals man ever got anywhere.

News conference, Durban, South Africa/
Newsweek, 9–21:57.

Haile Selassie
Emperor of Ethiopia

The apartheid government of South Africa and the racist white minority regime of Rhodesia have not yet realized the nature of the will and determination of the African people. We, therefore, believe that the time has come for both South Africa and Rhodesia to heed the Lusaka Manifesto, if reason is to prevail, lest they invite more disastrous consequences.

Interview, Addis Ababa, March 11/
The Dallas Times Herald, 3–11:AA8.

. . . Africa is a great continent with a great future . . . the countries are young, but they have their own traditions and their own history. We have sought to charter a path which other African countries can follow. What is disappointing is the fact that certain minority groups in Africa see fit to exercise minority regimes, racism and apartheid, especially in the southern part of Africa. This is very irritating, and humanity abhors it. By co-existing together, both whites and blacks would benefit; it would be fruitful and satisfactory.

Interview, Addis Ababa/
San Francisco Examiner & Chronicle, 11–15:A27.

As far as the United States is concerned, we have had a great link of friendship. But we are not bound and are under no obligation that would hamper us from managing our policy as we want. We can turn our face in any direction we want.

Interview, Addis Ababa/
San Francisco Examiner & Chronicle, 11–15:A27.

Ian Smith
Prime Minister of Rhodesia

Today (the country's first day as a republic) isn't such a tremendous day. We made our decision to become a republic quite a long time ago, and we are merely going through a process of formalization. Independence day is our great day—the day of that unique breakaway from Britain. That was an emotional thing, breaking the ties with people with whom we had been linked for so long. We did not want to do it, but when we asked our Queen if she would continue to be our Queen and the British politicians made her decision for her and said she wouldn't, what have we been since but a de facto republic? We have now turned ourselves into a de jure republic.

News conference, Salisbury, March 2/
The New York Times, 3–3:2.

I believe in a meritocracy. Our policy is a government in Rhodesia based on merit, where people won't worry whether you are African or European. Our policy is that people eventually won't look at you and say you are a black Rhodesian or a white Rhodesian, but that you are the best man for the job.

Quote, 5–3:424.

Jan Steytler
Leader, Progressive Party of South Africa

South Africa is multiracial and will remain so . . . No modern industrial state can hope to build its security on the denial of opportunity to its citizens. We begin by advocating education—free and compulsory—for all our citizens of whatever race or color up to standard sixth (eighth grade) . . . Once educated, the individual must be free to train for the best possible job and sell his labor in the best market. The industrial color bar and job reservation must go, and workers must be allowed to join recognized multiracial trade unions . . . We wish to adopt a qualified franchise and allow those who reach certain educational and economic standards to share with us the task of responsible government . . . in (a modern, rigid) constitution.

The Christian Science Monitor, 4–18:2.

Helen Suzman
Member of South African Parliament

I do not think there will be any change in South Africa in the foreseeable future. There is no revolution around the corner.

Interview, Newsweek, 4–27:49.

Most white people in this country meet Africans only on a master-servant relationship; and when you talk about allowing Africans the vote, or allowing Africans to sit in Parliament, they immediately think of their domestic servant. They think: "My God, he didn't come to work on Monday, he was drunk on Tuesday and he broke the soup tureen on Wednesday." They completely forget that there are Africans holding down responsible jobs in all walks of life.

Interview/Newsweek, 4–27:57.

Balthazar J. Vorster
Prime Minister of South Africa

We in the National Party stand for separate development, which means, firstly, the maintenance of a white identity in South Africa. Secondly, the policy of separate development stands for the creation of opportunities—opportunities for non-whites which never existed before and which cannot exist under any other policy . . . We have created opportunities for the black people, the colored people and the Indians, and we will create them whenever it is necessary to do so.

Election speech/
The Christian Science Monitor, 4–18:2.

. . . we are building a nation for whites only. We have a right to our own identity just as blacks and other non-whites have a right to theirs. Black people are entitled to political rights, but only over their own people—not my people.

The New York Times, 4–18:9.

Henry Winston
National chairman,
Communist Party U.S.A.

Ignorance, poverty, disease and other forms of national oppression are the fruits of imperialism. This act of nationalization (by the Sudanese government, of banks and foreign firms), along with many other radical reforms, gives new impetus to the struggle against these evils. The deafening ovation of the multitudes in the stadium when President Gaafar Mohamed Nimeri announced

(HENRY WINSTON)

the nationalization was an expression of the popular will of the Sudanese people. Progressive mankind throughout the world will also applaud such actions, for it is along this way that means will be found, the means to make it possible to wipe imperialism from the face of the globe.

Khartoum, Sudan, May 25/Daily World, 5–30:3.

Emile Derlin Zinsou
Overthrown President of Dahomey

I fear that there is more chance that this (continuous government changes and coup d'etats) will end in violence and tragedy than not. For the rest of the world, what is happening in Dahomey for now may look like farce. But it is my country, and, for me, it is a total tragedy.

The Washington Post, 3–29:B3.

Salvador Allende (Gossens)
President-elect of Chile

We have triumphed to definitely overthrow imperialist exploitation, to end the monopolies, to carry out a serious and profound agrarian reform and to nationalize banking and credit operations. And, in doing so, Chile will open a path that other peoples of America and the world can follow.

Following his election, Santiago, Sept. 5 /
Newsweek, 9-21:49.

We are not the mental colonists of anyone. What the Cubans have done is admirable; they have been able to turn their country from a floating house of prostitution into a land where there is a deep national feeling. But Chile is very different. Chile is the most politically developed country in Latin America. We have some problems similar to those of Cuba, but the methods we have chosen are very different. In Cuba there was a civil war. In Cuba there was a dictatorship. Here there is an elected government. I have been a candidate three times, and I have always accepted the results of the elections.

Interview, Santiago / Time, 9-21:35.

In essence, we want to be an economically independent country with the right to choose our own path. We are believers in self-determination of the people, and in non-intervention. We want to maintain the best relations with all the countries of the world, and we hope that the American government will understand that. Our revolution is within the right of a sovereign state.

Interview, Santiago / Time, 9-21:35.

The future government of Chile will not be a socialist government. It is unscientific to maintain the contrary. I have said repeatedly—and it could not be otherwise—that my government will be multiparty.

Interview, Santiago /
The Washington Post, 9-26:A7.

I can guarantee that at the end of my term in office there will be free elections in Chile, even freer and cleaner than the last ones.

Interview, Santiago /
The Washington Post, 9-26:A7.

I do not know any Latin American country—except Cuba, which is a matter apart because it is a socialist country—that has solved the essential problems of Latin American man . . . jobs, food, housing, education, health, rest and recreation.

Interview, Santiago /
San Francisco Examiner & Chronicle
(This World), 10-11:14.

. . . by its very essence, the "popular unity" is multipartied. Within it, the Communist Party is one of the parties and movements that form it. The participation of everyone in the government and in public administration will be the main characteristic of the future government. There will be no dominance or supremacy by any party.

Interview, Santiago /
San Francisco Examiner, 10-19:14.

Salvador Allende (Gossens)
President of Chile

We shall never make Parliament disappear. About this there should not be the slightest doubt. It is the essential form of Chilean democracy . . . In no way shall we create a climate ideal for the throwing of bombs. If reactionary violence is unleashed, we shall respond with revolutionary violence. It is clear that it will not be we who are the promoters of violence. We have set up a government through clean and unobjectionable democratic means.

Interview/Daily World, 11–5:2.

I promise . . . that, as long as I am President, Chile will never have a foreign military base on its soil—not of any country.

Interview, Santiago/
The Washington Post, 12–10:A19.

(Regarding nationalization of American-owned Chilean copper mines): I respect the American interests. But I respect the Chilean interests more. We can't live without copper in Chile. It is the air we breathe.

Interview, Santiago/
Los Angeles Times, 12–11:(2)10.

Juan Bosch
Former President of the Dominican Republic

For two years after the intervention (by American troops in 1965), I was very confused. I had never expected the U.S. to intervene. I thought the United States was a democracy. At base, I thought it was very good. Then I saw the real face of the United States. There is a picture in the world that shows the United States on the side of the weak and the helpless, on the side of right. We believed that propaganda. We were wrong.

Interview, Santo Domingo/
San Francisco Examiner & Chronicle, 6–7:A18.

Robert Bourassa
Premier, Province of Quebec, Canada

Quebec may be economically a part of North America, but culturally it is different. If you force Quebeckers to work in English, you will risk a social explosion. If you enable them to work in French, you will avoid unrest and revolution. You will also raise morale and increase production.

Before Quebec business leaders/
The New York Times, 9–13:(1)16.

Rafael Caldera (Rodriguez)
President of Venezuela

Liberty did not come easily to Venezuela; it was the product of Venezuelan sacrifice. Now, threats against it are no longer serious. The people are willing and ready to defend it and to see that it is not abused. We are happy that this is so, and know that, while the elections of 1968 meant victory for some and defeat for others, for Venezuela it was a conquest.

Television address, Caracas, Jan. 1/
The New York Times, 1–26:67.

Helder P. Camara
Archbishop of Olinda and Recife, Brazil

There is no monolithic capitalism or socialism; there are capitalisms and socialisms. Personally, I see no hope for Brazil or for Latin America in any capitalist or even neo-capitalist model. If you asked me, I'd say that, among the present models of socialism, none seem capable of being the solution for my country or my continent . . . I am always urging the youth of my country, the young university students and professors, to join interdisciplinary teams and to look for a model that will not be a servile copy of either capitalism or the present socialist models.

Interview, Recife/
The New York Times, 10–28:6.

Fidel Castro (Ruz)
Premier of Cuba

Cuba has not denied, Cuba will never deny support to revolutionary movements . . . Our position on the revolutionary movement is that, while there is imperialism, while there are fighters ready to fight imperialism, our peoples will give them help. Let this be very clear. We state and ratify that all those determined to fight imperialism will be able to count on our support.

Havana, April 23/
The Washington Post, 4–24:A21.

Unbreakable friendship links the peoples of the Soviet Union with Cuba. Without the

October revolution and the existence of the Soviet Union, Cuba would never have been able to liberate itself from imperialist domination and to become the first socialist state in the Western Hemisphere.

Havana/Daily World, 4-28:11.

Our enemies say we have problems, and in reality our enemies are right. They say there is discontent (in Cuba), and in reality our enemies are right. They say there is irritation, and in reality our enemies are right.

Annual address, Havana, July 26/
The Christian Science Monitor, 8-25:9.

We're going to suppose that elections (in Chile) may result in a triumph for the left. This occurrence and a Chilean revolution will depend on those who direct the leftist movement. I believe that conditions in Chile are different from those in Cuba, and I believe things can't be done there as they were here. Here we made a revolution by open struggle, using a small group of men to wage guerrilla war.

News conference, Havana, Aug. 1/
The New York Times, 8-23:(1)16.

. . . we are not one bit interested in improving our relations with the imperialists as long as that country (the United States) has a government of policemen and aggressors and criminals. And our ties with the Soviet Union will not be touched either! And if they can be strengthened, they will be strengthened! . . . Our disposition is to establish, if possible, even more military ties with the Soviet Union.

Aug. 24/The Wall Street Journal, 9-2:8.

Frank Church
United States Senator, D-Idaho

. . . economists know what is required within Latin America to move it into an era of adequate, self-sustaining economic growth . . . The impetus must come from within. Success or failure may be marginally influenced, but it cannot be bestowed from without—neither by the United States nor any other foreign power. It is also evident that the means adopted, the economic systems devised, the political forms chosen, will likewise have to be homegrown. Neither the leisurely evolution of modern capitalism, as it matured in northern Europe and the United States, nor the differing brands of Marxism, as practiced in Russia or China, offer models for Latin America that are really relevant to its cultural inheritance or its pressing needs. Even Cuban-style Communism has found a meager market in other Latin lands. Che Guevara's romantic excursion to spread Castroism to the mountains of Bolivia ended in fiasco and death. For Latin America, steeped in the Christian tradition and prizing the individual highly, Communism has little appeal. Indeed, those in the forefront of the struggle for radical, even revolutionary, reform in Latin America today are more likely to be found wearing Roman collars than carrying red banners.

Before the Senate, Washington, April 10/
Vital Speeches, 5-1:418.

Given the magnitude of our effort (in Latin America) during the '60s, we are left to wonder why it produced such disappointing results. We thought we were seeding the resurgence of democratic governments; instead, we have seen a relentless slide toward militarism. We thought we could remodel Latin societies, but the reforms we prescribed have largely eluded us. We thought our generosity would meet with gratitude; but we have seen antagonism toward us grow as our involvement in their problems has deepened. We pledged ourselves to goals which lay beyond our capacity to confer, objectives that could never be the gift of any program of external aid. By promising more than we could deliver, we have made ourselves a plausible scapegoat for pent-up furies and frustrations for which we bear little or no responsibility. Worse still, the kind of aid we have extended has tended to aggravate, rather than mitigate, these difficulties. Bilateral in character, administered on a government-to-government basis, our foreign-

(FRANK CHURCH)

aid program is embroiled in the internal
politics of both the donor and recipient
countries. The program's very nature has
made this unavoidable, but the consequences are contributing to a steady deterioration in relations.

> *Before the Senate, Washington, April 10/*
> *Vital Speeches, 5–1:419.*

John Diefenbaker
Former Prime Minister of Canada

This move by Canada (to recognize Communist China) will result in a loss of support for those who have stood against Communism in Southeast Asia . . . this will be
taken as approval of Communism.

> *Los Angeles Times, 10–14:(1)9.*

Jean Drapeau
Mayor of Montreal, Canada

Montreal is en route to becoming *The
City* of the world. Twenty years from now,
no matter what happens, it will have
achieved this position, and it will be referred
to in all parts of the world as The City.

> *Sports Illustrated, 9–28:76.*

Luis Echeverria (Alvarez)
President-elect of Mexico

The best defense against Communism in
the Americas is the strengthening of democratic institutions in those countries where
democracy is still alive.

> *San Francisco Examiner & Chronicle*
> *(This World), 11–22:2.*

Luis Echeverria (Alvarez)
President of Mexico

Those who maintain that we must grow
first in order to distribute afterward are
either mistaken or lying out of self-interest.
Employment and productivity must be increased more rapidly, and to accomplish this
it is indispensable to expand the domestic
market and share income more equitably.

> *Inauguration address, Mexico City, Dec. 1/*
> *The New York Times, 12–2:12.*

This will be a government of guarantees.
Those who come here to share the responsibility of investment and industrial production can remain calm. We have no expropri-
ation mentality.

> *Los Angeles Times, 12–11:(6)1.*

Gonzalo J. Facio
Foreign Minister of Costa Rica

The Marxist-Leninist tyranny that today
oppresses Cuba cannot be considered an isolated incident in the world panorama. It
counts on the efficient propaganda of the
Communist international movement and
has the economic and military support of
the super-powers, Russia and China. Because the Cuban government has made its
country the center of totalitarian conspiracy
against the free governments of the Americas, its action must be stopped through the
instruments available to the inter-American
system . . . The only effective solution that
I see to put an end to Castroite aggression
against its people and against the rest of
Latin America is to promote an internal up-
rising . . . The Castro regime has lost the
support which it once had among the majority of the population . . . the potential
of insurrection is there.

> *June 6/Human Events, 7–18:10.*

Jose Figueres (Ferrer)
President-elect of Costa Rica

I see very dark and dangerous days ahead
if the businessmen and labor leaders of this
country don't see that our problems can't be
solved if they don't work closely together for
common goals. I have told the labor leaders
that if they want to cut the heads off the
businessmen they can go ahead, but it will
mean 50 years of poverty for Costa Rica. I
tell the businessmen that if they don't take
responsibility for finding solutions to poverty and unemployment, they will not escape
another Cuba here.

> *Interview, San Jose/*
> *The New York Times, 2–4:8.*

I could get along here just fine devoting

my time to reading and to my businesses and to the children. But Costa Rica is really a pilot project in what can be done in a democratic way in Latin America, and I see a real opportunity to do something important in the next four years.

Interview, San Jose/
The New York Times, 2–4:8.

Eduardo Frei (Montalva)
President of Chile

I am sure that, whatever the situation the country will have in the future, the armed forces will continue to be the guardians of its internal and external security. Their patriotism, their discipline and high degree of professionalism are a guarantee of democratic stability and the exercise of individual rights. I always admired our armed forces before taking over this job. Now, at the end of my mandate, I have come to understand why the people see in them the true symbol of our fatherland.

Santiago, Sept. 17/Washington Star, 9–18:A3.

J.J. Greene
Minister of Energy, Mines and Resources of Canada

The new Canadian nationalism and determination to build something unique rests in the malaise that exists in your land (the U.S.)—what appears to many as the sudden and tragic disappearance of the American dream, which in some ways has turned to nightmare.

Before Independent Petroleum Association
of America, Denver, May 13/
Los Angeles Times, 6–25:(1A)6.

James R. Grover, Jr.
United States Representative, R-N.Y.

Our presence in strength in the Panama Canal Zone has an influence far more transcendent than the mere protection of the Canal operations. I am convinced that, if we are to withdraw, we will create a hemispheric power vacuum, and Castroism—the extension of the Moscow-Peking lust for worldwide domination—would move right in. The

American people should have learned by now that it is easy to be loved in international circles, but that it is far more important to be respected. Such respect can only be earned through the willingness to resist aggression. Nevertheless, there are many holdovers in the State Department who date back to prior Administrations, and they continue to urge that we give away our influential base in Panama. If this happens, the American people may well have cause to regret it. Some may call it colonialism, but I call it survival.

Human Events, 3–21:23.

W. Averell Harriman
Former United States Ambassador-at-Large

In no area in the world are freedom and democracy eroding more rapidly than in Latin America. The Nixon policy for Latin America has turned out to be a policy of retreat and abandonment.

News conference, Washington, Sept. 24/
The Washington Post, 9–25:A13.

Robert A. Hurwitch
Deputy Assistant Secretary for Inter-American Affairs, Department of State of the United States

Despite substantial Soviet assistance and (Cuban Premier Fidel) Castro's promises for a better life, our findings are that Cuba today is a drab place, with most of the trappings of a repressive police state. Long lines of consumers seek out the scarce essentials of life. An extensive block-warden system ensures that neighbor spies upon neighbor. And all are subjected to being uprooted at any time of day or night to pursue illusory goals, such as 10 million tons of sugar.

Before House Subcommittee on Inter-American
Affairs, Washington, July 8/
U.S. News & World Report, 7–20:50.

Cheddi Jagan
Former Prime Minister of British Guiana

It has been said that Latin America and the Caribbean are the backyard of the United States. It is important for those who

(CHEDDI JAGAN)

live in the house to know how those in the yard are getting along.

Interview, Moscow/Daily World, 11–14:M12.

Edward M. Kennedy
United States Senator, D-Mass.

Time and again over the past decade, we have seen the noble goals of the Alliance for Progress perverted by the cold-war philosophy symbolized by the Bay of Pigs . . . We stand silent while political prisoners are tortured in Brazil . . . Last year, despite continuing reports of terror and oppression, it was we who gave $19 million in military aid to the regime of the generals . . . When the United States is identified with those regimes through our economic and military assistance, we defeat our own political purposes and we are false to the ideals of the Alliance.

At University of Montana, April 17/
The Washington Post, 4–18:A6.

Rene Levesque
Leader, Quebecois Party, Canada

Our aim is to get Quebec the hell out of this Federal system. If we don't do it, we (French Quebec) won't survive. In the last 30 years, our birthrate has gone from one of the highest in the Western Hemisphere to about the lowest. Immigrants are learning to speak English rather than French. All this stuff about bilingualism will turn out to mean only bilingualism for the French. They will end up forgetting their own language . . . In 1974, I think it's possible that we will win a majority of the seats in the National Assembly. If we do, we will vote to secede from the federation (Canada). I don't know what will happen, but I suspect that Ottawa may try to prevent it by force of arms. Let them try! There's no power in Canada that could keep Quebec in if she made up her mind to get out.

Interview/
The New York Times Magazine, 12–6:151.

Malcolm Mackintosh
Consultant, Institute for Strategic Studie
London; Authority on Soviet policy

The Russians appear to have been con ducting a Caribbean probe to see whethe they could establish a naval facility in Cub for their ballistic-missile submarines. Thes submarines now must return all the way t the Soviet Union for repair and refittin periodically. The Russians undoubtedl would like to have a facility in Cuba tha would enable them to avoid that long voy age. But they seem to have put off this Carib bean probe for the time being—possibl because of the strong American reaction possibly because of complications on thei own side. But I think there may be anothe more ulterior, motive behind any Soviet de cision to establish a naval facility in Cuba The Russians never forget humiliations—o what they regard as humiliations. The Cu ban missile crisis of 1962 was the bigges humiliation they've suffered in the postwa period. They would always be on the look out to get their own back. They don't forgiv and forget. If they could in some way aveng the Cuban missile humiliation by establish ing some kind of naval facilities in Cuba, th political and emotional aspect of this woul certainly play a role in Soviet decision-mak ing.

Interview, London,
U.S. News & World Report, 11–2:69

Emilio G. Medici
President of Brazil

The revolutionary state will last as long as it takes to implant the political, adminis trative, juridical, social and economic struc tures capable of raising all Brazilians to a minimum level of well-being.

At Superior War College, Rio de Janeiro
March 10/The New York Times, 3–11:3

Charles A. Meyer
Assistant Secretary for Inter-American Af fairs, Department of State of the United States

The U.S. has no objection whatsoever to

Cuba's returning to the inter-American system, so long as its government respects the principle of non-intervention in the internal affairs of neighboring countries.

Plainview (Tex.) Daily Herald, 2-25:6.

G. Warren Nutter
Assistant Secretary for International Security Affairs, Department of Defense of the United States

Contrary to numerous recent news reports, we have discovered no evidence that strategic missiles have been reintroduced into Cuba, or that Cuba has any missiles that could be fired from Cuba and hit our mainland.

Before House Foreign Affairs Committee, Washington/Washington Star, 8-6:A13.

Juan D. Peron
Exiled former President of Argentina

I am ready. The day when I decide to go there (Argentina), no one will be able to stop me . . . To free the country like Fidel (Castro of Cuba), that is the solution . . . I will return at any moment I can be useful for something. I will return when the situation permits it. It is necessary for something to happen which makes my presence necessary.

Interview/The New York Times, 7-7:16.

Galo Plaza (Lasso)
Secretary-General, Organization of American States

The public in this country (United States) —largely uninformed about the magnitude of the Latin self-help effort and the actual terms of U.S. assistance—views the Alliance (for Progress) as a giveaway. The Latins— fully aware of their self-help effort and the fact that most U.S. aid is in the form of tied loans—question the sincerity of the U.S. commitment.

Before World Affairs Council, Los Angeles, Feb. 17/Los Angeles Times, 2-18:(2)5.

Latin America more and more looks toward Europe and other continents for mutually-beneficial relations to parallel those our countries have had with one another and with the United States. In this sense, Latin America is not, nor will it ever be, the private domain or the backyard of any power.

Before Atlantic Institute, Paris, Nov. 16/ The New York Times, 11-17:3.

Louis J. Robichaud
Premier of Province of New Brunswick, Canada

We have in Canada some very vocal nationalist groups and individuals who worry endlessly about American influence on our economy, on our television and on our foreign affairs. I am one Canadian who is more concerned about fostering the economic development of our nation than with making loud cries to protect what we have from influence and ownership to the south of us.

New York/ U.S. News & World Report, 6-15:80.

William P. Rogers
Secretary of State of the United States

There has been a rise in nationalism—no doubt about that. I think that is true all over the world, and it's probably a good thing. Certainly, it's a good thing in Latin America. In the past, there has been too much of a feeling of paternalism on the part of the United States. The fact that Latin Americans feel they are responsible for their own future and they take pride in their nationhood is a good thing. It's obviously natural that some of that national pride would manifest itself in anti-Americanism, because we have held ourselves out as the country that was going to do grandiose things for Latin America.

Interview, Washington/ U.S. News & World Report, 1-26:34.

Mitchell Sharp
Secretary of State for External Affairs of Canada

We have no intention of creeping under the friendship umbrella held up by the United States. We must find our own place to stand.

Los Angeles Times, 5-6:(6)5.

Hugh L. Shearer
Prime Minister of Jamaica

I can't think of a more inappropriate misnomer for misguided radicalism in the Caribbean than "black power" . . . When we who govern Jamaica today were being called young radicals, we fought against great odds for black opportunity, black rights, black equality. And, just after we won the fight and are making progress in the supreme struggle to bring a better life to all our people, a noisy bunch of malcontents started shouting "black power" . . . Separate and apart from their irrelevance and irresponsibility, I wish they were able to give some rational solutions to the problems that are disturbing the whole world today, black or white, and also red.

Washington/Washington Star, 8–13:A7.

J. A. Taylor
President, Canadian Chamber of Commerce

More than 50 per cent of world trade is now in the Pacific sector. Those are the countries with whom we are going to be competing more and more vigorously for the export markets for manufactured goods and raw materials alike that are vital for our future prosperity. We are making it tough on ourselves. Thirty-five per cent of our gross national product now goes to the upkeep of government in Canada. In New Zealand, a country that we have considered as being highly socialistic, the figure is only 31 per cent; in the United States, it is 28 per cent, including the costs of Vietnam; it is 21 per cent in Australia and 16 per cent in Japan. Thus, we are spending relatively much more than those competitors on the non-productive purposes of government, and, in doing so, we are taking away from the heavy and continuous infusion of capital that provides the production needed to supply our export trade. If Canada is to continue to develop its enormous resources, and if we are to provide jobs for the two million young people who come on the labor market during the seventies, we must maintain a climate that will encourage capital investment. The apparent lack of understanding of this basic economic premise by so many officials in Ottawa is disheartening indeed.

Before Annual Congress, Vancouver, Sept. 21/ Vital Speeches, 12–1:122.

James D. Theberge
Director, Latin-American studies, Georgetown University Center for Strategic and International Studies

A permanent Soviet naval presence in the Western Hemisphere would increase the political prestige and influence of the Soviet Union, which would now be capable of intervening, under certain circumstances, in onshore political developments, especially in the politically volatile Caribbean area. Unquestionably, it would seriously hamper the capacity of the U.S. to deal with future security problems in the area and increase the cost of a U.S. military response to a renewed emplacement of strategic missiles in Cuba. It would also tend to confirm something our Latin-American neighbors now suspect: that the power balance between the U.S. and the Soviet Union is shifting in favor of the Soviet Union, to the detriment of U.S. prestige and credibility.

U.S. News & World Report, 10–12:22.

Pierre Elliott Trudeau
Prime Minister of Canada

I'm afraid that there are a lot of people in this country who are bargaining that, "Oh well, the government can't act tough (to cure inflation) for too long because it will only get frightened if it sees unemployment go up to 6 per cent." If people think we are going to lose our nerve because of that, they should think again. Because we're not.

News conference/ The New York Times, 1–18:(1)25.

In the face of the U.S. giant, we feel we must have friends who share the same Western outlook—friends other than the United States. This is why we give high priority to our relations with Europe. In all fields, there is truly a community of interests between France and Canada.

Interview/Los Angeles Times, 2–21:(1)6.

I'm not afraid of the competition of ideas. If the teachers are good, I don't care if they're from Patagonia.

Commenting on U.S. professors in Canadian universities/ U.S. News & World Report, 2–23:19.

We cannot continue being present in all four corners of the globe and participating in every peacekeeping operation there is. We have to pick and choose. If it's a question of leverage, you can't have much leverage on world affairs if you try to exercise it in every country.

Look, 2–24:51.

It is a matter of deep regret and grave concern to me, as I am sure it is to all honorable Members, that the condition of our country makes necessary this proclamation. We in this House have all felt very strongly, I know, that democracy was nowhere in a healthier state than in Canada; that nowhere was there less need for frustrated men to turn to violence to attain their political ends. I still believe firmly that this is so. Yet, in recent years we have been forced to acknowledge the existence within Canada of a new and terrifying type of person—one who in earlier times would have been described as an anarchist, but who is now known as a "violent revolutionary." These persons allege that they are seeking social change through novel means. In fact, they are seeking the destruction of the social order through clandestine and violent means. Faced with such persons, and confronted with authoritative assessments of the seriousness of the risks to persons and property in the Montreal area, the government had no responsible choice but to act as it did last night . . . May I say . . . that no Canadian takes less lightly than I the seriousness of the present situation in Canada and the gravity of the measures which the govern-

ment has been asked to assume in order to meet that situation . . . I appeal to all Canadians not to become so obsessed by what the government has done today in response to terrorism that they forget the opening play in this vicious game. That play was taken by the revolutionaries; they chose to use bombing, murder and kidnaping.

Explaining his invoking of the War Measures Act, before House of Commons, Ottawa, Oct. 16/The New York Times, 10–17:12.

(Referring to criticism of his invoking the War Measures Act to deal with terrorism in Quebec): There are a lot of bleeding hearts around who just don't like to see people with helmets and guns. All I can say is go on and bleed. But it is more important to keep law and order in the society than to be worried about weak-kneed people . . .

News conference, Ottawa, Oct. 16/ The New York Times, 10–18:(4)1.

I've written often that the country is held together only by consent, not by force of arms. If any part of our country wants to leave Canada, I don't think force of arms will be used to prevent it. You can't hold a modern nation together by force. You have to hold it together by showing the people that their lot, their future, their destiny is better within the country than without. Because if they think they will be happier outside the country as individuals, they will leave; and if a whole province decides that it is happier outside the country, then *it* will leave.

Interview, Ottawa/ The New York Times Magazine, 12–6:146.

Gabriel Valdes (Subercaseaux)
Foreign Minister of Chile

Whether Cuba belongs or does not belong to the OAS is its own affair; but we believe that the widest possible continental unity is worthwhile . . . (Sanctions) cannot be eternal. Every country has a right to the government of its choice.

January/The Christian Science Monitor, 3–2:6.

Jose Maria Velasco (Ibarra)
President of Ecuador

(The) politicians, full of hatred and vengeance, have unceasingly fomented subversion and scandal . . . There have been added the incessant plans of terrorists and the conspiracy of the oligarchy. In the face of such grave circumstances, I cannot permit the republic to perish.

Radio address announcing his assumption of dictatorial powers, Quito/Newsweek, 7–6:47.

Eric Williams
Prime Minister of Trinidad and Tobago

No country of the hemisphere should be debarred from participation in the economic instrumentalities of the OAS . . . I refer to a consideration of the controversial question of the resumption of economic relations with Cuba. (By now) we should have learned the lesson that economic boycott is not the most productive attitude to be adopted with a country whose economic and social system we do not share.

At OAS conference on trade, Caracas, Feb. 3 Los Angeles Times, 2–6:(1)1.

Asia and the Pacific

piro T. Agnew
ice President of the United States

They (Asian governments) privately—in
ficial discussions—indicate a very strong de-
re for continued American presence and
ssistance. But from time to time—and this
oes not apply to each government—some of
nem have a tendency for their local domes-
c political consumption to indicate they're
ess than infatuated with our being there.

News conference, en route to
Canberra, Australia, Jan. 13 /
The Washington Post, 1–14:A14.

Let me make it very clear that, despite a
reat deal of speculation and rumor, we are
ot withdrawing from Asia and the Pacific.
Nations on the edge of the Pacific like Aus-
alia and the U.S.) may sometimes be
mpted to withdraw from this new commu-
ity, with its turbulence and uncertainties,
o seek tranquility and the enjoyment of our
lessings; but the ocean provides no sanctu-
ry for the rich, no barrier behind which we
an hide our abundance.

Canberra, Australia, Jan. 13 /
The New York Times, 1–14:8.

I feel one very prevalent opinion about
ne people of Asia is entirely misleading,
nd that is that they are inscrutable and
ather opaque. I find them, on the contrary,
xtremely forthcoming and relaxed and
illing to meet the issues head on.

San Francisco Examiner & Chronicle
(This World), 1–25:2.

. . . one event that went relatively un-
oticed here may . . . grow in importance
ith the years. That was our return of Oki-
awa to Japan. The world's greatest indus-
ial nation turned over a powerful and

strategic base to the world's third largest
industrial nation. That says a lot about
America to the Japanese and to all Asians.
This was done with no great outcry about a
loss of American security. That says a lot
about the leadership of a President and the
confidence of the American people in his
judgment about our security needs.

Before California Newspaper Publishers
Association, Los Angeles, Feb. 5 /
Congressional Record, 2–5:S1289.

The message I carried to Asia on behalf of
the President was this: That America stands
behind its friends, not in front of its friends,
in their defense of freedom. And the message
I brought back was this: As self-respect and
self-reliance increase among the nations of
Asia, respect for America will continue to
rise.

Before California Newspaper Publishers
Association, Los Angeles, Feb. 5 /
Los Angeles Times, 2–6:(1)3.

Kiichi Aichi
Foreign Minister of Japan

We are experiencing something new. Before, we were always a poor country. Once
we obtained foreign exchange, we held on
to it tightly. Now we have foreign currency.
We're like a man who suddenly finds he's
rich and doesn't quite know what to do with
all the money . . .

Interview, Tokyo /
The Christian Science Monitor, 9–11:6.

Felix Dias Bandaranaike
Minister of Public Administration and
Home Affairs of Ceylon

The United National Party has had its
last chance. The Sri Lanka Freedom Party
is having its last chance now. If the Freedom

311

(FELIX DIAS BANDARANAIKE)

Party fails, the parliamentary democratic system may not survive. You and I, gentlemen, may be hanging from parallel lamp-posts.

Before Ceylonese and foreign businessmen, Colombo/The New York Times, 10–18:(1)14.

David Ben-Gurion
Former Prime Minister of Israel

. . . it (is) ridiculous that America (does) not recognize the biggest country in the world, no matter what we think of Communism . . . I do not say America must accept Red Chinese ideas, but you must find a way to come closer to that country before it is too late. If you succeed in winning over Red China and returning the land to her that was stolen by the Soviets, you will have taken the biggest steps the world has known to secure peace. As it is now, I am afraid there could be an atomic war between China and Russia. If we can avoid that, and bring the U.S. and China and Russia to the peace table, I believe that permanent peace will be possible in the world in the next 50 years.

Interview, Sde Boker, Israel/ Los Angeles Herald-Examiner, 10–4:A16.

Norris E. Bradbury
Director, Los Alamos Scientific Laboratory, U.S.A.

The Chinese are a threat. I hope the danger will grow less with time, but they have so little to lose compared with everyone else, they might be tempted to start a war. The longer we can stave that off, the less likely it will become. As China becomes more of a "have" nation, she will find she has the same problems we do.

Interview, Los Alamos, N.M./ Los Angeles Times, 1–4:E6.

Leonid I. Brezhnev
General Secretary, Communist Party of the Soviet Union

The imperialist press has published a lot of various fabrications and slanders in which they claim the signing of the (Soviet-West German non-aggression) treaty united our hands in the East in order to put pressure on (Communist) China. Many Western people would like to set the Soviet Union against China; but these gentlemen are making miscalculations. In Peking, talks are continuing between the Soviet Union and China. The talks are going slow, but we are not losing hope. We displayed and will display a constructive and patient approach. We would like to hope that the Chinese side will respond in the same way.

Television address at 50th anniversary celebration of Kazakh Soviet Republic, Aug. 28/ Los Angeles Times, 8–30:A7.

Angie Brooks
President, United Nations General Assembly

. . . the UN believes we cannot continue to ignore 800 million people. The problem is that mainland China feels the Charter was signed on mainland China and yet the seat was taken by nationalist China . . . I agree there should be but one China, but it has to be conceded that to solve the problem we must have two Chinas.

Beverly Hills, Calif., Feb. 16/ Los Angeles Herald-Examiner, 2–17:B1.

Nicolae Ceausescu
President of Romania

(Communist) China is an important factor in international life today. This can no longer be denied by anybody. The development of an ample and multi-lateral international cooperation is no longer conceivable without China's participation.

Interview, Bucharest/ Los Angeles Herald-Examiner, 10–6:A10.

Chou En-lai
Premier of Communist China

The superpowers are keeping China under the menace of war—in the North and in the West by the Soviet Union, with a million men and missile forces; and in the East by the United States, allied with Japan, which is feverishly re-arming . . . The re-birth of Japanese militarism constitutes a menace for all Asia.

Interview/The Washington Post, 12–11:A12.

Il Kwon Chung
Prime Minister of South Korea

Russian military aid (to North Korea) will end in 1972, and Communist China will begin supporting North Korea with military and economic assistance at that time. This is a significant fact. Our view is that close relations with Communist China means that sooner or later North Korea will attack South Korea.

Interview, Seoul, July 13/
Los Angeles Herald-Examiner, 7–14:A4.

Frank H. Corner
Ambassador to the United States from New Zealand

We are the most geographically safe country of the world.

Before Rotary Club, Los Angeles, Sept. 18/
Los Angeles Herald-Examiner, 9–19:A5.

Douglas Ensminger
Former director, Ford Foundation in India

. . . I am leaving India with a very easy mind. I think India will be here two decades from now, still committed to democracy. I think one of the things we (in the United States) must face up to is that India is a distinctly different culture from ours. We must look at it in terms of what makes sense to India. I think India is going to have a good deal of things that the rest of the world is going to stop and look at—especially we in the United States with our high level of living that keeps our people on a treadmill. I think there are some values here that are worth adopting: their taking care of aged parents, for example, which *Time* magazine describes as our "unwanted generation." But I could feel more comfortable if India achieved freedom from the fear of hunger. This is achievable, but, as I said, it will take time. Instead of finding things wrong with India, let us look at what this country

achieved during the last two decades. The tragedy is that so many of the gains have been lost in the population increase.

Interview, New Delhi/
The Christian Science Monitor, 9–5:10.

Malcolm Fraser
Minister of Defense of Australia

We reject the concept of detachment . . . We do not believe there is any security in isolation. You do not make Southeast Asia or the Indian Ocean disappear by turning your back on them.

U.S. News & World Report, 8–31:21.

Takeo Fukuda
Minister of Finance of Japan

Not by military power but by economic power we can contribute to world politics and the world's peace. I believe firmly that Japan should not possess nuclear arms. With its famous Article 9 (the constitutional clause renouncing war and the maintenance of military power), Japan can take the strongest position against the nuclear problem because of the very fact that she has the power to have nuclear weapons.

Before Japan Reporters' Club, Tokyo,
Nov. 30/Los Angeles Times, 12–1:(1)13.

Indira Gandhi
Prime Minister of India

Our socialist policy means that our party is committed to left-of-center, but there is no question of aligning ourselves with the Communists . . . There is certainly a large area of common interest and agreement with Russia. It is this which accounts for the close ties we have with Moscow; but it is completely untrue that we have allowed the Soviet Union to influence our judgment on world issues.

Before National Congress Party/
The Christian Science Monitor, 1–27:3.

Lenin's name figures high amongst the great names of human history. To his own people he gave a revolution and a new social order. To oppressed people in other conti-

WHAT THEY SAID IN 1970

(INDIRA GANDHI)

nents he gave his sympathy and understanding in abundance. On the centenary of his birth, the people of India pay Lenin their warm tribute.

Daily World, 4–24:7.

The answer to Communists cannot be found in the right extremists. Any rightist trends on the part of upper classes may well force the poorer masses to left extremism. The Indian way is the middle of the road, which we follow—a way you would call slightly to the left of center.

Interview, New Delhi/
U.S. News & World Report, 5–25:66.

I do not think there is any serious threat to parliamentary democracy in India today. By and large, democracy has taken strong and permanent root here in the minds and hearts of Indians.

Interview, New Delhi/
U.S. News & World Report, 5–25:66.

Our plans do not call for socializing the entire economy, or even the greater part of it. We do want the commanding heights of the economy to be in the state hands—the basic industries, the defense industries and, to a large extent, the import trade. This is essential for India. In our country private capital, if left to itself, looks for quick profits and avoids the irksome but essential basic industries and infrastructure—concentrates on urban areas and ignores the countryside. State initiative is thus essential for the backward areas and poorer regions. We are a people in a hurry for progress, but we have chosen a mixed economy, with plenty of room and a real need for the private sector's initiative.

Interview, New Delhi/
U.S. News & World Report, 5–25:67.

Free sovereign India will never become a satellite of any country. This steadfast ad-

herence to non-alignment is non-negotiable

Before Parliament, New Delhi, July 29
Cleveland Plain Dealer, 7–30:A8

It is true that the people of India feel ver strongly (about resumption of U.S. militar aid to Pakistan), and I think they have caus to do so; because against whom can Pakistar use these war materials? It can only b against India.

Interview/Meet the Pres:
National Broadcasting Compan
Washington, 10–2:

Minoru Genda
Member, Japanese Diet (Parliament)

Japan and the United States should coop erate in keeping Asia out of the hands of th Communists. Asia and the Pacific are impor tant to the free world. This is the regio where nearly two-thirds of the world's popu lation live. When this area is fully deve oped, it will become the most importan market in the world. Japan cannot go i alone in the development of Asia and th Pacific because of her role in the last war And America cannot go it alone because sh is basically a white man's country. But Japar and the United States can do it together.

Interview, Tokyo
The Dallas Times Herald, 9–2:D:

Marshall Green
Assistant Secretary for East Asia and Pacifi Affairs, Department of State of the Unite States

In a way, I think we're beginning to se the end of Maoism. Mao is still the grea leader; but, in a way, he's been elevated t his mausoleum. In a way, he isn't there i the day-to-day decision-making in the de gree that he was, although he's still a re vered figure among the Communists i mainland China. More and more we see possibly, the people of a more pragmati state of mind, the less ideological and e> tremist state of mind, taking over.

Interview/Morning New
Columbia Broadcasting System, Nov. 17
The Washington Post, 11–18:A

Edvard Hambro
President, United Nations General Assembly

In my part of the world (Norway) we consider it rather unrealistic not to recognize that the government in Peking is today the government which has power in the greatest and most populous state of the world, and we believe also that it is slightly less than realistic to pretend that the government in Taiwan represents the people of China. In my country we are naive enough to believe that, even in politics, it is a good thing to act on realities and not ideology.

Interview/Meet the Press,
National Broadcasting Company, 10–18.

Edward Heath
Prime Minister of the United Kingdom

The (Communist) Chinese have recently adopted a more moderate and realistic attitude toward their foreign relations. This is all to the good, and it's a trend we would want to encourage. The more closely they are brought into the international community the better. They have not abandoned their support for subversive movements in Southeast Asia, but they do not seem to be contemplating any direct military intervention in the area.

Interview, London/
U.S. News & World Report, 12–21:26.

Keith J. Holyoake
Prime Minister of New Zealand

Do not underestimate the growing confidence of the nations of this Pacific and Asian area under the U.S. shield. Great changes are taking place. Japan, South Korea, other countries are making astonishing strides—economic, social and political. There is an increasing amount of interchange and contact. There is an awareness that, by far, the greater progress in all this area of Asia and the Pacific is being made by nations that are basically democratic nations, striving to govern themselves with freedom—far more freedom than is known in the Communist areas . . Count up our populations, our productive power, our energies and our common desires for a better life, and you will find that there is an impressive force in the Asian-Pacific areas moving forward together under your American shield.

Interview, Wellington/
U.S. News & World Report, 8–31:21.

Masamichi Inoki
Professor, Kyoto University

A nation not backed by nationalism is like a spineless man—but nationalism is a cancer cell at the same time . . . its virulence may prove fatal to this country (Japan).

San Francisco Examiner & Chronicle
(This World), 3–22:19.

U. Alexis Johnson
Under Secretary for Political Affairs, Department of State of the United States

Our basic objective in East Asia, as elsewhere in the world, is the establishment of a peaceful community of nations, each free to choose its own way of government and its own way of life, to develop its resources to the maximum and to have peaceful and productive relations with its neighbors. When this is stated, it so often sounds like a pious platitude. But it is far more than that. For it is only as we move toward that kind of a world that we will be able in our own country to sleep more easily at night and devote more of our resources to productive purposes . . . We are a Pacific power and we have learned that peace for us is much less likely if there is no peace in Asia.

Before Cleveland Council on World Affairs,
Cleveland, Feb. 28/Vital Speeches, 4–15:387.

There are some who look to Japan as a nation in this area with the potential to make the greatest security contribution. There are, no doubt, some Japanese who may think this way, but the large majority of the Japanese people now reject an overseas military role for Japan. Japan's policy is one for its leaders and people to make. As the President (Nixon) said last week, we shall not ask Japan to assume responsibili-

(U. ALEXIS JOHNSON)

ties inconsistent with the deeply-felt concerns of its people. Under present circumstances, Japan's most effective contribution may well be to take care of the local defense of its territory, including Okinawa when it assumes responsibility there, and continue to provide increasing economic cooperation with the other nations in Asia. Both we and Japan well recognize that security in the area is not just a matter of military power, but also very importantly the political, social and economic health of the countries of the area. To this, Japan's contribution can be very important.

Before Cleveland Council on World Affairs,
Cleveland, Feb. 28/Vital Speeches, 4–15:389.

Herman Kahn
Director, Hudson Institute

It seems quite plausible that Japan will pass the U.S. in gross national product per capita by the year 2000 and possibly pass the U.S. in total GNP. In any case, it would not be surprising if the 21st century turned out to be Japan's century.

San Francisco Examiner & Chronicle,
3–22:C11.

Thanat Khoman
Foreign Minister of Thailand

At one time, the Chinese thought they could unite all the developing nations in Asia and Africa—India included—against the developed nations, including the Soviet Union. But they have given up the idea. Neither the Asians nor the Africans are willing to be dominated by a backward regime. So now the Chinese are more concerned with their own problems, more inclined to leave us alone.

Interview, Bangkok/
U.S. News & World Report, 8–3:56.

One can say without hesitation that of all the countries in Asia—and perhaps the world—which have cooperated with the U.S., few have given so much in return for Ameri-

can generosity as the Thai government and people.

Before American Chamber of Commerce,
Bangkok/U.S. News & World Report,
8–24:52.

Jacques Kosciusko-Morizet
French Ambassador to the United Nations

There is truly no one among us who is not basically convinced that China will inevitably resume the place reserved in the Charter for her in the Security Council, in our assembly and in all the institutions of the United Nations. Therefore, why delay this inevitable event?

Before General Assembly, United Nations,
N.Y., Nov. 17/
The Washington Post, 11–18:A12.

Alexei N. Kosygin
Premier of the Soviet Union

The unalterable position of the Soviet Union is that it is in favor of normalizing our interstate relations with (Communist) China . . . It cannot be said we are satisfied with the development of Soviet-Chinese relations, but . . . progress here depends not on the Soviet side alone.

Interview, Moscow/
Memphis Commercial Appeal, 8–10:7.

Shankran Kristnamurthy
Director, Consumers Council of India

We are not concerned with pollution but with existence. The wealthy countries worry about car fumes. We worry about starvation.

Before International Organization of
Consumers Unions, Baden, Austria, July 2/
The New York Times, 7–3:2.

Owen Lattimore
Former Far East adviser to
U.S. President Franklin D. Roosevelt

I do not see any sign of Chinese expansion . . . I believe this is a myth.

Los Angeles Times, 3–18:(1)2.

Malcolm Mackintosh
Consultant, Institute for Strategic Studies,
London; Authority on Soviet policy

It's true that the Russians last year were quite hysterical about (Communist) China as a result of the border fighting and the confrontations. They are still deeply concerned about the long-term problems—China's numerical superiority, possible Chinese expansionism and Chinese missile nuclear power. But I think that Soviet planners now believe that, without a great deal of effort, they can for some time contain China diplomatically and politically. They can inhibit China economically by refusing to trade. They can exclude China from the comity of nations. Militarily they can control any activity on the border. And if the Chinese did decide, in a fit of irrationality, to take on the Soviet Union, then they (the Russians) certainly would come out on top.

Interview, London/
U.S. News & World Report, 11–2:69.

George S. McGovern
United States Senator, D-S.D.

If we look closer, we find that the gap between (Communist) Chinese rhetoric and actual aggression is sufficiently wide to indicate that their bellicose utterances may be born more of fear and damaged pride than of any serious intent or capacity to conquer the world. If we are concerned about Chinese missiles, why don't we admit China to the forums where we are discussing mutual arms limitation? We cannot guess what Peking's answer might be to such invitations, but we know that, so long as we bar the way to Chinese participation, there cannot be even the slightest hope that China will join the international community in dealing with problems that transcend ideology.

At Macalester College, St. Paul, Minn., Oct. 17/
San Francisco Examiner & Chronicle,
10–18:A18.

William McMahon
Minister for External Affairs of Australia

No one can doubt the horror of war that

is felt by the present generation of the Japanese people. They are wholeheartedly behind the renunciation of war enshrined in their Constitution, and they are determined that the affairs of their nation should never again fall into the hands of a military class. Although they have accepted that armed services should be established for the defense of the country, they are reluctant to assume any military power beyond this. Australia understands this attitude and, indeed, respects it.

Before Parliament, Canberra/
The Christian Science Monitor, 3–26:6.

The withdrawal of their (Britain's) permanent military establishment from Southeast Asia, which has already commenced, will remove an important factor for stability and will throw an added strain on the remaining countries which are cooperating for the security of the region. We, therefore, strongly hope that such withdrawal may be delayed and will not mean the disappearance of Britain's active interest and influence in the region.

Before Parliament, Canberra/
The Christian Science Monitor, 3–26:6.

Yashuhiro Nakasone
Director, Self-Defense Forces of Japan

As long as the United States deterrent functions, there is absolutely no possibility of our choosing to have nuclear weapons.

News conference, Washington, Sept. 10/
The New York Times, 9–11:10.

I am a nationalist and oppose Communism at home, but I am not anti-Soviet, nor am I anti-Peking. Least of all am I a militarist. I believe in peaceful coexistence.

Interview, Tokyo/
The New York Times, 9–11:10.

Siddhavanahalli Nijalingappa
President, National Congress Party of India

She (Prime Minister Indira Gandhi) has deliberately encouraged former Communist card-holders in the Administration and has acquiesced in the softening process that Communists favor. In fact, she has taken over some of their methods for her own use.

Before National Congress Party/
The Christian Science Monitor, 1–27:3.

Widjojo Nitisastro
Chief Economic Planner of Indonesia

We've reduced inflation from 650 per cent in 1966 to only 10 per cent last year. We've stabilized the rupiah and made it one of the freest currencies in the world, so that our own people are confident enough now to deposit their funds in local banks instead of sending them abroad. For the first time since independence, we have balanced the budget and set definite priorities on spending—mainly the repair of existing facilities, such as roads and harbors—before starting any new projects as we did in the old days. We inherited such economic chaos! Do you know the only factory going at full capacity before the coup was the money-printing plant?

Newsweek, 5–25:51.

We do not live in a vacuum. We must look to the whole Pacific region. If we compare ourselves to Malaysia, our neighbor, we realize what we are facing. Malaysia's exports now total $1.2 billion—more than ours —while their population is only one-tenth of ours. We are between two countries that are developing very fast: Japan and Australia. We feel we must be in even more of a hurry.

Newsweek, 5–25:52.

Richard M. Nixon
President of the United States

(The Nixon Doctrine) has as its goal not withdrawing from Asia, but providing the means whereby the United States will help other nations help themselves so that we can have a peaceful Pacific, with free nations in

Asia able to defend themselves against aggression.

News conference, San Clemente, Calif.
Aug. 22/The New York Times, 8–23:(1)1

We have no plans to change our policy with regard to the admission of Red China to the United Nations at this time. However, we are going to continue the initiative that I had begun—an initiative of relaxing trade restrictions and travel restrictions and attempting to open channels of communication with Communist China—having in mind the fact that, looking long toward the future—we must have some communication, and eventually relations, with Communist China.

News conference, Washington, Dec. 10
The New York Times, 12–11:3

Masaro Ogawa
Editor, Japan "Times"

Japan today is running like mad—but where are we *heading?* "Ask my feet" would probably be the most honest Japanese answer.

San Francisco Examiner & Chronicle
(This World), 3–22:1

Bruce Palmer
General and Vice Chief of Staff,
United States Army

(Gen. Douglas MacArthur) in a way could be called the father of modern Japan. It was MacArthur the statesman, MacArthur the humanitarian, MacArthur the educator—not MacArthur the conqueror—who transformed a feudalistic military state, ravaged by war, into what is now a true democracy and the third-ranking industrial nation in the world today.

Norfolk, Va., April 1
The Washington Post, 4–19:A

Chung Hee Park
President of South Korea

The North Korean Communists should desist forthwith from perpetrating all sort of military provocations—including the dispatch of armed agents into the South—and nnounce publicly that they renounce enceforth their so-called policies for communizing the whole of Korea by force and verthrowing the Republic of Korea (South orea) by means of violent revolution, and rove their sincerity by deeds . . . (I challnge North Korea to) a bona fide competion in development, in construction and in reativity to prove which institution—deocracy or Communist totalitarianism—an provide better living for the people and hich society is a better place to live in—inead of committing any further the crime war preparations at the sacrifice of the elfare of our innocent brethren in the orth.

At ceremony commemorating 25th anniversary of Korea's liberation from Japanese rule, Seoul, Aug. 15 / The New York Times, 8–15:9.

innathamby Rajaratnam
oreign Minister of Singapore

Can the United States hope to remain big, owerful, secure and prosperous by opting ut of the game—by building a new Great 'all from behind which it can passively obrve the rest of the barbarian world being aped and reshaped by others made of erner stuff? . . . Should military withdrawal om South Vietnam be the prelude to withrawal from the affairs of more than half of imanity? More important still, even if the mericans decide to leave Asia alone, would sia leave the Americans alone? . . . Can e United States really opt out of Asia? For opt out of Asia is to opt out of the Pacific. o opt out of the Pacific is to opt out of orld history. It can opt out politically and notionally, but it cannot remain unaffect-, for better or worse, by what happens on e other side of the Pacific. History will not me to an end merely because the Ameri-ns have withdrawn from the arena. It will made by others more determined to go on th the game—for the smaller countries, the me of survival; for the bigger countries, e relentless pursuit of global influence. he big powers with the will to carry on the uggle (Russia, China and Japan) will de-

termine the course of world history, even for those who think they have opted out.

Interview / Los Angeles Times, 5–22:(2)7.

John R. Rarick
United States Representative, D-La.

The peoples of civilized nations are utterly aghast at the reactionary announcement by the Indian government calling for the use of force by Britain to overthrow the Republic of Rhodesia. First, India's announcement is completely antagonistic to the lives and property of millions of Indians who live in Africa and have already been forced to flee from the north and midland sectors of Rhodesia, South Africa and Portuguese provinces for safety and sanctuary. Second, for the Indian politicians in power to attack the Rhodesians as being a "racist regime" is like the pot calling the kettle black. No country in the world has and maintains a stronger system of racial and religious apartheid than that to be found in India; nor do more citizens of any nation starve year after year. Yet no one has suggested isolating the segregated and ineffective government of India from the world community through economic sanctions, nor that England overthrow the Indian government to liberate the members of the "untouchable caste" or to feed the starving. In fact, applying the same standards of conduct and behavior against the Indians that they have accused the Rhodesians of, it would appear more rational for the civilized governments of the world to withdraw their diplomatic recognition from India rather than from Rhodesia. No Rhodesian troops occupy either Kashmir or Goa.

Before the House, Washington, March 31 / Congressional Record, 3–31:E2721.

Edwin O. Reischauer
Former United States Ambassador to Japan

If Japan becomes not only an economic giant but a military giant, then I see a very dangerous period in world history.

San Francisco Examiner & Chronicle (This World), 3–22:19.

319

William P. Rogers
Secretary of State of the United States

We have done everything we can to improve our relations with (Communist) China. They have given some indication they might like to improve relations, but so far the progress has been very slow. If the Communist Chinese have any interest in becoming a part of the world community, if they want to deal with other nations as the international community deals with itself—on a sensible basis, without threats and so forth—if it is willing to undertake its international obligations to be peaceful and not to threaten other nations nearby, then we could have no difficulty in improving our relations with Communist China.

Television interview, Tokyo, July 9/
Los Angeles Herald-Examiner, 7–9:A4.

Carlos P. Romulo
Foreign Secretary of the Philippines

We prefer a U.S. "commitment" instead of a U.S. military presence on land. Troops on land can cause irritations, misunderstandings and trouble—plenty of trouble. We have enough of that now.

Interview/U.S. News & World Report, 8–3:68.

Walt W. Rostow
Professor of History, University of Texas; Former Foreign Affairs Adviser to the President of the United States

There are some, I know, who regard Asia as primitive, in no way to be compared to Europe in potential importance to the United States. But as anyone who has recently been to Asia knows, it is a region on the march. We are all familiar with the extraordinary growth of Japan—now the third industrial power in the world and closing fast on a sluggish Soviet Union. But in South Korea and Taiwan, Thailand and Malaysia and Singapore, and in India, Pakistan and Iran as well, the modernization of these societies is moving forward swiftly. And Indonesia, too, is coming out of the chaos in which Sukarno left it . . . Sometime in the years ahead, the great natural gifts of the Chinese on the mainland will come to be focused on the modernization of that society in more or less rational ways. Round about the year 2000, then, we shall face across the Pacific almost 4 billion people who, by that time, will have acquired the capacity to use most of the then-existing technology. They will have reached—or be close to reaching—the stage of growth I have described as technological maturity . . . Right now, I believe, the kind of Asia that will exist in the year 2000 is being determined . . . It is being determined, above all, by the growing sense of regional cooperation that has emerged since the United States honored its commitment to South Vietnam in 1965, at a time of mortal danger to Southeast Asia . . . If we do not see it through to an honorable and stable peace in Southeast Asia, we could confront a very different and dangerous constellation of power across the Pacific which would alter the whole setting of American society and its inner life and pose dangers greater than those that came upon us at Pearl Harbor.

At Naval War College, Newport, R.I.,
June 19/Vital Speeches, 9–1:686.

Keiji Sakamoto
Japanese economist

If the U.S. produced a chart of where it wants Japan to go in the coming years, Japan would accept it. But whether it would follow the chart is another matter. We have an expression: "*Dosho imu*—Same bed, different dreams."

Time, 3–2:38.

Eisaku Sato
Prime Minister of Japan

(The nineteen-seventies will be) an era where Japan's national power will carry unprecedented weight in world affairs. (I call on my countrymen) to build such a nation as will have the whole world agreeing that the human race is richer for Japan's existence.

Before the Diet (Parliament), Tokyo, Feb. 14/
The New York Times, 2–15:(1)3.

Japan is not a country to play a role in world affairs by military means . . . in the Japan of tomorrow, we should be confident but not arrogant.

Before the Diet (Parliament), Tokyo, Feb. 14 /
San Francisco Examiner & Chronicle
(This World), 3–22:19.

Unless the United Nations or some international organization can come up with some kind of force to police the world, independent nations must look after their own security. We intend to strengthen our defenses; but to insure our security, we need the over-all nuclear protection provided by the U.S. under our security treaty.

Interview, Tokyo /
U.S. News & World Report, 2–23:56.

Japan is a neighbor of Communist China and cannot disregard the existence of such a large country. Realistic policies must be adopted. We will continue to maintain diplomatic relations with the Chinese Nationalists while remaining free to trade with the Chinese Communists and to exchange journalists, scientists and scholars. This we believe is a desirable, realistic approach to the China problem.

Interview, Tokyo /
U.S. News & World Report, 2–23:57.

It is entirely a new case that a country such as Japan, possessing great economic strength, has no significant military power and yet makes its presence felt throughout the world.

Before National Press Club, Tokyo, April 10 /
The New York Times, 4–11:10.

We have three non-nuclear principles. The first is "no manufacture," the second is "non-possession," the third is "no introduction." We shall steadfastly and faithfully observe these principles.

Interview, Tokyo /
San Francisco Examiner & Chronicle,
6–28:A22.

. . . historically, great economic powers usually become great military powers, too.

But I (state) emphatically that we (will) never again tread the path of the past by building up great military power. I realize the questions that will be and have been raised—whether we won't acquire nuclear power and weapons—but Japan is firmly determined to steer a new path—one away from war.

News conference, San Francisco, Oct. 25 /
Los Angeles Herald-Examiner, 10–26:A11.

Shin Bum Shik
Information Minister of South Korea

We have never consented to the withdrawal of 20,000 U.S. troops from Korea. There is no change at all in our basic position that the modernization of our armed forces must precede any U.S. troop cutback in Korea.

Seoul, Aug. 27 /
Los Angeles Times, 8–28:(1)6.

T.N.J. Suharto
President of Indonesia

Indonesia is still pursuing her active and independent foreign policy—correctly, dynamically and full of initiative—and remains independent from any country in the world.

Annual address to the nation, Jakarta,
Aug. 16 / The New York Times, 8–17:12.

Arthur B. A. Theunissen
Commissioner-general, pavilion of the European Economic Community, Expo '70

With the level of economy they now have achieved, it is time that the Japanese acted like big boys and stopped protecting themselves from foreign competition. If the Japanese will only grow up, they can reach any level of affluence they want.

Interview, Osaka /
The New York Times, 3–17:16.

Antonio J. Villegas
Mayor of Manila, Philippines

Of course they (dissident students) have grievances when a small minority in this country lives in authority and luxury while slavery and poverty is the lot of the majority

(ANTONIO J. VILLEGAS)

. . . the Philippine democracy has become "politocracy"—with a government of the politicians, by the politicians and for the politicians.

Interview, Manila, Feb. 21/
The New York Times, 2–22:(1)29.

Stephen M. Young
United States Senator, D-Ohio

Over the years, since the end of World War II, we Americans have been at a disadvantage in every respect due to the shortsighted policy of withholding diplomatic relations with Communist China. Furthermore, we have deprived ourselves of a listening-post at Peking; we have been forced to observe what is going on in Communist China through our consul at Hong Kong. There is no valid reason we should continue this shortsighted policy, while those lunatic-fringe extremists who desire to return to the witch-hunting, Communist-fearing days of Joe McCarthy still send out utterly false propaganda of a monolithic international Communist conspiracy on the part of the two great Communist nations, China and the Soviet Union. Time and events have proven how wrong these witchhunters have been and are.

Before the Senate, Washington, July 15/
Congressional Record, 7–15:S11326.

Huang Yung-Sheng
Chief of Staff, Armed Forces of Communist China

United States imperialism and its partners and lackeys have committed innumerable crimes in Asia, and this is clear for all to see. The attitude one takes toward the aggressive acts of the United States and Japanese reactionaries—whether it is one of opposition or non-opposition, whether it is genuine opposition or opposition only in words but encouragement and connivance in fact—that is the watershed distinguishing between those who are truly anti-imperialist and those who are spuriously anti-imperialist and between those who are true revolutionaries and those who are sham revolutionaries.

Pyongyang, North Korea, June 25/
The New York Times, 6–28:(1)5.

THE WAR IN INDOCHINA

Spiro T. Agnew
Vice President of the United States

In South Vietnam the morale of the U.S. troops is high. Just as important, there is a genuine and growing spirit of cooperation between U.S. troops and the men of the South Vietnamese Army. I have learned that "Vietnamization" is not just a word; more and more, it has become a fact; and it has stimulated the self-respect and self-confidence so necessary to any army in the field. After so many years of hopes that were raised and dashed, there can be expected to be a certain skepticism on the part of observers in South Vietnam. But even the most skeptical are becoming convinced that the process of shifting the burden of fighting is working, though much remains to be done. We are bound to hear more from those here at home who wanted us to pull out immediately and whose voices became muted after the President's November 3 speech. They are being proved wrong, and they don't like it one bit; obviously, they will seize upon any temporary setback to justify their own ideas of "peace now, worry about the price later." But the people—and the press—cannot be fooled about Vietnam in the Seventies. There is a new realism in policy, a new realism in news coverage, a new realism on the part of South Vietnam's leadership. I could sense that realism in my conversations with President Thieu and with Ambassador Bunker. Because the "iffiness" is gone from American policy, because President Nixon has a plan to end this war, you can actually feel a steadiness of purpose in Vietnam that was never there before. Importantly, the President's plan to end the war honorably is no isolated solution to a single difficult situation—it is a part of a total design, a strategy that is becoming known around the world as the Nixon Doctrine.

Before California Newspaper Publishers Association, Los Angeles, Feb. 5/
Congressional Record, 2–5:S1289.

To listen to the Party that sent over a half-million men to Vietnam decry the rate of our disengagement is a bit like lighting a fire and then criticizing the firemen.

St. Louis, Feb. 10/
The Dallas Times Herald, 2–10:A2.

You can take all of what (Senator J. William) Fulbright said in the last half decade, stack it up, slice it any way you want, and it still comes out as a blueprint for defeat in Vietnam and retreat from the world.

St. Louis, Feb. 10/
U.S. News & World Report, 6–8:39.

. . . I visited 10 nations in Asia, and there's not one of them that doesn't believe 100 per cent in the domino theory. I remember that President Kennedy believed in it. I know that there are a lot of people around now in international affairs that don't want to say they do because it's not very fashionable. I believe in it 100 per cent. I don't think there's any doubt that if a void were created in Southeast Asia—for example, if we withdrew everything from Vietnam and just ran out of there—I don't think that there's any doubt that the spread of Communism would continue—not only into Vietnam and Laos, but also into Thailand and Burma. And a weakening of our resolve to be a force in that area would just create a vacuum. The Australians believe it. The Malaysians believe it.

Interview, Washington/
The Christian Science Monitor, 3–12:3.

(SPIRO T. AGNEW)

The Laotian thing—well, here you have a situation where the total focus of most of our media is on, "Why do we have 600 people in Laos?" There's not been any question in the past of why the North Vietnamese have 67,000 combat troops there . . . Nobody faces the fact that the government that was set up with the consent of North Vietnam—the neutralist government of Souvanna Phouma—has called upon them to get out of Laos, has called upon *us* to help. And yet we're the ones who are criticized. I don't understand this body of opinion in the United States who looks only critically at us and says anything the enemy does is great with us. I don't understand it.

Interview, Washington/
The Christian Science Monitor, 3–12:3.

We are not going to heed the counsel of the Harrimans and Vances and Cliffords—who history has branded as failures—and we are not going to heed the counsels of a Kennedy, a McGovern, a Fulbright or an O'Brien. Most of them have admitted defeat so often and called for retreat so many times that one suspects they may now have developed a psychological addiction to an American defeat (in Vietnam).

Cleveland, June 20/
San Francisco Examiner & Chronicle, 6–21:A1.

When the United States went to the negotiating table at Paris in May, 1968, we were confronted by the toughest of negotiators—revolutionaries of a brutal Communist regime that had battled for power for a decade—the aces in Hanoi's diplomatic deck. Against them we dealt (W. Averell) Harriman and (Cyrus) Vance—a pair of deuces.

Cleveland, June 20/Human Events, 7–4.

I'm puzzled by the fact that not just among the media, but among certain elements of the political spectrum, they have this constant focus on what we're doing (in Vietnam)—are we being humane, are we being thoughtful, how many initiatives did we make this week for peace, are we really justified in each act we take—and yet never from these people, not once, will you ever find any examination of the attitudes of our enemies, or the outrageous acts against the prisoners they hold, the outrageous acts against the people they invade, the rejection of any reasonable peace settlement offers, their total intransigence, their foulmouthed accusations they make against anyone in this country who attempts to engage in some diplomacy.

Television interview, Los Angeles, July 25/
Los Angeles Times, 7–22:(1)11.

Should this proposed amendment (Hatfield-McGovern) become law, unless America declares war, President Nixon would be forced to end any military aid to Laos and to halt all military operations in South Vietnam—20 weeks from today. Every American soldier, sailor, marine and airman would have to be out of Vietnam by June 30 of next year—ten-and-a-half months from today. Hatfield-McGovern is a blueprint for the first defeat in the history of the United States—and for chaos and Communism for the future of South Vietnam . . . If adopted by the Senate and passed by the House, this publicized "Amendment to End the War" in Vietnam will go down in history as the amendment that lost the war in Vietnam and destroyed the chances for freedom and peace in Southeast Asia for the balance of the century. Nothing less is at stake . . . While I do not question the patriotism of the sponsors of this amendment, I do deeply question their wisdom, their judgment and their logic. They are horribly wrong. And if their grave error is enacted into law, generations of Asians and Americans will suffer for their tragic blunder.

Before Veterans of Foreign Wars,
Miami Beach, Aug. 17/
The Washington Post, 8–18:A11.

If South Vietnam collapses, then 285,000 Americans will have suffered and 43,000 will have died for nothing. An American Army, undefeated on the field of battle, will come home in humiliation because impatient pacifists in the Senate lost the war. What will be the reaction, then, when the American people wake up to learn that the thousands of lives and billions in taxes over a decade had been spent only to find national humiliation and disaster at the end of the road?

Before Veterans of Foreign Wars,
Miami Beach, Aug. 17/
The Washington Post, 8–18:A11.

When I speak out against anti-war demonstrators . . . I'm not speaking against their right to dissent. I'm speaking about the absurdity of what they are asking us to do. In other words, I'm dissenting to their dissent. But some people are sold on the idea that anybody who says anything against a dissenter is trying to stifle the right to dissent. And that's ridiculous. We're not trying to stop him from dissenting. We're merely trying to show how irresponsible his dissent really is.

Interview, Washington/
U.S. News & World Report, 8–24:35.

George D. Aiken
United States Senator, R-Vt.

The President had courage to assume the responsibility for the steps he has taken (attacking enemy sanctuaries in Cambodia). It has now become an expanded war, an American war and very probably it will now be known as Nixon's war. If the strategy is a complete success and it brings the war to an early end, the President will be a hero. But if the war drags on, I don't know; but he won't be a hero.

Washington, April 30/
Los Angeles Times, 5–1:(1)22.

To me, Vietnamization is first and foremost a recognition of past mistakes, particularly a recognition of the fact that self-determination in South Vietnam was never possible in the presence of half a million American troops and an American establishment in Saigon of such overwhelming size. Nearly half of these troops have now been withdrawn in an orderly manner, for which I give the President (Nixon) full credit. Vietnamization is apparently succeeding in other ways. Nearly two years ago, the Saigon government undertook to arm the peasantry in South Vietnam—an act of self-determination that cannot be minimized. Since then, the South Vietnamese Army has assumed a progressively larger role in the war and has done so with credit. A government that arms the peasantry, as Saigon has done, is not one to be trifled with. That is why I have joined the President in speaking out against those who advocate yet another intervention in South Vietnamese politics in order to impose a coalition government that might make peace more quickly. If, in the elections to come in South Vietnam in 10 months' time, the voters choose to change their government, so be it. We Americans should remain firmly aloof from that election, even if we have not always done so in the past. But we should also restrain ourselves from carping at *any* government in South Vietnam so long as Vietnamization is working. We should, in fact, continue to help that government overcome the mistakes we both made in the recent past.

Before the Senate, Washington, Nov. 24/
The Washington Post, 11–29:B6.

Raymond Aron
Professor of Faculty Letters, Paris University

To lose the war in Vietnam would not be the end of the world, not even the end of the United States. But the question is *how* you lose the war. I believe Nixon would be quite ready to lose the war five years after the departure of American troops. But now he does not dare to compromise the significance of the American commitment. Whether he is right or wrong is an extremely difficult question.

Interview, New York/
The Christian Science Monitor, 5–22:7.

Jonathan B. Bingham
United States Representative, D-N.Y.

How far will we go in Cambodia in pursuit of an elusive foe? Will we also invade

(JONATHAN B. BINGHAM)

Laos? What about North Vietnam itself? Whatever the answers to these questions, it seems clear that the President, by taking this step (attacking enemy sanctuaries in Cambodia) has plunged us deeper into the morass. If the President's major purpose was to protect American lives, there were many simpler and better ways open to him to accomplish that objective. If he was genuinely concerned about aggression in Cambodia, why has he not taken the case to the U.N. for decision on possible collective action? To me, the President's moves are a sign of desperation, a sign of belated recognition that his policy of Vietnamization of the war, without attempting to negotiate a compromise peace, was bound to fail.

Before the House, Washington, May 4 /
Congressional Record, 5–4:H3836.

Mme. Nguyen Thi Binh
Foreign Minister, National Liberation Front of South Vietnam-Viet Cong

The warlike and fascist Thieu-Ky-Khiem Administration (in South Vietnam), an instrument of the United States policy of aggression, is frantically opposing peace, striving to call for the intensification and expansion of the war and for the prolongation of the United States military occupation of South Vietnam, and are enriching themselves through the blood of the people. They are serving the United States imperialist aggressors who massacre their compatriots and devastate their country. They have stepped up the "pacification" campaigns to terrorize the people and hold them in the vise of their regime, set up a barbarous system of jails of the type of the "tiger cages" on Con Son and established a police regime of the utmost cruelty in South Vietnam. They carry out ferocious repression against those who stand for peace, independence, neutrality and democracy, regardless of their social stock, political tendencies and religions. They repress those who are not on their side. They increase forcible press-ganging and endeavor

to plunder the property of the South Vietnamese people so as to serve the United States policy of "Vietnamization" of the war.

At Paris peace talks, Sept. 17 /
The New York Times, 9–18:2.

The U.S. government still has not decided to enter into serious (peace) negotiations. This new peace maneuver (by U.S. President Nixon) has as its aim to camouflage the military enterprises and policies which the U.S. prepares in Indochina. Mr. Nixon has not changed and always had the intention of maintaining an important part of U.S. troops on our territory in order to pursue his plan of Vietnamization . . . We want a cease-fire, but only as a first step toward lasting peace; that is, a cease-fire which would be founded on a correct political settlement, on the guarantee of the fundamental rights of the Vietnamese people. (Once the U.S. declares its willingness to withdraw all its troops by June 30, 1971), immediately we will cease attacking American troops in the process of withdrawing. Immediately we will discuss liberation of all the captured (American) soldiers—a problem which Nixon uses all the time to mislead opinion and to cover the crimes committed by the United States.

Interview / Daily World, 10–13:2.

Daniel J. Boorstin
Director, National Museum of History and Technology, Washington

I think we ought to correct the idea that this is the first time Americans have ever been divided on a war. We've never been in a war which didn't stir up enormous opposition, and I suspect that the proportion of American people actively opposed to this war is no larger than was the case in some of our past wars. Take the American Revolution—John Adams said that the American people of that time were divided into three groups: one third in favor, one third against and one third that didn't care. I think you could say almost the same thing of most of our subsequent wars. This is not to say that the war in Vietnam is a "good" war, or that we ought to be in it. I pray for the end of the war as we all do. But we are being misled by those who tell us that the nation is in chaos simply because of Vietnam.

Interview, Washington/
U.S. News & World Report, 10–19:65.

Kingman Brewster, Jr.
President, Yale University

Most of us are torn apart by sorrow for the dead and by the anguish for the living. It is tempting to seek relief in blame and recrimination. It is hard to lower our voices when others raise theirs. It is hard to keep the faith when the repeated promises of victory and the promises of negotiated peace have not been fulfilled. But let us not make the equal mistake of saying that defeat is easy to take. If our country is to survive this wound, let us be more honest in the pursuit of peace than we have been in the pursuit of this war. If we make our choice for speedy withdrawal from Vietnam, let us speak in terms of candid confession rather than in terms of blame. Let us admit that it is not easy to stop short of victory in a cause for which so many have fallen in the line of duty. We were fooled by the false promise that this would be an easy war. Let us not fool our fellow countrymen into the belief that this will be an easy peace.

At University of Massachusetts commencement/
Life, 6–19:26.

Leonid I. Brezhnev
General Secretary, Communist Party of the Soviet Union

Comrades, look what is happening to the U.S. aggression against the Democratic Republic of Vietnam (North Vietnam) and the people of South Vietnam. No social system but socialism could have given the liberation struggle of the Vietnamese people such a scale, such organization, staunchness and tenacity. No political force but the Marxist-Leninist Party could have armed a fighting people with such a lucid understanding of the aims of the struggle and inspired them

to the performance of a mass feat. As a result of the heroism of the Vietnamese patriots, multiplied by the might of socialist solidarity and by broad assistance from the Soviet Union and other socialist countries, the U.S. adventure in Vietnam is suffering failure. The feat of Vietnam will go down in history. Honor and glory to the heroic Vietnamese people!

Before Soviet Communist Party and Supreme
Soviet, Moscow, April 21/
Vital Speeches, 6–1:493.

With the support of the Soviet Union and other socialist countries, the fighting people of Vietnam have thwarted the plans of the American military. American diplomats have to maneuver in every way somehow to distract the world public attention and the attention of the Americans, themselves, from the blind alley in which the U.S. finds itself. But deceptive political maneuvers to "legalize" in a roundabout way U.S. control over South Vietnam with the help of American puppets are doomed to failure.

At 50th anniversary ceremonies of Soviet
Armenia, Yerevan, Nov. 29/
Daily World, 12–1:2.

George Brown
United States Representative, D-Calif.

Any President who sends American boys to die in Cambodia, after what we've seen happen in Vietnam, should be ridden out of the White House on a rail. If he (Nixon) sends American soldiers into combat in Cambodia he will commit the utmost folly, and for that he should be impeached.

Before Business-Executives-Move-for
Vietnam-Peace, Washington, April 29/
Daily World, 5–1:1.

David K.E. Bruce
United States Ambassador to Paris peace talks

Hanoi and the Viet Cong must understand, in unmistakable terms, that their past and existing attitude on the prisoner-of-war question is intolerable. We will continue to

(DAVID K. E. BRUCE)

pursue the twin objectives of humane treatment and early release of our men by all means available to us. Our men and their families deserve nothing less.

News conference, Paris, Dec. 1/
The Christian Science Monitor, 12–3:18.

Gordon Bryant
Member, Australian House of Representatives

The situation is that a member of the United Nations (Cambodia) is being attacked by a non-member (North Vietnam), and the world—including Australia—is as silent as the grave . . . There's no doubt in my mind that North Vietnam is committing aggression in Cambodia.

Sydney, July 23 / The New York Times, 7–25:13.

Cheng Heng
Chief of State of Cambodia

Contrary to the situation in Vietnam, the North Vietnamese cannot and will never be able to live like Mao Tse-tung's "fish in water" amongst the Cambodian population . . . The Cambodian people will never cooperate with foreign aggressors who are racially, linguistically, culturally, totally different from us.

Before National Press Club, Washington,
Oct. 21 / The Washington Post, 10–22:A30.

Chou En-lai
Premier of Communist China

Recently, U.S. imperialism had openly instigated the Cambodian rightest clique to a coup d'etat against Norodom Sihanouk, Head of State of Cambodia. This is another frantic provocation made by U.S. imperialism against the peoples of Cambodia, Laos, Vietnam and other Asian countries. The Chinese people firmly support this stand taken by Norodom Sihanouk . . . We are deeply convinced that the Cambodian people, fighting shoulder to shoulder with the peoples of Vietnam and Laos, and supported by the people of the whole world, will cer-

tainly win complete victory in their just struggle against U.S. imperialism and its lackeys.

Pyongyang, North Korea, April 6/
The Dallas Times Herald, 4–6:A8.

Frank Church
United States Senator, D-Idaho

This war has already stretched the generation gap so wide that it threatens to pull the country apart. The new generation never saw in Vietnam the demons our generation perceived. Unlike American Presidents who were mesmerized by the "lessons" of World War II, our brightest young people never believed that Ho Chi Minh was Adolf Hitler in disguise, or that our failure to send in our own troops to fight for the government we subsidized in Saigon would amount to another "Munich." They knew that Vietnam really had nothing to do with the security of the United States, the safety of the American people or the well-being of our society . . . It does no good to tell these young people that "our will and character are being tested," that we shall not be humiliated or accept a first defeat. They do not believe a mistaken war should be won.

Before the Senate, Washington, May 13/
The Washington Post, 5–14:A5.

If we don't do something to establish legislative barriers upon the President's conduct of the (Vietnam) war, the students will be right to say that Congress is dead.

Interview/Newsweek, 5–18:36.

Any sizable economic assistance program (to Cambodia) will inevitably lead to a growing United States presence in Phnom Penh, which, in turn, will feed on itself . . . Once you get an aid contingent in there to administer the program, you need to find housing for them and bring in more marines to protect them, and on and on. We went through this cycle once in Vietnam and we don't want to do it again.

Washington, Aug. 21/
The New York Times, 8–25:3.

It really avails us little to discuss the relative merits of a timetable which would bring the American forces out (of Vietnam) by the end of this year, by the end of the following year or in six months . . . the average withdrawal has proceeded for nearly two years at the rate of 2,500 men a week. We may win many arguments with the President (Nixon). We may impose statutory restrictions and make them stick. But there is one argument we will never win with the President, and that is an argument over timetables, as long as he is making reasonable progress in withdrawing troops. That is why the heat has gone out of this debate on the war; that is why the Vietnam issue, so-called, has been defused—because the American people generally feel that the President is in the process of taking us out of the war, and his schedule is at least sufficient to satisfy them that it is reasonable. That is an argument we are not going to win. Why persist in it?

Before the Senate, Washington/
National Observer, 12–21:6.

Eldridge Cleaver

Information minister, Black Panther Party

You should know, if you don't know, that there's a war going on inside Babylon, inside the United States of America. Not a day goes by now that you don't hear about some pig getting knocked by a brother, or some brother or sister getting knocked by a pig, because our black people have risen up throughout the United States. We're trying to put together a black army so that we can take our freedom from these pigs . . . Instead of stumbling around down there until you get ripped off—and these cats will rip you off—you should desert. If you don't want to do it, you should start ripping off those Uncle Toms and those pigs who are giving you orders to kill the Vietnamese people. You should start blowing them away, throwing hand grenades at them and put that dynamite under their houses, under their jeeps, and rip off General (Creighton) Abrams (American Commander in Vietnam). Do something to let the people know that the

revolutionaries in the armed forces want this war brought to an end . . . All power to the people and revolutionary power to the soldiers, American soldiers in Vietnam who should be in the United States killing . . . Richard Nixon, Spiro Agnew and all other warmongers and dogs.

Radio Hanoi broadcast to American forces
in Vietnam/The Washington Post, 10–15:D23.

Clark M. Clifford

Former Secretary of Defense of the United States

Every American supports the President in his suggestion that there be a cease-fire (in Vietnam). If there could be a ceasefire, the fighting and dying would stop. But it's not how *we* react to it. The realistic test is how *Hanoi* looks at it. We must not be in a posture of offering only one plan of settlement, and if it's rejected, not have another one to offer.

Before Women's National Democratic Club,
Washington, Oct. 13/
Los Angeles Herald-Examiner, 10–14:A4.

Vietnamization is not a plan for peace. All it means is that we can gradually reduce our manpower there and turn the burden of the war over to the South Vietnamese. But the war goes on. Vietnamization is a plan for perpetual war.

Plainview (Tex.) Daily Herald, 11–8:6A.

The increased application of military force will not bring peace in Vietnam . . . I tell you what the bombing will do, if he (President Nixon) starts it again. It will mean more war and more destruction and more fighting and more dying.

Newsweek, 12–21:21.

James M. Collins

United States Representative, R-Tex.

What we have done in Vietnam is make the world's two greatest enemies—Russia and China—allies.

Before Navy League, Dallas, May 8/
The Dallas Times Herald, 5–9:A4.

Alan Cranston
United States Senator, D-Calif.

The Vietnam war, so costly to us in blood and treasure, has served no useful purpose: It has shattered some of our most cherished illusions about our role in the world and the nature of the threat that hostile powers pose to our national interest.

Before Western Electronics Manufacturers Association, Palo Alto, Calif., Jan. 15 / Congressional Record, 2–10:S1559.

The fact is that American combat troops in uniform have been fighting along the Ho Chi Minh Trail in Laos. Yes, we haven't sent in infantry divisions—yet. And yes, our men there are not in battalion strength—yet. But these men are there in Laos, where by treaty we promised they wouldn't be . . . Meddling American know-how seems hell-bent on making another bad little war into another bad big war.

Before California Democratic Council, Fresno, Calif., March 6 / Los Angeles Times, 3–7:(1)18.

Americans will die . . . in Cambodia for the purpose of saving lives in Vietnam, and I think this makes no sense at all.

San Francisco Examiner & Chronicle (This World), 5–10:12.

Let me tell you a shocking, little-known fact: Over half of the American boys who have died in Vietnam were not killed by frontline Viet Cong or North Vietnam troops. They were killed by South Vietnamese peasants—men, women and children—who planted mines and booby traps.

At California Democratic Party convention, Sacramento, Aug. 15 / San Francisco Examiner & Chronicle, 8–16:A10.

Eligio de la Garza
United States Representative, D-Tex.

I have had—and shall continue to have—the opinion that if you become involved in a military conflict you go out and win, using all the resources at your command. This has not been done in the past and it is not being done now. I do not trust the Communists and I never shall, so the idea of a negotiated peace (in Vietnam), as far as the Communists are concerned . . . is a futile effort. It has not worked in the past and it will not work in the future.

Before the House, Washington, Feb. 10 / Congressional Record, 2–10:H807.

Ronald Dellums
United States Representative-elect, D-Calif.

In the United States, the war in Indochina influences our every act and thought and is having a devastating effect upon our every political, economic and social program. This war threatens not only the survival of a tiny country (Vietnam) 10,000 miles away, but also the domestic tranquility and moral fibre of our people at home. There is a rising cry of outrage from our citizens, in increasing numbers, who view the war in Indochina as immoral, and the behavior of our country as America's great shame and humanity's extraordinary burden. Never have the intellectuals, the youth, the religious leaders, the educators, labor and racial minorities—yes, even some members of the armed forces and the U.S. government—been so vocal in courageous opposition to a national military undertaking. We reject as nonsense the "domino theory," which tries in vain to justify our military presence in Vietnam. We are injecting ourselves into a civil war there, in a covert attempt to replace France in Southeast Asia. Is it possible to find an honorable solution to a dishonorable act?

At World Conference on Vietnam, Laos and Cambodia, Stockholm, Nov. 28 / Daily World, 12–26:M2.

Thomas J. Dodd
United States Senator, D-Conn.

Whatever the intention of its authors and supporters, I say this amendment (the Cooper-Church amendment), if it were to become law, would guarantee a Communist takeover of all of Southeast Asia, and this in very short order . . . We all want peace

. . . But there would be no point in terminating the Vietnam war in a manner which invites more war and larger wars in the very near future. And it is this issue that lies at the heart of the current debate on Vietnam and on the Cooper-Church amendment. The distinguished columnist, Crosby Noyes, put the matter in these words: "These proposals are no more than the nose of the camel. The trend is toward the outright abdication of the United States as a major world power. If it prevails, the world is going to be a very dangerous place to live in—not only for Americans, but for everyone else as well."

Before the Senate, Washington/
Human Events, 6-20:3.

Pham Van Dong
Premier of North Vietnam

(The war in Vietnam) follows an implacable logic which serves us admirably. We are at ease, because we possess its secret, which (U.S. President) Nixon, the White House and the Pentagon cannot understand. This is the epoch of the decline of imperialism, including American imperialism. We play a role—we have played it, we are playing it, we will play it—and magnificently.

The Washington Post, 12-5:A15.

The Nixon people are scoundrels, really scoundrels, to talk of this (alleged mistreatment by Hanoi of U. S. prisoners of war). We Vietnamese know all too well what it's like being prisoners—under the French. Yet when they were our prisoners, we treated them well. Ask them. Ask the Americans in our camps. I swear to you these men are well treated.

Interview, Hanoi, Dec. 25/
The New York Times, 12-28:18.

Paul H. Douglas
Former United States Senator, D-Ill.

. . . the conditions under which we first operated (in Vietnam) and the assumptions which we made have not been fulfilled. We were believers in collective security—which I still believe in. I never dreamt we would get no help. I never dreamt that we were to do it all alone . . . I think we're going to get out. I don't approve of it, but I'm powerless to do anything about it. I think the ultimate results will be disastrous. It will be the popular thing for the next few years. But 25 years from now, the culmination of hostilities and aggression . . .

Interview, Washington/
San Francisco Examiner & Chronicle,
8-16:A25.

Ira C. Eaker
Lieutenant General, United States Air Force (Ret.)

. . . if we had fought World War II like we have Vietnam, Hitler would control all of Europe today and Japan all of Eastern and Southeastern Asia and the Pacific west of Honolulu. When a nation with the resources of the U.S. fails to accomplish a military mission against a nation the size of North Vietnam, it must be obvious to the most myopic that there have been errors in strategy, or tactics, or both.

Before Air War College graduating class,
June 5/Vital Speeches, 9-1:702.

We are now, tragically and incredibly, for the first time in our history, witnessing large-scale treason. A traitor traditionally is one who knowingly gives aid and comfort to the enemy. A considerable number of our citizens—some in high places—have been engaged in treasonable acts and statements (against the Vietnam war) for some time. They hide behind the legal fiction that we are engaged in an undeclared war and there is therefore no official enemy. I believe that when some historian of the future does the job on us which Gibbon did on Rome, he will find that the first certain evidence of our decline was our tolerance of treason.

Before Air War College graduating class,
June 5/Vital Speeches, 9-1:704.

Horst Faas
Journalist, Photographer

I will never be one of those guys who sit around and talk (about) the "good old days" in Saigon. There were never any good old days in Saigon. People were always getting killed.

Quote, 8–30:193.

Richard Falk
Professor of International Law, Princeton University

"No more Vietnams" seems to be an optimistic outlook when there is another Vietnam already in Laos. Except for no more troops on the ground, we're prepared, under the Nixon Doctrine, for unlimited Vietnams.

At Conference on War and National Responsibility, Washington, April 20/ The Washington Post, 2–21:A10.

Gerald R. Ford
United States Representative, R-Mich.

President Nixon is moving vigorously to end the American role in Vietnam and, hopefully, to end the war. He is winding down the war, and he is doing everything he reasonably can to achieve a breakthrough at the peace table . . . We certainly cannot stay in South Vietnam forever. If the Saigon government is to stand, it must learn to stand alone.

Before Menswear Retailers of America, Dallas, Feb. 10/ The Dallas Times Herald, 2–10:A1.

It is in Indochina that the Soviet Union has come closest to destroying the U.S. will to resist. We have seen a rise in pacifist sentiment, skillfully exploited by American subversives and revolutionaries. We have seen continuing demands that U.S. military spending be cut below the point of marginal risk. A strong wave of neo-isolationism has swept over a segment of the American people—notably many of our college students the growing feeling among the American gress. The basis for the new isolationism is the growing feeling among the American

people that the game has never been worth the candle in Vietnam.

At National War College, Washington, June 5/The Washington Post, 6–6:A11.

J. William Fulbright
United States Senator, D-Ark.

On the basis of their grudging, minimal contribution to the fighting in Vietnam, it would appear that our Asian and Pacific allies do not take the ostensible threat to their own security very seriously, or they are content to have the United States do the fighting for them.

U.S. News & World Report, 1–12:24.

What is the likelihood that the Viet Cong and the North Vietnamese will allow Vietnamization to proceed without trying to shatter it through a major new offensive? What will we do if Vietnamization fails, if the South Vietnamese Army, left on its own, should come near to collapse again, as in 1964? Would we then send American troops back in and re-escalate the war? Is that what President Nixon meant when he said last November 3, and again on December 15, that he would take "strong and effective measures" if the enemy took military advantage of the American withdrawal?

Before Senate Foreign Relations Committee, Washington, Feb. 3/ The New York Times, 2–4:10.

The Senate must not remain silent now while the President uses the armed forces of the United States to fight an undeclared war in Laos. Acquiescence now in even a limited use of air power in Laos will mean the Senate has surrendered one more legislative power to the executive.

Before the Senate, Washington, March 11/ The New York Times, 3–12:1.

We are fighting a double shadow in Indochina: the shadow of the international Communist conspiracy and the shadow of the old, obsolete, mindless game of power politics. Armed with weapons that have given war a new dimension of horror, and adorned with the sham morality of ideological conflict, the struggle for power and influence has taken on a deadly new intensity at exactly the time when it has lost much of the meaning it once had. All the old power-politics bromides—about "stability," "order" and "spheres of influence"—are largely without meaning to a global superpower armed with nuclear weapons. The world balance of power on which our security depends is a nuclear balance involving Russia, China, Western Europe and the United States. The preservation of a non-Communist—as against a Communist—dictatorship in South Vietnam is not going to protect us, or anybody else, from Soviet or Chinese missiles. It simply does not matter very much for the United States, in cold, unadorned strategic terms, *who* rules the states of Indochina . . .

Before the Senate, Washington, April 2/
Congressional Record, 4–2:S4929.

A disaster of great proportions to American foreign policy in Asia would induce a wave of recrimination at home, which in turn could set off a chain of events culminating in a disaster to American democracy . . . What a price to pay for the myth that Vietnam ever really mattered to the security of the United States.

Before the Senate, Washington, April 2/
The New York Times, 4–3:11.

The plain fact that comes out of the war in Vietnam—reinforced by recent events in Laos and perhaps Cambodia as well—is that, puny as it is by great power standards, North Vietnam is the paramount power in Indochina.

Before the Senate, Washington, April 2/
The Dallas Times Herald, 4–3:A4.

North Vietnam is far too small a power to have any serious hope of conquering all of Southeast Asia, much less of posing any kind of a threat to the United States.

Before the Senate, Washington, April 2/
The Dallas Times Herald, 4–3:A4.

It is up to all those of us who oppose this war (in Vietnam) to keep on boring and badgering our leaders until they make peace.

At Southeastern Massachusetts University,
April 26/Daily World, 4–28:3.

An American officer once said in Vietnam that we had to destroy a town in order to save it. The Administration is now arguing that it is necessary to widen the war (by attacking enemy sanctuaries in Cambodia) in order to end it.

Washington, June 6/
San Francisco Examiner & Chronicle, 6–7:A14.

It (Vietnamization) may make the war more tolerable for Americans by reducing the level of our own participation, but it will not extricate us completely. It will keep us involved indefinitely, while condemning the Vietnamese people to the bloodbath of continuing warfare.

Television broadcast, Washington, Aug. 31/
The New York Times, 9–1:4.

The Administration's request for (aid to) Cambodia represents a most serious and basic policy decision and should be considered by the Congress in that context. What is at stake is not just the support of the Cambodian government for just this fiscal year. It involves the creation of a client-government relationship, and undertaking almost total responsibility for support of that government for the indefinite future. It seems to follow so closely the pattern of our involvement in Vietnam.

Washington, Nov. 19/
Los Angeles Times, 11–20:(1)1.

There appears to be an effort on the part of some to imply that those who question our policies in Vietnam do not care about the (U.S. prisoners of war) . . . My position has always been that the only sure way to bring all our men home—including the prisoners—and to insure that the POW list does not grow, is to bring an end to the war. And I have dedicated myself to this purpose.

Los Angeles Herald-Examiner, 12–7:A4.

John Kenneth Galbraith
Professor of Economics, Harvard University

Politicians, businessmen, experts, intellectuals, students, unions, civil servants actively oppose the war. Who, then, is for the war? We remain in Vietnam, and we extend combat into Cambodia, because the military bureaucracy wants it. It is aided by those Congressmen and Senators—Mendel Rivers, John Stennis, Barry Goldwater—who are the parliamentary poodles of the Pentagon.

Before Americans for Democratic Action,
Washington, May 2/
The Dallas Times Herald, 5–3:A37.

John W. Gardner
Chairman, National Urban Coalition

Nothing we are doing to help or harm our friends or foes in Southeast Asia can compare with what we are doing to ourselves as a nation. The erosion of spirit that we have experienced is beyond calculation. Weighed against that erosion, any possible geopolitical advantages in the war (in Vietnam) must be seen as pitifully small.

News conference, Washington, May 14/
The New York Times, 5–14:22.

It would be extremely helpful, I think, if he (President Nixon) would finally relinquish the notion that the words "winning" or "losing" have any relevance whatever any more with respect to Vietnam. The whole relevance of those two words is a thing of the past now. If he would relinquish what appears to have been his conception in his last press conference that we might conceivably be the peacekeeper in the Asian world, I think we could move expeditiously to get out of Vietnam, and I think it would produce very considerable change in our national mood.

Interview, Washington/
The Christian Science Monitor, 6–8:10.

Vo Nguyen Giap
Minister of Defense of North Vietnam

The feverish acts of war expansion of Nixon decidedly are not signs of strength of the U.S. imperialists. Instead, they have revealed the utterly cruel and aggressive nature of the Nixon Administration, the inevitable failure of his "Vietnamization" program and the great confusion and passivity of the United States and its henchmen in South Vietnam, Cambodia and Laos.

May 8/The Washington Post, 5–10:A13.

Jacob H. Gilbert
United States Representative, D-N.Y.

The lingering war in Vietnam and the more recent events in Cambodia, as well as the resumption of the bombing of North Vietnam, all point out just how desperate our situation is in Southeast Asia. We cannot negotiate our way out, it seems; we cannot win a military victory; we cannot trust the government of South Vietnam to protect itself; the new Cambodian government cannot stand alone. We are simply trapped in quicksand in Indochina. The more we struggle, the deeper we go.

Before the House, Washington, May 4/
Congressional Record, 5–4:H3849.

Barry M. Goldwater
United States Senator, R-Ariz.

As we might have expected, President Nixon's courageous action in Cambodia (raiding Vietnamese Communist sanctuaries) has been met with weeping and wailing from the spokesmen for the political left. This mixed bag of liberals and anarchists just can't get over the fact that their theories and policies were soundly rejected by the American people in 1968.

Before Chamber of Commerce, Nashua, N.H./
The Dallas Times Herald, 5–6:A2.

This (Vietnam war) has been a wrong war. We never meant to win this war, and when you don't mean to win a war, for God's sake don't get into it. It has divided our country as no other war . . . It is a shame, a crime, and history is going to blacken the names of those Presidents who got us into this war and refused to do anything about it.

San Francisco Examiner & Chronicle
(This World), 9–6:2.

The men who cry doom every time the President and the Administration make a positive move in Vietnam are at it again—crying doom, because, of all things, the U.S. Army has tried to rescue some Americans held as prisoners by a cruel and vicious enemy (North Vietnam). These are the same people who went around crying that the sky was falling in when the President sent troops into Cambodia—an action that, as the President predicted, saved thousands of American lives and has made possible the large-scale withdrawal of Americans from South Vietnam. These are the same people who have fought bitterly—and vainly, thank goodness—for the privilege of leading the first surrender in American history. These are the same people leading a fight for unilateral disarmament; a fight that, if they win, will prevent the United States from ever trying to rescue anyone again—or even defend itself. These are the same kneejerk reactionaries who confuse cowardice with peace and surrender with victory . . . There was a time in our history when the nation would have risen up as a man to praise the daring soldiers who risked both life and liberty in an effort to help their fellows. One wonders what has happened to us. Are we too effete, too cynical, too sophisticated today to appreciate heroism? . . . the President of the United States fortunately comes from a tougher stock than the congressional doom-cryers and surrender-mongers.

Human Events, 12–5:5.

Charles E. Goodell
United States Senator, R-N.Y.

We have not Vietnamized the war; we have cosmetized it . . . We have painted a happy scene where Saigon prevails while we withdraw. Behind the facade of this Potemkin village, the facts of Vietnam remain as ugly as ever . . . The real war—the war going on there in Vietnam—has not been defused.

Before Senate Foreign Relations Committee, Washington, Feb. 3/Los Angeles Times, 2–4:(1)5.

The time has come for the Senate to be confronted by a Yes or No vote on the (Vietnam) war. The ultimate sanctuaries are in China and the Soviet Union. I wonder just how far we are going to go.

San Francisco Examiner & Chronicle (This World), 5–10:12.

Albert Gore
United States Senator, D-Tenn.

The tragic mistake was ordering the invasion (of Cambodia by U.S. forces), the crossing of the boundary of a small neutral country. When the reaction in this country and in the world was adverse, then, to placate the Congress, he (President Nixon) promises about 50 of us that he will not invade farther than 20 or 21 miles without the approval of Congress, and that all U.S. troops would be withdrawn from Cambodia by June 30, 1970. But now that the Congress wishes . . . to take his promise at face value, a lobbying effort is undertaken and the propaganda minions are unloosed to accuse those of us who wish to be strict constructionists of the Constitution where war or peace and the lives of American boys are concerned of being unpatriotic. Deplorable, perfectly deplorable.

Before the Senate, Washington, May 14/ Congressional Record, 5–14:S7185.

John Grey Gorton
Prime Minister of Australia

As President Nixon pointed out, they (the North Vietnamese) have embarked on a program to make Cambodia a vast enemy staging area and a springboard for attacks on South Vietnam along 600 miles of frontier. They have, in fact, begun a wider invasion and embarked on a course which poses greater military dangers to allied forces . . . The decision reached by the President of the United States (to attack enemy sanctuaries in Cambodia) was taken on operational military grounds and was designed to protect the lives of allied servicemen. Those who condemn this decision, as the government (of Australia) does not, must either argue

(JOHN GREY GORTON)

that there has not been an increased threat to allied forces as a result of the North Vietnamese action—which is scarcely arguable—or must hold that it does not matter whether there has been an increased threat or not—that allied forces should be left in greater danger from this flank and should not try to prevent that danger. We do not accept that.

Before Parliament, Canberra/
The Christian Science Monitor, 5–8:14.

Edward J. Gurney
United States Senator, R-Fla.

The strident cooing of the antiwar doves that this (U.S. attack on enemy sanctuaries in Cambodia) is a broadening of the war is pure bosh. A nation at war must take all actions necessary to defeat the enemy.

Before the Senate, Washington, May 1/
Los Angeles Times, 5–2:(1)10.

W. Averell Harriman
Former United States Ambassador-at-Large

After 18 months in office, his (President Nixon's) plan for peace in Vietnam only involves the withdrawal of less than half the troops there, and I think that's not good enough . . . This thing is going to be settled on a political basis, and everybody knows it.

News conference, Washington, July 8/
The New York Times, 7–9:4.

Whoever in the (Nixon) Administration thinks he can achieve things by force in Vietnam is wrong. This idea that you can impose your will on others by force doesn't go. Sorry to be so definite, but these people (Vietnamese Communists) have fought for 20 years. They're not afraid to take losses. They're not in a mood to be terrified by anything that we or anyone else threatens to do . . . The reality is that this war has already expanded to include Cambodia and Laos; it can be further expanded to include North Vietnam; then it will include China and even Russia, and we'll get to the world war which we want to avoid. This war cannot be won because it is supported by two large Communist powers.

Interview, Washington/
The Christian Science Monitor, 12–23:2.

I want to see this war ended. I want to see our prisoners home. I want to see those areas rehabilitated. I cannot help but feel unhappy every time I hear that our B-52s are out bombing—say, Cambodia. I wonder whether another community isn't being destroyed. Why do we want to continue to destroy? Why don't we stop this thing? Why don't we concentrate on ending the fighting and concentrate on how we can work toward reconstruction and trying to develop a decent life for the people we've been fighting in this period? Now, we didn't start this, and I realize that the North Vietnamese are aggressive, and I can say all the other things about their aggression. But we've got to be ourselves and be the carriers of mercy and goodwill, rather than waste and destruction.

Interview, Washington/
The Christian Science Monitor, 12–31:3.

Vance O. Hartke
United States Senator, D-Ind.

The President's action in sending troops into Cambodia amounts to a declaration of war against the Senate.

Newsweek, 5–11:25.

Mark O. Hatfield
United States Senator, R-Ore.

Vietnamization is put forth as a plan for ending the war. But it is nothing of the sort. Vietnamization means that the South Vietnamese will fight and die in increasing numbers instead of Americans . . . Vietnamization merely changes the nature of the conflict; it does not resolve political differences; it does not halt the loss of life; and it perpetuates the very political instability which dragged us into Vietnam initially.

Before the Senate, Washington/
The Christian Science Monitor, 9:1.

Warren E. Hearnes

Governor of Missouri

Call it Vietnamization, orderly withdrawal or anything you like, but the fact is that for the first time in our history the United States has lost a war. Consider the impact of that statement for a moment: We have lost a war. Perhaps it is impolite of me to phrase it in those terms. Perhaps the American people prefer to avoid the humiliation of that conclusion. President Nixon says he intends to Vietnamize the war. The news media call it an orderly troop withdrawal. Critics of this policy say we have failed to win the war. But if you define war by its historic terminology of either winning or losing, then we have lost the war.

At William Jewell College, Liberty, Mo.,
Feb. 19 / Vital Speeches, 3–15:336.

Edward Heath

Prime Minister of the United Kingdom

Like our predecessors in office, we have always held that Vietnam was not a war which could be won by military means. Lasting peace can come only through a negotiated settlement. For that very reason, I think President Nixon's efforts to get the Paris talks moving are right, and his recent negotiating offer seems very fair and reasonable. His other policy, Vietnamization, is realistic. The results on the ground are proving it so.

Interview, London /
U.S. News & World Report, 12–21:29.

Ernest F. Hollings

United States Senator, D-S.C.

I share the concern that the 42,118 killed, 278,006 wounded, 1,450 prisoners and 7,949 other casualties (in the Vietnam war) have not sacrificed in vain. But my immediate problem is that an *additional* 329,000 casualties not sacrifice in vain. If you're not seeking a military victory, if the policy is retreat, if, from elections, you will accept a Communist government, then what in the devil are we fighting for?

Quote, 7–5:1.

We never have come clean with a position on this war. The policy is retreat, but the rhetoric is attack. You ask why would anyone politick with war. We know that President Nixon would like to end it all in the next hour. But each President has feared the reaction of the home front when it learned we had failed at the battle front. No one has wanted to be in the chicken coop when the chickens come home to roost. Kenneth O'Donnell writes that President Kennedy's decision to get us out of Vietnam was delayed by his not wanting to face the reaction of the people on the heels of withdrawal. President Johnson thought he could politick it—it would be a painless war; there would be no threat of World War III because there would be no threat to annihilate the enemy; we would come with men and machines, bluff and gusto; but we wouldn't let the military really fight; we would minimize casualties so as to minimize complaints from home; no one would stay over a year; we wouldn't call up the National Guard or Reserve; we would have guns and butter both—business as usual; if the people at home didn't suffer, if they didn't feel any real impact of war, then this mandate for a Great Society in 1964 could be repeated in 1968.

At Blue Key Service Fraternity,
University of Georgia, Sept. 21 /
Vital Speeches, 11–1:38.

Harold E. Hughes

United States Senator, D-Iowa

(Vietnamization is) a semantic hoax. What it denotes is simply an extension of the Johnson foreign policy . . . It will not get us out of Vietnam. Rather, it will perpetuate our involvement.

Before Senate Foreign Relations Committee,
Washington, Feb. 3 /
The New York Times, 2–4:1.

The idea of years of involvement in another bloody Asian war is too ghastly to stand.

The Dallas Times Herald, 3–6:A2.

Hubert H. Humphrey
Former Vice President of the United States

Maybe history will say we were wrong (to involve ourselves in Vietnam), that we never should have been there. But it is my view that we made the only decision that we could have made at the time, that it was a responsible decision in light of the evidence.

Interview, St. Paul, Minn./
Los Angeles Herald-Examiner, 1–12:A4.

I think his (President Nixon's) program must be based on systematic and accelerated (troop) withdrawal. It must not depend on Saigon or the actions of North Vietnam. It must be based upon our national interest . . . I am convinced in my own mind the President will have to withdraw these troops. The politics and the economics of the situation at home will dictate it . . . The public has soured on the war; they really want out.

News conference, Washington, Feb. 9/
Los Angeles Times, 2–10:(1)5.

. . . Vietnam is like a bunch of mosquito bites on your arm. And when Nixon went into Cambodia, he scratched them and spread the misery.

Interview, Minneapolis/
Los Angeles Times, 8–18:(2)7.

One thing's for sure: Nobody's going to be elected President (of the United States) by trying to win that stupid war (in Vietnam). Two people have learned that—Lyndon Johnson and Hubert Humphrey—and a third (Richard Nixon) is learning it right now.

Interview, Minneapolis, Sept. 16/
The New York Times, 9–18:19.

I had a President (Lyndon Johnson) who was absolutely paranoid about the war—beyond his ego, which we all know about, which he certainly had, which any man does have who is President. But beyond that, you've got to remember he had two sons-in-law who were over there. Why, anybody who said the *slightest* thing to him about change

in Vietnam—why, my Lord!

Interview/The New York Times Magazine,
10–11:26.

David Ifshin
President-elect, United States National Student Association

The Vietnam war is a racist war of colonization . . . that is not simply an error, but is a manifestation of how American society is structured.

Interview, St. Paul, Minn., Aug. 19/
The Washington Post, 8–20:A4.

Andrew Jacobs, Jr.
United States Representative, D-Ind.

. . . it is my duty today to announce the discovery of a new "domino theory" that says, in essence: If you disregard the advice of General Douglas MacArthur and go into the quicksand of an Asian country, like a domino you will fall into the quicksand of another Asian country.

Before the House, Washington, May 14/
Congressional Record, 5–14:H4373.

Jacob K. Javits
United States Senator, D-N.Y.

(If there are) U.S. interests in Laos which justify our combat involvement there, the Administration should have no hesitancy in making its case to the Congress and to the people. (But) present U.S. policy actions in Laos have not been specifically authorized as such by Congress and are, it is charged, even masked from public and Congressional scrutiny by a continuing policy of non-disclosure.

San Francisco Examiner & Chronicle
(This World), 3–15:12.

We went into Vietnam to help a small nation get self-determination. It *has* self-determination. That is what everybody argues about. They say the government (in South Vietnam) is good, bad, indifferent; but it actually had an election, and this is their elected government. They have an elected assembly functioning, et cetera. Now, do you have to stay in forever and be their guardian? Is there any national honor or national victory or defeat in that; or is it only a disguised way to destroy yourself in your own country, which is what we are doing—economically, incidentally, beyond anything else—and to paralyze ourselves from being able to conduct a policy of vigor which will bring peace . . . in the world.

Interview/Issues and Answers,
American Broadcasting Company, 6–21.

Lyndon B. Johnson
Former President of the United States

. . . I agonized, I explored every possible way, I tried to get these people (the North Vietnamese) to talk reason. I tried to keep them from coming in attacking our camps, and killing their people. I tried to get them not to infiltrate. But they were determined to do one thing, and that's take over this little country (South Vietnam). And if they take that one over, they were determined to take over others, in my judgment, just as Hitler was.

Television interview, Johnson City, Tex.,
Feb. 6/The Washington Post, 2–7:A10.

It was a shame somebody didn't think of calling it (the Tonkin Gulf resolution) the Fulbright Resolution, like the Fulbright Scholars thing, because Senator (J. William) Fulbright introduced it with his knowledge, with his approval, with his consent.

Television interview, Johnson City, Tex.,
Feb. 6/The Washington Post, 2–7:A10.

I hoped for a great deal more than has been achieved (in Vietnam). I was desperately trying to show that I was reasonable, that our country would prefer to talk rather than fight, that we were determined not to let aggression take over Southeast Asia, but that we would try to negotiate it out rather than fight it out. Now we haven't made any progress (at the Paris talks)—and my hopes have faded away, and my dreams have not been realized.

Television interview, Johnson City, Tex./
Columbia Broadcasting System, Feb. 6.

I hope the President (Nixon) and all the hundreds of good men under his command will have the prayers and support of all the people (in his decision to attack enemy sanctuaries in Cambodia)—he has mine. God knows Presidents need it, and I know because I have been there . . . I know from personal experience that his problem and our problem tonight is getting Hanoi to listen, and I hope that our President's voice will not be drowned out by other voices who may not have all the facts and who do not have the responsibility of making these dangerous and agonizing decisions . . . We can only have one President at a time . . . I have seen in this country over the years that it hurts our country, it hurts every citizen in our country for America to ever present an image of a divided land . . .

Chicago, May 1/
Los Angeles Times, 5–2:(1)2.

Edward M. Kennedy
United States Senator, D-Mass.

(President Nixon has) fallen prey to the same illusions that drove another from power—victory in Southeast Asia . . . Today we are in error (in attacking enemy sanctuaries in Cambodia). Men will die, and we will reap the harvest of this error with dissent and turmoil.

Boston, May 1/
Los Angeles Herald-Examiner, 5–1:A6.

Thanat Khoman
Foreign Minister of Thailand

We convinced General Lon Nol (Premier of Cambodia) that as long as they can afford not to rely on foreign soldiers, it is better not to. We said, "Defend yourself, and we will give you everything that we can spare, and we will help you train your soldiers" . . . It is only in the last extremity—when the question is absolutely life and death—then, of course, we will reconsider.

Interview, Bangkok/
The Christian Science Monitor, 9–12:13.

Henry A. Kissinger
Assistant to the President of the United States for National Security Affairs

What is needed now is a national recognition that only the President can take us out of the war (in Vietnam). The time has come for an act of national commitment to the Presidency, even an act of love.

Washington/Time, 6-1:10.

Edward I. Koch
United States Representative, D-N.Y.

Candidate Nixon had a secret plan to end the war in Vietnam. President Nixon has a secret timetable for withdrawing our troops from Vietnam. Because his plans and time-tables are secret, the Administration now will not even tell us what the war will cost in fiscal year 1971. We know the human cost; 100 American men are being killed almost every week in Vietnam. The Administration cannot hide that fact, though I am sure they would like to if they could. We are told that the budget has been censored for security reasons. The conduct of a war that has consumed $100 billion and 40,000 American lives now becomes so secret that the American people who must pay for it are no longer entitled to know its cost. I suspect the real reason that the budget has been censored is to avoid any setback in the President's public relations effort. The so-called "silent majority" is apparently supposed to trust the President, pay its taxes and not ask questions. Well, let me say there are still plenty of Americans who do *not* trust the President, who pay their taxes and want some answers . . .

*Before the House, Washington, March 11/
Congressional Record, 3-11:H1667.*

Foy D. Kohler
Former United States Ambassador to the Soviet Union

I'm convinced that Moscow decided long ago that there was no chance of a Communist military victory there (Vietnam) and felt that a political settlement would be acceptable—a settlement as favorable to the Communists as possible, of course, but still a settlement. However, Moscow has refused consistently to play an active role in seeking a settlement, the reason being that the Chinese accuse them of being ready to sell out "little brother"—the North Vietnamese Communists. The Russians are very sensitive Moscow are determined to look more militant than the other in supporting Communist causes around the world.

*Interview/U.S. News & World Report,
6-22:26.*

Alexei N. Kosygin
Premier of the Soviet Union

President Nixon's statement that they (the Americans) are defending United States honor in Cambodia is more like a travesty of the word "honor." To reckon that, by annihilating the peaceful population in Cambodia, by annihilating towns and villages, by plundering a peaceful country, one is defending the honor of the United States—well, I think that does not need any comment.

*News conference, Moscow, May 4/
The New York Times, 5-5:2.*

We are trying to do everything possible to stop the aggressive war in Indochina which was unleashed and which is being waged by American imperialists . . . The Soviet Union supports a political solution of the problem, with strict respect for the rights of the peoples of Indochina to settle their affairs without foreign interference.

Interview, Moscow/Milwaukee Journal, 8-10:4.

William M. Kunstler
American civil rights lawyer

If the war in Vietnam is wrong, indecent, immoral and unjust, then the system that started it should be destroyed; and anyone who says anything else is evading the issue.

*At Catholic University, Washington/
Human Events, 11-28:16.*

Nguyen Cao Ky
Vice President of South Vietnam

I wish to make it clear that we will not let

our hands be bound by anyone any more
. . . Some people put forth a hypothesis
that if some day the Americans leave Cambodia, then the South Vietnamese will have
to follow them out of Cambodia, too. This
is a silly argument of silly people.

At National Defense College, Saigon, May 21 /
The New York Times, 5–22:7.

Three years ago, when I stepped down and
became Vice President, I decided not to create additional problems for (President
Nguyen Van) Thieu. For the last three
years, he's been in control. For the last three
years, I've been silent . . . But recently I've
begun to speak out because of the many
problems. I've told the President what is the
situation and what is my opinion. Most of
the time he agrees with me, but he does not
act. As Thieu told me: "Ky, you and I both
have many of the same ideas. But we are both
like race-car drivers. I like to go slow; you
like to go as fast as you can. You will probably win the race, but you forget that if you
go too fast, accidents can happen." But if
you wait too long, you come to a day when
it will be too late. If the South becomes
strong and peaceful, then I'll quit politics.
But if in a year there's still a big internal
problem, then I don't know whether I will
run (for President), but I'll consider it. I
must serve my country.

Interview, Saigon/Newsweek, 6–1:49.

After these (Cambodian) operations, I
think that American ground troops can
leave Vietnam by '71, because now everyone
can see the fighting spirit of the Vietnamese
and their capacities. They are not so weak
as rabbits as some people think. I've been
around all the corps areas and with the
ground troops, marines, navy and the air
force. Everywhere I see big, big spirit. For
years our troops have not clearly seen the
reason why they could not destroy the
enemy. But now they realize that the enemy
are Vietnamese just as we are. We can prove
to ourselves that we are capable of destroying
the enemy.

Interview, Saigon/Newsweek, 6–1:49.

We have no deadline (for withdrawing
Vietnamese troops from Cambodia) because
I think Cambodia and Vietnam we are like
lips and teeth.

Interview, Saigon/Newsweek, 6–1:49.

Villifying the Yankee gives me pleasure.

News conference, Saigon, July/
Los Angeles Herald-Examiner, 8–27:A3.

Because American aid policies are wrong
and because aid procedures are complicated
and arbitrary, United States aid has not
helped Vietnam toward self-sufficiency and
has clearly not been entirely helpful to the
South Vietnamese people . . . Worse yet, a
small minority of local capitalists, specula-
tors and middlemen have profited by the
program, thus creating a new class of profi-
teers who have contributed to an increase in
social injustice and conflicts within Vietnamese society.

Before South Vietnamese newspaper
publishers, Saigon, July 4/
The New York Times, 7–5:(1)3.

They (1967 South Vietnamese elections)
were only useful to elect a regime which is
wrong and corrupted and weak, and would
fall immediately with a revolution. It is hard
for me to say so because I share the responsibility of those elections . . . but I recognize evil where the evil is . . . (Americans)
don't like me because I tell them what I
think, and I accuse them of lying . . .
Americans are not here for democracy or
freedom; they are here to defend their interests.

Interview/Washington Star, 9–28:A11.

We would have no objection to a (U.S.)
congressional deadline for American withdrawal of troops from Vietnam, with one
condition: that knowing that deadline, the
Communists will agree to discuss with us
sincerely a solution to the political problems
of Vietnam.

Washington, Nov. 25/
The Washington Post, 11–26:A2.

(NGUYEN CAO KY)

I can tell you that the Vietnamese newspapers have more freedom than any press in any country in the world today. Saigon itself has more than 15 new daily newspapers, and it is very hard to find some who are not against the government.

Television interview, Washington, Nov. 29 /
Los Angeles Herald-Examiner, 11–30:A4.

Our side has repeatedly declared we are ready to discuss any problem without trying to eliminate anyone, without order of priority on the subjects, and in any form of meetings. (But) for freedom we are determined to fight on if war is still imposed upon us, even if we have to fight alone . . . I feel that one should still fight on to the last limits of our strength, and, if one should die, then death may be better than life without freedom.

Before Commonwealth Club, San Francisco,
Dec. 1 / San Francisco Examiner, 12–2:6.

Melvin R. Laird
Secretary of Defense of the United States

This trip (to Vietnam) has convinced me that Vietnamization continues to make solid progress, that we face formidable but manageable problems ahead and that we and the South Vietnamese people, together with other free-world forces, can press ahead with Vietnamization and the goal of self-determination for the Republic of Vietnam, as we continue to hope for a breakthrough in the Paris talks.

Los Angeles Times, 2–15:A2.

. . . we've had problems with Cambodian sanctuaries during the 15 months I've been Secretary of Defense—and my predecessors had them, too. In the past, the enemy enjoyed a tremendous opportunity to operate from privileged sanctuaries in Cambodia against not only the Mekong Delta region but also the area stretching north of Saigon. And the supplies that were funneled through Cambodia to enemy forces in South Vietnam were substantial . . . If the North Vietnamese were to control Cambodia, they would have free access to ports and beaches there, and could move supplies without restriction. So it would not be correct, by any stretch of the imagination, to think that such a situation would benefit our Vietnamization program. This supply question is easily understood. The sanctuary matter has been far less well understood by the American public, but, over the long run, it is even more important.

Interview, Washington /
U.S. News & World Report, 5–11:64.

. . . we have a job which was started there (Vietnam) years ago, and we're going to complete that job. Through Vietnamization or negotiation or some combination, we are going to achieve our objective of self-determination for the South Vietnamese people. We are going to protect their right to make their own political choices without having those choices forced on them by North Vietnamese bayonets or Viet Cong terrorists controlled from Hanoi. It doesn't do any good to debate whether or not we should have gone with large ground forces in the first place. Since I've been Secretary of Defense, I've tried to get the debate away from "Why Vietnam?" to "Why Vietnamization?" Vietnamization is one of the cornerstones of the Nixon Doctrine, and I believe that it will succeed.

Interview, Washington /
U.S. News & World Report, 5–11:66.

. . . there is one fact that should be widely and clearly understood: The military pressure on and harassment of the Cambodian government in Cambodia is not coming from Cambodians. It is coming from North Vietnamese Army units which include some South Vietnamese Communists or Viet Cong. If Hanoi wants to expand Communist influence in Cambodia, it must use North Vietnamese Army troops to do so. There is no ethnic Cambodian Communist movement of any real size or consequence in Cambodia.

Interview, Washington /
U.S. News & World Report, 5–11:67.

The President's bold and decisive move into Cambodian sanctuaries (of the Vietnamese Communists) was greeted initially by some skepticism. This skepticism, nurtured by too many prior years of unrealized hopes and unfounded optimism, is a legacy hard to overcome. I think the way to restore credibility is to promise only what you can deliver—and then deliver it. Our record on this score is, in my judgment, both significant and visible with regard to the war in Vietnam.

At United States Air Force Academy
commencement/Life, 6–19:27.

Pham Dang Lam
South Vietnamese Ambassador to
Paris peace talks

Despite your repeated denials in the past, it is no longer possible for you now to deny that you are violating the sovereignty and territorial integrity of the kingdom of Cambodia. In the past few days, tens of thousands of Cambodians have demonstrated continuously in Phnom Penh to express the indignation of the Khmer people for the blatant violation of their country by your side. With every passing day, public opinion has fully realized that, in spite of your fine words of peace and fundamental rights, it is precisely your side which constitutes a threat to peace and to the national fundamental rights of the peoples of South Vietnam, Cambodia and Laos.

Addressing Communist representatives at
Paris peace talks, March 19/
Los Angeles Times, 3–20:(1)7.

(The South Vietnamese government) has the sincere conviction that free elections, open to all political parties and groups in Vietnam, including the National Liberation Front (Viet Cong) . . . would constitute the best and . . . most rational way for the South Vietnamese population to exercise genuinely its right of self-determination.

At Paris peace talks/
National Observer, 10–19:2.

John V. Lindsay
Mayor of New York

Our hold on the future is very frail. That future—all that we are and all that we can be—dies a little bit each day the (Vietnam) war goes on; and it dies whenever we succumb to the easy conclusion that the contestants there or here are gooks or devils, bums or pigs. We must not forget that we all bleed.

At New York University, May 6/
The New York Times, 5–7:24.

The ones I have unending admiration for are the guys who say, "I simply will not serve in the Army of the United States in Vietnam, and I am willing to take the consequences for it . . ." These are the guys who are heroic.

At University of Pennsylvania/
Newsweek, 5–11:65.

The violence that started long ago in some obscure Vietnamese village, reinforced and magnified by years of folly and killing, has done to America what no enemy has done for 100 years. It has turned our land into a battlefield.

Quote, 7–5:1.

Louis B. Lundborg
Chairman, Bank of America

If a company in private business were guilty of making such a bad judgment as we have made in Vietnam, and then of pursuing that judgment until so large a part of its total resources were committed to the ill-starred project, the management of the company would be under attack by the directors and ultimately by the shareholders of the company . . . In my judgment, it is time the shareholders of America—the people—begin to call for an end to the squandering of American blood, morale and resources on what is in essence an Asian war of nationalism.

Before Senate Foreign Relations Committee,
Washington, April 16/
San Francisco Examiner & Chronicle
(This World), 4–26:13.

(LOUIS B. LUNDBORG)

An end to the war (in Vietnam) would be good, not bad, for American business. War is, as we would say in business, a low-yield operation.

Plainview (Tex.) Daily Herald, 8–9:6A.

Lester G. Maddox
Governor of Georgia

We didn't lose our war in Southeast Asia; we lost it here in Washington. Only by making it clear to our enemies—both at home and abroad—that we are strong, determined and fearless can we bring the shooting and bombing to a halt . . . Now, I'm not talking about sending more troops to Vietnam or turning this stinking little war into a nuclear holocaust. There is no need to bring out the elephant guns to swat a fly.

Washington, April 4/
The Washington Post, 4–5:A8.

Norman Mailer
Author

Jail sentences are becoming routine. Anyone associated with the antiwar movement has to expect one nowadays. It's almost an honor to go in (to jail) today because we have a President who is the living embodiment of . . . Uriah Heep—the veritible cathedral of hypocrisy.

Alexandria, Va., May 5/
The Washington Post, 5–6:A3.

Mike Mansfield
United States Senator, D-Mont.

. . . the only glimmer of hope . . . is that the tide is out in Vietnam rather than in as far as our own people are concerned. But I would like to see something done so that we could move out of Vietnam and all Southeast Asia, lock, stock and barrel. Give up all the bases we have. Let the Vietnamese govern themselves. Let the South Vietnamese—all groupings—get together to create a coalition government, which I think is going to come any-

way. And let these people, all of whom are South Vietnamese, decide what their own future will be.

Interview, Washington/
The Christian Science Monitor, 1–26:2.

For years, Cambodia was in the eye of the Indochina hurricane; now it is swept up in the full fury of a racial, ideological and militarist storm . . . Some may find it difficult to resist an appeal for aid to this country. Some may find the present military government . . . more "worthy" of aid. (Some may argue that without aid it) will topple under the domino theory (and) some may note that it is just some arms aid that is being sought, not American forces. If these observations sound familiar, it is because they are the siren's songs which have beckoned us time and again ever deeper into the morass of Southeast Asia.

Before the Senate, Washington, April 16/
The Washington Post, 4–17:A13.

The President (Nixon) reached a conclusion (to attack enemy sanctuaries in Cambodia) which was his to reach as Commander-in-Chief of the Armed Forces under the Constitution. I respect his decision even as I regret it and am deeply concerned by it. I hope that, as he expects, his decision will reduce American casualties, speed the withdrawal of American troops from Vietnam and hasten the end of the war. I would be less than honest, however, if I did not express the grave doubts which I have expressed today on these expectations. There is nothing in past experience in Indochina to suggest that casualties can be reduced by enlarging the area of military operations. There is nothing in past experience to suggest that the way out of the Vietnamese conflict follows the road of a second Indochina war. Indeed, that road may well meander throughout all of Southeast Asia and end nobody knows where.

Before the Senate, Washington, May 1/
The New York Times, 5–2:5.

Sisowath Sirik Matak
Deputy Premier of Cambodia

We are more determined than the V.C. (Viet Cong). We understand why we fight, while the Viet Cong and the North Vietnamese are fighting (in Cambodia) for indefensible reasons they cannot understand. At the present levels of enemy activity, United States troops are not needed. All we need now is military equipment. We must carry out this war ourselves and not create another burden for our American friends.

Interview, Phnom Penh /
The New York Times, 9–10:3.

Charles McC. Mathias, Jr.
United States Senator, R-Md.

The reports I get, the information I get, is that we have very large numbers of troops there (Laos). The fact that we have troops on the ground there—this is the very point of the whole thing: that when we have troops on the ground there, that when there are battles raging there and that when our troops are cheek by jowl with local troops who may be engaged in fighting, it is almost inconceivable that we won't be drawn into some of it or some phase of this. And once the first shot is fired, who knows where the end of it will be.

Interview, Washington /
The Christian Science Monitor, 3–2:3.

Eugene J. McCarthy
United States Senator, D-Minn.

Even if through a resurgence of morale and a reduction of corruption the South Vietnamese Army could be made into an effective military force, there would still be the question of whether Vietnamization would be desirable. Asians would be killing Asians with American arms. Defoliation and destruction of crops would continue; villages be destroyed; refugees be "generated"; casualties be continued.

Before Senate Foreign Relations Committee,
Washington, Feb. 19 /
The Washington Post, 2–20:A2.

The Administration is now saying we're fighting because of the prisoners in North Vietnam. (Threatening to resume bombing is really) saying we're going to get the prisoners out of North Vietnam by the very thing that got them in.

Television interview, Dec. 27 /
San Francisco Examiner, 12–28:4.

Paul N. McCloskey, Jr.
United States Representative, R-Calif.

We see our government as the protector of individual freedom, but our policy in Vietnam has led us to a way of making war that is repugnant to the ideals of democracy. We executed war criminals at Nuremburg for the same crimes we are committing in Vietnam—destruction of villages. A policy of massive destruction of people and villages by aerial firepower through impersonal technology amounts to cowardice . . .

Before Emergency Committee Against
Escalation, Palo Alto, Calif., Dec. 20 /
San Francisco Examiner, 12–21:6.

John W. McCormack
United States Representative, D-Mass.

Few people realize that Southeast Asia is the first line of defense in the Far East for the United States. If we are forced out, it will be only a short time until we will be driven back to a continental defense line, which is Hawaii and Alaska. Some people can laugh that off. I cannot.

Interview, Washington /
U.S. News & World Report, 7–27:58.

Gale W. McGee
United States Senator, D-Wyo.

Cambodia is not that strategically important either to Hanoi or to South Vietnam. It's the marginal regions that they share in common that become the keys. Obviously from our point of view, I would suppose, it would be better if the present government did not collapse; but it's not fatal if it does.

Radio interview, Washington, Aug. 23 /
Los Angeles Times, 8–24:(1)4.

George S. McGovern
United States Senator, D-S.D.

Now, if we want to see this war come to an end on a more humane and rational basis than simply arming the Vietnamese to fight it out among themselves, I would say that we ought to Vietnamize the government in South Vietnam by easing off our embrace, by easing off our support for (President) Thieu and (Vice President) Ky and, in doing so, create the kind of political situation where they would be forced to go out and form a much broader coalition government —where they would have no other alternative except to embrace many of the political groups whose leaders are now imprisoned in Saigon, and to perhaps invite some of the exiles to return and form what would amount to a transitional peace government in Saigon that would have the credibility to negotiate a settlement with the Viet Cong. That's really the way to end the war—on a negotiated basis and on a more enduring political basis that would hold out the hope for real stability and peace in South Vietnam.

Interview / The Christian Science Monitor,
1–5:2.

The policy of Vietnamization is a political hoax designed to screen from the American public the bankruptcy of our needless military involvement in the affairs of the Vietnamese people . . . How can we justify before God and man the use of our massive firepower to continue a slaughter that serves neither our interest nor the interest of the Vietnamese?

Before Senate Foreign Relations Committee,
Washington, Feb. 4 /
Los Angeles Herald-Examiner, 2–4:A4.

. . . the blunt truth (is) that there will be no resolution to the war so long as we cling to the Thieu-Ky regime . . . We can continue to pour our blood and substance into a never-ending effort to support the Saigon hierarchy, or we can have peace. But we can-

not have both General Thieu and an end to the war.

Before Senate Foreign Relations Committee,
Washington, Feb. 4 / Daily World, 2–5:2.

Vietnamization is basically an effort to tranquilize the conscience of the American people while our government wages a cruel and needless war by proxy.

Before Senate Foreign Relations Committee,
Washington, Feb. 4 /
U.S. News & World Report, 2–16:10.

It is absolutely incredible that a great nation such as ours could be waging a major military operation in a foreign country without the knowledge of either its citizens or its Congress. The secret war we are waging in Laos is repugnant to the principles and security of a free society.

Before the Senate, Washington, March 3 /
Daily World, 3–4:2.

Now, what is he (Vice President Agnew) talking about on (some Senators) being "addicted to defeat"? Does he mean he thinks we are going to score some kind of victory in Vietnam? The President doesn't hold to that view; he is not talking about military victory; he is talking about getting out; he is talking about withdrawing forces. That is not the way to victory. We wouldn't be withdrawing if we didn't know we had made a mistake in going; and I suspect 90 per cent of the Congress wishes we weren't involved in Vietnam. What I am "addicted" to is peace and to ending this war.

Interview / Issues and Answers,
American Broadcasting Company, 6–21.

If, as (Vice President) Agnew claims, the Cambodian invasion was "the finest hour in the Nixon Presidency," God save us from whatever might be the worst hour.

Washington, Aug. 17 /
The Washington Post, 8–18:A4.

. . . our interests in this war are different from the interests of our ally in Saigon. We had hoped from the beginning that the South Vietnamese rulers would carry out reforms that would bring to them the support of their own people. But instead, the politicians and generals of Saigon have feathered their own nests with American money and bribes demanded from their own people.

Television broadcast, Washington, Aug. 31/
The New York Times, 9–1:4.

The longer we stay in Vietnam, the more we play into the hands of the Communists and weaken our society. The two great centers of Communist power in the world are Russia and China. Yet, while we have poured our substance in Vietnam for 10 years, not one Chinese or Russian has been expended in that conflict. If Peking or Moscow had been in charge of American foreign policy for the past decade, they could not have devised a policy to hurt us more than the one we have chosen for ourselves.

Television broadcast, Washington, Aug. 31/
Los Angeles Times, 9–1:(1)12.

Every Senator in this chamber is partly responsible for sending 50,000 young Americans to an early grave; and, in one sense, this chamber literally reeks of blood. Every Senator here is partly responsible for that human wreckage at Walter Reed (Hospital) and all across this land . . . If we don't end this damnable war, those young men will some day curse us for our pitiful willingness to let the Executive carry the burden that the Constitution places on us.

Before the Senate, Washington, Sept. 1/
The New York Times, 9–2:10.

He (President Nixon) has whatever ego satisfaction comes from demonstrating that he's running the show, that he's running the war (in Vietnam). But he has the great political hazard of making a decision that at best is going to be controversial and unpopular. There's no way to back out of this war now and look graceful about it. You can't settle a war that we're going to settle short of victory without setting off a lot of cries of

anguish in the country. If I were the President, I would want to share that decision as broadly as possible, and I think he's making a mistake carrying the full load himself.

Interview after defeat of Hatfield-McGovern
"end the war" amendment,
Washington, Sept. 1/
The Dallas Times Herald, 9–2:A1.

If tying the President's hands is the only way we can stop him from tying our country down to an indefinite war in Indochina, then we indeed should tie his hands and force an end to this conflict.

Before the Senate, Washington, Nov. 23/
San Francisco Examiner, 11–24:4.

William McMahon
Minister for External Affairs of Australia

Ho Chi Minh (late President of North Vietnam) was a Vietnamese nationalist, a towering figure, and he liked to make decisions himself, without reference to Peking, if he wanted to. Since his death, I think the control of the Indochinese Communist Party has moved to the Secretary General, Le Duan, who is Peking-oriented; and I'm sure that since he has become the de facto leader in Hanoi the control of the Indochinese Communist Party has moved from Hanoi to Peking, and now they do as they are told.

Interview, Hong Kong/
San Francisco Examiner & Chronicle
7–12:A17.

John N. Mitchell
Attorney General of the United States

This Administration took office pledging to end the war in Vietnam in a way that would permit the people of South Vietnam to decide their own form of government. The basic measure of our involvement in that war is the number of our troops in that country. There are 115,000 fewer American troops there than were before. That, I submit, is a track record. When the President pledges to withdraw 150,000 more in a year's time, you can look to that track record for full confidence that he will do what he says he will do.

Cleveland, Miss., May 19/
U.S. News & World Report, 6–1:40.

Walter F. Mondale
United States Senator, D-Minn.

I do not think that our national interest can possibly justify the introduction of ground troops in Laos. But if there are national interests which are somehow at stake, I have every confidence in the ability of Congress and the American people to decide upon the proper course of action . . . The Congress must regain control over this situation. We need to know what the CIA is doing in support of General Van Peo's secret army and how this involvement can be justified in the light of clear prohibitions against ground involvement in Laos. We need to know about the bombing sorties being flown in support of the Laotian Army. We need to know what the Administration plans to do if the North Vietnamese and the Pathet Lao move southward. Will "honor" and "commitments" again escalate our involvement from a handful of advisers to a half-million men? And we need to know, above all, how long we must wait until we can recall our secret army and restore to Congress its constitutional responsibility for making such vital decisions.

Before the Senate, Washington, March 9/
Congressional Record, 3–9:S3286.

This (U.S. attack on Communist sanctuaries in Cambodia) is not only a tragic escalation which will broaden the war and increase casualties but is an outright admission of the failure of Vietnamization.

The Dallas Times Herald, 5–1:A2.

Thomas H. Moorer
Admiral, United States Navy;
Chief of Naval Operations

The young American there (in Southeast Asia) is willing to fight for his country rather than loudly condemn someone else for its shortcomings. He works to solve our problems. He appreciates our blessings. It is seldom that we see him blame or seek credit. He has dealt courageously with a war which has taken the lives of more than 40 thousand of his kind. By any standard of historical reference, no American soldier, airman, sailor or marine ever had more of a challenge. Demands on his knowledge, courage and technical expertise are the greatest we have ever known. He is fighting in an unorthodox and unpopular war with too little vocal or moral support. He is wearing a uniform that too many would hope to demean. In spite of such demands and what has been defined as a negative minority attitude, he has performed superbly and his deeds deserve the attention we see directed elsewhere.

Before American Legion Security
Commission, Washington, March 4/
Vital Speeches, 4–15:392.

George Murphy
United States Senator, R-Calif.

The war in Laos and the war in Vietnam are substantially elements of the same conflict. The troops bent on aggression in Laos are not the indigenous Communists, the Pathet Lao. They are playing a minor, almost insignificant, role. The enemy in Laos is North Vietnam . . . the fact is that the war in Vietnam and the war in Laos are one and the same war. Both are being primarily fought—not by citizens of the country under attack—but by North Vietnamese. Let us make this crystal clear once and for all: This is not a civil war. These regular soldiers—and that is what they are—are being supported and supplied by Red China and the Soviet Union . . . I repeat, it is all part of the same war. It is part of the same Communist plan, drawn in Moscow and in Red China and activated through their puppets in Hanoi.

Before the Senate, Washington, March 31/
Congressional Record, 3–31:S4712.

Edmund S. Muskie
United States Senator, D-Maine

The cruel irony of Vietnamization of the war is that, even if it succeeds as a military strategy, it succeeds only in perpetuating the killing of Vietnamese by Vietnamese. And, by so doing, it perpetuates American involvement in the war, American deaths and the diversion of needed American resources. The President's plan cannot bring peace because it is essentially a military strategy intended to win what is primarily a political struggle . . . Given the prospect of our indefinite stay in Vietnam, Saigon has no incentive either to improve militarily or to bargain away its own power at the peace table.

Washington, March 5
The Washington Post, 3–6:A13.

We have bought the Vietnamese five years of time, and I don't think we can afford to buy them any more. I am confident the Vietnamese can fight their own war.

The Dallas Times Herald, 5–2:A1.

We started out with a few advisers (in Vietnam). Then, by 1965, 250,000 troops. That didn't win it. Then 500,000 troops. That didn't win it. We dropped more bombs than in all of Europe in World War II. That didn't win it. How many lives are you willing to invest in the jungles of Southeast Asia for victory? How many more American lives are you willing to invest?

At Democratic fund-raising party, Lincoln,
Maine/The Washington Post, 10–19:A5.

We'd like, beneficently, to influence the affairs of people living in adverse conditions all over the world. But, unfortunately, our power to do so is goddamn limited. We're beginning to understand that whatever influence we're going to exert in Southeast Asia is going to have to be of a different kind from what we have now. It's going to have to be a lot wiser and more sophisticated than it has been. And, goddamn it, I'm afraid that in Southeast Asia we're not going to have any influence at all for many years to come because we've banged up those countries so badly.

Interview/The New York Times Magazine,
11–22:136.

Henri Navarre
Former Commander, French Armed Forces in Vietnam

Vietnamization is an old idea. It was the basis of my own plan when I was sent to Indochina in 1952. In my days, the South Vietnamese did not fight well. Now, the situation seems to have changed. The South Vietnamese regime seems to have a more solid base. The key question is whether they will be able to hold on once the Americans pull out. The question would be different if the Americans merely withdrew to bases. But announcing, in advance, evacuation withdrawals . . .

Interview, Vence, France, May 9/
The New York Times, 5–10:(1)20.

Gaylord Nelson
United States Senator, D-Wis.

In a little more than eight years, the United States has sprayed more than 100 million pounds of assorted herbicide chemicals (over Vietnam. That is enough) to amount to six pounds for every man, woman and child in that country . . . If our role is to defend Vietnam, how can we risk destroying the environment in which they must survive when we leave?

Before the Senate, Washington, Aug. 26/
The New York Times, 8–27:14.

Richard M. Nixon
President of the United States

The major immediate goal of our foreign policy is to bring an end to the war in Vietnam in a way that our generation will be remembered, not so much as the generation that suffered in war, but more for the fact that we had the courage and character to win the kind of a just peace that the next generation was able to keep.

State of the Union address, Washington,
Jan. 22/Los Angeles Times, 1–23:(1)20.

WHAT THEY SAID IN 1970

(RICHARD M. NIXON)

I hope that a genuine quest for peace in Indochina can now begin. For Laos, this will require the efforts of the Geneva Conference cochairmen and the signatory countries. But, most of all, it will require realism and reasonableness from Hanoi. For it is the North Vietnamese, not we, who have escalated the fighting. Today there are 67,000 North Vietnamese troops in this small country (Laos). There are no American troops there.

Key Biscayne, Fla., March 6/
Los Angeles Herald-Examiner, 3–6:A2.

I realize that in this war there are honest and deep differences about whether we should have ever become involved in Vietnam. There are differences as to how the war should be conducted. But the decision I announce tonight (the attacking of enemy sanctuaries in Cambodia) transcends those differences. For the lives of American men are involved. The opportunity for 150,000 American men to come home over the next 12 months is involved. The future of 18 million in South Vietnam and seven million people in Cambodia is involved. The possibility of winning a just peace in Vietnam and the Pacific is at stake.

Radio-TV address, Washington, April 30/
Los Angeles Times, 5–1:(1)31.

Let me briefly review . . . the principles that govern our view of a just political settlement: First, our overriding objective is a political solution that reflects the will of the South Vietnamese people and allows them to determine their future without outside interference. I again reaffirm this government's acceptance of eventual total withdrawal of American troops. In turn, we must see the permanent withdrawal of all North Vietnamese troops and be given reasonable assurances that they will not return. Second, a fair political solution should reflect the existing relationship of political forces within South Vietnam. We recognize the complexity of shaping machinery that would fairly apportion political power in South Vietnam. We are flexible; we have offered nothing on a take-it-or-leave-it basis. And, third, we will abide by the outcome of the political process agreed upon. President Thieu (of South Vietnam) and I have repeatedly stated our willingness to accept the free decision of the South Vietnamese people. But we will not agree to the arrogant demand that the elected leaders of the government of Vietnam be overthrown before real negotiations begin.

Radio-TV address, San Clemente, Calif.,
April 20/U.S. News & World Report, 5–4:62.

We were told repeatedly in the past that our adversaries would negotiate seriously—if only we stopped the bombing of North Vietnam; if only we began withdrawing our forces from South Vietnam; if only we dealt with the National Liberation Front as one of the parties to the negotiations; if only we would agree in principle to removal of all of our forces from Vietnam. We have taken all these steps. The United States over a year and a half ago halted all bombing of North Vietnam. Long ago we agreed to negotiate with the National Liberation Front as one of the parties. We have already withdrawn 115,500 American troops. Tonight I have announced a decision to reduce American force levels by a quarter of a million men from what they were 15 months ago. We have offered repeatedly to withdraw all of our troops if the North Vietnamese would withdraw theirs. We have taken risks for peace that every fair and objective man can readily recognize. And still there is no progress at the negotiating table. It is Hanoi—and Hanoi alone—that stands today blocking the path to a just peace for all the peoples of Southeast Asia.

Radio-TV address, San Clemente, Calif.,
April 20/U.S. News & World Report, 5–4:62.

The enemy has failed to win the war in Vietnam because of three basic errors in their strategy: They thought they could win a military victory; they have failed to do so.

They thought they could win politically in South Vietnam; they have failed to do so. They thought they could win politically in the United States; this proved to be their most fatal miscalculation. In this great, free country of ours, we debate, we disagree—sometimes violently—but the mistake the to-talitarians make over and over again is to conclude that debate in a free country is proof of weakness. We are not a weak people. We are a strong people. America has never been defeated in the proud 190-year history of this country, and we shall not be defeated in Vietnam.

Radio-TV address, San Clemente, Calif.,
April 20/U.S. News & World Report, 5–4:62.

I would rather be a one-term President and do what is right than a two-term President at the cost of seeing America become a second-rate power and see this nation accept the first defeat of its proud 190-year history.

Radio-TV address, Washington, April 30/
The Washington Post, 5–1:A1.

It is not our power but our will and character that is being tested . . . The question all Americans must ask and answer . . . does the richest and strongest nation in the history of the world have the character to meet a direct challenge by a group (North Vietnam) which rejects every effort to win a just peace, ignores our warning, tramples on solemn agreements, violates the neutrality of an unarmed people (Cambodia) and uses our prisoners as hostages? If we failed to meet this challenge, all other nations will be on notice that, despite its overwhelming power, the United States, when a real crisis comes, will be found wanting.

Radio-TV address, Washington, April 30/
The Dallas Times Herald, 5–1:A11.

We will not allow American men by the thousands to be killed by an enemy from privileged sanctuaries . . . Any government that chooses to use these actions (U.S. attacks of enemy sanctuaries in Cambodia) as a pretext for harming relations with the United States will be doing so on its own responsibility and on its own initiative, and we will draw the appropriate conclusions.

Radio-TV address, Washington, April 30/
Time, 5–11:14.

Everything that I stand for is what they (protesters) want . . . They are trying to say that they want peace. They are trying to say that they want to end the draft. They are trying to say that we ought to get out of Vietnam. I agree with everything they are trying to accomplish.

News conference, Washington, May 8/
Los Angeles Herald-Examiner, 5–9:A1.

I have pledged to end this war, and I shall keep that promise. But I am determined to end the war in a way that will promote peace rather than conflict throughout the world. I am determined to end it in a way that will bring an era of reconciliation to our people —and not an era of furious recrimination. In seeking peace, let us remember that at this time only this Administration can end this war and bring peace. We have a program for peace, and the greater the support the Administration receives in its efforts, the greater the opportunity to win that just peace we all desire. Peace is the goal that unites us. Peace is the goal toward which we are working. And peace is the goal this government will pursue until the day we reach it.

Radio-TV address, Washington, June 3/
U.S. News & World Report, 6–15:79.

It isn't just the case of seeing that the Americans are moved out (of Vietnam) in an orderly way. If that were the case, we could move them out more quickly. But it is a case of moving American forces out in a way that we can at the same time win a just peace. Now, by winning a just peace what I mean is not victory over North Vietnam; we're not asking for that. But it is simply the right of the people of South Vietnam to determine their own future without having us impose our will upon them, or the North

WHAT THEY SAID IN 1970

(RICHARD M. NIXON)

Vietnamese, or anybody else outside impose their will upon them. Now, when we look at that limited objective, I'm sure some would say, "Well, is that really worth it? Is that worth the efforts of all these Americans fighting in Vietnam, the lives that have been lost?" And I suppose it could be said that simply saving 17 million people in South Vietnam from a Communist take-over isn't worth the efforts of the United States. But let's go further. If the United States after all of this effort, if we were to withdraw immediately—as many Americans would want us to do—and it would be very easy for me to do it and simply blame it on the previous Administration. But if we were to do that, I would probably survive through my term; but it would have, in my view, a catastrophic effect on this country in the cause of peace in years ahead. Now I know there are those that say, "Well, the domino theory is obsolete." They haven't talked to the dominoes. They should talk to the Thais, Malaysians, to Singapore, to Indonesia, to the Philippines, to the Japanese and the rest. And if the United States leaves Vietnam in a way that we are humiliated or defeated, not simply speaking in what are called jingoistic terms but in very practical terms, this will be immensely discouraging to the 300 million people from Japan clear around to Thailand in free Asia. And, even more important, it will be ominously encouraging to the leaders of Communist China and the Soviet Union who are supporting the North Vietnamese. It will encourage them in their expansionist policies in other areas. The world will be much (less safe) in which to live.

Television interview, Los Angeles, July 2 /
The New York Times, 7–3:4.

If the people of South Vietnam, after they see what the Viet Cong, the Communist Viet Cong, have done to the villages that they have occupied, the 40,000 people that they have murdered, village chiefs and others,

the atrocities . . . if the people of South Vietnam under those circumstances should choose to move in the direction of a Communist government, that, of course, is their right. I do not think it will happen.

Television interview, Los Angeles, July 2 /
The Washington Post, 7–3:D8.

When we came into office, we found 500,-000 Americans in Vietnam. There was no plan to bring them home. There was no plan to end the war. There was no peace plan that had been submitted. And what have we done? Let me tell you. We have implemented a plan to bring Americans home, and during the spring of next year half of the men that were there in Vietnam when we got there will be coming home . . . We wound down the fighting by the strong stand that we took to clean up the sanctuaries in Cambodia. We have cut American casualties to the lowest level in 4½ years . . . We have presented to the North Vietnamese, over national television, and I am sure many of you heard it, a far-reaching peace plan . . . As I stand before you today, I can say confidently the war in Vietnam is coming to an end—and we are going to win a just peace in Vietnam.

Republican campaign speech,
Burlington, Vt., Oct. 17 /
The Washington Post, 10–18:A11.

At a time when we are withdrawing . . . from South Vietnam, it is vitally important that the President of the United States, as Commander-in-Chief, take the action that is necessary to protect our remaining forces, because the number of our ground combat forces is going down very, very steadily. Now, if, as a result of my conclusion that the North Vietnamese, by their infiltration, threaten our remaining forces—if they thereby develop a capacity and proceed possibly to use that capacity to increase the level of fighting in South Vietnam—then I will order the bombing of military sites in North Vietnam, the passes that lead from North Vietnam into South Vietnam, the military complexes and the military supply lines. That will be the reaction I shall take.

News conference, Washington, Dec. 10/
The New York Times, 12–11:32.

The quarter-billion-dollar aid program for Cambodia is, in my opinion, probably the best investment in foreign assistance that the United States has made in my political lifetime. The Cambodians—a people seven million only, neutralist previously, un-trained—are tying down 40,000 trained North Vietnamese regulars. If those North Vietnamese weren't in Cambodia, they'd be over (in South Vietnam) killing Americans. That investment of $250 million in small arms and aid to Cambodia, so that they can defend themselves against a foreign aggres-sor—this is no civil war, there's no aspect of a civil war—the dollars we sent to Cambodia save American lives and enable us to bring Americans home.

News conference, Washington, Dec. 10/
The New York Times, 12–11:32.

Lon Nol
Premier of Cambodia

Both North Vietnam and the revolution-ary government of South Vietnam (Viet Cong) make much of their legality, their will-ingness to respect the Geneva Accord and past agreements. We have appealed to the International Control Commission, and more recently to the United Nations Secur-ity Council, to send observers to establish beyond doubt the extent of this foreign oc-cupation of our soil. The Vietnamese (Com-munists) will then either get out or all the world will see how they violate the agree-ments they pretend to respect.

Interview, Phnom Penh/
U.S. News & World Report, 4–13:31.

You do not reform a nation after a dicta-torship overnight. But we have no fears of the outcome. Our unity as a team drawn from all sectors of the Cambodian popula-tion is solid and secure. You will see we must build; it is not enough to liberate.

Interview, Phnom Penh/
U.S. News & World Report, 4–13:31.

We may have to grit our teeth for a while, but that is easy. The enemy thought Cam-bodia would be a quick mouthful. He has been wrong until now. He will be wrong in the future.

Los Angeles Times, 12–17:(2)6.

Lawrence F. O'Brien
Chairman, Democratic National Committee

The possible consequences of our offen-sive in Cambodia are grave and real. By our own violation of the neutrality of Cambodia, together with our continued involvement in the struggle in Laos, we have given North Vietnam a pretext for more open and sus-tained military activity in both of these countries. Will their response be to put pres-sure on Phnom Penh and on the capital of Laos at Vientiane? In such event, will we send American troops to defend those be-leaguered cities? Or will we accept their fall as a consequence of our own military escala-tion? Having developed the domino theory to explain our presence in Southeast Asia, are we now, through our own action, to put it into practice?

Milwaukee, May 9/
U.S. News & World Report, 5–25:97.

Claiborne Pell
United States Senator, D-R.I.

I believe that there is only one way to get out of Southeast Asia, and that is to accept the fact that the damage caused by our con-tinued military presence there to our true national interests and to our economy and social structure far outweighs the question-able advantages that result to our national interest by maintaining the corrupt, inept Thieu-Ky government in South Vietnam, or even maintaining the division of Vietnam into two countries.

Before the Senate, Washington
Daily World, 6–30:2.

H. Ross Perot
Industrialist, Philanthropist

As a nation, the North Vietnamese have an inferiority complex. If you really pressure them on this issue, they will react. When I first began talking to North Vietnam (about U.S. prisoners of war), everybody told me to be polite. I was, and nothing happened. Finally, I told them, "You are nothing but animals." At that point, we started talking business, because they wanted to assure me that they were really humane people, a first-class nation, and they wouldn't mistreat these men. Making the treatment of our men a visible issue in the United States will bring the North Vietnamese to their knees.

May/National Observer, 9-21:22.

Souvanna Phouma
Premier of Laos

People talk too much about the bombing by American planes in Laos. I only know one thing: There are North Vietnamese troops here, and people don't talk enough about this.

Interview, Vientiane, Feb. 25/
Fort Worth Star-Telegram, 2-26:A3.

Georges Pompidou
President of France

I know—because France has experienced it—how difficult it is to end such conflicts (Vietnam) and that the stronger a people, the greater the effort required, but also the greater the honor won. Allow me, as a friend, to tell you that the end of the war in Vietnam for the United States will be the most precious of victories—a victory won first over oneself.

Before joint session of Congress, Washington,
Feb. 25/Daily World, 2-26:2.

. . . it would be desirable—and here I'm not talking about Southeast Asia as a whole, but just those states of former Indochina: Laos, Cambodia, North Vietnam and South Vietnam—it would be desirable if each were independent; that is, that no attempt be made to associate or reunify these countries by force . . . Whatever their economic or social regimes, these countries must be neutral; that is, there must be no bases, no troops, no foreign military presence of any kind on their soil—not Chinese, Russian or American—and not in North Vietnam or in South Vietnam, not in Laos and not in Cambodia. I believe these countries will acquire a taste for their independence, that they will want to escape from the influences which threaten them from all sides, and that consequently this state of neutrality will suit them.

Interview, Paris/
U.S. News & World Report, 3-2:44.

. . . there will be no prospects for peace in Indochina until the day when the United States has taken, by itself and voluntarily, the firm resolution to evacuate Indochina. That is the basis for everything, and, starting from that, one can hope that intervention and all interference of all kinds will cease and that each of these unhappy states of Indochina will recover the possibility of life, of peace and of independence—and, I hope, of neutrality. And since everybody makes appeals, if I had one to make, well then, as for me, I would say: pity for the Vietnamese people; pity for the Cambodian people; pity for the Laotian people; pity, perhaps tomorrow, for the Thai people; and let these unhappy people no longer be made the subject and the victim of rivalries that go beyond them and don't even concern them. That is the policy of France.

News conference, Paris, July 2/
The New York Times, 7-3:3.

Enoch Powell
Member of British Parliament

American military power cannot secure any specific political result in Southeast Asia. This is a war in which the United States can win, if it wishes, every battle; but it is a war which the United States is bound to lose. I have no doubt that the United States forces can eliminate the Viet Cong base which has so long flourished—of course it has—in Cambodia. But when the operation is over, the underlying facts of the situation reassert themselves like the tide washing out footmarks in the sand. The ultimate fact reasserts itself: The Americans do not live there; everyone knows that their presence is destined to be temporary; everyone knows the realities which will prevail over them.

The New York Times, 5–9:24.

John R. Rarick
United States Representative, D-La.

The Hanoi Reds have now given their Swedish Santa Claus the list of the "humanitarian" aid which they can use. This "humanitarian" aid to our enemy is the $45 million which had been previously promised for a 3-year period, and the current Swedish budget includes the first $15 million installment. Of particular interest is the request of the enemy for $1 million—in U.S. currency. This surprisingly frank request points up with undeniable clarity two important facts. First, that Sweden acquires American dollars only by selling goods to Americans. Americans who buy Swedish goods from this day forth must understand that their dollars are going to be given to Hanoi—to aid the enemy. Second, Hanoi needs American dollars only to purchase American goods—from our so-called friends who trade with the enemy, or to finance its world-wide propaganda and support its "dear American friends" in their fifth-column activities in this country.

Before the House, Washington, Jan. 26/
Congressional Record, 1–26:E329.

Abdul Razak
Prime Minister-designate of Malaysia

Our policy in regard to Cambodia, Vietnam, Laos and all countries is clear: We would like the people of these countries to be left alone to settle their internal affairs themselves. We made it clear at the Jakarta conference that all foreign troops, regular or irregular, in Cambodia should be withdrawn—the same with Vietnam—so that the Vietnamese people and the Cambodian people can determine their future themselves. This is the view of nonaligned countries, of which we are a member.

News conference, Kuala Lumpur, Sept. 5/
The New York Times, 9–7:2.

William P. Rogers
Secretary of State of the United States

We recognize that if we get involved in Cambodia with our ground forces, our whole program is defeated. I think the one lesson that the war in Vietnam has taught us is that if you are going to fight a war of this kind satisfactorily, you need public support and Congressional support.

Before House Appropriations Subcommittee,
Washington, April 23/Time, 5–18:11.

More than 40,000 North Vietnamese and Viet Cong troops have invaded and now occupy Cambodia . . . A more explicit and unprovoked violation of the fundamental provisions of the charter of the United Nations, and of additional specific international obligations to respect the territory of others, could hardly be imagined. The flouting of international agreements, which were freely entered into by Hanoi, is not just a problem for the parties to the agreements. It a problem for the world community.

Before American Society of International Law,
New York, April 25/San Francisco
Examiner & Chronicle, 4–26:A1.

I've been very much impressed with the attitude of the Saigon government toward a settlement. I've seen a real flexibility on their part. If you ask me if I think they would be interested in a negotiated settlement, my answer would be, "Yes." If you ask me if I think North Vietnam is interested, my answer is, "Absolutely no. Absolutely zero."

Before Senate Appropriations Subcommittee,
Washington, Dec. 8/
Los Angeles Times, 12–9:(1)22.

George W. Romney
Secretary of Housing and Urban Development of the United States

(American involvement in Vietnam was) the most tragic event in our history . . . We continued to adhere to the containment policy when the world has fundamentally changed. We made the mistake of seeing red at a time and under circumstances when that did not exist . . . In my opinion, the mistakes we have made there have helped to create most of the very conditions that we assumed existed there when we went in.

Before general assembly of United Presbyterian Church, Chicago, May 26/ The New York Times, 5–27:13.

Walt W. Rostow
Professor of History, University of Texas; Former Foreign Affairs Adviser to the President of the United States

We used military force (in Vietnam) . . . when it was judged by those who bore constitutional responsibility that danger of Asian hegemony by a power potentially hostile to the U.S. had emerged, and there was no nation in Asia—and no extra-Asian nation—able and/or willing to deal with it if the U.S. did not act.

Panel discussion before American Historical Association/Newsweek, 1–12:42.

Clearly, the war (in Vietnam) has diverted substantial resources from private and public purposes; but I do not believe it is primarily responsible for the slackening in allocations to the cities or education or for the present state of racial tension. The net cost of the war in Vietnam—what we would actually save by abandoning the effort—is less than 2 per cent of GNP (gross national product). The figure is declining, not rising. At a normal 4 per cent growth rate, it is less than half the annual increment in GNP we should have available to allocate to new private or public purposes. I regret every nickel of it, as I regret, even more, every casualty of the war. But with a GNP approaching a trillion dollars, we obviously command the resources in the United States to do far more in the public sector if we manage the economy well and generate the political will to allocate those resources wisely. And while the war in Vietnam is not irrelevant to the problem of bringing the Negro to full citizenship in our land, I do not believe for one moment that it is a critical variable.

At Naval War College, Newport, R.I., June 19/Vital Speeches, 9–1:687.

Dean Rusk
Former Secretary of State of the United States

I feel anxious about the talk that this (the Vietnam war) is too far away, not our business, that we should forget about these problems and stay at home. This kind of talk sent another generation of students into a world war.

San Francisco Examiner, 6–7:2.

It would be unseemly for me to be a grandstand quarterback or throw brickbats because he (President Nixon) cannot find the answers to that to which we (in the Johnson Administration) could find no answers ourselves . . . We are all in the same canoe in turbulent waters. I pray for wisdom and compassion for those lonely men in Washington who try to find the answers.

At forum on Law and the Cambodian Incursion, Washington, June 17/ The New York Times, 6–18:11.

William F. Ryan
United States Representative, D-N.Y.

The interesting thing about numbers is that they so readily lend themselves to comparative thinking. Ten apples seem like a lot until one sees 10,000. Then the ten appear inconsequential. "Numbers" is the name of the game being played these days in Vietnam. A hundred soldiers killed this week, 90 the next, 120 the next—these tend to be overshadowed by announcements in June of a withdrawal of 25,000 men, in September of 35,000 and in December of another 50,000 by April 15. It would be very comforting if only we could ignore and then forget the "small" numbers. But this easy solution—this balm to soothe the tensions of a nation now at full war for five years—is a chimera. Death is too final. It is too ultimate a fact to be discounted and disregarded. *The Washington Post* this morning reports that, in the last 24 hours alone, 40 American soldiers have been killed and 190 wounded in Vietnam. And for the two-day period starting Tuesday, U.S. deaths were listed as 61. It is interesting to note that this story appeared on page 22 of the newspaper. Obviously the public interest is being successfully channeled by the Administration.

Before the House, Washington, April 2/
Congressional Record, 4–2:E2780.

William J. Scherle
United States Representative, R-Iowa

I have not seen the so-called "tiger cages" (in South Vietnam). If they are what they are touted to be, they are an outrage. But that is beside the point. The point is that those who want Communism to win in Southeast Asia and those who want the United States to lose have erected another strawman. Those who cry most loudly about the "tiger cages" have been the quiet ones when it comes to demanding redress against the North Vietnamese for keeping American soldiers in bamboo cages, pulling out their nails and otherwise torturing them. Where have their cries of outrage been over the Hue massacre, over the tens of thousands of South Vietnamese killed, kidnaped and tortured by the Communists? We cannot hear them. They are silent, because none of these things serve their purpose—which is to bring on a U.S. retreat and defeat. Yes, let them call for humane treatment of South Vietnam's prisoners. But let them also call for humane treatment for North Vietnam's prisoners and every other human being held against his will. That will be a sign of true outrage. That will be the time when we know they are sincere.

Before the House, Washington, July 14/
Congressional Record, 7–14:H6657.

Jean-Jacques Servan-Schreiber
Journalist; Member, French National Assembly

We were stunned by the Cambodian decision (U.S. attacks on Vietnamese enemy sanctuaries in Cambodia). Until then, there was a favorable prejudice toward Nixon in France. He was seen as a sober, rational man. Now, there is no confidence.

News conference, Washington/
San Francisco Examiner & Chronicle
(This World), 8–30:24.

Norodom Sihanouk
Chief of State of Cambodia

I am going to tell these two great capitals (Moscow and Peking) that there will very probably be a trial of strength between me—representing the vast majority of Cambodians who want neutrality—and the right, which seeks to outflank us. So I shall warn these two friendly capitals as follows: You must choose between trying to communize Cambodia—which is a utopian idea, for Cambodians do not like Communism—or support Cambodia's neutrality, which for you would be the lesser evil.

Television interview, Paris, March 12/
Los Angeles Times, 3–13:(1)5.

I am sure this serious event (anti-Communist demonstrations in Cambodia) was willed and organized by certain personalities trying to irremediably destroy the friendship Cambodia (has) with the socialist camp, and to throw our country into the arms of an imperialist capitalist power . . . I am returning to our country to address the nation and the army and to ask them to make their choice. If they choose to follow these personalities along the road which will make of Cambodia a second Laos, let them allow me to resign.

Paris, March 12/Daily World, 3–13:2.

In all Asia, this departure (U.S. withdrawal from South Vietnam) would be interpreted, without exception, as a defeat, an avowal of the weakness of the American

(NORODOM SIHANOUK)

giant. And all Asia remains persuaded that the domino theory would come into play against the Americans . . . If the Americans quit Vietnam, Asia will stir, first the Philippines and Thailand; already the U.S.S.R. is installing itself in India more solidly than America; Pakistan still plays neutralist but becomes more and more friendly to China.

The New York Times, 3–15:(4)16.

I'll keep maneuvering as long as I have cards in my hand. First a little to the left, then a little to the right. And when I have no more cards to play, I'll stop.

Plainview (Tex.) Daily Herald, 3–30:4.

Norodom Sihanouk
Former Chief of State of Cambodia

I am not a red prince, but my present hope is to become a pink prince.

News conference, Peking/
The Dallas Times Herald, 5–6:A2.

Howard K. Smith
News commentator, American Broadcasting Company

(Senator J. William) Fulbright maneuvered the Gulf of Tonkin Resolution through —with a clause stating that Congress may revoke it. Ever since, he's been saying: "This is a terribly immoral thing." I asked him: "If it's that bad, aren't *you* morally obligated to try to revoke it?" He runs away! And yet, Mr. Fulbright is not criticized for his want of character. He is beloved by reporters, by every one of my group which is left-of-center. It's one of the mysteries of my time.

Interview, Washington/TV Guide, 2–28:10.

Many have described Ho Chi Minh (late President of North Vietnam) as a nationalist leader comparable to George Washington. But this advent to power in Hanoi in 1954 was marked by the murder of 50,000 of his people. His consistent method was terror.

He was not his country's George Washington—he was more his country's Hitler or Stalin . . . I heard an eminent TV commentator say: "It's an awful thing when you can trust Ho Chi Minh more than you can trust your President." At the time he said that, Ho Chi Minh was lying! He was presiding over atrocities! And yet, an American TV commentator could say that!

Interview, Washington/TV Guide, 2–28:10.

Benjamin Spock
Physician, Author

I campaigned hard for him (Lyndon B. Johnson) because he promised he would not escalate the war. Among others, I helped to get him elected. A day after his election, he telephoned me and said that he hoped he could live up to my faith in him. Then a few months later he did escalate the war. I'm very ashamed that I worked for him. But I suppose that a man can be a humanitarian at home even if he's a warmonger in Vietnam.

Interview/Family Weekly, 4–26:7.

Adlai E. Stevenson III
Democratic candidate for United States Senate from Illinois

I think we must continue with the withdrawal of troops in South Vietnam. And I believe the spokesmen for the Administration when they say the withdrawals are irreversible. But I think we should recognize that at some point we will have, through the withdrawal of troops, pulled the props from under the Thieu-Ky regime and that regime will collapse. It can't win a war alone that it couldn't win with the support of 500,000 well-equipped, well-trained American troops.

Interview, Chicago/
The Christian Science Monitor, 5–11:2.

Olin E. Teague
United States Representative, D-Tex.

We can knock out (North Vietnamese) power plants, the harbor at Haiphong and agricultural dams—without killing people —and put them in one helluva shape. It is foolish and immature to think they will come to any reasonable terms by negotiation.

The Dallas Times Herald, 12–25:A26.

Ton Duc Thang
President of North Vietnam

The U.S. aggressors' failure is evident, but they still are reluctant to give up their design of aggression against our country. Their Vietnamization-of-the-war plan is precisely a plan to prolong the war and their occupation of South Vietnam, to cling to the puppet army and administration, to use Vietnamese to fight Vietnamese in order to materialize U.S. neocolonialism.

Hanoi, Jan. 1 /
Los Angeles Herald-Examiner, 1–2:A4.

Nguyen Van Thieu
President of South Vietnam

Coalition is suicide and self-poisoning . . . if we agree to a neutralist coalition arrangement with (Communists), they will cut our throats. The advocates of coalition and neutralism are people-killers and traitors to the nation.

Vungtau, South Vietnam, Jan. 13 /
The Washington Post, 1–14:A14.

There are naive people who have asked why Mr. Thieu got elected (in 1967) with only 37 per cent of the total votes and concluded thus: that the government needs to broaden its base to have a more representative character. Those critics, willingly or not, have forgotten that in the Presidential elections of 1967 there were 11 tickets in the race. In a democratic election, with that number of tickets, it is difficult to have the majority of votes on the first ballot. Nevertheless, the winning ticket had double the number of votes of its runner-up.

Before Vietnamese Newspaper Editors
Association, Saigon, Jan. 26 /
The New York Times, 1–27:3.

Life in democracy and freedom has just begun to develop here and therefore cannot be compared with 100-year-old European

and American democracy. Do not expect babies who just learned to walk to run with adults.

Saigon / The Dallas Times Herald, 1–27:A2.

. . . in this war we are not just dealing with North Vietnam only, but we also are dealing with the whole Communist supply system. Even the Communist guerrillas in the countryside have the most modern weapons from Russia and China and Czechoslovakia and other countries of the Communist bloc. They are fighting a conventional war and a guerrilla war, but both with very modern means.

Interview, Saigon /
U.S. News & World Report, 3–16:72.

Many people now say that the "domino theory" is not valid any more—that in case South Vietnam falls under Communism, the other countries will stand. That is wrong. I maintain that the domino theory still applies. If South Vietnam falls into the hands of the Communists, Laos, Cambodia, Thailand and the other countries in this part of the world also fall. Even the United States will see Communists in its land—not Russian or Chinese, but American Communists, because the Communists are very clever to wage their war by proxy. When all of Asia falls into the hands of the Communist bloc, what will happen to Africa, South America and to the United States? Bear in mind that Cuba is not that far from your mainland. If you sit idle and let the Communist bloc have a free hand in the other countries, then you will be squeezed between them. This is the old doctrine of Mao Tse-tung: to take the countryside, as represented by the small countries, in order to surround the city, as represented by the United States. The Communists seek to implement that strategy throughout the world. This is why the United States—for its own future—should have a responsibility in this part of the world.

Interview, Saigon /
U.S. News & World Report, 3–16:73.

(NGUYEN VAN THIEU)

I think here we have a very clear position: We have not invaded North Vietnam. We have not demanded any concessions from them—no territory, no seat in the Hanoi government and no surrender from the North. But I have made clear that we will not surrender to them and that they can never defeat us. So it is better for Hanoi to cease its aggression. Then there can be some relationship between the North and the South, as two temporary Vietnams with two temporary administrations—two temporary parts of the country.

Interview, Saigon/
U.S. News & World Report, 3–16:74.

The Vietnamese people have never believed it is the policy of the U.S. troops to massacre Vietnamese people anywhere, in any battle. They know that in wartime there are individuals—sometimes many individuals—who are so nervous or so foolish that incidents occur. They know this can happen with any troops—that this can happen with any individual soldier on the battlefield. The most important fact is that the Vietnamese people have never said that any incident—whatever did occur—is the behavior and the policy of the whole United States Army. But I agree that those individuals involved in any atrocity—if there was an atrocity—should be punished.

Interview, Saigon/
U.S. News & World Report, 3–16:75.

Cambodia, under Prince (Norodom) Sihanouk's regime, was not really neutral. Sihanouk, under the appearance of neutrality, favored the Communists . . . Like the Sihanoukville port, the Sihanouk Trail, like the supply of rice, the support by the Cambodian Army to the Communist troops, the support from the people to the Communist troops and many sanctuaries along the border . . . The Lon Nol government would like to keep Cambodia really neutral and to keep out the external invasion. They don't want to have Communist domination. They are very quiet people. They are principally Buddhist; they cannot live under a Communist regime. And so they react—and they have the right to react because, even though they are neutral, they would like to be independent.

Interview, Saigon, April 29/
Newsweek, 5–11:26.

It will be a long war (in Cambodia). Vietnam has no intention of waging it in place of the Cambodians; but a more effective, more methodical long-range aid must be considered for the Cambodian government to be able to hold fast militarily, economically, socially . . . We must help Cambodia as we must help ourselves.

Interview/The New York Times, 6–14:(1)22.

We cannot have peace overnight, and we are not going to accept peace at any price. There must be peace with conditions, and that peace will come with the strength of our army, the determined anti-Communist spirit of the government and the people. I am ready to smash all movements calling for peace at any price because I am still much of a soldier. We will beat to death the people who are demanding immediate peace, in surrender to the Communists.

Caolanh, South Vietnam, July 15/
The New York Times, 7–16:9.

We are not against peace. The man who talks about peace the most in Vietnam is President Thieu himself. The man who has the most initiatives of peace is President Thieu. Who talks about peace was not in jail. Who talks about coalition government should be put in jail. It's very clear.

Interview/Face the Nation,
Columbia Broadcasting System, July 19.

You know, I cannot always criticize Americans. But I do not care if you (newsmen) do.

News conference/
Los Angeles Herald-Examiner, 8–27:A3.

To the Communists, peace that does not bring forth their ultimate goal is always a temporary peace, restored under circumstances favorable to them so that they continue their aggression and agitation leading to their ultimate purpose—that is, a takeover. It goes the same way with coalition. Coalition is a word that has never existed in the Communist policy. Only simpleminded people believe that coalition is a political solution to end the war and restore peace; whereas the Communists use coalition only as a ruse to fool innocent people and to achieve a silent takeover.

Before National Assembly, Saigon, Oct. 31/
The New York Times, 11–1:(1)1.

Robert Thompson
Authority on guerrilla warfare

The whole point of Vietnamization is psychological improvement, not just military improvement. Psychological dominance has long been a key to North Vietnamese success. They were confident and the people knew it. Now this operation (attacking Communist sanctuaries in Cambodia), as an unintended side effect, has given the South Vietnamese confidence.

Interview, New York/
The New York Times, 6–16:7.

Nguyen Dang Thuc
South Vietnamese author and philosopher

If, in the future, the American presence (in South Vietnam) could return to the form it took during the early Diem period, when the Americans acted as advisers and civilians dominated policy, much could be shared. As Vietnam is a small nation in the midst of giants, ties with Americans would allow us to balance larger powers and maintain our own independence.

Interview, Saigon/
The New York Times, 11–12:6.

Strom Thurmond
United States Senator, R-S.C.

Let us not make the U.S. Senate a war room from which we dictate tactics and strategy to a Commander-in-Chief (President Nixon) who has pledged to Vietnamize this war. He has kept every pledge made concerning Vietnam. Some 150,000 of our troops have been successfully withdrawn and another 150,000 will be out by next spring. The previous Administration kept saying the war would end soon. President Nixon has made no such pledge, but he has pledged to gradually reduce our involvement. He does not desire an expansion of the war. He favors the opposite.

Before the Senate, Washington, May 14/
Congressional Record, 5–14:S7190.

Xuan Thuy
Chief delegate to Paris peace talks from North Vietnam

Particularly with regard to the American people's anti-war movement, we are delighted to note that, in spite of the Nixon Administration's policy of repression and maneuvers of concealing the truth, the American people throughout last year did not sit quiet and let the U.S. government commit in their name acts of intervention and aggression and crimes in Vietnam and in many other places, impairing their honor and fine tradition of the American nation. Last year, the American people's movement against the Vietnam war was marked by important events so far unknown in American history. The Moratorium Day and the demonstrations on November 13, 14 and 15, the opposition to the Chicago (conspiracy) trial, the denunciation of U.S. troops' crimes in South Vietnam, the anti-draft movement, the opposition to the war budget, the statements made inside and outside the Congress against the Nixon Administration's policy and innumerable other actions of support to the South Vietnamese people were warmly hailed and responded to by the Vietnamese people and the world's people.

At Stockholm Peace Conference, March 28/
Daily World, 5–23:M2.

If the United States continues the war, we must continue to fight. If the U.S. intensifies

(XUAN THUY)

the war, we must face this intensification. But we are certain that violence can never defeat a just cause.

News conference, Paris, Dec. 13/
The New York Times, 12–14:12.

Nguyen Duy Trinh
Deputy Premier and Foreign Minister of North Vietnam

If Vietnamization is to be used as a basis of negotiations, negotiations cannot possibly make progress. We've often said Vietnamization does not mean ending the war but prolonging it. The United States is withdrawing its troops by driblets in order to calm down public opinion against the war . . . The American hope is to build strength of the puppet (South Vietnamese) army and to use Vietnamese to fight against Vietnamese to satisfy American bellicose circles. The United States government hopes if it prolongs the war the Vietnamese people will encounter more difficulties and we will have to accept American terms. But this can't happen. On the contrary, the more that the war drags on, the greater the difficulties that will be encountered by the United States. That's why we say the Vietnamization policy is doomed to fail.

Interview, Hanoi, Feb. 27/
San Francisco Examiner & Chronicle, 3–1:A1.

Huang Tung
Editor, "Nhan Dan," Hanoi

It Vietnamization means that some more millions of us must die to make Vietnam free, we will accept it. Mr. Nixon has forces made up of steel and iron. Our forces are made of water. Water is not so aggressive and violent as steel and iron, but water rusts iron and cools down steel.

Interview, Hanoi/
The New York Times, 1–3:3.

John V. Tunney
United States Representative, D-Calif.

. . . I find this great apathy about Viet-

nam. The people seem to think it's over, or at least ending. Well, it isn't. Mr. Nixon's so-called "Vietnamization" program has to be exposed for what it is—a farce, a fraud. Mark my words: Vietnam will be the Number One issue again inside of six months, when the public finally awakens to the fact that we're not pulling out at all.

Interview, San Francisco/
San Francisco Examiner & Chronicle
(Sunday Punch), 2–15:1.

It is clear to me that, as in Vietnam, the ruling junta of Cambodia has no broad base of popular support. Their support comes from the strengths of their army, from the velocity of their bullets. When their power wanes, it could well be that their support would then come from the strength of *our* Army.

At Diablo Valley College (Calif.), April 15/
Los Angeles Times, 4–16:(2)5.

Sim Var
Member, Political Council of Cambodia

The United States is tired of fighting in Vietnam because it is a civil war—Vietnamese fighting Vietnamese. But here it is not so. We have been invaded by foreigners, and if the South Vietnamese fought like the Cambodians, the Vietnam war would have been over in two years . . . The Thais give us a lot of support, but only with words. When they suddenly find the VC at their door, perhaps they will react.

Interview, Phnom Penh, Aug. 5/
The New York Times, 8–6:3.

Lewis W. Walt
Assistant Commandant, United States Marine Corps

I believe if we were to go into this (Vietnam) type of war again, and, knowing that, if we could let the American people understand the nature of the war, we would have had better backing back here. And I think the backing is very important. This has been a very psychological-type war. The enemy has done everything he could in the field of propaganda to try to get the American people to put pressure on the Administration to pull out of Vietnam . . . And you can't blame the people. It's just been a lack of innate understanding of the war and the fact that the understanding has been further clouded by the propaganda the enemy has continuously put out . . . I suppose all of us must take some of the responsibility. I know that we in the military didn't define the war in the terms that we could have. I know some of the press men didn't understand the war, and reported it out of context many times . . . I think we all have to recognize that if we get into another war like this—and I hope we don't—but if we do, that it's a very complicated war; it's something that you can't show on television screens and expect people to understand it.

News conference, Washington, Nov. 18/
National Observer, 11–23:19.

Earl Warren
Former Chief Justice of the United States

. . . so long as youth carries the burden of the war while their elders seem in no hurry to end it—and, indeed, seem to profit financially from it—they have a right to complain; and as long as their elders are not responsive to their complaints, we may expect to have a generation gap that widens every day.

New York, May 19/
The New York Times, 5–20:18.

Edward G. Whitlam
Leader, Australian Labor Party

So far as Australia is concerned, this war has become solely the war of a political party, the Liberal Party. It is no longer possible to depict or defend this war in terms of the freedom of the Vietnamese people or the people of Indochina, as a war for freedom, a war against China, or a war to maintain the American alliance or any of the other definitions which have been used to extenuate and extend our commitment. It is a war of a party. It is not a war of this nation.

The Christian Science Monitor, 5–2:4.

Koun Wick
Foreign Minister of Cambodia

Our problem is very simple: We have been attacked by foreign (North Vietnamese) troops. The solution to our problem is very simple: That is, they have to get out of Cambodia.

News conference, Phnom Penh, Sept. 1/
The New York Times, 9–2:4.

Lee Kuan Yew
Prime Minister of Singapore

I had hoped that this disengagement from the military conflict (by the U.S.) would be ordered at a pace which could be seen to have given the South Vietnamese the opportunity to decide their future for themselves . . . But for political goals in Southeast Asia, where success or failure is related to qualitative and not quantitative factors, the fixing of dates for achieving intermediate targets may not be the best way of achieving final goals. If you (U.S. Vice President Agnew) can bring back to Washington an appreciation of the different time scales in which the peoples of this region live, work and fight and of the fact that they are . . . not yet amenable to programming and time-tabling, you would have done a service to the people of Southeast Asia.

Singapore, Jan. 10/
The Washington Post, 1–11:A22.

Stephen M. Young
United States Senator, D-Ohio

For many years, these veterans (of the Vietnam war) will be living relics of the bitterest and most terrible blunder ever made by a President of the United States and by his advisers, such as (former Secretary of State) Dean Rusk and the generals of the Joint Chiefs of Staff representing the military-industrial complex. They are the ones responsible for involving our nation in a civil war in a little country of no importance whatever to the defense of the United States. They are guilty of bringing about a national insanity which resulted in sending more than 2,100,000 young Americans at

WHAT THEY SAID IN 1970

(STEPHEN M. YOUNG)

different times, from 1964 to 1970, to fight in a small Asiatic country, 10,000 miles distant from our shores, an immoral and unpopular undeclared war in our unjustified intervention in a civil war in Vietnam.

Before the Senate, Washington, Feb. 9/
Congressional Record, 2–9:S1406.

. . . I wish to say that Laos is just about the most undeveloped country that I have ever visited. That country is certainly not worth the life of one American soldier.

Before the Senate, Washington, March 2/
Congressional Record, 3–2:S2731.

. . . Americans have reason to feel outraged that their President is sending thousands of draftees to fight in Vietnam following basic training of 4 months, when seven divisions of highly-trained, largely professional career officers and enlisted men are living the good life in West Germany. The officers, from captain up to the generals, never had it so good. They are living high on the hog with their wives and youngsters, with servants to spare and enjoying their Mercedes automobiles, skiing in Germany and Switzerland and traveling by air and automobile to the various spas and famed vacation areas in Italy, Spain and elsewhere.

Before the Senate, Washington, March 2/
Congressional Record, 3–2:S2744.

Dean Acheson
Former Secretary of State of the United States

The essential difference between our problems and Russia's is that ours are almost entirely related to being constructive, while theirs are concerned with letting things go to pot in order to pick up the pieces. The Russians win by everyone else losing . . . The worse things get, the better off they themselves are.

Interview, Sandy Spring, Md./
The New York Times, 9–20:(4)16.

Giovanni Agnelli
Chairman, Fiat Company of Italy

As a businessman, I must consider the fact that the East European markets are development markets belonging to the industrialized world; that these countries have worked out a model of economic organization which has a profound influence on the non-industrialized countries; that those of East Europe are countries where consumption, production and commerce are in full evolution, as the consequence of the emergence of a new generation of managers and administrators. As a European, I cannot forget that these countries are a significant part of Europe, at least from the cultural standpoint. As an individual who believes that economic relations help the cause of peace, I cannot lose sight of the fact that detente today is more important than eventual competition for the markets of the Third World.

Before Economic Club, Detroit, Oct. 12/
Vital Speeches, 11–15:96.

Andrei Amalrik
Soviet author

. . . if one could at least partly explain the struggle against heretic ideas in the Middle Ages as religious fanaticism, everything taking place now (in the Soviet Union) can be explained only as the cowardice of a regime that regards as a danger the spreading of any thought, any idea alien to its top bureaucrats . . . Neither the witch hunt carried out by the regime, nor this particular example—this trial—arouses in me the slightest respect nor any fear. I understand, however, that such trials are counted on (to) frighten many; and many will be frightened. But all the same, I think, the development of ideological emancipation, having begun, is irreversible.

At his trial on charges of defaming the
Soviet state, Moscow, Nov. 12/
The New York Times, 11–15:(1)12.

It seems to me that the main task of my country just now is to throw off the burden of the heavy past, and for this my country needs free criticism, not self-glorification. I think that I am a better patriot than those who shout about their love for the motherland and who mean by that love for their privileges.

At his trial on charges of defaming the
Soviet state, Moscow, Nov. 12/
The Washington Post, 11–15:A20.

Howard H. Baker
United States Senator, R-Tenn.

We assume that the United States and the Western world are superior to the Russians. (But) the leadership of a nation is a broth consisting of intellectualism, emotionalism and animal instincts. When these three elements are combined, I am not really sure that the Russian leadership is inferior to Western leadership.

Before Senate subcommittee on national
security and international operations,
Washington, Jan. 26.

Raymond Barre
Vice president, Commission of the European Communities

Today, the European currency is in fact the dollar; the Federal Reserve System (of the United States) is in fact the lender of last resort to European central banks; there is no European capital market, but rather a market of the Eurodollar. European industrial structures tend to be more and more shaped by the investments of American firms; European technology is too dispersed to enter into competition with (American) technology.

Before French Chamber of Commerce of Brussels, Jan. 14/ The Christian Science Monitor, 1–29:10.

Hale Boggs
United States Representative, D-La.

There is a danger that Europe will be so involved over the next few years in working out its own internal trade and economic relationships that it will completely neglect its relationship with the outside world.

Quote, 5–31:505.

Willy Brandt
Chancellor of West Germany

We maintain that the Federal Republic (West Germany) and the German Democratic Republic (East Germany) are not foreign countries to each other. We also maintain that international recognition of the GDR is out of the question for us.

Before Parliament, Bonn, Jan. 14/ The New York Times, 1–15:1.

I want to say one thing in all clarity: A treaty between us and East Germany can never be a wall of fog, behind which no changes are made in the conditions which burden the people . . . Between our system and theirs, there can be no mixing, no rotten compromise.

Before Parliament, Bonn, Jan. 14/ The Washington Post, 1–15:A28.

We are watching very carefully what potential dangers a reduction of the American military engagement (in Europe) could bring in the period that lies before us. You can depend on it that the Federal government (West Germany) will do everything in its power in order to secure the military presence of the United States in Europe until one day a new peace order is created with the cooperation of East and West.

Before Parliament, Bonn, Feb. 25/ The Washington Post, 2–26:A30.

. . . the European Economic Community (Common Market) should not be an inward-looking autarchic entity. Rather, it should contribute more than before to international exchange and rising prosperity. There is nothing in the Common Market structure that would prevent the community from introducing suitable forms of cooperation with individual states in Eastern Europe or a whole group of states.

Interview, Bonn, April 2/ The New York Times, 4–4:10.

The efficiency of the Atlantic Alliance continues to depend essentially on maintaining the military presence of the U.S. on the European continent. No European effort can be a substitute for this. There is still no security for Europe without the United States. I am sure that the interpretation of America's own interests will arrive at the same conclusion.

Before National Press Club, Washington, April 10/U.S. News & World Report, 4–20:80.

Just as NATO is a reality, as West Berlin with its relationships with the Federal Republic (West Germany) is a reality, so is the Warsaw Pact, so are the two states in Germany, so are the frontiers of Poland. We have to start from these realities if we want to improve relations with the Soviet Union, seek reconciliation with the Polish people and mitigate the distressing division of our country.

News conference, Washington/Time, 4–20:15.

I am convinced that one day reconciliation between Germany and Poland will have the same historical importance as reconciliation between Germany and France has had —equal importance and weight.

Interview, Bonn/Look, 4–21:84.

We remember them all (the victims of Nazi terror) with reverence. The sorrow that their deaths brought and the sorrow that the war caused impel us not to forget the lesson of history and to regard the search for peace as the foremost objective of our political work.

Before Parliament, Bonn, May 8/
The Washington Post, 5–9:A16.

Our readiness for a good, neighborly relationship between the two German states cannot be taken to mean that we are hoisting the white flag in the ideological argument. We can have the same political rights without having the same political style.

Before Social Democratic Party, Saar Brucken,
West Germany, May 13/
The New York Times, 5–14:7.

(Commenting on West German-Soviet agreements): . . . we are right in step with NATO detente attempts. We have no illusion that our role will compare with that of America. Even in a friendly alliance all animals are equal, with some more equal than others. The U.S. has been much more equal and we less so. By becoming a bit more equal we can add a significant voice to the strategic debate. Germany can perhaps cease to be quite the problem child it's been. Up till now, whenever East-West relations were discussed, they always bogged down on the "German problem." Now, by working in the framework of East-West relations, we hope to ease the burden on the alliance.

Interview, Bonn/Newsweek, 8–10:33.

It (Soviet-West German non-aggression treaty) is a decisive step toward the bettering of our relations with the Soviet Union and our Eastern neighbors—a quarter-century

after the catastrophe that forced untold sacrifices on the peoples of the East as well as the West. The treaty endangers nothing and no one. It should help to open the way forward . . .

Television address to West Germany from
Moscow, Aug. 12/The Washington Post,
8–13:A1.

Europe neither ends on the Elbe River nor on the Polish eastern border. Russia is inextricably interwoven to Europe—not only as an opponent and a danger, but also as a partner—historically, politically, culturally and economically. Only if we in Western Europe recognize this partnership, and only if the people of Eastern Europe see it too, can we balance our interests.

Television address to West Germany from
Moscow, Aug. 12/Time, 8–24:16.

The question of a reduction of American troops in Europe has long been a subject of discussion in the United States . . . We will negotiate with the Americans, and, together with the other North Atlantic Treaty Organization countries, will try for a reasonable distribution of the burden.

Interview/The Washington Post, 8–18:A10.

I am Chancellor of West Germany when I visit Moscow. I am Chancellor of West Germany when I visit Washington. How can I not be Chancellor of West Germany when I visit West Berlin?

To Soviet Communist Party Chairman
Leonid Brezhnev, Moscow, August/
Los Angeles Times, 10–14:(1)19.

History alone can show whether the Polish-West German treaty will fulfill our hopes and be the beginning of actual reconciliation as we have already achieved it, fortunately, with our French neighbors. The issue at stake is a serious attempt, a quarter-century after the war, to put an end politically to the chain of injustice.

Bonn, Nov. 20/The New York Times, 11–21:11.

(WILLY BRANDT)

The Treaty of Warsaw is supposed to close the book on the sufferings and sacrifices of an evil past. It is supposed to build a bridge between both states and both nations (Poland and West Germany). It is supposed to open the path for divided families to get together again, to make frontiers less divisive than before. Just the same, this treaty could be signed only after earnest reflection. We did not have light hearts in deciding to do it. We are too much formed by memories and marked by destroyed hopes. But one must proceed from what exists. This also applies to the western frontier of Poland. Nobody forced us to this insight. We are adults. It involves proof of our maturity and the courage to recognize reality.

Broadcast to West Germany, from Warsaw, Dec. 7 / The New York Times, 12–8:6.

Gregorio Lopez Bravo
Foreign Minister of Spain

Spain is not interested in joining NATO ... Things have changed. NATO is different now. All of Southern Europe is now vulnerable to attack. We have to look somewhere else.

Washington / Time, 6–8:36.

Leonid I. Brezhnev
General Secretary, Communist Party of the Soviet Union

To any attempts by anyone to ensure military superiority over the U.S.S.R. we will reply with a proper increase in military might, guaranteeing our defense. We cannot act otherwise.

Kharkov, U.S.S.R., April 14 / Daily World, 4–15:11.

Soviet society today is friendship and cooperation between all classes and social groups, all nations and nationalities, all generations; it is socialist democracy, which actually assures the working people of a part in the administration of all the affairs of state and society; it is advanced socialist science and culture, which belong to the mass of the people. Soviet society today is the real embodiment of the ideas of proletarian, socialist humanism. It has placed the production of material values and the achievements of spiritual culture, the whole system of social relations, at the service of the man of labor. The Soviet people have already come to accept as fact that the growth of production and the development of culture in our country lead to better conditions of life for the working people, for the whole people. This appears to be quite natural; it is not given too much thought; it is sometimes even forgotten. But, after all, it is, essentially, one of the basic distinctions between our system and capitalism, under which production is expanded to enrich the property-owner and not to improve the life of the working man. One of the greatest achievements of socialism is that every Soviet man is assured of his future. He is aware that his work, his abilities and his energy will always find a fitting use and appreciation. He is sure that his children will be given a free education and the opportunity of developing their talents. He knows that society will never abandon him in misfortune, that in the event of illness he will be given free medical treatment, a pension in the event of permanent disability, and security in old age. Everything we have, everything we live by and take pride in is the result of the struggle and working endeavor of our working class, peasantry and intelligentsia—of the whole Soviet people.

Before Soviet Communist Party and the Supreme Soviet, Moscow, April 21 / Vital Speeches, 6–1:487.

Today we live as well as we worked yesterday. Tomorrow we shall live as well as we work today.

Time, 5–4:36.

Manlio Brosio
Secretary-General, North Atlantic Treaty Organization

The Soviet Union has now caught up with and even overtaken the United States as regards the number and yield of intercontinental ballistic missiles, while it has created a navy which can sail the seven seas and which comprises the most powerful submarine force in the world.

Before Western European Union, Paris, Nov. 17/Los Angeles Times, 11–18:(1)19.

Zbigniew Brzezinski
Director, Research Institute on Communist Affairs, Columbia University

Russia's present ruling group is unquestionably the oldest, man for man, in any nation of importance in the modern-day world. As a group, it is uncertain, cautious, ambiguous, mired in party dogma, and moribund. In some ways, it is a throwback to the Curia of the Vatican—that ancient clerical bureaucracy that deteriorated into a body of venerable reactionaries. At the same time, the Soviet bureaucracy has developed into a deeply conservative institution—preservers of the *status quo* of Russian Communism. Moreover, it is so loaded with bumbling incompetents as to be a favorite butt of Russian jokes —and serious criticism.

Interview/U.S. News & World Report, 4–20:71.

McGeorge Bundy
President, Ford Foundation; Former Assistant to the President of the United States for National Security Affairs

The Soviet purpose in negotiating with non-Communist powers is not always benign, and Soviet alertness for a one-sided advantage is proverbial.

Time, 4–20:23.

David A. Burchinal
General, United States Air Force; Deputy Commander-in-Chief, United States European Command

As a military man looking at the security problems in Europe, I think that the size of the U.S. commitment to our security in Europe is about what is required today to maintain the stability that we have had for the past 21 years. I look at our allies, and I think that, rather than we doing less, it is essential

that they do more to maintain this in the years ahead after 1970.

Before Senate Foreign Relations Committee, Washington, May 25/ The Washington Post, 12–25:A14.

Luis Carrero (Blanco)
Vice President of Spain

Communism has sought to influence the course of justice by orchestrating abroad a campaign of calumny and insults against our country, making us out as a barbarous land where there are no judicial safeguards in the conduct of trials. Spain has laws and is ruled by them. Spain will not bend to pressure from abroad, whatever its source, which reflects on Spain's dignity or sovereignty.

Before the Cortes (Parliament), Madrid/ The Christian Science Monitor, 12–24:13.

Emilio Colombo
Premier of Italy

The recent events (rioting) in Poland and the embarrassed reactions of the Italian Communist Party to the ruthless use of violence (by Polish authorities) remind us again of the inadmissibility of cooperation with the Communist Party.

Television address to nation, Rome, Dec. 27/ Los Angeles Herald-Examiner, 12–28:A4.

Robert Conquest
Author; Authority on the Soviet Union

The Soviet Union is a very strange and idiosyncratic polity, not to be understood or dealt with without a considerable conscious effort. The Soviet leaders are not to be treated as though their motives and conceptions were, in our sense, natural and rational. The particular leadership now in control in Russia—one which is thoroughly representative of the ruling class as a whole—derives from a tradition which is alien in both aim and method to our own. But it is also, and this is a major point for us today, intellectually third-rate, even within that tradition.

Before Senate Subcommittee on National Security and International Operations, Washington/Christian Science Monitor, 2–2:2.

William Craig
*Former Home Affairs Minister
of Northern Ireland*

I'm striving to get rid of this government (in Northern Ireland), which has committed the country to policies which have made law and order a laughing stock.

*Radio interview, Belfast, Aug. 10/
The Washington Post, 8–11:A11.*

Josef Cyrankiewicz
Premier of Poland

It is a moral obligation of our generation —the generation which has survived the Second World War—that the problems resulting from that war not be left to the young generation, seemingly open, unsettled, with glowing and sometimes fanned embers of future conflicts . . . (The Treaty of Warsaw, between Poland and West Germany), which we signed today, has already been received in all Europe and in the international world community as a new and important step forward in the removing of the crust of the cold war in Europe, the region crucial for peace. With this act, we are contributing to extinguishing one of the potentially most dangerous tension centers.

*At reception honoring West German
Chancellor Willy Brandt, Warsaw, Dec. 7/
The Washington Post, 12–13:B6.*

Citizens, I am speaking to you at a serious time. As I am sure you are all aware, we have all felt very deeply the events (rioting) in Gdansk and on the coast. But the duty of the representatives of the people's power—representatives of the state—the supreme duty, irrespective of grief, is to think in terms of the state, to be guided by the interests of the state as an entity, of the nation as an entity, to be guided by the interests of our country's future and to serve these supreme interests with determination . . . For the last three days, Gdansk and the coast have been the scene of street disturbances and violations of authority and public order. Dur-

ing these events, many public buildings were demolished and set on fire, many shops looted and ransacked, many cars destroyed. During these events, militiamen and soldiers—standing guard over order, public and private property, and the security of the citizens—have been attacked and shot at. Tragic clashes followed in which the forces of order were compelled to use arms. There were casualties, a number of dead in the tens, several hundred wounded —militiamen and civilians. Here are the painful consequences of the lack of prudence and sense of responsibility by those who abandoned work and went into the streets, providing an opportunity for scum, adventurers and enemies, for vandalism, looting and murder. Each of us must realize that these events have not only brought vast material and moral losses to the country, but have also become a feeding ground for the enemies of People's Poland . . . In order to create the achievements of which we are proud today, we needed more than 25 years of difficult effort by the entire nation. To build a house is difficult; it requires work and great efforts. To burn and destroy is easy. It is our sacred duty to defend these achievements by all necessary means. Where order has been violated, it is already being restored; and it will be maintained right to the end.

*Broadcast to nation, Dec. 17/
The New York Times, 12–18:8.*

Clelio Darida
Mayor of Rome

To say I have problems would be an understatement. Like other Italian cities, Rome has just grown too fast. In other places, cities spread out and gradually gobble up smaller communities on their outskirts. Rome has no such problem. It just eats up the countryside while still revolving around one single center. This city has now become a terrible *polenta* (Italian cornmeal) of three million people.

Interview, Rome/Los Angeles Times, 2–15:A.

Michel Debre
Minister of Defense of France

Let no one doubt that France continues to be a part of the Atlantic alliance, even if it has quit the (integrated military) organization. Our military policy is based on the notion of independence, but, as an independent state, we shall be—if need be—a more solid ally than certain countries which prefer integration.

Before French National Assembly, Paris/
The Washington Post, 10–10:A13.

Suleyman Demirel
Prime Minister of Turkey

We have developed true democracy, and we are developing our economy. My government has plenty of problems; but we continue to reflect the majority will in spite of all the noise you hear. We will make it. By "we" I mean Turkey. Maybe I won't make it; but that doesn't matter. Turkey will make it.

Interview/The New York Times, 8–5:12.

Bernadette Devlin
Member of British Parliament
from Northern Ireland

I am in Parliament with the intention of using it for my own ends.

Time, 11–9:34.

Milovan Djilas
Author; Former Vice President
of Yugoslavia

In 30 years, everything will be changed in Russia—its economic and social relations with the West, its government and party structure. The spirit inside the party will change. I believe democracy will come to Russia. In the beginning, maybe something on the order of Yugoslavia will be set up. That would be a good start. But it has to come. It cannot be stopped.

Interview, Belgrade/Life, 5–1:64.

There is so much America can do. It should liquidate all economic discrimination (against Russia) and go forward with trade, credits, investment, and not be afraid of such things as reciprocity or mutual trust. America is strong enough and Russia needs it desperately. Her economy is more and more inefficient. Comecon (the Communist-bloc trade organization) is a failure. Russia will be forced to cooperate with the West because she cannot afford to remain isolated.

Interview, Belgrade/Life, 5–1:68.

There are no ideals—neither ideology nor idealism—holding our country together today. The only thing that keeps the nation together is (President) Tito's authority . . . and Tito's authority holds no idealism.

Interview, Belgrade/Los Angeles Times,
11–15:A4.

Alec Douglas-Home
Foreign Secretary of the United Kingdom

To suggest that Britain has a racialist outlook because she trades with South Africa is, on the record of the creation of the Commonwealth of independent nations, patently absurd.

Quote, 9–20:265.

The Soviet military machine has grown out of all proportion to the traditional strength of Russia. A new factor in defense planning for the future is that the Soviet Navy has become oceanic in its range. When I say "new," I mean that literally. This is a development of the last three or four years. This is a new fact of life with which we must reckon; or, if we do not, we may pay a price that is unacceptable at some future time. For, quite simply, it is not safe—whether it be in the Mediterranean now or in the Indian Ocean soon—to leave the Communists as undisputed masters of all military activity in an area where British interests lie.

At Conservative Party convention, Blackpool,
England, Oct. 9/
The Washington Post, 10–10:A10.

Elizabeth II
Queen of England

The strength of the (British) Commonwealth lives in its history and the way people feel about it. All those years through which

(ELIZABETH II)

we have lived together have given us an exchange of people and ideas which ensures that there is a continuing concern for each other . . . These matters of the spirit are more important and more lasting than simple material development. It is a hard lesson, but I like to think that we in the Commonwealth have perhaps begun to understand it.

TV-radio broadcast, London, Dec. 25/
The Washington Post, 12–26:A11.

J. William Fulbright
United States Senator, D-Ark.

. . . one of the most hopeful and impressive things to me is what the (West) Germans have done (signing non-aggression pact with the Soviet Union), and I am not sure that we had anything whatever to do with that. It is a rather ridiculous posture we have of keeping 300,000 men in Germany and see the Germans go off to Moscow and make peace and make a treaty with the Russians. I am glad they did . . .

Interview/Meet the Press,
National Broadcasting Company,
Washington, 8–23.

One of these days, they (the present Greek government) will be thrown out and you (U.S. State Department) will be thrown out with them. I think you are very shortsighted in this policy of thinking that it is in our interest to go to bed with the Papadopouloses.

At hearings of Senate Foreign Relations
Subcommittee on United States Security
Agreements and Commitments Abroad,
Washington/The Washington Post, 10–5:A3.

Edward Gierek
First Secretary, Communist Party of Poland

A quarter of a century ago, our nation entered the road of socialism. We entered it after the most tragic experiences in our history. No hostile forces are in a position to lead or turn us back from the road of socialism. In brotherly and cordial cooperation,

we shall continue to consolidate the friendship and alliance with the Soviet Union. For us, this is a fundamental question, a basic guarantee of independence, security and development of our country. In accordance with the internationalist traditions of our nation, with the Marxist-Leninist ideology of our Party, Poland is, and shall remain, a lasting link of the forces of socialism, democracy and peace.

After assuming his new post as First Secretary,
Warsaw, Dec. 20/The New York Times,
12–21:15.

Eduard Goldstucker
Visiting professor, Sussex University,
England; Former member, Czechoslovak
Parliament

. . . what we tried in 1968 will never be lost in history. For those who will come after us, either in Czechoslovakia or anywhere else, our experience in 1968 will serve as a very important textbook—to know what to do and what to avoid. It will not be lost. We could not have avoided the so-called Brezhnev Doctrine no matter what we did or omitted to do. I can understand the Soviet apprehension as they followed the developments in Czechoslovakia after January, 1968, because they were confronted with something new within the socialist camp, different from what happened in Hungary in 1956, different from what happened in Poland in 1956, and every new phenomenon of that sort creates, as the first reaction, mistrust, apprehension . . . And I think, looking back, that the Soviet Union had really only two possibilities in dealing with the Czechoslovak problem. They could either come to some sort of *modus vivendi*, or crush the country . . . I am absolutely certain that if the Soviet Union had found some sort of *modus vivendi* with Czechoslovakia, we would have been prepared to do much not to irritate the Soviet Union. If the Soviet Union had found the possibility of such *modus vivendi*, we would have been its most faithful ally out of the free will of the whole nation.

Interview/Los Angeles Times, 8–30:F3.

. . . when you try to weld together a number of nations, without guaranteeing them their equality in that new formation, you build into that new formation elements of its future disruption. And that is what, to my mind, is the great danger for the future —that the nations of the socialist community of Eastern Europe, with the exception of Yugoslavia and Albania, are welded together not as equals with full rights, but under the domination of one of the superpowers of the world. This cannot work in the future; it is absolutely impossible.

Interview/Los Angeles Times, 8–30:F3.

Andrew J. Goodpaster
General, United States Army; Supreme Allied Commander-Europe

Soviet military power exceeds anything the world has ever previously seen . . . Before our very eyes, but with too little recognition of the consequences, a shift in the balance of security is occurring.

Human Events, 11–7:14.

Gunter Grass
Author

Germany was the only country in Europe where, up to 1966, there was no anti-Americanism. That has changed. Not only because of Vietnam, about which we in Europe are largely powerless, but even more because of Greece—as an affair of American responsibility that is close to us. America's large capital of moral credit is now lost, and the policy of backing the Greek government is directed against America's own interests.

Interview, New York/
The New York Times, 3–19:58.

In spite of the opulence they see around them, the young people in Germany are bored by the kind of success that has been achieved by their fathers. They merely accept it as something given, a fundamental condition. They have no memory of it being different. What the radical young need most today is resistance, rational resistance. This provokes discussion, and that is what we need most. There is at present a great deal of confusion among Germans of the young generation. There are many splinter radical groups. But those—the great majority—who could not be called radical, have now withdrawn to wait and see what will happen. This last group is important. It is the electorate of the future.

Interview/National Observer, 10–19:22.

Andrei A. Grechko
Minister of Defense of the Soviet Union

The construction of Communist society in our country is being conducted in an acute and tense international atmosphere. The United States imperialists fan the flames of war in Southeast Asia. With the support of international reactionaries, Israeli aggressors stage more and more brazen provocations against Arab countries. Revenge-seeking and neo-Nazi forces are being activated in West Germany. In these conditions, the Communist Party of the Soviet Union and the government are steadily bringing peaceful Leninist foreign policy to life, and are taking the measures necessary to ensure the security of the motherland, to strengthen the combat might of the army and the navy. Soldiers of our armed forces will always be found vigilantly guarding the great gains of socialism.

Minsk, U.S.S.R., March 15/
The New York Times, 3–16:4.

Andrei A. Gromyko
Foreign Minister of the Soviet Union

The talks (concerning the Soviet-West German non-aggression treaty) ended with results that will be positively assessed by both sides. The Soviet government is convinced that the results will work toward the expansion of cooperation between our two countries and in the interest of relaxing tensions and promoting European security. I am greatly satisfied.

Moscow, Aug. 7/The Washington Post, 8–8:A13.

W. Averell Harriman
Former United States Ambassador-at-Large

(All through the Roosevelt-Truman-Churchill talks with Stalin) it became obvious to me that the Russians were going to build a navy. Now, God didn't make the Mediterranean an American sea. Neither did God make it a Russian sea. We have to accept this. And we've got to relax about it. The countries around the Mediterranean—the countries of West Europe and of North Africa—have an enormous interest in it, as well as the United States and its international responsibilities and the Soviet Union. I've said since '45 that there are some very deep differences between us and the Soviet Union and that some of them are irreconcilable. But it was our obligation to compose our differences in order to live in peace on this small planet. We've got to recognize they've got a right to place their vessels there . . .

Interview, Washington/
The Christian Science Monitor, 12–30:5.

Denis Healey
Minister of Defense of the United Kingdom

There is no real possibility of defending Western Europe against an all-out Soviet conventional attack, and, therefore, if we ever face such an attack, we would have to use nuclear weapons early.

Quote, 5–10:433.

Edward Heath
Prime Minister of the United Kingdom

I have always had in my mind's eye a vision about the people of this country. I have always wanted to see them look up instead of always looking down.

Norfolk County, England, July 4/
The Washington Post, 7–5:A19.

Leadership is a quality which creates a feeling in those who support the leader. It's not a technique or style; it's a human quality made up of character and practical wisdom. That is the kind of leadership I shall try to give—the kind that would make people say in retrospect: "He always told us the truth; he always did what he thought was right; he put principle above power; and he worked as hard as anybody else alive."

After his election, London/
U.S. News & World Report, 7–6:60.

There is to be no more permanent large-scale (non-white) immigration into this country.

Quote, 8–2:97.

We are leaving behind the years of retreat. We are determined to establish the reputation of Britain once again, a reputation as the firm defender of her own interests and the skillful and persistent partner of all those who are working for a lasting peace.

At Conservative Party convention,
Blackpool, England, Oct. 10/
The Dallas Times Herald, 10–11:A17.

(His government's strategy) is to ensure that government withdraws from all those activities no longer necessary . . . because they are better done outside government or because they should rightly be carried on, if wanted at all, by individual or by voluntary effort . . . It is to reorganize the functions of government, to leave more to individual or to corporate effort, to make savings in government expenditure, to provide greater incentives to men and women and to firms and business. Our strategy is to encourage them more and more to (make) their own decisions, to stand on their feet, to accept responsibility for themselves and their families.

At Conservative Party convention,
Blackpool, England, Oct. 10/
The Washington Post, 10–11:A17.

If we can win the hearts and minds of the people, we can permanently change the outlook of the British nation. Our strategy is clear: to reorganize government, to provide savings and incentives. Not what kind of government is important, but how much government. We need less government and of a better quality . . . Get used to the idea of change, because it is going to be the pattern of this government. We in government have accepted the challenge, and I warn the nation there is no alternative.

At Conservative Party convention,
Blackpool, England, Oct. 10/
The Christian Science Monitor, 10–14:4.

It was in freedom, not in reliance upon the state, that Britain achieved greatness. It was the acceptance of personal responsibility, not dependence upon the central government, that made this small island, with its comparatively small population, so dominant in the world.

At Guildhall, London, November/
The New York Times, 12–17:5.

We are not out to destroy the welfare state. The social services will always be there for those who need them. But, since the war, individuals in this country have come to lean too much on the government. I want the British to learn again to stand on their own feet.

Interview/Newsweek, 12–21:49.

Without substantial American forces in Europe, we could not achieve the necessary level of operational units to maintain the validity of NATO's present strategy and, thus, the credibility of the ultimate Western nuclear response. For obvious reasons, American forces also have a special psychological importance. Even if they could be replaced by European troops, their departure would cause an immediate crisis of confidence.

Interview, London/
U.S. News & World Report, 12–21:25.

We could never go back to the little England of centuries ago. Nor can we be a superpower in the sense that America is today. We shall be ourselves: an outward-looking people, a nation with worldwide interests and responsibilities, a medium power of the first rank. We shall set our own order of priori-

ties. Our own interests must come first—that is the responsibility of any government— then Europe's and those of the North Atlantic Alliance. We shall make a full contribution to the world's debates and to the resolution of international problems. We shall be contracting in—not contracting out. None knows better than the British that you simply cannot afford to stop the world and get off.

Interview, London/
U.S. News & World Report, 12–21:25.

Gustav Heinemann
President of West Germany

The names of Bergen-Belsen, Dachau, Auschwitz, Theresienstadt, Mauthausen and Schirmeck have lost none of their horror. Nothing can mitigate them; no rhetoric can dissipate them. They cannot and must not be relegated to oblivion.

Time, 5–4:54.

Hubert H. Humphrey
United States Senator-elect, D-Minn.; Former Vice President of the United States

When you're withdrawing from other parts of the world, you better have an anchor in Europe. Those Soviet leaders are not a bunch of kindly social workers, you know.

News conference, Washington, Dec. 10/
The Washington Post, 12–11:B17.

Gustav Husak
First Secretary, Communist Party of Czechoslovakia

Not even the bourgeois world is today putting a question mark over Czechoslovakia and, although it uses the situation as a basis for insults and slanders, it takes it as a firm fact that Czechoslovakia belongs where it wants to belong—to the Socialist camp— and the political position of the Czechoslovak Socialist Republic will no longer be decided by accident.

Interview/Los Angeles Times, 1–6:(1)8.

We do not wish to destroy or to do people in. Our party will never lower itself to con-

(GUSTAV HUSAK)

trived trials, contrived accusations—not even against political adversaries.

Newsweek, 2–9:44.

Czechoslovakia is essentially a rich state. With good organization, there should be no special problems. But what kills us is an almost general disorder for which the blame should be placed not on the working man but rather on all these superstructures and mechanisms which create the confusion . . . If somewhere people are loafing, it is because management does not know how to organize work.

Before Czechoslovak Trade Union Council,
Prague, Feb. 12/
Los Angeles Times, 2–13:(1)13.

The traditional bonds of friendship and cooperation between our people and the Soviet people have been restored. We can say that Czechoslovakia is once again firmly in the common front of the socialist states, in firm alliance with the Soviet Union.

Prague, May 5/Los Angeles Times, 5–6:(1)19.

Why was (former First Secretary) Alexander Dubcek expelled from the ranks of our party? He was expelled from the ranks of our party because, in the relatively short time that he headed it, he brought our party to a disintegration such as it had never known. He led our society, our social organizations, trade unions and youth to such a degree of disintegration, and our economy to such a wave of inflation and to such disorganization, that we stood on the brink of economic bankruptcy. In the sphere of international relations, he destroyed relations with the Soviet Union and the other allied states, and Czechoslovakia became isolated on the brink of great perils and dangers. Is that not enough?

Television address, Prague, July 5/
The Washington Post, 7–6:A1.

Henry M. Jackson
United States Senator, D-Wash.

The Soviet Union is now, for the first time in Russian history, a *global military power.* Looking ahead, the somber prospect is a Soviet Union increasingly bolder in its policies and more disposed to throw its military weight around to support its great power interests and to extend Soviet influence into new areas of the world.

U.S. News & World Report, 7–27:39.

Foy D. Kohler
Former United States Ambassador to the Soviet Union

The United States is a constant in Soviet thinking—just as the devil is a constant to the church. We have to be—by the Marxist dogma—the main enemy.

Interview/U.S. News & World Report, 6–22:26.

Alexei N. Kosygin
Premier of the Soviet Union

There have been all kinds of reports in the Western press lately about supposed changes in the U.S.S.R., be it in the economy, policy or leadership . . . this is something we know nothing about.

News conference, Moscow, May 4/
The New York Times, 5–5:2.

We attach considerable importance to this treaty (Soviet-West German non-aggression treaty), and hope that it will serve to improve our relations with the F.R.G. (West Germany) and that it would strongly promote a detente to Europe. The understanding reached between the U.S.S.R. and the F.R.G. shows that even in the complicated conditions of international relations in Europe, mutually acceptable decisions could be bound in the interests of consolidating peace on a bilateral as well as a multilateral basis. The understanding between both countries constitutes, in our view, a major political event, and it should serve the end of stabilizing the situation in Europe and in the world at large.

Interview, Moscow/
Milwaukee Journal, 8–10:4.

Melvin R. Laird
Secretary of Defense of the United States

When you look at an SS-9 (Soviet) missile, it just dwarfs the size of anything we have. When you realize the cost of each of those—when you look at their tremendous submarine-construction program, their surface-ship construction program and all of their other military programs—you must conclude there is some incentive for them to seek some sort of arms-limitation agreement, some sort of understanding. Remember, the Soviets have only one half the gross national product of the U.S.

Interview, Washington/
U.S. News & World Report, 5–11:68.

As Secretary of Defense, I don't believe it is appropriate for me to try to assess the intentions of the Soviet Union. My responsibilities are to consider their real and potential capabilities, particularly in relation to our own policy of deterrence. However, I believe this much is clear: They do not want to be in the position they found themselves in when they were confronted with the power of the United States at the time of the Cuban missile crisis.

Interview, Washington/
U.S. News & World Report, 5–11:68.

Lyman L. Lemnitzer
General, United States Army (Ret.); Former Supreme Allied Commander-Europe

During the period that I was Supreme Allied Commander, 1963 to 1969, United States forces in Europe were reduced from 408,000 to 300,000. In my opinion, our forces are now at the minimum level consistent with the assigned mission and the known enemy capability. Indeed, in some areas they are already below troop level. I firmly believe that until there is an agreement by the Warsaw Pact

and NATO for the mutual reduction of forces . . . any further unilateral reductions by the United States would be the wrong action at the wrong time.

On receiving George Catlett Marshall Medal
from Association of the United States Army,
Washington, Oct. 14/
Washington Star, 10–15:A5.

Malcolm Mackintosh
Consultant, Institute for Strategic Studies, London; Authority on Soviet policy

In the Soviet Union—and, indeed, in Russia before the Revolution—there has always been a strong tendency to believe that the biggest and strongest power in any grouping should have a natural predominance over the smaller powers. The Russians believe that, by natural law, they should have paramount influence not only over Eastern Europe but also over Western Europe, which in a sense they regard as part of their parish.

Interview, London/
U.S. News & World Report, 11–2:68.

I see no danger in talking to the Russians on any subject at any time. But when the Russians call for talks, go, listen more than talk, and make it clear that there is a point beyond which you are not prepared to make any concessions. There is absolutely no sense, when one is negotiating with the Russians, to make any concessions or offer concessions in order to improve the atmosphere. This only convinces them that the donor is on weak grounds and leads them to pocket the concessions and demand more.

Interview, London/
U.S. News & World Report, 11–2:69.

Iain MacLeod
Former Colonial Secretary of the United Kingdom

I have been responsible for bringing independence to more countries than any other man that ever lived.

The Dallas Times Herald, 6–22:A2.

377

Neil H. McElroy
Former Secretary of Defense of the United States

By my evaluation, the Russian is a great tester of resolution. If he tests you and you run, then he will test you again and see whether you will run further. If he tests you and you don't run and he tests you again and you don't run, then he lets you alone for a bit. He thinks he has learned something.

Interview, Cincinnati /
Nation's Business, Aug. 62.

William McMahon
Minister for External Affairs of Australia

We need have no illusions that the policies and actions of the Soviet government are motivated by anything other than the interests of the Soviet government and of that part of the Communist network which it still effectively controls.

Before Parliament, Canberra /
The Christian Science Monitor, 3–26:6.

Mike Mansfield
United States Senator, D-Mont.

I believe that, a quarter of a century after the end of the Second World War, it is time that this nation (United States) changed its policy, recognizing that Europe is now fully rehabilitated and reconstructed and is quite capable of undertaking a greater share of its own defense, both in manpower and in cost, and that we should change with the times . . . I hope that, on the basis of the Nixon Doctrine, there will be a substantial withdrawal of (American) troops and dependents from Europe and that we will get away from this vested policy of a quarter of a century ago—this outmoded and invalid policy— and that we will recognize that we are, indeed, considered . . . as hostages held for the security of some other country. I firmly believe in NATO—but not to the extent of 600,000 men and dependents, and not to the extent of $14 billion to $15 billion a year.

Before the Senate, Washington, Feb. 20 /
Congressional Record, 2–20:S2060.

The initialing of this agreement (Soviet-West German non-aggression treaty) may well point toward a full European diplomatic reconciliation . . . It is urgent that this nation (United States) readjust its policies to the changing realities of Europe, and notably as they involve a massive and costly U.S. troop deployment in Western Europe . . . The $14 billion annual drain on U.S. resources is made even more anachronistic by the latest developments in West German-Soviet relations.

Washington, Aug. 10 /
The Washington Post, 8–11:A5.

Golda Meir
Prime Minister of Israel

I think (the Russians) are very careful. It isn't true that they just rush into something. First, they put in one foot—"How's the water? Is it all right?" The next one goes in. There is one wave—"When it is passed, then we can go on to the next one." That is their mentality; that's how they work. And I am horrified to see how the free world sits back. It isn't that they don't understand; that's nonsense. They just don't want to see.

Interview, Tel Aviv, Dec. 19 /
The New York Times, 12–27:(1)1.

Melina Mercouri
Actress

. . . the Russians have many similarities to Americans. They slap you on the back like Texans, and they admire and imitate Americans. I once said in a speech that a flirtation has started between the Soviet Union and America. Now, after working there (in the Soviet Union), I am ready to say this flirtation will become a great love. And I think this great love will be very constructive for world peace. The Russians adore Coca Cola, and the Americans adore vodka.

Interview, Paris /
The Washington Post, 12–6:E11.

Riccardo Misasi
Minister of Public Instruction of Italy

The Italian school system is tied to an organization and a conception of education that are greatly behind the times . . . Statistically, we know that among the persons getting high school diplomas—and this is even more so in the case of those obtaining university degrees—the number who come from peasant families is infinitely less than the number from worker families. And we know that the sum of these two is much less than those coming from professional families and from the bourgeoise. This is what we must change. I do not mean to create a leveling of education. But we must correct the selection process so that it is not based on social origin but only on the natural capacity of the student.

Interview, Rome/
Los Angeles Times, 4–26:H5.

Slawomir Mrozek
Polish playwright-in-exile

Can you imagine all information sifted and repressed? In Poland, if you want to have your personal card printed, it must go through censorship first. I am not joking; this is how far it reaches. Yes, it's an insane society. But you wouldn't go insane under such a system. You would get adjusted. But you would suffer terrible schizophrenia because you would have to convince yourself in order to survive. And that's worse. So everything is controlled. When people meet together, it's already suspect . . . To think that there is a sense of community in a Communist society is the greatest mistake people make here (in the West). Society does not exist as such. There is only the power and the atomized people.

Interview, Washington/
The Washington Post, 4–5:F5.

Gunnar Myrdal
Swedish economist and sociologist

Young Swedes do not remember that the United States helped to destroy Hitler. They do not recall Marshall Plan aid. They see only the ugliness in America.

The Christian Science Monitor, 10–12:5.

Richard M. Nixon
President of the United States

One of the primary principles of American foreign policy is to maintain the necessary strength in the Mediterranean to preserve the peace against those who might threaten the peace . . . The Mediterranean is the cradle of many great civilizations of the past, and we are determined that it shall not be the starting place of great wars in the future.

Rome, Sept. 27/
The New York Times, 9–28:1.

Considerable concern, I find, has arisen among many of the NATO nations . . . as a result of some comments by political figures in the United States, as well as some of those commenting upon the American role in the world, that the United States might not meet its NATO responsibilities and was on the verge of reducing its contribution to NATO. I stated categorically to the NATO commanders, and I do here publicly again, that the United States will, under no circumstances, reduce unilaterally its commitment to NATO. Any reduction in NATO forces, if it occurs, will only take place on a multilateral basis and on the basis of what those who are lined up against the NATO forces—what they might do. In other words, it would have to be on a mutual basis.

Ireland, Oct. 4/
The Washington Post, 10–9:A2.

Franco Nogueira
Former Foreign Minister of Portugal

We have only one neighbor—who will always be larger, richer and stronger than . . . Portugal. Remember that our connections with Europe must inevitably pass through Spain—with all the disadvantages this implies.

The Christian Science Monitor, 5–27:3.

Ian Paisley
Member of Northern Irish Parliament

I am going to Stormont (Parliament) as . . . the voice of Protestantism; and I am

(IAN PAISLEY)

going there to say, "No surrender." We will keep Ulster Protestant, and we will keep Ulster free.

Newsweek, 4–27:61.

I'll make it so hot for the Prime Minister (of Northern Ireland, James Chichester-Clark), he'll want to retire.

Time, 4–27:43.

Olof Palme
Prime Minister of Sweden

Sweden does not excite any tremendous international interest. We tend to exaggerate the interest we sometimes attract abroad as well as magnify the importance of what is said about us. By some observers, we are described as a country where all essential problems have been solved. We are impeccable, but very dull—relieved only by occasional fits of collective neurosis. To others, we are a nightmare state where private initiative is allowed only in the field of morals to an extent at which suicide comes as an inevitable end to a pitiful existence. Neither of these pictures is very accurate. Sweden is a technically advanced country enjoying a fairly high standard of living. We devote a bigger proportion of our total resources than other countries to employment policy, education, housebuilding, social security and medical care. Consequently, we also pay higher taxes. Industry is mostly privately owned, but the importance of the public sector is growing. We are beset by the familiar problems of rising prices, the credit squeeze, imbalance in our foreign trade, etc. But it is fair to say that, basically, we have a strong economy.

Before National Press Club, Washington, June 5/Vital Speeches, 7–15:580.

Our neutrality has never condemned us to silence. If it did, we could never take any position on any question. We could never vote in the United Nations. We could not protest against the Berlin Wall, or against the invasion of Hungary, or against suppression of the black people in South Africa, as we have done. We have criticized Communist countries of the East on a large number of occasions. So it cannot be regarded as un-neutral when we take a different position from that of the U.S. on Vietnam. That is basically in line with our neutrality policy.

Interview, Washington/ U.S. News & World Report, 6–22:48.

We have had Swedish troops all around the globe on peace-keeping operations—the Congo, Korea, Cyprus, Lebanon, the Middle East—everywhere. We are slowly beginning to learn that we are involved in international questions—disarmament and the environment, for instance. So, while neutrality is supported by nearly 100 per cent of our people, we—especially the young generation—are very determined that neutrality should never mean isolation.

Interview, Washington/ U.S. News & World Report, 6–22:48.

George Papadopoulos
Premier of Greece

Only I, as the bearer of the people's mandate, will decide when the time is right for a safe return to parliamentary life in accordance with the Constitution.

Address to nation, Athens, Dec. 19/ The New York Times, 12–20:(1)3.

James B. Pearson
United States Senator, R-Kan.

I simply reject the notion that the political bonds of NATO are so weak that they will be broken by the withdrawal of a substantial number of American troops. If, indeed, NATO is so fragile, it is, then, inherently too weak and too ineffective to be of any great value, even if our present force levels were to be doubled.

Quote, 11–29:515.

Charles H. Percy
United States Senator, R-Ill.

The time has come for a tough reassessment of the U.S. commitment to NATO—both the level of that commitment and the costs associated with that commitment. Today, 25 years after the end of World War II, 1.2 million American troops are overseas—310,000, or more than 25 per cent, are in Europe. Of the troops in Europe, about 220,000 are in West Germany. Along with our troops in Europe are 235,000 dependents and 14,000 U.S. civilian employes—a total of 569,000 Americans in Western Europe. This represents a larger military presence than the United States currently has in Vietnam, where an actual war is going on. To support this military presence in Europe, a tremendous drain is placed on the U.S. budget. It costs $14 billion annually to support our troops in NATO. In addition, associated with the military commitments, is a $1.5 billion balance-of-payments deficit in Germany alone. The United States can no longer afford this commitment of men and money, considering our pressing domestic needs . . . The time has come for the Europeans to do more in their own defense. I foresee a grave threat to the U.S. commitment to NATO unless the whole structure of NATO is reassessed and Europeans make a greater commitment to their own common defense.

Before the Senate, Washington, Feb. 20/
Congressional Record, 2–2C:S2058.

Richard Pipes
Professor of History and Director, Russian Research Center, Harvard University

Legitimacy of some kind is essential to every political authority to justify the right of some men to order others about. The Soviet government is no exception. Unable to obtain a popular mandate, it seeks to obtain it in a variety of other ways, of which nationalism is the handiest. By appearing as the protector of Russian national interests from internal and external enemies, the regime can identify itself with the people. But

to be able to do so, it must have enemies, and it conjures them up as the need arises. The atmosphere of crisis is essential to the Soviet elite and can be counted on to remain an instrument of Soviet policy as long as the present elite remains in power.

Before Special Subcommittee on Strategic Arms Limitation Talks of the Senate Armed Services Committee, Washington, March 18/
Vital Speeches, 9–15:730.

The Soviet citizen today is poor, not only in comparison with his counterpart in other European countries, but also in comparison with his own grandfather. In terms of essentials—food, clothing and housing—the Soviet population as a whole is worse off than it was before the Revolution and in the 1920s. If one considers such intangibles as access to information and the right to travel as elements of the standard of living—as they should be—then the Soviet citizenry is positively destitute.

Before Special Subcommittee on Strategic Arms Limitation Talks of the Senate Armed Services Committee, Washington, March 18/
Vital Speeches, 9–15:730.

Nikolai V. Podgorny
President of the Soviet Union

France in the West and the Soviet Union in the East form a kind of natural "pillars of security" in the area of the globe where the two world wars broke out in the past.

At dinner honoring French President Pompidou, Moscow, Oct. 6/
Los Angeles Times, 10–7:(1)14.

Georges Pompidou
President of France

As far as we are concerned, we have no plans to resume membership in the integrated NATO organization. We do, on the other hand, intend to pursue our relationship as allies with contact and, of course, certain arrangements which now exist or may exist in the future. As for bilateral cooperation between France and the United

381

States, I personally doubt that the United States wants this.

Interview, Paris, Feb. 10/
The New York Times, 2–15:(1)22.

Among the positions taken by (West German) Chancellor (Willy) Brandt, there is one which I particularly approve . . . that the question of German reunification is not today's problem; I feel this problem of the relationship between the two Germanys requires a long-term, progressive and prudent approach.

Interview, Paris, Feb. 10/
The New York Times, 2–15:(1)22.

. . . France and America have a fundamentally sentimental relationship which is bound to swing between fondness and exasperation.

Interview, Paris/Life, 2–20:37.

There have been times—there are times, there will be times—when we (France and the United States) are not always of the same opinion on all matters. Our interests may sometimes diverge. It may be that to us America seems overwhelming and that France to America seems of slight importance . . . But the important thing is to feel within ourselves the profound conviction that we are united as regards the essential. The essential in our world is peace, which depends more on the strong than on the weak and lays particular responsibility on the former.

Before National Press Club, Washington,
Feb. 24/Los Angeles Herald-Examiner,
2–24:A3.

We wish deeply that the presence of United States troops in Europe would become unnecessary, because on that day we would have not only a detente but an "entente." But this day has not yet come. And

this presence must be significative and not symbolic.

Before National Press Club, Washington,
Feb. 24/The New York Times, 2–25:12.

My chief preoccupation is to make of France a modern country. This means many things. It means the transformation of agriculture, industrialization, the opening of frontiers, scientific and technical research. It also means an intellectual—I might almost say "moral"—transformation in the university and in relations between people at a time when it is plainly evident that former society, with its definitely established framework, has been swept away by events.

Interview, Paris/Time, 3–2:18.

Outside of the problems particular to Britain—its geographic location, its economy—I think that it's more difficult to unify seven than six, eight than seven, or ten than nine. Consequently, each new member of the European Community (Common Market) creates the possibility of—if not disassociation, that's too strong—but of loosening of that Community. That's precisely why I consider that, in the negotiations with Britain, the nature of the Community ties be emphasized.

Interview, Paris/
U.S. News & World Report, 3–2:45.

The Soviet Union and France are very close to each other in many respects . . . Traditional relations of friendship exist between our two people, which explains the fact that, despite differences, we consider contacts between leaders of the two countries useful and valuable. The French government remains committed to the policy pursued by President de Gaulle, which is in keeping with the deep and abiding interests of our two countries. France wants Franco-Soviet cooperation as an essential element for peace and stability in Europe and an important factor in world peace.

Paris, June 2/Daily World, 6–4:2

We are and we remain the allies of one side, cooperating at the same time with the others, without depending on anybody. (French policy intends) to repudiate none of its Western alliances and friendships, while desiring to enlarge its cooperation with the Eastern countries.

Before French Cabinet, Paris, Oct. 14/
The Washington Post, 10–15:A17.

Frenchmen, Frenchwomen. General de Gaulle is dead. France is a widow. In 1940, General de Gaulle saved our honor. In 1944, he led us to liberation and victory. In 1958, he saved us from civil war. To present-day France, he gave its institutions, its independence, its place in the world . . . Let us measure the duties which gratitude imposes on us. Let us promise France not to be unworthy of the lessons which have been given us. And may de Gaulle live eternally in the nation's soul.

Address to the nation, Paris, Nov. 10/
The Washington Post, 11–11:A2.

Enoch Powell
Member of British Parliament

The future of Britain is as much at risk now as in the years when imperial Germany was building dreadnoughts or Nazism rearming. Indeed, the danger is greater today just because the enemy is invisible or disguised. Other nations before now have remained blind and supine before a rising danger from within until it was too late . . . "Race" is billed to play a major, perhaps decisive, part in the battle of Britain, whose enemies must have been unable to believe their good fortune as they watched the numbers of West Indians, Africans and Asians concentrated in her major cities mount toward the two million mark.

Birmingham, England, June 13/
The New York Times, 6–14:(1)25.

Stanley R. Resor
Secretary of the Army of the United States

The record of Soviet military involvements since World War II shows that they are opportunists. They will use military forces as needed when they think they can do so without interference from the West. Incidents from the invasion of Hungary in 1956, to the Berlin crisis of 1961, to the Cuban missile emplacements in 1962, to the invasion of Czechoslovakia in 1968, forcibly demonstrate this. Were we to remove or significantly reduce our forces defending Western Europe, we would present the Soviets with new temptations. If we did, we could not predict precisely what would happen. But there surely would be a greater likelihood of threats, blackmail and attempts at domination, such as increased pressures on Berlin or on individual members of the NATO Alliance. Each such probe would carry with it the dangers of miscalculation, over-reaction and war. Without the presence of our forces, new power adjustments would have to be made. The course of readjustments would be dangerous. The ultimate result surely would be less favorable to the West . . . Soviet military forces could dominate Europe without ever being used, if there were no substantial forces to oppose them. No doubt the Soviets would prefer this. The case of Finland is an example. That sort of domination, rather than armed invasion, would be the most likely outcome of our unilateral withdrawal.

Before Los Angeles World Affairs Council,
April 10/Vital Speeches, 5–15:457.

Elliot L. Richardson
Under Secretary of State of the United States

A precipitate reduction of United States forces in Europe would . . . not only fail to stimulate additional European effort (for their own defense), it would probably produce the contrary effect. The bulk of any substantial reductions in U.S. forces would have to be made up by West Germany, the most populous and wealthy of our NATO allies. But the German people do not relish an enlargement of their country's military establishment. Nor, certainly, does a Soviet Union still highly emotional about its 20

(ELLIOT L. RICHARDSON)

million World War II dead and enormously sensitive on the subject of German "revanchism." Indeed, it would give pause even to some of Germany's allies. Any significant rise in the German defense effort could thus . . . halt the attempts to lay the foundation for a settlement of the issues still dividing Europe.

Before Chicago Council on Foreign Relations,
Jan. 20/The New York Times, 1–21:4.

When there is no more threat to the security of the nations of Western Europe, there will be no more need for NATO. And only when the confrontation in Europe truly ends and a genuine peace replaces the always precarious peace of mutual deterrence will the role of our troops be finally accomplished.

Before Chicago Council on Foreign Relations,
Jan. 20/The New York Times, 1–21:4.

Ironically . . . there exists among a younger generation of Europeans the . . . suspicion that the United States and the U.S.S.R. are collaborators in the defense of the status quo. But we intend to do everything possible to allay such fears and suspicions by sticking strictly to our pledge to consult closely with our allies and take their interests into account as talks go forward. Only by such close consultation can we quiet the Cassandras who see every effort at U.S.-Soviet rapprochement, or even minor moves to adjust force levels, as evidence of betrayal.

Before Chicago Council on Foreign Relations,
Jan. 20/Vital Speeches, 2–15:259.

William P. Rogers
Secretary of State of the United States

The goal of this decade is to heal the division between East and West which has been left over from the cold war. The division of Europe is, after all, an unnatural deed 25 years after the end of World War II. The time has surely come to end it.

San Francisco Examiner & Chronicle
(This World), 5–31:2.

Andrei Sakharov
Soviet physicist

Now, at the start of the '70s, we see that, having failed to catch up with America, we lag farther and farther behind.

Time, 5–4:35.

Walter Scheel
Foreign Minister of West Germany

With it (Soviet-West German non-aggression treaty) a new page should be opened in the relations between the Soviet Union and the Federal Republic of Germany (West Germany). At the same time, we are striving for better relations between East and West Europe. We made clear from the beginning that we were not only concerned with representing the interests of the Federal Republic. We want to contribute to a relaxation of tensions which will benefit all the peoples of East and West Europe. Our goal is to make possible more security and a flourishing good neighborliness. We are leaving Moscow with the feeling that we have created a solid foundation for achieving these goals.

Moscow, Aug. 7/
The Washington Post, 8–8:A1.

Ernst Scholz
Deputy Foreign Minister of East Germany

West Berlin is situated on the territory of the Deutsche Demokratische Republik (East Germany). Look at the map. We must recognize West Berlin is a political entity for itself. It didn't belong to West Germany. It doesn't belong to West Germany. And it will never belong to West Germany.

Interview, East Berlin/Look, 6–16:53.

Jean-Jacques Servan-Schreiber
Journalist; Member, French National Assembly

Those who govern Greece are the CIA and the American military.

Paris/Newsweek, 4–27:21.

Happily, the world is no longer as polarized as it used to be. Strong centrifugal forces are at work both in the East and in the West. Russia, no less than America, is learning the limitations of military might and developing dangerous internal cracks. The empire over which it presides is discovering the inevitable link between economic progress and human freedom. This is the tender sword which will open the East. In the last few years, the Eastern countries have given evidence of their desire to become integrated into the world economy. Communist planners are groping for new techniques to improve the competitive position of their economies and the standard of living of their people. Under these new conditions, international cooperation becomes imperative. If the Eastern countries wish to participate in the feast of industrial development, they can no longer afford the luxury of splendid isolation and the suppression of creative freedom. This process must be helped along, for it can help to reopen the East.

Before Congressional Foreign Economic
Policy Subcommittee, Washington, July 30/
The Washington Post, 8–2:B4.

The American commitment to defend Europe should be absolutely sacred, and I think it is. I think, for instance, to take one precise case, Berlin, to America and to all of us, is a sacred place to defend. This commitment, nobody really questions it, and this is good. But all the military bases, all the ground forces, all the divisions—why? It is costing money to America. It is making counter-American reaction in public opinion. It is not needed. It is useless technically. You don't need them to defend Europe. We don't need them.

Interview/Meet the Press,
National Broadcasting Company,
Washington, 8–2.

Leonard Shapiro
Professor, School of Economics and Political Science, University of London

Soviet policy is unremittingly dynamic. It is not directed toward achieving equilibrium, or balance of forces, or peace, or collective security, or certain specific concrete objectives; its ultimate aim is "victory," which means Communist rule on a world scale.

Before a United States Senate subcommittee/
U.S. News & World Report, 7–27:38.

Theodore C. Sorensen
Former Special Counsel to the President of the United States

. . . the Soviet Union should not keep in adherents of the Jewish faith who have been invited to settle in the state of Israel. I do not raise this question of Jewish emigration in order to embarrass the Soviet government. My advice to any government faced with this problem in any part of the world is simply this: However contrary such a desire to emigrate may be to your wishes, your customs, the desires of a majority of your population, or even your laws—let them go.

Moscow, April 13/
The New York Times, 4–14:2.

Paul-Henri Spaak
Former Premier of Belgium

Europe cannot be Europe without Britain. All we would have without her is the "little Europe" of the six (Common Market). None of us ever invisioned a Europe without Britain.

Interview, Brussels/
The Christian Science Monitor, 3–9:9.

I am amazed when (U.S. President) Nixon says he wants to reduce American dominance in Europe. When did the United States ever force us to do something in Europe we did not want to do?

Interview, Brussels/
The Christian Science Monitor, 3–9:9.

Willi Stoph
Prime Minister of East Germany

I wish to make a strong point of this: Recognition of the German Democratic Republic (East Germany) and of the status quo in

(WILLI STOPH)

Europe by the Federal German Republic (West Germany) . . . is a basic requirement of peace and security in Europe.

Kassel, West Germany, May 21/
The Washington Post, 5–22:A21.

We stick to realities. The destruction of the unity of the nation (Germany)—caused and completed after 1945 by the imperialist forces of West Germany in alliance with U.S. imperialism—cannot be made undone by any construction of ideas alleging a fictitious continued existence of the "unity of the nation."

Kassel, West Germany, May 21/
The Christian Science Monitor, 5–23:1.

Franz-Josef Strauss
Former Minister of Finance of West Germany

If we should offer to the Russians to throw the Americans out of Germany, to pull out of NATO, to reduce the Bundeswehr to 100,000 men and to equip them with nothing more than rifles, and if we offered not to discuss reunification until the year 2000 and agreed to give Soviet industry one billion marks of investment credit in West Germany, then they still would say that all these things had merely served as a good basis for further discussions.

The Washington Post, 4–19:A25.

This regime (of Chancellor Willy Brandt) must turn back or disappear. In the long run, its policies will destroy European unity and lead to the expansion of Soviet hegemony over Europe.

Bonn/Los Angeles Times, 6–2:(1)28.

Lubomir Strougal
Deputy First Secretary, Communist Party of Czechoslovakia

The mass media must ensure that there is only one line of thought in the country. There is no place for individual opinion.

Time, 2–9:28.

Mikhail A. Suslov
Secretary, Central Committee, Communist Party of the Soviet Union

Our country has made and will make the utmost effort to strengthen and preserve the general peace. But taking into account the continued activity of aggressive imperialist forces, the Communist Party and the Soviet government will demonstrate vigilance in all questions concerning the security of our state, will expose and short the perfidious designs of the imperialists, will tirelessly perfect and arm the Soviet Army and Navy with the most modern weapons, in order to give a crushing rebuff to anybody who dares attack the sacred frontiers of our homeland.

On eve of anniversary of Bolshevik
Revolution, Kremlin Palace of Congresses,
Moscow, Nov. 6/The Washington Post,
11–7:A12.

Ludvik Svoboda
President of Czechoslovakia

The Czechoslovak Army is well-trained, politically-conscious and loyal to the principles of proletarian internationalism. It stands shoulder-to-shoulder with the Soviet Army.

Karlovy Vary, Czechoslovakia, Aug. 18/
Daily World, 8–20:2.

Josip Broz Tito
President of Yugoslavia

We have no other interests than good relations as far as Albania is concerned. It has always been our wish to make our relations as good as possible. True, our systems are different; but this should not be a reason for poor relations on the frontiers.

Zabljak, Yugoslavia/
The New York Times, 8–23:(1)8.

. . . the status of Yugoslavia as an independent, non-aligned and socialist country is the unalterable basis of our entire policy and of our approach to international relations and problems.

Belgrade, Sept. 30/
Los Angeles Herald-Examiner, 10–1:A3.

Willem den Toom
Minister of Defense of the Netherlands

There is agreement among us (NATO members) that the U.S. must be kept in Europe, and we know that we should lighten their burden. Some elements in the United States are urging a cut-down of the U.S. effort in Europe. It is also known that the (Nixon) Administration is against this. But we have found the situation imperative enough to get together on the cost problem. We have reached no decision, but the result is that everybody is positive toward burden-sharing—even those who cannot go beyond a symbolic gesture.

Brussels, Oct. 1 / The Washington Post, 10–2:A16.

Helen Vlachos
Former Greek newspaper publisher

Does it matter if one is caged in a blue cage instead of a red one? He is still caged. The junta (now ruling Greece), instead of wiping out the underground, wiped out the overground—the establishment, businessmen, bankers, royalty. They literally hijacked the government like a strike of lightning. The army—our protectors—moved in on us. How can you protect yourself against your protectors? It was as if the bank guards took over the bank.

Interview, Los Angeles /
Los Angeles Times, 5–24:E1.

Otto von Hapsburg
Former heir-apparent to the throne of the Austro-Hungarian Empire

The nation-state is a thing of the past. We need to shape a new system for Europe that will go beyond national borders. Both monarchies and republics will have to change. Anyway, Europe's monarchies are crowned republics, and her republics are uncrowned monarchies.

Newsweek, 3–16:20.

Arthur K. Watson
Chairman, International Business Machines World Trade Corporation

In Western Europe, through the instrument of trade, we have forged physical bonds of interdependence and spiritual bonds of understanding that those nations had never known in all of history. Cooperation has replaced war. The writer, Peter Drucker, has called this world market the one enduring creation of the postwar period. I concur. It is this market, with all of its political and social implications, which we must nurture and perfect.

Before Joint Congressional Subcommittee
on Foreign Economic Policy, Washington /
The Wall Street Journal, 1–27:14.

Waldemar F.A. Wendt
Commander in Chief, United States Naval Forces-Europe

In just over 10 years, the Soviet Union has transferred herself from a maritime nonentity into a major sea power . . . Their excellence in naval missilery, electronics, fire control and hulls design is a fact Western experts must acknowledge . . . The swimming Russian Bear is not yet 10 feet tall, but he is five feet and growing rapidly. He has not yet wrested supremacy on the seas away from the free world, but he is making a very determined effort to do so.

Before Association of American Correspondents, London / San Francisco Examiner &
Chronicle, 3–1:A2.

Earle G. Wheeler
General, United States Army; Chairman, Joint Chiefs of Staff

I think if you start pulling back substantial numbers of (U.S.) troops from Europe, you're going to destroy NATO. It has been very evident over the years that the United States is not only the leading ally, the leading partner in NATO, but it is the American forces that are the cement that holds the NATO forces together. If you substantially reduce the number of American forces, I think that you're going to find an almost inevitable reduction in European NATO forces, because they will take the attitude: "Well, what's good enough for the United States is certainly good enough for us." As a

387

(EARLE G. WHEELER)

result, NATO would become an ineffectual instrument of a policy for peace.

*Interview, Washington/
U.S. News & World Report, 4–20:36.*

Wilfrid Hyde White
Actor

This precious stone set in the silver sea, this realm, this England, is nothing more than a floating casino.

Time, 4–20:28.

Harold Wilson
Prime Minister of the United Kingdom

If I were a football manager, I would be more worried about job security than I am as Prime Minister.

*London/The Christian Science Monitor,
4–4:B9.*

I am still fairly young, by Downing Street standards. Some of my most distinguished predecessors—for example, Attlee and Mac-

millan—began their premiership when they were 10 years older than I am today. I do not want that to be misconstrued as a threat.

*San Francisco Examiner & Chronicle,
5–10:A18.*

They (newly-elected Prime Minister Edward Heath and the Conservative Party) will have the strongest economic position of any Prime Minister who has taken over in living memory.

London/Los Angeles Times, 6–21:A7.

Stephen M. Young
United States Senator, D-Ohio

Throughout the last 24 years, the United States has girded its military power against international Communism. With the recognition that there is no longer even a hint of a monolithic Communist conspiracy to conquer the world, the last vestige of reason for us to maintain armed forces in Western Europe no longer exists.

*Before the Senate, Washington, March 2/
Congressional Record, 3–2:S2744.*

Mawlud Kamal Abed
Minister of Agriculture of Iraq

We are not Communists and we are not the opposite. We try to take the good from the Communists and the good from the capitalists. But we make our own rules.

Baghdad / The New York Times, 3–13:3.

Yigal Allon
Deputy Prime Minister of Israel

As long as Egypt doesn't shoot, we don't shoot. It has nothing to do with the agreement of August, 1970. We consider the cease-fire of 1967 still valid. In fact, we consider the cease-fire of 1948 still valid. Our willingness to stop fighting did not have to be reaffirmed by the American peace initiative.

Interview, Tel Aviv /
Washington Star, 10–6:A8.

Cleveland Amory
Author, Lecturer

What manner of madness is this in our (United States) State Department? What kind of muddle-headed, mealy-mouthed men are they? Well, I've been there, and I can tell you. They have a lot of so-called "Arabists" there. There's a so-called Egyptian desk, and a Jordanian desk, and a Syrian desk, and a Libyan desk, and so on. And, oh yes, there is also an Israeli desk. But when the chiefs of these desks move into the awesome offices of Secretary of State Rogers—well, it's very much, apparently, like a United Nations meeting. Because they all, evidently, have a vote. And the score comes out something like Arabists 12, Israelis 0 . . . In the sands of the Middle East, where there is, for the first time in recorded history, not just a real political democracy, but a true democracy of the human spirit—for this, America cannot even spare planes we had promised. Not give

them, mind you, nor lend them—not even, for God's sake, *sell* them . . . In a world where there is no Israel I do not wish to live, you do not wish to live and the United States of America does not *deserve* to live.

At Hadassah convention, Washington, Aug.
18 / Hadassah Magazine, 9:21.

Yasir Arafat
Leader of Al Fatah

We are just beginning to get ready for what will be a long, long war (with Israel)—a war that will run for generations. Ours is not the first generation to fight; the world tends to forget that in the '20s our fathers were already struggling against Zionist invaders. They were weak then, alone facing a strong opponent who had the support of the British, of the Americans, of the imperialists of the world. But we are strong now. Since January, 1965, the day Al Fatah was formed, we have become a very dangerous adversary for Israel. The fedayeen are acquiring experience, they are improving their guerrilla methods and their numbers are registering a phenomenal increase.

Interview / The Washington Post, 3–29:B1.

As Napoleon and Hitler were drowned in the snows of Russia, the sands of our deserts will swallow the Israelis. Our people can put up with many invasions. It is better to die as fighters than to die of hunger in the refugee camps. It is enough that, after 20 years in the tents, children born in the tents are still pointing their guns toward Haifa.

Interview / Time, 3–30:32.

American imperialism and its agents were responsible for the attempt to crush the Palestine Arab revolutionary movement . . . American intelligence thought that by

(YASIR ARAFAT)

threatening us with the 82nd Airborne Division they could frighten Arab resistance. If they are still thinking of sending the 82nd Division, we tell them, "Welcome to another Vietnam."

*News conference, Amman, Jordan /
San Francisco Examiner & Chronicle
(This World), 6–21:14.*

We don't want to oust King Hussein (of Jordan) because we don't want to be encumbered with the tasks of administration . . . We feel that elements in the government should resign themselves to the fact that we are here to stay and that they should cooperate with us rather than squash us, because they cannot do that.

*News conference, Amman, Jordan /
San Francisco Examiner & Chronicle
(This World), 6–21:14.*

(What militant Palestinians want is) a democratic, non-Zionist, secular state where we would all live in peace and equality as we did for thousands of years. If the Zionists would accept this principle, we could share power on a democratic basis. We would not insist on having an Arab majority.

Interview, Amman, Jordan / Time, 12–21:28.

Something is cooking in the international kitchen, but we are not going to be a sandwich. They are not going to give us a federation and then say that the Palestine question problem is solved, and forget about us. We are going back to Palestine some day—all of Palestine.

Interview, Amman / Time, 12–21:29.

Thomas L. Ashley
United States Representative, D-Ohio

In the Middle East, Israel is the outpost of democracy and freedom. It is in trouble because it is a free nation which respects the dignity of the individual man. If these precepts are driven from this rehabilitated cradle of civilization, they will be threatened all over the world. The democracies of this planet must mutually aid and support each other. When one is destroyed, all are threatened.

Quote, 11–8:445.

Anton Atalla
Foreign Minister of Jordan

I admire them (Palestinian guerrillas). I think most of them are sincere. However, few are realists. The fighting is not just between Palestinians and Jews. The two great super-powers (the United States and the Soviet Union) are determined to prevent a confrontation that is bound to come if the fighting continues and accelerates. And the acceleration is due to the fact that the United States is supporting Israel, not defensively as the Soviet Union is doing for Egypt, but offensively.

*Interview, Amman /
The New York Times, 8–20:3.*

Nureddin al Attassi
President of Syria

The knife which we have been swallowing for the past three years (since the 1967 Arab-Israeli war) shall be withdrawn, and we shall throw it in the face of anyone trying to touch the Arab revolution and the Syrian people. This is our battle, and we shall place all the potential of this country at the disposal of the Palestinian revolution.

*At trade union rally, Damascus, Sept. 20 /
Los Angeles Herald-Examiner, 9–24:A10.*

David Ben-Gurion
Former Prime Minister of Israel

Without Russia, no war is possible in the Middle East—and no peace either.

*Interview, Tel Aviv /
The Christian Science Monitor, 5–23:1.*

They (the Soviets) want to get the two oceans, the Atlantic and the Pacific. So, first of all, they must have the Mediterranean, and it is not easy to get that without the Arabs. They want the Arabs, but not because they like the Arabs. I do not think they are interested in destroying Israel, because if they do the Arabs will not need them.

Interview, Tel Aviv / Time, 6-1:20.

I blame (Egyptian President) Nasser more severely than I do any other Arab ruler, as I believe he at one time had the capacity, the vision and the means to improve his people's condition and to stop this futile merry-go-round of war.

Interview / The Washington Post, 10-12:A3.

Landrum R. Bolling
President, Earlham College, Richmond, Ind.

Israelis are deeply divided over the policies of their government since the end of the June war of 1967—on questions of boundary lines, on issues having to do with the rights of the Arab refugees and on the whole problem of how to attain security. Those Americans who make quick trips to Israel, talk to a few high officials and come back saying the Israelis are 100% behind (Prime Minister) Meir and all the Israeli government policies on matters having to do with war and peace don't know what they are talking about. The strength and diversity of dissent inside Israel is one of the best kept secrets about that country.

Before House Subcommittee on the Near East, Washington, July 24 / Daily World, 7-25:9.

Leonid I. Brezhnev
General Secretary, Communist Party of the Soviet Union

There is only one way to the peaceful solution in the Middle East—withdrawal of aggressor troops from the territories they occupy. It is necessary to make Israel respect decisions of such a lofty international body as the United Nations Security Council. The sooner the leaders of the United States realize how pointless and dangerous is their connivance with the Israeli aggressor, the sooner this can be achieved. The Arab peoples will never agree to capitulation and will never agree to perpetuation of occupation

of their lands; and this must be understood by all.

Kharkov, U.S.S.R., April 14 / The New York Times, 4-15:17.

The real goal of the Israeli aggression and of the policy pursued by the U.S. imperialist circles backing it is to abolish the progressive regimes in the U.A.R., Syria and a number of other Arab countries and to ensure conditions for the unhindered exploitation of the oil and other wealth of the Arab East by foreign monopolies. But powerful popular forces are now rising against the conspiracies of the imperialists. The Arab peoples are actively and staunchly defending their just cause. On their side are the Soviet Union and other socialist countries, and the communist and democratic movements of the whole world. One can confidently say that the cause of the imperialists is doomed and that the cause of the freedom of peoples is unconquerable!

Before Soviet Communist Party and Supreme Soviet, Moscow, April 21 / Vital Speeches, 6-1:496.

It is very important now for the peace forces in the Middle East not to let go of the initiative in settling the (Arab-Israeli) conflict, and not to allow the foes of peace to blow up the (cease-fire) agreement reached or use it to cover up their aggressive designs . . . There are opportunities now for approaching the settlement of the Middle East conflict from the position of realism and responsibility. What is needed now is not new provocations and subterfuges designed to circumvent or violate the cease-fire agreement, but an honest observance of the agreement reached and real steps in favor of peace.

Alma-Ata, U.S.S.R., Aug. 28 / The New York Times, 8-29:1.

George Brown
Deputy leader, British Labor Party; Former Foreign Minister of the United Kingdom

(Israeli Prime Minister Golda Meir is) a tough politician—I love her very much. But

391

I'm fond of Nasser, too. If you want peace, you have to love both peoples. The Jews are wrong to attack Nasser. I think he is an honest man.

London / Time, 3–2:41.

Michael Bruno
Chairman, Economics Faculty, Hebrew University, Jerusalem

The hawks in the Egyptian government pick up the hawkish positions of Israel to prove that nothing can be done. Just as the hawks in Israel point to their counterparts on the other side to prove that there is no alternative to the present impasse.

Newsweek, 4–20:57.

Jacques Chaban-Delmas
Premier of France

Our policy, which is aimed at peace, is carried out uniquely in the framework of the interests of F-r-a-n-c-e. We are neither pro- Israeli or pro-Arab, but pro-French.

Paris, Jan. 21 /
Los Angeles Times, 1–22:(1)10.

John H. Chafee
Secretary of the Navy of the United States

With the (Suez) Canal open, it was only 7,000 miles from Odessa (U.S.S.R.) in the Black Sea to Haiphong (North Vietnam), and the round trip took about two months. They (Russia) were able to put about 47 merchantmen a month into Haiphong. With the Canal closed, the 14,000-mile voyage around Africa takes about 72 days, the round trip nearly five months, and the number of Russian ships in Haiphong each month has been cut in half . . . Access to the Suez Canal means more to the Russians than it does to practically any other nation.

At Navy Day luncheon, Philadelphia, Oct. 27 /
Los Angeles Herald-Examiner, 10–28:A4.

Burhan Dajani
Palestinian writer on economic development

Until attitudes change, there is no way out of the impasse (Arab-Israel conflict). They (Israel) are the more dynamic force, the victors; and we the vanquished. We are the ones who need reassurance. So the initiative must come from the other side—and the Jewish intellectuals said so themselves. Westerners are always saying to us: "Be moderate; reassure them." But a moderate Israeli is someone who is less expansionist, while a moderate Arab is one who is more submissive. A substantial difference. We are not about to play the role of quislings during the German occupation of Europe. Our attitudes are very logical, not irrational.

Panel discussion, Beirut / Newsweek, 4–27:53.

Moshe Dayan
Minister of Defense of Israel

As far as military objectives are concerned, there are no limitations . . . all of Egypt is a field of battle, the theatre of our operations.

San Francisco Examiner & Chronicle
(This World), 2–1:14

I distinguish between a de facto state of peace and a signed peace treaty. I don't deprecate a peace treaty, but I also don't see it as a panacea. For instance, the Egyptians are signatories of the Geneva Convention on the treatment of prisoners of war; yet they refuse to let the Red Cross visit our pilots. But as to the question of the prospects of peace, even without any full formal and diplomatic expression of it, I assume that the present policy of the Arab governments will not pay off and that in two or three years the Arabs will have to take account and adopt a change of policy. They will soon reach the conclusion that they have no choice but to change from a policy of fighting us to a policy of peace.

National Observer, 2–2:10

The Soviets are not physically active in combat operations against us, and thank God. I'd be happier if it did not come to that. If the Soviet Union became actively involved in combat operations against Israel then the power to confront them would be the United States.

News conference, Jerusalem, June 23 /
Daily World, 6–24:2.

Suleyman Demirel
Prime Minister of Turkey

Our debts are high, but our credit is good. I would rather be a prosperous man with a debt and a future than a poor man free of debt and with no future.

Interview / Time, 7–27:21.

Abba Eban
Foreign Minister of Israel

Never in the history of Russia . . . has there ever been any regime like the Nasser regime (in Egypt) with a similar disposition to get the Russians into the Mediterranean. This is such an enormous service to Soviet strategy that, if Nasser didn't exist, the Soviet Union would want to invent him. He is a precious asset to the Soviet Union in terms of their broader strategy, which is not aimed in the first place at Israel but at getting the United States out of the Mediterranean and outflanking the European defense system. The Arab-Israeli struggle is a marginal expression of a much broader struggle.

Interview, Jerusalem, Jan. 21 /
Los Angeles Times, 1–22:(1)9.

Soviet penetration of the Mediterranean is carried out by exploiting the Arab-Israeli conflict. And, if that's true, it follows logically that the least hopeful way to try to solve the Arab-Israeli problem is through discussions with the Soviet Union.

Interview, Jerusalem, Jan. 21 /
The Washington Post, 1–22:A26.

France has become, with the Soviet Union, the most active element in upsetting the balance of security and peace in the Middle East. The answer is to look to the United States for equipment and loans and to increase our own self-sufficiency.

Before the Knesset (Parliament), Jerusalem /
Newsweek, 1–26:54.

The word "non-negotiable" is not in our vocabulary.

At Belgian Royal Institute for International
Relations, Brussels, Feb. 19 /
The New York Times, 2–20:47.

I know that all countries in Europe and the Federal Republic of Germany (West Germany) desire to strengthen their relations with other Middle Eastern states. But here is the difference: Israel does not interfere with the development of German-Arab relations. Alas, our neighbors try to interfere with the development of German-Israeli relations. And for this we have no other suggestion than that which I always give to all your compatriots, official and unofficial—to preserve our relationship in a watertight and separate and independent compartment.

Before German-Israeli Society, Bonn, Feb. 23 /
Abilene (Tex.) Reporter-News, 4–24:B2.

Provided that our security is maintained and our defense is not harmed, Israel is prepared to make an extra effort and make concessions (to the Arabs) that would startle the world.

Jerusalem, May 6 /
Los Angeles Times, 5–7:(1)2.

The relationship of this problem (Egyptian violation of current cease-fire) to peace talks is very direct . . . peace would depend, to some extent, on the confidence placed by the contracting states in the integrity and validating of their signed commitments. The violation of an Egyptian signature on an existing agreement does not create a good atmosphere for talks on another, more far-reaching agreement. The six-day war (of 1967) is a case history on the fragility of international guarantees, commitments, assurances.

News conference, Jerusalem, Aug. 17 /
The Washington Post, 8–18:A12.

My diagnosis is that they (the Soviet Union) are in an expanding, dynamic mood and that they want to achieve certain objectives not all connected with the Middle East. They want to outflank the defense system of Europe in the south, which means the position in the Mediterranean. They have obtained a military foothold in Egypt, which, after all, is part of Africa. They are trying to change the whole international equilibrium between themselves and the U.S. The United States and the West should understand the need to put roadblocks in the way of that policy.

Interview/Los Angeles Herald-Examiner, 10–13:A8.

We can't go around saving everybody's face except our own. If one says that to violate an agreement (Egyptian violation of Middle East cease-fire) creates a situation whereby to respect the agreement (to admit to the violation) is a loss of face, then we reach a point of moral anarchy. We cannot accept the idea that honoring an agreement is a loss of face whereas violating an agreement is a legitimate indulgence of face. If we were to reconcile ourselves to this violation, we would lose not only face but security and honor. We would reduce the peace dialogue to absurdity because the principle at stake is the integrity of agreements.

Interview/San Francisco Examiner, 10–14:14.

The United States must help us maintain our strength; it must see we are not crushed economically; it must continue to maintain that we do not have to withdraw from the Arab-Israeli truce line without peace; and the United States must deter the Soviet Union intervention so as not to risk confrontation.

Before Commonwealth Club, San Francisco, Nov. 14/ San Francisco Examiner & Chronicle, 11–15:A22.

Israel wants total peace without total withdrawal, while Egypt wants total withdrawal without total peace.

Time, 12–14:30.

Arie L. Eliav
Secretary general, Labor Party of Israel

True, our forefathers lived here and in Jordan. But so did the Arabs. The solution has to be that two states can live equally together. There is ample place for a Jewish state as big as Holland, with 10 million people, and an Arab state as big as Belgium, with 9 million. I think we should recognize a legitimate Arab national movement.

Interview, Tel Aviv/Time, 1–26:26.

Faisal (Ibn Abdel Aziz al-Saud)
King of Saudi Arabia

. . . Zionism and Communism are working hand in glove to block any settlement to restore peace (in the Middle East) . . . It's all part of a great plot, a grand conspiracy. Communism is a Zionist creation designed to fulfill the aims of Zionism. They are only pretending to work against each other in the Mideast. The Zionists are deceiving the U.S. into believing they are on their side. The Communists, on the other hand, are cheating the Arabs, making them believe that they are on their side. But actually, they are in league with the Zionists.

Interview, Riyadh, Saudi Arabia/ Newsweek, 12–21:43.

Mahmoud Fawzi
Prime Minister of the United Arab Republic

We (Egypt) are menaced by ignorance in a world where there is no dignity or power without scientific development . . . and no false pretensions of pride should close our eyes to this fact . . . Ultimately, we shall be free from Israel's threat, and, when we do that, we will be facing up to the bigger threat —ignorance.

Interview/Los Angeles Times, 11–2:(1)7.

J. William Fulbright
United States Senator, D-Ark.

. . . it wasn't too long ago that the Arabs and the Jews got along very well. They used to live together . . . They are both of a

Semitic background. And if the Germans can make up with the Russians, why in the world can't the Arabs make up with the Jews, if given proper circumstances and some adjustment to the obvious injustices that have taken place in this area? Goodness knows, I don't minimize the provocation on both sides . . . but I think it is possible that this can be worked out. I mean, we see now the French and the Germans aren't so apprehensive; but, above all, this recent move between Russia and Germany—why, every time I have been over there in Eastern Europe, they all still hated the Germans no end, and they feared them. Now, it looks as if progress is being made. So we have to have some confidence in human nature . . .

Interview/Meet the Press,
National Broadcasting Company,
Washington, 8–23.

The myths that shape events in the Middle East are the oldest myths of all. Some derive from religion. The contested land is a "holy" land; more than a place for raising crops and building cities, it is a "sacred soil" for three great religions. Neither can hold exclusive title to the city (Jerusalem) without also owning the other faith's shrine. Now, as in the days of the crusades, religion exacerbates the issue; because, now as then, the behavior of the belligerents is more affected by the zeal with which they hold their beliefs than by the humane ethics taught by their respective religions. Now, as in the past, it is hard to strike a bargain over sacred soil.

Before the Senate, Washington, Aug. 24 /
The New York Times, 8–23:(1)22.

For reasons of varying merit, Israel has indicated on numerous occasions a lack of confidence in the United Nations. In order to accommodate this attitude and provide Israel with an added assurance of security, I for one would be willing to supplement a United Nations guarantee with a bilateral treaty—not an executive agreement, but a treaty consented to by the Senate—under which the United States would guarantee the

territory and independence of Israel within the borders of 1967.

Before the Senate, Washington, Aug. 24 /
The New York Times, 8–23:(1)1.

The weight of evidence indicates that the Russians do indeed want a compromise settlement in the Middle East (of the Arab-Israeli conflict). They would welcome the re-opening of the Suez Canal, relief from the heavy costs of arming Egypt and a reduction of great-power tensions . . . I believe that they've come to their senses.

Before the Senate, Washington, Aug. 24 /
San Francisco Examiner & Chronicle,
8–23:A1.

I have never fully understood why some of our statesmen feel that it would be a heinous crime for external parties to "impose" a solution (to the Arab-Israeli conflict). Under the United Nations Charter the Security Council has full authority—possibly even the obligation—to impose a settlement upon warring parties who fail to make peace on their own. I think it would be a fine thing, a useful step forward for civilization, if, in the absence of a voluntary settlement by the parties, the United Nations were to "impose" a peaceful settlement in the Middle East.

Before the Senate, Washington, Aug. 24 /
The New York Times, 8–23:(1)22.

The Middle East, in geo-political terms, is something far more abstract than an oil-rich desert contested by feuding Semitic peoples. Beyond that, it is the "gateway to the East," "the Hinge of NATO" and the crucial cockpit of the historic Russian drive toward warm water.

Before the Senate, Washington, Aug. 24 /
The New York Times, 8–23:(1)22.

Barry Goldwater, Jr.
United States Representative, R-Calif.

The future stability of both Israel and the entire free world depends in part upon the continued strength of the Jewish state. With the aggression being demonstrated by the Soviets in the Middle East, I believe it extremely important for Israel to become a member of NATO . . . The only position the Communists respect is military power; and I believe the admittance of Israel to NATO will clearly demonstrate the free world's resolve to back up this small, free Middle East nation in its battle for survival.

Before Encino B'nai B'rith, Studio City, Calif., Oct. 21 / Los Angeles Herald-Examiner, 10–22:A16.

George Habash
Leader, Popular Front for the Liberation of Palestine

In this war Israel is not our only enemy. Our enemy is Israel, plus the Zionist movement that controls many of the countries which support Israel, plus imperialism. I mean, specifically, British imperialism from 1918, and American imperialism from 1948 on. If we had to face Israel alone, the problem would have been almost a simple one.

Interview, Amman, Jordan / Life, 6–12:32.

The attacks of the Popular Front are based on quality, not quantity. We believe that to kill a Jew far from the battleground has more of an effect than killing 100 of them in battle; it attracts more attention. And when we set fire to a store in London, those few flames are worth the burning down of two kibbutzim. Because we force people to ask what is going on, and so they get to know our tragic situation. You have to be constantly reminded of our existence. After all, world opinion has never been either with us or against us; it has just kept on ignoring us.

Interview, Amman, Jordan / Life, 6–12:33.

We have to stand against whoever supports Israel economically, militarily, politically, ideologically. This means . . . the U.S. and almost every country in Europe . . . Our struggle has barely begun. The worst is yet to come. And it is right for Europe and

America to be warned now that there will be no peace for them until there is justice for Palestine.

Interview, Amman, Jordan / The New York Times, 9–13:(4)1.

We (Palestinians) do not wake up in the morning as you (non-Palestinians) may, to have a cup of milk or coffee and then sit for half an hour in front of a mirror or think of flying for a month's vacation somewhere. We live daily in camps. Our wives wait to see whether they will get water at 10 o'clock or 12 o'clock or 3 o'clock in the afternoon. We cannot be calm as you, think as you think. And we have been living in these conditions not for days, or weeks, or months, but for 23 years. If any one of you can come to live in one of these camps for only two weeks, you will never be the same again.

Before a group of his former hostages, Amman, Jordan, June / The Christian Science Monitor, 9–16:2.

We do not want peace. Peace would be the end of all our hopes. We shall sabotage any peace negotiations in the future.

Interview / Time, 9–28:24.

Raymond A. Hare
Former United States Ambassador to the United Arab Republic; Chairman, Middle East Institute

(U.A.R. President) Nasser's death will be a serious blow to our (peace) efforts. Here was a man of great prestige among the Arabs, who had accepted the U.S. peace proposals. Suddenly, with these efforts already resisted by the Palestinians, this man vanished from the scene. Nobody, really, is going to replace him. He was unique. Nasser came up from the people with a strong sense of dignity as an Arab, plus a strong sense of shame in the state of the Arabs' economic and social condition. He had an ability to transmit his feelings to his fellow Arabs, to be one with them. To the day of his death, this never changed. No matter what Egyptian succeeds

Nasser as President, he will not have what Nasser had. This does not go with the job.

Interview, Washington/
U.S. News & World Report, 10–12:20.

Mohammed Hassanein Heikal
Editor, "Al Ahram," Cairo

Speaking frankly as an editor, and not as an official, let me stress that Egypt's defeat in 1967 was not entirely an Israeli victory. One of the things that the Israelis really succeeded in convincing us of was our mutual Arab destiny. Before the war, we used to talk about one destiny, but that was mostly sentimental nostalgia. The Israelis changed that. They made the Egyptian people realize that their own land is threatened, that they are subjected to the same dangers that have eaten at Palestine bit by bit. Now, for the first time, the Egyptians are fighting because they are defending themselves—it's happening to them.

Interview, Cairo/Newsweek, 6–29:36.

In our fight, we are indebted very much to Soviet know-how—but less than the Israelis are indebted to the Americans. After all, we were not created by the Soviet Union as Israel was by the big powers . . . Our independence is not for sale, neither to you (the United States), nor to any other nation. The independence of Egypt is not for hire, not for lease, not for anything.

Interview, Cairo/Newsweek, 6–29:36.

Charles Helou
President of Lebanon

It is truly strange that in the late 20th century Zionists resort to napalm to explain prophecies about a state (Israel) that run counter to the course of history . . . It is truly strange that a people (the Jews), who have tasted the bitterness of persecution outside the Arab world, have become the persecutors.

Before World Conference of Christians for
Palestine, Beirut, May 7/
The Christian Science Monitor, 5–11:7.

The enemy (Israel) alleges that its aim is to halt resistance activities undertaken by Palestinians . . . and to seek revenge from Lebanon which permits these activities. The world has learned from history that attempts to strike at resistance forces only increase their violence. Israel is aware of this. In every Arab country, and even in the territories it occupies, it faces increased resistance every time it increases the violent measures which it takes to crush this resistance.

Before Lebanese Cabinet, Beirut/
The Christian Science Monitor, 5–14:1.

Hussein I
King of Jordan

The power of the (Palestinian) commandos is our power. And our power is their power.

News conference, Amman, Feb. 14/
The New York Times, 2–16:8.

Basically, we have two requirements for peace: (1) Israeli withdrawal from all territories occupied in 1967—and that includes Jerusalem; (2) The right of self-determination for the Palestinian people. As far as Jerusalem goes, we would be willing to accept its internationalization as outlined by the 1948 United Nations plan. But it would have to be internationalization of the entire city, not just of its Arab part. Internationalizing merely Arab Jerusalem would be totally unacceptable to us. I've always said that the Israelis can have either peace or territory, but not both.

Interview, Amman/Newsweek, 8–31:36.

I was fooled by the intelligence services—consciously, no doubt. Honeycombed with sympathizers or agents of the Palestinian (guerrilla) organization, they presented me with an idyllic picture of the situation (the guerrilla-government war in Jordan), assuring me that we would overcome the resistance in a few hours. At the beginning of operations, I realized that the enemy knew perfectly the plans for intervention which the general staff had made in case we should have to resort to force. And, progressively,

(HUSSEIN I)

I realized that the state, from top to bottom, was infiltrated by the commandos. I was shocked to learn a few days ago that my own chauffeur, to whom I confided my children, was a terrorist. He was arrested just as he was firing a mortar at my palace . . . I have just discovered, moreover, that my cook occupies important functions in one of the Palestinian organizations . . .

Interview, Amman/
The Washington Post, 9–26:A1.

I have no intention, at least in the foreseeable future, of calling on the world of politicians (to form a civilian government). I have had enough of those who make a career by presenting themselves as conciliators; men who call themselves, at the same time, friends of the throne and of the fedayeen, while, at the same time, telling the latter that we have no other idea in mind than to destroy then . Besides, our country needs a disciplined, active, effective government, which only the Army can provide until there is new order.

Interview, Amman/
The Washington Post, 9–26:A16.

It is not pleasant to be in my position. The responsibility is very heavy. I feel the weight of it all the time. And also the fears; the fears that I might not succeed in one particular objective: creating for Jordan a system that can last independent of an individual—in this case, myself.

Interview, near Amman/Life, 11–20:50.

. . . unfortunately, the Israelis have suspicions and continue to seek "secure" and "recognized" boundaries. Recognized boundaries well and good. But secure boundaries in this time and age do not exist, except if there is justice and a desire on both sides to maintain a state of peace.

Television interview/
San Francisco Examiner, 12–14:8.

Henry M. Jackson
United States Senator, D-Wash.

If there were no Arab-Israeli conflict, the Soviets would invent one. The flagrant exploitation of the tragic conflict between Arabs and Jews ranks high among the cynical designs of Russia's postwar policy.

Washington, Dec. 21/
Los Angeles Times, 12–22:(1)16.

Alexei N. Kosygin
Premier of the Soviet Union

Let the Israeli extremists be under no illusion that they will be able to gain something for their consent to a peaceful settlement in the Middle East. Nobody asks from Israel and its imperialist patrons peace at any price. The principles the peoples are guided by in the struggle for their national liberation, independence and freedom, cannot be bought or sold. This should be learned well by the Israeli aggressors.

Moscow, Dec. 21/
The New York Times, 12–22:8.

John Law
Member, International Staff, "U.S. News & World Report"

It's certainly by no means irrevocable (Soviet hold on Egypt). I don't think the Egyptians, because they're getting all this help from the Soviets, desire or expect to be permanently dependent on them. Which is all the more reason, of course, why it might be in the Soviet interest to make sure the Arabs never do destroy Israel, because this keeps the Arabs dependent on having the Soviets on hand. (Egyptian President) Nasser is fond of saying—only partly in jest—that the creditor is really dependent on the debtor, rather than the other way around, because the creditor is always afraid the debtor might say: "I won't pay." In any case, even after all these years of Soviet presence, the Egyptians are still basically oriented toward the West. Most of the people who run Egypt have had their education in Western-type institutions, or even in the West itself. English is their second language, not Russian. They love to go to American movies. You don't find crowds lining up in front of the Soviet movies in Cairo.

Interview/U.S. News & World Report, 6–29:55.

Yakov Malik
Soviet Ambassador to the United Nations

If Israel did not receive a single bullet for a year, they would still be sufficiently armed to fight the Arabs.

The Dallas Times Herald, 4–17:2A.

Mike Mansfield
United States Senator, D-Mont.

Israel is going to have to get down off its high horse . . . We have no commitments in that part of the world.

Before National Press Club,
Washington, July 10/
Los Angeles Times, 7–11:(1)2.

George S. McGovern
United States Senator, D-S.D.

The feeling of the Palestinians that they have unjustly lost their homes and property is perhaps the most important single source of tension and conflict in the Middle East. A unilateral act of Israel recognizing that fact could be the greatest single step toward peace.

Before the Senate, Washington, July 18/
The New York Times, 7–21:2.

Golda Meir
Prime Minister of Israel

Nasser (President of the UAR) is frustrated, not because Egypt has the lowest income and the highest infant mortality rate in the world, but because he tried three times to throw us into the sea and the poor man did not succeed.

Los Angeles Herald-Examiner 1–13:A3.

The most that any one of them (Arabs) ever said is, "Peace in the Middle East—that would be very nice, if it weren't that there were three wars between the Arabs and Israel." Not one of them has come out with a statement that they want peace and to live

in peace with Israel. There must be a specific "We want peace with Israel; we want to live with it in peace." Next best, in the meantime, "No shooting" . . . We say to the Arabs, "All right. You don't want to have peace, you don't want to negotiate—but in the meantime, let's just stop the shooting; let's just stop the killing on both sides."

Interview, Tel Aviv, Feb. 2/
The Washington Post, 2–27:A12.

We never asked for equality with Arabs in arms. We don't even dare ask for that. We never said plane for plane and tank for tank. But there is a certain point where the imbalance is such that it's suicide.

Interview, Tel Aviv, Feb. 6/
The New York Times, 2–8:(1)32.

Not out of weakness and not out of the pride of victors we appeal to the Arab nations and their rulers to end this chapter of bloodshed and to enter negotiations for peace—peace between equals, preserving national honor, respecting the sovereignty of all the states in the region. As long as there is no peace, we repeat the call to observe the cease-fire; in other words, to stop the killing. We are ready.

Before the Knesset (Parliament), Jerusalem,
Feb. 17/The New York Times, 2–18:3.

The lesson of Czechoslovakia must not be forgotten. If the free world—and particularly the United States, which is its leader—can pass on to the next item on the agenda without any attempt at deterrence, when the Soviet Union, in its selfish policy, reaches such a degree of involvement in a dispute with which it has no connection, then not only Israel is endangered by that involvement, but no small or even medium-sized nation can dwell in safety within its frontiers.

Before the Knesset (Parliament), Jerusalem,
May 26/The New York Times, 5–27:3.

With them (the Arabs) we have to live and, therefore, with them we have to negoti-

(GOLDA MEIR)

ate. If they do not want to negotiate with us, how can they be expected to live with us?

Jerusalem, June 22/
The Washington Post, 6–23:A16.

If I thought I had let even the smallest chance for peace get away, I could not in all conscience today hold the post of Premier. We've done everything—do you hear me?—everything.

Interview/Los Angeles Times, 7–13:(1)4.

The ultimate aim of Soviet policy in the Middle East is actually to take possession of the entire area, and even not to stop there. From there to Europe, North Africa, the Indian Ocean, and so on, is their ultimate aim. The Soviets have been testing the Western world for the last few months. When they brought in the SAM 3's (missiles)—with Russian personnel to operate these very complicated, sophisticated weapons—they stopped and listened. Nothing happened. So they kept on, took another step. Pilots were brought in. Again they stopped and listened. Again, nothing happened. Now they are moving closer to the canal. I am sure they don't want war with the Western world. That's the one thing they don't want. But if the West doesn't tell them, "thus far and no further," they will just go on. They now seem to believe—I hope without any justification—that they can go on because it's only little Israel.

Interview, Jerusalem/
Los Angeles Herald-Examiner, 7–16:A10.

It would be naive to think that we and the Arabs could sit at a table and that we could reach a peace agreement in a couple of hours. It will probably take days, maybe weeks, maybe months. But we can reach agreement if the Arabs are willing to live in peace with us. But when the Arabs say, "We can't sit with you in the same room, or at the same table," and somebody else says the delegations should be in different hotels—God for-

bid that we should be in the same hotel—this is not the kind of procedure to be followed by two peoples who really want peace. If the Arabs can't bear to be with us in one room, then they are not prepared to live with us, and negotiations, no matter what the procedure, are meaningless.

Interview, Jerusalem/
Los Angeles Herald-Examiner, 7–16:A10.

It is too glib to say that the current struggle in the Middle East is one between two rights and that one side can only flourish at the expense of the other. Had the Arabs not striven so zealously to destroy the Jewish State since its establishment by international consensus, our dream of peaceful cooperation with our Arab neighbors might have been achieved to the profit of the whole Middle East. For we compromised again and again in the interests of peace, but no concession was enough.

Interview, Jerusalem/
Los Angeles Herald-Examiner, 8–30:B7.

There have been many people in the world that have lost wars, whose countries have been invaded and taken over by foreign powers. It is tragic, extremely unpleasant. But the people remained; and, therefore, there was always a hope and an attempt made that some day they will throw out the foreign power and they will be themselves again on their own soil. This isn't what awaits Israel if it should come out of this (conflict with the Arabs) defeated. Because what our enemies promise us is not merely an invasion of the country and overtaking the rule of the country and so on, but the expulsion from the country. And since we know of that twice in our history before in olden times, we are certainly not going to do this, no matter what happens. We have no choice. We have to protect ourselves to the very end . . .

Interview/Issues and Answers,
American Broadcasting Company, 9–20.

The question we all face—Israelis and

Arabs alike—is whether we forfeit our right to decide our own destiny. That question will only be resolved in the measure that the people of the Middle East succeed or fail in making peace among themselves by themselves, without hindrance or intervention of any outside power. Recent events in the Middle East have proven yet again that resort to substitutes and alternatives for direct peaceful solution of the conflict creates fertile ground for breaches of promise and mutual suspicion.

At United Nations, N.Y., Oct. 21/
Los Angeles Times, 10–22:(1)4.

A French paper asked whether I would consent to negotiate with Arafat (Yasir Arafat, leader of the Popular Front for the Liberation of Palestine). I said, "Arafat, head of a terrorist movement whose aim is to kill Jews, no. If Arafat becomes the head of Jordan or Palestine, call it anything he wishes, I would negotiate with him. I was prepared to negotiate with (Egyptian President) Nasser, not because of my special love for Nasser —may he rest in peace—but we are interested in peace with our neighbors and will negotiate with any representative of any Arab state —not with terrorist organizations."

New York, Oct. 25/Hadassah magazine, 12:7.

With all our skepticism about the negotiations under (Gunnar) Jarring's auspices, there is hope that, maybe, it could lead to peace. This depends entirely on whether the other side is really interested and prepared to come to a peace agreement which will do away with future wars. This is really the basic condition. If this desire on the part of the Arab governments exists, then there is hope. If they are coming to the Jarring talks in a mood of serving us ultimatums and timetables, this is the blueprint for the failure of the talks.

Interview, Tel Aviv, Dec. 19/
The New York Times, 12–27:(1)18.

With the changing of the guard in Egypt, we hope the new leadership will follow the path of peace. I call again on the Egyptian leaders to open a new page in relations between our states. The Israeli government is ready for this with all its heart.

Before the Knesset (Parliament), Jerusalem,
Dec. 29/Los Angeles Times, 12–30:(1)18.

Gamal Abdel Nasser
President of the United Arab Republic

France stood by our side in its demands for justice and refused to help the aggressor (Israel, in 1967 war), unlike the U.S. which supplied him with weapons, arms and soldiers. France asked for total evacuation of Arab territory. Because of all this, we consider that France is in the position of a friend . . .

At Sudan's 14th independence anniversary,
Khartoum, Jan. 1/
The Christian Science Monitor, 1–5:4.

We seek peace and not surrender, and there's a great difference between the two.

U.S. News & World Report, 1–26:14.

The Arab nation has no other alternative but to pursue its fight (to recover Israeli-occupied Arab territory)—no matter what the sacrifices . . . The Arab nation is facing a crisis unparalleled in modern history. It is a crisis of human conscience, the crisis of mankind which has been able to conquer space and to reach the moon but has been unable to bring justice to earth.

Before an international parliamentary
conference, Cairo, Feb. 2/
The New York Times, 2–3:7.

You can have a collection of my speeches, my interviews—there is no single word about sending the Israelis into the sea.

Interview, Cairo, Feb. 8/
The Dallas Times Herald, 2–8:A23.

If really everyone wants peace, we want peace. But what is peace to us? Peace means the complete evacuation of the occupied territory (by Israel), as I said, including Jerusalem; and, after that, the recognition of Israel

(GAMAL ABDEL NASSER)

to exist, the freedom of navigation in the Suez Canal. Then there will be peace. There will be no need of police forces, no need of demilitarized zones; because if we solve the refugee problem, and Israel agrees to borders without expansion, there will be a solution. This problem went on 20 years because there was no solution of the refugee problem, and if there will be no solution it will continue for another 20 years. I hope you understand me.

Interview, Cairo, Feb. 13/
The New York Times, 2–15:(1)18.

The United States does what the Israelis say. The Israelis say they want direct negotiations with the Arab states; that's what the United States has said. The United States has said it wants to negotiate secure and recognized boundaries; that's what the Israelis said, too. The United States wants to see negotiated agreements about the Gulf of Aqaba; that's what the Israelis have said.

Interview, Cairo, Feb. 13/
The New York Times, 2–15:(1)18.

The American position, as exposed by (U.S. Secretary of State William P.) Rogers, entirely adopts that of Israel. The delivery of heavy bombers to Tel Aviv is the proof that Washington wants Israel to break Arab resistance. The Americans have sought to overthrow the Egyptian regime since 1965. Their strategic objective is to provoke the fall of progressive Arab governments, especially since the revolutions that occurred last year in the Sudan and Libya. They are using Israel as the instrument of their policy.

Interview, Cairo/The New York Times, 2–19:2.

Why didn't the United States negotiate after Pearl Harbor? The Japanese asked you to do so, but you refused. You refused because you were being invited to a table of capitulation and surrender, not to negotiations. That's just how we feel today. No Arab can negotiate with Israel when they occupy

one seventh of our territory, our Egyptian territory.

Interview, Cairo/
U.S. News & World Report, 5–18:60.

. . . we must understand who these (Palestinian) commandos are. These are the people, or their sons, who were expelled from their homes in 1948 and in 1967. These are the Arabs who lived in the Palestine which Mrs. Meir (Prime Minister of Israel) says no longer exists. These are the people who want to go back to their homes or want to be given just recompense for the loss of their homes . . . How can any Arab leader deny justice to these Arabs? You ask whether Arab governments can "control" them. We cannot seek to "control" them if this means denying them the right to seek justice. It is Israel alone that can right this wrong.

Interview, Cairo/
U.S. News & World Report, 5–18:61.

The Israeli leaders always portray us as people who want war. This is not so. We not only want peace, we are the ones who accept UN resolutions about peace. They are the ones who reject them. Understand this: Nasser wants peace. I want peace. I do not want war for war's sake. I am not a bloodthirsty military conqueror. I have not been an active soldier for 18 years. Before that time, I learned to hate war as much as, or more, than any man. In 1948 I saw enough war. I buried my Egyptian comrades in the field. I buried Israeli men, too. I do not like war; I hate it. The Israelis tell you: Nasser does not want peace. I certainly do. But what I want is not the peace of capitulation and surrender to expanding Israeli power. I want peace with dignity, a peace that can be obtained between reasonable men.

Interview, Cairo/
U.S. News & World Report, 5–18:63.

. . . I have absolutely no hope for a settlement, because I read all the statements made by Israeli officials and they all want expansion (of Israeli territory). I also read the statements made by American congressmen and governors and they all want modification of Israel's borders—in other words, expansion. I will never surrender one inch of Arab territory—whether in Egypt, Syria or Jordan—because this is not my right and it is not possible.

> *At Arab Socialist Union Congress, Cairo,*
> *July 24/Los Angeles Herald-Examiner,*
> *7–25:A2.*

For Israel to be able to fly its airplanes over Cairo any time it wants is as humiliating to me as it would be to you (an American) if the Cubans were able to fly over Washington and your armed forces were powerless to stop them.

> *Interview/The Washington Post, 10–1:A14.*

Western papers say that I am going to become another Czechoslovakia. How do you think these Russian technicians are going to seize power? I have my army, my police and no Communist Party. What are they going to do—march on Cairo?

> *Time, 10–12:26.*

Gaafar al Nimeiry
President of Sudan

I would say that the first enemy of the Arab nation is Zionism, represented by the state of Israel. The state of Israel has many expansionist aims against the Arab state. The state of Israel is an agent of the United States, which acts in cooperation with Israel in the plot against the Arab people.

> *News conference, Cairo, Sept. 26/*
> *The New York Times, 9–27:(1)28.*

Richard M. Nixon
President of the United States

The United States stands by its friends. Israel is one of its friends . . . The United States is prepared to supply military equipment necessary to support the efforts of friendly governments, like Israel's, to defend the safety of their people. We would prefer restraint in the shipment of arms to this area. But we are maintaining a careful watch on

the relative strength of the forces there, and we will not hesitate to provide arms to friendly states as the need arises.

> *Jan. 25/U.S. News & World Report, 6–15:30.*

I've noticed several recent stories indicating that the United States one day is pro-Arab and the next day is pro-Israel. We are neither pro-Arab nor pro-Israel. We are pro-peace. We are for security for all the nations in that area.

> *News conference, Washington, Jan. 30/*
> *The New York Times, 1–31:14.*

Once the balance of power shifts where Israel is weaker than its neighbors, there will be a war. Therefore, it is in the United States' interests to maintain the balance of power . . . we will do what is necessary to maintain Israel's strength vis-a-vis its neighbors—not because we want Israel to be in a position to wage war, that isn't it; but because that is what will deter its neighbors from attacking it.

> *Television interview, Los Angeles, July 1/*
> *The New York Times, 7–5:(4)10.*

Bertram L. Podell
United States Representative, D-N.Y.

France has now joined Russia as a major purveyor of arms to the Arabs. French duplicity has shocked the civilized world. Her recent actions speak louder than her past professions of Liberte, Egalite and Fraternite . . . There must be some explanation when a highly-civilized nation, a nation that inspired the American Revolution, betrays a friend. We would be wrong to conclude that the people of France have suddenly become anti-Semites. But we can be quite correct in assuming that the Pompidou government of France is following the cynical, two-faced policy of Charles de Gaulle—and is going even a step further. France is not motivated by hatred of Israel; nor is her policy attached to any easily-recognizable ideals. Rather, her foreign policy is being determined by oil. In this case, justice is being compromised for oil. For this reason, France is ready to build

(BERTRAM L. PODELL)

up the military power of the radical and aggressive Arab states against Israel. The French government is not motivated by considerations of peace or of honor. French policy is based on false dreams of grandeur, power and wealth—which she is willing to achieve at any price . . . France is also motivated by a dream of empire in the Mediterranean . . . France dreams of dividing power with Russia in the Mediterranean. But this will be only illusionary power. The French will sell out freedom and gain nothing but contempt in return. The smile will be on the face of the Russian bear—and Paris may once again burn.

Before the House, Washington, Jan. 28/
Congressional Record, 1–28:H479.

Georges Pompidou
President of France

Anyone can see that France is always seeking ways to reconcile the assertion that Israel has an absolute right to exist, to function freely and to live in peace within safe, recognized borders, with our refusal to recognize Israel's right of military conquest. Everyone should understand that France has not forgotten the Nazi martyrdom of European Jews, including French Jews, whose courage during the ordeal earned the admiration of all our people. However, France also intends to maintain and develop its ancient ties with most of the Moslem world and, more particularly, with the Arab countries. In the Middle East crisis, France wants and seeks only peace—a peace which I believe is indispensable to everyone, and first of all to Israel.

Interview, Paris, Feb. 10/
The New York Times, 2–15:(1)22.

The capital of France is not Cairo, but I must say it isn't Tel Aviv either . . . we seek peace in the Mediterranean and peace in general. We are not against Israel. We had extremely close relations with it. When I read of the Israeli air superiority over the Arabs, I must note that it is the French Mirages that fly in the skies; and they are Israeli.

Before National Press Club, Washington,
Feb. 24/The New York Times, 2–25:12.

Judging its existence threatened, the state of Israel has started a preventive action which has brought it undeniable success on the battlefield. France has indicated her position in terms which have often been criticized or misunderstood. Faithful to the United Nations resolution for which our two countries voted, I reaffirm here the right of the state of Israel not only to existence but also to security and the free exercise of all the rights of an independent and sovereign state. But who cannot see the precarious and, in the long run, sterile nature of the victories gained? Who does not understand that there is no assured future for Israel outside a lasting entente with the world which surrounds it—entente which implies renunciation of military conquest and the solution of the Palestinian problem? Such a result, in a situation where feelings and fanaticism are increasing daily, should, to be quickly reached, proceed from United Nations action and in particular from the agreement of the four permanent members of the Security Council to define and propose the general conditions for a settlement and to provide the guarantees for it. Believe me, France's intention in the face of these different conflicts has never been to be detrimental to any nation nor to serve another. We seek, we want, only peace, a peace that is sound and just because it is founded on the will of the peoples and the right of all men to a home and homeland.

Before joint session of Congress, Washington,
Feb. 24/National Observer, 3–2:2.

William Proxmire
United States Senator, D-Wis.

A so-called "balanced policy" in the Middle East, which will enable us to gain respect with the Arab states as well as with Israel, is not impossible. But I emphatically reject the concept of a balanced policy if it implies we weaken our support for Israel. Our continued resolve to maintain our strong support for Israel must not even come into question, for in so doing we encourage miscalculations as to our intent and vital interests in the Middle East. Such miscalculations could lead to broader conflagration and might involve the United States.

Before the Senate, Washington, Jan. 26/
Congressional Record, 1–26:S542.

Middle Eastern oil has long been used as a bogeyman by the oil industry. On one hand, they claim it is too insecure a source to rely upon, thus we must limit its importation. On the other hand, they claim it is too important to us to alienate the Arab states, thus we must not be too friendly with Israel. About the only consistent thread running through their argument is that which keeps their pocketbooks full.

Before the Senate, Washington, Jan. 26/
Congressional Record, 1–26:S543.

Roman C. Pucinski
United States Representative, D-Ill.

I have said time and again that the Israelis do not want a single American soldier or any other American personnel to help in this crisis. The Israelis only want the sinews with which to defend their homeland, and they themselves will supply the manpower. But, as encouraging as Mr. Nixon's statement was yesterday, the statement made by Ron Ziegler (White House Press Secretary) today raises some serious questions. Mr. Ziegler emphasized that while the President would be agreeable to providing additional arms to Israel, such arms could be provided only on a purchase basis. I think the country ought to know that the Soviet Union has provided the Arab states with whatever equipment they need to wage aggression, without any financial exchange. In other words, the Soviets are *giving* the Arabs everything they need while the American administration says that it will be glad to *sell* Israel whatever she needs. This does not appear to me to be a realistic policy. I hope Mr. Nixon will reconsider and agree to lend-lease Israel

whatever hardware she needs to defend herself from Arab aggression.

Before the House, Washington, Jan. 26/
Congressional Record, 1–26:H237.

Yitzhak Rabin
Israeli Ambassador to the United States

I won't deny that we are strong enough now to deter war. But the problem is not about today . . . the decision to supply Israel with arms has to be made today, or else the balance of power will be upset within one-and-one-half to three years, and by then it will be too late.

Before National Jewish Welfare Board,
Washington, March 20/
The Washington Post, 3–21:A11.

I believe that the main aim of the Soviet Union in the Middle East is to gain hegemony and a predominant role in that part of the world. If, to achieve it, they will have to come into military confrontation with Israel, they will not hesitate to do so.

Interview/Meet the Press,
National Broadcasting Company, 7–19.

The Soviet Union has exploited the Arab-Israeli conflict and used it as an entry into that part of the world. To eliminate the Arab-Israeli conflict would eliminate the reason for Soviet existence there, and I don't see that they would want that. They can't survive without tension. They only supply arms and more arms, which does not encourage peace.

News conference, Los Angeles, Oct. 19/
Los Angeles Herald-Examiner, 10–20:A5.

Mahmoud Riad
Foreign Minister of the United Arab Republic

The rule of the (UN) Charter makes it incumbent upon the United States to stand by the countries that are victims of aggression and not to support Israel, the aggressor. By taking this hostile position toward the Arab peoples and by supporting Israel, the aggressor, the United States obstructs the

(MAHMOUD RIAD)

realization of peace in the Middle East, endangers world peace and encourages the use of force in international relations.

Before United Nations General Assembly,
N.Y., Oct. 26/
Los Angeles Herald-Examiner, 10–26:A1.

Abraham A. Ribicoff
United States Senator, D-Conn.

It is clearly in the interest of the Soviet Union to aid and encourage Arab hostility against Israel, short of armed confrontation with the United States, in order to extend Soviet influence in the Mediterranean and in the Arab world. It is in the interest of the Arab rulers to stoke the fires of hatred against Israel in order to conceal their own shortcomings in caring for the needs of their peoples, and in order to provide the only consistent basis for Arab unity. It is in the interest of the Arab terrorists to perpetuate the illusion of the Middle East as a continuing powder keg, unless their demands for the dismantlement of Israel are met, since of all the parties concerned they have the least to lose. It is in the interest of Great Britain and France to preserve the illusion they are on a par with the United States and Russia in the "Big Four" talks while seeking to preserve and expand their own narrow interests in the area. And, to put it bluntly, it is in the interest of Israel to survive as a nation.

Before the Senate, Washington, Jan. 26/
Congressional Record, 1–26:S533.

France's entire role in the Middle East since the 1967 war has been outrageous, given the yawning gap between its protestations of neutrality and peaceful intentions and its deeds. At least the Russians are more candid in their support of the Arabs. French conduct toward Israel has been scandalous, and toward the United States only slightly less so.

Before the Senate, Washington, Jan. 26/
Congressional Record, 1–26:S534.

Elliot L. Richardson
Under Secretary of State of the United States

The Soviet Union should realize that any immediate gains it might make by attempting to take advantage of the troubled Middle East situation are far outweighed by the danger of stirring up a wider conflict. When in such an area, one of us—in this case the U.S.S.R.—involves itself militarily, it is inevitable that the other will take notice and react.

U.S. News & World Report, 5–11:53.

L. Mendel Rivers
United States Representative, D-S.C.

On one of these fine mornings we are going to be told by the Russians—in the most unmistakable terms—to get out of the Mediterranean . . . At the rate we are going now, considering the condition of the Sixth Fleet . . . we would be forced to back down.

Before the House, Washington, Sept. 28/
U.S. News & World Report, 10–12:19.

William P. Rogers
Secretary of State of the United States

It's in our best interest to be sure that Israel survives as a nation. That's been our policy and it will continue to be our policy. So we have to take whatever action we think is necessary to give them the assurance that they need that their independence and sovereignty is going to continue. At the same time, we want to do it in a balanced and measured way so that we don't signal to the Arabs that we are so behind Israel that we will support them no matter what they do.

Interview/Face the Nation,
Columbia Broadcasting System, 6–7.

We have, I think, in our relations with Israel, convinced Israel that they should have no concern about our support for their continued existence; and we have made that clear by word and by deed.

News conference, Washington, Dec. 23/
The New York Times, 12–24:2.

Burnett Roth
National vice chairman, civil rights committee, Anti-Defamation League

As Americans, we must remember that our first concern must be for the security of our nation—what is best for the United States. And I say to you, as a student of the Middle East for more than 40 years, that the preservation of a democratic state in the Middle East is of prime concern to us as Americans. There is no dichotomy between concern for Israel and patriotism as an American. The present position of the United States . . . is frightening and is a diplomatic blunder which as Americans we must criticize. Let me make it clear that I believe the mistakes being made by this Administration are not willful mistakes, but based upon a naive belief that the United States can make friends with money and other people's rights.

Before B'nai B'rith Luncheon Club,
Miami Beach, Jan. 13/
Vital Speeches, 5–1:444.

Anwar el Sadat
Vice President of the United Arab Republic

You should have been here on June 5 this year, on the third anniversary of the 1967 war (with Israel). You should have seen our President (Nasser) riding through the streets of Cairo in an open car, surrounded on all sides by thousands of Egyptians shouting, "Never capitulate! Never capitulate!" Then you should hear the comments we hear from the other side—from Israel—where they say, "There is a mood of despair (in Egypt) because of their high casualties and because they don't see any end to this war." And you would finally understand: The Egyptian war of attrition is succeeding. Yes, whatever casualties we have suffered, we can absorb—as we have absorbed so many times before throughout the 7,000 years of Egyptian history. The Israelis don't understand this; they still think they can bring us to our knees. But we can take this war for hundreds of years. What is our strength? The people as a whole support us . . . There is a 100 per

cent unity in this country. And if you don't believe this, it is because you don't know Egypt well enough.

Interview, Cairo/Newsweek, 6–29:36.

The United Arab Republic, the Arab nation and all mankind have lost one of the most precious men, most courageous and most sincere men, President Gamal Abdel Nasser, who passed away at 6:15 this evening while he was standing on the field of struggle, striving for the unity of the Arab nation and for the day of victory . . . Gamal Abdel Nasser was more than words. He is more immortal than any words. Nothing can describe him except his record in the service of his people, nation and humanity—a struggler for freedom, for humanity, a struggler for truth and justice, a fighter for honor to the last moment of life. No words are sufficient to express condolences for Gamal Abdel Nasser. The only thing that can be commensurate with his righteousness and esteem is that the entire Arab nation should stand patient, steadfast—a steadfast, solid, heroic and able stand so that it can realize the victory for which the great son of Egypt and the hero of this nation, its man and leader, had lived and was martyred.

Radio-TV broadcast, Cairo, Sept. 28/
The New York Times 9–29:17.

Anwar el Sadat
President of the United Arab Republic

In spite of the fact that our revolution is 18 years old, the United States does not understand the revolution or the Egyptian people even now. The Baghdad Pact represented part of this material and psychological misunderstanding. We are a simple, modest people, but we are fierce and stubborn if a big power tries to apply pressure on us. And you (the U.S.) lack understanding of this fact.

Interview, Cairo, Oct. 19/
The New York Times, 10–21:6.

It is regrettable the United States has not learned the lesson it received at the hands

(ANWAR EL SADAT)

of the Vietnamese people. Despite its formidable weapons arsenal, the United States has been unable to conquer the will of a small, helpless people because the peoples' will is derived from God's will. If the United States failed to learn this lesson in Vietnam, it will learn it here and at the hands of our generation.

Cairo, Oct. 28 /
San Francisco Examiner, 10–28:1.

The Soviet Union is an honest and honorable friend. It always stands by us in time of difficulty and sorrow and never tries to exploit the situation.

Before Arab Socialist Union, Cairo, Nov. 12 /
The New York Times, 11–13:3.

By passing a decision on the resumption of contacts through (Gunnar) Jarring, before the United Nations Secretary-General submits his report to the Security Council, Israel wants to avoid the censure of its policy. We shall not allow this maneuver to be a success. If we see that Israel really is sincerely striving for full implementation of the Security Council resolution, we shall do all that is required of us. But we shall not allow any maneuvers aimed at the prolongation of the occupation of our territory, denying us the right to liberate our land . . . If we allow again and again this situation (continuation of the cease-fire) to remain unchanged, this might go on for the next twenty years. I am ready to go to the ends of the earth in the name of peace. But we shall not cede one inch of our soil, and we shall not go back to our decision (not to renew the cease-fire).

Before a delegation of the World Peace
Council, Cairo, Dec. 29 /
Daily World, 12–30:2.

Saeb Salam
Prime Minister of Lebanon

United States interests urgently require a rapprochement with the Arab peoples, from the Arabian Gulf to the Atlantic Ocean.

Support in arms or money for Israeli aggression means the destruction of these American interests throughout the Arab world. This is what the Americans should understand. They are not only departing from rules of right and justice, but are intensifying their hostility, thus injuring American interests, protection of which, after all, is the final objective of United States policy. We hope that the voice coming from Lebanon and expressing the feelings of all Lebanese will cause an awakening of the conscience of Americans.

Christian Science Monitor, 11–24:9.

Richard S. Schweiker
United States Senator, R-Pa.

So long as Israel is strong, and so long as it is clear that the Israeli forces can turn back any Arab threats, the threat of war in the Middle East is reduced. But as soon as Israel appears weak, and as soon as the United States lessens its firm support of the Israeli position, then the prospects for war increase. The best insurance against another full-scale Middle East war, therefore, is to keep Israel strong and to fully support Israeli bargaining positions.

Before the Senate, Washington, Jan. 26 /
Congressional Record, 1–26:S541.

Hugh Scott
United States Senator, R-Pa.

We cannot dictate peace (between Israel and the Arabs). We must assure a peace initiated, enforced and adhered to by the peoples whose nations and lives are affected . . . Certainly, the United States should not seek to impose its own desires upon Israel, but, rather, Israel and the Arab parties should be encouraged to develop their own negotiating positions. The cause of peace can be better served if Russia also realizes that the sovereign Arab governments must be allowed to seek their own destiny. The great powers cannot merely negotiate among themselves in order to dictate a false, deceptive and temporary solution.

Before Hadassah convention, Washington,
Aug. 16 / Los Angeles Times, 8–17:(1)5.

Haile Selassie
Emperor of Ethiopia

The friendship between Israelis and Ethiopians was not something that was created yesterday. We have had a long-standing friendship for many centuries. Now, in the crisis which is taking place in the Middle East, we have made it clear to both parties that it is not our interest to support or condemn one side or the other.

Interview, Addis Ababa/
San Francisco Examiner & Chronicle,
11–15:A27.

Yosef Tekoah
Israeli Ambassador to the United Nations

The question is, can Egypt, Jordan and other Arab governments be brought to abide by their international responsibilities? . . . The Middle East today is under a wave of lawlessness. I think there is a clear pattern here—a feeling in Arab capitals that they can stand in utter disregard of international law.

News conference, United Nations, N.Y.,
Sept. 8/Los Angeles Herald-Examiner, 9–8:A2.

Jacques Torczyner
President, Zionist Organization of America

Israel is the touchstone and the symbol of what America will do in the world. If, after all the promises that were made, all the statements, all the letters that were written, America should abandon Israel, we are back where we were in 1938, the era of appeasement.

Before Zionist Organization of America,
New York, Sept. 3/
The New York Times, 9–4:16.

Tarik Zafer Tunaya
Professor of Political Science,
Istanbul University

Turkey is a field on which gasoline has been poured. Watch your cigarette.

Time, 7–27:20.

Joseph D. Tydings
United States Senator, D-Md.

. . . there can be no lasting peace in the area until all of the parties to the conflict truly want peace. And as the Israelis have properly pointed out, willingness to negotiate directly is certainly a reasonable test of sincere commitment to a peaceful resolution of differences. In the meantime, until a permanent peace is possible, it is essential that the United States provide Israel with the economic and military assistance she needs to survive. I believe we must do so, for two principle reasons: First, the United States is morally committed to the preservation of Israel as a Jewish homeland. History has made tragically clear the necessity for a place to which Jews may turn in the face of the persecution which has continued to infect Western history . . . Second, until a meaningful peace settlement is possible, the best deterrent to open conflict in the Middle East is an Israel strong enough to maintain a regional balance of power vis-a-vis her Arab neighbors.

Before the Senate, Washington, Jan. 26/
Congressional Record, 1–26:S530.

Geoffrey Wheeler
Former director, Central Asian Research
Center; Authority on the Middle East

If Russia's aim is to displace Western influence in the Middle East with Russian influence—political, cultural and economic—it cannot claim to have been very successful. Banking and insurance, the two most vital elements in the economy of the area, are still under Western control or influence. Culturally, no one is studying Russian. Politically, the Russians have had to abandon the idea of forcing Communism on the Arabs . . . The Russians have a long record of failures in the Middle East dating back to 1921. If I had to guess, I would say that eventually they will be counted out in the Arab world simply because they are no more successful in controlling the Arabs than were the British or French.

U.S. News & World Report, 4–6:55.

Elie Wiesel
Author

I think our generation is privileged and cursed. We are privileged to be a witness—to be able to say, "I was there; I saw it; I was at Sinai; I was in Jerusalem when it was liberated." Our generation is the link between the holocaust and Israel. Like Job, we are cursed and haunted by what has happened to us, but—like Job—privileged, because it has happened to *us*.

Interview, New York/
The New York Times, 2-10:48.

Charles W. Yost
United States Ambassador to the
United Nations

When Ambassador Malik (of the Soviet Union) wishes to negotiate seriously, when he has authority from his government to engage in the normal give-and-take of diplomatic negotiation and political settlement, he speaks in a quiet, businesslike manner. When, however, his government has decided not to make any accommodation whatsoever, to dig its heels in and insist that the Soviet position be adopted 100 per cent, and hence to bring effective negotiations to a halt, then he endeavors to conceal this fact by throwing up a smokescreen and indulging in a torrent of bombast and invective . . . This is, I may say, a very bad sign for peace in the Middle East.

At United Nations, N.Y./
The Christian Science Monitor, 5-22:13.

Stephen M. Young
United States Senator, D-Ohio

I oppose firmly all pressures by Nixon Administration leaders upon Israeli leaders to surrender territories taken by this valiant little nation fighting against Nasser's aggression—at least until security from Arab aggression is pledged in face-to-face negotiations . . . This issue is not territorial expansionism by Israel. The prime concern is security for the valiant people of Israel. Return to the 1967 lines means retreat to 1967 close-range exposure of Israeli civilians to terrorism and siege. It is an open invitation to future aggression by the Arab leaders.

Before the Senate, Washington, Jan. 26/
Congressional Record, 1-26:S540.

PART THREE

General

The Arts

Spiro T. Agnew
Vice President of the United States

Just today, the lameduck (Presidential) Commission on Obscenity and Pornography weighed in with its final report. Its views do not represent the thinking of the Nixon Administration. This commission was not named by President Nixon. No sir, your honor, it's not our baby . . . As long as Richard Nixon is President, Main Street is not going to turn into Smut Alley.

Salt Lake City, Sept. 30/
Los Angeles Herald-Examiner, 10–1:A4;
Human Events, 10–31:12.

Thomas Hart Benton
Artist

When art reveals life, it becomes a form of history of the most vivid kind—permanently valuable to men.

Interview, Kansas City/
Los Angeles Times, 3–15:B7.

Charles Buckley
Director, St. Louis City Art Museum

Art museums in the United States are slowly being strangled by their own success in attracting ever-increasing numbers of visitors who come to seek services that museums have promised to provide but which now, for lack of funds, are either not forthcoming or are offered only in token form . . . I doubt if the art museum as an institution will vanish from the scene, but its chronic undernourishment will surely reduce many of them to mere shadows.

Before House Subcommittee on the Arts,
Washington, Feb. 5/
The Washington Post, 2–6:B15.

Marc Chagall
Artist

In art and in love there is as little begin-

ning and end as there is in the holy books. Art which one can explain, as one can explain that two and two are four, is not art.

Zurich, Sept. 5/
The Christian Science Monitor, 9–25:7.

Barry M. Goldwater
United States Senator, R-Ariz.

There is no longer any question that the arts constitute an important dimension of American life and represent a legitimate subject for governmental concern and interest. So long as the government's role is limited to providing a climate in which the arts can grow, to engaging each local community in the cultural currents flowing across the nation and to bringing the arts to the people, I intend to support the program and commend it. I cannot see anything wrong with preserving our cultural treasures fully as much as other natural resources.

Before the Senate, Washington/
Variety, 2–25:2.

Dan Greenburg
Author

I think paintings should be rated like movies—"R" means if you're under seventeen you can only look at certain pictures with an adult present; "X" means you're not allowed to look at them at all until you're old enough to handle it. Museums should be rated this way, too. I can tell you there aren't too many art galleries in this town that would get a "G" rating.

Interview, New York/
The Washington Post (Book World), 1–4:10.

E. Y. Harburg
Music lyricist

. . . our music has become noise, our literature has become grunts, a play is called a

(E. Y. HARBURG)

property, a theatre is real estate and a show is just a packaging job.

Interview/Newsweek, 6–22:10.

John Cardinal Heenan
Archbishop of Westminster, England

All forms of censorship are abhorrent. If people want to wallow in filth, that is their responsibility.

*At London School of Economics, Nov. 17/
The Washington Post, 11–18:A3.*

Thomas Hoving
*Director, Metropolitan Museum of Art,
New York*

This place (the Museum) used to be the living room of the very rich. Now it belongs to everyone—and we must see to it that no special group takes it over ... again.

New York/Newsweek, 4–27:73.

George M. Irwin
Chairman, Associated Council of the Arts

In our concern to develop new audiences for the arts, we must take advantage of every 20th century technique and not continue to delude ourselves that 19th century procedures or art forms are necessarily relevant to audiences today. A re-direction and re-thinking is necessary if we are to properly take arts programs and experiences to the people and not expect them to come to the museum or concert hall in the same old way. What corporation today would be successful without a research and development division? New arts patrons must be found, as the arts cannot be expected to pay their way at the box-office. Yesterday's single patron is today being replaced by large numbers of donors, by government at all levels and, in more recent years, by corporations. Cooperative funding today is vital to the continued existence and growth of our arts institutions. Just as our leaders in business, industry and education look to the future and plan for tomorrow, so arts managers have a major responsibility to seek the best talent and think-

ing available, not only for problems of today, but for the continuing security of tomorrow.

*Before Conference on Business and the Arts,
Atlanta/The Wall Street Journal, 3–6:8.*

Edward I. Koch
United States Representative, D-N.Y.

The fact that we will give a tax break to the inventor of a hair curler but not a composer of a musical score speaks poorly for the values of our society.

Washington, Jan. 29/Daily Variety, 1–30:1.

Rouben Mamoulian
Former motion picture director

All through history there has never been a high civilization or culture that didn't have a highly diversified theatre—ancient Greece, Italy, Britain, you name it. The theatre is the most authentic reflection of the well-being of a nation—as long as the theatre is prosperous and vigorous, you don't have to worry about that state of the country. When the other causes fail, it's different; but with the arts, we still have hope. When they fail, we have great reason to worry, not only for the state of the nation, but for the state of the world.

*Interview, Los Angeles/
Los Angeles Times (Calendar), 4–5:16.*

John N. Mitchell
Attorney General of the United States

In the area of pornographic literature, I couldn't care less what they do with it—as long as it is not made available to the young. If somebody wants to look at dirty pictures, that is their business—if they're old enough and have a mind of sufficient stature to make this determination. But it's the spreading of pornography through the mails and into the homes where it falls into the hands of the young that is particularly disturbing. That is why the Administration has asked for laws to keep this material away from youngsters.

*Interview, Washington,
Nation's Business, June:37.*

Paul VI
Pope

Art must have an educational function. It must not be merely pleasing and interesting —much less frivolous, seductive or capricious —but must be aware of its ethical and social responsibility.

Vatican City/Quote, 6–21:579.

Man Ray
Artist

People ask me, "What about your recent paintings?" I say, "I never painted a recent painting in my life." Life is an instant, a one-day insect; there's no time to do two things alike. This confuses the galleries; they say, "You don't have a style." I say, "Leonardo didn't have a style, but if you look at the signatures you will see that they all look alike."

Interview, Saint-Paul de Vence, France/ The New York Times Magazine, 9–6:25.

Nelson A. Rockefeller
Governor of New York

To consider a society without the arts . . . celebrated orchestras, museums, libraries and other cultural entities, is to imagine a culture without pride or inspiration for our citizens.

State of the State address, Albany, Jan. 7/ The New York Times, 1–8:30.

Aline Saarinen
Author, Journalist

I like order. I like form. I like ground rules. That's why I like sonnets. It's why I like art.

Interview, New York/TV Guide, 4–25:30.

William J. Scherle
United States Representative, R-Iowa

It is ironic that at the very time there is no money in the budget for the school milk program for next year, veterans' burial benefits are being reduced, the agricultural conservation program is being cut back and other high-priority national interests are being curtailed—all in the name of economy—

that funds for the Foundation on Arts and Humanities should be doubled to $40 million. Culture should not be fed to an effete elite at the expense of the general public. If seven-letter poems turn on some people, then they should pay for that joy rather than force hard-working taxpayers to subsidize their exotic cultural tastes.

Human Events, 4–25:15.

Muriel Spark
Author

The power and influence of the creative arts is not to be belittled. I only say that the art and literature of sentiment and emotion, however beautiful in itself, however striking in its depiction of actuality, has to go. It cheats us into a sense of involvement with life and society, but in reality it is a segregated activity. In its place, I advocate the arts of satire and ridicule. And I see no other living art form for the future. Ridicule is the only honorable weapon we have left. If someone derides me, I don't like it. But at least I can begin to understand the mentality of the mocker. And I can mock back in such a way that he might understand mine. And so there may be room for a mutual understanding.

At American Academy of Arts and Letters, New York, May 26/National Observer, 6–15:15.

Roy Strong
Director, National Portrait Gallery, London

I am sick to death of education as the prime function of museums. I think we have got to get across the idea of the wonderful and marvelous. Education comes later.

Interview, Washington/ The Washington Post, 10–7:B1.

Mikis Theodorakis
Composer

Whether art is music or cinema or whatever, it really is art only when it is in touch with the people—forced to respond to their agonies, their joys and their aspirations. And, if art expresses the feelings of the people properly, then inevitably it is political.

(MIKIS THEODORAKIS)

Because of this, art always has helped the people to overcome problems and find solutions to their collective difficulties.

Interview, New York/
The New York Times, 8–16:(2)11.

Jack Valenti
President, Motion Picture Association
of America

It is absurd, really, to put the judgment of creative works in the all-powerful hands of one man or a group of men. Personal opinion plays such a high role in the recording of taste that it is impossible for a small group to classify a work of art for their peers and make it a final measure.

Before Commonwealth Club, San Francisco/
National Observer, 1–12:16.

If we ever allow legislation to create boards or commissions or groups armed with the bludgeon of the law to tell their fellow citizens what they can see or read or hear or think, we will have swallowed cultural hemlock.

Before House Judiciary subcommittee,
Washington, Jan. 28/
The Washington Post, 1–29:D1.

Mr. Blackwell
Fashion designer

Let us try to forget the mid-calf, little-boy look, paper dresses, baby dolls, sack freaks, cut-outs, moon styles, topless, mini and maxi as fast as possible . . . Perhaps the '60s will be long remembered as the period in which women did not look into their mirrors. And in which they must have abandoned their sense of humor—and just plain style sense. May the '70s return loveliness and beauty to raiment.

Interview, Los Angeles/
Los Angeles Herald-Examiner, 1–7:A15.

Donald Brooks
Fashion designer

Fashion is not an abstraction. A designer's clothes must please someone or they serve no function. When there have been men on the moon and you know someone will be dancing on Mars tomorrow, 18th-century art that serves no function seems absurd.

Interview, Los Angeles/
Los Angeles Times, 8–24:(4)11.

The midi isn't a fad, except that some manufacturers and designers are tasteless, weak-willed and mentally-deficient enough not to design it right.

The Washington Post,/10–15:C7.

Richard Burton
Actor

I have no concern for fashion. And men who do nothing but sit around talking about fashion all day are not my type of men. I'm not in favor of the Beau Brummells of the world. His is not a character I would like to play.

Interview, Beverly Hills, Calif./
Los Angeles Times 4–8:(4)1.

Johnny Carson
Television talk-show host

I've never been one for the wild clothes. I like "little touches," like the buttoned flaps on the pockets. Although I have wildly-garbed guests on my show, I feel that people should not be conscious of what you wear, but conscious of the fact that you are well-dressed.

Dallas, Feb. 8/
The Dallas Times Herald, 2–9:A5.

Coco Chanel
Fashion designer

Miniskirts are indecent—an exhibition of meat.

Quote, 4–19:384.

Tony Curtis
Actor

I haven't worn a tie for two years. As long as a man keeps his figure he can get away with dressing young for years. Clothes today are designed to show off a man's figure to advantage. In the old days, they were designed to hide it.

Interview, London/
San Francisco Examiner & Chronicle
(Women Today), 8–23:5.

Erte
Fashion designer

There's nothing more frustrating than designing fashions when nudity is "in." You have to do so much with so little space. In the end, you put a bracelet on the arm, something on the toe—and voila, there it is!

The New York Times, 12–13:(4)8.

Rudi Gernreich
Fashion designer

Fashion as we know it is going to end be-

(RUDI GERNREICH)

cause of our changing social structures. We are going into a period of functionalism, as we are involved in too many other problems to play around. Right now, we are in a rather confused period. That's why there's so much dress up and spoofing and reverting (to other eras).

Interview, Los Angeles /
Los Angeles Herald-Examiner, 1–6:A10.

People who are stressing romantic and nostalgic clothes are not facing the problems of the world—those of pollution and over-population. Clothes should be totally utilitarian to represent the age we are living in. Fashion has become an expression of social and political attitudes toward life.

Panel discussion, New York, Jan. 7 /
The Washington Post, 1–8:C2.

(During the 1970s) basic clothing will become much more understated. Our aesthetics will change and focus more on the body than on its adornment. Nudity will be much more prevalent . . . The problems of overpopulation, pollution and so forth are going to intrude in some ways on all our lives and change our everyday involvements. Clothes will just not be that important any more.

Los Angeles / Time, 1–26:39.

I'm not out to kill fashion. It's already finished. The word has no meaning. It stands for all the wrong values: snobbism, wealth, the select few. It's antisocial. It isolates itself from the masses. Today, you can't be antisocial, so fashion is gone. Even the word has become a little embarrassing. Clothes, gear—these are the words of today.

Interview, Los Angeles /
Los Angeles Times, 11–25:(4)1.

Robert L. Green
Fashion director, "Playboy" magazine
When society recognizes that masculinity is not determined by the clothes you have

on, but (by) what you do when you take them off, menswear will be truly liberated.

Los Angeles / Los Angeles Times, 11–18:(4)1.

Rupert Lycett Green
Fashion designer
Today's man needn't be in a mold. He should dress to fit his mood and environment, but he can be colorful in any line of work. Wouldn't it be great to see workmen on a high-rise building in bright orange uniforms as well as hard hats? Even a banker need not be dull. After all, a dark suit doesn't mean that a man is virtuous or trustworthy. Personally, I dress according to my mood. Maybe I'm lucky, as I'm the boss in my stores, and no one can complain about what I wear.

Los Angeles Times, 3–18:(4)7.

Edith Head
Motion picture fashion designer
I've survived a long time, dressing as many men as women. If I had to do it over again, I'd do only men. Every woman is basically a designer, only they suppress it. Men are much more cooperative. Cary Grant agrees to every idea. Paul Newman just wants to know if it's comfortable. The fashion psyche is so different between men and women that there will never be a "unisex" look.

Interview, Los Angeles /
Los Angeles Times (Calendar), 10–11:24.

Fashion is the only art, craft, science, whatever you want to call it, not gearing to the future. I think designers are going backward because they don't know what to do. There must be something that's romantic, dramatic and modern.

Interview, London /
The Christian Science Monitor, 11–13:8.

Marshall McLuhan
Professor of English, University of Toronto
The miniskirt will never die. It's a tribal costume. It is *fashion* that is dead.

The Washington Post, 9–27:H11.

Martha Mitchell
Wife of the Attorney General of the United States

The style industry has killed itself; it has really missed the bet. If they want to promote styles and fashion, they should see to it that a woman—no matter what her age or figure—looks well. I'm not going to buy clothes just because someone dictates to me that I should have a mini or maxi or midi. Why is it that American women do not sit and analyze themselves and try to dress according to their needs?

Interview, Washington, March 21/
The New York Times, 3–22:(1)74.

W. C. Newberry
Professor of Education, Southwest Texas State University

Little children naturally cling to their mothers' skirts, but today's have to be five years old before they can reach them.

Before Texas Future Teachers of America,
Fort Worth/The Dallas Times Herald,
2–15:A12.

Emilio Pucci
Fashion designer

Fashion is a reflection of its times, and the trends of the times set the fashion trends. We live in a society which values youth and regards age as undesirable. Men and women used to be old at 60. They aren't anymore. They play golf and tennis; they ski; they think young; they flirt. Women exercise and diet, and their young figures don't require the slimming help that longer lengths give.

Dallas, April 30/
The Dallas Times Herald, 5–1:C1.

Mary Quant
Fashion designer

The mini has served the purpose of proving that woman is emancipated; that's now accepted. Now we can get back to normal—to cool elegance.

Quote, 8–9:128.

Fashion is going into a gentler, calmer, easier period. The arrogance is going out of it. That arrogant attitude—that was the beginning of true emancipation. But once that was achieved, fashion didn't have to say it any more; it was taken for granted. It's all reflected in the fashions we're seeing right now.

Interview, London/
The Washington Post, 10–3:C2.

Yves Saint Laurent
Fashion designer

All that—a new shape, a new length—is false now. For me, fashion today is much more a state of spirit . . . and image . . . colors.

Paris/The Washington Post, 6–20:C1.

Jane Trahey
President, Trahey-Wolff advertising; Advertising Woman of the Year

Most fashion ladies are the dowdiest bunch of broads in history. They all look like mice.

Interview, Los Angeles/
Los Angeles Times, 2–25:(4)1.

Mae West
Actress

Clothes can put a woman in any mood she wants them to. If you look good to yourself, you not only feel good, but you make the people around you feel good. It's every woman's duty to look beautiful. But I don't think clothes should ever dominate a woman. I don't want people to say, "What a beautiful dress she's wearing." I want them to say, "What a beautiful woman."

Interview/Look, 3–24:50.

Journalism

Elie Abel

Dean, Columbia University Graduate School of Journalism

(Vice President) Agnew is trying to build public pressure in favor of suppressing reality. That is not really new. It has a long history—from the time the medieval kings beheaded the herald who brought bad news, to the campaigns of Governor (George) Wallace, who berated newsmen as point-headed intellectuals.

> *San Francisco Examiner & Chronicle*
> *(This World), 3–15:2.*

Spiro T. Agnew

Vice President of the United States

This is my favorite time of the year in Maryland—that wonderful time when the (Baltimore) *Sun*papers are on strike.

> *At Republican fund-raising dinner,*
> *Essex, Md., Jan. 30/*
> *The Washington Post, 1–31:B5.*

(Law-abiding Americans) need a strong voice to penetrate the cacophony of seditious drivel emanating from the best-publicized clowns of our society and from their fans in the Fourth Estate.

> *Atlanta, Feb. 21/*
> *The Dallas Times Herald, 2–23:B20.*

Our media would be well advised to recognize a new dimension of their responsibility to critically examine our enemies which have no free press to criticize them. Pulitzer Prizes are not won by exposing the evils of Communism as rapidly as discrediting American elective officials. Tons of tons of innuendos designed to smear officials are printed every day.

> *St. Thomas, Virgin Islands, March 19/*
> *The Dallas Times Herald, 3–20:A19.*

Lately, you have been exposed to a great deal of public comment about Vice Presidential rhetoric and how I should "cool it." The President is getting this advice daily from many quarters . . . some of them inside the government. But mostly it has come from persons who have been in the target area of some of my speeches. Nowhere is the complaint louder than in the columns and editorials of the liberal news media of this country—those really illiberal, self-appointed guardians of our destiny who would like to run the country without ever submitting to the elective process as we in public office must do.

> *At Republican fund-raising dinner, Houston,*
> *May 22/The Washington Post, 5–23:A14.*

It does bother me . . . that the press—as a group—regards the First Amendment as its own private preserve. Every time I criticize what I consider to be excesses or faults in the news business, I am accused of repression, and the leaders of the various media professional groups wave the First Amendment as they denounce me. That happens to be *my* amendment, too. It guarantees *my* free speech as much as it does *their* freedom of the press. So I hope that will be remembered the next time a "muzzle Agnew" campaign is launched. There is room for all of us—and for our divergent views—under the First Amendment.

> *At Republican fund-raising dinner, Houston,*
> *May 22/The Washington Post, 5–23:A14.*

The price for not presenting both sides of a story is loss of credibility as a public institution. It is a heavy price to pay for a fleeting exercise in power or influence. Because a

420

newspaper, like a politician, has lost every-thing when it loses its credibility.

Before International Federation of
Newspaper Publishers, June 15/
Human Events, 6–27:8.

. . . I find there is an odd vacuum, any effort by the free media in this country, to show conditions as they are in North Viet-nam, within China, in (the) Soviet Union, in Communist Cuba. They always seem to paint these places as some sort of heaven. Well, if they were so good, I would imagine most of our people would be beating down the gates trying to get into those countries, instead of vice versa.

Television interview, Los Angeles, July 25/
Los Angeles Times, 7–22:(1)11.

You can write about anything two ways. The liberal media says not that a bunch of kids violently threw over a hot dog stand and stole the man's products, but that they "liberated" his hot dogs.

Interview, Washington/
San Francisco Examiner & Chronicle
(Women Today), 8–23:2.

. . . I believe that the great majority of the people want a conservative and respon-sible government. But I pick up the Eastern "liberal" newspapers, and it's like going to a Greek tragedy—there's something wrong with the country on every page, and the United States isn't worth a damn, and the people in it are "insensitive" and all that. You get a completely distorted view.

Interview, Washington/
U.S. News & World Report, 8–24:36.

. . . the people who are watching that (TV) tube have a right to know what your (news commentators') opinions are if you happen to be a man who is telling the news every night, because you can select what parts of the news you want to emphasize, and by your language you can convey a point of view that is not an editorial and yet is colored by your own viewpoints. Now, I think the people ought to know what those viewpoints

are . . . It would be very interesting to have a show, a panel-type show, where Senators from either party, Representatives I suppose, maybe a couple of governors, could sit down with someone who has a national reputation as a commentator . . . and just examine him in depth on where he stands personally on the issues he talks about every day.

Interview/Kup's Show,
WMAQ-TV, Chicago, 9–20.

I have not the least doubt that the United States has the most self-demanding, least self-satisfied, most ingenious, least inhibited, best informed, least controlled, most professional, least subjective, most competitive, least party-line, fairest and finest journalist com-plex in the entire world. I have found news-casters and reporters, in large majority, as fair and objective as they are emotionally and psychologically able to be, and I have found the great preponderance of them con-scientious in their calling. I have found most news accounts of my deeds and words accu-rate and factual. Indeed, time and again, I have found surprisingly complimentary coverage of my viewpoint by journalists who I happen to know do not suffer from ardor of Agnew.

Before Associated Press Managing Editors
Association, Honolulu, Nov. 20/
Denver Rocky Mountain News, 11–21:34.

Howard H. Baker
United States Senator, R-Tenn.

Opinion-formers in this country are not limited to governmental officials. News-media personalities are opinion-formers as well; and I believe it is fortunate that non-governmental sources, such as Vanderbilt University in Nashville, Tennessee, is now, for the first time, taping all of the morning and evening network news programs so that commentators today and scholars in the fu-ture can examine them and determine for themselves whether or not they represent objective reporting or subjective interpreta-tion.

Before the Senate, Washington, May 5/
U.S. News & World Report, 5–18:93.

Bernard Beguin
Editor-in-chief, "Journal of Geneva"

Journalists should not be mirrors, but men of action who also know how to evaluate the position of the opposition.

> *At Monte Carlo International Television Festival/Hollywood Reporter, 2–19:12.*

Winton M. Blount
Postmaster General of the United States

The fortunate thing about America is it doesn't happen to be oriented around the New York-Washington axis. You get out around the country, and you don't feel the sense of despair you get around the East. The columnists are trying to say this country is in a helluva fix, and it isn't true.

> *Time, 6–1:8.*

David Brinkley
News commentator, National Broadcasting Company

(Commenting on co-commentator Chet Huntley's retirement to Montana): From now on, when somebody stops me in the street and says, "Aren't you Chet Huntley?" I'll say, "No, ma'am. He's the one out West on a horse."

> *Television broadcast/ Huntley-Brinkley Report, National Broadcasting Company, July 31.*

Harry F. Byrd, Jr.
United States Senator, D-Va.

The press is a bulwark of liberty. Anyone —inside or outside the government—may question the judgment, the taste or the accuracy of individual press accounts. But it would be a sad day in this country if the press were to be held accountable to the government.

> *Before the Senate, Washington, Feb. 5/ Congressional Record, 2–5:S1252.*

Liz Carpenter
Former White House staff director and press secretary to Lady Bird Johnson

The time has come to re-evaluate our out-

moded definitions of news. Is news, indeed, only the failure, the conflict? Or is it really what is happening, good and bad? Isn't it what 200 million people are seeking and achieving? Or is it what 400 people yell and scream about?

> *Before Texas Daily Newspaper Association, El Paso, Feb. 15/ The Dallas Times Herald, 2–16:A16.*

We all heard Vice President Agnew's statement critical of news media loud and clear. I was disappointed that most of the people in our trade—most of the press organizations—answered only with instant tantrums.

> *Before Texas Daily Newspaper Association, El Paso, Feb. 15/ The Dallas Times Herald, 2–16:A16.*

Turner Catledge
Former executive editor, "The New York Times"

If we ever get to the point where we lose believability, first thing will happen, we will just go back into a candidly partisan press— not partisan in party terms, but in terms of ideas. Whether this is an internal verity—objectivity—I don't know. Don't forget, it's comparatively new to newspapers. There wasn't a great deal of it around at the time Adolph Ochs came up from the South (in 1896 to become publisher of the *Times*). Mr. Hearst and Mr. Pulitzer were the kings of their day, and they did fancy things like stirring up a war between Spain and the United States. Mr. Ochs just started printing the news, printing the news, printing the news. It turned out to be damned good business.

> *Interview, New Orleans, April 3/ The New York Times, 4–6:36.*

George Christian
Former Press Secretary to the President of the United States

If any major force in our society—and that includes the press—should ever be immune from criticism, or, equally bad, should it ever be insensitive to criticism, then God save the Republic.

Before Texas United Press International Editors Association, Dallas, Jan. 17/ The Washington Post, 1–18:A3.

Walter Cronkite
News commentator, Columbia Broadcasting System

We teeter now on the brink of a communications crisis that could undermine the foundation of our democracy, which is a free and responsible press . . . Today, under the drumfire assault of the hysterical Establishment and the painful complaints of a frightened populace, there are many in our business who believe we should tailor our news reports to console our critics. They would have us report more good news, play down the (Vietnam) war, revolution, social disturbance . . . (When) "Give us the good news" becomes a euphemism for "Don't give us the bad news," the danger signal must be hoisted.

At Sigma Delta Chi convention, Chicago, Nov. 12/ Los Angeles Times, 10–13:(1)18.

The trouble is that we (broadcast journalists) are not free; we are government-licensed. The power to make us conform is too great to forever lie dormant. The ax lies there temptingly for the use of any enraged Administration—Republican, Democrat or Wallaceite. We are at the mercy of the whim of politicians and bureaucrats, and, whether they choose to chop us down or not, the mere existence of their power is an intimidating and constraining threat in being. (Today, television news) finds itself carrying the brunt of the attack against our freedoms . . . not, I am convinced, because of our performance, but mostly because of our impact . . . I don't think it is any of our business what the moral, political, social or economic effect of our reporting is. I suggest we concentrate on doing our job of telling it like it is and not be diverted from that ex-

alted task by the apoplectic apostles of alliteration.

At Sigma Delta Chi convention, Chicago, Nov. 12/ San Francisco Examiner, 11–13:2.

We in radio and television, with our greater impact and our numerous outlets, have forced many of our print competitors out of business. It is a rare American city today that has more than one newspaper. And yet, I think most of us will acknowledge that we are not an adequate substitute for the newspapers whose demise we have hastened. If we do our jobs thoroughly, however, we can be a superb monitor on the monopoly newspaper to assure that it does not, by plot, caprice or inadvertence, miss a major story.

At Sigma Delta Chi convention, Chicago, Nov. 12/ The Dallas Times-Herald, 11–13:A3.

From time to time, CBS has suggested that I do commentaries or analyses, but I have always refused. Should I take a position with analysis or commentary, then the public would decide that I am prejudiced in editing the news. The public does not understand journalism. They do not know how we work. They do not believe that we can hold strong private thoughts and still be objective journalists. So I choose to do only unbiased reporting. I give you the news, and I don't help you make the judgment. You make it all alone.

Interview/Look, 11–17:58.

The reason why the Establishment does not seem so concerned about the press, but would like to put clamps on television, is that the people in America do not really read the newspapers; they watch TV—especially the illiterate, the poor, the underprivileged. And the reason why the Establishment would welcome clamps on television is that we disturb the status quo of these people, because we impose on them what they can ignore when they read—or don't read—the newspapers. You can pass by a headline, even if dramatic, but you cannot close your eyes

(WALTER CRONKITE)

to a dramatic picture that appears on TV, right? So here is what we do: We take the troubles of the world and we transfer them to their homes, nightly, and we oblige them to watch. But they don't want to watch. They want to escape such troubles; they want to hide their heads in the sand. And they are brought to agree with politicians who would like us to shut up.

Interview/Look, 11–17:60.

Gardner Cowles
Chairman, Cowles Communications, Inc.

There *is* a place for the mass general magazine in the future, particularly if it's a magazine of personal advocacy, of in-depth investigation of the issues that affect us all —a magazine like *Look* . . . If *Look* should ever become bland, it'll die—and I won't let that happen . . . My heart is in *Look*; it's my baby. I founded it 33 years ago. I'd sell everything to keep it going.

Interview/Newsweek, 9–14:73.

Keith Davey
Canadian Senator

I think Mr. Agnew (U.S. Vice President) wants to shift control of the press from what he calls a few people in New York to a few officials in Washington. We are not trying to give Ottawa control of the press, but we want to make sure press freedom is not considered a privilege by publishers, but a public trust.

Ottawa/The New York Times, 3–10:12.

Joseph T. Dembo
General manager, WCBS Radio, New York

We have the tools, the writers, the producers to effectively tell people what the function of a free press is. We need, in effect, a primer on the First Amendment, and we need to spell out this constitutional guarantee in clear, arresting terms . . . Help us prove to your listeners and ours that we are not egotistically preaching, that an under-

standing of and a willingness to protect press freedom is, in the final analysis, *their* duty and in their own best interest.

Before Connecticut Broadcasters Association, Bridgeport, May 19/Variety, 5–20:39.

Reuven Frank
President, National Broadcasting Company News

If we do our job well, it is to be expected that almost everybody with a special interest he holds important will find something wrong with what we do . . . But they all insist we do it on purpose. Each believes that we set out to do him in. I submit it is not possible. It cannot be our conscious intention to destroy everybody on every side of every subject . . .

Omaha, Jan. 12/Variety, 1–14:46.

Fred W. Friendly
Professor of Journalism, Columbia University; Former president, Columbia Broadcasting System News

We live in a time when facts alone will not tell the story; for when all facts are taken as equal and left unexplained, we contribute to organized chaos.

The Christian Science Monitor, 3–12:5.

Anyone who doubts the ability of newsmen to interpret the news should ask himself who has done the better job of helping the American people understand that Vietnam war—the last two Administrations, or the journalists?

The Christian Science Monitor, 3–18:11.

The journalist fails when he allows himself to be diverted by the tactics of a skilled sleight-of-hand artist like the Vice President (Spiro Agnew).

Before American Jewish Congress, Washington, May 22/ The Washington Post, 5–23:A2.

The media have finally come to realize that all-white newsrooms cannot properly cover their communities. It is essential that more minority-group members become newsmen and, with much-needed new perspec-- tives, help to cover and explain the complex issues of our times.

New York, Aug. 28/
The New York Times, 8-29:11.

Otto Fuerbringer
Vice president, Time, Inc.

One way (to restore confidence in the news media) may be to give the word "objectivity" a renewed status. Objectivity was once the hallmark of American journalism, embraced by editors and taught in all journalism schools. It became an article of faith, a stamp of purity. It fell from high esteem because it became a rigid dogma. Carried to its extreme, it inhibited writers and led to insipid reporting. The revolution against it was successful. By common consent, most journalists today agree that objectivity is impossible to achieve, that complete objectivity is an illusory goal. But, it seems to me, a parallel doctrine that could be dangerous has now sprung up: the feeling that, since it is impossible to achieve objectivity, it is nonsense to try for it. The operative word today is "fairness," a desirable quality that should certainly be high in the lexicon of all reporters and editors. But fairness is, after all, subjective. One man's fairness can be another's subtle attack. On the other hand, objectivity, while it cannot be precisely defined, nevertheless has about it the quality of an absolute which all men can recognize and strive for, even though they cannot achieve it.

Before Sigma Delta Chi Headline Club,
Chicago/The Wall Street Journal, 1-23:6.

J. William Fulbright
United States Senator, D-Ark.

Communication is power; and exclusive access to it (by a President) is a dangerous, unchecked power.

Before Senate Communications Subcommittee,
Washington, Aug. 4/
The New York Times, 8-5:1.

Barry M. Goldwater
United States Senator, R-Ariz.

I think it's time to ask just who these TV news people are. If one of their employes has information or material that would be useful to (a) grand jury or a district attorney in legal proceedings, why shouldn't he be asked to produce the items requested? Are we to take Mr. Goodman's (Julian Goodman, president of the National Broadcasting Company) word for the fact that the news media is above the law?

Before Young Republican Leadership
Training School, Washington, March 12/
The New York Times, 3-13:13.

If the TV industry is seriously worried about the freedom of the press, I suggest it look to its own performance. Because I believe the most serious threat to freedom of the press is the media's own biased attitude.

Before Young Republican Leadership
Training School, Washington, March 12/
The New York Times, 3-13:13.

Henry B. Gonzalez
United States Representative, D-Tex.

If (U.S. Attorney General John) Mitchell is concerned about news accuracy, then he should assure the press its full liberty; for, in the end, if the press is inaccurate its stories will be rejected by the people who read them. It is a controlled press that cannot be contradicted; it is a controlled press that cannot expose facts needful of exposure; and it is a controlled press whose falsehoods cannot be denounced.

Variety, 2-18:34.

Julian Goodman
President, National Broadcasting Company

If every TV camera went blind, not one problem in this country would disappear. If all the media reported only happy news, not a single issue would fade away. They would fester in darkness, and they would erupt. But the public would be ignorant of the causes and not sufficiently aware of the consequences to take effective action.

Before Hollywood Radio and Television
Society, Los Angeles, Jan. 13/
Daily Variety, 1-14:22.

(JULIAN GOODMAN)

What man will talk in confidence of things he knows if his name becomes common property and he is exposed to retribution? What organization will speak to the press if its disclosures turn up as the case for the prosecution? What if reporters and cameramen become linked in the public mind with the police apparatus, as has already happened? Can the press fulfill its function with these handicaps? Will it be believed? The use of government writ to compel newsmen to act as agents of the government or as witness for the state is destructive of our freedoms and offensive to our democratic institutions.

At University of Texas at Austin, March 10/
The New York Times, 3–11:75.

Not since 1798—when newsmen were sentenced to prison under the Sedition Act for statements displeasing to the government—has American journalism been under greater attack. It began with television news. It has moved to newspapers, news magazines and other periodicals. The intent of the attackers doesn't matter, but the effect does. It can limit legitimate news coverage. It can narrow the range of the newsman's sources. It can dry up the flow of information to the public. If the pressure continues, they create a clear and growing danger to the freedom of information secured by the First Amendment.

At University of Texas at Austin, March 10/
The Dallas Times Herald, 3–12:B9.

(Former Vice President Hubert H. Humphrey) does a disservice to thousands of dedicated electronic journalists when he says rating competition leads to unnecessarily spectacular news coverage. His suggestion that the public would be served better if TV news programming were removed from the regular commercial rate structure is based on a false assumption that there is some public-interest distinction between sponsored and unsponsored programming. The FCC has held that there is not. The networks' ability to attract commercial support for regular

and special news programs has, in fact, stimulated the growth and progress of network news operations, and the public has benefitted accordingly. Since advertising provides the only financial support for network programming, removal or restriction of commercial sponsorship of news can only damage, not enhance, the networks' ability to maintain and improve their service to the public through enterprising and comprehensive news coverage.

Before National Association of Broadcasters,
Chicago, April 6/Daily Variety, 4–7:13.

The real competition in journalism is to present events and issues factually, fairly and comprehensively, so the public will understand them. It is a competition to win the public faith, not . . . to win public attention through sensationalism.

Before National Association of Broadcasters,
Chicago, April 6/Variety, 4–8:34.

There is no question that the news media —especially radio and television—are under pressures—official and unofficial—that are perhaps greater than at any time in our history. But it should be apparent that the push will very quickly become a shove if we show signs of knuckling under . . . Of course, we have to keep out of any trouble that threatens our ability to do our jobs and to stay in business. But we will keep out of trouble in Washington the same way we keep out of trouble anywhere else—by going about our work carefully and responsibly. Our mandate as broadcasters and journalists is to provide service to the American public that no one else can offer. And, as broadcasters and journalists, we must stand firmly behind our responsible professional judgments when we know we are right and when we are conducting ourselves in the public interest.

At NBC Radio affiliates convention,
San Francisco, Oct. 19/Variety, 10–21:26.

Katharine Graham
Publisher, "The Washington Post"

We owe the Vice President (Agnew) something, for he has declared open season on the news media, and in so doing he has provoked an important debate and generated some constructive criticism and forced us to reappraise ourselves, which is not something which always comes easy to the news business.

At Sigma Delta Chi convention,
Chicago, Nov. 12/
Los Angeles Times, 11–13:(1)18.

H.R. Haldeman
Assistant to the President of the United States

Somewhere in the jungle labyrinth of Manhattan Island there is a secret nerve center where, every Sunday afternoon, an enormously powerful group of men gather to decide what the "Eastern Establishment Media" line for the coming week will be. A week or so ago, it was "Desperate Gamble," then last week it was "Crisis of Leadership." (This is) "Isolation of the President" week.

At University of California, Los Angeles/
Time, 6–8:41.

Louis Harris
Public opinion analyst

. . . people have a genuine, deep and abiding interest in the substantive problems going on around them, and want more, rather than less, reporting on TV about them. Perhaps more than anything else, people want TV to be something more than a blotter of the contemporary scene and to put some shape and form around the substance of what is shown. The fact is that what the American people want more than anything else today is leadership which will not back off the hard truth of what is happening, but which will be willing to assume the gigantic burden of tackling the problems in substantive terms, rather than turning tricks of rhetoric and then thinking the issue will go away when the words have ended. The media must be willing to stick its neck out by a willingness to take these major substantive areas and to report them, research them, explain them, and even take stands on where

we ought to go to solve them, albeit giving wide open access to all those who disagree. Leadership is not simply to reflect, but to be prepared to go that step beyond the present and spell out the implications, the costs and the sacrifice and pain involved in going through the crucible of genuine betterment of mankind.

At International Radio and Television
Society Newsmakers' Luncheon, New York,
Oct. 8/Variety, 10–21:35.

Palmer Hoyt
Editor and publisher, "Denver Post"

We (the press) can criticize everybody else, so we can and must take it ourselves. And maybe the TV people could take a little, too. However, any restriction on freedom of expression must be viewed with alarm. So far, I don't see any harm that has come from the controversy (criticism of the press) and maybe it has done some good.

Before American Newspaper Publishers
Association, New York/
The New York Times, 4–23:32.

Harold E. Hughes
United States Senator, D-Iowa

Never have we seen anything like the concentrated program of the Nixon Administration—with its bevy of propaganda specialists—flexing its muscles against those elements of the news media who present the information which conflicts with the official Washington version.

San Francisco Examiner & Chronicle
(This World), 8–9:2.

Chet Huntley
News commentator, National Broadcasting Company

A reporter can use good judgment, but if he sounds like Moses writing on the tablets of stone, the message is distorted.

At Oklahoma Broadcasters convention,
Tulsa, Feb. 6/
The Dallas Times Herald, 2–8:A36.

(Patriotism) is not our business. Truth, information, facts and ideas are our business;

(CHET HUNTLEY)

and if these verities, these commodities, are permitted to flourish . . . then the patriotism of all of us is on substantial foundation and flourishes in a benign climate.

At George Polk Memorial Awards luncheon, New York, March 24/Variety, 3–25:43.

Journalists were never intended to be the cheerleaders of a society, the conductors of applause, the sycophants. Tragically, that is their assigned role in authoritarian societies, but not here—not yet.

New York/Newsweek, 4–6:53.

(Discussing his leaving the Huntley-Brinkley news program): I wanted to get these headlines off my neck. Jesus, six nights a week, night after night after night . . . the noise . . . the clamoring for attention . . . the divisions in our society . . . When you deliver it night after night, you start feeling almost *responsible* for it . . . I'm not running away from things; I'm running away to think. Maybe where there's clarity of air, there's clarity of thought.

Interview/Life, 7–17:33.

Nicholas Johnson
Commissioner, Federal Communications Commission of the United States

I believe this wave of government subpoenas, together with other manipulations of the press, have placed the freedom and integrity of this country's news media in serious jeopardy. What will happen to freedom of news gathering—and therefore the public's access to vital information—if news sources know that the material they give in confidence can be subpoenaed by the government for use in public courts of law? The answer, I think, is clear: Sources of news and information will dry up.

Before former Neiman Fellows, Washington, Feb. 12/ The New York Times, 2–13:18.

Never in my tenure as an FCC Commissioner have I seen such serious threats to the integrity of the news media as I think we have witnessed from certain departments of government during the past few months . . . Whether or not the government's recent actions be called "censorship," they have clearly had that result.

Before former Neiman Fellows, Washington, Feb. 12/ The Dallas Times Herald, 2–13:A4.

Recent incidents of television media acquiescence to government demands leaves one with the uneasy feeling that the networks, at least, will not do much fighting for freedom of the press . . . No one has charged a "deal," and I do not. But the results are very much the same as if there were a government-media agreement that the media will take care of the Administration's image, if the Administration will take care of the media's balance sheets.

Washington/Hollywood Reporter, 2–16:1.

John Kauffmann
President, "Washington Star"

I am not concerned with the comments of our Vice President (Agnew), for he has every right to criticize the press as we criticize him . . . What I am suggesting is that big government—with the finest of intentions and, seriously, with a concern for the public interest—is in reality, and without meaning to do so, negating the First Amendment . . . To a major extent, we have brought this situation upon ourselves. We seem to have lost touch with our audience. I speak of all major media. Instead of looking to us to protect them from big government, they (the public) seem to be looking to big government to protect them from the excesses of the press.

Before International Circulation Managers Association, Denver, June 29/ The Dallas Times Herald, 6–30:C3.

Herbert G. Klein
Director of Communications for the President of the United States

A lot of people have made a lot of speeches about the press in various ways, including almost all of the officials (of television) who have been critical of (Vice President) Agnew. I've been a critic of the press as well as a member of it. We've looked at a lot of things, and I think we've improved a lot of things from the press standpoint. But I think the sharpness of Mr. Agnew's attack has done more to focus the industry's attention on itself than anything else has done in the past decade or more. And the question now before us is whether the introspection is healthy. I think that the (Vietnam) war will not continue and that the introspection will result in a better press—and I mean by that a fairer press.

Interview, Washington/
The Christian Science Monitor, 1–8:5.

When there is a demonstration or a riot on campus, those normally quoted are from the minority who have led the disorder. We should know, also, about the students who made the decision not to participate . . . When we neglect the silent majority in the black community, how can we pretend to understand the feelings of those who in the long run will be most likely to lead their neglected area to greater progress, economically and socially? Who understands the man who didn't participate in the Watts or Detroit riots, or the black small businessman, or the silent black teacher? In the old days, many newspapers attempted to reach the views of the silent majority by running "voice of the people" columns. Most of those have been abandoned. Perhaps they became dull. But if so, the fault seems more likely to have been the technique than the subject.

Before Sigma Delta Chi,
Oklahoma City, April 25/
The Dallas Times Herald, 4–26:A31.

I think . . . that our policy represented in the government today is that the key to freedom is to retain a greater free press—a greater and vigorous press that is free to criticize, free to report and free to interpret this very complex age in which we stand. I've heard a lot of comment as to whether there's an effort to intimidate the industry

itself. And I can only say that, as one who has answered reporters' questions, I haven't yet found a good reporter who has been intimidated by a government official.

At 50th anniversary of radio station WWJ,
Detroit, Aug. 20/Milwaukee Journal, 8–21:2.

Frederick B. Lacy
United States Attorney for New Jersey

If mob millions can, as they do, buy souls of otherwise decent people in the public life, can the newspaper profession smugly assume that the slimy tentacles of organized crime will not at least attempt the corruption of the press? . . . It would not be surprising if the mob had tried to distort news by alliances with underpaid reporters, or had tried to get to inside men—like rewrite men or even editors.

Before Sigma Delta Chi, Irvington, N.J.,
Jan. 22/The New York Times, 1–23:18.

John V. Lindsay
Mayor of New York

The license to broadcast in the public interest is not an invitation to mirror the public mood. I am convinced that frank criticism and constructive analysis, openly labeled as editorials and comment, are logical extensions of (broadcasting's) resources and power . . . Satisfying our curiosity is not enough. You and your partners in news have a responsibility larger than conveying the raw facts. The media must point the way, not wait to report that someone else has found it . . . All of this requires the media to risk the wrath of those bruised by candor and frankness. But if you are to fulfill your role in a free society, I hope you will ignore complaints of officials and interests who want the media to serve only them . . . I am suggesting that interpretive radio and TV journalism is not only right; it is also consistent with financial success. There are few occasions when self-interest and conscience coincide; this is one of them.

By phone, to WINS Radio, New York,
fifth anniversary celebration, April 15/
Variety, 4–22:38.

Mike Mansfield
United States Senator, D-Mont.

If the government intimidates reporters or uses the powers of government to suppress their activities or to cut the press off from its sources of information, our press will in fact be controlled, our people will have lost their right to know the truth—and it is the truth that makes men free.

Variety, 2–18:34.

•George S. McGovern
United States Senator, D-S.D.

When the political leaders of our nation set themselves up as judge and jury, freedom of the press is in danger. That is why the deliberate effort of the Nixon-Agnew Administration to harass and intimidate the press is a serious threat (to) our free society. What we are witnessing is an incredible paradox in which the Administration seeks to silence its critics in the media while exploiting the use of the media for its own message to an unprecedented degree.

Before Association for Education in Journalism, American University, Washington, Aug. 18/ Los Angeles Herald-Examiner, 8–18:A4.

Thomas J. McIntyre
United States Senator, D-N.H.

Slowly, almost imperceptibly, our mass communications media are falling into fewer and fewer hands. Unless we face up to the dangers such concentration entails, we may soon lose the diverse and antagonistic voices on which the welfare of our nation depends.

Washington, Jan. 15/ The Washington Post, 1–16:A4.

W. Walter Menninger
Psychiatrist; Member, National Commission on the Causes and Prevention of Violence

Regardless of their performance, the media will never be able to assure the non-violent resolution of conflict; but they can assure the violent resolution of conflict.

The New York Times, 2–5:26.

Abner J. Mikva
United States Representative, D-Ill.

I am concerned, as many of us are, about an insidious situation which is developing between the institutions of government and the press—a situation which has threatening implications for the right of each of us to learn and to know. Censorship is not the issue. I know that American journalists have too much energy and too much integrity to ever allow overt censorship to stifle the flow of their news. What concerns me, instead, is intimidation of those journalists—directly or indirectly—which brings about a censorship of its own: a self-censorship—the reluctance of a newsman to write or report information because he must be wary of personal, legal or financial consequences to himself, his employer or his sources. It is this situation—a government-inspired mind-set which inhibits the journalist's work—which disturbs me, and should disturb all of us.

Before the House, Washington, March 9/ Congressional Record, 3–9:E1759.

John N. Mitchell
Attorney General of the United States

. . . we are not in any way conceding our constitutional and statutory power to request a court to subpoena the press—or anyone else—in any case where, in our opinion, the fair administration of justice requires it . . . We will not permit an innocent man to be convicted or a guilty man to be freed because we declined to subpoena a newsman who had information vital to the case . . . (The) government views subpoenas to the press as an authorized and proper exercise of the Federal grand jury power to obtain facts tending to prove or disprove allegations of criminal conduct.

Before American Bar Association, St. Louis, Aug. 10/ The Washington Post, 8–11:A7; Los Angeles Times, 8–11:(1)7.

Bill Moyers
Publisher, Long Island "Newsday"; Former

Secretary to the President of the United States

I do not fear for the sanctity of the press. We are quite able to protect ourselves . . . But I am less certain that the country as a whole can protect itself from the forces (Vice President) Agnew appears to be rallying. As Owen Glendower boasted in Shakespeare's *Henry IV* (Agnew appears to be saying), "I can call spirits from the vastly deep." Those of us in the press who, like Senator (J. William) Fulbright, have received venomous and threatening letters since Mr. Agnew's speeches, believe we have been hearing from some of those spirits, and they pose a far greater threat to the nation than the grumblings of an unfriendly press.

Before Advertising Club of Washington, Jan. 13 / The Washington Post, 1–14:C4.

George Murphy
United States Senator, R-Calif.

From early morning until late at night we are besieged, boomed at and bombarded by experts who admittedly sell some products, but, between the commercials, give us all the news of the day. Now I want you to understand that I'm gung ho for information. I want it to be full, flowing and factual. There is nothing more important in the lifestream of our nation than a free press. But it must have a certain respect for fact and truth, and an understanding of the various subjects is highly recommended.

At California State College, Los Angeles, April 3 / Los Angeles Times, 4–4:(2)10.

Richard M. Nixon
President of the United States

. . . I've noted with interest that several members of the press corps have indicated a desire for more (Presidential) news conferences. And let me be quite candid as to what I feel about this . . . First, I believe that I have a responsibility to members of the press. I go by that press building of yours about 11:30 at night from the EOB (Executive Office Building). I see most of you still working there. I, as President, have a responsibility to

help you do your job. But I, as President, also have a primary responsibility to do *my* job. Now, my job is, among other things, to inform the American people. Now, one of the ways to inform them is through a press conference like this. Another way is through making reports to the nation, as I did on several occasions about the war in Southeast Asia. Another is an interview—an hour's interview with the three anchor men of the three (TV) networks, which mainly dealt, you may recall, upon Southeast Asia. I feel that all of these are useful ways to inform the American people. I think the American people are entitled to see the President and to hear his views directly, and not to see him only through the press. And I think any member of the press would agree with that.

News conference, Washington, Dec. 10 / The New York Times, 12–11:32.

Everett C. Parker
Director, Office of Communications, United Church of Christ

A key element in the quality of life in any society is the state of its criticism. If criticism of the mass media and the arts comes to be no more than puffery and cheap praise, there is danger of a public lulled into noncritical acceptance of the banal, the sentimental or the simply untrue.

News conference, New York, March 16 / The New York Times, 3–17:70.

Paul VI
Pope

There are no longer newspapers that inform, but newspapers that deform.

Quote, 5–24:481.

Eugene C. Pulliam
Assistant Publisher, Indianapolis "Star" and "News"

Without a free press, man would face the agonizing problems which plague the world today practically without a prayer.

Accepting William H. White Award for Journalistic Merit / Quote, 3–15:241.

George E. Reedy
Former Press Secretary to the President of the United States

Politicians and political types invariably regard the press as an implacable enemy.

At Princeton University, Oct. 6/
Los Angeles Times, 10–8:(1)2.

Richard S. Salant
President, Columbia Broadcasting System News

Selective perception is more of a problem in television, because in print people can skip over what they don't want to read. But *we* cram it down their throats.

The Christian Science Monitor, 3–18:11.

I think most people find the dinner-hour news is a convenient and—relatively—painless way to catch up with events. I think Walter (Cronkite) gives people a certain reassurance. Sure, there has been a bad plane crash, and Nixon said—, and Vietnam goes on. But at least we're still alive and nobody has started the final war. Walter is there and he seems to be saying that we've made it through another day and we'll probably still be around tomorrow.

San Francisco Examiner & Chronicle
(Datebook), 5–31:15.

Although it would be an exaggeration to say that there is significant explicit repression of electronic journalism, the portents are disturbing . . . If newsmen do not tell the truth as they see it because it might make waves, or if their bosses decide something should or should not be broadcast because of Washington or Main Street consequences, we have dishonored ourselves and we have lost the First Amendment by default. All that is easy to say, but it's mighty hard to do. It takes an awesome amount of guts . . . the problem—as we who live with it so often see —is government's trying to enforce . . . eminently sound journalistic principles. The notion of government enforcement is, literally, like seduction—creeping seduction. It all starts innocently; but, as can readily be

seen from the growing body of regulations and decisions, one thing leads to another. A benign government smile, a benevolent introduction—and where it ends, nobody knows. Or perhaps, more accurately, everybody knows *exactly* where it ends.

Before Tennessee Association of Broadcasters,
Gatlinburg, Oct. 16/Variety, 10–21:26.

Aline Saarinen
Author, Journalist

I'm especially concerned about Vice President Spiro T. Agnew's attack on the media. We in the media aren't evil people, as he seems to believe. We try to be impartial, but what do you do if you have five minutes in which to give the news? Do you tell about the little boy who found a puppy or report that so many more boys were killed in action (in Vietnam)? You have to make decisions when you have just so much news to report and so much time and space to do it in. The very process of choice becomes a form of editorializing, particularly in television where you have sight and sound.

Interview, New York/
The Christian Science Monitor, 5–29:4.

Thomas W. Sarnoff
Executive vice president, National Broadcasting Company

We welcome constructive criticism, but we do not welcome intimidation. It is no longer proper for government disagreement to become government pressure on a federally licensed medium of news. Our nation's problems wouldn't be easier to solve if TV just ignored them. The specter of censorship has clearly been raised.

Before Idaho State Broadcasters Association,
Boise, Jan. 28/Daily Variety, 1–28:17.

Rene Schenker
Director, French television services in Switzerland

The true journalist must not only report the truth of the event he has reported, but he also has a duty to make spectators understand what he has said.

At Monte Carlo International Television Festival/Hollywood Reporter, 2-19:12.

Glenn T. Seaborg
Chairman, Atomic Energy Commission of the United States

A good and conscientious journalist faces an incredible task today. He is operating in a world of increasingly rapid change, flooded with torrents of events generated by a growing number of "activists." He is confronted by new complexity created by a scientific-technological culture that speaks a new language he must learn more of every day. He is challenged to be objective and subjective, factual and fascinating, respectful and provocative, patriotic and apolitical all at one and the same time. He is charged to be all this in a country filled with conflicting ideas and facts espoused by seemingly knowledgeable and sincere people, as well as by a number of attention-getting individuals who make news by their public "put-ons." And he is asked to capture public attention in a society saturated with information and entertainment from competing media, that is often stimulated by them to the point of either frenzy or stupor . . . For all their problems, newsmen do a remarkable job and one that I'm sure is not fully appreciated by most of the American public.

At Associated Press Managing Editors convention, Honolulu/ The Dallas Times Herald, 11-24:A18.

Eric Sevareid
News commentator, Columbia Broadcasting System

The bad news is what's news because you assume normalcy. If you assumed nothing but upheaval, then only good news would be real news.

Interview/TV Guide, 3-14:10.

(Vice President) Agnew wants to know where we (news commentators) stand. We stand—or rather sit—right here, in the full glare. At a disadvantage as against politicians. We can't cast one vote in committee, and opposite vote on the floor; can't say one thing in the North, and opposite thing in the South. We hold no tenure, four years or otherwise, and can be voted out with a twist of the dial. We can't use invective and epithets; can't even dream of impugning the patriotism of leading citizens; can't reduce every complicated issue to yes or no, black or white; and would rather go to jail than do bodily injury to the marvelous English language. We can't come down on this side or that side of each disputed public issue because we're trying to explain far more than advocate and because some issues don't have two sides; some have three, four or half a dozen, and in these matters we're damned if we know the right answers. This may be why most of us look a bit frazzled while Mr. Agnew looks so serene.

Commentary, CBS Evening News, Oct. 21/ The Washington Post 10-26:A22.

The central point about the free press is not that it be accurate, though it must try to be; not that it even be fair, though it must try to be that; but that it be free. And that means, in first instance, freedom from any and all attempts by the power of government to coerce it or intimidate it or police it in any way.

San Francisco Examiner & Chronicle (This World), 11-1:2.

Frank Shakespeare
Director, United States Information Agency

With news, (the *Voice of America* has) to present the things that really happen, even though some of them are unpleasant, merely for credibility. If all you talk about is beauty, truth and motherhood, no one would believe you, and you'd end up like *Radio Moscow*, which is a joke. However, in my view, the presentation of these things has a very positive effect, because we thus show to foreign people that we are a free and open society. In our films and TV programs, we try to provide people in foreign lands with a frame of reference for these events. We who live here in the U.S. have our own frame of reference built in. But people in Poland, in Chad, in Thailand or in Ecuador don't.

Interview, Washington/TV Guide, 12–5:13.

Howard K. Smith
News commentator, American Broadcasting Company

Our liberal friends (in the news media) today have become dogmatic. They have a set of automatic reactions. They react the way political cartoonists do—with oversimplification. Oversimplify. Be sure you please your fellows, because that's what's "good." They're conventional; they're conformists. They're pleasing *The Washington Post*, they're pleasing the editors of *The New York Times* and they're pleasing one another.

Interview, Washington/TV Guide, 2–28:8.

Newsmen are *proud* of the fact that the middle class is antagonistic to them. They're proud of being out of contact with the middle class. Joseph Kraft did a column in which he said: "Let's face it, we reporters have little to do with middle America. They're not our kind of people." Well, I resent that. *I'm* from middle America.

Interview, Washington/TV Guide, 2–28:8.

As reporters, we have always been falsifying issu: by reporting on what goes wrong in a nation where, historically, most has gone i .;ht. That is how you get on page one; that is how you win a Pulitzer Prize. This gears the reporter's mind to the negative—even when it is not justified.

Interview, Washington/TV Guide, 2–28:11.

I. Norman Smith
Editor, "Ottawa Journal"

In a frantic world, everyone feels he can criticize. The press is not so popular that we can continue to hide behind the shield of freedom of the press. We dish it out and we can take it. Today we have to.

Interview/The New York Times, 3–10:12.

Frank Stanton
President, Columbia Broadcasting System

The question of the extent to which news-gathering organizations and reporters can be required in certain criminal proceedings to provide materials gathered in the course of news functions, but not published or broadcast, is an immensely important one. Broad, unrestricted access to reporters' notes, notebooks and other materials not published or broadcast can have a direct and seriously adverse effect on the free flow of information and access to news sources.

New York, Feb. 3/Daily Variety, 2–4:1.

Lowell Thomas
News commentator, Columbia Broadcasting System

I've always considered myself as an observer of the human shadow show. I've never been a special pleader, but I've always been concerned. But as an observer I've always tried to avoid the gloomy. I've always been at the same time, which is the dinner hour, and I didn't want to destroy the digestive system of America.

Interview, New York, Oct. 21/
Los Angeles Times, 11–5:(4)24.

Fletcher Thompson
United States Representative, R-Ga.

One would have to be half blind and extremely naive to think that newsmen are not human and that at least some could have a personal financial interest in legislation and attempt to influence it through the pressure of their news reporting.

Cleveland Plain Dealer, 8–12:B2.

Melba Tolliver
News commentator, WABC-TV, New York

People expect a woman TV reporter to be a combination of Raquel Welch and Eric Sevareid. It gets pretty discouraging when you do a story on air pollution and the next day you get a letter from a woman who liked the ribbed sweater you were wearing.

Interview, New York/
The New York Times, 2–9:43.

Sander Vanocur
News commentator, National Broadcasting Company

It is our job to keep the government honest.

At Harper College, Palatine, Ill./
Variety, 7–22:1.

. . . when you have the Vice President (Agnew) slapping at network brass who depend upon the government for their charters, that isn't a threat, it is intimidation. It is the rawest form of blackmail. The Nixon Administration cannot stand dissent. I have never in my life seen such flagrant pressure put on the united press as in this Administration.

At Harper College, Palatine, Ill./
Variety, 7–22:51.

Nick B. Williams
Editor and executive vice president, "Los Angeles Times"

Very broadly . . . what ought to be the purpose in editing a newspaper? . . . The first purpose, I think, should be to preserve the best of the past while reaching for the potential best of the future. The purpose should be to reconcile the basic constitutional goals of individual liberty and individual happiness with the philosophical goal of the greatest good for the greatest number. The purpose, that is, should be to seek justice, in every sense of that word, for all men and for every man, in an age as revolutionary as that in which the Constitution itself was phrased; an age in which technology and the sheer mass of the world's exploding populations have made justice seem at best impersonal and vague, and at worst have made individual justice unattainable; and have made violence seem, if not a sure path to justice and happiness, its own rational necessity; a revolutionary age, in which the physical conveniences of our lives have made our institutions seem no longer adequate and no longer unchallengeable, although the original needs for these institutions do persist. All this implies the dangerously-abrasive nature of the controversies of this century, beyond our nation and within it. And the purpose in editing a newspaper then becomes, in this kind of age, to speak with tolerance when we can, and with passion when we must, but always to speak out—to take risks with caution, but to take them. To take them in a world and an age that is moving.

Accepting Distinguished Achievement Award
of Journalism Alumni Association,
University of Southern California,
Los Angeles/Los Angeles Times, 11–15:F3.

Ronald L. Ziegler
Press Secretary to the President of the United States

I have a lot of respect for the press. The key to this job is a willingness to understand the problems that the press faces and to work at those problems—recognizing, of course, that I don't work for them; I work for the President.

Interview, Washington/
Los Angeles Times, 2–22:E1.

Our democracy is working because our people are well-informed.

Before Radio-Television News Directors
Association/The Dallas Times Herald,
9–25.A2.

Literature

Richard Armour
Author

At some point, children are turned away from poetry. When they are little, they love it; but the teachers, or perhaps because the lines don't mean anything to them . . . something turns them off. Like Arnold Bennett once said: "The thing that clears a room faster than anything but a fire hose or a swarm of bees is for someone to say he's going to talk on poetry." I'm trying to get children and adults back on poetry. I think it should be clear, understandable, rather than obscure and, for the young, not sentimental.

Interview/Los Angeles Herald-Examiner,
10–14:C3.

W. H. Auden
Poet

If you take two poems by one man and read them, and you can't tell which was written first—that is a minor poet.

At Downstate Medical Center, Brooklyn,
N.Y., Dec. 15/The New York Times, 12–16:43.

Saul Bellow
Author

We have better writers than we ever had before. But so many of them are gnarled and tangled up in irrelevancies. They all—or most of them—have their gimmick, and they think that gimmick is sufficient.

San Francisco Examiner & Chronicle, 2–1:B4.

I don't want to join the jet set like (Gore) Vidal or (Truman) Capote. If (Norman) Mailer wants to be the Joe Louis of literature, fine. I don't want to be a public figure or go on TV. I'm not trying to free the middle-class mind from sexual repression . . . I'm just an old-fashioned writer.

Interview/Time, 2–9:82.

Robert L. Bernstein
President, Random House

I believe the chances of a (writing) talent emerging today are much greater if the power and the financial assets of a big publishing house are behind that talent. It is difficult enough for a writer to get a work published without having to take the chance that his publisher may not have the means or the staff to promote his work—or even to stay in business.

Interview/The New York Times Magazine,
8–16:14.

Paul L. Briand, Jr.
Professor of English, State University of New York at Oswego

. . . fifty-three per cent of adult Americans have not read a book since they left school. What, indeed as Mark Twain says, is the difference between the man who cannot read and the man who can read and doesn't? There is none. Clearly, then, we are graduating from our schools thousands upon thousands of technical illiterates every year.

Convocation address at summer session,
College of Arts and Sciences, S.U.N.Y.
at Oswego, July 8/Vital Speeches, 9–1:676.

Bennett Cerf
Chairman, Random House

I may be remembered as the only publisher who could have gotten along with John O'Hara. John was the master of the fancied slight. Anything remotely like a snub or insult could set him off . . . He could be the most charming man when he wanted to; the only trouble was that he turned it off as quickly as he turned it on . . . Underneath that childishness, John was a really good man—and probably the most under-recognized writer of the generation. He accused me of all sorts of shenanigans to my face, but behind my back he was as loyal as he could be. I prefer that to the authors who are gentle and nice to your face and stab you in the back.

Los Angeles/Los Angeles Times, 4–27:(4)9.

John Creasey
Author

In the beginning, I wrote 38 novels and couldn't publish one of them—perhaps because I was writing on subjects I knew something about. So I switched and began to write of things I knew nothing about—and everything I have written since then has been published.

Santa Fe, N.M./
The Christian Science Monitor, 8–6:13.

John Fowles
Author

Doing fiction well is like eating or making love. If you don't want to do it with your whole self, then there is something wrong with doing it. But I cannot tell you how the mood comes. If I only knew!

Interview/Life, 5–29:57.

Yasunari Kawabata
Author; Winner, 1968 Nobel Prize for Literature

. . . it seems to me that people do not necessarily need to read. It might be enough just to observe nature and people. But I can't imagine who could get along without reading at all. If there should be anyone, it would be very interesting . . . Reading and watching are two different ways of learning. I would like people to do both.

Interview/The Washington Post,
Book World, 1–11:2.

Anatoly Kuznetsov
Soviet author

Since the age of 14, I have been published in Russia. For these 25 years, not one of my works—starting with a minuscule novella and ending with a big novel—was published the way I wrote it—not one. Now (in the West, after his defection), everything is being published, down to the last dot. Fantastic!

Interview, London/
The Christian Science Monitor, 12–3:11.

Lewis Mumford
Author

Writing an honest autobiography is so difficult. Not just because one doesn't want to say everything one can say about oneself, but because it involves other people. As long as they're alive, one can't just speak with absolute freedom about them—not unless one's a heel.

Interview, Amenia, N.Y./
The New York Times, 10–20:89.

John O'Hara
Author

Loafing and excuse-making are occupational diseases related to unfinished work, and all three affect the honesty of a writer's writing. The man who has made a financial success of writing is in the worst danger of all, and it is hardly a secret that I am one of those who have made money. But I believe, and I suppose I have always believed, that the writer who loafs after he has made a financial success is confessing that the money was all he was after in the first place. That was never my idea. Much as I like owning a Rolls Royce, for instance, I could do without it. What I could *not* do without is a typewriter, a supply of yellow-second-sheets and the time to put them to good use.

Quote, 5–3:425.

S.J. Perelman
Author

As a glittering generality, reality has overtaken fantasy. One great problem for comic writers is that life today surpasses any fantasy you can think of. Almost everything is so bizarre . . . When you see your exterminator riding in on the train with you, carrying his English attache case, wearing a hat that looks like a cone of ice cream, and those great flowing sideburns—what fantasy could one write that's any funnier?

Interview, New York/
The Washington Post, 10–18:E4.

(S. J. PERELMAN)

The dubious privilege of a freelance writer is he's given the freedom to starve anywhere.

Interview, New York/
The Washington Post, 10–18:E4.

Erich Maria Remarque
Author

The task of an author whose first book was successful is much more difficult than the work of a writer whom critics can scrutinize, and comment on (his) progress and development. A writer who succeeds in gaining quick popularity hardly escapes the envy of his colleagues.

Interview, Lake Maggiore, Switzerland/
The Christian Science Monitor, 5–14:13.

Leo Rosten
Author

(How he does his writing): Well, I fill a fountain pen with my blood, work 12 to 15 hours a day, and write the first draft in longhand. Then I rewrite, using scissors and Scotch tape. I embroider, perhaps keeping one line or several paragraphs, or start over. I get great pleasure out of it (rewriting). It's like the jeweler who doesn't have to mine, but loves polishing the stones or adding facets. Unfortunately, of course, I also have to do the mining.

Telephone interview/Look, 12–15:Sec.M.

Karl Shapiro
Professor of English, University of California at Davis

The downhill speed of American poetry in the last decade has been breathtaking for those who watch the sport. Poetry plunged out of the classics, out of the modern master, out of all standards, and plopped into the playpen. There we are, entertained with the fecal-buccal carnival of the Naughties and the Uglies, who have their own magazines and publishing houses, and the love-lorn alienates, nihilists, disaffiliates, who croon or "rock" their way into the legitimate publishing establishment . . . Entertainment is a healthful and life-giving diversion of the masses, and even the high-decibel howls of the pseudo-poets deserve a niche in the wall of time. But the deliberate obtrusion of the howler or the rocker-crooner upon the literate minority can serve no other purpose than to destroy the sensibilities of everyone concerned. Discrimination is a dirty word in the vocabulary of politics, but in literature it is one of the holiest of concepts. Without it, all is offal. Publishers, even those who formerly prided themselves on the quality of their publications, are now miring themselves in the dismal swamp of the adolescent revolution.

Before California Library Association,
San Francisco/Human Events, 7–11:10.

We are experiencing a literary breakdown which is unlike anything I know of in the history of letters. It is something new and something to be reckoned with. We have reached the level of mindlessness at which students and the literate public can no longer distinguish between poetry and gibberish. Ten years ago, nobody would have dreamed of comparing Robert W. Service or Edgar Guest—poor Edgar—or even Joyce Kilmer with Andrew Marvell or Robert Browning. But today I read in a California paper that a "serious critic . . . has likened the Beatles' lyrics to Shakespeare's work." I read that Bob Dylan is "the major poet of his generation." Arrogance and ignorance always go hand in hand, and now we are having both shoved at us from all sides: from publishers, from professional saboteurs and from many dog-in-the-manger professors as well.

Before California Library Association,
San Francisco/Human Events, 7–11:10.

Isaac Bashevis Singer
Author

There are five hundred reasons why I began to write for children, but to save time I will mention only ten of them. Number 1: Children read books, not reviews. They don't give a hoot about the critics. Number 2: They don't read to find their identity. Number 3: They don't read to free themselves of guilt, to quench the thirst for rebellion, or to get rid of alienation. Number 4: They have no use for psychology. Number 5: They detest sociology. 6: They don't try to understand Kafka or *Finnegan's Wake*. 7: They still believe in God, the family, angels, devils, witches, goblins, logic, clarity, punctuation and other such obsolete stuff. 8: They love interesting stories, not commentary, guides or footnotes. 9: When a book is boring, they yawn openly, without any shame or fear of authority. 10: They don't expect their beloved writer to redeem humanity. Young as they are, they know it is not in his power. Only the adults have such childish illusions.

Accepting National Book Award for children's literature/The Wall Street Journal, 3–10:16.

Elizabeth Speare
Author

Children need textbooks for the heart as well as for the mind. The enduring values of life—courage, devotion, compassion, forgiveness—none of these can be absorbed entirely by the mind, but must instead be received into the heart. These values are the raw material of fiction.

Receiving the Newberry Award/ Quote, 5–10:435.

Roger Straus
President, Farrar, Straus & Giroux

. . . what has really happened is that there has been a management breakdown in publishing. There has been an enormous turnover in editors. Authors and their agents are in a state of anxiety. They don't know who is where anymore or even if it matters. The situation in so many publishing houses today is that there has been no continuity of thoughtful management that is beamed to the literary product and not to somebody's idea of an instant market.

National Observer, 11–30:23.

Jacqueline Susann
Author

The bad reviews don't bother me, as long as the public is reading the book. Critics are usually people who have tried writing and failed.

Interview, Dallas/ The Dallas Times Herald, 7–24:B1.

Albert Szent-Gyorgyi
Biologist

It (his book, *The Crazy Ape*) is a revolutionary book because it's only 40 pages. It can be read in two hours. The trouble with books is that they cannot be read. Who the hell has time to read 300 pages? There is nothing you can't say in two hours if it is essential.

Interview, Woods Hole, Mass./ The New York Times, 2–20:37.

Dalton Trumbo
Author

All a writer needs is a pencil and a sheet of paper and he's in business . . . A director needs material to direct; an actor needs lines to deliver. But there's no way to stop a writer, even when he's in jail or in exile.

Interview, San Francisco/ San Francisco Examiner, 11–20:27.

Kurt Vonnegut, Jr.
Author

It's a lot of fun (being a famous writer). It really is. The money is nice. I'm only sorry it happened now. I wish it had happened a hell of a lot earlier. Most writers—myself included—would just settle for a fixed income so they can do their work. But, for some reason, that's not the way it works. It comes in practically not at all or in crazy amounts. Nothing in between.

At press conference with student editors, New York/National Observer, 10–12:21.

Robert Penn Warren
Author, Poet

Concerning literature . . . the most obvious question is: What subject matter is ap-

(ROBERT PENN WARREN)

propriate for our time? . . . it is hard to tell at any given moment what is relevant. The thing so advertised is likely to be as unrelated to reality as the skirt length is to the construction of the female anatomy—to be relevant, to change our metaphor, merely to a symptom and not to the disease. The question is not that of the topicality of a subject. It is that of the writer's own grounding in his time, the relation of his sensibility to his time and, paradoxically enough, of his resistance to his time. For there must be resistance. And the good work is always the drama of the writer's identity with, and struggle against, his time.

Accepting 1970 National Medal for Literature,
Washington, Dec. 2/
The Washington Post, 12–6:C3.

Elie Wiesel
Author

. . . on the whole, the French public is more literary-minded than the American audience . . . They take literature very seriously there. Anyone who gets an award sells. Here (in the U. S.), most bestsellers are disputed on their literary merits. In France, at least 50 per cent of the bestsellers are truly literary works.

Interview, The Washington Post
(Book World), 2–8:2.

Medicine and Health

Spiro T. Agnew
Vice President of the United States

I find another virtue in the pursuit of science—namely, as a channel into which the youth of a nation can pour its impressive strength to create a better world. Although I in no way challenge the right of youth, and indeed the obligation of youth, to make their voices heard responsibly in the corridors of political power, I would draw their attention to the challenges of the laboratories of science as well. I would urge more young men and women to join in the difficult but challenging course of action, exemplified by the activities of every individual at this meeting. The solution to the problem of cancer will take diligent research, long-term investment of time and energy, an optimistic faith that the problem can be solved, and a dedication to the improvement of human life. Is this not what our youths are demanding, and is this not a proper battle for them to join?

*Before International Cancer Congress,
Houston, May 24 /
Los Angeles Times, 5–25:(1)5.*

I propose that the nations of this world—plagued by many ills, some admittedly of our own making, some born of nature—that these nations, which occupy only a very small portion of the universe, declare the next 10 years to be a decade against disease. Let us join in any manner open to us—by increase in the exchange of cooperative research information, by joining in projects, by avoiding unnecessary duplication of unusual and expensive facilities, by examining the health hazards in our environment, by committing funds when we can and, most important, by rising above narrow self-interest—let us join together in a determined venture to make life and health the birthright of all children

born from this day on, regardless of nationality, race or religious beliefs.

*Before International Cancer Congress,
Houston, May 24 /
Los Angeles Times, 5–25:(1)8.*

George W. Albee
Professor of Psychology, Case Western Reserve University

I think part of the widespread willingness to write off psychoanalysis, to say it's useless and dead, is a continuing reaction against the analytic insight that one's adult behavior is largely determined by one's childhood experience. The whole Western, or at least Protestant, ethic was that one had freedom of choice and could choose to behave this way or that, and that if you wanted to be saved, you acted in certain consistent ways. So, along comes Freud and a field which says that you are really not free to choose; that you are behaving in ways that are determined. Then, we are no longer able to choose salvation and are just another part of the empty universe, bodies in motion, with no eternal hand guiding us.

Interview / The Washington Post, 11–22:B2.

Christiaan Barnard
Heart transplant surgeon

To be honest, I enjoy my popularity. But I remind myself of all the people who contribute to a single success in a field like heart surgery. It's like an orchestra—one man takes all the bows.

Time, 5–11:49.

Larry Alan Bear
Commissioner, New York City Addiction Services Agency

Heroin addiction is not a new problem. With increasing experimentation, kids are

(LARRY ALAN BEAR)

making decisions at 12 years old. Peer-group pressure forces them to try soft drugs, and we are going to find ourselves with a far greater problem of drug usage that will make the present heroin problem look like a picnic. We have to address ourselves to the kids who are not yet using soft drugs at all. They need interference therapy before they go on into the drug scene.

Interview, New York/
The New York Times, 3–13:24.

Howard Bierman
Clinical Professor of Medicine, Loma Linda (Calif.) University School of Medicine

People worry about the Hong Kong flu that comes every year and, in a relatively serious outbreak, claimed 2,000 or so lives in the United States. But one patient dies of cancer in the United States every minute—about 1,400 a day and about half a million a year. If the public and government got as uptight about cancer as they periodically do about flu, the death toll from cancer could be cut nearly in half during the 1970s.

Los Angeles, Feb. 19/
Los Angeles Times, 2–20:(1)31.

Richard Blum
Director, Psychopharmacology Project, Stanford University

Chemicals can help people become normal for a while if there is something wrong with them, if they have a pain, for example. But I don't think anybody has discovered a drug that scientists say makes you any better than you were at a point where you were already operating normally and effectively. There will be no solution to our drug problems until we put our minds in order; until, really, what we decide our minds are for.

Look, 4–7:61.

Walter C. Bornemeier
President, American Medical Association

For the past 25 years, more and more of our medical school graduates have been withheld from the productive practice of medicine for two to five or more years in order to pursue their education in a specialty. Today there are about 35,000 of these licensed doctors of medicine, graduates of schools in the United States, in residency training programs. A high percentage of these are over 30 years of age. These young men and women would have been in the active practice of medicine under our system of training 25 or 30 years ago . . . In addition to these 35,000 residents, there are an estimated 5,000 of our best physicians who have quit practice to take positions as medical educators in the full-time employment of the hospital for the purpose of teaching the residents . . . No wonder we have a doctor shortage.

Inaugural address, Chicago/
Human Events, 12–6:9.

Jim Brown
Actor

One thing they're never going to get me for is marijuana. I hate it. And it's getting worse. There's always somebody doing it—it's so "in." And a non-smoker feels guilty saying, "No, I don't do it." They act like, "This guy is looking down on us." You can't tell them not to, because then you're preaching and you're square. I think it's harmful because it's a crutch. I'm talking about young people. They lose their ambition to do healthy things. You have to have a certain amount of discipline. I have a choice of getting out of bed every morning and going to work, or a I can be lazy and seek out thrills and just die away.

Interview, New York/
Los Angeles Herald-Examiner, 2–27:A23.

Dmitri F. Chebotarev
Director, Institute of Gerontology, Soviet Academy of Medical Sciences

If anyone thinks that life is like the unwinding of a clock and that, if you can find a way to rewind it, you can live longer, he is wrong. Aging is a genetic process.

News conference, Kiev, U.S.S.R./
The New York Times, 2–22:(1)2.

Leo Cherne
Executive director, Research Institute of America

Pot and hashish will long before the end of this century have fallen into disuse, simply because they're inefficient drugs. Whatever the debate about habituating qualities or the harm they cause, one can't escape the clear fact that among the least productive tier of nations are the hashish-smoking countries of northern Africa.

Before Business Publications Audit meeting,
Chicago, Feb. 18 / Vital Speeches, 4–15:410.

Robert B. Choate
Nutrition authority

The cartoon maker, the jingle writer and the box-label designer, the food broker and the supermarket manager are helping to shape our food habits . . . Junior is off at the TV set being misinformed by various ads, while mother is slicing open a plastic package to save time and trouble. Rather than being the world's best-fed nation, we are the world's most misfed nation.

Before House Democratic Study Group panel,
Washington, Sept. 18 /
Los Angeles Times, 9–19:(1)4.

Ramsey Clark
Former Attorney General of the United States

Our clearest duty is education—that's the essential part of any drug program. Kids wouldn't take drugs such as speed—that is, amphetamines—if they really believed it would hurt them. We are dealing with very skeptical young people, and part of the reason is the crazy way we've handled the marijuana problem. We've just never done the research. I tried for two years to get doctors to tell me about the effects of marijuana and I couldn't. Now, we're in the situation where we cried wolf about marijuana, and the kids don't believe us about other drugs. But there are some real wolves around.

Interview, New York /
Los Angeles Herald-Examiner, 11–29:A15.

William Clay
United States Representative, D-Mo.

He (President Nixon) can live with a budget that appropriates $400 per person for defense, but he can't live with a bill that appropriates $13 per person for health. He says that's inflationary.

Television broadcast, Feb. 8 /
The New York Times, 2–9:1.

Luther Cloud
President, National Council on Alcoholism

I don't think marijuana is any more a problem than going to the movies on Saturday afternoon is a problem. Ours is an alcohol-oriented culture, not a marijuana-oriented one.

San Francisco Examiner & Chronicle
(This World), 3–22:16.

Charles Max Cole
President, Texas Medical Association

. . . the Medicare and Medicaid programs were politically conceived and designed at the national level. The programs are being continually manipulated and hampered by new federal regulations and directives. The simple fact is that the federal government has promised more than it can deliver and more than the taxpayer is willing to pay for. It is not surprising that the Medicaid program throughout the country is costing three times more than had been estimated. It is inappropriate and morally wrong for government to promise medical care and then ask the providers of services to subsidize it.

The Dallas Times Herald, 2–13:A27.

Alex Comfort
Director, Group on Aging, University College, London

The age of sinility today is exactly what it was at the time of Moses. What medicine has achieved so far, in conjunction with social betterment, is to enable more people to reach old age. No amount of conventional effort—cancer research, spare-part surgery, or welfare—can do more than rearrange the distribution of death to make it more common at ages 75 to 80. In privileged societies we are already pushing that limit.

San Francisco Examiner & Chronicle (This World), 5–31:19.

Denton Cooley
Chief surgeon, Texas Heart Institute, Houston

The public is becoming discouraged, after looking at the record of (heart) transplants. The public was oversold on the prospects for the patient after the first operation . . . Out of the 150 such operations in the past 2½ years, there are nine men alive today, seven of whom have lived more than a year . . . If I have a recipient and a proper donor, however, I will perform another transplantation at any time.

News conference, Los Angeles/ Los Angeles Herald-Examiner, 2–24:A9.

The initial experience with cardiac transplantation has been encouraging. In fact, nothing has been encountered which was not anticipated from the outset. The remarkable prolongation of life and restoration of good cardiac output has been most encouraging and somewhat beyond expectation. In the future, the challenge remains with the prevention of rejection. Once this and other obstacles are overcome by the immunologists, then cardiac transplantation will hold greater promise.

Family Weekly, 3–22:7.

Michael DeBakey
President, College of Medicine, Baylor University

The truth is that medical care today goes where the money is.

Quote, 7–26:73.

Gerald D. Dorman
President, American Medical Association

The profession resents the fact, the inference, that (any physician) who made over $25,000 in a single year is padding or doing

something illegal . . . Most doctors across the country are working 65 to 70 hours a week . . . A steelworker who put in that many hours would be making over $40,000 a year, and a carpenter who worked that many hours would receive about $30,000. But if we put doctors on a 40-hour week, we would need 50 per cent more doctors.

News conference, Los Angeles, March 3/ Los Angeles Herald-Examiner, 3–4:A3.

If we continue to pattern our activities on the requirements of yesterday and on the conditions of yesterday, we shall find ourselves reliving yesterday over and over again.

Before American Medical Association, Chicago/The Dallas Times Herald, 6–23:A2.

Charles C. Edwards
Commissioner, Food and Drug Administration of the United States

Yesterday's adolescent fads—goldfish swallowing and hula hoops—have given way to the frightening fad of the "high." All elements of society, and especially those of us in the health profession, must mobilize to rid ourselves and our children of this idea of chemical nirvana.

Before National Association of Retail Druggists, Atlantic City, N.J., Oct. 21/ Los Angeles Herald-Examiner, 10–22:A6.

Roger O. Egeberg
Assistant Secretary for Health and Scientific Affairs, Department of Health, Education and Welfare of the United States

If we voted some kind of universal health insurance program right now, we would make the people think that this year or next year, or at the latest the year after, they are going to get a doctor just by clicking their fingers. And it won't happen. Therefore, I think the people will be resentful against the government and against the doctors.

Interview, Washington/ The Dallas Times Herald, 11–19:A8.

R.S. Farr
President, American Academy of Allergy

It is my opinion that a study is needed to

help doctors decide whether aspirin should be a prescription item, prudently given under the same watchful eye we now give such preparations as penicillin, digitalis and the barbiturates.

Before American Academy of Allergy,
New Orleans/Los Angeles Times, 2–24:(2)2.

Joseph W. Gardella
Dean of student affairs, Harvard University Medical School

They've a greater sense of social awareness (today's medical students), a real sense of compassion, a great concern for injustice and a seriousness of purpose I haven't seen in any other generation—so much, in fact, that it often impairs their sense of humor. Today's medical student will devote infinite time and energy to achieving his purposes if he thinks they are just and right . . . My generation of doctors was concerned with social success. It was a fun-loving, elitist society, interested in a more material, highly organized way of life which provided for security, comfort and success. The present-day students are impossible to understand if your concepts and standards are of a former generation.

Interview, Boston/
The Dallas Times Herald, 10–7:A8.

William Glasser
Psychiatrist

. . . coming under the influence of drugs is an attempt to escape from a reality which many young people who feel failure judge too painful to endure. The fact is that they *can* feel better for a short time by using drugs, so it is useless to criticize them as being immoral—any more than you can criticize someone for taking aspirin for a headache. We have to help them to succeed, to get rid of the pain—or we will never reduce narcotic use.

Interview/U.S. News & World Report,
4–27:42.

John J. Hanlon
Assistant Surgeon-General, United States Public Health Service

It is fine and wonderful to heal the sick, to repair the ravages of illness and injury. But this does not, of itself, get at the root cause of human health problems, which are dependent more and more on environmental determinants. It is not enough to treat chronic respiratory disease—and then to send the victim back into smog-filled air, or to the fumes and dust of an unwholesome work environment. It is not enough to treat the ghetto mother and her sick, undernourished child—and then hope that others will somehow clean up the toxic, filthy, rat-infested kennels that house the poor in an environment where disease and death are bound to flourish . . . (The doctor's) voice should be heard loud and clear at the time when it matters most—that is, when public policies that affect the environment and life are being formulated.

At Clinical Convention of American Medical
Association, Boston, Nov. 30/
The New York Times, 12–1:20.

Harold E. Hughes
United States Senator, D-Iowa

We cannot wish narcotics and mind-altering drugs out of existence; we cannot legislate them away; we cannot enforce them into oblivion. But we can do something about healing sick people and about preventing others from incurring the illness. We are properly concerned about protecting society from crime induced by drugs. But the protection is a delusion, unless we get at the problem of addiction itself. Somehow, public programs and policies get diverted from the central point, the need for salvaging human beings—both for the protection of society and for simple humanity. Armed with this understanding, I am convinced that we can meet the drug problem sensibly and be a stronger and better society for so doing.

Before the Senate, Washington, March 9/
Congressional Record, 3–9:S3222.

John E. Ingersoll
Director, Bureau of Narcotics and Dangerous Drugs, Department of Justice of the United States

Comparing marijuana to alcohol is not a valid concept. The two are used for different purposes. People smoke marijuana specifically for the purpose of getting "high." I would say that the vast majority of people who consume alcohol don't do it for that purpose. Alcohol is a depressant. Marijuana is a hallucinogen.

Interview, Washington/
U.S. News & World Report, 5–25:40.

Jacob K. Javits
United States Senator, D-N.Y.

It is now clear that some form of mandatory prepaid health care for all Americans is an idea whose time has arrived.

The Dallas Times Herald, 4–14:A2.

John Kirklin
Chairman, Department of Surgery, University of Alabama Medical School

I think the whole (heart) transplant thing has been blown up way out of proportion to its importance in terms of solving the health problems of the American public, and to the contribution it makes to our fundamental knowledge. It has done nobody any good; it has raised a lot of false hopes; it has degraded the American surgeon in many people's eyes.

Interview, Birmingham, Ala./
The Dallas Times Herald, 3–25:AAA4.

Harry Klenda
President, American Dental Association

Within the decade, people will be immunized against cavities by swallowing a pill.

Before American Academy of Dental Practice Administration, St. Louis/
The Dallas Times Herald, 6–22:A2.

Samuel Kountz
Transplant division, University of California at Berkeley Medical Center

Someone asked me the other day if it wasn't true that all we were doing by transplanting organs was extending human life. All I could think of to say was, "Yes, I guess that's what we're doing, all right."

Interview/San Francisco Examiner & Chronicle
(California Living), 3–22:16.

Art Linkletter
Television entertainer

I can't talk to kids any more. They just turn off now. Sure, they know I'm a good guy and sincere, but every time I go to college campuses to speak about drugs, they ask: "Did you ever try it?" When I say no, I lose them.

Chicago, Feb. 3/
Los Angeles Times, 2–5:(4)5.

Donald Louria
President, New York State Council on Drug Addiction

If you think your problem with heroin is serious now, you wait. Because, at the rate we're going now, within a couple of years every high school and every college in the country will be inundated by heroin. I'm flabbergasted by this myself; but all of a sudden, unpredictably, this dangerous, addictive drug has grown in frightening popularity.

New York, Feb. 5/
The New York Times, 2–6:33.

Jean Mayer
Professor of Nutrition, Harvard University

In that year (1966), American people had spent 44 billion in medical care as compared to 11 billion in 1949; by 1969, the figure was 62 billion. If present trends continue, medical care will soon be *the* largest consumer of manpower. Surely, with expenditures of this magnitude, it is readily understandable that the public should expect impressive results. In fact . . . we are certainly getting "health services" for those tens of billions, but in terms of what we expect from these services—longevity, health and happiness or, as they are often expressed in the negative, postponement of death, freedom from discomfort and disability, and freedom from apprehension and worry—the results are much more doubtful.

At Charles Allen Thomas Science Symposium, St. Louis, March 5/Vital Speeches, 4-15:403.

Mary C. McLaughlin
New York City Commissioner of Health

Malpractice litigation is a hidden cost factor often forgotten in private and government efforts to constrain spiraling (medical) costs . . . Physicians are beginning to view each patient as a potential malpractice claimant and, as a result, practice "defensive" medicine.

Before State Senate hearing, New York, Sept. 28/The New York Times, 9-29:30.

Margaret Mead
Anthropologist

We're endangering people terribly with heroin, with LSD, with "speed." We're endangering people permanently. We tell them that pot (marijuana) is one of these. Then they try pot, and they find that nothing happens; and they're not addicted. And they don't trust the adult world any more when they say that "speed" is dangerous, that LSD is terribly dangerous and that heroin is a terrible habit to have. They don't trust their elders, because their elders have lied to them about pot. So that's the reason I want to separate pot off from the others and repeal the laws against pot and put it in another box.

"Anatomy of Youth" program, American Broadcasting Company/ San Francisco Examiner & Chronicle (This World), 12-27:26.

George Meany
President, American Federation of Labor-Congress of Industrial Organizations

Among the industrial nations, America ranks 13th in the death of infants during their first year and 17th in the death rate for young mothers in childbirth. There are 35 nations where 10-year-old boys can expect to live longer than American boys, and 10 nations whose 10-year-old girls will outlive the daughters of Americans . . . (America) can and does provide the finest medical treatment on earth—for those who can get access to it and those who can afford it. What we want is for that standard of excellence to be available to all at a cost that all can afford. We look on the right to a decent standard of health as a basic human right.

Before Senate Labor and Public Welfare Committee on National Health Insurance, Washington, Sept. 24/ San Francisco Examiner, 9-24:2.

William Minkowski
Senior public health physician, Los Angeles County Health Department

We cannot categorize everyone who pops a pill or smokes marijuana as drug abusers. We must separate those who do it out of curiosity, to flaunt authority or enjoy taking risks. Such people may experiment only once or twice. We (the medical profession) have to focus most of our therapeutic attention on those who have made drugs a way of life.

Los Angeles Herald-Examiner, 1-22:B1.

John N. Mitchell
Attorney General of the United States

If the House of Representatives takes much longer (in acting on Administration drug-abuse legislation), it will paralyze our whole coordinated assault against narcotics . . . Frankly, I find this delay appalling. Each day another three or four addicts in New York die of heroin overdose; each day 100,-000 more addicts spend an average of $45 each to support their habits, with many resorting to crime for their funds; and each day a countless number of boys and girls will, for the first time, pop brightly-colored pills in their mouths, smoke pot or jab a filthy needle into a waiting vein.

Before Florida Bar Association, Bal Harbour, June 19/The New York Times, 6-20:8.

We should not be hung up like some doctors who say on TV that marijuana is no worse than alcohol. Alcohol can kill you. And if you look at all the problems that alcohol produces, with suggestions from Congress that hundreds of millions of dollars be spent on dealing with its problems, there is no reason to open the doors to marijuana and compound the problem.

Interview, San Clemente, Calif./
Newsweek, 9–7:22.

Walter F. Mondale
United States Senator, D-Minn.

We must strip narcotics of their illusive, murderous glamour. We must give our young people the ammunition of facts and common sense to ward off the peer or pusher who might otherwise lure them to tragedy.

Quote, 10–18:361.

American medical care is the best in the world—for those who can find and afford it. But soaring costs, the demise of the general practitioner and the flight of doctors from the small towns, rural areas and inner city are increasingly putting this care out of the reach of those who often need it most.

Quote, 12–20:575.

Frank E. Moss
United States Senator, D-Utah

. . . the drug culture finds its fullest flowering in the portrait of American society which can be pieced together out of the hundreds of thousands of advertisements and commercials . . . It is advertising which mounts so graphically the message that pills turn rain to sunshine, gloom to joy, depression to euphoria, solve problems and dispel doubt.

Washington, May/
The New York Times, 7–26:(1)45.

Ralph Nader
Lawyer; Consumer rights advocate

. . . there have neither been the full-fledged Congressional hearings, nor the enforcement of adequate Federal and state standards, nor the administrative inquiries and disclosures that are needed to reduce

the institutional violence and cruelty that are rampant (in nursing homes for the aged).

At Senate hearing, Washington, Dec. 17/
The New York Times, 12–18:23.

Richard M. Nixon
President of the United States

One of the great tragedies of the past decade has been that our schools, where children should learn about the wonder of life, have often been the places where they learn the living—and sometimes actual—death of drug abuse. There is no priority higher in this Administration than to see that children —and the public—learn the facts about drugs in the right way and for the right purpose, through education.

March 11/Quote, 4–19:361.

David Pryor
United States Representative, D-Ark.

This is where our government made a mistake. It made nursing-home care a profit-making industry, a housing program instead of a health program. Our nation has no goal, no policy with regard to where the nursing home industry is heading today.

Before the House, Washington, Feb. 24/
The Dallas Times Herald, 2–24:A6.

Robert F. Rushmer
Director, Center for Bioengineering,
University of Washington

There are more technological advances in the kitchen than in doctors' offices across the country.

The Dallas Times Herald, 4–14:A2.

Saul Schepartz
Chief, cancer research program,
National Cancer Institute

Through the history of medical research, more new drugs have come through random investigation than through what people like to call a "rational approach."

Newsweek, 8–31:48.

Norman E. Shumway
Heart transplant surgeon,
Stanford University

No one who does heart surgery has any illusion about the heart. It's just a very active muscle. I guess the heart is a thoroughly admirable organ. It's the only one that does something. It jumps around. The others just lie there.

Interview/San Francisco Examiner & Chronicle
(This World), 8-2:19.

Neil Solomon
Secretary of Health and Hygiene
of Maryland

To say outright, at this point, that the drug (marijuana) is only psychologically habituating and there are no serious side effects is wrong. It's an unpredictable drug, used by unpredictable people, which brings about unpredictable reactions.

Jan. 7/The Washington Post, 1-8:D7.

Edward Stainbrook
Professor of Human Behavior, University of
Southern California School of Medicine

Much of mental disease is not disease at all in the basic medical sense of something wrong in the brain or body causing symptoms. Many mental disorders are the result of how the person has learned to be human. They are failures of social learning. If someone has learned to be ineffective and unresourceful as a person, he or she can unlearn his or her disease and relearn more effective ways of behaving. The consequences of calling all behavioral problems "disease" is that such a decision may lead to inappropriate efforts to reduce or prevent such problems.

Before American Academy of General
Practice, San Francisco/
Los Angeles Herald-Examiner, 10-12:A15.

Jesse L. Steinfeld
Surgeon General of the United States

The time is ripe for government and voluntary groups to mount a more vigorous program on all fronts to portray (cigarette) smoking as what it really is—a dirty, smelly, foul, chronic form of suicide.

At National Conference on Smoking and
Health, San Diego, Sept. 10/
The Dallas Times Herald, 9-11:C1.

The greatest thing for the collective health of this nation would be for everyone to stop smoking. I'm convinced it's one of the causative factors in lung cancer, emphysema and heart disease. I've rarely seen a patient with lung cancer who didn't smoke.

Washington/Los Angeles Times, 11-8:G3.

Strom Thurmond
United States Senator, R-S.C.

A society whose youth seek escape from the world's responsibilities through drugs, or whose poor seek escape from the misery of poverty through drugs, or whose suburbanites seek escape from the monotony of daily responsibilities is not a great society. It is a sick society.

Before the Senate, Washington, Jan. 26/
Congressional Record, 1-26:S606.

Thomas J. Watson, Jr.
Chairman, International Business Machines

I have become increasingly appalled to read of a country which, during the last two decades, has dropped from seventh in the world to sixteenth in the prevention of infant mortality; in female life expectancy from sixth to eighth; in male life expectancy from tenth to twenty-fourth; and which has bought itself this unenviable trend by spending more of its gross national product for medical care—$1 out of every $14—than any other country on the face of the earth. The country I am talking about is our own U.S.A. —the home of the free, the home of the brave, and the home of a decrepit, inefficient, high-priced system of medical care. I know experts disagree over our precise international standings. I realize that medical problems here and abroad are not identical. I know American medicine has scored many brilliant triumphs. But, on the evidence, we are clearly moving in the wrong direction, fail-

(THOMAS J. WATSON, JR.)

ing to fulfill for all our people the first right set down in the Declaration of Independence: the right to life . . . We can take pride in our system of universal public education, social security and work laws. The time has now arrived for us to have a system of universal public medicine, to do for us what the Scandinavian and British systems have done for those countries: put them medically at the top of the world. We must bring the fullness of American medical care to all the American people. As the greatest nation in the world, I believe we can do no less.

At Mayo Foundation's Industry Day,
Rochester, Minn./
The New York Times, 12–19:27.

Louis J. West
Chairman, Department of Psychiatry,
University of California at Los Angeles

Just because alcohol is bad doesn't mean that marijuana is good. Just because people have been lied to about the dangers of marijuana doesn't mean it is safe . . . What I have seen is not schizophrenia, not rebellion against the establishment, but what I believe to be biological changes in brain function because of the use of marijuana . . . I would feel remiss if I didn't voice these suspicions. At the same time, I am afraid to because I don't want them used as a basis for more punitive legislation. The law should protect the kids, but the present ones only complete the downhill trend begun by the smugglers.

Los Angeles, Feb. 4/
Los Angeles Times, 2–5:(1)3.

Paul Dudley White
Physician

Millions upon millions of Americans own cars and television sets. So they sit in front of their sets and watch others exercising. They have cars, so they won't even walk to the corner for a newspaper or a loaf of bread. Wives won't even let their children walk to school. Moreover, they tend to overfeed their children and their husbands. Machines have re-

placed the hand, the arms and the back at many jobs that could only be done by manual labor years ago. The younger generation is revolting against the wrong thing. It should revolt against the bad habits their fathers have, not against the fathers themselves.

Interview, Boston/
San Francisco Examiner & Chronicle
(Travel), 2–15:14.

(Heart) transplants are improving. Thousands of them may be needed in any given year . . . but perhaps not all who need them should be given someone else's heart. I don't know—but it doesn't seem practical or logical to put a strong, young heart into a body that is otherwise so ailing that the person will die in a relatively short time anyway. But that's an ethical and moral matter, and I don't think the time has come to discuss it. However, I will say that it makes sense to me to give a heart transplant to a child or a young adult in otherwise good health.

Los Angeles Herald-Examiner, 2–22:A10.

Nobody under the age of 70, or really 80, should have a heart attack. The importance of stress is overstressed. Many people are well at 80 who have always been under stress. If hard work and little sleep is that dangerous, I should have been dead 30 years ago.

Sports Illustrated, 7–6:7.

John Cardinal Wright
Prefect, Congregation of the Clergy,
Roman Curia, the Vatican

. . . we look upon abortion as murder. Sometimes the public-relations people tell us to be careful about the use of this ugly word. But I use the word, nevertheless. The destruction of life is murder, and, as Cal Coolidge said about sin, "We're agin it."

Interview, Vatican City/
U.S. News & World Report, 8–31:58.

Ralph W. Yarborough
United States Senator, D-Tex.

The President has been very quick with

the veto pen. He vetoes health bills and asks more money for Cambodia. I think it is at least as important to care for the health of the American people as to kill people in another nation.

San Francisco Examiner & Chronicle, 12–27:A8.

Robert Young
Actor; Star of TV medical series

What we now call orthodox medicine— surgery and so forth—will become unorthodox, and the much-doubted field of psychiatry will be the orthodoxy of tomorrow. Today you have a headache and you take two aspirins; but you never treat the *source* of the headache. That's where the really skillful general practitioner can use his intimate knowledge of his patients better than the specialist. What we have to do in the future is to train people not to become sick, to learn to control their energy levels and emotional attitudes. I know this is contrary to present thinking in medicine, but not so long ago people were shocked to discover that the world isn't flat.

Interview / TV Guide, 6–6:25.

The Performing Arts

MOTION PICTURES

Robert Aldrich
Director

(I am) a better director than most people think I am; a less commercial director than they think I am . . . but in this town (Hollywood), you are the sort of director *they* think you are, not the sort of director *you* think you are.

Interview, Los Angeles/
Los Angeles Herald-Examiner, 10–11:F3.

Alan Arkin
Actor, Director

I think anybody who can actually get a movie done deserves a tremendous amount of points; it's such an extraordinary amount of work. If they had ever put Hitler behind a movie camera, he never would have needed to conquer the world. He wouldn't have had the time or the energy or the inclination. Because, in making a film, you are making a whole world.

Interview, New York/
The New York Times, 6–21:(2)9.

Samuel Z. Arkoff
Chairman, American International Pictures

In a sense, we are at the end of an era. One of the basic reasons we are has been the attitude that you can buy an audience by spending big gobs of money. What the (film) companies forgot was that the reason *The Sound of Music* was a big success was because it appealed to a big audience, not because it cost a lot of money to make.

Before film exhibitors, Dallas/
The Dallas Times Herald, 2–8:F1.

It's all right for a (Federico) Fellini or an (Michelangelo) Antonioni, with years of ex-

perience and public acceptance behind them, to project a personal point of view in films; but for the new artist and craftsman it is wise to proceed slowly in this area. The key to such individualistic expression rests in public recognition and audience acceptance. There will come a time, as you pursue a successful course in motion pictures, when you will receive this recognition and will be free to personally express your point of view.

At University of Southern California,
Feb. 27/Daily Variety, 3–2:6.

James T. Aubrey, Jr.
President, Metro-Goldwyn-Mayer

The older stars are going to have to play older roles if they want to work with us. We can't make a picture with Burt Lancaster and Deborah Kerr groping with each other any more. That's obscene. It's like watching a couple of grandparents pawing each other.

Time, 2–9:58.

I don't think the film-going audiences we have now will ever leave us. Their heads are right, and we've got to catch up to them. They don't care about our point of view—not yours, not mine. We've got to realize this and cater to theirs. Mr. Nixon's silent majority stays home and uses television as a soporific. Its mediocrity and banality has driven the young away from television to the movies . . . I'm upbeat about this business. We simply have to recognize that a change—no, not change—a revolution—has taken place, and we've got to deal with it.

Interview, Los Angeles/
Los Angeles Times (Calendar), 2–15:14.

Martin Baum
President, ABC Pictures Corporation

Only if you discuss cost are musicals not

452

doing well. *Hello Dolly* and *Paint Your Wagon* would be considered smash hits if they hadn't cost so much.

Interview, Los Angeles/
Los Angeles Herald-Examiner, 6–22:B5.

Ingrid Bergman
Actress

I am happy for Goldie (Goldie Hawn, "Oscar" winner for best supporting actress), naturally, but also a little sad. She will always miss that special enjoyment of getting one, after years of *working* for it. That she will regret. You saw how John Wayne had to brush away a tear. I don't think Goldie would have been crying.

Knoxville, Tenn./
The Dallas Times Herald, 4–14:A21.

Charles Bluhdorn
Chairman, Gulf & Western Industries/
Paramount Pictures

You get from these big stars a document of conditions on how many hours they'll work, how many days a week, what they'll do and won't do. Well, who needs them?

Los Angeles Herald-Examiner
(California Living Magazine), 5–17:5.

Richard Boone
Actor

There isn't any (film industry). It's ceased to exist. The film industry is a guy, with a camera and some actors, who goes out to make a picture. Maybe that's the way it always should have been.

Interview, Honolulu/
Los Angeles Times, 1–6:(4)12.

Marlon Brando
Actor

Seriously, why should anybody be interested in what I have to say? Why should anybody care about what any movie star has to say? A movie star is nothing important. Freud, Gandhi, Marx—these people are important. But movie acting is just dull, boring, childish work ... movie stars are nothing

as actors. There's no Duse, no Chaliapin. There's not even a Robert Donat any more. I guess Garbo was the last one who had it.

Interview, Marrakesh, Morocco/
Life, 3–13:Sec.R.

Albert R. Broccoli
Producer

It is important to our industry to encourage one another and say, "Well, goddammit, we can make money in this business," to get some spirit in it ... Christ, I'm *happy* when anybody does a big gross on a picture. I think this is the whole thing our business is based on. It depresses me to see what's been going on at MGM and these other studios. (A couple of major studios) at the moment aren't grinding a bloody camera. It's depressing.

Interview, Los Angeles/
Hollywood Reporter, 1–12:3.

Richard Brooks
Director

I'll tell you about those men (the old movie moguls). They were monsters and pirates and bastards right down to the bottom of their feet, but they *loved* movies. They loved *making* movies, they loved *seeing* movies and they protected the people who worked for them. Some of the jerks running the business now don't even have faces. Not one of them has ever been on the back lot or rummaged through the vaults or walked through their stockpiles to see what they *bought!* I listen to them talk, and I don't even know what they're saying. All they want to know is what did it cost and what will it gross and how much can they dump it for ... These guys today should be running gas stations.

Interview, Los Angeles/
The New York Times, 1–18:(2)13.

Genevieve Bujold
Actress

As soon as they say "Action," I can smell in the first two seconds whether I am going to get on the wave or not. And if you don't get on, you have this disastrous feeling. I can tell you—it's like love without climax.

Time, 3–30:92

Veljko Bulajic
Director

We (in Europe) would rather have an "Oscar" than win the Czech, Moscow or Berlin film festival prizes ... "Oscar" is the biggest, most important award ... In Europe, everybody knows exactly what the "Oscar" is. "Oscar" is not given by a committee of nine or ten people, but by 3,000 people—all in the film industry in different fields. Therefore, it is much respected.

Interview, Los Angeles/
Hollywood Reporter, 3–20:32.

Richard Burton
Actor

There was an article . . . recently where some producer said that the Burtons and the Waynes and the Pecks, the rest, were finished. All (they) want is young people, young people. They're the only ones who make money. But I notice in the boxoffice things this year, Elizabeth (his wife) was still in the top ten and I was still number five. So what's happening? There must be two groups.

Interview, Beverly Hills, Calif./
Hollywood Reporter, 3–18:18.

Ultimately, the main thing about acting is luck: to be born with the proper set of shoulders; to be as enormous as John Wayne, who is six-foot-five; to be beautifully ugly, as Humphrey Bogart was; as short, squat and vital as Jimmy Cagney; as solid as Eddie Robinson. Most importantly, you must have that particular compulsion for an audience, and it is productive if you can tell the imagination of that audience.

Interview, Los Angeles/
Hollywood Reporter, 3–19:22.

The "Oscars" this year are in the generation gap. To presume that either the Duke

(John Wayne) or I is the Establishment is ridiculous. But there it is. It amuses me. It's the old guys against the young guys, and I'll tell you what: the old guys are going to win. There's still a tentacle, a touch, that goes out from us and reaches people.

Interview, Beverly Hills, Calif./
Los Angeles Times (Calendar), 3–22:15.

. . . everybody falls into the rut of typecasting. Once you're established as a king or a prince or a saint, it's bloody hard to get producers to see you without a crown or a halo on your head.

Interview, London/
Los Angeles Times (Calendar), 12–27:20.

John Calley
Executive vice president in charge of production, Warner Bros. Pictures

If there's a trend in films now, it's less a budgetary thing than it is the emergence of the director as the prime force. Studios have started to unravel. Television is now the manufacturing process that the studios once were. The producer-as-powerhouse has in the main been replaced by the director, and in some instances by the collaboration of the director and writer. The archaic idea that the director is a filmic stenographer who transfers a story to film is disappearing. A film, after all, is a director's vision.

Interview, Burbank, Calif./
The Washington Post, 5–9:C7.

Lee J. Cobb
Actor

When you're young, you look for the romance in it all (acting). You set out to slay the dragon. You're like a young medic who knows he'll find a cure for cancer. It isn't till later, much later, when you're in it and it's too late to get out, that the romance flies out the window.

Interview, Torreon, Mexico/
San Francisco Examiner & Chronicle
(Datebook), 6–21:7.

If some of the people who are lauded

around in movies were indispensable, this business would fall on its face.

Interview, Torreon, Mexico/
San Francisco Examiner & Chronicle
(Datebook), 6–21:7.

James Coburn
Actor

People like to think of you as that great superhuman figure on the screen doing all those giant things. In the end, a lot of actors get to thinking they are like that. It kills them when they find they can't live up to it. I'm not bothered by it. I just feel sorry for those guys. First we've got to learn to be human beings. Then we can become actors or writers or whatever. We mustn't just be our profession.

Interview, Guadalajara, Spain/
San Francisco Examiner & Chronicle
(Datebook), 9–20:3.

Tony Curtis
Actor

I'll tell you this, pal. There are bodies flung all over the hills of Beverly. No one's working. It's a blight, a bloody blight! If you got no place to go in the morning, you are poor, you are very poor. And there are lots of poor people staring at their swimming pools.

Interview, London/
The New York Times, 8–23:(2)15.

Saul David
Producer, Director

The only time I worked with an established star was Frank Sinatra. I paid him a hefty sum and a percentage. Stars tend to be stars because they are valuable. But they can sink a picture under the weight of their salaries.

Los Angeles/
San Francisco Examiner & Chronicle, 3–1:B4.

Bette Davis
Actress

In our day, stars had it lucky. The studios built our careers with care and bought ve-

hicles or created them especially for us. Today's stars must take what comes to them. And if they make the wrong choices, they're dead.

Interview, Los Angeles/
The Dallas Times Herald, 10–20:B5.

Ossie Davis
Actor

The American public—the theatregoing public, the whites—has not really made up its mind what it wants to do about the black folks in our country—which means that the very presence of black on the screen can be a disturbing fact to a large number of people. Just standing there, black, is enough to cause a man to make a conscious readjustment. How to create an image that reflects the reality of black life and black people and at the same time do it in such a way that the whole world—white and black—will at least stop and look at it, is one of the problems the artist faces.

Interview, New York/
The Christian Science Monitor, 9–1:11.

Kirk Douglas
Actor

When Julie Andrews made *Mary Poppins,* nobody thought she was overpaid. When she made *Sound of Music,* was she overpaid? I never heard of a star going up to the head of a studio and putting a gun to his head and demanding a million dollars. These men are supposed to be businessmen and know what someone is worth. I personally don't think the creative people are paid enough.

Los Angeles/Daily Variety, 3–27:20.

. . . I don't believe you can give prizes for works of art. Prizes only make sense at agricultural fairs. I mean, one cow gives so many more gallons of milk than the others, so you give her the blue ribbon; that's logical. But I don't think one work of art, like . . . films . . . can be valued as being better than all the others.

Cannes, France/
Los Angeles Times (Calendar), 5–31:41.

(KIRK DOUGLAS)

A performer should be judged on a body of work, not a single picture, or even two or three . . . The test of any artist is partly his failures. One of mine was *The Arrangement*. What a magnificent failure it was . . . I can look at all 50 of my pictures and recognize that a few of them were good, and one or two were damn good . . . You judge a man as an actor like you would a fighter—on his record.

Interview, Beverly Hills, Calif./
The Dallas Times Herald, 8–25:C5.

Roger Ebert
Film critic, Chicago "Sun-Times"

You can take any film and criticize it for what it is not. But I believe each movie has to be judged on the level of its own ambitions. If you try to apply the same yardstick to the new Godard and the new John Wayne, you're probably missing the point of both films.

Time, 3–30:59.

Henry Fonda
Actor

. . . when you're making a film, you get a call from an assistant director and he tells you you're going to do scenes 92 and 93 tomorrow. You read them the night before, rehearse the scenes in the morning and before lunchtime, they're done to the satisfaction of the director and that is your performance. The next day, you do one or two scenes, usually out of sequence, and that's the way it is—bits, 30 seconds at a time, over a six-week period. Then the director puts it together, and you may turn out just fine. But no matter how many awards you win for that picture, you have no recollection of ever creating the character.

Interview, Los Angeles/
San Francisco Examiner & Chronicle
(Datebook), 6–14:14.

Jane Fonda
Actress

European directors study American movies with a seriousness that American film directors don't. Truffaut or Godard are essentially outcroppings of American film making. What Truffaut wants to make is a Hitchcock picture. But they can't do our stuff, and that is why our stuff impresses them so much. It makes me mad when people get discouraged about American movies.

Interview, Los Angeles/Time, 2–16:61.

Glenn Ford
Actor

I can't look back on the old times (in motion pictures) as bad times. We were young and innocent and perhaps believed that we lived in a different world from other people. But it wasn't honest. The world has changed. Things like men on the moon have made it more miraculous, and things like war have made it more bitter and sad. Only honesty counts now in every field, including stars and public. Who is to say it is not a better relationship?

Interview/San Francisco Examiner, 10–12:28.

John Forsythe
Actor

This is the day of the anti-hero—the Steve McQueens, the Dustin Hoffmans, the fellows who look more like bartenders than movie stars . . . Ty Power would have had a rough time.

Interview, Los Angeles/TV Guide, 6–20:26.

Dominic Frontiere
Composer

Since Burt Bacharach's *Butch Cassidy* score and the success of "Raindrops," producers are now realizing that contemporary music can be written even though the action takes place in the past. No longer do they insist on 70 minutes of wall-to-wall music and tom toms during the Indian fights. The freedom is great. No producers are saying to me before anything else, "Where's the song in the picture and who can we get to record it?" Music on film should be put there to add another dimension. You don't need the heavy violins in the background saying "I love you" anymore. "Moon River" is a perfect example of a song that added another dimension. The viewers learned more about Audrey Hepburn (in *Breakfast at Tiffany's*) in those three minutes than they did in the rest of the movie.

Interview, Los Angeles/
Hollywood Reporter, 6–12:6.

Cary Grant
Actor

I can't think of anything that keeps our family (Hollywood) going more than the Academy Awards.

Daily Variety, 4–7:2.

Richard Harris
Actor

. . . I can see the difficulties of making a movie. Directors and producers have to put up with a lot of rubbish from temperamental actors.

Interview, New York/
The Dallas Times Herald, 11–27:C7.

Charlton Heston
Actor; President, Screen Actors Guild

It's perfectly true that many films that would have been shown in the back of a barroom only a few years ago are now being exhibited in theatres to enormous profits. I don't think, however, that filmmakers as a group can be held responsible for their production anymore than the public as a whole can be held responsible for their success. The public will get, by and large, those films it has shown it will pay to see.

Los Angeles, May 4/
Hollywood Reporter, 5–5:4.

Trevor Howard
Actor

Good God, some of (the new crop of young actors) say they don't know whether they want to be actors or not! I cannot understand this. To me, it is like saying you can't make up your mind whether or not you love a certain woman. If you don't, then take a

walk. In acting, as in love, there is no place for indifference.

Interview, Beverly Hills, Calif./
Los Angeles Herald-Examiner, 10–25:G3.

Ross Hunter
Producer

I will never pay a million dollars to any star. They are going to gamble with the rest of us, or we'll make new stars. Deborah Kerr, Doris Day and Lana Turner gambled with me on profits and made fortunes.

Los Angeles/
San Francisco Examiner & Chronicle, 3–1:B4.

"Make movies for the young," they say. "They're the only ones going to the movies these days," they tell us. You know why? Because we're not making any films for adults, who don't want to see *Easy Rider* or *Hell's Angels* or *Alice's Restaurant*. They want to be entertained. Anyway, who the hell are the youngsters to dictate to us? They only happen to be the mass of (the) ticket-buying public because there's nobody else being catered to.

Interview, Los Angeles/
Entertainment World, 3–13:16.

The screens are being flooded by sexploitation films. That is why the mass audiences of yesterday are staying at home now watching old movies on television. It is not the sex movie, the movie that drags nudity in by the heels, that attracts a mass family audience. People want to be moved emotionally. The only excitement of sex is mystery. Sex made too explicit becomes sexless.

Interview, New York/
Plainview (Tex.) Daily Herald, 5–12:6.

I'm really sick to death of people who knock Hollywood. And I'm fed up with Hollywood for turning its back on the attacks. We should fight back. You know who the biggest star is in Europe? It's no one with a name or anything like that. The biggest film star in Europe is the word "Hollywood," and you better realize that's where

(ROSS HUNTER)

40% of the gross comes from. The money we're taking out of Europe on *Thoroughly Modern Millie* you wouldn't believe. What, may I ask, is wrong with superior technicians and a good, happy, escapist movie?

Interview, Los Angeles/
Los Angeles Times (Calendar), 6–21:19.

I like to consider myself a rebel, a producer who insists on bucking the trends. That's why I made *Pillow Talk* with Doris Day and Rock Hudson at a time when sophisticated comedy was boxoffice poison. That's why I made *Magnificent Obsession* and *Madame X* when Hollywood said audiences wanted war dramas, westerns and gangster films. I believe every type of movie should be made—even those dull, dreary exhibitions of pornography which I consider ideal for screening in damp cellars for lonely social misfits. I'm not sure what my next film will be, but I hope I can choose a vehicle that will be the only one of its kind at the time it reaches the screen.

Interview, Los Angeles/
The Dallas Times Herald, 8–31:A20.

Nudity and sex are like the fads of wide screens, 3-D, monster pictures and motorcycle movies. The worthwhile, artistic elements will survive. The rest will die out. And that's as it should be.

San Francisco Examiner & Chronicle, 12–20:B4.

Arthur P. Jacobs
Producer

I don't know of any star worth a million dollars. They should be on a percentage basis. Nobody's paying Elizabeth (Taylor) and Richard (Burton) a million anymore. I still believe in the star system, but no star is a guaranteed boxoffice attraction.

Los Angeles/
San Francisco Examiner & Chronicle, 3–1:B4.

Leo Jaffe
President, Columbia Pictures Industries

We shall make pictures at any price that makes sense to us. We cannot subscribe to the policy of several of our competitors that success can only be found in making pictures at a low budget. We believe there is a market for every type of picture, made as economically as possible and based on a considered judgment as to the potential of each picture with the public.

Daily Variety, 3–6:22.

We at Columbia are far from pessimistic. We do not share the expression of the prophets of doom who predict that the industry is on the wane, that Hollywood is a thing of the past, that a cycle of depression will hit every facet of our industry in the years ahead. In our opinion, these fears are unfounded.

Daily Variety, 3–6:22.

Thomas H. Kuchel
Former United States Senator, R-Calif.

The motion picture is not only of major economic importance to this country—bringing many millions of dollars from abroad to contribute to the favorable side of our balance of payments—it is an invaluable factor in the culture of the nation. Other governments throughout the world nurture their native film industries. They provide everything in the power of government to give, to keep those industries alive and give them the opportunity to reflect the good face of those countries to the rest of the world. The time has come in this country for some substantial, helpful recognition of the value of the American motion picture industry to the nation.

Los Angeles, March 1/Daily Variety, 3–2:8.

Buzz Kulik
Director

Technically, the movie industry is the most anachronistic industry around today. As an example, they are still using the old parallex camera. You can buy a $10 Kodak camera in a store that lines up a picture better. Although the studios have spent millions of dollars on ridiculous things, they have spent very little on technical research.

Interview, Los Angeles/
Hollywood Reporter, 2–11:11.

Mervyn LeRoy
Director, Producer

There's nothing wrong with the picture business that a good picture can't cure.

Interview, Los Angeles/
Los Angeles Herald-Examiner
(California Living Magazine), 4–5:25.

Joseph E. Levine
President, Avco Embassy
Pictures Corporation

I think that in the next 10 years there will be a prosperity for those making motion pictures that is undreamed of today . . . The prosperity will come not only from the thousands of bright young people who are learning about film, but because of technological advances. The appetite to absorb motion pictures is inexhaustible.

Interview/San Francisco Examiner & Chronicle
(Datebook), 5–10:3.

With the coming of cable and pay-TV, cassettes and such things as the laser beam and 3-D films, we are going to have the greatest revolution ever in the history of entertainment. This is the beginning of a fabulous era for producers and directors. The new cassettes, and all the other coming things, will bring enormous new business to filmmakers. In my opinion, the ability to fill the rapacious appetite of theatre, cable-TV, (and) cassettes will never be satisfied.

Boston/Variety, 8–19:27.

Jerry Lewis
Actor, Director

I think that *Myra Breckinridge* is the death knell of the dirty-picture cycle. To think that a major Hollywood studio would turn out such a piece of junk is incredible. People who see this movie will get so disgusted with what they see, they will start a revolution to bring back the movies as we all know them—the movies that featured entertainment, not smut: Clark Gable and Claudette Colbert in *It Happened One Night, Dinner at Eight* and the rest of the great products our industry turned out.

Interview/Los Angeles Herald-Examiner,
7–5:F3.

Robert L. Lippert
President, Transcontinental Theatres

The low-grossing houses are those for the most part in church-oriented, civic-minded communities where sensual-savage films keep the majority away from the boxoffice. These people are not the trend-followers. They may be the silent majority the politicians talk about. They are conservative by nature, and their film tastes were dictated years ago when movies were truly family affairs . . . It's true that while the costs of production are met by the returns from the big first runs, it is the steady dribble of money from these low-grossing houses that provide the profit cream. Soon the market will be sated with sex films, and they will have jaded and lost their audience by then. They certainly can't be booked into the small provincial houses. Audiences for these theatres automatically reject them.

Daily Variety, 3–17:16.

Jack Lord
Actor

Something happens to an actor on location. The smell of reality does something to a guy. I think it transmits itself to the screen —the smell of reality.

Interview, Honolulu/
San Francisco Examiner & Chronicle
(Datebook), 1–18:16.

Shirley MacLaine
Actress

The "Oscar" means one thing—an added $1 million gross to the picture. It has nothing to do with "acclaim of your peers." It's a big publicity contest, and Suzie Schlitz wins because somebody spends $75,000 for her publicity. Oh, the voting is legitimate, but

(SHIRLEY MACLAINE)

there's the sentimentality. One year when I was a candidate, when Elizabeth Taylor got a hole in her throat, I canceled my plane.

New York/
Los Angeles Herald-Examiner, 4–3:A13.

When I see the amount of money flung into that cauldron called Hollywood, I feel not one ounce of guilt about what I get ($800,000 a film). Producers have always grumbled about the money they pay us, but they keep coming back. Lots more stars are going to start making their own pictures outside the studios, taking no money, but owning the film in the end. Then we'll be saying to the studio heads: "So who needs you?"

Interview, London/Variety, 4–8:30.

Rouben Mamoulian
Former director

About what goes on on the screen . . . today, where all the defenses are down, I feel that a real filmmaker . . . must have a ruthless built-in censorship—in other words, be able to censor himself. But just like in all the arts, there's a fringe interested only in the buck. They take the easiest way—a lot of mechanical form, nudeness, sex and violence; no story or characterization. It's not a question of morality, but that it's all in such incredible taste—and most utterly amateurish.

Interview, Los Angeles/
Los Angeles Times (Calendar), 4–5:16.

Abby Mann
Producer, Writer

. . . the writer is more important than ever, because kids today care about what a picture is and not who is in it. I think films ought to dare more than ever with the raw meat of our times.

Interview, Los Angeles/
Hollywood Reporter, 4–29:15.

James Mason
Actor

I love "Oscars." It's a great prize and a wonderful public relations gimmick; but it's not a very good way of evaluating talent. When I'm not nominated, I'm always delighted to note that others who were equally good that year were also overlooked.

Interview, Los Angeles/
Los Angeles Times (West Magazine), 4–19:7.

Stan Margulies
Producer; Vice president, David L. Wolper Pictures

From announcements being made by everybody, it appears all want to make contemporary satire. I hope not too many do, because it's like eating fried chicken: How much can you take of it, regardless how it is prepared?

Los Angeles/Hollywood Reporter, 3–27:8.

Marcello Mastroianni
Actor

They come for you in the morning in a limousine; they take you to the studio; they stick a pretty girl in your arms; sometimes they earn something off you and give you some of the profits. They call that a profession?—come on!

Interview, Padua, Italy/
The New York Times, 6–21:(2)16.

Walter Matthau
Actor

These are unsettling times in the (film) business, and there's a lot of grabbing for the fast buck. But for those who can read, the writing on the wall is very clear. The films making the big, big money this year are *Patton, Airport, The Out of Towners,* to mention a few. The best selling novel is *Love Story.* Americans have a talent for pulling out and righting things, and, wait and see, so has Hollywood.

Interview/
Los Angeles Herald-Examinter, 10–20:D1.

Arne Mattson
Director

My main purpose is to entertain. I make my films to fill theatres, and I don't think the critics should chop your head off because your films are comprehensible. Not that the art film shouldn't be made and respected. On the contrary. The Swedish government is finally developing a plan to build and subsidize a series of small theatres for the sole purpose of showing art films. The Swedish critics, though, tend to take the position that if they are "entertained" at a screening, the film must be bad. One of the most financially successful films of the past decade was MGM's *Where Eagles Dare,* but one critic advised his readers to stay home and go to bed early, thus saving themselves from this terrible bore. Something's wrong somewhere.

Interview, New York/Variety, 4–1:3.

Steve McQueen
Actor

Actors have a bad handle on the world. I'll tell you, in my own mind, I'm not sure acting is a thing for a grown man to be doing.

Interview/Look, 1–27:52.

Russ Meyer
Director

I agree with the President's Commission on Obscenity. There should be no censorship at all. I know that there are sincere, honest people who think the production of sexploitation films is harmful to the country, but I don't think they have the right to impose their ideas on the majority. I understand the parents' fear that children will be corrupted, but children are not exposed to these films, and most of them aren't interested in them anyway. The theatres that play sexploitation movies are filled with middle-aged couples.

Interview, Los Angeles/
Los Angeles Herald-Examiner, 11–15:F5.

Ann Miller
Actress, Dancer

In those (early) days, you belonged to the studio. They were concerned with keeping your name before the public all the time. They made my name a household word. Even when you weren't actually working on

a picture, they released photographs and information about you—pictures in Easter bonnets, in Fourth-of-July outfits, that sort of thing. Now, stars flash into attention only when their current movies are good; between times, most are forgotten.

Interview, Culver City, Calif./
Los Angeles Herald-Examiner, 3–30:B5.

Ron Miller
Executive producer, Walt Disney
Productions

These days, so few movies are made that give us competition—ones people can take their kids to—that we even get credit for the movies we *don't* make. You should see the letters we have thanking us for *Oliver!*

Interview, Los Angeles/
Los Angeles Times (TV Times), 3–22:2.

Paul Monash
Producer

The "X" rating can be used as a convenient cover for the production of crude, pornographic films, the manufacturing of which —and manufacturing is the word for it—does a total disservice to the entire film industry. Hollywood used to cater to the taste of the country; now it is pandering to the sick fantasies of the perverted. I hate the very idea of censorship, and I am dismayed to see major studios inviting—even requesting—its imposition. Perhaps films like *Myra (Breckinridge)* or *Beyond the Valley of the Dolls* will squeeze out some profits, but they will be drops of blood sucked from the corpse of our industry.

Los Angeles, June 25/Daily Variety, 6–26:17.

Roger Moore
Actor

Basically, there are two types of heroes. One of them has the world against him. He usually gets the "Oscar" and everyone says that's great acting. The other type of hero— the romantic action type—has the most absurd dialogue and situations. The job then

(ROGER MOORE)

is keeping the grin off your face. That's acting, too, isn't it?

Interview, London/
The New York Times, 8–23:(2)15.

John Mortimer
Playwright, Screenwriter

Everybody talks about *Midnight Cowboy.* But who talks about the writer of *Midnight Cowboy?* You know, actors can't be brilliant without writers.

Interview, Los Angeles/
Los Angeles Herald-Examiner, 1–13:A14.

James H. Nicholson
President, American International Pictures

For varied reasons, which we can charge off to progress and development and changing times, the motion picture industry comes up against a crisis every several years. But history has proven, each time, the somewhat battered but virile and sturdy gladiator rises from the canvas at nine to deliver the kayo punch. With judicious cost controls, elimination of outdated studio overhead, an uninterrupted flow of production and augmented sales impetus, today more than ever before in our history the film industry has to come up a winner. In my opinion, any business that can gross $1,100,000,000 at the boxoffice annually is not a dead industry. It's not even very sick. It just has some economic symptoms.

At American Cinema Editors Awards,
Los Angeles, March 14/
Hollywood Reporter, 3–16:6.

Richard M. Nixon
President of the United States

One of the reasons (for the durability of the movie Western) is perhaps—and this may be a square observation—the good guys come out ahead in the Westerns, the bad guys lose.

Denver, Aug. 3/The New York Times, 8–22:28.

Peter O'Toole
Actor

In this business we're always celebrating a

wake. Do you think that movies cost $30 million because of the actors? Rubbish! That's all bull. We brought *Lion in Winter* in for $4 million—and Kate (Hepburn) and I don't come cheap. It's all crap about actors being too highly paid. It's simply a matter of getting your priorities right, seeing where the money runs out to.

Interview, Dragon's Mouth, Venezuela/
San Francisco Examiner & Chronicle
(Datebook), 5–24:11.

Today, the film business is run by tuppeny-ha'penny bird-brain morons. They excuse their own failure by spreading the propaganda that actors cost too much. That is one of the most delightful pieces of pulp fiction I ever heard.

Interview, Puerto Ordaz, Venezuela/
Los Angeles Times (Calendar), 10–18:27.

George Peppard
Actor

(Commenting on athletes becoming actors): You can't get a job in the movie business today unless you've won the Cy Young Award, the heavyweight championship, led the NFL in yards gained from scrimmage, or won one for the Old Gipper. The Screen Actors Guild looks like the *Rams'* locker room. Even the directors wear cleats. They cast pictures out of the sports pages. I expect the Academy Award will be won by the same guy who won the Davis Cup or the British Open any year now.

Interview, Los Angeles/
Sporting News, 9–19:40.

S. J. Perelman
Author

The "professionalism" of young moviemakers is a source of sardonic pleasure. They're all so much more technical, talk of truck shots and whip shots. Then what turn out are what we called "chasers"—snow melting, a little Chopin tinkling behind it. They're sort of playing at it and giving themselves enormous seriousness about the whole thing.

Interview, New York/
The Washington Post, 10–18:E4.

Jacques Perrin
Producer, Actor

. . . you must be vulgar and give a hard-sell to films. The French do not know how to exploit films with showmanship as you do, and can, here in America. It takes an awful lot of hard work to bring a film to its audience, and that is largely an unknown art in France.

Los Angeles/Hollywood Reporter, 4–2:9.

Eugene Picker
*President, National Association
of Theatre Owners*

The reality of the matter is that we cannot make up for diminishing attendance by raising admission prices ad infinitum, because eventually we will reach the point where we will price ourselves out of the mass market, which has historically been the sustenance of this industry.

*Before Theatre Equipmnt Dealers Association
and Theatre Equipment Supply and
Manufacturers Association, Monterey, Calif./
Daily Variety, 2–3:6.*

Most of us have heard the catch-phrase, "Half the population is under 25"—a statement used as justification for the direction of much of our current filmmaking and advertising effort. But I ask you bear in mind the corollary to this: Half the population is over 25. And that is the half which spends 90% of the consumer dollars. And let us also remember this: Almost half the people who are under 25 are less than 10 years old.

*At Show-A-Rama 13 convention, Kansas City/
Variety, 3–11:4.*

Otto Preminger
Producer, Director

Many, if not most, films are made today by individuals, not the big corporations of old. They make a picture and stand or fall on it.

The days of a big company turning out 20 a year, and hoping to get six or eight winners, are on the way out. I think most pictures in the future will be individually financed, such as Broadway plays are. I believe the old system of distribution will disappear, too. A group will make a picture and invite the country's theatre owners to come to New York to bid for it, just as the dress industry operates. The rights to show the picture will go to the highest bidder. Why shouldn't theatres buy direct, by auction? Why must we maintain that distributing apparatus that has cost us countless millions of dollars?

*New York/
Los Angeles Herald-Examiner, 2–19:A13.*

If a 5-year-old kid came up to a box office today and plunked down his $3 for a ticket to see a picture rated "X," the management would see him as 45 years older and take his money. Only the parents can police their children.

*New York/
Los Angeles Herald-Examiner, 2–19:A13.*

I think it would be very good if theatre owners and film producers would get together from time to time and examine the market and determine what people in the various communities, large and small, really want to see in their motion picture theatres. The reactions of the film customers and the theatre owners are much more important to the future of filmmaking than the generalizations of the big conglomerates that now control distribution. These big companies really are much more worried about the stock market than they are about either my films or your theatres.

*Before Michigan Theatre Owners, Detroit/
Variety, 4–22:7.*

I don't think films are that powerful. They only reflect what's happening; they are a mirror of our times. I wish it were true that they could make people change their attitudes; it would make me feel more important.

*News conference, Boston/
The Christian Science Monitor, 9–5:12.*

463

Anthony Quinn
Actor

I am often asked, "Why have you stayed in pictures so long? You're not a leading man; you're not a pretty fellow; you're not a star. Why?" Is it possible that I'm a good actor?

Interview, Los Angeles/
San Francisco Examiner & Chronicle
(Datebook), 7–26:12.

Styles of acting have changed . . . When I started, Barrymore's style of acting was popular. Then we had Brando and the inarticulate school. We have now come to a time when the environment is so important. Today, if you are caught "acting," it is terrible.

News conference, Albuquerque, N.M./
The Dallas Times Herald, 12–6:E1.

Robert Radnitz
Producer, Director

I get very uptight when I read that you have to make a film for the teenage group or the adult group or any other group. Why aren't the non-members of these groups *not* going to see films? What is it that we can do to get them to attend? Why is it that when *National Geographic* does a TV special, it knocks everything else out of the box? Because people want to be informed. If you can commingle your story with showing them a part of the world they've never seen before, you'll get them. The market is there.

Interview, New York/Variety, 3–25:26.

Most motion picture companies do not make films for children. When they do, they make them with their left hand and sell them with their left foot. Then, when it flops at the boxoffice, they say, "See—I told you so."

Interview, Washington/
The Washington Post, 12–19:B6.

Robert Redford
Actor

They throw that word "star" at you loosely, and they take it away loosely if your pictures flop. *You* take responsibility for *their* crappy movie, that's all it means.

Life, 2–6:44.

Rex Reed
Film critic, "Holiday" magazine

Hollywood is suicidal. They make all these big-budget films and they're all disasters. The directors are kids who've never seen a camera, and they make films which are incomprehensive. And if that makes me old-fashioned, then I hope I stay that way.

Interview, New York/
San Francisco Examiner & Chronicle
(Datebook), 6–28:12.

Harold Robbins
Author

I'll agree that nudity for nudity's sake may be moving off center stage. It can become tiresome and slightly ridiculous. If it is a prediction you're after, I say the next cycle for books and films will be sadism—the merging of sex and violence, as in the highly successful *M-A-S-H* . . . There will be others.

Interview, Los Angeles/
Los Angeles Herald-Examiner, 2–22:G3.

Cliff Robertson
Actor

I'm 43, and I've been around so long I feel 65. This isn't exactly a stable business. It's like trying to stand up in a canoe with your pants down.

Los Angeles Times (West Magazine), 2–22:20.

Edward G. Robinson
Actor

We're an art that's also an industry and an industry that's also an art—depending on whether you're in the front office or on the stage.

Los Angeles/Daily Variety, 2–4:2.

Richard Roud
Director, New York Film Festival

Whether we like it or not, the "political" film is here to stay . . . In the cinema, a more direct confrontation of art and politics cannot be avoided.

The Christian Science Monitor, 9–28:1.

Waldo Salt
Screenwriter

The worst thing for a screenwriter is to have to write with a specific personality in mind. You wind up reinforcing an image that was created by another writer. Doing a Humphrey Bogart role, for example, means rehashing Dashiel Hammett. Thankfully, the film itself has replaced the personality as the star. It won't be long before the film business becomes the kind of art form painting is. You can't sell the work of a painter unless it's good—the ultimate fusion of commerce and art. What's true of painting will eventually hold true for motion pictures.

Interview, New York / Variety 3–25:61.

Aubrey Schenck
Producer

We are in a business based on one thing—enthusiasm. Ever since P. T. Barnum, show business has depended as much on enthusiasm as (on) anything else. But today there is much pessimism apparent in the various areas of show business, and the film business can do a great deal in clearing this up. People have enough money to buy color television sets, so they can certainly afford to go to theatres. You'll never see a damper in the automobile business, even when things are bad, but we cry doom and let the public know how bad things are. We must stop this and build, or at least restore, the enthusiasm that the film business, and all other forms of show business, require to survive.

Interview, New York / Variety 1–28:78.

Let me say at the outset that I am optimistic about the future of Hollywood. I think the whole town will convert to a United Artists operation, where independent producers will come in and make pictures under studio financing and distribution, but have complete control of the product. No more will there be 24 hairdressers charged to a picture when only two or three are needed—but the others must still be paid because they are on the studio staff, working or not. There can be no more jurisdictional disputes among the unions. Why should four men take three hours to pull a barge across a river while 75 men watch idly by . . ? In the future, we must all chip in and cut down costs.

Interview, Los Angeles /
Los Angeles Herald-Examiner, 3–15:G3.

. . . I predict that there will be a whole reversal of the star system. The big names will be on TV, while the director and the story and good actors who are right for the part will dominate the movies. About 70 per cent of the movie audience is under 30. They don't want to see some old guy on Medicare making love to a young girl.

Interview, Los Angeles /
Los Angeles Herald-Examiner, 3–15:G3.

George Seaton
Writer, Director

(I'll) never make a 100% message film. The reason is that no one goes to them except people who already know the problem and who agree with the movie's point of view. I think the idea is to attract people who need informing and persuasion.

Interview, Minneapolis / Variety, 4–1:7.

I think nudity in most cases is unnecessary. Ernst Lubitch was able to make a sexier scene out of a closed bedroom door and the squeaky shoes of the butler than today's directors can do with total fornication. A lot of filmmakers today are simply not making use of their imaginations.

Los Angeies Herald-Examiner, 12–24:B8.

Peter Sellers
Actor

How can any one person say that he is worth $500,000, $750,000 or a million dollars to a picture? In the old days that might have been true. I can recall, when I was a movie nut as a boy, I went to many bad films just because my favorite stars were in them.

(PETER SELLERS)

But that's not true today. The younger audience goes to see the end product, not the stars. They wouldn't care if God himself was in the picture; they wouldn't go unless they were interested in the story.

Interview, Los Angeles/
Los Angeles Herald-Examiner, 3–1:F2.

Melville Shavelson
President, Writers Guild of America-West

In a year in which the major studios managed to lose $137,000,000, they also produced some of the finest motion pictures in recent memory; and the national boxoffice, as indicated by federal tax receipts, reached the highest total in years. The only conclusion to be drawn . . . is that some of the most imaginative writing in Hollywood is being done by bookkeepers.

Los Angeles/Hollywood Reporter, 1–19:1.

Edward Small
Producer

It (censorship) has been waiting in the wings ever since performers started taking off their clothes, indulging in explicit sex scenes and throwing around four-letter words usually heard on the San Francisco docks . . . While a handful of producers kept within the boundaries of good taste, while still being adventurous and experimental with their product, it was obvious that a large group of tasteless exploiters were catering to base and crude audience demands.

Los Angeles/Daily Variety, 3–23:8.

Maggie Smith
Actress

In the past, an "Oscar" was a very valuable career asset for a performer . . . But an actress shouldn't take a bit of success too seriously. It's easy to be a star today and a nonentity two years from now. But at the moment, like Miss Brodie, I'm in my prime.

Interview, Rome/
San Francisco Examiner & Chronicle, 5–24:B6.

Robert Stack
Actor

Being called a "star" gives you one of the greatest luxuries in God's world: You can choose your parts. An actor can't; an actor can see a part he knows he's born for—and hasn't got a prayer of getting. If you're a star, you go through the front door carrying the roses, instead of going through the back door carrying the garbage.

Interview, Los Angeles/
San Francisco Examiner & Chronicle
(Datebook), 7–5:9.

Rod Steiger
Actor

When someone says, "I want to be an actor," I ask them if they *need* to be an actor . . . If you *need* to be an actor, you will be one, whatever happens.

Interview/
Los Angeles Herald-Examiner, 5–3:F3.

James Stewart
Actor

I disagree that people won't go to see what has wrongly been called "a family picture." I *hate* that term. There is proof that this isn't true. All those prophets of doom who say that Hollywood is a ghost town . . . I've never heard one of them mention Walt Disney. That stock is higher than it's ever been, and one of their pictures, *Love Bug*, was in the top five grossers last year. Right now, Disney is absolutely in full production. They couldn't do that if nobody went to see their pictures.

Interview, New York/
The New York Times, 2–22:(2)5.

I don't want to sound like "give-me-the-good-old-days." But, to be realistic, the big studios were an ideal way to make pictures, because they were a home base for people. When you were under contract, you had a chance to work at your craft all the time. You would have big parts in little pictures and little parts in big pictures. It was exciting, with writers, producers and directors around all the time. But the whole thing became too expensive. It's just a whole different world today.

Interview, New York/
The New York Times, 2–22:(2)5.

I think there's too much of it (pornography). I think that our business has got to have variety. There's got to be all kinds of pictures, because the medium can stand it. When they say people won't go to family pictures—well, that's not true. Because if it were, Disney wouldn't be in business. On the other hand, you need other things than Disney. I think our business is indestructible. We're in danger only if we cultivate a cultish, strange industry bordering on the obscene. If we cater to just that segment of the population, then we're finished.

Interview, New York/
Los Angeles Times (Calendar), 3–15:17.

They say the old-timer doesn't go any more. Well, maybe. Kinda resented it a little when they said Duke Wayne's "Oscar" was just a sentimental award. Know what I figured? I figured he gave the best performance of the year.

Interview, Beverly Hills, Calif./
TV Guide, 5–16:43.

Raymond St. Jacques
Actor

The movie business has made all-black films before, but none of them has been profitable—*Porgy and Bess, Carmen Jones, Cabin in the Sky,* etc. The reason for their failure is that such films were always white Hollywood's idea of the black experience. They were directed by men who claimed to understand the blacks—"Some of my best friends are colored," they said. But only a black director . . . can really portray it on the screen.

Interview, Los Angeles/
The Dallas Times Herald, 8–2:E8.

Joseph Strick
Producer, Director

The public and critics are fully capable of choosing acceptability of their films. They're not idiots who need film companies to tell them, branding their pictures by foolish symbols. The rating system is destructive to film art and business.

New York/Variety, 2–18:6.

David Susskind
Producer

I'm going to make boxoffice movies; I'm going to make people want to come to see them. In the great list in heaven, there are terrific marks beside my name for all my "statement" films. But now the scorecard is full, and God, I want to make films that people will stand in the heat and freezing cold to see.

Interview, Toronto/
San Francisco Chronicle, 9–26:36.

Donald Sutherland
Actor

(Movies are) a director's medium. It all happens in the cutting room. As an actor, you can only bring so much to a film. As a director, there is almost no limit.

Time, 2–2:41.

Danny Thomas
Actor, Comedian

I don't think it's necessary for talented people to use four-letter words on the stage or to show their bodies on the screen. I am against that garbage. And I think it will be very exciting some day if a picture begins with a nude person who's putting his clothes on, and keeps them on for the rest of the picture.

At Golden Apple Awards luncheon of
Hollywood Women's Press Club,
Beverly Hills, Calif., Dec. 13/
Hollywood Reporter, 12–15:11.

Sir John Travelyan
Head, British Board of Film Censors

I've had enough of American, German, Scandinavian and Italian sex films. Sex is a marvelous human activity—but merely to watch other people doing it is not my kind of entertainment.

Resignation statement, London/
San Francisco Examiner, 12–30:22.

Francois Truffaut
Director

A few years ago, the scripts for Hollywood films may have been less intelligent, less *adult* than they are now, but at least the directorial techniques corresponded to the content—because the directors were *better* then. But today—take a picture like *M-A-S-H;* an excellent script, disastrous direction . . . *In the Heat of the Night* also had a screenplay that was interesting; but the direction was absurd.

Interview, New York/
The New York Times, 9–27:(2)13.

Ten or fifteen years ago, all pictures were for everyone. They told stories; they were generally chronological; their differences were in plot, dialog, execution. The function of the critic was to show which films were better than others. But films have been more varied from 1959 on. Now the function of the critic really is to tell the public what a film looks like.

Interview, New York/
National Observer, 10–12:20.

Lawrence Turman
Producer

I've never made a film with a movie star. I told Dustin Hoffman when he did our picture (*The Graduate*) he destroyed the star system while becoming a star in the process.

Los Angeles/
San Francisco Examiner & Chronicle, 3–1:B4.

Roger Vadim
Director

Something bothers me about the "New Wave" in general today. When I directed *And God Created Woman,* France was in a strange situation. The "Old Wave," if we

may say that, was really building walls, barriers, against anything from outside. Everything was so codified, so difficult for young directors, when suddenly the walls were broken down. Suddenly, only young directors were making films. That was a great influence all over the world. That was wonderful. But it was like the process of a revolution, when there has been a tyrant who was very strong and there was no liberty. The moment the new people take over the responsibility, they become repressive also. The "New Wave" was a fantastic moment, heaven knows—something fantastic. But it has become a tyrant. I'm not talking specifically about directors but their supporters, about critics who support their heroes and become completely intolerant of all others. They have their rules and they like only what meets their test. They do not respect anything they don't like.

Interview, Los Angeles/
Los Angeles Times (Calendar), 8–23:10.

Jack Valenti
President, Motion Picture
Association of America

The fastest way to ruin the movie business is to run sex films in downtown and neighborhood houses. Exhibitors booking a sex product for a quick buck will, in the long run, lose their audiences, and the serious filmmaker will have no place left to show his work.

Before House Subcommittee on Obscenity,
Washington, Jan. 28/
Entertainment World, 2–6:4.

Gore Vidal
Author

The innocence is gone from films, because there is no longer such inspired vulgarity as Harry Cohn and Louis B. Mayer so generously possessed. The new movie makers have been to college, for better or worse—usually worse.

Interview/
Los Angeles Herald-Examiner, 10–20:D1.

Good directors sometimes make bad pictures, but bad directors *always* make bad pictures.

Interview, Los Angeles/
San Francisco Examiner & Chronicle, 11–1:B5.

Luchino Visconti
Director

I used to breed and train horses professionally prior to becoming a director, and that was the best preparation for this. Actors are not much different from pure-bred horses: They are also full of exposed nerves and deep sensitivity. *Difficili! Molto difficili!* One tiny mistake and they are gone from your control forever. Therefore, I never let go when I work. I believe in discipline and method.

Venice, Italy/
Los Angeles Times (Calendar), 5–31:1.

Hal Wallis
Producer

New people in pictures cost less money and can become great successes. Why give a million to an actor and then struggle to break even?

Los Angeles/
San Francisco Examiner & Chronicle, 3–1:B4.

John Wayne
Actor

I don't think my pictures are violent. The characters are usually rather likeable. Fights with too much violence are dull. The violence in my pictures is lusty and a little bit humorous, because I believe humor nullifies violence.

Interview, Los Angeles/
The Washington Post, 4–8:B1.

The Jack Warners, Harry Cohns and Louis B. Mayers were men with a certain integrity, whether for business reasons or not, and they cared about the future of the industry. When gangster pictures were cleaning up at the boxoffice, those men realized the bad effect they were having on youth around the country and the reaction that was bound to set in against the industry, and they saw that Hollywood stopped making gangster pictures. But one by one they've left the scene, and they have not been replaced. The raiding stock manipulators and bankers have taken charge, and they apparently don't care about the industry's future. Now we're afflicted with fast-buck producers cashing in on pornography and depravity, and there's no leadership to stop them.

Interview, Tucson, Ariz./
Hollywood Reporter, 5–5:5.

When everybody stops shivering and shaking, a lot of these new people running things are going to find out you can't make movies like you make pants. You can't say to writers, directors, actors, as you might to your tailor: "Sam, run me off a batch of money-making movies, and don't make the money too long." Can't be done. This business is an art as well as a commercial venture. A good picture must cost what it *needs* to cost. Making little pictures just to be making little pictures could very well make little audiences.

Interview/
Los Angeles Herald-Examiner, 10–19:B3.

Richard Widmark
Actor

We're hung up on this "cult of the directors." There's a handful of *artists,* and a double handful who deserve the designation *director.* The rest are self-serving bums.

Interview, Los Angeles/
Los Angeles Times, 11–30:(4)23.

Billy Wilder
Director

In today's market, familiar star faces keep audiences away. They know what's coming from these people. They know what to expect. They're tired of the same old characterizations. The element of expectation has died. Today's audience no longer cares about spectaculars or production values. Nobody in Kansas City says, "Let's go to see such and such a film—it has a cast of thousands and cost $20 million." They couldn't care less.

Interview, London/Parade, 5–10:5.

Michael Winner
Director

Lunacy is a very important quality (in being a successful director). Most of the top directors are quite a bit batty. That's what makes them great. They can conceive fantasies beyond the normal mind. Another important quality is just keeping alive. It is quite remarkable that no director yet has been murdered in cold blood on a set.

*At National Film Theatre, London/
Los Angeles Herald-Examiner, 9–30:C7.*

Robert Wise
Producer, Director

Personally, I prefer to base my pictures in the U.S. I think most American producers share my dislike of so-called "runaway" production. We know why American producers continue to make their films abroad. We know other countries offer financial inducements for production on their foreign shores, which greatly reduce the economic risks to U.S. investors who back such production . . . I am convinced Hollywood and other U.S. film production centers can be restored to their rightful place in the world of picture-making. This can be accomplished if all segments of our industry will join hands in asking the President and the Congress for a realistic form of government support for films made in this country, and if we join hands in a realistic re-evaluation of the basic economics of our business and determine what we all can do to make Hollywood truly competitive in the world market . . . The U.S. film-making industry should be repatriated before it is lost to this country as an important American medium of expression and communication. Hollywood is at the crossroads. I hope our friends in Washington can help us to get on the right road home, at last.

*Interview, Los Angeles/
Hollywood Reporter, 12–3:15.*

Darryl F. Zanuck
*Chairman, 20th Century-Fox
Film Corporation*

I have seen a resurgence over the past 40 years in this business. It has gone up and down, from triumph to crisis and back again. Maybe we have ourselves to blame for our own problems. Maybe, in our eagerness to beat the competition of that small screen (television), we've gone overboard and spent too much on our product. But I tell you something: As long as there is show business, there will be problems, there will be fluctuating audiences and critics who complain. There is nothing wrong with the business as long as we who make films keep on listening and thinking and readjusting our attitudes.

*Edinburgh, Scotland, Aug. 31/
Daily Variety, 9–4:1.*

A great percentage of our audience today is young. We must satisfy their demands. We must try to understand what it is they ask of the cinema, and we must try to do it without resorting to the easy way out—the exaggerated shock, the exaggerated sex, the perversion of the art to the point where we lose our identity. This is a sure way to disaster.

*Edinburgh, Scotland, Aug. 31/
Daily Variety, 9–4:6.*

Franco Zeffirelli
Director

The movies in Hollywood are going through a structural change long overdue, I feel, because, after all, the cinema is a delicate thing; it was an idea in someone's head; around this idea grew a colossus. When it becomes overburdened, too heavy with executives, with too many restrictions, it cannot survive. I have had a taste of this while doing *The Taming of the Shrew* and was amazed how Hollywood could have survived in that state for such a long time. Things are changing for the better. A new cinema is emerging already. You see, the so-called "digestive cinema" days are gone—when people went to the movies after dinner and before retiring. Today, they still go to the movies, but are more selective; they go to see a *certain* film. It has to be good; it better be good! So that eliminates a lot. Thank Heaven!

*Interview, Rome/
Los Angeles Times (Calendar), 7–26:15.*

Adolph Zukor
Chairman emeritus,
Paramount Pictures Corporation

It (sexy films) comes and goes. I've seen it happen two or three times in my life. Pictures that shouldn't ever be made get made, draw some business, but the trend fades.

Interview/The Christian Science Monitor, 3-7:12.

MUSIC

Spiro T. Agnew
Vice President of the United States

They (rock groups) are not interested in anything but the dollars they are getting. They are really exploiting the kids and they have great contempt for them. They don't show up for their concerts on time; they treat them (the kids) as serfs; they don't do the things usually done by performers, such as autographing and giving pictures.

Interview, Washington/
San Francisco Examiner & Chronicle
(Women Today), 8–23:2.

Eddy Arnold
Singer

When I first started in the business, you couldn't get a "country" record played on a big-city radio station outside the South no matter what you did. If you were lucky, you might find a station where the morning man would play a couple around 6 a.m., but that was it. Now you can't turn a radio on without hearing . . . the same kind of music we couldn't get on the air.

Interview, New York/
Milwaukee Journal, 8–12:4.

John Barry
Composer

There's not that much separation between art and business in the '70s. One has to be aware of what's going on to protect oneself and do as one wants. I don't do both the same day; there are writing days and business days. Actually, the composer image is poetic and innacurate. Beethoven was one of the original music publishing hustlers. He was a first-rate wheeler and dealer, one of the first to collect advances. And Mahler—he was involved in the Vienna Opera House right

down to the decor and costumes. He knew boxoffice.

Interview, Los Angeles
Los Angeles Times (Calender), 2–22:18.

Leon Barzin
Conductor

Between the wars was the great time for musical directors. Despite his temper, we loved Toscanini. We loved Furtwangler. We loved Bruno Walter and Mengelberg. In these men intellect and emotion emerged. They knew the difference between clarity and coolness, between self-discipline and severity. A conductor as musical director is important because he feeds music to his public, and in that way leads it forward. But now, I see a growing pattern based on a checker game of guest conductors. The idea of musical director is dying. In the past, a musical director needed to know between 3,000 and 6,000 works. Today, a guest star conductor can live on 35. If he knows six programs well, he can fly around and subsist on just these.

New York, September/
The New York Times, 11–15:(2)19.

Harry Belafonte
Singer

. . . it is not correct to say that music influences the times. The times influence music. Take the carefree days of the '20s. They produced the happy music of jazz. The depression of the '30s brought the sentimental Cole Porters and Irving Berlins, and other composers wrote songs like "Brother, Can You Spare a Dime?" and "I Can't Give You Anything But Love, Baby." The prosperous '50s and early '60s produced jive and the high speed beat music. Along 'round the mid '60s, the whole world started coming unglued and the music began to speak of soul-searching and the quest for meaning in life. No, music does not bring on conditions—it reflects them.

Interview, Beverly Hills, Calif./
Los Angeles Herald-Examiner, 8–2:F2.

Tony Bennett
Singer

Music should be good for the appetite, for the mind and for the spirit.

Chicago Daily News, 8–8:18.

Leonard Bernstein
Composer, Conductor

In the decade surrounding 1940, the key to musical expression was nobility. We still had a form called the symphony, the noble symphony. We had the Shostakovich Fifth for the first time, the Prokofieff Fifth for the first time, Copland's Third, towering symphonic works by Hindemith, Bartok, Roy Harris, Bill Schuman, and what may have been the last of them all, Stravinsky's great Symphony in three movements. All this music was heroic music; it spoke of struggle and triumph; it reflected the basic nobility of man. Now, today, all that is gone. New music has splintered into dozens of movements, groups and experiments, ranging from the most didactic super-serialism to the most frivolous dada. Some of it is fascinating, some is titillating, some of it is touching and even beautiful, and some merely opportunistic. But one thing it almost never is is *noble*. And this negativism ranges right across the arts into almost all thinking disciplines.

Before students, Berkshire Music Center/
The New York Times, 11–25:37.

Anshel Brusilow
Conductor, Dallas Symphony Orchestra

The young people of the "now" generation are really listening to Beethoven—only with a different beat. It is very possible that you will be hearing more Beethoven in the popular vein in the near future. Beethoven,

on his 200th birthday, is now just about coming into his own.

Los Angeles Times, 12–16:(1A)4.

Petula Clark
Singer

As soon as I start to sing, something happens to me. I have an intensity of feeling. Rhythm isn't just the snapping of fingers and telling yourself you're really grooving. It comes from the inside. Even without a rhythm section, you have an inner sense of rhythm. It seizes hold of you. It's the kind of rhythm people don't hear but feel.

Interview/Los Angeles Herald-Examiner
(TV Weekly), 12–6:7.

Van Cliburn
Pianist

Great art is timeless and it is changeless and it is forever. So what do Beethoven and his music offer the world today? The same as when he was alive and as 100 years from today: a spiritual value. When you're dealing with great music, it is the most universal of all music, because it appeals to every generation and belongs to no one.

New York/Los Angeles Times, 12–16:(1A)4.

Aaron Copland
Composer, Conductor

All composers hope to reach an audience. But there's a limit to what you're prepared to do. We all know how to get a hand at the end of a piece by making a loud noise on a big drum. But that's not the point . . . With today's advanced composers, there's not much interest in writing music that *anybody* can understand; it's written for more cultivated listeners. Even some of mine—piano works such as the "Sonata," "Variations," the "Fantasy"—are not designed to appeal to a large public which can only like "Rodeo" or "Billy the Kid."

Interview/Newsweek, 11–23:139.

Richard Dufallo
Conductor

As for the young and as for rock—well,

(RICHARD DUFALLO)

rock is a pill that offers an instant "high." Rock has produced a drugged atmosphere. And rock has done something else. It has done away with mystery. There is no mystery in a rock piece. It's played, and right away you "get it." The young are not patient, and with contemporary music you've got to have *some* patience. You must really *want* to be intrigued by it. And if you're intrigued enough, the rewards are usually very high. When I conduct an aleatory score of one sort or another, I try to communicate its essential mystery, as well as its scheme, its architecture, its form.

Interview, New York/
The New York Times, 7–12:(2)13.

"Duke" Ellington
Musician

Typing and labelling is a stifling restriction on the creative arts. I have always believed that there are really only two kinds of music—good music and the other kind.

Telephone interview, Houston/
Los Angeles Herald-Examiner, 11–9:D1.

Arthur Fiedler
Conductor, Boston Pops Orchestra

We are forced to listen to too much music —in airplanes, elevators, restaurants. I'd like to have music be like fresh air. Now it's like pollution.

Interview, Washington, Feb. 2/
The Washington Post, 2–3:B1.

Pops has brought a lot of people to classical music. They go from rock-and-roll to pops and then to the classics. Thirteen-year-olds listen to rock and buy the records, but by the time they're 17, it's old hat. Then they discover there is other music. They go into pops music. That in turn opens their ears for really fine classics. I've been given credit for bringing more people to good music than anyone else.

Interview, San Francisco/
San Luis Obispo (Calif.) Telegram-Tribune,
8–29:11.

Rudolf Friml
Composer

I pity this generation of voiceless singers snapping their fingers to the eternal 4/4 beat. Music has gone to the devil. How can they write good music if they've never heard it?

Interview, Los Angeles/
Los Angeles Times, 9–25:(4)6.

Goeran Gentele
General manager and director, Royal Opera House, Stockholm; General manager-designate, Metropolitan Opera, New York

For 400 years, the opera has been in crisis. I think that is good. The patient always survives. It must be that way in any kind of art, or else it dies. The ideal opera company never existed and never will exist. When it does, it will be dead.

Interview, New York, Dec. 10/
The New York Times, 12–11:54.

What would I say was an ideal (opera) season? There is no such thing. A season is like a menu, and you have to vary what you serve from one year to the next. A year is related to the one before and the one after. When I plan a season, I'm always thinking in terms of four or five years.

Interview, New York/
The New York Times, 12–20:(2)19.

For the very reason that I am Swedish, I will fight for Americans in opera. There are so many exceptional American singers and craftsmen. European opera houses are full of American singers. Why should the Met be full of European singers?

Newsweek, 12–21:67.

Jakob Gimpel
Pianist

The whole process of work is refreshing the memory of the fingers. The finger has to respond to the slightest wish, which is controlled by the ear—and fingers develop their own memory. Some things you remember in your mind, but the fingers will carry on while there is a blank spot in the mind, so the process is achieving constant coordination. And one has to cultivate one's God. You have to weed, sow. You have to water. The only thing you can pray for is rain and sunshine.

Interview, Los Angeles/
Los Angeles Times, 2–12:(4)3.

Paul Horgan
Author

Where I halt (in his appreciation of music) is at the threshold of those sonic articulators of contemporary decibels who have recourse to other than musical resources and solutions of esthetic form. The aleatoric, so far as I am concerned, has nothing to do with the work of artists.

Interview, New York/
The New York Times, 9–1:34.

Marilyn Horne
Opera singer

We (opera singers) carry our instrument in our body, so if your big toe hurts, you feel it in your voice. The body is really the sounding board for the vocal chords.

Interview, New York/
The New York Times, 3–5:45.

Gene Kelly
Actor, Dancer, Choreographer

When I was a young man, you danced with a girl as a form of courtship—you touched her, and it was beautiful. In a discotheque today, a partner is a mere formality.

Interview, London/
San Francisco Examiner, 11–14:8.

Tikhon N. Khrennikov
General secretary, Soviet Union of Composers

It is necessary to safeguard Soviet music in every way from alien ideological influences . . . Soviet music is called upon to oppose the ideas of bourgeois society and to assert the socialist outlook and way of life. A composer's individuality is inseparable from his civic position.

Before Soviet Union of Composers, Dec. 2/
The New York Times, 12–3:16.

Dorothy Kirsten
Opera singer

So many opera companies are trying to be "groovy" and "now," and some critics have criticized the antiquity of opera. Why, that's what opera *is*. Opera is velvet and crystal chandeliers.

Interview, Los Angeles/
Los Angeles Herald-Examiner, 12–20:E4.

Josef Krips
Conductor

You can tell an orchestra only on the classics; that is, on works where you can hear every note. There you can build an orchestra. An orchestra which is not built on the classics is not worth five cents—in my opinion. When you judge an orchestra, you will judge it on how well it can play the Eroica, or how they can play a Brahms symphony—not how they do Shifrin or Imbrie. And I tell you something: I conduct many things by Stravinsky, but I don't conduct the "Rite of Spring"; it is not a piece for me. Everybody has his things. This kind of all-around—it's not so good. You don't expect a doctor, a specialist for ears, to take out an appendix.

Interview, Los Angeles/
San Francisco Examiner & Chronicle
(California Living), 8–30:18.

Music is not an entertainment . . . Music is uplift and consolation . . . Music is the language of the soul. And nobody should say, "I can't go to a concert; I don't understand." What have you to *understand*? Go there; sit down and be willing to listen. Everybody has to get out something. Everybody! But not entertainment. And I can tell you, if the government would ever understand what they could do with music, they would spend *fifty* times as much money as they do now. Somebody who loves a Schu-

(JOSEF KRIPS)

bert symphony will not be a murderer. No!

Interview, Los Angeles/
San Francisco Examiner & Chronicle
(California Living), 8–30:19.

Liberace
Entertainer, Pianist

You may as well stay home and listen to a recording as watch a dark-suited piano player.

Los Angeles Herald-Examiner, 2–27:A23.

Goddard Lieberson
President, CBS-Columbia Group; Former president, Columbia Records

We all must feel for the future of our symphony orchestras. How can we guarantee the success of that future? I know you must be sick of hearing it, but I believe the future success of symphonic music is in the hands of the youth of today. Further, I believe we have been on the wrong track in reaching for that future. We have wasted our money and our energies on children's concerts, illustrated lectures, piano and tuba lessons, and to appeals to the finer feelings of our children, which, as far as I know, have never been scientifically isolated or identified. My solution, on the other hand, is inexpensive, direct and, I believe, foolproof. It is this: We simply place outside our concert halls a sign which reads: "No one under 21 years of age admitted." Then, after an appropriate period of picketing and window-smashing, we allow the youth of our land to attend concerts. The only risk we run in this plan is the possibility of later finding *ourselves* barred by a sign which says: "Persons over 30 years of age allowed only if accompanied by a child." It's a risk worth taking.

Before Friends of the New York Philharmonic/
The Wall Street Journal, 12–30:6.

Henry Mancini
Composer, Musician

I think the ideal contemporary-classic composer is being formed now. He's probably coming out of the colleges. His vocabulary will be different from mine. He'll think in terms of new instruments. But, and this is essential, he has to come up through the system. He must take what he wants from the system, throw out the rest and develop his own language. The language of tomorrow will include a large orchestra; but along with it you might see four huge amps, an electric fiddle, a flute wired up for sound, amplified bassoon—all of which will be natural to the composer, because he's been brought up with them. I don't know how long it's going to take, but somebody like this is going to be our next Gershwin.

Interview, Los Angeles/
Los Angeles Times (Calendar), 6–21:45.

Zubin Mehta
Musical director, Los Angeles Philharmonic Orchestra

I suppose the top six (orchestras) are really Philadelphia, New York, Boston, Chicago, Cleveland and Los Angeles. But why is that so important, all those numbers? In every issue of *High Fidelity,* in the "Musical America" section, they have the first five or six. In Europe, there are no such Olympics.

Interview, New York/
The New York Times, 10–18:(2)15.

I just don't think women should be in an orchestra. They become men. Men treat them as equals; they even change their pants in front of them. I think it's terrible.

Interview, New York/
The New York Times, 10–18:(2)33.

Yehudi Menuhin
Violinist

Pop (music) in a way is a very good thing —it's captivating and spontaneous and reflects our times. Music must speak of universal sensations and thoughts, and a lot of contemporary (classical) composers have lost that. They don't speak of the big emotions —love, or faith, or fear, or humor. Curiously enough, it is in pop music that these things find a home.

Interview, London/
Los Angeles Times (Calendar), 5–10:28.

I think great music will be written for a very long time to come. As long as people suffer, as long as they face great anxieties, as long as they cherish hopes and experience visions, great music will be produced. The soil for it is so fertile; it has been well watered with blood and tears and prepared by suffering.

Interview, London/
Los Angeles Times, 12–16:(1A)4.

Gregor Piatigorsky
Cellist

Because I do not wish to play every day everywhere, they say I'm in semi-retirement. But I'm more active than ever—in a different way. Let the young talents do what I did in my youth—play everywhere. Heine said, "Everyone is a fool who does not live according to his age." I play in public only concerts which have a special meaning to me. Heifetz and I suddenly decided to play in Israel. No one even invited us. We invited ourselves. Can we come and play? we asked. We were very happy that they said yes. Here (in New York) I came to play with the Philharmonic first because all the conductors I played with here in 40 years—Toscanini, Reiner, Bruno Walter, Rodzinski, Barbirolli, Mitropoulos —are dead now. I have a terrible habit of continuing to live with my friends, dead or alive.

Interview, New York/Newsweek, 11–9:87.

Jean-Pierre Rampal
Flutist

The music you make must be a sung expression. All music must have something voice-like about it. That's when it really works. And that is why I say that when playing the flute you must be involved not only with flute playing but with other instruments as well.

Interview, New York/
The New York Times, 2–22:(2)19.

Artur Rubinstein
Pianist

All my life I have been on my knees before the art of music.

TV documentary of his life/
National Observer, 6–1:16.

William Schuman
Composer

. . . all a composer has to do is be honest. He has to write from the gut, from inside himself. I feel such a sense of sorrow for any composer who thinks he has to be fashionable, because that's absolutely the one true way of going out of date.

Interview, New York/
The New York Times, 1–28:48.

Pete Seeger
Folksinger

The musicians down here play essentially by ear, and that's the way I play. Up in New York, it was always cut and dried. They'd get ready and then they'd point at you from behind a glass and you'd play and that would be pretty much it.

Nashville/Variety, 2–18:57.

Kate Smith
Singer

Good music has never been away, and, therefore, will not have to replace any other kind of music.

Quote, 11–29:505.

Isaac Stern
Violinist

Obviously, the raucous rhythms of rock 'n' roll are captivating the young. The pressures of our time demand speed. They get their kicks out of immediate satisfaction. By contrast, the artistic process requires discipline and a period of learning and gestation. To break through the mass of information and the immediacy of popular styles, art has to resort to shock techniques—loudness, weirdness and unthinking rejection of past efforts and standards.

Interview, New York/
The New York Times, 7–29:30.

(ISAAC STERN)

Sometimes I think musicians should be world leaders. We have to learn how to get along in rehearsal.

Quote, 9–6:217.

Vilem Tausky
Musical Director, British Broadcasting Corporation Concert Orchestra

It (opera) is such a challenge to a conductor because his performance depends so much on the singers, the live material on the stage—their moods, their health, whether they got out of bed on the right side that morning. So you are some kind of liaison between the orchestra and the singers—and that is stimulating, exciting and sometimes frightening.

Interview, London/
The Christian Science Monitor, 4–6:15.

I can't imagine a world without music. It will always be the one medium which joins people together, no matter where you are. And that is noble, no?

Interview, London/
The Christian Science Monitor, 4–6:15.

Mikis Theodorakis
Greek composer

To me, the song is the atom. I've tried to use its energy to progress to a higher level—to where it could have an impact similar to that of Greek tragedy . . . To the extent that my music expresses a deep feeling of unhappiness of the people, yes, it's political. Most of my songs are devoted to the great and small incidents in the life of my people . . . I would have no interest in taking part in a purely musical event unconnected with the Greek struggle for freedom. If people consider me more a fighter for freedom than a composer, that pleases. I believe politically uncommitted artists are an abnormality.

Interview, London/Newsweek, 7–13:103.

THE STAGE

Edie Adams
Actress, Singer

I would like to do a Broadway show, but I can't afford to. You can earn about three times as much in summer stock as you can on Broadway. Isn't that ironic?

Interview, New York/
The Washington Post, 3–20:C3.

Jean Anouilh
Playwright

I write plays as a chair-maker makes chairs. Chairs are made to be sat and plays are made to be played to give actors work and the public entertainment. But aside from practical purposes, a play, like a chair, may be designed with artistry. Styles in plays change as they do in furniture. But one thing in the theatre never changes: the avant-garde. It is just where it was in 1896 when Jarry wrote *Ubu-Roi.*

Interview, Paris/The New York Times, 9–23:38

I have been accused of "theatrical" theatre. What a ridiculous charge! Critics seem anxious to transform the theatre into something it is not: a lecture hall, a reform school.

Interview, Paris/The New York Times, 9–23:38.

Peter Brook
Director

In this enormous body of work called the plays of Shakespeare, somehow something as close as possible to the real world was invented, in that his plays allow for endless interpretations, just as life does. Behind the surface is something, and something else is behind that. And this is why people have been finding fresh meanings for 400 years.

Washington/The Washington Post, 3–14:C3.

Gower Champion
Director, Choreographer

I feel that musical-comedy theatre, my particular interest, has reached a dead end. The new musicals have nothing to do with the surge of rock, country and western or folk music now going on. This is an enormous loss to Broadway. *Hair* comes close to using today's music. I can't think of any others.

Panel discussion, Los Angeles, Oct. 21/
Los Angeles Times, 10–23:(4)1.

Noel Coward
Actor, Playwright

A stageful of very attractive young people undressed could be pleasant, but I think it rather holds up the action.

Interview, New York, Feb. 10/
The New York Times, 2–11:42.

Danielle Darrieux
Actress

The stage is taking more from your life in three hours of work than one whole day in the (film) studio. On stage, you are a prisoner, even though it is a lovely prison.

Interview, New York/New York Post, 8–29:13.

Hilton Edwards
Founder, Dublin Gate Players

Most popular Irish plays are like an incestuous love affair of the Irish with the Irish.

Los Angeles/Daily Variety, 3–20:10.

Thomas C. Fichandler
Executive director, Arena Stage, Washington

Theatres are johnny-come-latelies to the field of patronage. Whatever individual fortunes there are that are available to support

(THOMAS C. FICHANDLER)

the arts have long since been pre-empted by the symphony orchestras, opera and ballet. Theatres, therefore, must look to government for substantial aid if they are to survive.

U.S. News & World Report, 5-4:82.

Christopher Fry
Playwright

The theatre asks for a kind of simplification because of the time limit you have in a play and because an audience is hearing things for the first time. I think one should always fight simplicity. If one is trying to get at the truth, complexity is language and action is part of it. But you've got to make the complexity immediately understandable. Part of the conflict in writing is an endless effort to make things plain.

Interview/Newsweek, 7-27:79.

John Gielgud
Actor

I'm sick of all the stories about me. I've come to dislike the past with a passionate loathing. I'm not interested in whether Hamlet is or is not, was or was not, my greatest role. There's no point in trying to relive one's past achievements. In that they are past, they are safe—so why disturb their memory? Also, one has got to play parts of one's age. Prospero, Lear. The repertory is small in number but gigantic in concept. To have lived as richly as they and to have suffered, and then to recreate that in the theatre . . . *this* is the kind of challenge that confronts me now.

*Interview, London/
The New York Times, 11–15:(2)1.*

. . . nudity on stage seems to me just a fashion that will pass. I find it neither important nor interesting as a dramatic device. Often, it is an excuse for the poverty of the playwright's imagination. I've no objection to watching naked bodies on the stage, but they must be beautiful. And usually those with really beautiful bodies can't act; so what's the point?

*Interview, London/
The New York Times, 11–15:(2)5.*

Jed Harris
Producer, Director

I think it (the theatre today) stinks; it's pathetic. The theatre on the whole is fairly dismissable.

New York/The New York Times, 7–8:40.

Helen Hayes
Actress

I think the most important thing I've learned from all those long years in the theatre is to use every means possible to keep your courage up. That's all I know about acting—isn't that terrible? Because when an actor loses his courage, that's the beginning of all the bad mistakes.

Interview/Look, 10–6:Sec.M.

How can I explain to young, ambitious performers that they must plan to be at the right place at the right time?

*Television program marking her 70th birthday;
National Educational Television, Oct. 8/
The Dallas Times Herald, 10–9:A2.*

Alan P. Herbert
Former member, British House of Commons; Author, Playwright, Composer

The people who present it (nudity on stage) should be made to prove before the law that it is a dramatic necessity and a work of art. If someone suddenly starts to caper about stark naked in a busy street or on a beach, they would soon be locked up. But now it can be done on a public stage without any let or hindrance . . . You have a captive audience in the theatre. You can always throw a book away or switch off the radio and television. It's not so easy to get up in the middle of a performance under the gaze of hundreds and walk out.

*Interview, London, Aug. 26/
Los Angeles Times, 8–27:(1)15.*

Jerry Herman
Composer

The only thing that disturbs me is when someone says the musical theatre must go in such and such a direction—that the only way is *Hair.* I admire rock and I admire Burt Bacharach, but all I want to do is my own thing. I don't want to do anybody else's. My thing is simple, melodic. I care desperately about polished, intelligent lyric writing, and I don't think it's time to throw it all out of the window. I believe very strongly that an audience deserves to be able to hum something on the way out after paying $15 a ticket. I believe in theatricality and in positivism in a time when that is not fashionable. Even if I turn out to be the only person left doing this sort of musical, I still believe it can exist alongside the protest musical.

Interview, New York /
National Observer, 2–2:18.

Sol Hurok
Impresario

If I would be in this business for business, I wouldn't be in this business.

Interview, New York /
The New York Times, 8–28:14.

Somegoro Ichikawa
Actor

I find many striking parallels between the techniques used in *(Man of) La Mancha* with those of Kabuki, the classical theatre of Japan. The shifting back and forth of time and space, for instance, all on the same stage. The quick changes of costume as the actor alternates between Cervantes and his creation, Don Quixote. The use of song, dance and declamation. The use of actors on stage as prop men. Kabuki is old, *La Mancha* is new. Yet there are these common elements.

Tokyo / The New York Times, 2–18:42.

William Inge
Playwright

The main fault of the American theatre is that it's too commercial. We're not as mature as the English about it. The theatre is a part of their lives. With us, it's a business. In London, the theatre has a definable, consistent audience. In New York—our largest theatre market—there is no real audience that grows along with the theatre. The New York audience is comprised mostly of expense-account men. We simply don't have a theatre public that is purely and simply interested in the welfare and growth of the theatre and its artists . . . Someone once said the American theatre has an "edifice complex." All over the country you have these marvelous, million-dollar community theatres—and nothing, practically nothing, is happening in them.

Interview, Los Angeles /
Los Angeles Times, 7–30:(4)19.

Danny Kaye
Actor

The secret of staying fresh in a show is to remember that the audience you're playing for that night has never seen it before.

Interview, New York / Parade, 10–18:19.

Gene Kelly
Actor, Dancer, Choreographer

A choreographer takes an idea out of his head and transposes it on people's anatomy.

Interview, Los Angeles /
Los Angeles Herald-Examiner
(TV Weekly), 1–11:6.

Jack Lemmon
Actor

There is no longer a case that Broadway is "it." Off-Broadway is probably as important as Broadway; and local, regional and traveling companies are blossoming. It's marvelous, and adds immeasurably to the country's total theatrical culture.

U.S. News & World Report, 5–4:82.

The changes in the theatre in the last five years have driven some people away and awakened others. Content is often sacrificed for the sake of technique and cleverness. Nothing's left.

Panel discussion, Los Angeles, Oct. 21 /
Los Angeles Times, 10–23:(4)4.

Myrna Loy
Actress

You know, it's funny about this play (*Dear Love*). When people hear it's about Elizabeth Barrett and Robert Browning, they assume that it will be a certain kind of entertainment—low key, so to speak. Just like movie audiences these days, theatregoers aren't all that much interested unless there's something sensational in a play. A little old lady came up to me when we were playing in Phoenix . . . She introduced herself and told me how much she enjoyed my pictures . . . When I asked her if she was going to see *Dear Love,* she made every excuse in the world about why she probably wouldn't get to it. But then I told her that Elizabeth was a drug addict. Well, her eyes lit up. "I never knew that," she said. "You know, I must see that play. Imagine! A drug addict."

Interview, Los Angeles/
Los Angeles Times, 11–18:(4)1.

Marcel Marceau
Mime

Mime is physical—it strikes to the heart. It deals with basic—I would say, extreme—situations and states of mind. It makes the invisible visible, the abstract concrete. Life is a cycle, and mime is particularly suitable for showing fluidity, transformation, metamorphosis. Words can keep people apart; mime can be a bridge between them.

Interview, Los Angeles/
Los Angeles Times (Calendar), 3–22:28.

Davey Marlin-Jones
Artistic director, Washington, D.C., Theatre Club

Most of the excitement in the American theatre is now found outside New York. There is more original drama and more experimentation. It's the wave of the future.

U.S. News & World Report, 5–4:80.

Raymond Massey
Actor

To me, theatre should be enchantment,

make believe, let's pretend. Today, it's sex, obscenity and squalor. We don't seem to have entertainment any more. The stage has become a dissecting table, and I'm sure people don't want to be insulted by the vulgarity of the permissive theatre . . . I don't mean it's got to be all light comedy . . . (But) somewhere we've lost the theatre of enjoyment.

Interview, London/
Los Angeles Times, 6–12:(4)14.

David Merrick
Producer

There are some musicals that have $15 seats on the weekend. I think that's probably a factor in keeping some of the patronage away, but not the major reason. I find that the price of a ticket is not important. If they want to go to the theatre, they'll go.

Interview/U.S. News & World Report, 5–4:83.

I am violently opposed to it (nudity and obscene language). I think it's just vulgar pornography that most of those Off-Broadway shows are selling to the public. There's always a large audience of voyeurs who want to go look at nudity and depravity on the stage . . . I think there should be more of an interpretation of the law on the subject, so that there are some guidelines for the authorities to follow. Some of these shows and films should be closed. If that sounds like censorship, I don't intend it to be. On the contrary, I'm afraid what has been going on will bring about censorship. I'm certainly opposed to that. In the long history of Broadway, the top 50 long runs have been clean shows. The family-type show is the one that does best. Look at them: *My Fair Lady, Life With Father, The Sound of Music, Hello, Dolly!* and *Mame.* Some of them are mine.

Interview, U.S. News & World Report, 5–4:84.

I don't think much of television and radio (theatre) critics, because I think they're rather selected at random. They're not trained journalists. Worse than that, they're given 60 seconds to review a play, which includes the commercials and all sorts of things. So they can only say that the play is dull, hilarious or something like that. That's not a review. I would just as soon eliminate all the radio and television critics.

Interview, U.S. News & World Report, 5-4:84.

The best creative people are snapped up by the movies now. There are just three men who account for 60 per cent of all the shows: Hal Prince, Neil Simon and myself . . . And all three of us are turning to films . . . because there just isn't enough action in New York any more; we just aren't getting the audiences . . . The real threat, though, is that we've lost the young people; they don't even attend *Off* Broadway—and it isn't ticket prices, because there are plenty of balcony seats for what they spend to go to a movie . . . The writers and directors who speak to them are working in films.

Interview, New York/
The New York Times, 9-6:(2)3.

. . . we are surrounded today by mediocrity. Everything is mediocre, from the phones to the plays. I've asked critics, separately, "Do you think there are any masterpieces around that the theatre's neglecting?" They've all said no, and I've replied, "Then I think you fellas are going to *have* to praise the higher grade of mediocrity, which may find an audience and bring in the tourists and make enough money that we can afford to produce the occasional good, noncommercial play. If you don't, there won't be any Broadway at all." I mean that, and I think I've begun to make my point.

Interview, New York/
The New York Times, 9-6:(2)3.

Arthur Miller
Author, Playwright

. . . Broadway hasn't come to terms with the present. There are now two audiences, the majority audience and the alienated audience. The basic, economic fact is that our drama is not mass entertainment any longer. Broadway cannot exist as it has.

Broadway has become the mark of a square play. It has become an economic thing, a matter of competing with industry for the price of land. The theatre—that poor, crippled art—has to ward out industry for its very space.

Interview/
Los Angeles Times (Calendar), 3-1:26.

Rudolf Nureyev
Ballet dancer

Life really revolves around performance. Everything offstage should be channeled for that short experience. Here on tour, I dance four and five times a week. I love that. It is not just the indulgence of being on stage, or of public adulation. You might even grumble and feel very tired and wish it wouldn't happen. But what you remember is the great privilege, the sense of accomplishment, and that time goes very fast and you must not waste a second.

Interview, New York/Newsweek, 5-25:117.

. . . when one goes on stage, it should be something extraordinary; it should be like a sacrifice. You cannot go on stage as if you were going to the office. Still, many dancers do this. Yes, they can do wonderful turns; but still, it seems as if they go on stage to do office work.

Interview, New York/
The New York Times, 6-21:(2)23.

Arthur O'Connell
Actor

. . . the stage is vital to an actor. On the stage, a performance is all yours. Nobody can edit you or cut you out. Actors need the stage for the rejuvenation of their abilities and equipment.

Interview, Los Angeles/
Los Angeles Herald-Examiner, 12-4:C3.

Laurence Olivier
Actor, Director

Between the ages of 30 and 40, there's very little limit to what you can do. You can probably play Romeo. You can even play a

(LAURENCE OLIVIER)

boy. And you can certainly play King Lear. But as you get into the sixties, you can't play Romeo. The field contracts. Your gifts of imagination, observation, intuition, must stop somewhere. Therefore, your means of invention are narrowed. You cannot go on being different. You can't do much except gently, slowly and rather despondently get a little, little, little more like yourself in almost everything.

Interview/Look, 1–27:23.

A national theatre has to be state-supported. In (the United States) a lot of things are not state-supported, but are—dare I say?—millionaire-supported. Well, I don't know the future of millionaires, but in our country (Britain) destiny seems to have looked after that little problem, and we haven't got many. The government is really the sugar daddy of our profession.

Interview/Look, 1–27:23.

I'm not so artistic that I despise profit.

Newsweek, 2–2:57.

When I first played New York in 1929, there were 74 theatres alight! There aren't anymore. The audience is staying home. They are staying home because a great majority of the hours taken up by television—the Box—have to do in some form or another with drama; from some classical play down to *Peyton Place* and *Perry Mason* down to the westerns which, in England anyway, are absolutely permanent. People will go to the opera or the ballet, because these are very rare on the Box, but not to the theatre.

Interview, Los Angeles/
Los Angeles Times (Calendar), 2–22:1.

Geraldine Page
Actress

. . . name me one character in literature or drama who can't be described as neurotic. Everyone in the beginning of my career would say to me, "What dreadful people you play!" I'd ask, "What kind of people do you want to see on the stage?" and they'd say, "Nice, normal people like we know." Well, it sure would deplete dramatic literature if we only played nice, normal people. But the point is we wouldn't want to know the people we go to see on the stage. How would you like to have Medea for dinner? Or Macbeth slurping your soup? Or Oedipus, with his bloody, blinded eyes dripping all over your tablecloth?

Interview, Los Angeles/
Los Angeles Times, 7–10:(4)17.

Estelle Parsons
Actress

The theatre is full of dopes. The smart people are in TV and movies. Oh, I don't believe in "culture." I see a theatre audience dozing and fanning itself and yawning. Afterward, they yell "Bravo" and "Wasn't it delightful?" They should say, "Wasn't it a bore?"

Interview, New York/
Los Angeles Herald-Examiner, 6–19:A12.

Otto Preminger
Motion picture producer-director

I go to a lot of Off-Broadway plays these days because I find the audiences there livelier and more responsive to a serious idea. On Broadway, a serious play is a terrific risk. Broadway theatregoers appear to love musicals and comedies. But it is my opinion that Off-Broadway and Broadway will merge.

New York, Feb. 17/
The New York Times, 2–18:42.

Ellis Rabb
President, APA Repertory Company,
New York

For the National Theatre in England, Sir Laurence Olivier gets a certain amount from the British government. What he gets is one-third of what the Swedish government provides for its national theatre, and Sweden has one-third the population of Great Britain. In other words, on a per capita basis, citizens are making nine times the contribution in Sweden than in England. In the U.S., government subsidy for theatre does not at present look promising . . . In America, repertory companies have a chance to restore the good name of the Establishment by presenting respected plays. If the Establishment will recognize that fact, a company like ACT (American Conservatory Theatre) can be immeasurably helped.

Interview/San Francisco Examiner &
Chronicle (Datebook), 2–22:3.

Cyril Ritchard
Actor, Director

I . . . think "relevancy" is becoming boring. You've got to have a rest; you've got to have a coffee break. And the theatre should be just that. A great deal of it should be sheer enjoyment, not always having problems bashed into your head.

Interview, Washington/
The Washington Post, 11–15:K1.

Barbara Rush
Actress

My play, *Forty Carats*, is a commercial play, which does not go down well in certain quarters. There's no message in it whatsoever. I think there's a place for this kind of play. But young people are hostile; they want a crusading play. This I resent. Theatre should be exciting, but it should be entertaining, too.

Panel discussion, Los Angeles, Oct. 21/
Los Angeles Times, 10–23:(4)1.

George C. Scott
Actor

All actors feel insecure at times. Just try doing a play eight times a week and you'll find out how good and how bad you can be. There's no guarantee in this business that things will go right. You're on top one minute and the next minute—*zappo!* It's a cruel and capricious profession and you've got *nothing* to fall back on. So actors find shields to hide from their insecurity and pain. Sometimes mine is a bottle.

Interview, South Salem, N.Y./
The New York Times, 3–29:(2)15.

This nudity crap. Most of it is trash and in spite of all those naked actors' claims, there is very little freedom in it. I don't think that kind of tastelessness will pay off for long. Dirty jokes are only fun for half an hour. I have not seen *Oh! Calcutta!* or *Che* or any of that garbage. I have no interest in it. I've seen all the stag films I want to see. They're like the old Moon Mullins books we used to hide in our desks at school. It's called turning a fast buck.

Interview, South Salem, N.Y./
The New York Times, 3–29:(2)20.

Lee Strasberg
Director, Actor's Studio, New York

A good deal of the nudity in the theatre is just a fad and will vanish. To some extent, it may extend the range. But so far as I can see, the way the theatre has used it, nudity is pure opportunism. It is used mainly for exhibitionism. I have not yet seen any dramatic scene in which nudity was used for artistic reasons.

Interview, New York/
The New York Times, 12–25:34.

Edward Villella
Ballet dancer

I am paid the highest salary of anyone in the New York City Ballet and that just about pays my expenses to get on stage—chiropractors, masseurs, whirlpool baths, practice clothes, the proper food—after all, I have to have a steak tonight, not a ham sandwich. But it's important that parents know that this can be a fantastic, profitable life if you're good. You have to work like hell, but you can end up with a brownstone in New York and a sports car.

Interview, Washington/
The Washington Post, 3–22:K6.

Dale Wasserman
Playwright

The one thing I'm certain of . . . is that I don't want to become involved in a series of pre-Broadway tryouts on the East Coast.

(DALE WASSERMAN)

I'm through with that. There's just too much agony involved. The death-watchers come to those tryouts and send their lethal little reports back to New York before you've had a chance to get the show on its feet. By the time you get to Broadway, everyone is preconditioned to a failure. It's an unhealthy, unfair situation. And, on top of that, you waste time and money moving from town to town when you could be spending both on the show itself.

Interview, Los Angeles/
Los Angeles Times, 2–4:(4)9.

A lot of critics attacked me, some with violence, about *Man of La Mancha*. They called it intellectually pretentious. I think they're just not ready to treat the musical as serious theatre.

Interview/
Los Angeles Herald-Examiner, 2–27:B2.

TELEVISION AND RADIO

James T. Aubrey, Jr.
President, Metro-Goldwyn-Mayer

You cannot attract the young and talented into television. They recognize it as a formula medium, censored and mediocre. It's quantitative, not qualitative.

Interview, Los Angeles/
Los Angeles Times (Calendar), 2–15:15.

Richard Boone
Actor

I feel the (TV) ratings should be in the hands of the Federal Communications Commission or a public group . . . Depending upon where ne (Nielsen) puts the 1,200 rating meters for the United States, he can absolutely control TV programming. If he, for example, quite wrongly puts meters only in the homes of Ph.D's, you will get one kind of rating. If meters are placed only in the homes of illiterates, you would obviously get quite another reaction.

Interview, Honolulu/Variety, 2–25:34.

Daniel J. Boorstin
Director, National Museum of History and Technology, Washington

I think television's main consequence on American life may be that it has reinforced what I see as a serious problem of our society: the tendency to dramatize the explosive, the disruptive, the disconnection from the past.

Interview, Washington/
U.S. News & World Report, 10–19:19.

Paul L. Briand, Jr.
Professor of English, State University of New York at Oswego

The television industry—a powerful monopoly of three networks, a triploly—solicits and receives two and one-half billion dollars a year on the claim that by information and entertainment it can change human behavior—and so it does. As some critics have claimed, television tears down in the evening, from 4:00 to 7:00 PM and later, what school systems all over America are spending $52 billion a year trying to build up in the classroom. Every night, television teaches cheap solutions to life's most difficult problems: Success?—Easy; Conflict resolution?—Destroy the enemy!; Answer to frustration?—Aspirin, cigarettes, beer!; Sex appeal?—Lotions, unguents, creams, underwear! And all of this, of course, WITH THE VOLUME TURNED UP! If, as (FCC) Commissioner (Nicholas) Johnson says, the TV manufacturer is legally liable for the physical harm that can come from the radiation in the set, why not the networks for the psychic harm radiating from the same set?

Convocation address at summer session, College of Arts and Sciences, S.U.N.Y. at Oswego, July 8/
Vital Speeches, 9–1:678.

Les Brown
Radio-TV editor, "Variety"

(A) myth I would bury at once is the myth that television is a medium still in its infancy; it is the broadcaster's cop-out, and nothing more. As long as we sustain the myth, the broadcaster will have a reason not to mature . . . Television, at very least, is voting age—old enough to be responsible for what it does. It is even older than that, because as an industry it is an outgrowth of radio, so that it has had 45 years to deal with its problems of service to the public. Furthermore, I would double or triple that age because through sheer experience television has more mileage than most newspapers or magazines. A newspaper has to answer for itself only once or twice a day, a magazine once a week. But television is on the air 18 hours or more a day. For sheer volume of output and experience before the public, a couple of years of television may well be equivalent to a lifetime for many publications. So television is not an infant; it is not even a juvenile. And to insist that it is will only retard it. I don't buy the alibi and never will, although it is one the industry still loves to use when it is caught doing something that is unconscionable.

Before National Association of Television Program Executives, Miami Beach, Feb. 25 / Variety, 3–4:39.

Dean Burch
Chairman, Federal Communications Commission of the United States)

Many sex scenes are introduced into movies solely for shock or commercial purposes. Some producers make no bones about the "X" rating—they look forward to publicizing it . . . Should a similar trend develop in broadcasting, it would be, in my opinion, a public cancer, and the time for effective and swift action to prevent such occurrence is now.

San Francisco / Hollywood Reporter, 2–2:1.

Commercial broadcasting must be encouraged and permitted to continue its development, so that its service will continue to benefit the millions of viewers and listeners. Non-commercial educational broadcasters must be given the resources to make good on its great promise. CATV (cable TV) must be given leeway to bring its contribution of diversity of programming material into the home. Over-the-air pay-TV should be given a fair chance. The development of satellite communications and new terrestrial broadband capacity into the home must be facilitated. The job in the next few years will be to find the proper mix of all these diverse elements—so

that each can be allowed to "do its own thing," and in so doing bring the American people a new richness of communications service.

Before California Association of Broadcasters, Palm Springs, Feb. 13 / Hollywood Reporter, 2–16:9.

. . . (the FCC) will not protect the minimal operator against competition. The responsible broadcaster is perfectly safe. The broadcaster whose only charm is to get by with as little service to the people as possible is in danger. He must run on his record, without upgrading when the competitors appear on the scene; and he must run the risk of losing (his license) to a better applicant.

Before National Association of Broadcasters, Chicago, April 8 / The Washington Post, 4–9:A2.

I think it's inherently unhealthy for three organizations (the networks ABC, NBC, CBS) to control 96.5% of what people can see in prime time.

Los Angeles / Los Angeles Times, 6–22:(4)1.

Johnny Carson
Television talk-show host

I would agree that TV doesn't take many forward steps. But you go out on the street and ask the average person what's wrong with television. He doesn't want to sound like a dummy, so he'll say, "It's all pap; we need more news, information and culture." But he watches the pap. Sure there's a lot of garbage on TV, but most people's tastes are fairly plebeian. Put *Gilligan's Island* on next to the Bolshoi Ballet and who do you think is going to get the ratings? Bolshoi? No way. No *way*.

Interview / Life, 1–23:52.

This is an insecure business. You're only as good as your last show. It's not like going to the office every day and knowing that after 20 years they'll give you the goddam watch.

Interview / Life, 1–23:52.

Kenneth Clark
Art historian

I don't know much about television over here, but all I can tell you is that I watch television almost every day of my life in England, and there are very few days that I don't find something of interest or don't learn and enjoy myself.

Interview/Meet the Press, National Broadcasting Company, Washington, 11–15/ The Washington Post, 11–16:C1.

Mike Connors
Actor

The way things are going now, in another two years we'll be seeing most movie stars on television. You can't think of an actor today who hasn't been on TV, whether it's in a movie, a series, or a variety show. Besides, I think people who make the distinction between movie and television actors are unrealistic. Acting is acting.

Interview, Los Angeles/ Los Angeles Times (Calendar), 2–1:13.

Michael H. Dann
Senior vice president in charge of television programming, Columbia Broadcasting System

. . . TV entertainment of the '70s will have greater relevance to the real world. Young people are interested in the world around us and want to interpret it in their own way. Beyond that, all I'm sure of is that shows like *Laugh-In* and *The Smothers Brothers Comedy Hour* will look very traditional 10 years from now.

TV Guide, 1–3:17.

Michael H. Dann
Vice president, Children's Television Workshop; Former senior vice president in charge of television programming, Columbia Broadcasting System

TV's product today is derivative, not distinctive; we imitate instead of innovate; we program defensively, not substantively. The result is, by and large, bland where it should be bold, poor where it should have

power . . . Unless the industry's leaders introduce other values than profits into their operating formulae, they may end up with long-term leases on a network of coaxial cables that are of little or no value to anyone. The network heads, then, are facing their moment of crisis. They must not forget the responsibility of leadership is to lead. The alternative is to squander the most powerful force for good at a time when it is most desperately needed. This is an unacceptable alternative for both the industry and for our society.

Before Hollywood Radio and Television Society, Beverly Hills, Calif., Oct. 13/ Daily Variety, 10–14:8.

James Day
President, National Educational Television

We who serve in public broadcasting must be mindful of the limits of our role as well as the opportunities. We are not the surrogate consciences of our public, determining what they shall have because we feel it best for them. But neither are we the surrogate voices of our public, telling others what that public wants and will have. That public—cantankerous, radical, thoughtful, timid, conservative, diverse, generous—will speak for itself in a million voices. We must interpret those million voices. But we must not permit the loudest to be taken for the whole. Above all, we must not protect that public as though its taste was not as good as ours, its intelligence as keen, its judgment as wise.

TV Guide, 1–31:2.

We discovered more than 20 years ago how powerful television can be in moving merchandise out of stores and into homes. Ever since then, those of us who signed on with non-commercial television have been trying to harness that power to improve the quality of life. More often than not we have failed . . . I think we have failed because our approach has been wordy, dark brown and humorless. To improve the quality of life you need an audience; and to get an

(JAMES DAY)

audience you must be entertaining. I don't care how earth-shattering the issues are which public broadcasters examine. If nobody is watching, nobody can care about those issues.

New York/The New York Times, 12–29:53.

James E. Duffy
President, American Broadcasting Company Television

(Television is) a medium that has evolved into both educator and entertainer every day and every night of the year; a medium that has become as much an art form as it is a theatre for the masses; a medium that has changed the entire economy, that has reshaped advertising; a medium that has become this nation's most popular stage as well as its most potent forum.

Before Hollywood Radio and Television Society, Los Angeles/ Los Angeles Herald-Examiner, 9–21:A14.

Vince Edwards
Actor

The movie star trend may not necessarily work in TV. In pictures, you never really know where you stand—if it's you or the picture that made it. TV is a very personalized medium. People have got to like *you*.

Interview, Los Angeles/Daily Variety, 7–1:12.

Federico Fellini
Motion picture director

Some think that television gives a greater intimacy. But it is really too broad, too distracted. When you think of all those people watching while they argue or eat or put the children to bed, it's very upsetting. TV people told me I would have to repeat things to get them across. That's like telling a writer to say the same thing every third page, because his reader is not paying attention.

Interview, Rome/ The New York Times, 7–19:(2)13.

Henry Fonda
Actor

What seduced me into this (doing a TV series) was not one thing but a lot of things . . . The big advantage is the time off it gives you to do other things—a play, a movie, a tour . . . But that isn't the only thing. I feel an actor has to function through exposure, and a professional exposes his work in every possible way, whether a Broadway play or a television commercial.

Interview, Los Angeles/ Los Angeles Times, 11–16:(4)21.

Frederick Ford
Former Chairman, Federal Communications Commission of the United States

Cable TV is where the action is . . . Nobody really knows where it's all going. We don't yet know where the big entrepreneurs will put their money. There's no prototype for what's happening. It's a frontier. This is indeed a revolution in communications.

Interview, Washington/TV Guide, 1–3:10.

Reuven Frank
President, National Broadcasting Company News

. . . television has more power than any previous medium in history. This is an accurate statement of fact, but when it is stated as criticism it is unwarranted. Every new medium has been the most powerful medium of its time—up to that time. Each of them has widened the reach of the previous media, or the impact of the information presented, or both: movable type, news magazine, picture magazine, radio, newsreel. I have no idea what follows television in the evolution of media-of-communication, but it will, by definition, be the most powerful in history.

At Yale University, Feb. 17/ Vital Speeches, 3–15:333.

David Frost
Television interviewer

I do believe that programs that arouse

people are not a danger to the status quo or the state of health of the nation, that the danger is programs that send people's minds to sleep . . . perhaps forever. The aim of a television program ought to be to leave people a little more awake, a little more aware, a little more alert than they were at the beginning. That can be done by a genuinely life-enhancing situation comedy or an Anne Bancroft special. It doesn't have to be a rather noble thing on the extinction of the Ubongo tribe or hydroelectric power in Sweden—which is one of my favorite non-topics—or the Common Market—that's a real drag.

Interview, New York/
The Christian Science Monitor, 4–15:11.

Dave Garroway
Radio-TV personality

There used to be television. There's no television now. What you have is pretty much a movie projector. I think of television as an instrument to let you know what's going on somewhere else. That's really gone. The money people took it over and turned it into a flaccid, safe product. The quality of the show wasn't the decisive thing; the ratings were. So, if you're two points below somebody else, you're out of business.

Interview, Los Angeles/
Los Angeles Herald-Examiner, 10–29:A18.

Julian Goodman
President, National Broadcasting Company

. . . I am opposed to exploiting fractional ratings differences for narrow promotional purposes. I am against helping our detractors claim that television is only a scramble for meaningless numbers.

Before NBC affiliates, New York, May 21/
Los Angeles Times, 5–22:(4)24.

(People) attack television entertainment, claiming that it aims below the average level of taste and interest, instead of uplifting the audience. Those who make this claim have never before confronted a medium that's designed for the tastes and interests of other people—of all the people. They don't watch television very much, and they don't try to select from it what matches their own interests. Instead, they want everything on television to be tailored to *their* tastes. Television is, at one time or another, the medium for all seasons, all ages, all levels of education and interest. My father, who is 86, would like to see *Gunsmoke* every night *Bonanza* is not on. My wife prefers news documentaries and panel discussions—but not when the *Mets* are playing. My seven-year-old son would be willing to watch *The Pink Panther* on a loop day and night, and my barber wants coverage of the six-day bicycle races. Television must provide reasonable satisfaction to the interests of the main audience elements. It must not allow majority tastes to suppress minority interests. Nor must it frustrate majority interests by converting a mass medium into a specialized one.

Before Rocky Mountain Broadcasters
Association, Jackson Hole, Wyo., June 23/
Vital Speeches, 8–15:658.

The public, which supports television with its viewing, should now support it with its voice. The millions of viewers who enjoy television and rely on it should be clear in their support—just as the much smaller number of detractors are loud in their attacks. The press is open to praise of programming as well as criticism. Congressmen, who are constantly petitioned to curtail some vital television freedom, can just as easily be encouraged to sustain it. There are many more constituents who favor television than there are who oppose it . . . I think it's time television's silent majority became vocal.

Before Rocky Mountain Broadcasters
Association, Jackson Hole, Wyo., June 23/
Vital Speeches, 8–15:659.

There is a general misconception that, when people speak of television, it represents their actual response to the medium. Every professional researcher knows through experience—and study after study

491

(JULIAN GOODMAN)

—that what people *say* about television and what they *do* about television are often poles apart. Put them before a questionnaire and they will profess a craving for serious, educative, uplifting programs—like ballet, for example. Put them before the television receiver in the privacy of their living rooms and you can't pry them loose from *Laugh-In*.

Before Rocky Mountain Broadcasters Association, Jackson Hole, Wyo., June 23/ Vital Speeches, 8–15:659.

Tom Gries
Writer, Director

Ten years ago, there was more to TV than just the excitement of experiment and learning. There was the satisfaction of good work, sometimes even significant work. At that point in time, television was far ahead of motion pictures in techniques, far ahead in the ability and willingness to make relevant statements. During that period, television hurt movies not just because it was free, but because there was so much to be said . . . so many things that audiences rarely, if ever, could see in their local theatres. Now, the balance has shifted. Cinema, movies, call them what you will, are the relevant medium. They speak to the people. For a lot of us, gut satisfaction has gone out of TV; and that's why writers and directors who are given a chance to say their piece in motion pictures just don't want to go back. Why? Turn on any dramatic show tonight in any series—*any* dramatic show—and I promise you that from the first three minutes' viewing you'll know all the character relationships, all the plot convolutions to come, and about half the lines of dialog. And whatever the conflicts, there will be no catharsis, no dramatic release—because network fears and government pressures have smeared the tube with chicken fat.

Before Phoenix (Ariz.) chapter, National Academy of Television Arts and Sciences/ Variety, 10–14:40.

Merv Griffin
Television talk-show host

Imagine three grown men (Johnny Carson, Dick Cavett and himself) and three billion-dollar networks fighting over nothing (late night TV). That's all that's out there—nothing! There's no audience. The same old insomniacs watch year after year. The only other people awake are those doing things they shouldn't—and they aren't watching television.

Interview, Los Angeles/ Los Angeles Times, 2–2:(4)16.

Edmund Hartmann
Producer

There is a patronizing air in Hollywood about situation comedies. I find that in the (TV) business the reaction is that a family show is easy to do, compared with a show of social comment. My point is that it's harder to keep a situation comedy interesting than broad comedy, western or whatever. The inference that situation comedy is easy is ridiculous. It's much more difficult to maintain interest in the narrow range of family life, where the whole thrust is believability.

Interview, Los Angeles/Daily Variety, 3–17:22.

When I was working on Broadway years ago, status required saying I never saw a Broadway show, but read books instead. When I worked in movies, I said I never saw movies, but read books and saw plays. In TV, they say they never watch TV, but watch movies instead. I'm always one medium behind.

Interview, Los Angeles/Daily Variety, 3–17:22.

Van Heflin
Actor

All we did in radio was anonymous. No name was connected with it. If the voice was recognized, we could always deny it.

Interview, Los Angeles/ Los Angeles Herald-Examiner, 3–4:B7.

Charlton Heston
Actor

. . . in commercial TV we are working not

in an entertainment medium, but in what might be called an adjunct or subsidiary of the advertising business. The economic structure is purely based on its effectiveness as an advertising tool to promote the sale of products . . . the dollars and cents are not enough to pay the cost of time, talent, material and the use of capital required to produce quality entertainment.

Before House Subcommittee on Communications and Power, Washington/ Hollywood Reporter, 1-7:10.

Nicholas Johnson
Commissioner, Federal Communications Commission of the United States

A nation is the mirror that reflects what is on its television screen.

Interview, London/ The Christian Science Monitor, 2-3:2.

Television does to your mind what cotton candy does to your body. It attracts your attention, makes you want it and then leaves you with nothing but an empty feeling and a toothache.

The Wall Street Journal, 3-3:24.

In a majority of the television homes at any given time, the choice most Americans make is to turn the television set off. Startling, but obvious once you think about it . . . More sets are now turned off than ever before. Indeed, some people have kept their sets off for so many hours that the picture tubes are lasting longer, and they don't need to replace their sets so often. Equipment manufacturers report set sales have hit new lows in the past few months. Some may miss the tingle of excessive x-ray radiation given off by their sets, but so far I haven't heard many complaints.

Before American Women in Radio and Television, New York/Variety, 3-11:39.

. . . I think almost everyone would concede—(both) those in and out of the industry—that television has failed. Not only has

television failed to make of us a better race of men, it has actually made us worse than we were before. The former condition would be indictment enough. The latter is simply intolerable.

At University of California at Berkeley, Nov. 5/ San Francisco Examiner, 11-6:40.

William Johnson
Associate editor, "Sports Illustrated"

After all these months pondering TV, I can no longer suspend my disbelief about the business. I disbelieve that there are millions of us life-sized, grown, middle-aged, responsible men sitting around in the dark staring for hours at eensy-weensy mosaics made of electronic dots. I disbelieve that there are highly paid people who are paid highly simply because they believe that if they show for the 10 trillionth time a commercial in which two guys stand in two bathrooms talking to each other through a jointly-held medicine cabinet, all of us middle-aged people will buy vats of underarm deodorant. I disbelieve anything I see or know about television because it's all too damned absurd. And what I disbelieve most about it is what I know the best: that it is all true.

Sports Illustrated, 1-26:4.

Charles Martin Jones
Executive director of children's programming, American Broadcasting Company Television

There's too much sameness in current kid shows; too many are still "illustrated radio," relying on voice imitations and outmoded cartoon techniques. Kids' minds work in delightfully different ways than those of adults—and discovery is the key to their growing process. Three factors should govern children's programming—education, entertainment and, above all, stimulation. There are thousands of ways of stimulating the interest of a child in the right way—I want to get some of them on TV.

Interview, New York/Variety, 4-1:45.

Pierre Juneau
Chairman, Canadian Radio and
Television Commission

For God's sake, let's try new things; let's not condemn a new policy just because it goes against the status quo. Let's put some excitement into broadcasting.

Variety, 2-18:37.

Buzz Kulik
Director, Producer

The (TV) networks are still pandering to the lowest common denominator, and there is no real intention on the part of the networks to uplift the standards of the quality of the programs. They make occasional attempts with specials, but that is all. The networks have brainwashed the sponsors and producers into this thinking with the criteria of a rating system that is nebulous, tenuous, faulty and, at best, unscientific.

Interview, Los Angeles/
Hollywood Reporter, 2-11:11.

That's how we killed television drama. We gave it a body blow from which it never recovered. It's on our heads. We killed an art form. We tried to top each other, and that killed it. I taped a show on top of a mountain. So (John) Frankenheimer flooded a studio and turned it into the Mississippi River. And George Roy sank the *Titanic* on television. Television is people. Its drama is close-ups, faces. Albert McCleery's "cameo" technique, with just faces and no sets, was brilliant television. But that wasn't good enough for us. We had to do big, massive productions, with scenes and sets that don't mean a damned thing on that little screen. Our drama was kitchen drama. Four walls and people. Out of necessity, we created an art form. Then we had to get bigger and bigger, pushing costs up and up until we destroyed the kind of television we created.

Interview, Los Angeles/
Los Angeles Times, 6-12:(4)19.

Perry Lafferty
Vice president for West Coast programming,

Columbia Broadcasting System Television

They (today's young people) are the mobile society. They get into their cars and go to the movies. They move and are not interested in "G"-rated films—which are what TV shows are basically . . . It's the kids from 18 to 20 who are seeing the movies in theatres today—such films as *Easy Rider, Midnight Cowboy, Getting Straight, M-A-S-H, Woodstock* and other "R" or "X"-rated films; this is the kind of stuff they want to see. We (in TV) can't make "R" or "X" shows, and that's what the kids are interested in . . . In other words, what I'm trying to say is TV cannot design its shows for teenagers in the mobile society.

Interview, Honolulu/
Hollywood Reporter, 6-23:5.

Ann Landers
Newspaper columnist

Television has proved that people will look at anything rather than each other. The importance of television in the American home is a symptom of our national disease—boredom.

Before Massachusetts State Federation of
Women's Clubs, Boston/
The Christian Science Monitor, 2-6:8.

John W. Macy, Jr.
President, Corporation for
Public Broadcasting

By and large, they (commercial networks) are doing—and doing very well indeed—what they must do under a system which measures survival and success in terms of mass audience ratings that respond more to the stimulus of entertainment and excitement than to information. Coverage of a moon shot or any other momentous event is appropriate and appealing under this system, and even the most severe critic cannot deny the networks high marks for magnificent, understandable and in-depth coverage. But to expect them to provide sustained coverage of many sides of complicated public issues such as hunger, environmental destruction, or even a local school bond controversy—to expect them to provide air time for citizens to become involved in these controversies—is to expect too much.

Before National Press Club, Washington,
Jan. 15/Vital Speeches, 2–15:287.

... I agree with E. B. White when he told the Carnegie Commission on Educational Television several years ago: "I think television should be the visual counterpart of the literary essay, should arouse our dreams, satisfy our hunger for beauty, take us on journeys, enable us to participate in events, present great drama and music, explore the sea and the sky and the woods and the hills. It should be our Lyceum, our Chautauqua, our Minskys and our Camelot. It should restate and clarify the social dilemma and the political pickle." We have not yet measured up to Mr. White's prescription. We are determined to do so. What's more, we are determined to fill the desperate need of the American people today to become involved in the examination and definition of the problems that beset them and the search for solutions.

Before National Press Club, Washington,
Jan. 15/Vital Speeches, 2–15:288.

Marcel Marceau
Mime

People have the idea that television is ideal for mime. No. On television you can see the expression on the performer's face, but there is no feeling of depth. I have seen Nureyev on TV, and there is no sense of virtuosity at all, just geometric patterns.

Interview, Los Angeles/
Los Angeles Times (Calendar), 3–22:28.

Raymond Massey
Actor

I have a great respect for TV. Even if so much of it, particularly in America, is junk, I'm not one of those actors who look on it as slumming ... you get a wonderful chance to develop the character—something you can't have in movies or the theatre, which

are just a one-shot thing.

Interview, London/
Los Angeles Times, 6–12:(4)14.

Donald H. McGannon
Chairman, Westinghouse Broadcasting Company

It is my opinion that TV has lost its compelling quality—that is, the reason for the public to view. This fact, coupled with the relatively old age of the top programs and the rising irritation on the part of the public to the proliferating of commercial interruptions and messages, has already alienated segments of our society ... The programming has not kept abreast of the evolution of values and the social crises of the '60's, and to that degree TV programming is not relevant to our times.

Before Federal Communications Commission,
Washington/TV Guide, 5–2:2.

Ricardo Montalban
Actor

Television destroyed a way of life in Hollywood, and at first I resented it. For old-line movie people, TV killed the red carpet. And yet it is to TV that I owe my freedom from the bondage of the "Latin lover" roles. Television came along and gave me parts to chew on. It gave me wings as an actor.

Interview/TV Guide, 1–24:10.

Craig W. Moodie
Vice president for advertising,
Armstrong Cork Company

Millions of Americans are tuning out TV (because the networks are offering) pablum programming ... Any differences in personality or programs that existed between the networks disappeared in the struggle for each other's rating points. Television's power over the communications industry became absolute. Absolute power corrupts, and network television as we know it today is corrupting itself.

At Building Products Distributors convention,
Lancaster, Pa./Los Angeles Times, 4–11:(2)3.

495

Malcolm Muggeridge
Author, Editor

You simply cannot expound ideas in a visual medium such as television, and ideas are the essence of human life. And I think, too, that newspapers and magazines have wrongly tried to fight television on its own terms, by adopting the televised style. Yet their real strength is in the written word, the ability to expound ideas. I've clung to that, and I believe it still. But television, this fantasy projection—what is it, anyway? I think it is a symptom and not a cause. All right, then: What is the disease? That's the question.

Interview, Robertsbridge, Sussex, England/
National Observer, 7-20:21.

Vincent Price
Actor

Television's talk and game shows are a great boon to the performer. Talk-game shows attract all but the most rarified personalities. Actors have come to realize the need of the very public appearances television affords them. They can display another side of their often type-bound careers and can decide for themselves just how much they have been able to retain of their humanity, their identity with other human beings.

The Dallas Times Herald (TV Times), 12-20:29.

Cliff Robertson
Actor

Actors who got their breaks in TV shouldn't look down their long, imperious noses at it.

Los Angeles Times (West Magazine), 2-22:20.

Eugene V. Rostow
Professor of Law, Yale University

The worst scenario for the future I can imagine would be one in which cable television would be completely absorbed and integrated into the existing communications oligopoly. The best would be what I have tried to sketch here today: of cable television evolving freely within a legal and economic environment structured to encourage experiment and to prevent concentration—an environment that made many channels accessible to citizens' groups as common carriers and made it impossible for government or business or labor or any segment of any industry to dominate the national mind.

Before National Cable Television Association,
Chicago, June 8/Variety, 6-10:34.

Elton H. Rule
President, American Broadcasting
Company

We are in the midst of a cultural revolution that is tied to a social revolution. The moods, manners and mores of our viewers are changing constantly. In television we cannot follow the change. We must be with it or ahead of it. Following a trend in an industry which moves as fast as television is a waste of energy, a waste of resources and a waste of money. We must know not only who's in our audience today, but whom we must reach next year and the year after—four years from now. We have to know what kind of program material will appeal to them. A paper company must plan as far ahead as 40 years—they deal in trees. IBM uses a five-year plan. As our network planning division creates more sophisticated means of forecasting, and as research teaches us more than we know now, our range will become longer. Two years is a long time today. But in the future, five years won't be long at all.

Before Association for Professional
Broadcasting Education, Chicago/
Variety, 4-8:34.

Thomas W. Sarnoff
Executive vice president, National
Broadcasting Company

Television is a mass medium that must offer a service most people will find interesting and useful most of the time. Though it is true that commercial broadcasters have an obligation to their audiences, nothing could be more fatal, nor futile, for television than to get so far ahead that it cannot or will not be seen.

Before Idaho State Broadcasters Association, Boise, Jan. 28/Hollywood Reporter, 1–29:16.

George C. Scott
Actor

TV has got to realize it can't all stop with *Petticoat Junction*. It is going to either be the savior of the world or send us all to hell fast. It's the most powerful communications device since the discovery of language, and it is full of bull. We're still in the horse and buggy stage with television. In the next decade, I believe the networks as we know them now will be obsolete, just as the Hollywood studios crumbled under the changing of the times. Too many forces are hammering at them now. The marketplace is too competitive for them to stay in control. The Mike Danns (programming vice president at CBS) of the world will become as archaic as dinosaurs.

Interview, South Salem, N.Y./ The New York Times, 3–29:(2)20.

William Self
President, 20th Century-Fox Television

With all the manpower which has applied itself to the new shows (this season), all the ASI tests, the surveys, the big salaries paid writers, directors and others involved, when you're all done, you come up with shows the public doesn't want . . . The networks test a concept, a pilot, the episodes on every show. TV has become too computerized, too subject to analysis.

Interview, Los Angeles/ Daily Variety, 10–27:14.

Eric Sevareid
News commentator, Columbia Broadcasting System

I don't think a President of the United States, unless he's declaring war, or some other terribly critical thing, ought to have all three networks at the same time. We've given too *much* time, and as a result anyone

in power thinks of TV as an open conduit for his use.

Interview/TV Guide, 3–14:11.

Robert Stack
Actor

When I made *Written on the Wind*, everybody thought I had it made. After *The High and the Mighty*, John Wayne said, "You've got it made, kid." I've had it made so many times! In movies you're always waiting from picture to picture. You go to all the stupid Hollywood parties, hoping a producer will notice you—they never do—and, while you're there, you keep going to the men's room to look at yourself in the mirror. On television, you get real, honest-to-God love. After *The Untouchables* became a hit, I felt like a candy-hungry kid who suddenly got himself a candy store.

Interview, Los Angeles/TV Guide, 10–31:16.

Barry Sullivan
Actor

When you go to a play in the theatre, that's your entertainment for the night. You think about it, digest it. But on TV, it's only one item in a whole night of viewing. Your critical and perceptive sense is so diluted the play cannot register as it should. Too often it becomes just another program.

Interview, New York/ The Washington Post, 8–11:B6.

Lionel Van Deerlin
United States Representative, D-Calif.

CATV (cable television) is an idea whose time has come. All the armies of the world couldn't stop it.

Time, 6–1:71.

Willard E. Walbridge
Chairman, National Association of Broadcasters

If I were a revolutionary seeking first to limit and then destroy the democratic process of this nation, and then the individual freedom of its people, I would begin my attack with a frontal assault on that institu-

(WILLARD E. WALBRIDGE)

tion which has contributed in this day the most to that process and to those freedoms. I would attack the people's media—the ones that tell them fairer and faster—the ones that they trust the most. I would attack broadcasting on the basis of its content—its structure—and, of course, its economic viability . . . I cannot remember a time when broadcasting's service to the American public was better. That's just another way of saying that there has been no time when we deserved the criticism and calumny less than we do today—yet we are getting more than ever. What is it all about?

Before National Association of Broadcasters board meeting, Maui, Hawaii/ Hollywood Reporter, 1–27:6.

(Broadcasting is, in the public eye, the) fastest, the best, the most reliable, the most believable source of information of the world around them. Of all broadcasting's achievements, this alone dwarfs the sum total of the others into insignificance.

Dallas/Hollywood Reporter, 3–23:12.

Somewhere and sometime someone first wrote or uttered the phrase, "The Public's Airwaves." May his soul rest in peace; he has left us none. For there is no phrase so apt for the glib detractor, so useful for the demogogue, so sly for the covetous competitor, so relevant for the cynical militant revolutionary.

Before Broadcast Advertising Club, Chicago/ Variety, 4–8:34.

Vincent T. Wasilewski
President, National Association of Broadcasters

We are accused of money-grubbing and indifference to the public interest. Yet automobile manufacturers do not give away cars. Appliance makers do not give away stoves and refrigerators. The telephone company does not give away free service. But broadcasters do, in enormous amounts.

A contribution not only of our product—time—but the aid and assistance of our people and such highly-tangible items as tape and film and the use of production facilities. It is indeed ironic that the industry which is most generous in contributing its sustenance to the public good seems to receive the least credit for it.

Before National Association of Broadcasters, Chicago/Variety, 4–8:34.

Caspar W. Weinberger
Chairman, Federal Trade Commission of the United States

(Television is the) greatest single force we have for demonstrating . . . what our system of freedom really means, and the unbelievable wonders it has accomplished and the wonders yet to come.

Before Columbia Broadcasting System affiliates, Los Angeles, May 6/Daily Variety, 5–7:12.

Mae West
Actress

TV *should* be censored. You can't have those awful sex movies on TV. It's repulsive. You can get sick to your stomach watching them . . . And the four-letter words in these movies—TV is *right* to censor them. Why, you couldn't pay me to say those words. TV should stay just the way it is and keep this kind of thing off the air—because you've got children listening, and a lot of people who live very properly. If you didn't have them, the world would go to pieces in no time. You've got to have *some* people with dignity. So I think TV should stay that way. *Something* should stay that way.

Interview, New York/TV Guide, 8–22:16.

Richard Widmark
Actor

. . . it's so fruitless and frustrating in television. How can you do drama? Never have I been really moved by television. Too many distractions: interruptions from commercials to flushing toilets and ringing telephones. None of the concentration that is so necessary! Television is for things happening: football games, walks on the moon —you can't beat it. But its drama is a dead pigeon.

Interview, Los Angeles/
Los Angeles Times, 11–30:(4)23.

Michael Winner
Motion picture director

I don't like television. I think it is a shoddy medium for drama. It has very few writers who have contributed anything worthwhile, with the exception of Harold Pinter. TV is best at documentaries, sports and covering live news stories like riots, fires, earthquakes and parades. But for drama, the stage and screen are far superior.

At National Film Theatre, London/
Los Angeles Herald-Examiner, 9–30:C7.

Robert D. Wood
President, Columbia Broadcasting
System Television

The acid test is programming. But do you know how hard it is to find and schedule a series? We read and considered 2,100 ideas and projects in script form, of which eight were made into pilots, from which we scheduled three . . .

Interview, Los Angeles/
Los Angeles Times, 5–13:(4)15.

We are determined that we will resist being sucked into the annual ratings rat race, where long-range advantages are sacrificed for short-term gains. We are going to lift our sights from the narrow focus of last week's ratings report, or next quarter's, or next season's.

Before CBS affiliates, Los Angeles/
Los Angeles Times, 5–22:(4)24.

Vladimir K. Zworykin
Scientist; Honorary vice president,
RCA Laboratories

From the beginning, American television networks and their producers acceded to the public taste for trivia because of commercialism. Television had the chance to become the greatest social force for good in this century. But the networks subscribed to what Mr. Nixon now calls the "silent majority."

Interview/Newsweek, 1–19:12.

Personal Profiles

Edie Adams
Actress, Singer

I always have to be working hard at something. I suppose it's the Pennsylvania Dutch in me. I'm kind of like the old-time farm women. You know, drop the baby, and pick up the plow.

Interview, New York/
The Washington Post, 3–20:C3.

Ruth M. Adams
President, Wellesley College

If you tell people how to do things, they tell you you ought to do them yourself, and that's how I became president of Wellesley.

Interview, Dallas/
The Dallas Times Herald, 10–20:B1.

Mario Andretti
Auto racing driver

Why do I race? I've thought about it a lot, believe it or not, and I don't know. I really don't. I don't think anybody, except me, can understand it. Whenever I get bored with racing, I start thinking again about how much I wanted to be where I am now. I would give up everything—my home, my family, everything I've gained—to stay in racing.

Interview/Sports Illustrated, 5–11:46.

Pietro Annigoni
Artist

That is how I see her (Queen Elizabeth II): regal, but inevitably solitary, a mature woman of great experience who carries what must sometimes be burdensome responsibilities. In painting the queen, I had 18 sessions with her and was able to study her changing expressions. She is an extremely kind and considerate person. When she talks, a smile transforms her face. But in repose, the expression is thoughtful, grave. After all, she is not a film star who must always be seen to smile.

London/The Christian Science Monitor, 3–2:10.

Eve Arden
Actress

I've worked with a lot of great, glamorous girls in movies and the theatre. They would always give their last ounce to get where they wanted to go. And I'll admit, I've often thought it would be wonderful to be a femme fatale. But then I'd always come back to thinking that if they only had what I've had—a family, real love, an anchor—they would have been so much happier during all the hours when the marquees and the footlights are dark.

Interview, Hidden Valley, Calif./
Los Angeles Times (Calendar), 5–17:24.

Elizabeth Ashley
Actress

... I'm a hopeless extrovert. Every single morning I wake up and tell myself I'm going to be a totally different type of person—mysterious, aloof, serene. But then my son does something or my husband does something, and I blow it. My new personality doesn't make it through the first cup of coffee.

Interview, Los Angeles/
Los Angeles Herald-Examiner, 12–6:F4.

W. H. Auden
Poet

One always enjoys imagining what one might have been if one had not become what one is. I like to think that if I hadn't been a poet I might have become an Anglican bishop—politically liberal, I hope;

theologically and liturgically conservative, I know.

At Downstate Medical Center, Brooklyn, N.Y., Dec. 15/The New York Times, 12–16:43.

Charles Aznavour
Actor, Singer

I'm always surprised about my success. Every day I am surprised. And I think the day I'm not surprised, I'm finished.

The Washington Post, 1–31:C2.

Lauren Bacall
Actress

I get the greatest kind of soaring feeling from this work (acting on stage in *Applause*). I don't mind rehearsing at all. It gives you the good discipline. You get the feeling that you're making good use of yourself, and nothing makes you feel better than that. It's exhilarating, and it's coming at such a crucial time for me. I've had fourteen years of bad luck, and I mean pretty desperately bad luck. But now I feel the cycle of life changing. It's like a second chance, as if my life is beginning again. My eyes are open, my ears are open, all my senses are at work. I'm counting on this for a lot, because, believe me, I'm *due*. I'm *overdue*.

Interview, New York/Life, 4–3:53D.

Carroll Baker
Actress

Looking back, I can't believe some of the things they (the film industry) got me to do. Arriving at a premiere in a car with two huge dogs next to me . . . dressing up as Harlow to go across the Atlantic on the *Queen Mary* . . . wearing the see-through dresses that caused such a rumpus . . . I didn't feel like a human being any more. I wasn't leading any sort of a normal life. I was so jittery . . . in the end it led to a kind of nervous breakdown. When I came out of it I realized I was faced with two choices: the way out that Marilyn Monroe took, or to run away. I just ran.

Television interview, London/ San Francisco Examiner & Chronicle (Datebook), 2–15:2.

Thomas Hart Benton
Artist

Money has made no difference in my life. Rita's (his wife) still in the kitchen; I'm still in the studio. I'm just lucky—extremely lucky—that financial success came late in life rather than early. A young man might view it the other way around. But if I had been successful when I was young, I might not have done anything, seen anything, gone adventuring. That's not necessarily so, of course. Cezanne was rich and made his own experiences. But I think the tendency would be not to.

Interview, Kansas City/ Los Angeles Times, 3–15:B6.

Claude Berri
Motion picture director

I am afraid I'm not a "cinephile." I love to make films, and to see them, but not to sit and talk about them. (Francois) Truffaut, for example, is a very good friend of mine, but life for him is only film. He organizes his life with film. Me, I make business, I make love, I make a film every two years or so, then I go on to something else.

Interview, New York/ The New York Times, 1–18:(2)11.

Dirk Bogarde
Actor

I'm very much a loner. I don't go out a lot. I'm not seen at restaurants. If you want to be "famous," you have to be "one of the gang" . . . Nobody knows me but the public.

Interview, Venice, Italy/ San Francisco Examiner & Chronicle (Datebook), 7–12:9.

Ray Bradbury
Author

I love my work and love the world with all its nonsense and hydrogen bombs. I'm not a blind optimist; I see the evil. I circumvent it when I can and warn people where I can warn them. But I don't know how to cure morons; the only thing I can do is be honest —and take a trip on my imagination when it seizes me and says, "Run away."

Interview, Los Angeles/
Los Angeles Times, 3–15:E18.

Charles Bronson
Actor

Do you know what it is like to work in the coal mines? No, you don't. Very few people do. I remember seeing movies on miners with actors like Paul Muni, and I just looked and I looked and didn't know whether to laugh or to cry. Nobody really knows, unless you are part of it, what it is to live down there underneath the surface of the world, in that total blackness, live on your knees, breathe that dust and be unable to shake it off even when you do go home. It took me years to get it out of my pores, and maybe I'll never get it out of my system . . . During my years as a miner, I was convinced that I was the lowliest of all forms of man. Then I was drafted, became a machine-gunner in the tail section of a bomber, and suddenly discovered the world. I suddenly discovered that I was not the dumbest, the lowliest among men. I suddenly felt that the others around me were no better than I was.

Interview, Nice, France/
Los Angeles Times (Calendar), 10–25:69.

Richard Burton
Actor

There are two bones of contention between Elizabeth (his wife) and myself. She is never on time and she loves films. Of course she was educated in Culver City, and that is a very different matter than South Wales . . . I'd rather read. Elizabeth loves to queue up.

Interview, Beverly Hills, Calif./
Hollywood Reporter, 3–18:18.

I've never pretended to be—though the press has sometimes pretended that I've pretended to be—one of the "major actors" or anything like that. I don't think I have the dedication to be a major actor. I mean, I don't enjoy my job with the same passion that most top-class actors do.

Interview, San Felipe, Mexico/
Los Angeles Herald-Examiner, 9–20:G6.

It seems fairly ridiculous for someone 45 or 50 to be learning words written by other people, most of which are bad, to make a few dollars. I'm not dedicated; I never was. In a sense, I'm totally alienated from the craft that I employ so superficially and successfully.

Interview, Bracknell, England/
The New York Times, 12–6:(2)9.

James M. Cain
Author

. . . I don't read other novelists, because I'm afraid I'll start writing like those guys.

At Catholic University panel discussion,
Washington, March 12/
The Washington Post, 3–13:B7.

Michael Caine
Actor

At one time I was concerned with living a life of luxury. Not now. I have freedom from worry about money; this is good. But I'm not sumptuous; I'm modest in demands. I don't think success has changed me much.

Interview, New York/
The Dallas Times Herald, 7–3:D6.

Glen Campbell
Singer

They call me an "overnight success," but my night's been 15 years long. That's just about how long I've been struggling in this business. I'm getting some of the gravy now, but it sure hasn't been a picnic.

Interview, Los Angeles/Parade, 2–8:5.

Diahann Carroll
Actress

The moneyed people, the managers, know they can deal with me. I'm "acceptable." In fact, I'm sure that's why I got the part of Julia (in the TV series). I'm a black woman with a white image. I'm as close as they can get to having the best of both worlds. The audience can accept me in the same way and for the same reason. I don't scare them.

Interview, Los Angeles/TV Guide, 3–14:27.

I worked hard to get where I am. I took the best jobs I could get. I'm doing it for money and power, because money *is* power in this country, and power means freedom. I want the freedom to do what *I want to do,* and you can't do that in this business or in this country without money or power.

Interview, Los Angeles/TV Guide, 3–14:27.

Johnny Carson
Television talk-show host

What do I want to do? What a dumb question! I'm *doing* it.

Interview/Life, 1–23:53.

George Christian

Presidential Press Secretary during Lyndon B. Johnson Administration

I do like him, but strong people like Johnson can intimidate you. Those guys are different from ordinary human beings . . . Everything about Johnson was magnified. When he was unhappy, he was the most unhappy man in the world; and when he was happy, it was the same way. He could love someone and go to excesses and bestow sainthood on him. He always said, "You know a man by the enemies he makes," and, "Show me a man with no enemies and I'll show you a man with no friends." He had enemies and they were clearly defined and he didn't mind talking about them. He was like Roosevelt that way. He felt that if you accepted the fact that you were going to be bruised, you had to learn how to adapt. A super-sensitive person could never have survived working for Johnson. He could make you feel like the biggest idiot in the world—and he would forget it the next day.

Interview, Washington/
The Washington Post, 8–18:B1.

Lee J. Cobb
Actor

Mine have always been strong-man roles. And I've had a rich life playing them. But they don't come close to my character at all. I'm really a very shy person. I can't be indicted by what the public thinks. But I wouldn't want to be thought of only as the strong actor with the Stetson and the sneer.

Interview, Torreon, Mexico/
San Francisco Examiner & Chronicle
(Datebook), 6–21:7.

Bing Crosby
Singer, Actor

My greatest weakness, the fact that I was never trained for any of the things I do, is my greatest strength. I was always able to remain myself. But that really shouldn't be the key to success. A good actor should be many people, capable of transporting himself into whatever personality a role requires. I still want to find out for myself if I can play good character roles. And that's why, you see, I'm still not a success.

Interview, Hillsborough, Calif./
San Francisco Examiner & Chronicle
(Datebook), 1–18:11.

Kim Darby
Actress

I protect myself by using my waif quality a lot because I am vulnerable. Some people think of me only as a kind of melancholy character, but I'm not when I'm around people I know care about me. I'd like to stop giving this impression of shyness, and it's only now that I'm beginning to learn about myself. In the last 18 months, I've been divorced twice and become a mother. I guess for me to be standing up and existing at all is something. Deep down inside, I'm really made of steel.

Interview/Life, 5–29:40.

Alain Delon
Actor

I am not a drinker, and I am not a gam-

(ALAIN DELON)

bler—except with life, not cards. I can count the friends I have on the fingers of one hand. I'm not a dancer, and I'm not a nightclubber, and I really don't like to go out. What I like to do is stay home with people I love. But if I do go out, I don't like the fashionable places, because I am not polite when I am out of my home. Most of the time I think it is very false to go around and kiss people and shake hands and say, "Hi, my dear."

Interview, New York/
The New York Times, 8–16:(2)10.

Sometimes I think seriously about quitting acting. My nature and my mentality and my understanding of life and people don't make me out to be an actor. The only part of an actor's life that I like is the 20 seconds between when they say, "Roll it," and "Cut." I hate all the rest—the mentality of the people, the facilities, the reporters. They're all against my nature.

Interview, New York/
The New York Times, 8–16:(2)10.

Life is a constant fight, but beautiful. You fight every day for what you believe, but it is worth it. It is all too short, anyway. It is a race run so fast it is a shame. I want to live for myself and the few people I love. I want to do only the things I believe in deeply, so that I can look in the mirror at my face and not be ashamed.

Interview, New York/
Plainview (Tex.) Daily Herald, 8–21:6.

Bernadette Devlin
Member of British Parliament from Northern Ireland

I'm not a socialist because of high-flown intellectual theorizing. I'm a socialist because life made me one. When I was elected, people asked me if I was a Marxist. To my eternal shame I had to say I hadn't even read Marx. In the past year I've bought books on politics and history, but I haven't had time to read them. But I'm not a moron. I have an intelligent enough brain. I have an important contribution to make. I have something which makes people listen to me. I can put into words what 500 people are thinking but can't express. I can talk about change, but my trouble is that I don't really know the mechanics of how that change is brought about.

The New York Times Magazine, 8–9:20.

Fifi D'Orsay
Former actress

If you don't know who I am, ask your mother. Better yet, ask your father.

The Dallas Times Herald, 7–22:A2.

"Duke" Ellington
Musician

My talent is painting. My compulsion is playing the piano. My occupation is listening.

Interview, New York/
The New York Times, 8–11:26.

Jane Fonda
Actress

You must admit my father (Henry Fonda), with the kind of image he had, produced peculiar offshoots. He's always been the all-American liberal democratic good solid citizen—look at all the Presidents and Senators he's played—and here his son (Peter) is, a pot-smoking hippie, whatever that means, and his daughter—I don't know *what* she is! But we've all made it our separate ways. We're sort of a combination of *Grapes of Wrath, Easy Rider* and *Barbarella*.

Interview, New York/
The New York Times, 1–25:(2)15.

Glenn Ford
Actor

As my career has advanced, I have found it a great antidote to self-adulation to visit the Santa Monica neighborhood where I washed the windows of a drug store and swept out the stock room of a dry-goods store.

The Washington Post (TV Channels), 10–11.

Jean Genet
Poet

Legally, I am a Frenchman. But the destiny of France does not touch me at all. I would be happy any place in the world—Japan, Guatemala, America—where revolutionary acts are taking place.

Interview, San Francisco/Look, 6–16:Sec.T.

Stewart Granger
Actor

Friday night, when we're through (with his TV series), it's such a relief that I usually get loaded. Saturday I spend nursing my hangover and Sunday I spend being depressed at the thought of working again on Monday. That's my weekend. But what the hell—the money's good.

Interview, London/
San Francisco Examiner, 2–10:27.

George Hamilton
Actor

(For) too many years I was being what others wanted me to be under a studio contract, and what's come out of it is everyone thinking I'm something I'm not. And now I walk around with somebody—me—and can sit back and watch other people talk, because they're not talking to me, they're talking to what they think I am. It's a marvelous thing to see. It's like being an 8 by 10 glossy. If I met George Hamilton, I'd think he was without much depth and dresses well, from all you read in the newspapers and magazines.

Interview, Las Vegas/
Los Angeles Herald-Examiner, 6–20:B7.

Noel Harrison
Actor, Singer

I've learned to live life as it comes. If it all falls apart and I have to go back to playing my guitar at deb parties, then I'm quite pre-

pared to do it. I now have the strength and the will, and they alone will take me quite nicely through life.

Interview, London/
The Christian Science Monitor, 3–25:17.

Hugh M. Hefner
Publisher, "Playboy" magazine

Next to beautiful women, I think I like gadgets best.

Los Angeles Times (West Magazine), 3–22:10.

Katharine Hepburn
Actress

Really, I'm rather square. But it's the squares who carry the burden of the world, and the bores who become heroes.

Interview, Madrid/San Francisco Examiner
& Chronicle (Datebook), 9–27:4.

Walter J. Hickel
Secretary of the Interior of the United States

This job is very challenging. I enjoy challenges. I get totally involved. I commit myself and move. I never dreamt I'd be here. I don't move toward goals. I solve *problems*. People who set goals set them too low; reach them too quick. Then they lean back. I've never had fear of anything. Never. People say I'm naive. But I say I have utter confidence. Perhaps they are the same thing. You must ask what motivates men. My motivation is not political, not economic, not social. I'm motivated by seeing the job to be done and then doing it. I brought Alaska its first escalator. That was in 1959. I built a supermarket and decided to put in an escalator. Why? Because the challenge was there. It took two 40-foot flatbed trucks to get it up the highway. But I did it. Now there are four escalators in Alaska.

Interview/Life, 8–28:48B.

Eric Hoffer
Author, Philosopher

No more columns, no more television, no more pictures, no more teaching. I'm going to crawl back into my hole where I started . . . I have become a professional scold, and it is not really me.

The New York Times, 2–22:(4)5.

Tom Jones
Singer

Women when they pass the age of 30 are still full-blooded women, and they like full-blooded men. That's what they get from me. No one's come along for the real women in America until me. They've never had anyone to scream over. All you've got is Dean Martin, Frank Sinatra, Andy Williams—adults. Strict adults. Bobby Darin is a very slick performer; you can look at him and say, "That's good." But nobody is going, "Aaahhhhhggggggwhoooooooomp!"

Interview/TV Guide, 1–24:16.

Kirk Kerkorian
Financier

Well, I guess they think I got rich overnight . . . But getting rich has been gradual for me. Like 1941 was a good year, '50 was a good year too!

Los Angeles Herald-Examiner (California Living Magazine), 2–1:13.

Clark Kerr
Former president, University of California

I left the presidency as I entered it—fired with enthusiasm.

The New York Times, 3–3:24.

Hedy Lamarr
Actress

I'm a water person. In my next incarnation, I'm going to be a fish—a whale, I think.

Interview, New York/ The New York Times, 8–23:(2)16.

Louis L'Amour
Author

I could sit in the middle of Sunset Boule-vard and write with my typewriter on my knees. Temperamental I am not.

Interview, Los Angeles/ Los Angeles Times, 7–12:G1.

Angela Lansbury
Actress

. . . it's very hard for an actress . . . to be a star. When it happens, it's difficult to believe. Then you're expected to live up to what people expect of you as a star. The battle against you by yourself is endless. Do I do star parts or parts I want to do as an actress? . . . To put it another way, I got up this morning to come here and do an interview. My first instinct was to be a star, all dressed up. I put on false eyelashes. Then I looked into the mirror and I thought, "Who are you fooling—yourself?" So I decided, to hell with the eyelashes, and I haven't dressed up either.

Interview, Los Angeles/ Los Angeles Times (Calendar), 6–14:18.

Peter Lawford
Actor

I have many weaknesses, (such as) procrastination and not nearly enough drive. In some ways that's good—I've enjoyed life more and lived it according to my own styles where possible—and in other ways it's worked against me. Some actors have that drive that makes them forget everything else. I take my time to do things; I've almost surfed my way out of show biz. I never spend the time looking for things for myself that are necessarily lasting. I go for the moment.

Interview, San Francisco/ San Francisco Examiner & Chronicle (Datebook), 9–6:12.

Janet Leigh
Actress

I don't know what it is I exude. But whatever it is, it's whatever I am!

Interview, St. Moritz, Switzerland/ San Francisco Examiner & Chronicle (Datebook), 3–8:6.

John V. Lindsay
Mayor of New York

I'm Dutch and I'm stubborn; I'm Scotch and tight; and I'm Irish and angry.

Chicago Daily News, 8–20:35.

Sophia Loren
Actress

Oh, I am very insecure. That is, I am very vulnerable. I can be the most secure person and at the same time the most insecure. It is enough for me, for example, while I work, to spot a member of the crew who is indifferent. Maybe he yawns or just couldn't care less. It bothers me. I will do the scene next time doing my best to involve him. In other words, I need reassurance all the time, as all of us do. It is only human. I am proud of it.

*Interview, Marino, Italy/
Los Angeles Times (Calendar), 4–26:17.*

I never worked to be a sex-bomb. They made me one—the papers, the publicity, all that. I always wanted to be an *actress*. But in the beginning, it's impossible to choose. Anyway, people think I have 100% sex appeal, but it is only imagination. Maybe 50% is what I've got. The other 50% is their fantasies working on it.

*Interview, Padua, Italy/
San Francisco Examiner & Chronicle
(Datebook), 8–2:12.*

Shirley MacLaine
Actress

All I want out of life is freedom. Freedom for me. Freedom for everyone . . . I believe so strongly in freedom that it underlies all my thinking. That's why I'm always getting in all sorts of trouble.

*Interview, Los Angeles/
Los Angeles Herald-Examiner, 1–4:E5.*

Mike Mansfield
United States Senator, D-Mont.

In Montana, the forests reach out from high mountains to the places of people. Their endless depths beckon with a promise of peace and purpose. As a youth, I heard the call but did not respond to it as I thought to do. Instead, I find myself in the thickets of government in Washington. Yet I still cherish a sense of longing for what might have been.

Interview/Nation's Business, Aug.:48.

Lee Marvin
Actor

I've spent my life in the saddle, and it's darned uncomfortable. But with a face like mine, it's inevitable. It's basically the Western face: lantern jaw and a horsey look. Somebody's got to be the black-hearted rat in movies.

*Interview, London/
San Francisco Examiner, 11–21:9.*

Marcello Mastroianni
Actor

I am (a) very lazy, passive man—an observer, not a man of action. I am a man at the window, looking out at others. I am a very negative man. In *La Dolce Vita, 8½, Leo the Last, The Stranger*—in all my good films—I played all men who don't act but *react*. I feel more comfortable in parts like those.

*Interview, Padua, Italy/
The New York Times, 6–21:(2)13.*

From time to time, I think of old age and I don't picture it as a happy time for me. I earn money now, but somehow I just can't put any of it away for my old age. It's strange. Somehow a person who has been poor all his life should know how to put money aside for a time when it will be needed. But all the money I have ever earned I have just spent like water, as if it didn't belong to me.

*Interview, Padua, Italy/
The New York Times, 6–21:(2)16.*

I have never really loved anyone, at this point am inclined to believe that I am unable to love profoundly. Yet, I cannot be without the stimulus of a love affair: It is and has

(MARCELLO MASTROIANNI)

always been the focus of my life; it fills me with energy toward my work and toward everything. I simply cannot be without a love affair . . . My relationship with a woman is always a game, a beautiful fantasy that enriches me in every way.

Interview, Padua, Italy/
The Washington Post, 6–28:F5.

Walter Matthau
Actor

I can look at all my movies and tell you which ones I made while betting heavy on the horses. I always had one ear off-stage, listening for the call from the bookie.

Interview/
Los Angeles Herald-Examiner, 9–27:F2.

Steve McQueen
Actor

My world is really very small. All I really know about are motorcycles and cars. I travel a lot, but I like to get back. I guess I live in a world of men. My wife gets uptight because I don't take her out. But I don't like to go out.

Interview/Look, 1–27:51.

Dina Merrill
Actress

I can't seem to get away from that label (socialite actress), and it irritates the hell out of me. It implies I'm a dilettante. I study the classics. I don't play bridge. I work hard at whatever I do. I am not some mindless lady who serves tea to a bunch of other mindless ladies. I'm not that kind of person; I resent any implication that I am.

Interview/
Los Angeles Times (West Magazine), 2–22:18.

Anna Moffo
Opera singer, Actress

I do what I like, and it's my credo in life and art that you'll do well only what you

can draw some fun out of. This goes for my singing and acting, and a great many other things besides, such as dancing, playing the piano, composing jazz music or even teaching cooking on TV. As a completely normal woman, I enjoy being in the nude. It does to me something as it probably will many other females. Like them, I often feel a vague need for some kind of psychoanalytic treatment; but then, by dropping clothes, I think I drop not merely the so-called moral inhibitions but also a few others which cause me relentless timidity, lack of confidence, inferiority complexes. Be that as it may, stripping means mental recovery—to me in any case.

Munich/Variety, 2–18:68.

Ricardo Montalban
Actor

The press has always considered me pleasant but colorless. No night clubs, no scandals, no jet-setting, no divorces. Only as a performer do I create some illusion of flamboyance. I have a temper, but I usually control it. I am a Catholic, and what I used to accept emotionally from my religion I now acknowledge intellectually as well. Altogether, I am a happy actor.

Interview/TV Guide, 1–24:12.

Lewis Mumford
Author

I've never tried to evade age. When I was young, I had the beginnings of TB. The fact that I lived beyond 40 was something of a surprise. At the age of 60, I thought I won't try to amass any more intellectual capital, but rather live on what I had. I never suspected that fate would play a very happy trick on me, and that three of my best books would be the product of this last 10 years. One knows that at 75 one must look forward to declining powers, and things will dwindle. But it was sheer good luck that I've lived to write these books, and I can't expect that kind of luck from the future.

Interview, Amenia, N.Y./
The New York Times, 10–20:89.

Joe Namath
Football player, New York "Jets"

Everything that's been written about me is a lie.

News conference, Hempstead, N.Y., Aug. 18/
The New York Times, 8–19:46.

Pat Nixon
Wife of the President of the United States

I just want to go down in history as the wife of the President.

Interview/The New York Times, 1–26:16.

I can get along with anyone. I have found that a smile and a warm handclasp go a long way. Even on our many trips . . . even if I couldn't speak the language, people look in your eye and they can tell you care.

Interview, Washington/
Washington Star, 7–31:D2.

Richard M. Nixon
President of the United States

Everybody is two persons. Even though I'm supposed to be an extrovert—because I'm a political animal and can get up before an audience—I'm basically reserved.

Interview/Los Angeles Times, 5–22:(4)2.

Lloyd Nolan
Actor

I'm lazy. I don't have much drive at all. I'm a great procrastinator. I have very little ambition . . . I'm much more comfortable and brazen on the screen than in real life.

Interview, Los Angeles/
Los Angeles Herald-Examiner, 1–7:D12.

Rudolf Nureyev
Ballet dancer

. . . I must tell you that for me being on stage is really very abnormal. There is something very artificial about it. I must *give* more, and so my emotions run very high. *Because* I feel so alien on the stage, I have a need to be on it more, and more, and more. I find it difficult to get used to each time. For some dancers, being on stage doesn't matter so much—their heart-beat doesn't change; nothing really changes them. But for me, just standing in the wings, before going on, I am already exhausted, dead. Already my knees are shaking. It's extraordinary how terrified I am.

Interview, New York/
The New York Times, 6–21:23.

(On the possibility of marriage): Oh, come on—it would never be an honest or sincere relationship. I would *only* think of myself. I would *only* think of my being up there, on the stage. Who has the guts to really share that? I don't think anybody does. And believe me, I don't want surf-riders. I don't want anybody riding the surf from the waves I make.

Interview, New York/
The New York Times, 6–21:23.

Aristotle Onassis
Shipowner; Business executive

If a quarter of what reporters have written about me were true, I would already be ruined, abandoned and so depressed by my misadventures that I would be on the point of shooting myself.

Interview/The Washington Post, 10–1:B9.

Peter O'Toole
Actor

To be honest, I hate publicity. My trouble is keeping *out* of the papers. I wouldn't care if people didn't want to know about me any more. I think they must be sick to death of me by now, anyway. But if they didn't go to see my films or plays . . . ah, now, that would be very sad.

Interview, Dragon's Mouth, Venezuela/
San Francisco Examiner & Chronicle
(Datebook), 5–24:11.

It's painful for me to act—sheer hell while I'm doing it. I live a role . . . for three months, and every day is agony. I can never hang a part up on a peg when I go home.

Interview, Dragon's Mouth, Venezuela/
San Francisco Examiner & Chronicle
(Datebook), 5–24:11.

J. C. Penney
Founder, J. C. Penney Company

(Regarding his age, 95): My eyesight is impaired, but not my vision. My vision is greater than ever.

Plainview (Tex.) Daily Herald, 12–13:A12.

Pablo Picasso
Artist

Everyone is the age he has decided on, and I have decided to remain 30 years old.

Interview, Cannes, France/Time, 12–7:49.

Katherine Anne Porter
Author

Anybody who wants can have my rights. I want my privileges. I want to be able to say to a husband or to anybody else: "I can't do the cleaning now; I can't do the shopping or the cooking. I have to write a short story."

Interview, College Park, Md./
The New York Times, 4–3:39.

Harold Robbins
Author

I never *planned* to be a writer. I never really *planned* anything. Of course, when I was a kid I believed all that stuff they told me about work hard and brush your teeth and study, go to Sunday school. I never went *that* far, but I did all the rest. Then I noticed that the guys who had what I wanted—the racketeers and the politicians—didn't seem to do any of those things, and they all had a black Cadillac limousine, a diamond wrist watch and a beautiful blonde.

Interview/TV Guide, 4–11:44.

Chi Chi Rodriguez
Golfer

I have 13 dependents. All of them have 140 IQ or better, except me. I'm under 100 and I support them all.

Sports Illustrated, 4–27:10.

Aline Saarinen
Author, Journalist

I like people who act with consistency and dignity, people who aren't *flabby*. I don't like self-indulgent people, people who go endlessly to psychiatrists. I'm intolerant of a certain kind of weakness—*everybody* has had awful things that have happened in their lives. I like people who handle their problems well, people with *gallantry*. I think laziness, *sloth*, this whole out-of-control business are *evil*.

Interview, New York/TV Guide, 4–25:30.

Francoise Sagan
Author

I am not an intellectual, but I am left wing. I am also a Gaullist, which is not a contradiction . . . If I take a stand on anything, the attitude is, "What is little Sagan meddling with? Why doesn't she look after her Ferraris and her whiskey bottles?"

Interview, Paris/
The Dallas Times Herald, 10–12:B3.

George C. Scott
Actor

The happiest time of my life was when I was laying bricks.

Interview, Beverly Hills, Calif./
Los Angeles Times (Calendar), 3–22:1.

Rod Serling
Writer

I used to be one of those irascible, angry young men. But I'm middle-aged now. I'm waiting for the next generation of angry young men.

Interview/The Dallas Times Herald, 7–22:A2.

Jean-Jacques Servan-Schreiber
Journalist; Member, French
National Assembly

I am not a great orator. I am not a great worker. I can't work 14 hours a day. I am not a great writer, just a good journalist. My only talent is as a catalyst. I know how to organize teamwork.

News conference, Washington/
San Francisco Examiner & Chronicle
(This World), 8–30:25.

Omar Sharif
Actor

At the bridge table I feel I am the captain of my soul and the master of my fate.

The Dallas Times Herald, 1–30:A2.

Bernard (Toots) Shor
Restauranteur

I'll never retire. I'm going to stay in business 50 more years, just to aggravate my friends.

Interview, New York/
The Washington Post, 1–31:C2.

Barbra Streisand
Actress, Singer

There are so many things to do in life. Art galleries to visit, museums to go to, books to read—and it's so overwhelming that I'd rather just make the movie and be busy from 10 to 6 and not have to think of all the things I should be doing. And actually, the real, *real* reason I like to be in movies is because it's an easy place to have my hems done. There's always a seamstress on the set. And if you break a chair, they can fix it—they have people who do everything. Chair people, hem people.

Interview/Life, 1–9:94.

I am terribly lazy . . . I can't even stand to bend down and pick up the birds in badminton. That's why I love being in movies. I'm performing all over the world—while I'm sitting home taking a bath.

Interview/Life, 1–9:94.

Barry Sullivan
Actor

I'm so lazy that when I get a new role I ask myself, "Can I do the part without shaving?"

Interview, New York/
The Washington Post, 8–11:B6.

Jacqueline Susann
Author

I don't care about the baubles. I don't want the world's biggest diamond. I like name clothes and, yes, I like mink coats—but jewelry for its sentimental value. Yes, I like I've also got a sheepskin coat I adore.

Interview, Dallas/
The Dallas Times Herald, 7–24:B1.

David Susskind
Motion picture-stage-television producer

I suppose you would say I'm a sociological liberal and a personal conservative. I'm really an old-fashioned man in a new era.

Interview, San Francisco/
San Francisco Examiner & Chronicle
(Datebook), 5–10:15.

Danny Thomas
Actor, Comedian

Let me tell you about the night Senator Robert Kennedy was killed. I was playing the Sands in Las Vegas, and the first person to call and tell me about the tragedy was my pal, Buddy Hackett. He was bawling like a baby. He said, "Danny, you can't go out for your late show. You gotta call it off." I thought so, too. I called Jack Entratter (of the Sands) and said, "Let's cancel out. Nobody will be in for the late show." He said, "Then why is the room oversold to standing room only? Danny, everyone in town now knows about this tragedy. But they want to be lifted out of themselves, want to forget for just a minute this black tragedy." When I walked out on the stage, I couldn't believe it. Faces turned up to me as though saying, "Help us not remember for a moment. Make us laugh, we are badly hurt." Never in my life have I made such an effort to be funny, and I've never known such a feeling of being needed, that my nonsense was medicine, that my songs and stories were therapy. And I know that every entertainer in the country working that awful night felt the same thing from his audience. Baby, this is the sort of thing that makes Danny Thomas, and all the others, run.

Interview, Los Angeles/
Los Angeles Herald-Examiner, 8–30:F3.

Harry S. Truman
Former President of the United States

I can hear anything I want to hear, and being 86 years old I guess I've heard enough anyway.

Independence, Mo., April 12/
Newsweek, 4–27:63.

John Wayne
Actor

I would like to be remembered—well, the Mexicans have an expression, feo, fuerte y formal, which means: He was ugly, was strong and had dignity.

Interview, Los Angeles/
The Washington Post, 4–8:B9.

The Duke of Windsor
Former King of England

The Duchess and I are a little past the age of being what they call "with it" today. But don't for one moment imagine that we weren't "with it" when we were younger. In fact, I was so much "with it" that it was one of the big criticisms that was leveled against me by the older generation.

Television interview, Paris, Jan. 13/
Los Angeles Times, 1–14:(1)19.

Gig Young
Actor

The only way I'll get married is with a Ford Foundation grant.

Los Angeles/Daily Variety, 2–4:2.

Robert Young
Actor

When I began in the theatre, I thought that I was an introvert in a field of extroverts. (But) they're all terrified, frightened, insecure people who have found this remarkable outlet of playing all these characters who are not themselves. They don't want to be themselves, and neither did I for a long time. I am convinced that I drank for the same reason that other people do self-destructive things. You can call it many names: anxiety, depression, loneliness, boredom, emptiness, or a sense of lack of fulfillment. But there is only one word which can do justice to that inner feeling: terror . . . fear. The root of all disease is fear. Fear of what? Fear of yourself. If you can become unafraid of yourself, then it is axiomatic that you lose your fear of other things. I'm not that far along myself, but I've had a great deal of experience with this kind of transformation.

Interview/TV Guide, 6–6:26.

Philosophy

Spiro T. Agnew
Vice President of the United States

Protest is every citizen's right, but that does not insure that every protest is right.

Quote, 2–1:97.

Every view is a proper target for rational challenge; every challenge is a proper target for criticism and rebuttal. No view has a claim on truth by virtue of wide acceptance; no view has a claim on truth by virtue of limited acceptance. Every partisan has an obligation to present his position forcefully, factually and fearlessly; every partisan has an obligation to admit to the possibility of error. Every man has a right to be heard to the extent he shows a willingness to listen; no man should interpret a willingness to listen as a commitment to follow. No argument is fair that appeals exclusively to emotion; no argument is realistic that rules out all emotion. No age group or minority group or income group has a monopoly on wisdom; no majority has the obligation to be silent, or the right to overwhelm dissent. And finally, the 13th rule of rhetoric for our times, and the most painful one of all: Provided he acts without violence and within the constitutional law, every man has the right to disagree with, and to break, every one of these "rules."

Detroit, June 15/
The New York Times, 6–16:26.

John Joseph Akar
Ambassador to the United States
from Sierra Leone

We Africans . . . know that "Black is Beautiful" is not a synonym for "White Is Ugly." Whether we like it or not, as regards black and white, each needs and is needed by the other. God, in his inscrutable wisdom, has taken the white of Europe, the black of Africa, the brown of the Middle East, the yellow of Asia and the red of the American Indians to weave into a beautiful and sacred tapestry called humanity. Let us not soil it with our prejudices.

San Francisco Examiner & Chronicle
(This World), 11–8:2.

Muhammad Ali (Cassius Clay)
Former Heavyweight Boxing Champion
of the World

If a building caught fire with 100 men and 100 women in it, the women would run to the men. When death is around, women depend on the men to save them. God made man to be the boss.

Interview/
Los Angeles Herald-Examiner, 10–20:C1.

George Allen
Football coach, Los Angeles "Rams"

Every man was born with the ability to do something well. Every man is a born salesman, accountant, football player, farmer or artist. The individual who uses the ability he was given when he was put on this earth—who works to the very limit of that ability—is doing what the Lord intended him to do. This is what life is all about.

Interview/Sports Illustrated, 9–7:35.

Salvador Allende (Gossens)
President-elect of Chile

For you (America), to be a Communist or a socialist is to be totalitarian. For me, no. I believe that man is freed when he has an economic position that guarantees him work, food, housing, health, rest and recreation. I am a founder of the Socialist Party, and I must tell you that I am not totalitarian; and I think socialism frees man.

Interview/Time, 10–19:29.

Svetlana Alliluyeva
*Daughter of late
Soviet Premier Josef Stalin*

What is this bra-burning business? I don't understand this. I am a conservative, a convinced conservative. I think to be a wife is a good job to have. I don't agree with women that it's not enough.

*Interview, Spring Green, Wis./
Los Angeles Times, 8–16:A.*

Raymond Aron
*Professor of Faculty Letters,
Paris University*

I see a difference . . . in what is happening in the East and in the West. In the Eastern countries, the youth revolt is libertarian. There, the youth would be happy with what our youth already have. In the Western countries, the revolt seems to be libertine. Young people already have what they want, and I find it difficult to imagine their being more successful in their quest for liberty. These young people have good sentiments; I don't dispute their good will. But they really can't conceive of the better society that they talk about, as Marx once did. So some of them create marginal societies, like hippie communes. Unfortunately, some of the others dream of destroying contemporary society altogether, without knowing what will replace it.

*Interview, Paris/
The New York Times Magazine, 4–19:95.*

Elizabeth Ashley
Actress

Marriage is just not something you pick up and do when it's convenient. It's a responsibility. You work very hard at it. There's nothing more difficult than living in that peculiar kind of intimacy and passion and emotional dependency with another human being. It's very hard. Just because so many people are doing it doesn't mean they're doing it well. They're doing it bloody awful.

*Interview, Los Angeles/
Los Angeles Herald-Examiner, 12–6:F4.*

Charles Aznavour
Actor, Singer

What can you tell about happiness? But about sadness there is much to say. It is real and more interesting than gaiety.

Washington/The Washington Post, 1–31:C2.

Lucille Ball
Actress

The days in my iife that stand out most vividly are the days I've learned something. There is a feeling I get. It's so exciting, I can't describe it; but I get goose bumps when I've realized I've learned something real important. All the good things in life come hard; but wisdom is the hardest to come by.

*Interview, New York/
San Francisco Examiner & Chronicle
(Datebook), 5–24:15.*

Saul Bellow
Author

In the way the young declare the obsolescence of the old, there's a kind of totalitarian cruelty, like Hitler's attitude toward Jews or Stalin's toward kulaks. These kids, I predict, will face a lot more trouble than their elders. If I were an enterprising real estate man in California, I'd buy a colony— not for the old, but for the soon-to-be-senile young.

Interview, Yale University/Life, 4–3:60.

Thomas Hart Benton
Artist

We have all these machines, and there is no question that we produce more as a result of them. But they also separate us from our natural environment. They allow us to control nature. Anyone who can control nature loses his respect for it.

*Interview, Kansas City/
Los Angeles Times, 3–15:A.*

Great individuals are accidents. Only rarely does an Alexander or Shakespeare or Michelangelo turn up. The only individual who stands out in my lifetime is (former President) Harry S. Truman. If there is an ounce of vanity in that man it has yet to show itself.

Interview, Kansas City/
Los Angeles Times, 3–15:B7.

Martin Berezin
Psychiatrist, Harvard University
Medical School

What is virility at age 25 is lechery at 65.

Plainview (Tex.) Daily Herald, 4–13:4.

Busby Berkeley
Former motion picture director

Age doesn't mean anything to me. I claim that a person doesn't grow old by living a certain number of years; a person grows old by deserting his ideals. In my book, you're as young as your faith, and as old as your doubt. You're as young as your self-confidence, and as old as your despair.

Interview, New York/
The New York Times, 3–17:42.

Bruno Bettelheim
Professor of Psychology and Psychiatry,
University of Chicago

Everybody wants to strike blows for freedom. It is such a nice thing to do, you know. So what do we mean by freedom? Let's look at the long hair and the beard, shall we? So if you look at them, you see that the same fashion has occurred and reoccurred. So what's new and original about that? As a matter of fact, wigs are back. So what is so great an innovation that people wear wigs? It's just the flow of fashion. Do men wear colorful dress and jewelry? Well, my God!— we are back in the 18th century. We are not yet back to lace collars, but they will come. They will come. And they will go again. Let's not mistake custom for real progress.

Interview, Chicago/
The New York Times Magazine, 1–11:108.

Jacqueline Bisset
Actress

What makes a person sexy is liking the opposite sex. It's more mental than physical. There are a lot of birds around who dress in a sexy fashion but who aren't at all sexy in their minds. They are just doing a narcissistic trick in their heads. A Frenchwoman, even if plain, is attractive because she is aware of being a woman and feels like a woman. That makes a man feel more masculine.

Interview, New York/
The Washington Post, 6–17:C4.

Winton M. Blount
Postmaster General of the United States

When we (adults) see war as a political reality, they (the young) see peace as a moral imperative. When we speak of making the world safe for democracy, they speak of making the world safe for humanity. When we point to history and the lessons of past wars, they point to the future and answer with the hope that we can put wars by. When we point to what has been accomplished, they point to what remains to be accomplished. It is a simple matter to see in our differences that the young are naive, that their view of the world suffers from a superabundance of idealism and a lack of reality and the hard lessons that come with responsibility. And if we see only in these terms, then we miss the most important fact that beyond our differences we share a vast community of interest . . . It is from this base that we can reach out and help the young to grow and come to civic maturity. And it would be wrong to ignore what has already been accomplished here, both with and for the young.

Wilmington, Del./
The Washington Post, 5–21:A18.

Ray Bradbury
Author

If we are lucky, we die in the right year of our lives. No one should live beyond creativity and active participation in the world. I hope my loved ones will excuse me, but I want to choose that moment for myself.

Interview, Los Angeles/
Los Angeles Times, 3–15:E18.

Kingman Brewster, Jr.
President, Yale University

Perhaps the greatest contribution we can make is to reaffirm, in the face of those who would seek to coerce conformity, that practical progress relies most of all on the evolution of the better by the survival of the fittest among ideas tossed in the blanket of debate, dispute and disagreement.

At Yale alumni banquet/Time, 3–30:42.

Leonid I. Brezhnev
General Secretary, Communist Party of the Soviet Union

The peoples of the world are seeing with increasing clarity that imperialism has created a vast production machine, but that this machine serves only to increase the wealth and power of a tiny handful of capitalist magnates. In the sphere ruled by world capitalism, tens and hundreds of millions are suffering from hunger and poverty. Imperialism uses the greatest achievements of technology to intensify the exploitation of millions of working people and to prepare for piratical wars. Mankind pays for the existence of imperialism with hundreds of thousands of lives—the victims of these wars and the victims of ruthless exploitation . . . What prospects does this inhuman system hold out for the ordinary man? Only one thing: more blood and sweat, more prisoners in the jails, more maimed and killed, and a still greater menace to the very existence of entire nations. Modern capitalism is a society without ideals, a society without a future. Hence its moral disintegration, spiritual hollowness and stupefying philistinism that is encouraged by a philistine pseudo-culture specially created for this purpose. Hence the monstrous crime wave in the Western countries, the black torrents of drug addiction and pornography, and the sea of perverted feelings and mutilated souls.

Before Soviet Communist Party and Supreme Soviet, Moscow, April 21/ Vital Speeches, 6–1:495.

Genevieve Bujold
Actress

Any dishonest person angers me. My God, life is so short. There's no time for crap. It's like the accumulated anger we women are so full of. Truth is a balm for that, like oil on a cut.

Interview/Life, 5–29:45.

Richard Burton
Actor

I hope to live long enough to see the next generation gap. Like when my sons are my age. My oldest son is now 17. When he is, shall we say, 40, I want to see the gap between him and his son, when he is 17.

Interview, Los Angeles/ Hollywood Reporter, 3–19:22.

I think the most perfect kind of fame . . . is an anonymous fame. Like, for instance, I have a friend, Graham Greene, who's a famous writer. Now, his kind of fame is marvelous, because the public doesn't know what his face looks like. He can travel on a train or go on a bus or fly tourist class on a plane, and all the time he's able to observe and not be bothered. Whereas, for a famous actor, a famous politician or even a famous writer like Hemingway, who was recognized like a film star, then everybody puts on an act for you because you're famous. Nobody is, strictly speaking, himself anymore. Instead of a woman sitting at the next table in a restaurant behaving as she normally would, she puts on an act because she's aware of the fact that there's a famous actor in the room. The same think happens with my wife (Elizabeth Taylor). They all behave like cockatoos when she's around. So apart from the fact that you, yourself, are not behaving normally because you're well known, others don't behave normally either, for the same reason. So you lose touch with reality.

Interview, San Felipe, Mexico/ Los Angeles Herald-Examiner, 9–20:G6.

Kofi Busia
Prime Minister of Ghana

I don't like hypocrisy—even in international relations. A lot of trouble in the world today is going on because we've developed what we call diplomacy—which really means the art of nearly deceiving all your friends, but not quite deceiving all your enemies.

Interview, Accra/Los Angeles Times, 2–1:A18.

Helder P. Camara
Archbishop of Olinda and Recife, Brazil

There is a primary violence, the mother of all violence, which is the injustice that exists almost everywhere. In underdeveloped countries, this violence takes the form of internal colonialism. There are small groups of privileged families whose riches are maintained by the misery of millions of fellow citizens. I call injustice violence, because, in fact, misery kills more than the most bloody wars.

Interview, Recife/
The New York Times, 10–28:6.

Emanuel Celler
United States Representative, D-N.Y.

When we consider how easily the adolescent attaches himself to causes, (how he sees) in patterns of black and white without shadings, lest he falter . . . we can readily understand why the demagogue and the dictator and the hypnotic orator have been able historically to capture the youth of the land. Witness the regimes of Hitler and Mussolini. There are sound psychological reasons why the age of 21 has been considered the beginning of maturity.

Newsweek, 3–30:29.

Leo Cherne
Executive director,
Research Institute of America

As I look toward the year 2000, I must present a panorama of unbelievable progress, of unimaginable affluence, of unprecedented size, of growth for many of your businesses that will dwarf your wildest expectations and raise challenges that will test your utmost capabilities. But I must also present a tapestry of crisis beyond all precedent in human history, of change so great, of wealth so large, of mass so dense, of technology so be-

wildering that the crisis of the past decades will seem minor claims upon human courage and wisdom.

At Business Publications Audit Meeting,
Chicago, Feb. 18/Vital Speeches, 4–15:407.

Mark Clark
General, United States Army, Retired

When I went into Austria as High Commissioner of the General Commander, I found that the Communists serve their friends vodka from one bottle while they are drinking only water from another vodka bottle. This is only the beginning of their conniving . . .

Dallas/The Dallas Times Herald, 4–14:A14.

J.V. Clyne
Former Justice,
Supreme Court of British Columbia

If instant reforms are not provided for all mankind's chronic ills, it is alleged to be the fault of the Establishment, which is seen standing foursquare against progress, freedom, peace and all things good. One of the conveniences of using the Establishment as a whipping boy is its characterization as a great impersonal "they" to whom all sins can be ascribed without the necessity of a bill of particulars. Arrayed against this wicked "they" is a great collective "we," who are invariably righteous and noble-minded. This is according to the popular liturgy.

At Town Hall, Los Angeles/
The Wall Street Journal, 1–13:16.

. . . we in the Western world—old and young alike—are still moved by ideals, whether or not we agree on what they are. The young, in fact, believe themselves to be more idealistic than the old, and it is a fact that necessary reforms have been brought about by the ideals of youth. But the one irreplaceable attitude necessary to hold these ideals aloft—the pursuit of excellence—is being ignored. The negative cults of confusion and whimsy are honored in its place.

At Town Hall, Los Angeles/
The Wall Street Journal, 1–13:16.

Wayne A. Danielson
Dean, School of Communications,
University of Texas at Austin

The young people I deal with seem to be characterized by their candor and their courage. How about their intellectual abilities? What are their strong and weak points? Well, it seems to me that we were better verbally and they are better visually. They have not read much, but they have seen a great deal more. They are lousy spellers, but good photographers. Their headlines are sloppy, but their page designs are often fresh and intriguing. They can't understand a simple balance sheet, but they can "see things" in a psychedelic painting. No one remembers the things they say at their rallies, but their symbolism—like carrying the limbs of the chopped-down trees to the main building—is often deeply compelling. Why do they have demonstrations in the first place? I think they want to see something happen. They are not content to read about it. They want to be there.

Before Austin Society of Industrial Editors/
National Observer, 1–12:16.

Alain Delon
Actor

In my office in Paris, I have a photograph of the earth taken from the moon. Whenever I get depressed, I look at it and it gets me out of it. It helps me have the right values. I may be a great big movie star down here, but from up there I am nothing, and we all are nothing. Diamonds and rubies and emeralds are nothing and Da Vinci paintings are nothing . . . so what the hell are we doing fighting all the time? It's like the Bible says: "For dust thou art, and unto dust shall thou return."

Interview, New York/
The New York Times, 8–16:(2)10.

A statesman, a scientist or a writer can put his stamp upon his time, but not an actor. There is a difference between creativity and interpretation . . . A famous painter might paint your portrait, and it would be eternal —but *you* wouldn't be eternal. It is only the creation that is eternal. It remains. The individual is dead.

Interview, New York/
Plainview (Tex.) Daily Herald, 8–21:6.

Lord Alfred Denning
Master of the Rolls,
Royal Court of Justice, London

Freedom we have stressed for centuries. But we are coming to think that equally important is the security of decent people. What good is any man's freedom to him if his home is invaded, his womenfolk assaulted, his security in jeopardy? The problem is to find the balance between the freedom of the individual and the security of a civilized society.

Before California Bar Association,
San Francisco/Tulsa Tribune, 4–24:C24.

Milovan Djilas
Author; Former Vice President
of Yugoslavia

Nobody today really believes in Communism. Maybe only (East Germany's) Ulbricht or (Poland's) Gomulka. When we talk about Communists, we are talking about phantoms. The Communism of old is dead. Only the structures it created remain behind.

Interview, Belgrade/Life, 5–1:64.

Everett Dulit
Director, Adolescent Psychiatry Clinic,
Jacobi Hospital, Albert Einstein
College of Medicine

Adolescents have always rebelled, but there was a character growth out of pushing against a well-defined other way of life in which adults were sure of their values. There is no character growth pushing against a cream puff.

The New York Times, 2–20:48.

Erhard Eppler
Minister for Economic Cooperation
of West Germany

There is not a "third world," a "second world" or a "first world"—but just one, the only one we have. Man has the capability and the power either to destroy or to develop it. To destroy it may be easier and—please forgive me for being cynical—even less expensive. To develop it is far more complicated, and it takes more courage. But it is worth trying.

Plainview (Tex.) Daily Herald, 11–29:A4.

Jane Fonda
Actress

Isn't it sad? Children are so alive and awake and they listen and see and touch and experience so fully. Then they grow up and become dead. They've stopped changing; they've decided, "This is what I am," and that's death. Things should be in perpetual change.

Interview, Los Angeles/
The Dallas Times Herald, 6–24:AAA2.

Ford C. Frick
Former Commissioner of Baseball

We are living in an era of doubt and controversy. And the thing that is needed most of all is continuity—something that has gone on for years and years, something to cling to . . . Today is only 24 hours, but behind us are thousands of yesterdays. Anything that connects yesterday to today and today to tomorrow is important because it means continuity . . . Without memories of the past, there could be no dream of the future. Without those yesterdays, there could be no bright tomorrows.

At his induction into Baseball Hall of Fame,
Cooperstown, N.Y., July 27/
Sporting News, 8–8:5.

Milton Friedman
Professor of Economics,
University of Chicago

People often talk . . . nonsense about how the value placed on life is infinite or immeasurable. On that basis, nobody would ever cross the street. The thing that baffles me about the members of the human race is what a low value they place upon life. You don't have to pay people much extra to get them to be drivers in the Indianapolis 500, yet that surely increases the chance of their loss of life. Even more impressive is that there is no demagogue so absurd and stupid that he cannot persuade some people to throw away their lives in pursuit of a silly cause. If you read in the newspapers about riots in which people get killed, it just seems incredible that people value their lives at such a low price.

Interview, Chicago/Human Events, 4–25:13.

J. William Fulbright
United States Senator, D-Ark.

At the risk of being accused of every sin from racism to Communism, I stress the irrelevance of ideology to poor and backward populations. Someday, perhaps, it will matter, in what one hopes will be a constructive and utilitarian way. But, in the meantime, what earthly difference does it make to nomadic tribes or uneducated subsistence farmers, in Vietnam or Laos or the north of Thailand, whether they have a military dictator, a royal prince or a Socialist commissar in some distant capital that they have never seen and may never even have heard of?

Before the Senate, Washington, April 2/
Congressional Record, 4–2:S4929.

Allen Funt
Television and film producer

I think it's about time that we stop breathing so hard about sex in films and relax a bit. We must try to make other things obscene besides sex. When we find out what's really obscene, then sex will find its proper place.

San Francisco Examiner & Chronicle
(This World), 3–22:2.

Zsa Zsa Gabor
Actress

If you (wives) wear the pants in the family, your husband's mistress is going to wear the sables.

San Francisco Examiner, 10–7:38.

WHAT THEY SAID IN 1970

Indira Gandhi
Prime Minister of India

My theory is that men are no more liberated than women. I suppose that leadership at one time meant muscle; but today it means getting along with people.

San Francisco Examiner & Chronicle
(This World), 11–1:2.

John S. Gibson
Professor of Political Science,
Tufts University

The young people of today are no worse than we were; they just have more ways of making fools of themselves.

Quote, 2–8:137.

Jackie Gleason
Actor, Comedian

All through an actor's life, failure is snapping at his heels like a giant mongrel dog. But because conceit is an actor's courage, he refuses to recognize that dog as anything more than a puppy who really can't harm him. Without conceit, an actor couldn't get anywhere; and maybe this applies to anyone who wants to get to the top in any profession.

Quote, 11–22:485.

Paul Goodman
Author

Stop talking about "the quality of life." Leave the quality of life to poets and lovers. Keep government planning to the minimum level of the tolerable. Give the people bread and let them make their own circuses.

Aspen, Colo./The New York Times, 9–2:32.

Billy Graham
Evangelist

Modern youth are rebellious. There was a time when I put most of the blame on adults, the home, the church, the government, for young people in trouble. But now I have become convinced that a large proportion of these young people must be held responsible. They have deliberately chosen to be rebels against society and God.

Before World Baptist Congress, Toyko, July 18/
The Dallas Times Herald, 7–19:A3.

Wife, mother, homemaker—this is the appointed destiny of real womanhood. It can be embroidered on and supplemented; but the fabric underneath must be preserved.

Newsweek, 11–30:49.

Ralph R. Greenson
Clinical Professor of Psychiatry, University
of California at Los Angeles

Hate must be recognized as an integral part of life and living . . . You cannot love without hating. The opposite of love is not hate; it is indifference. The more you love, and this is particularly true of romantic and sexual love, the more susceptible you are to being hurt, and if you are hurt the natural response is anger and hate in some form and fashion. If you believe that people can love, then you must also believe we all can hate.

Los Angeles/Los Angeles Times, 5–3:G7.

Arlo Guthrie
Singer, Composer

What youth is leading up to is a revolution—an earth revolution that has nothing to do with what color you are. And the black people and the purple people and the pink people are insignificant in terms of what's going down. We're all God's kiddies. No more nationalism, countryism, land-of-the-free-ism. It's world-of-the-free-ism, universe-of-the-free-ism. We're thinking big. We're changing life styles. I don't believe that there's nothing new under the sun. Everything's new under the sun.

Interview, Washington, Mass./
San Francisco Examiner & Chronicle
(Datebook), 1–25:5.

Gabriel Hauge
President, Manufacturers Hanover
Trust Company, New York

The core values that have sustained our society over many generations are three: the urge to excel, the acceptance of change, and spiritual concern for our fellow man. The survival of our civilization depends on their sure transmission from one generation to the next. The urge to excel is the heart of the sometimes-disparaged Puritan work ethic, which converts millions of individualists into a competitive society. The acceptance of change, with all that it entails in hazard and loss, makes a competitive society dynamic. Concern for our fellow man makes a competitive society compassionate and channels the pursuit of excellence to beneficial and humane needs. For excellence and competition alone can be antisocial; concern for our fellow man alone can result merely in sympathy without sustenance.

Before Bankers Club of Chicago/
The Wall Street Journal, 6–2:18.

August Heckscher
New York City Administrator of Park, Recreation and Cultural Affairs

If you are fearless and honest, as I believe you are, you must think about the hidden future as one of more and fiercer wars; bombs dropped upon the innocent, overcrowding on the planet; the slow exhaustion of resources—and for cold comfort, only the thought that scientific progress will somehow rescue us from the worst of dooms, though at the cost of increased regimentation and loss of human values.

At Ulster Community College commencement, Stone Ridge, N.Y., June 7/
The New York Times, 6–9:24.

Lewis B. Hershey
Former Director, Selective Service System of the United States

Between a fellow who is stupid and honest and one who is smart and crooked, I will take the fellow who is stupid and honest. I won't get much out of him, but, with that other guy, I can't keep what I've got.

San Francisco Examiner & Chronicle (This World), 2–8:2.

Stephen Hess
National Chairman, White House Conference on Children and Youth

Young people are conditioned to rapid change. It is all they have known; it is their personal history, just as evolution and gradualism is mine. Thus, youth are emotionally able to grasp, though often inarticulately, the implications to its generation of nuclear war, uncontrolled population growth, unbridled pollution of earth and atmosphere and other consequences of the technology their parents created. They know, almost as a condition of their birth, as Kenneth Keniston of Yale has said, that "all youth are linked by their common vulnerability to technological death." Which leads me to the belief that one cannot simply dismiss the (division) between youth and adult today with the reassuring thought that there has always been a generation gap. Of course I was convinced that my parents didn't understand me, and of course my parents were right that it was only a Huck Finn-Penrod phase that I was going through before I would become a useful citizen in their image. This is cold comfort, because today's generation gap is a different type and a different magnitude and hence demands especially hard work on the part of both adults and youth to bridge it.

Before South Dakota Governor's Committee on Children and Youth/
The Wall Street Journal, 5–29:6.

Walter J. Hickel
Secretary of the Interior of the United States

When man appeared on the earth, he was relatively helpless, in a hostile environment. His primary need was security—for himself and his family—and security has remained our main concern right up to 1970. Although the average citizen spends very little time defending himself personally, a large percentage of his wealth is still dedicated to that end. But now we are at a point where we must move beyond this fortress thinking. Let's go on with the job of learning to live, instead of just developing our capacity to destroy.

At University of Alaska, April 22/
Sports Illustrated, 5–4:28.

Perhaps because of my Alaskan heritage, I think a great deal about the need for a personal kind of ecology—call it the ecology of

(WALTER J. HICKEL)

the mind and spirit of man. Most of us are aware of what a walk in the hills does for us. There is a mystery attached to the variety and perfection of nature—a mystery that stirs the wonder in a child and gives a grown man perspective. We are learning about ecology as the balance in nature which keeps the body of a man or an animal healthy. There is also a balance that has to do with the mind and the soul . . . If we helped refresh the *inner* man, we could begin to answer such real problems as those of the inner city. Yes, at stake is man's very habitat—and also man's mind and soul.

The Wall Street Journal, 6–7:5.

Eric Hoffer
Author, Philosopher

The young are slovenly and stoned, decked out in nightmarish masquerade, on its way to the ashcan.

*Interview, Berkeley, Calif./
The Dallas Times Herald, 10–22:A16.*

There is an American hidden in the soil of every country and in the soul of every people. It is our task to help common people everywhere discover their American at home.

Plainview (Tex.) Daily Herald, 12–1:6.

Jeanne M. Holm
Colonel, United States Air Force; Director, Women in the Air Force

It is high time we stopped telling children that girls don't have the aptitude for mathematics, engineering, science, etc. Most girls are still raised with a romantic idea of life—school, marriage, family—and they live happily ever after. But Cinderella is dead!

Quote, 5–10:437.

John A. Howard
President, Rockford College

This is a scary world. We now have in college a generation that has grown up with television from their first lucid moments.

When the Vietnam war, Biafra or riots in the cities are put in your face in moving pictures, it is something different from hearing about it on the radio or reading it in magazines or newspapers. If the young only talk to each other about the things that frighten and frustrate them, it is no wonder that brighter students have looked at the world and have become cynics, or revolutionaries who want to tear it all down, or hippies who choose to withdraw. It is my belief that the only hope of affirmative leadership among the young is to have them in productive, creative activities with older people who have lived through wars, survived difficult personal reversals and still see joy in life, hope in life and some reason to stand up against difficulties.

*Interview, Rockford College/
The Christian Science Monitor, 4–11:B8.*

Hubert H. Humphrey
Former Vice President of the United States

Great decisions are not made by majorities —majorities confirm decisions . . . Great movements of change come as a result of militant, active, positive minorities; and it is the majority that provides the consensus, the reaffirmation.

*Interview, Waverly, Minn./
The Washington Post, 6–4:H3.*

Eugene Ionesco
Playwright

One may scorn success, but one would miss it. Being talked about is a bad habit one picks up. Anonymity is depressing; so is fame.

Los Angeles Times (Calendar), 1–18:26.

Burl Ives
Actor

The trouble is, life today is so easy. We get so much from the outside in. If we want music, we don't have to sing, because just by pushing a button we can get Sinatra. We don't even have to cook any more. Things are carried from the outside in with such ease. But I believe that the only thing about man that is worth a damn is what comes from the inside out. The Chinese understood all this; and they still knew that nothing stands still. Like even that shadow, right on the table here. You can't point to that and say that's where it is, because in the second it takes you to say it, the shadow has moved.

Interview, Los Angeles/TV Guide, 4–18:36.

Arthur Koestler
Author

Human sacrifice has existed from the very beginning of civilization, in all cultures . . . The same goes for loyalty—loyalty to the tribe, to the country, to the flag. This loyalty is an infernal dialectic, because it is out of loyalty that we fight national wars, civil wars, religious wars. Man doesn't make war for his individual interest. Nobody makes war because he hates the enemy. The altruism of the individual makes for the egoism of the crowd. This infernal dialectic has been present from the beginning.

Interview, Paris/
The New York Times Magazine, 8–30:24.

Language is man's greater glory. But it is also one of his greatest enslavers, since it builds barriers between different groups. Man's greatest glory is thus the greatest cause of pathogenesis, since it creates conflicts. Do you know the etymology of the "barbarian"? Someone who barks like a dog: arf, arf, arf, grr, grr, grr . . . The foreigner barks like a dog—people don't understand him. These language conflicts exist within a single nation. In Belgium, in Canada . . . And look how in England formidable hostility develops between the working class which doesn't pronounce the h's and those who have Oxford accents. Without language, there is no war. War is fought for words, not for living-space or food. Without slogans, no war. Communism against capitalism: The conflict has to be put into words to make war.

Interview, Paris/
The New York Times Magazine, 8–30:26.

Jacques Kosciusko-Morizet
French Ambassador to the United Nations

It is not confidence that creates negotiation. It is negotiation which creates confidence, when each side is in a position to test the good will, the desire for peace, of the other side.

At United Nations, N.Y., Oct. 30/
The Washington Post, 10–31:A13.

Stanley Kramer
Motion picture producer

The real definition of the "generation gap" is that none of the activists today think that anything that happened more than three weeks ago really took place. They know or care nothing about the Depression or World War II.

Interview/
Los Angeles Herald-Examiner, 2–25:B6.

John Cardinal Krol
Archbishop of Philadelphia

As we seek more and more to cure the ills of society with merely material remedies, we run the danger of adopting, certainly not by design but by default, the false principles of the totalitarian societies whose actions we abhor.

Washington, April 5/
Los Angeles Herald-Examiner, 4–6:A10.

Charles Y. Lazarus
Chairman, F. & R. Lazarus Company

Is there an Establishment? Of course there is. Not merely one Establishment, but many establishments—including the "military-industrial complex" that President Eisenhower warned us about. Establishments exist because, unless we are to live in anarchy, there must be people with the power to run things. In our own time and throughout history, different establishments have been variously arrogant, sensitive, concerned, lazy, industrious, stupid, enlightened, naive, sophisticated. Is it accurate, then, to say that "*the* Establishment" is evil or that all establishments are evil? Only, I believe, if one takes

(CHARLES Y. LAZARUS)

for truth the half-truth that man himself is evil, which I do not.

At Bowling Green State University, Ohio,
April 15/Vital Speeches, 6–1:498.

John Lederle
President, University of Massachusetts

We hear that the government, the establishment, the military-industrial complex, have their earphones turned off where youth is concerned. If it is true, it is bad. But listening is not a one-way proposition. Youth also often appears not to listen. It is youth's right, of course, to challenge the old. But closed youthful ears reflect an arrogance that deserves the same condemnation we rightly direct toward a nonlistening older generation. The notion that only youth has the answers to our problems is reduced to absurdity when a student revolutionary wakes up on the morning of his 30th birthday.

At University of Massachusetts commencement/
Life, 6–19:26.

Sam Levenson
Writer, Humorist

A home should smell like a home. Children have got to touch, feel, see that they are home. Mothering requires smothering. Children whose senses come alive at home do not need to take a trip in search of what is so freely available to them.

New York/Los Angeles Times, 8–27:(4)4.

Walter Lippmann
Author; Former newspaper columnist

While the right to talk may be the beginning of freedom, the necessity of listening is what makes that right important.

San Francisco Examiner, 9–24:34.

Bernard J.F. Lonergan
Philosopher

A philosophy is an individual becoming himself.

At St. Leo College, Tampa, Fla./Time, 4–20:59.

Konrad Z. Lorenz
Director, Max Planck Institute for Physiology of Behavior, Seewiesen, West Germany

If you were to ask me if I'm a monist or a dualist, I would reply: "The devil if I know." When I look with emotion upon the inorganic world around us, the beauty of a sunset, I think I'm a monist. At such a time, I am convinced that there are universal laws that reign over the entire universe, and that among them the laws of life are merely special cases. But when I see the struggle of organic life, so fragile, so vulnerable, against the eternal forces of the inorganic world, my vision of that struggle is something like a photograph of the Galapagos Islands: an immense torrent of frozen lava in the midst of which is a hole no bigger than the palm of your hand—and from this tiny hole rises a minuscule flowering cactus!

Interview/
The New York Times Magazine, 7–5:30.

Lee Marvin
Actor

The American dream obviously can't be true. Success always brings bitterness. The old performer, who has been acting 45 years, tells you it's all been fun. I don't believe him. Success can only make you realize you could have done so much more. You could have, and you hate yourself for not having done it. If you build your own pyramid, do it right.

Interview, Los Angeles/
Los Angeles Herald-Examiner, 3–30:C8.

Groucho Marx
Comedian

Man wasn't made to live alone. Neither was woman. I've tried being single. It doesn't work. You sit at a table alone, eating.

Interview, Beverly Hills, Calif./
The Dallas Times Herald, 2–8:F5.

David Mathews
President, University of Alabama

What may be happening in our society is that the adult generation is so willing to assume the guilt for their offspring—this is the

"Oh, where did we fail?" phenomenon—that the younger generation never has the opportunity to feel guilty. As one senior said to me, "I've learned to feel guilty about everyone and everything—except myself and what I do." Most seriously of all, uncritical praise of the "now" people tends to rob them of their capacity for concerted, uncompromising, and yet balanced and persistent attacks on the problems of our times.

At University of Tennessee at Chattanooga/
National Observer, 8–24:13.

Robert S. McNamara
President, International Bank for Reconstruction and Development

If development becomes a social as well as an economic objective, if it aims squarely at an end of grinding poverty and gross injustice, I believe it has a constituency waiting for it among the emerging generation of young adults. These young men and women are looking for goals beyond their own personal affluence. Human development is surely a challenge that can command their dedication—provided it is a development not simply in goods and gadgets but in the self-respect and dignity of man.

At Columbia University Conference on
International Economic Development,
New York, Feb. 20/
Los Angeles Times, 2–21:(1)9.

The dilemma that faces the wealthy nations of the world is not whether they should devote more of their GNP to solving domestic crises, and less of it to helping eliminate inhuman deprivations abroad; but, rather, whether they are going to seek a more equitable balance between private opulence and public responsibility. Private wealth cannot be preserved and public responsibility cannot be met by a heedless indifference to common crises that, in the end, will touch rich and poor alike.

At Columbia University Conference on
International Economic Development,
New York, Feb. 20/Vital Speeches, 3–15:339.

In setting the objectives, planning the programs and measuring the progress of development in the '70s, we must look to more than gross measures of economic growth. What we require are relevant "development indicators" that go beyond the measure of growth in total output, and provide practical yardsticks of change in other economic, social and moral dimensions of the modernizing process . . . If we achieve the "quantity goals" and neglect the "quality goals" of development, we will have failed.

February/Vital Speeches, 8–15:650.

George Meany
President, American Federation of Labor-Congress of Industrial Organizations

I don't hold with the idea that this generation of kids is exceptional, except in the sense that they have had greater educational opportunities. And the mere fact that they have had greater educational opportunities doesn't indicate to me that they have got the answers that the older generation haven't got . . . To these people who constantly say you have got to listen to these young people, they have got something to say, I just don't buy that at all. They smoke more pot than we do, and if the younger generation are the hundred thousand kids that lay around a field up in Woodstock, N.Y., I am not going to trust the destiny of the country to that group.

News conference, Washington, Aug. 31/
The New York Times, 8–31:43.

When I think of the contrast of our world and the world behind the Iron Curtain, where there are no (golf) courses, it tells a great story.

Napa, Calif., Oct. 21/Daily World, 10–23:12.

Ann Miller
Actress, Dancer

The hippies are at the core of all this drug-taking; and so are the Communists. The Beatles share the blame, too. I love their music, but they are a terrible image for young boys and girls. It's all so ugly—the

(ANN MILLER)

orgies, the dope. It's wrong. I think the whole fad of lady stars having babies out of wedlock is wrong. They ought to retire, drop their foals somewhere private and shut up about it. The way we're going, the only thing left is to climb back into a tree with a banana in your hand.

Interview, Los Angeles/
Los Angeles Times (Calendar), 3–29:24.

Roger Moore
Actor

Youth always accuses the generations ahead of them of being intolerant. There's nothing more intolerant than youth. Young people have lots of knowledge crammed into them now. But they can't assess it—that's wisdom.

Interview, Los Angeles/
Los Angeles Herald-Examiner, 3–31:A14.

Daniel P. Moynihan
Counsellor to the President of the United States

It has been the fashion of social scientists to see themselves as a slightly beleaguered group, taking risks on the edge of social innovation. Actually, for the past generation they and their students have been anything but. To the contrary, they have been part of an exceptionally secure elite community earning high salaries, and passing out privileges in the manner of elites anywhere.

Before American Jewish Committee, New York,
May 15/The New York Times, 5–16:29.

Barry Nelson
Actor

Everybody thinks there's some secret out there (in the world), but I've looked and I know there isn't. As long as you go on thinking it's there, the longer you miss the nice things in life—the smell of a bakery, the laughter of friends, things like that.

Plainview (Tex.) Daily Herald, 12–3:8.

Richard M. Nixon
President of the United States

There are those who protest that if the verdict of democracy goes against them, democracy itself is at fault—who say that if they don't get their own way, the answer is to burn a bus or bomb a building. Yet we can maintain a free society only if we recognize that in a free society no one can win all the time; no one can have his own way all the time, and no one is right all the time. Whether in a campaign or a football game, or in debate on the great issues of the day, the answer to "losing one" is not a rush to the barricades, but a study of why, and then a careful rebuilding—or perhaps a careful re-examination of whether the other fellow may have been right after all.

At Kansas State University, Sept. 16/
Los Angeles Times, 9–17:(1)16.

Aristotle Onassis
Shipowner; Business executive

If you aspire for success, do not squander your time reading about the things others have done. It is better to get on living your own life than to concern yourself with what others have done.

Interview/The Washington Post, 10–1:B9.

Thomas P. O'Neill, Jr.
United States Representative, D-Mass.

. . . since the time of Christ, the male species has worn long hair and beards about 90% of the time. The Western world turned to short hair and clean-shaven faces only after the Prussian victory over France. All the great heroes of America have worn long hair. It's nothing for Americans to get alarmed about.

Time, 8–17:37.

Olof Palme
Prime Minister of Sweden

The older generation has to realize that there is no point in young people working for goals their parents have already won. And young people must respect what their parents won through struggle.

Plainview (Tex.) Daily Herald, 10–19:6.

Paul VI
Pope

We see prevailing in ever more harmful manifestations nowadays an attempt to make the body the beginning and end of life . . . arriving to the point, in these very days, of naturalistic and obscene displays, and of the exhaltation of nudism, eroticism and pan-sexualism.

Castel Gandolfo, Italy, Aug. 16/
San Luis Obispo (Calif.) Telegram-Tribune,
8–17:12.

Exaggerated nationalism, racism engendering hate, the lust for unlimited power, the unbridled thirst for domination—who will convince men to emerge from such aberrations? Who will be the first to break the circle of the armaments race, ever more ruinous and vain? . . . Will man, who has learned how to harness the atom and conquer space, finally succeed in conquering his selfishness?

Before conference of United Nations Food and
Agriculture Organization, Rome, Nov. 16/
Los Angeles Herald-Examiner, 11–16:A4.

. . . what emptiness (is) in the human heart. What a temptation there is to fill its place with counterfeits, some of which—such as self-centered hedonism, eroticism and many others—lead, in the end, to contempt for man; and do not, for all that, satisfy his profound restlessness. Man's heart is made for God.

Celebrating High Mass, Sydney, Australia,
Dec. 1/San Francisco Examiner, 12–1:6.

Around us and throughout the world, there are so many poor, so many in need of life's basic necessities—while we fill ourselves to overflowing.

Rome/San Francisco Examiner, 12–14:9.

Richard W. Peck
Assistant director, Bulletin of the Council for Basic Education

The trouble with Utopias is that they are invariably devised by people who will not have to endure them.

Plainview (Tex.) Daily Herald, 3–27:6.

S.J. Perelman
Author

. . . the great phenomenon of our age: the decline of reticence. Everyone has got to express everything. There are no secrets any more. This is particularly true of sexual relations. We've reached the point where it's like supermarket goods. I believe in reticence in all things.

Interview, New York/
The Washington Post, 10–18:E4.

H. Ross Perot
Industrialist, Philanthropist

I didn't want to leave a vast estate to my children—I don't want to deny them the advantages I had, which come from making your own way in the world. Consequently, I'm not leaving them anything—except, I hope, a better America in which they can make their way.

Interview, Dallas/
Los Angeles Times (West Magazine), 3–22:22.

Georges Pompidou
President of France

. . . we must restore a meaning to men's actions, a meaning that is not only materialistic and utilitarian. Economic wealth must remain a means and not become an end in itself for society or for the individual. We need faith more than reason, a community spirit more than individualism, hope more than negation.

Before Commonwealth Club of California,
San Francisco, Feb. 27/
Los Angeles Herald-Examiner, 3–1:A2.

Katherine Anne Porter
Author

(To youth): You have only one time the great gift of balanced strength and health, and it's a great shame to waste it on drugs and drink and sexual hoodlumism. You're wasting your life, and it's not going to be given back to you. Use what you have more gracefully and gratefully. What is there about life that's so terrible that you have to throw it away?

Interview, College Park, Md./
The New York Times, 4–3:39.

J.B. Priestley
Author

Like its politicians and its wars, society has the teenagers it deserves.

Quote, 5–17:472.

Anthony Quinn
Actor

Most people try to get along in life in the easiest way. I read a study recently about the energy contained in a human being, and it said that a man like Einstein used only 15 per cent of his energy capacity, while average human beings use only 4 per cent. One of my big theories is that all human beings do not need to sleep eight hours every day, do not need to eat three meals a day, do not need to go to the toilet every day. I believe in putting time to good use. Somebody once said that if you put Tony Quinn on a desert island, he'd collect rocks. They're right.

Interview, New York/
The New York Times, 9–20:(2)23.

Martin Rackin
Motion picture producer

You all want to be different, but you're all the same. You wear the same uniform—long hair, moccasins and jeans. If you were all ordered to wear them, you'd come to school with haircuts, white shirts and ties. You're the biggest copouts I ever saw! . . . If you were rushed to the hospital, would you want a 19-year-old surgeon to operate on you—or an 11-year-old pilot to fly your plane across the Atlantic? Sure, young people should have a chance—but under experienced hands.

Before students, McGill University, Montreal/
Variety, 4–8:2.

Walter P. Reuther
President, United Auto Workers of America

(The auto workers) have been in the forefront of every basic struggle in this country, and we have learned some very simple, fundamental truths—that you can't solve a human problem by pitting one human being against another human being . . . We have learned that the only way you can solve human problems is to get people to join hands and to find answers to these problems together. We reject the voices of extremism in America, whether they be white or black, for there are no separate answers. There are no white answers to the problems. There are no black answers. There are only common answers.

At U.A.W. convention, Atlantic City, N.J.,
April 20/The New York Times, 4–21:27.

Eddie Rickenbacker
Aviator

If a thing is old, it is a sign that it was fit to live. Old families, old customs, old styles survive because they are fit to survive. The guarantee of continuity is quality. Old-fashioned hospitality, old-fashioned politeness, old-fashioned honor in transaction and work had qualities of survival. They will come back.

Quote, 3–8:232.

Hyman G. Rickover
Vice Admiral, United States Navy; Director, Division of Naval Reactors, Atomic Energy Commission

Liberty is never gained for once and for all. Each generation must win it anew. Each must defend it against new perils.

Before Western Society of Engineers, Chicago/
National Observer, 4–20:15.

Simon H. Rifkind
Former Judge, United States District Court for the Southern District of New York

We are told to listen to the young, that they have an important message to deliver; and I heartily agree. Everywhere, I meet young people who are earnest, intelligent, well-informed, thoughtful, and whose views are rich with wisdom. But in not a single instance have I encountered such positive performance from the exhibitionists, the impudent loud-mouths, the stone-throwers and the window-smashers. It is my earnest belief that the world has undergone a period of foolishness like in the days of the Children's Crusade in the thirteenth century. Now it is time to stop the nonsense. It won't be stopped by college presidents who can't make up their minds whether cheating and promiscuity are vices or permissible forms of behavior. It won't be stopped by professors who look upon violent coercion as a valid mode of securing academic change. The nonsense that I believe can and should be stopped includes these notions: the proposition that the way to improve the human condition is to extirpate all of the operating institutions of society; that force and violence are appropriate means by which to accomplish the restructuring of our universities and other social institutions; that the right of dissent includes the right to shout down and drown out the voice of those with whom you disagree; that the life of the scavenger pigeon is appropriate for civilized human beings—that is, to sleep where you pause, to feed on the bread others have labored to produce and to practice none of the arts of civilization except the art of self-indulgence; that sexual morality, family integrity and responsibility for child-rearing are obsolete vestiges of a repressive society, no longer relevant to modern life; that public decisions should be taken, not by the constitutional organs of a democratic government, but by reference to a community sentiment as determined and expressed by self-appointed oracles. The failure to stop this nonsense will bring, in its train, first revulsion and then reaction; that reaction will appear in fascist trappings and will avow fascist goals. I do not believe that the way to paradise is through the jungle of Hippieland; I do not believe that a free society is achieved by drowning out disagreement; I do not believe that an open society can be achieved by self-segregation.

Before Lawyers Division, American Jewish Committee/National Observer, 12–14:14.

John D. Rockefeller III
Philanthropist

My very simple thesis is that society faces overwhelming problems, and we're not doing as effective a job as we could to meet them. At the same time, we have young people who are our future, who are our leaders of tomorrow, concerned about the problems. They want to be involved, to be relevant to the problems of our time, to have a part in decision-making. We of the older generation need their fresh ideas, their feeling for change; and I think it's right for older people to be pushed to re-think, both personally and institutionally.

Interview, New York/ The New York Times, 12–6:(1)65.

Jerry Rubin
Organizer, Youth International Party

The first part of the Yippie program, you know, is kill your parents. And I mean that quite seriously. Because until you're prepared to kill your parents, you're not really prepared to change the country, because our parents are our first oppressors.

At Kent State University, Ohio/ Human Events, 9–5:3.

Giuseppe Saragat
President of Italy

Serious, grievous, difficult human problems require, in order to be resolved, fatigue, work, a sense of responsibility and sacrifices. To believe that they may be resolved through acts of violence is absurd.

Address to nation, Rome, Dec. 31/ Los Angeles Times, 1–1(1971):(1)25.

Maximilian Schell
Actor

Women love to fight with a man; but they

(MAXIMILIAN SCHELL)

love it more to be beaten in the fight . . . They love to lose, to be sat on, conquered, vanquished . . . to be bossed.

Interview, New York/
San Francisco Examiner, 9–26:31.

William J. Scherle
United States Representative, R-Iowa

If you look at what young people are reading these days, it is not hard to see where the ideas come from. One popular writer is Herbert Marcuse, who attacks big, rich organizations as "de-humanizing" and "totalitarian" because, he believes, they control people's lives without their consent, or even their knowledge. Under this heading, he lumps big business and big government, especially the military. Obviously, this doctrine has a lot of appeal to a young man fearful of exchanging the freedom and individualism he has known as a student for the regimented life of the Army or a large corporation in a nine-to-five job. It is easier to condemn the establishment than to accept the hard realities of adult responsibilities.

Before the House, Washington, May 4/
Congressional Record, 5–4:E3848.

Charles R. Schroeder
Director, San Diego Zoo

There are no juvenile delinquents in the animal world. Animal parents don't permit it.

The Dallas Times Herald, 7–6:A2.

George C. Scott
Actor

I played (General George S.) Patton because I liked the man. He was a professional, and I admire professionalism. And for whatever else he was—good or bad—he was an individual. That's what's most important to me today—when everybody else around seems to be some kind of damn ostrich.

Time, 2–9:78.

Glenn T. Seaborg
Chairman, Atomic Energy Commission of the United States

I believe that one of the characteristics of the human race—possibly the one that is primarily responsible for its course of evolution—is that it has grown by creatively responding to failure. We have always experienced times when we have been dissatisfied, unhappy with ourselves and our conditions and lamented them profoundly before we took new steps to change them.

Before House Select Subcommittee on
Education, Washington, Feb. 4/
The New York Times, 2–5:1.

Jean-Jacques Servan-Schreiber
Journalist; Member, French National Assembly

By far the greatest challenge (in the world today) is the passion of youth—admirable in its motivation, dangerous in its frustration. The quest of the young for dignity, sincerity and truth in our generation is one of the two great sources of human energy. The other source is industry. Both are highly progressive and liberating forces. If we allow them to remain as they are today, on a collision course, the future will be dark. If we forge their alliance by reform, then we shall have met the challenge of our generation.

Washington/
The Christian Science Monitor, 8–7:2.

Dan Seymour
President, J. Walter Thompson Company

Bad news always did travel fast; now it travels instantaneously. But gloom isn't the only thing that travels freely across the borders of the world. Today, under the big eye of television, with the busy satellites whirling overhead and the telephone lines and pipelines and airports endlessly connecting people and things, the world has been pulled tightly together. Not only are the countries connected by roads and wires and pipes; they are connected by policies and pacts and agreements and commerce and matters of health and information and money and currencies and trade. Not only diseases are epidemic today; the words on a picket sign, the graffiti words on a wall, a college slogan, a phrase in a speech, an insult—all these ideas are flung around the world immediately. A dramatic picture or newsreel is seen around the world within hours. No nation can escape this wonderful and terrible new immediacy. And no nation or institution has yet really learned how to use this wonderful and terrible new power of mass international communications. The prime fact is that we could never say things like this before. It would have been nonsense to claim that there was a general world view on anything. You could not know what the whole world felt or thought because the countries got the news at different times—or never got the news at all. But we have had television for years; and it is television which instantly joins cultures, customs, habits, races, lifestyles. Almost all the world joins day and night in international moments of emotion, from grief and anger to pleasure and pomp. Millions of people see a soldier talking, a President talking; they see the soldier and the President shot; they see them both buried. What we have, therefore, as the result of all the connections, and through television, is a new kind of international unity. It is fragile; it is formless; it shifts like water; it has no body or structure; but it is there—it is really there. It is the start of the formation of world opinion, of a world audience. And it is momentous, because it is the beginning of the first true unity the world has ever had. And I think we ought to realize that this is one of the tremendous new facts of our times.

Before International Advertising Association,
New York, June 9/
The Wall Street Journal, 7–17:8.

Edgar F. Shannon
President, University of Virginia

The mind is man's primary human attribute, and reason has been his chief means of advancement. Reason, of course, is the ultimate source of authority in any university or college and in a dynamic nation—and (is) supplanted with naked power and repression.

At Bridgewater (Va.) College commencement/
Quote, 10–25:396.

Karl Shapiro
Professor of English, University of California at Davis

It appears that the modern student enters the university with a contempt for the university, a contempt for society, a contempt for literature and a contempt for himself. Where did he learn this? Not from his own school; not from the library. I don't think so. He learned it from what the new illiterates call the Media: TV, radio, magazine and paperback bookstore. He learned it from what the new illiterates call their "counter-culture"; he learned it from his contemporaries and the exploiters of cults. For the first time in history, the illiterates have a literature of their own: op-pop-camp-kitsch-existential-occult-nihilist sweepings and swill. Armed to the teeth with this quasi-literature, it is little wonder that they slam the textbook on the floor and stomp out to their cars, barefooted.

Before California Library Association,
San Francisco/Human Events, 7–11:9.

Fulton J. Sheen
Former Bishop of Rochester, N.Y.

History? The British never remember it; the Irish never forget it; the Russians never make it; and the Americans never learn from it.

Quote, 10–25:385.

Civilization is always in danger when those who have never learned to obey are given the right to command.

Quote, 11–29:505.

Lord Shinwell
Life Peer, British House of Lords; Former Member, House of Commons

I think the world has gone crazy. We're just drifting along. We don't have any definite purpose. It doesn't reside in politicians, nor in the church, nor in governments. People have got to make up their minds what they want, what their objective is. We need a world purpose, a civilized purpose.

Interview, London/
The Christian Science Monitor, 9–2:15.

R. Sargent Shriver
Former United States Ambassador to France

The politics of death is bureaucracy, routine, rules, status quo. The politics of life is personal initiative, creativity, flair, dash, a little daring. The politics of death is calculation, prudence, measured gestures. The politics of life is experience, spontaneity, grace, directness. The politics of death is fear of youth. The politics of life is to trust the young to their own experiences.

Berkeley, Calif., Aug. 4/
San Francisco Chronicle, 8–5:9.

Jean Simmons
Actress

. . . even when two people are beautifully suited, a marriage needs working on, and to keep things running smoothly is a woman's responsibility. This obligation is the essence of femininity—a word that needs re-examination today because women have outgrown the mold of chattel. But to what extreme do they want to carry their emancipation? A woman with an active sense of our femininity appreciates and enjoys men much too much to want to compete with a potential lover. A frontal attack is unfeminine. With understanding of the situation and with sufficient discretion not to provoke controversy, a woman can gain her end. Subtlety is the key to femininity.

Interview, Los Angeles/
Los Angeles Times, 1–18:E15.

James B. Somerall
President, Pepsi-Cola Company

The teenager today is striving for a new image that's quite different from that of his immediate predecessor of the late 1950s—the delinquent rebel lost in an uncomprehending and uncaring adult society. He no longer takes as his role model the late James Dean or the early Marlon Brando. Today's teenager is very conscious of his numerical strength and of his real potential to influence change in an adult world that's finally beginning to take him and his attitudes seriously. Today's young people are aware of being virtually a new social class in themselves, rather than just a group in transition from one age to another. It may surprise and shock and even anger you to hear this word, but the image being sought by the youth of today is one of nobility. And what large numbers of these young would-be noblemen are searching for, believe it or not, is nothing less romantic than glory . . . But they know that ours is a complex society that withholds the winning of true glory from most people until they're well over thirty. And today's kid doesn't want to wait that long. He wants access to it now. He's tragically wrong, in a way. He hasn't learned—or hasn't accepted—that glory is something that's won by long, hard work. He demands instant gratification . . . instant glory.

At seminar of Retail Management Institute
of New York University/
The Wall Street Journal, 3–9:12.

Muriel Spark
Author

I think the world is absurd. Our old ideas about good and evil belong more to mythology than to history . . . I don't believe there are really bad men—just a great deal of absurdity.

Before American Academy of Arts and Letters,
New York, May 26/
Los Angeles Times (Calendar), 8–16:10.

Maurice H. Stans
Secretary of Commerce of the United States

The next time you hear someone say conditions in the world are bad, ask him just one question—compared to what? Compared to 60 years ago when I was born? Compared to the world of 100 years ago? Compared to the Dark Ages of the past? More progress has been made in my lifetime than in all mankind's history before us. But we have seen only the beginning of the possible.

Quote, 5–10:445.

Gloria Steinem
Author

. . . this is the year of Women's Liberation, a major revolution in consciousness—in everyone's consciousness, male or female. Our first problem is not to learn but to unlearn, to clear out some of the old assumptions: patriotism means obedience, age means wisdom, black means inferior, woman means submission. They just don't work any more. Women's Liberation is men's liberation, too. No more alimony; fewer boring wives; fewer childlike wives; no more so-called "Jewish Mothers," who are simply normally ambitious human beings with all their ambitiousness confined to the house; no more wives who fall apart with the first wrinkle because they've been taught their total identity depends on their outsides; no more responsibility for another human being who has never been told she is responsible for her own life, and who sooner or later says some version of, "If I hadn't married you, I could have been a star." And, let's hear it one more time—no more alimony.

At Vassar College commencement/Life, 6–19:26.

Leopold Stokowski
Orchestra conductor

The main thing in life is to have an intense interest in something. It is like traveling in a car at high speed and very straight—not turning any corners. When life is straight and simple like that, one has time to enjoy things. There are no complications.

Interview, New York/
The New York Times, 12–13:(2)15.

Igor Stravinsky
Composer

If old people look dour and cantankerous, experience is probably a lesser cause—reasonable as that would be—than physiological degeneration: Circe's terrible island of change. Thus, the narrow pursing of lips—the lockjaw look—is due in greater measure to dental vacancies and instabilities, it seems to me, than to bitterness and enmity. Likewise, the silence of the elderly must be attributed more to poor hearing than to critical disapproval; and their fitful speech to difficulties of enunciation, rather than to ill humor, for old age tongue-ties. So, too, if the aged are annoyingly finical and complain of every perturbation, physiological weakness is the primary reason. Thus, the two antediluvian spinsters at the next table, who appeared to be greatly concerned with the beverages on mine, may not have been the Brothers Grim at all but quite genial (and thirsty) old souls, whose countenances . . . simply did not register any semblance of their "inner dynamics." So I would like to believe, anyway, since I agree with Madame De Nino, that "after the age of eighty, all contemporaries are friends."

Interview/The Wall Street Journal, 10–30:14.

Albert Szent-Gyorgyi
Biologist

Man is a very strange animal. In much of the world, half the children go to bed hungry, and we spend half a trillion on rubbish —steel, iron, tanks. We are all criminals. There is an old Hungarian poem: "If you are among brigands and you are silent, you are a brigand yourself."

Interview, Wood's Hole, Mass./
The New York Times, 2–20:37.

U Thant
Secretary-General of the United Nations

. . . there must be on the part of governments a radical change from present power politics to a policy of collective responsibility toward mankind . . . A successful management of the world . . . depends on the behavior of nations. The justice, peace, security, prosperity, health, cleanliness and the beauty of our world must become the prime preoccupation of governments. The world is too small, its people are too intelligent and the mass problems that lie in store for us are too frightening to allow continued blind acceptance of the sacrosanct concept of "national interest." World affairs are no longer foreign affairs of governments. They have become internal affairs of all.

At 25th anniversary of UN Charter signing,
San Francisco, June 26, Vital Speeches, 8–15:653.

In a world of many billions of people, who are divided into highly industrialized societies as well as regions of extreme poverty, each with (its) own culture and special problems, there can be no universal recipe or system. Nations must, therefore, enrich each other with what has proved good in the art of governing man. Private initiative may be the solution in one case, public initiative may be the answer in another. Many countries have demonstrated that the two can coexist and that one can admirably complement or even correct and stimulate the other.

At 25th anniversary of UN Charter signing,
San Francisco, June 26/Vital Speeches, 8–15:654.

I do not wish to seem over-dramatic; but I can only conclude from the information that is available to me that the members of the United Nations have perhaps 10 years left in which to subordinate their ancient quarrels and launch a global partnership to curb the arms race, to improve the human environment, to defuse the population explosion and to supply the required momentum to development efforts. If such a global partnership is not forged in the next decade, then I very much fear that the problems I have mentioned will have reached such staggering proportions that they will be beyond our capacity to control.

Los Angeles Herald-Examiner, 10–24:A10.

Nguyen Dang Thuc
South Vietnamese author and philosopher

There is no essential contradiction between the rural, agricultural society of the Orient and the industrial and urban society of the West. If there is a difference, it has been the basic Western error of opposing man to nature, separating reason and sentiment, spirituality and materiality, considering reason and faith as two things that cannot coexist.

Interview, Saigon/
The New York Times, 11–12:6.

Lionel Tiger
Author; Social anthropologist

Males are very fragile. They can only operate in very fantasy structures—like the Pentagon and like the U.S. government—with seals and all the wings and eagles. They have this fantastic panoply that males create. Males are always in drag, in a sense, even if they're in the Pentagon, always constantly elaborating these highly mythical structures. The thing the females do, of course, is break them—which is why it's a very desirable thing, often, to have females in the structure to laugh at the funny men in their Shriners' costumes.

Interview/Time, 8–31:21.

Josip Broz Tito
President of Yugoslavia

When you get older, whiskey is much better for the blood than milk.

The Dallas Times Herald, 10–2:A2.

Hugh Trevor-Roper
Historian

I think at all times there are some people who will say these are the worst times. I know of no period when this has not been said; so I don't take it too seriously. I am optimistic about what is ahead for the world . . . I don't think any situation today is desperate.

News conference, San Francisco, Dec. 3/
San Francisco Examiner, 12–3:20.

Robert C. Tyson
Chairman, Finance Committee, United States Steel Corporation

. . . I bow to no man in love of freedom,

but I believe we should ever be mindful of the fact that no man is free to do *anything* he likes. After all, freedom involves morality; it involves discipline, an inner discipline, a conscience within the individual ever reminding him that his freedom stops where the other fellow's freedom begins, that no man is really free if he renders another man less free. And it makes no difference who lessens freedom, whether he is in the private or public sector. To be sure, there are great social problems gnawing at our body politic —violence, crime, poverty, inflation, environment and others—but irresponsible "powers" and "freedoms" are not the answer in my book.

Before Independent College Funds of America, Palm Springs, Calif., March 3 | Vital Speeches, 4–15:416.

Roger Vadim
Motion picture director

The trouble with female companionship is this: If a woman is intellectual, she begins to compete with the man and becomes aggressive; if she is not intellectual, she is boring to be with. That's a man's fate; he is doomed to be aggressed or bored.

Interview, Los Angeles | Plainview (Tex.) Daily Herald, 8–5:8.

Jack Valenti
President, Motion Picture Association of America

. . . when one is in his 20s, time is casual coin. There is so much of it yet to be minted.

Interview, Nation's Business, Aug.:50.

Sander Vanocur
News commentator,
National Broadcasting Company

There's a problem that bothers me about the young. I can really understand a lot of the things they don't like. But where I fall out with them is their unwillingness, or inability—I think it's both—to struggle with the definition of their goals. I'm not saying it's incumbent on you to come up with definitions—but try to *work* with me about what

you're talking about. Don't give me the *grunt*. Give me complex thoughts in simple declarative sentences. Or complex thoughts in complex sentences. *Think!*

Interview, New York | TV Guide, 7–4:36.

Kurt Vonnegut, Jr.
Author

Everything is going to become unimaginably worse and never get better again . . . We would be a lot safer if the government would take its money out of science and put it into astrology and the reading of palms. I used to think that science would save us. But only in superstition is there hope. I beg you to believe in the most ridiculous superstition of all: that humanity is at the center of the universe, the fulfiller or the frustrator of the grandest dreams of God Almighty. If you can believe that and make others believe it, human beings might stop treating each other like garbage.

At Bennington (Vt.) College commencement | Time, 6–29:8.

(A) great swindle of our time is that people your age are supposed to save the world. I was a graduation speaker at a little preparatory school for girls on Cape Cod a couple of weeks ago. I told the girls that they were much too young to save the world and that, after they got their diplomas, they should go swimming and sailing and walking, and just fool around.

At Bennington (Vt.) College commencement | Time, 6–29:8.

Walter H. Wheeler, Jr.
Chairman, executive committee,
Pitney-Bowes, Inc.

I think it (humor) is a very important thing. It's the oil or the grease of human nature. Lord help you if you can't laugh, at yourself and others. Humor was one of (former Soviet Premier) Kruschchev's great assets. I wish he had lasted a while longer— I think we and the Russians would have gotten along much better.

Interview | Quote, 3–15:250.

Lynn White
*Professor of History, University of
California at Los Angeles*

Historians don't romanticize the past.
They know about the past. They're more
willing to live in the present. I never met a
historian who wishes he had lived in some
past period.
*Interview, Los Angeles/
Los Angeles Times, 2–24:(1)17.*

Flip Wilson
Comedian

Being a comedian is like being a con man.
You have to make 'em like you before you
can fool 'em.
Interview/Look, 5–5:Sec.M.

Kendrick R. Wilson
Chairman, Avco Corporation

If you spend every waking hour on business, it probably is not good for you or the
business.
Interview/Nation's Business, April:68.

Franco Zeffirelli
Motion picture director

Sometimes I get annoyed with my friends
who don't want to grow old. The idea of
everybody wanting to stay young! Ridiculous—the 50-year-olds with their long mous-
taches, sideburns and mod clothes, who refuse to be old. Sometimes I think that the
"youth movement" has been taken over by
the middle-aged! If I were young, I'd be
pretty upset about this theft! How silly. It's
like saying the day is only beautiful in the
morning . . . Ridiculous! The afternoons
can be fabulous! And how about the nights?
They can be absolutely smashing!
*Interview, Rome/
Los Angeles Times (Calendar), 7–26:15.*

Ronald L. Ziegler
*Press Secretary to the President
of the United States*

I'd suggest that the equal and opposite
slogans, "never trust anyone over 30" and
"never trust anyone under 30," both miss the
mark. I'd suggest that a better formulation
would be, "Beware of any mix that doesn't
include both."
*At Muskingum College, New Concord, Ohio/
The New York Times, 6–14:(4)2.*

Religion

Spiro T. Agnew
Vice President of the United States

(Today we have) children dropped-off by their parents at Sunday school to hear the "modern" gospel from a "progressive" preacher more interested in fighting pollution than fighting evil—one of those pleasant clergymen who lifts his weekly sermons out of old newsletters from a National Council of Churches that has cast morality and theology aside as "not relevant" and set as its goal on earth the recognition of Red China and the preservation of the Florida alligator.

Fort Lauderdale, Fla., April 28/Time, 5–11:20.

Hans Dieter Betz
Professor of Religion,
Claremont (Calif.) College

Why do books that carry so little significance get so much publicity? First, there was this book, *The Passover Plot* (claiming that Christ was a fraud), then a book about Jesus and his followers using psychedelic mushrooms, and now we've got a book claiming the possibility that Christ was married. What's next?

Los Angeles Herald-Examiner, 11–21:A7.

Alexander Carter
President, Canadian Catholic Conference

If government and business find it necessary to institute think-tanks to work on prospects for the next 20 years, the church in its own way and with its own scope must strive to attempt to shape a form of community that will allow the people of God to live in Christ in a computerized society.

Before House of Delegates of the National Association of Priests' Councils, San Diego, Calif., March 9/ The New York Times, 3–10:20.

William Sloane Coffin, Jr.
Chaplain, Yale University

Ministers, priests and rabbis hear this time and time again—that we shouldn't meddle in politics. And I bet Pharaoh said that to Moses.

Plainview (Tex.) Daily Herald, 11–27:6.

Donald Connolly
Coordinator, National Catholic Office for Radio and Television

Some clergymen have become so involved in contemporary problems that they have ended up thinking that to be a minister or a priest is to be a sociologist or a social worker . . . We must start going into the world with *religious* answers.

TV Guide, 6–13:13.

John Tracy Ellis
Roman Catholic church historian

Nearly a century ago, John Henry Cardinal Newman made the prophetic utterance that we would be coming into a time when the Church would be faced for the first time with a world that was simply irreligious, that believed in nothing. I wonder if we have not arrived at the time when Cardinal Newman said we would be afflicted by "the plague of infidelity."

U.S. News & World Report, 3–23:44.

Leonard Fein
Professor of Political Science, Massachusetts Institute of Technology

(Today's Jew asks himself): Why do I need to be a Jew? To be ethical? Humanistic? Liberal? Back in the '40s Jews had an instinct that they were the only liberals. Now Jews are rich and the (Christian) church is looking good on civil rights. In any objective sense, it would be easier not to be Jewish.

(LEONARD FEIN)

But what options are open? Historically, to become a Christian meant joining the enemy. Now, your motives would be questioned—are they just base, careeristic motives? To join the country club?

National Observer, 3–16:14.

Joseph H. Fichter
Sociologist, Harvard University

In many instances, clergy and laity are moving apart. The laity often feel that they have been the victims of a "clerical mystique." Some of them are going their own way, and they "couldn't care less" what the priests say. Then the clergy, themselves, have been victims of the "episcopal mystique," treated like children, allowed to be seen but not heard except to murmur pious approval and give polite applause to whatever directives come down from above. They, too, are walking away in spectacular and increasing numbers, and they are giving their reasons loud and clear.

Before House of Delegates of the National Federation of Priests' Councils, San Diego, Calif,. March 9/ The New York Times, 3–10:20.

Louis Finkelstein
Chancellor, Jewish Theological Seminary, New York

There was no real revival of religion in the deepest sense in the 1950s and 1960s. But I see hopeful signs today, particularly among students, which suggest that the next 10 years will bring a new sense of religion in terms of charity, love, kindness and pursuit of peace.

U.S. News & World Report, 3–23:44.

William Fore
Executive director, Broadcasting and Film Commission, National Council of Churches of Christ

We've gone too far in embracing the secular world. There's been a kind of emphasis in the church on guys who are "hip" and "with it"—each one saying, "I can be more secular than thou"!

TV Guide, 6–13:8.

Richard Gilbert
Chairman, Division of Mass Media of the Board of National Missions, United Presbyterian Church

If you take the entire religious world, about one-third are intensely secular and liberal; one-third are intensely pietistic, evangelical and conservative; and one-third are utterly indifferent. In terms of those who are active in the church, it's a 50-50 split.

TV Guide, 6–13:12.

Jackie Gleason
Actor, Comedian

Religion's not supposed to be gravy. It's not supposed to be a Valhalla. It's not supposed to be something that makes you jump up and scream, "Hallelujah!" It's supposed to hurt you. It's supposed to stick you with a pin every time you do something wrong; and when you do do something wrong, you get stuck with that pin, and you think it over. Now, if you want to get stuck with that pin again, and it's worth that, then you sin again.

Interview, New York/ The Dallas Times Herald, 8–16:C12.

Billy Graham
Evangelist

. . . (youth) feel alienated and are looking for something which they can only find through God . . . The organized church has not taught them that you can have an "experience" with God, so they're trying to find it through drugs . . . Today's youth are asking questions that are basically religious questions.

Quote, 4–5:329.

Some of the radical groups in the country are being led by so-called clergymen. Where many of these men get the "reverend" in front of their names, I do not know. Certainly they don't get it from God.

At Southern Baptist Convention/ Newsweek, 7–20:55.

Gerald H. Kennedy
Bishop, United Methodist Church

I wouldn't be surprised if before the decade of the '70s is over, everything is going to be Gung Ho on evangelism . . . I am pretty sure in my own mind that the church is a necessary institution in the world, and we are not close to getting along without it.

Los Angeles Times, 1–4:E12.

Bernard J.F. Lonergan
Philosopher

The Church always arrives on the scene a little breathless and a little late.

Time, 4–20:59.

Konrad Z. Lorenz
Director, Max Planck Institute for Physiology of Behavior, Seewiesen, West Germany

What bothers me about religions is that the priests are on such intimate terms with God. To me, it's blasphemous to be so intimate with God. God isn't an individual. If He exists, He is everywhere—maybe in me.

Interview/
The New York Times Magazine, 7–5:30.

Edgar F. Magnin
Rabbi, Wilshire Boulevard Temple, Los Angeles

You hear religion faces a revolution. That's a lot of baloney. It is true that, up to a point, it faces defiance. There is more defiance in every department of life. But, actually, there is not so much rebellion as people think. The good professional men, the honest houses of business, the worthy places of worship—they have no trouble. People come for what they want, and they find religion as necessary as sex. Adolescents always did wander away, although they were not so vocal in the past as now. Most of them come back. Except those who take drugs and go insane. Where the leadership is right, the people will come, those who want religion. Some, of course, will never go for it. Some won't go for art, either—does that mean all art should be junked? Some have no feel for music—does that mean symphonies are out? Of course not.

Interview, Los Angeles/
Los Angeles Times, 6–28:H6.

Timothy Manning
Coadjutor Bishop of Los Angeles

We are deeply concerned that the Church must make her own needs the social needs of the world of men, their griefs and anxieties. The Church is constantly progressing in its attempts to meet the needs of our times.

U.S. News & World Report, 2–2:12.

Calvin Marshall
Chairman, Black Economic Development Conference

If we (black people) were nothing here, at least we were children of God. At some far-off point in time, all these things would be rectified and we would get our golden slippers. Our religion *had* to mean more to us. We had to emote; we had to lose ourselves in it. We had to sing and shout, and after it was all over we had to have a big meal and have something going on Sunday afternoon. Because when Monday came, it was back out into the fields, or back to the janitor's job, or back in Miss Ann's kitchen scrubbing the floor.

Time, 4–6:71.

Martin E. Marty
Professor of Modern Church History, University of Chicago Divinity School

. . . the more anti-modern, anti-ecumenical and authoritarian a church is, the more likely it is to be growing.

The Wall Street Journal, 4–24:12.

Many . . . clergymen look at political office-seeking as a chance to enlarge their ministry and gain a broader impact. They are seeking the satisfaction of doing something about the social and political problems that are directly related to national morality—war, poverty, race, the youth question and others. As more and more come to feel this way, you can expect increasing numbers to seek political office as an answer.

U.S. News & World Report, 8–10:21.

Marcello Mastroianni
Actor

The church has more strength in Italy than in other countries, but I do not think the Italians are so superstitious any more. Only the peasants are close to the church. When you get a little money, you break away from religion. As a parent, I no longer feel the need to send my daughter to church . . . My daughter, Barbara, and her friends are so busy they don't have time for St. Peter and madonnas and mysterious symbols and philosophies. They find a Divinity, like God or Buddha or Lenin, in themselves. Now they go less to priests and more to psychiatrists. Church is old fashioned.

Interview, Padua, Italy /
The New York Times, 6–21:(2)13.

Kilian McDonnell

Executive director, Institute for Ecumenical and Cultural Research

Especially for a generation which is concerned about personal fulfillment and personal relationships is the sense of (divine) presence important. Though the evangelicals have their problems of relevancy, their sense of presence corresponds to real needs. An experience-oriented generation will not buy a God who is "the great absent one."

U.S. News & World Report, 10–19:86.

Thomas R. McDonough
Archbishop of Louisville, Kentucky

We have come a long, long way. The second Vatican council was almost revolutionary in bringing in new ideas and new hopes. The church is on the move . . . More doors are open for dialogue, and that means chancery doors. We must close our ranks and think as one—bishops, priests, religious and laity. Unity is the key word.

Before National Federation of Priests'
Councils, San Diego, Calif., March 10 /
The New York Times, 3–11:22.

Uneasy lies the head that wears a miter.

Before National Federation of Priests'
Councils, San Diego, Calif., March 10 /
The New York Times, 3–15:(4)5.

James Francis Cardinal McIntyre
Former Archbishop of Los Angeles

A priest's job is to bring the knowledge and love of God to people—to say mass, hear confessions, to be available to the people in his parish. It is not a job really, it is a vocation, as he is a priest 24 hours a day. If you were sick and called me at midnight, I would be there.

Interview, Los Angeles /
Los Angeles Herald-Examiner, 1–22:A6.

Humberto S. Medeiros
Archbishop of Boston

(Christian-Jewish relations) have to be the most cordial and the most candid and sincere precisely because the members of the Jewish faith really are our forefathers in the faith. In the long run, we are all children of Abraham, are we not?

Interview, Boston /
The Christian Science Monitor, 11–12:3.

William Metcalfe
Anglican Rector of Bottesford, England

If the church were to try to communicate successfully today, its buildings would have to be psychedelic, its choir girls topless, its hymns bawdy, prayers replaced by pot and the vicar a well-known pop singer.

Plainview (Tex.) Daily Herald, 10–27:10.

Richard M. Nixon
President of the United States

I have studied the lives of all the Presidents of this country, of both parties. They came from different religions; some were better church-goers than others. But there is one thing I have noted about every man who has occupied this office, and that is, by the time he ended his term in office, he was more dedicated and more dependent on his religious faith than when he entered it. And that tells me something. This is a great office, and I am proud and humble to hold it. This is an enormous responsibility, and I accept the responsibility without fear, but with also great respect. But I can also tell you America would not be what it is today—the greatest nation in the world—if it were not a nation which has made progress under God. This nation would not be—this would not be the great nation that it were—unless those who have led this nation had each in his own way turned for help beyond himself for these causes that we all want for our young people —a better life, the things that we may not have had ourselves but we want for them.

At University of Tennessee, May 28/
The New York Times, 5–29:8.

Levi A. Olan
Rabbi, Temple Emanu-el, Dallas, Tex.

It has been suggested that, in view of what we know about the universe today, we must revise our understanding of the nature of God. To keep on insisting that He is omnipotent and good in the face of senseless tragedies of life is to alienate ourselves from a living God who has meaning for life today. Let us think of God as a father. When we are children, our fathers seem to be all-powerful . . .When the child becomes an adult, he sees his father with his limitations and views him with even greater love . . .

The Dallas Times Herald Sunday Magazine,
10–11:21.

Albert O. Outler
Professor of Theology,
Southern Methodist University

The church is always most vital when concern for the here-and-now and the "sweet bye-and-bye" are intermingled, where the finite and infinite interact. The church cannot hope to return to its unquestioned pre-eminence of a former age—but it might turn out that human concern about the mysterious dimensions of our existence will reassert itself once we run out of the audacious promises of technology. Then the church can say: Here is where man's understanding and highest hopes are centered.

U.S. News & World Report, 3–23:46.

Paul VI
Pope

. . . ecclesiastical celibacy (is) a supreme testimony to the kingdom of God, a unique sign that speaks of the values of faith, of hope, of love, an incomparable condition of full pastoral service, a continuous asceticism of Christian perfection. Yes, it is difficult; but it is just this aspect that makes it attractive to young and ardent spirits, and it is more than ever valid for the needs of our time. We will say more: It can become easy; it is happy, it is lovely, it is Catholic. We must conserve and defend it.

Vatican City, Feb. 1/
The New York Times, 2–2:8.

The Church must be poor. Not only this, the Church must *appear* poor.

Vatican City/
The Dallas Times Herald, 6–25:A2.

Today, 100 years after Rome was united to Italy, the relations between church and state are such that one can say never before has the sovereignty of the Italian people been in more perfect harmony with the sovereignty of the Catholic Church.

Vatican City/
The Dallas Times Herald, 9–21:A2.

People ask themselves: Are religious truths and dogmas changing? Does nothing permanent exist? (An answer must be found) if only to avoid the catastrophic consequences which would arise from admitting that no norm, no doctrine, can remain forever, and that all changes, however radical, can be adopted as a method of progress, contestation or revolution. If we do not want civilization to end in chaos and the Christian religion to lose all justification in the modern world, we must all make clear . . . that something remains and must remain in the passing of time.

Vatican City/
The Dallas Times Herald, 10–29:A9

The best reply that can be given to those who see the Catholic Church as a strictly

(PAUL VI)

European organization is this: The Church is Catholic—that is to say, universal.

Jakarta, Indonesia, Dec. 3/
Los Angeles Times, 12–4:(1)6.

Arthur Michael Ramsey
Archbishop of Canterbury

Just now the ecumenical movement has become so familiar, so well established, that it is in danger of becoming complacent and conventional. Once it was new and adventurous and brave to be ecumenical. Now it has become the established thing. This is dangerous, for God calls us ever to new ventures. It is time for new things to be happening in the ecumenical cause.

London, Jan. 20/
The New York Times, 1–21:15.

Fulton J. Sheen
Former Bishop of Rochester, N.Y.

Remorse results in worry, jealousy, envy, indignation; but sorrow related to God results in expiation and hope.

Quote, 12–27:599.

James D. Watson
Moderator, New York City presbytery,
United Presbyterian Church

I see the ministry in terms of social action, not in terms of preaching or the rest of the nonsense we went through years ago. In our day, we are more concerned about man than God. God can take care of himself.

U.S. News & World Report, 3–23:44.

Cynthia Wedel
President, National Council of Churches
of the United States

The growing concern about the role of women in the Roman Catholic Church—on the part of many influential men as well as on the part of women—is one of the most fascinating aspects of the fundamental change and renewal in that church. As a Protestant, I see the Roman Catholic Church

moving faster and more vigorously in most areas of renewal than the Protestant churches today . . . I am thoroughly aware of all the counter-renewal forces which exist, and which have probably been strengthened by the rapid and radical changes. But I feel safe in predicting that no one—including the Pope himself—can put the lid back on the life of the church. Because fundamental rethinking is being done by Roman Catholics —and especially by many extremely sound Biblical and theological scholars—I predict that the question of the ordination of women will be resolved in the Roman Church before it is in the Orthodox or Anglican churches.

At gathering hosted by Franciscan Friars
of the Atonement, Garrison, N.Y./
The New York Times, 11–13:23.

John Cardinal Wright
Prefect, Congregation of the Clergy,
Roman Curia, the Vatican

The idea of celibacy in the Church is a very old one. As a matter of fact, contrary to many things widely said, it is a discipline, a custom which has foundations in Scripture—where both Christ and Saint Paul speak of remaining unmarried, as they say, "for the sake of the kingdom." Well, if there was ever a period in history when it was necessary to do whatever one can "for the sake of the kingdom," that period is right now.

Interview, Vatican City/
U.S. News & World Report, 8–31:58.

. . . the Church needs the total devotion, the total love of any man who offers himself to the priesthood. It is not an exaggeration to say that he has to be prepared to work 24 hours a day, 7 days a week, 52 weeks a year. Even a woman who marries a doctor who has that kind of idealism has problems enough on her hands. No one has any right to ask a woman to marry a man who is thus committed, with his full heart, to the kingdom of God.

Interview, Vatican City/
U.S. News & World Report, 8–31:59.

Space · Science · Technology

Alan L. Bean
United States Astronaut

We have a tendency to overestimate the other guy and underestimate ourselves . . . Let us not be so concerned about what the other guy is doing with unmanned spacecraft until he touches what we have done with manned exploration. He is not coming close yet.

News conference, Washington, Nov. 19/
Los Angeles Times, 11–20:(1)13.

Harvey Brooks
Dean of engineering and applied physics,
Harvard University

Not only is less importance attached to material progress as a condition of a viable society, but also there is an obsessive preoccupation with the bad side effects of technology while taking its benefits for granted. If we assume even a moderate degree of persistence in this present mood, the outlook for technological change appears rather dim.

U.S. News & World Report, 2–9:31.

Aristedes Calvani
Foreign Minister of Venezuela

. . . the arrival of man on the moon gives to all human endeavor a new perspective. Earth has ceased to be the only place for man's activity. Mankind has now arrived in the cosmos, hence human existence has achieved a new and vital dimension. This fact, still barely assimilated, places the concept of humanity in an unusual projection. Earth, growing ever smaller, makes men feel even closer. One can understand, or perhaps one should say one can "feel," more readily the need for solidarity among nations.

At United Nations, N.Y./
The New York Times, 1–26:69.

Leo Cherne
Executive director,
Research Institute of America

The deep-seated fear of mushrooming technology has inherent in it exactly the right mixture of the valid and the emotional, the real and the exaggerated, to be the most explosive issue any society has ever faced. If technology is the evil and the scientist the villain, then the entire industrial process is a perfect target for anxiety, for hostility, for nihilistic revolution.

Before Chamber of Commerce of the
United States, Washington/
The Dallas Times Herald, 5–1:A30.

Alex Comfort
Director, Group on Aging,
University College, London

There are many gifts which a scientific nation could give to humanity . . . I can think of few achievements for which an epoch, an administration or a people might more wish to be remembered than this: lengthening of the useful and vigorous life of man.

San Francisco Examiner & Chronicle
(This World), 5–31:19.

Lee A. DuBridge
Science Adviser to the President
of the United States

If you are going to have a space program at all, it is going to cost three and a half billion or more dollars a year . . . This is a small price to pay for the tremendous worldwide lift that is given to people all over the world, for the tremendous advance in our knowledge which is provided to us—knowledge about the solar system, about space and the nature of matter, the origin of the solar system and of the earth . . . All of this is worth the investment many times over.

The Christian Science Monitor, 1–17:2.

Lee A. DuBridge
Former Science Adviser to the President of the United States

One reason the *Apollo* program went off so well, despite its size, was that while it was a political decision in the beginning (to go to the moon), from then on it was a technological program ... What made it work and not bog down in politics was that once the political decision was made, there was no political interference.

Interview, Washington/ The Christian Science Monitor, 9-4:7.

Paul R. Ehrlich
Professor of Biology, Stanford University

(The National Academy of Sciences is) another part of the never-take-a-stand science establishment. It would be unable to give a unanimous decision if asked whether the sun would rise tomorrow.

Interview/Look, 4-21:42.

Thomas Gold
Professor of Astronomy, Cornell University; Member, Science Advisory Committee to the President of the United States

(The cancelling of two moon flights) is like buying a Rolls-Royce and then not using it because you claim you can't afford the gas.

Sept. 3/The New York Times, 9-4:9.

Chet Huntley
News commentator, National Broadcasting Company

Most astronauts are dull as hell—nice guys, mechanics. The only ones who had a mind of their own didn't last long.

Interview/Life, 7-17:36.

George Low
Acting Administrator, National Aeronautics and Space Administration of the United States

There is almost nothing in manned space flight I would justify on the basis of science. Science is an adjunct to manned flight.

Apollo is a good example of this. If the nation's sole purpose for going to the moon had been to bring back a lunar sample, I'm not sure we shouldn't have done without men, like the Soviet Union's *Luna 16.* But we went with men, and what the scientists quickly forget is that we are now reaping the scientific benefits from having gone with men.

Interview/The Washington Post, 9-27:B3.

In a little more than 60 days, the Soviet Union has launched 22 space missions, including *Luna 16,* which gathered and returned a lunar sample to earth, and *Zond 8,* which carried extensive photography in lunar orbit. Now, *Luna 17,* with its remote-controlled Lunokhod 1 vehicle, has added to the list in a clear demonstration that the Soviet Union is operating with an advanced state of technology and is exploiting it for a broad range of objectives.

Los Angeles Times, 11-18:(1)7.

Salvador E. Luria
Biologist

The problem of how the fruits of science are going to be used is an ethical rather than a scientific problem—a problem of values, of wisdom, of responsibility. For the first time in his history, man has learned enough about his environment, with which he is engaged in an unending game, that he may deal his own hand. But he has not learned enough about himself. Man is like a card player engaged in a game for high stakes without being sure of his own nerves and, even worse, without reliable knowledge of the rules of the game ... We may gamble on the wrong card and face nuclear and biological disaster. Or we may stumble on the right play, and then the only reward will be to go on playing ...

Aspen, Colo./ The New York Times, 9-2:32.

H. E. Markley
President, Timken Company

Technology is moving faster than people can grasp and use. It is questionable whether we can stand 20 more years of technical improvements without improving the people who operate and utilize the equipment.

Before Farm and Industrial Equipment Institute, Toronto, Sept. 16/ Vital Speeches, 12–15:145.

William D. McElroy
Director, National Science Foundation

If I were to name the single most praiseworthy aspect of science, it would be its working methods, not its accomplishments. It is not the technological translation of science into more comfortable lives, it is not landing on the moon or discovery of nuclear energy. The greatness of science lies in the testimony science offers to the marvelous capacity of the human mind—the power to reason, to perceive order in apparent chaos, to understand the universe and control our corner of it . . .

Interview, Washington/ The Christian Science Monitor, 9–4:7.

Richard M. Nixon
President of the United States

I thought the most exciting day of my life was the day I was elected President of the United States. I thought perhaps next to that was the day that *Appollo 11* completed its flight and I met it when it came down to sea in the Pacific. But there is no question in my mind that for me, personally, this is the most exciting, the most meaningful day that I have ever experienced.

On safe return to earth of crippled "Apollo 13," Washington, April 17/ Los Angeles Times, 4–18:(1)18.

Thomas O. Paine
Administrator, National Aeronautics and Space Administration of the United States

I think those that take the position that the space program is holding up advances in the cities or welfare or poverty simply do not understand that the space program is much less than 1 per cent of our gross national product. We spend more than twice as much on tobacco, four times as much on alcoholic beverages, on racetracks.

The New York Times, 1–12:82.

We applaud the increase in sewage disposal plants. But we certainly hope this doesn't mean that the nation has taken its eyes off the stars and put them on the sewers.

Plainview (Tex.) Daily Herald, 3–4:6.

Cooperation with the Soviet Union is not limited so much by technical considerations as by political considerations on the Soviet side. Soviet spokesmen have themselves said that political questions preclude more extensive cooperation with the U.S. In our experience, the Soviets have limited space cooperation to scientific and theoretical, rather than technological and operational, matters. They have not been prepared to talk about their plans and to look with us at what might be accomplished. Thus, many intrinsically meritorious proposals for cooperation have little prospect of gaining Soviet acceptance. The success of our efforts with other nations in space is a measure of the difficulty of cooperating with the Soviet Union.

The Christian Science Monitor, 4–7:16.

John O. Pastore
United States Senator, D-R.I.

Why do we have to keep going to the moon? What is it we're looking for up there that's more important than providing education for our children on earth and housing for the elderly and all the rest?

Before the Senate, Washington/ The Dallas Times Herald, 7–8:A2.

Rocco A. Petrone
"Apollo" Program Director, National Aeronautics and Space Administration

There's no question that space exploration must ultimately involve men. Because no matter what you find there, you're going to want to put a man's brain, eyes, hands and feet up there to use the instruments you've got.

The Washington Post, 11–18:A14.

Paul D. Saltman
Biochemist; Provost, Revelle College,
University of California at San Diego

Archibald MacLeish has called for a moratorium on science until the humanists are able to sort things out and bring us back to "normality." MacLeish, and many other humanists, feel so alienated, and so apart from, and so unknowing of, science and technology, as to believe that we can declare a moratorium. They speak of the technological plagues which scientists have brought to the earth, and absolve themselves and society of any responsibility. The reason for this is that they have failed to see the intellect of man as a single coherent circle, a continuum that encompasses all of man's creativity. Until we do, we have to respond to the anti-intellectuals who wring their hands and cry, "Wait until we humanists can straighten it out."

Lecture/Los Angeles Times, 9–13:D2.

Leon T. Silver
California Institute of Technology

Our ultimate objective is to understand the moon in its context with the solar system. It stands up there quite different from the earth—a sort of frozen record book.

U.S. News & World Report, 4–20:46.

Harry G. Slater
Senior vice president, Niagara Mohawk
Power Corporation

Most scientists and technicians read novels, listen to music, worry about social problems, watch television and generally know something about what is going on in the nontechnical world. But the lay public is virtually illiterate as far as understanding the basics of today's science and technology . . . Probably no more than one in ten educated, nontechnical members of the public could describe what is meant by "mass" or "acceleration"—which is the scientific equivalent of saying, "Can you read?" From the technical man's point of view, this represents an ignorance and, more distressing, a lack of interest in what is going on in the world today. We hear members of the public demanding that we tell it like it is in referring to social and political conditions, but many have no desire to learn the principles behind a very important element of our society—the scientific and technological advancements that have revolutionized virtually every aspect of industry, government, education and our day-to-day lives. Without at least a rudimentary understanding of the principles of electronics, propulsion, nuclear fission and other advanced technologies, the public today cannot really evaluate or even cope with our complex society.

Before American Nuclear Society,
Toronto, Feb. 5/
Vital Speeches, 4–15:400.

Stewart L. Udall
Former Secretary of the Interior
of the United States

For too long the American scientific community has sought a special status for itself but has restricted its sense of responsibility. To put it briefly, some leaders of science have seemed to assert that their profession merits public support without public accountability, public support without any assurance of value returned, public support without any guarantee that such largesse will be used in the long-term national interest . . . There is no doubt that, in the main, science has returned good value in terms of scientific results. But as we all know today, science, lacking any foresighted ethical or social vision, can be a menace to man as well as a beneficence.

At annual meeting, American Association for
the Advancement of Science, Chicago, Dec. 30/
The New York Times, 12–31:6.

James Van Allen
Professor of Physics, University of Iowa

Some persons have compared the landing of *Apollo 11* on the moon to the landing of Columbus in the West Indies. I personally believe that is essentially a false analogy. I think it might properly be compared to the explorations of Amundsen and Peary and Byrd in the Arctic and Antarctic, or perhaps

Lindbergh flying the Atlantic. These are great achievements, heroic achievements, but the general potential of the moon in its relationship to human life on a large scale is by no means obvious to me. I don't think any competent person has found a significant, economic, human use for the moon.

At University of Iowa/
National Observer, 6–15:15.

George Wiley
Executive director, National Welfare
Rights Organization

When I left science it was because I found no way in my 21 years of studying, learning, teaching and pursuing chemistry that had any relation to the liberation of myself and millions of other black people who are degraded and humiliated every day in this country. Since then, I have slowly realized that this was the profession that made war and oppression possible . . . In the black community, we have a word for those who sell their souls for a pittance. We call them "Uncle Toms." I say that the vast majority of the scientific community are "Uncle Toms." They have sold their souls to the Defense Department and the Federal Government for small grants, status in the intellectual community. Others have sold their souls to industry. We have blindly exchanged our dignity for a house in the suburbs, a $15,000-a-year job and two cars in the garage. There must be a renaissance, indeed there must be a revolution, in science where people with technical experience say to themselves that today my brain power, manpower, skills and energy will not be used any longer to exploit oppressed people in this country and throughout the world.

At symposium entitled, "Science and Human
Needs," before annual meeting, American
Association for the Advancement of Science,
Chicago/The New York Times, 12–30:8.

Sports

Hank Aaron
Baseball player, Atlanta "Braves"

In football and basketball, you go to college and you're ready for the pros. Baseball is different. Even the connotation of "big league" is different. In baseball there is something electrifying about the big leagues. I had read so much about Musial, Williams and Robinson . . . I put those guys on a pedestal. They were something special . . . I really thought that they put their pants on different, rather than one leg at a time.

Interview, Atlanta/Sporting News, 5-23:3.

Muhammad Ali (Cassius Clay)
Former Heavyweight Boxing Champion of the World

I have proven to be superior in speed, skill, looks and brains to any other heavyweight in the world. I came out with no scratches. I'm well invested. I beat boxing. Boxing didn't beat me.

Kingston, N.Y./
San Francisco Examiner & Chronicle, 3-29:A22.

I'm not just fightin' one man (Jerry Quarry on Oct. 26); I'm fightin' a lot of men, showin' a lot of 'em here is one man they couldn't defeat, couldn't conquer, one they didn't see get big and fat and flat on his back. Lose this one and Quarry'll be a movie star. By beatin' me, he'll be so valuable. He'll be in big cinemas, probably playin' in a top Western—the man who defeated Muhammad Ali. Like the man who shot Liberty Valance. He'll be a great man. It won't be just a loss to me. So many people'll be rejoicin' and jumpin' up and down and hollerin' and just rollin' under beds and chairs. Then again, so many faces throughout the world will be sad, so sad they'll feel like *they've* been defeated. All of this, just over a bout. If I lose,

I'll be in jail for the rest of my life. If I lose, I will not be free. I'll have to listen to all this about how I was a bum, I was fat, I joined the wrong movement, they misled me. So I'm fightin' for my freedom.

Interview, Miami/
Sports Illustrated, 10-26:19.

What prestige can I get from beating Frazier? Technically, he's the champion, but technical stuff don't mean too much in this country. People rebel against technical stuff. That's just a name: Joe Frazier, the champion. I've got the title now that I'm boxing again.

News conference, Atlanta, Oct. 27/
The New York Times, 10-28:37.

Joe Frazier was the active champion. I am back now and I am the champion. And if you don't believe it let's take a walk down Broadway and you'll need 30 police cars to keep order when people come around to see me. Remember, I've never been whupped.

Quote, 12-27:619.

George Allen
Football coach, Los Angeles "Rams"

If you can accept defeat and open your pay envelope without feeling guilty, then you're stealing. Winning is the only way to go. I've heard that the average NFL player draws a salary of $25,000, but I can't think of a thing this money will buy that a loser could enjoy. Losers just look foolish in a new car or partying it up. As far as I'm concerned, life without victories is like being in prison.

Sports Illustrated, 9-7:35.

The way to win is to get good athletes, get them in shape and have great morale . . . The biggest thing is to love the game, play it with enthusiasm and emotion—and love to hit people.

Sports Illustrated, 9–7:36.

Rich Allen
Baseball player, St. Louis "Cardinals"

(Commenting on artificial turf): If a horse can't eat it, I don't want to play on it.

Sports Illustrated, 9–14:40.

Don Anderson
Associate editor, "Sports Illustrated"

Many people don't realize that a whole new generation of golfers and golf fans has come of age in the years since Arnold Palmer began dominating the tour. And I don't think people realize how many really excellent golfers are competing on the circuit today. One of these days there's going to be a breakthrough—another Palmer, Nicklaus or Player—and we're going to see another golden era.

Sports Illustrated, 4–6:4.

Sparky Anderson
Baseball manager, Cincinnati "Reds"

When I was in the minor leagues, I used to hear people say, "up here," all the time (referring to the major leagues). Well, what's "up here"? There are managers in class A who are as smart as I am . . . To me, baseball is baseball. The minor leagues are the same as the major leagues. Myself, I am not overwhelmed by all the gay lights.

Interview, Pittsburgh/
The Dallas Times Herald, 10–3:A4.

Mario Andretti
Auto racing driver

Technology is outstripping the driver. At Indianapolis this year, the pole car will average 175 mph; at Michigan International Speedway two years ago I ran 183 mph; and at a new track in Texas this season we'll be averaging 195. Things happen before you can react. It used to be that when you blew an engine, for example, you had time to pop

the clutch, but now you're into the wall, backward, before you realize what's happened. I don't know whether we need a cutback in engine sizes or higher minimum weights, but something's got to be done.

Interview/Sports Illustrated, 5–11:40.

Frank Beard
Golfer

When I talk about certain players being obsessed with winning, I don't mean that winning precludes everything else in their lives—family, friends, religion, fishing and other recreation. But they have a need to win. If you guaranteed them $20,000 for second place, they wouldn't take it. They must have the opportunity to win. If I were offered the same money, I'd grab it and stay home and watch the tournament on television.

Interview, Rancho La Costa, Calif./
Sporting News, 5–9:47.

Bernie Bierman
Former football coach, University of Michigan

I did not say that football is better now just because it is more complicated. Sure, in the main it's a better game. There are more boys to choose from, and statistics prove that they have gotten bigger from one decade to the next. But I have not seen a team anywhere—in person, on film, on television—that is better than my 1934 team. It was my best team, my favorite team, and it could do anything you'd want a good football team to do.

Interview, Laguna Hills, Calif./
Los Angeles Times, 1–25:C5.

Lou Boudreau
Former baseball player and manager

I've waited 12 years for this. It's a dream. It's something you keep within yourself. You just keep hoping, but you never really say it to anyone. It's worth waiting for. This is a very happy moment. This is a very happy day. This is reaching the top. That's what we all strive for no matter what profession we're in. I feel that my life is fulfilled now.

On his admission to baseball's Hall of Fame,
Cooperstown, N.Y., Jan. 20/
The Washington Post, 1–21:D1.

August A. Busch, Jr.
Owner, St. Louis "Cardinals" baseball club

Much to my disappointment, I have to admit that I am fed up. The fans are getting disappointed, too. With the pension plan the players have, I don't understand how they still think we're (the owners) a bunch of tight-fisted bums.

St. Petersburg, Fla., March 12/
The New York Times, 3–13:46.

Wilt Chamberlain
Basketball player, Los Angeles "Lakers"

I think in American sports there has been too much emphasis placed on winning. All the accolades go to the winners, and I don't think this is very fair. Sports fans are too callous to those who finish second. I think everyone should be given credit.

Interview, Los Angeles/
Los Angeles Herald-Examiner, 5–7:C2.

Roberto Clemente
Baseball player, Pittsburgh "Pirates"

I don't understand why so many players say they like artificial turf because they will always get a true hop. If all the errors were taken out of baseball, the game wouldn't be the same. Ballplayers can't expect everything to be perfect on the field.

Sporting News, 8–8:41.

Bob Cousy
Basketball coach, Cincinnati "Royals"

Contracts today are ludicrous. The players should get as much as they can; but when it reaches a point where it harms the game, it's time to take a stand. Give the players all the money they deserve, but don't guarantee it. Don't tell them they don't have to work for it. When you eliminate motivation, you

eliminate competition, you eliminate accomplishment.

Sports Illustrated, 11–9:9.

Joe Cronin
President, American (Baseball) League

It (the reserve clause) is necessary to maintain the integrity of the game. If everyone were free to sign with the highest bidder, all the great players would jump to the wealthiest clubs. There wouldn't be any point in playing the schedule; you would know before you started who would win.

National Observer, 1–19:13.

Frank Crosetti
Baseball coach, Minnesota "Twins"

What they're playing on those (artificial turf) fields isn't baseball. I'm glad I didn't have to play on it. The people who invented baseball intended that it be played outdoors on the good earth and under the sun. It's what I call "a natural game"—on infields and outfields of grass.

Sports Illustrated, 9–14:45.

Al Davis
President, Oakland "Raiders" football team

In the military, they say war is hell. To be honest about the damn thing, football is hell.

The Washington Post, 1–4:B4.

Win Elliott
Sports announcer

Our culture doesn't include horse racing to the degree some others do. Queen Elizabeth owns a stable, but could you see President Nixon attending a yearling sale?

Interview/The Washington Post, 2–11:D8.

Chuck Fairbanks
Football coach, University of Oklahoma

(College) football has to make money. It has to support the spring sports. I can show you how to have a heck of a wrestling team. Let me recruit the guys who'll get us on top in football and we'll have good everything.

Sports Illustrated, 9–14:48.

Chub Feeney
President, National (Baseball) League

I've got to remind myself that I'm the only guy in the ball park who is there to root for the umpire.

Sports Illustrated, 4–6:17.

John Ferguson
Hockey player, Montreal "Canadiens"

I start hating the minute I wake up in the morning. That's the only way to play this game. That's how you have to play it.

Interview, March 15 | Daily World, 3–17:12.

Robert H. Finch
Secretary of Health, Education and Welfare of the United States

The best thing we've found so far for the population explosion is a 24-hour schedule for athletic events on TV—all year round.

Before National Press Club, Washington |
Time, 1–26:30.

Curt Flood
Baseball player, St. Louis "Cardinals"

I knew players were traded and sold, but I cannot describe the kind of shock I felt when I got this cold notice that I, a human being, was the property of one team one day, another the next and had no say, if I had to be property, whose property I'd like to be. And I decided it was never going to happen to me again . . . Because I'm well paid, does that mean I have no rights?

National Observer, 1–19:1.

A lot of people don't understand how you can make a lot of money and complain. And I think all players ought to take a closer look at their contracts. I was guilty of not doing that until somebody, my lawyer, sat me down and spelled it out to me in terms that a layman can understand. The contract is all in favor of the owner, not the player.

Interview, St. Petersburg, Fla., Nov. 17 |
The Washington Post, 11–18:C1.

Everybody thinks of baseball as a sacred cow. When you have the nerve to challenge it, people look down their noses at you. There are a lot of things wrong with a lot of industries . . . baseball is one of them.

Interview, St. Petersburg, Fla. |
Los Angeles Times, 11–19:(3)9.

Bob Gibson
Baseball player, St. Louis "Cardinals"

Too many people think an athlete's life can be an open book. You're supposed to be an example. Why do I have to be an example for your kid? *You* be an example for your own kid. The newspapermen come around and want to know about your private life. They say the public wants to know. Hell, I think just *they* want to know. You might get 100,000 people out to see a game some day, but you wouldn't get 15 come to hear what I did last night.

Sports Illustrated, 3–30:15.

Bob Goalby
Golfer

We (golfers) drink too much. We live too good. I don't consider myself an athlete because I'm not in good shape. Arnie Palmer's not in good shape. Bob Murphy sits on a walking cane between shots. Julius Boros could be one hell of a player, but he's 20 pounds overweight and he doesn't want to fight it.

Sports Illustrated, 7–20:11.

Arthur J. Goldberg
Former Associate Justice, Supreme Court of the United States; Attorney for baseball player Curt Flood

(Curt Flood's case against the reserve clause) is not designed to cripple or harass baseball. He desires to be treated as a free man. The chamber of horrors about the end of baseball if antitrust applies is dispelled by reference to other activities. Football, boxing, theatres have similar situations—and they seem to do all right under antitrust.

In Federal Court, New York, Feb. 3 |
The New York Times, 2–4:50.

Lefty Gomez
Former baseball player,
New York "Yankees"

When I first signed with the *Yankees*, the regulars wouldn't talk to you until you were with the team three or four years. Nowadays, the rookies get $100,000 to sign and they don't talk to the regulars.

Sporting News, 7–25:4.

Hank Greenberg
Former baseball player and club owner

We need more harmonious relations between players and owners, and we need to repair baseball's image with the public. The reserve clause has been in the news since 1923, and has brought objections from players and confused the public. We must recognize that times have changed and must go forward harmoniously, and the first step —the last step—is to abolish the existing reserve clause and work out a substitute. I'd rather see the owners do it voluntarily than in court, but it has to be worked out somehow. I can't see anything detrimental happening to baseball without it.

At Curt Flood's "reserve clause" trial,
New York, May 21/
The New York Times, 5–22:22.

Tom Haller
Baseball player, Los Angeles "Dodgers"

. . . we steadfastly believe that there should be modification—not abolition—of the reserve clause and that in matters that demand arbitration, the arbitrator should not be the commissioner, a man who is paid by the owners.

Interview, Vero Beach, Fla., March 5/
Los Angeles Times, 3–6:(3)2.

Woody Hayes
Football coach, Ohio State University

. . . consider the fact that in football there are 11 men moving at the same time. Other sports have the same thing—to a degree. But even though you've got nine men in baseball, for example, the emphasis is on nine

men stopping one batter. In football—well, it's 11 against 11 . . . Now I don't mean that the football player necessarily has to be more talented than those in other sports. He probably does not. But he is part of a more highly coordinated group. If the play is to succeed, every man has to do his job. I think football is the most intricate game that's ever been invented.

Interview/
The Christian Science Monitor, 10–21:11.

Bob Hope
Actor, Comedian

I never played golf with President Roosevelt because of his physical handicap. Harry Truman played cards, not golf. For some reason, I never got a game together with President Kennedy. And President Johnson preferred riding horses. But President Nixon hits the ball right down the middle. Come to think of it, that's the way he got elected.

Interview, North Hollywood, Calif./
The Washington Post, 1–21:B10.

Willie Horton
Baseball player, Detroit "Tigers"

There is a quota system in baseball . . . only so many blacks per team, please. Coaches, managers, scouts laugh when you mention it.

Interview, Lakeland, Fla./Daily World, 3–5:12.

Ralph Houk
Baseball manager, New York "Yankees"

Times change. We used to talk baseball a lot—I mean, players among themselves, and coaches and managers to players—on long train trips. And we used to sit around hotel lobbies and do a lot of talking. You don't see that any more. The air travel doesn't bring you together the same way, with everyone sitting strapped in his own seat. And with television sets in hotel rooms, you don't find guys hanging around the lobby . . . But there is a lot in baseball that can be learned by talk.

Interview, Fort Lauderdale, Fla./
The New York Times, 2–20:50.

The mental approach to pinch-hitting—to walking up there cold—is so different to playing regularly that it takes a special talent. Some of the game's greatest haven't been able to handle it. Yet, men with lifetime .220 batting averages have been murder when sent up off the bench. I'll tell you this much: It's one of the toughest pressure jobs in baseball, because most of the time it means the ball game.

The Christian Science Monitor, 5–29:6.

One of the hardest things to manage is an All-Star Game. To begin with, 50% of your players don't want to be there. And 75% want you to get them in and out as quickly as possible so they can catch a plane to someplace. Then the guy you plan on pitching comes to you and says, "I pitched Sunday and I got this little bit of stiffness here in the elbow. If you really need me, well, maybe I can go an inning at the most."

Time, 7–27:33.

Carl Hubbell

Farm director, San Francisco "Giants" baseball club; Former player

(Football is) all right as a sideshow, but it doesn't bring out the whole man. How can you really identify with a sport that has specialists for the hand, the foot and the shoulder? Baseball is the only game that calls for every skill from normal-sized people. If you can't throw, run, catch and hit, you're not a major-leaguer. Fans identify with baseball, and they'll continue to do so when other meteoric sports have had their innings.

Sports Illustrated, 12–7:14.

Lamar Hunt

Owner, Kansas City "Chiefs" football team

Pro football must become more efficient as a business. The cost spiral has gone up. We've got to economize and yet offer the fans an interesting package. I don't think any business can stand still, and I think this is the problem with some teams in pro football today. The owners are still running clubs like a hobby.

Dallas/The New York Times, 1–4:(5)3.

Al Kaline

Baseball player, Detroit "Tigers"

I think that 95 per cent of the players in the game today would have a hard time making the money outside that they do in baseball. But still, a lot of players gripe about the owners and the conditions under which they work—as if the conditions were slavery. All I'm saying is that, when it comes to the reserve clause, I'm on the side of the owners. I think about the tremendous investment they have in players. Some clubs send boys through college. I think of the farm systems that cost so much money. I can't see a player coming into the majors and then becoming a free agent after a couple of years. I think it would destroy the game.

Washington, Dec. 10/
The Washington Post, 12–11:D3.

Bob Kehoe

Soccer coach, St. Louis "Stars"

I don't want for one minute to give the impression we are as polished as those teams who employ predominately foreign-born players. We are not as classy and have to work harder and take longer to get the job done. For one thing, Americans have to learn to play rough, aggressive soccer. They start the game as gentlemen, playing the ball and staying away from body contact. We have to learn to play as aggressively as foreign players.

Washington/The Washington Post, 7–5:E1.

Robert K. Kerlan

Physician; Consultant to major league sports clubs

If athletes resort to medication to improve the mood, where do you stop? If a greenie (pep pill) makes you feel great, opium will make you feel greater. And you can go to cocaine and morphine, too. If this thing continues on its present course, you are going to find sports played by a bunch of dope fiends.

Sporting News, 7–4:16.

Billie Jean King
Tennis player

The public thinks that tennis is rich people out on their lawns going pitter-pat, pitter-pat. As a result, the only ones who watch tennis are those who participate in the sport.

Time, 4–27:53.

There are three differences between the men's and women's game in tennis: Men hit harder, because they're stronger, but otherwise we're just as good; men get more good business deals, because the game is run by men; and men tank more matches than women do—I guess we just have more pride.

The New York Times, 9–3:41.

Fred Koenig
Baseball pitching coach, California "Angels"

Times have changed drastically in the relief business. There used to be nothing but old heads out there (in the bullpen). Today, it's full of kids who are earning their major-league letters. But what better place for a boy to learn? The pitchers may be young, but the coaches are experienced. A reliever has plenty of time and opportunity to improve himself under game conditions. It's the road to a starting berth.

The Christian Science Monitor, 9–11:12.

Sandy Koufax
Former baseball player, Los Angeles "Dodgers"

I can't believe that Babe Ruth was a better player than Willie Mays. Ruth is probably to baseball what Arnold Palmer is to golf. He got the game moving. But I can't believe he could run as well as Mays, and I can't believe he was any better an outfielder. It's like being a second husband to a widow—you

never can compete with a legend. Very few people remember the bad, only the good.

Interview, New York/
Los Angeles Times, 4–19:C8.

Bowie Kuhn
Commissioner of Baseball

I don't like comparisons with football. Baseball is an entirely different game. You can watch a tight, well-played football game, but it isn't exciting if half the stadium is empty. The violence on the field must bounce off a lot of people. But you can go to the ball park on a quiet Tuesday afternoon, with only a few thousand people in the place, and thoroughly enjoy a one-sided (baseball) game. Baseball has an esthetic, intellectual appeal found in no other team sport.

Interview, TV Guide, 10–10:16.

Bob Lemon
Baseball manager, Kansas City "Royals"

Everybody is aware how important bullpens have been this year in the American and National Leagues, and will be right down to the wire . . . In fact, every time an important game or series is played these days, a bullpen will probably win it . . . Starters years ago had to learn to rate themselves over nine innings. Now the manager says, "Go as far as you can and the bullpen will pick you up." It's a different game. Nothing makes a manager look better than having a key reliever come in and do the job right.

The Christian Science Monitor, 9–11:12.

Vince Lombardi
General manager and head coach, Washington "Redskins" football team

I'm training people to be two things: Hopefully, I try to make each one into a man, and then into a football player. It's my job to see how they react under pressure. If they can't put up with my pressure, how are they ever going to stand the pressure from 60,000 people?

*New York/
Los Angeles Herald-Examiner, 5-27:D1.*

Al Lopez
*Former baseball manager, Chicago
"White Sox"*

The youngsters coming up now just go through the motions necessary to make the play. They should bounce around a little, show some life and zip. It adds a little action and gives the fans something to look at—rather than the monotonous routine, no matter how perfectly the play is made.

Interview, Chicago/Sporting News, 8-22:22.

Lee MacPhail
*General manager,
New York "Yankees" baseball club*

This thing of a club jumping from the lower parts of the standings to the top will continue. It has been happening since 1966 and will continue because of the fine balance baseball has attained. There are three reasons for this balance: the coming of the free-agent draft, the unrestricted major league draft, and expansion. It is no longer possible for any one club to have an oversupply of major league players.

Paramus, N.J./Sporting News, 2-14:39.

William C. MacPhail
*Vice president,
Columbia Broadcasting System Sports*

I hate to admit this, because we (at CBS) don't have baseball, but all this talk that football has superseded baseball as the national pastime is malarkey. Whenever baseball is opposite football, it kills us in the ratings.

Sporting News, 1-17:4.

Mickey Mantle
*Former baseball player,
New York "Yankees"*

During my 18 years (as a player), I came to bat almost 10,000 times. I struck out about 1,700 times and walked maybe 1,800 times.

You figure a ballplayer will average about 500 at-bats a season. That means I played seven years in the major leagues without even hitting the ball.

Sports Illustrated, 12-7:14.

Willie Mays
Baseball player, San Francisco "Giants"

I don't kid myself. Iron rusts. I see that ball as well as I ever did, but I don't respond the way I should. Age tells. Some day a kid will come up and beat me out of my job, but I don't think the time is now.

*San Francisco Examiner & Chronicle
(This World), 1-25:2.*

Sam McDowell
Baseball pitcher, Cleveland "Indians"

Managers are mostly ex-hitters, and they seldom have any respect for pitchers. They don't understand that all pitchers are unique and have to be handled differently. Most managers think pitchers are dumb because we like to do our own thing. Yet we couldn't be too dumb, because every year they're changing the rules of baseball to make life easier for the hitters.

Sports Illustrated, 8-17:40.

Denny McLain
Baseball player, Detroit "Tigers"

All I can say now, because I'm under orders from the Detroit grand jury and my lawyers not to discuss the case, is that I have done nothing to hurt baseball. Some of those allegations carried in that *Sports Illustrated* magazine article about my bookmaking activities and other incidents are absurd, and they're going to hear from me and my lawyers. Yes, that means I'll sue. But I want to add that (baseball) Commissioner (Bowie) Kuhn did the right thing in suspending me. I would have done the same thing in his place. I'm glad of one thing—Kuhn is a lawyer. He is not likely to get emotional, as some other people are doing. He will weigh the facts and I'll abide by his judgment.

*Interview, Lakeland, Fla., Feb. 20/
The Dallas Times Herald, 2-21:C1.*

Charlie Metro
Baseball manager, Kansas City "Royals"

Bases are a hazard. They are an obstacle, a trap. They add nothing to the game except injury, fluke hits and botched double plays . . . For eight years I've been trying to get people to do something about the bases. Why not bury the edges, take away those corners and make it like an upside-down plate with only an oval sticking up above the ground? You could still see it, but you wouldn't fall over it.

Interview, Kansas City/Sporting News, 5–2:22.

I think 25 players are too many. There's no way you can use them all, and the ones sitting on the bench are always dissatisfied. I don't blame them; nobody likes to sit. If you had only 21 players, everybody would get plenty of work. And it would force us to do a better job of managing. We'd have to conserve our pinch hitters, go longer with our starters, save our relief men until they were really needed. It would make more players available for the weaker teams, and I don't think it would hurt the general caliber of play at all.

Sports Illustrated, 5–25:16

Gerald Micklem
British golfer

It is time something was done about the slow play of Americans. What they do in their own country is their own affair; but American tourists play the game (golf) all over the world now, and everywhere they go there are complaints of their keeping people waiting on the course. With so many people waiting to play the game, this could become a real menace.

Sports Illustrated, 5–11:19.

Marvin Miller
*Executive director, Major League
Baseball Players' Association*

Baseball has maintained a facade which it has sold to a good part of the public, and part of the press, that these reserve rules are somehow God-given, and that, if you change one comma, Yankee Stadium falls down. Team stability? Baseball, of all sports, has led the way in moving whole teams. Some stability!

*Interview, New York/
National Observer, 1–19:13.*

Chuck Mills
Football Coach, Utah State University

. . . football is the great American game. It is a game where you sacrifice; respect each other and yourself; work together—regardless of backgrounds, political, social or religious differences—for a common goal; and suffer, cry, laugh, wonder together. Football is a micro form of the American adventure.

*Logan, Utah/
The Dallas Times Herald, 9–30:B4.*

Byron Nelson
Golfer

Putting affects the nerves more than anything. I would actually get nauseated over three-footers, and there were tournaments when I couldn't keep a meal down for four days.

Time, 4–27:53.

Bill Nicholas
General manager, Los Angeles Coliseum

Comparatively, Russia has a history of snubbing other nations' athletes in the Olympic village, of failing to show up for international track-and-field meets after tickets had been sold and of supporting the threatened black boycott of the Olympics. They have agitated far more, than contributed to, the Olympic ideal of free men in friendly competition.

*Los Angeles/
Los Angeles Herald-Examiner, 2–15:A6.*

Len Okrie
*Bullpen coach,
Detroit "Tigers" baseball club*

Relief pitchers are separated from everything. They're so far back, all they have to look at are fences and other relief pitchers. In some parks, you can't see the hitter at all. Relievers are the most neglected people in the game. It's tragically wrong, because there are so many young pitchers in today's relief corps. The old-time reliever has disappeared, probably forever. A bullpen is not stocked with green youngsters who are striving to pitch themselves into starting roles ... But each time they build a new stadium, the bullpen seems to get farther from home plate. Today's reliever might as well warm up across the street from the ball park.

Interview/
The Christian Science Monitor, 8–25:12.

Walter F. O'Malley
President,
Los Angeles "Dodgers" baseball club

If there was no reserve clause, then many of the best players would come to us. They would all want to play here. After all, we are a successful team with an excellent reputation, and we play our games in a fertile area economically. Selfishly, we would benefit by removal of the reserve clause. Realistically, there would be such imbalance that the game couldn't exist.

Interview, Los Angeles/Sporting News, 3–7:7.

Wes Parker
Baseball player, Los Angeles "Dodgers"

Everybody in baseball, or any other game or business, has a lot more potential than he even dreams he has. No hitter hits as well as he should, but if he considers himself a .240 hitter he'll hit .240. If he considers himself a .300 hitter, he'll narrow the margin between potential and performance.

Interview/Los Angeles Times, 1–23:(3)5.

Players believe the mystique about big-league baseball probably more than kids or fans do. It's those two words that are not applied to any other sport—big league.

Sports Illustrated, 4–20:27.

Joe Paterno
Football coach, Penn State University

I don't think an athlete (today) will buy this business that they'll do something just because you have "Coach" in front of your name. Football is a product of a culture and it's got to adapt to society; society isn't going to adapt to football.

Sports Illustrated, 9–14:64.

Lefty Phillips
Baseball manager, California "Angels"

Even before I got this job, it used to surprise me when I read that certain clubs showed favoritism toward its star players. I believe that's a mistake. You should treat them all alike. As a matter of fact, why shouldn't a $100,000 a year player give 100 per cent? In my opinion, he should give 110 per cent. He should be the leader. He should set an example for the others.

The Christian Science Monitor, 4–17:6.

Grading hitters is about like making out report cards. You can rate just about all the hitters in baseball on a scale from A to F. There aren't many A's around, and the guys who get A-plusses, well, they're just plain rare.

Interview, Anaheim, Calif./
Sporting News, 5–2:5.

Gary Player
Golfer

When you play (golf) for fun, it's fun. But when you play golf for a living, it's a game of sorrows. You're never happy.

Rancho La Costa, Calif., April 23/
Los Angeles Times, 4–24:(3)1.

Paul Richards
Vice president,
Atlanta "Braves" baseball club

I've been in baseball more than 40 years, and anyone who says he can watch a player and tell you what he's going to do in the big leagues is simply lying. You usually can

(PAUL RICHARDS)

tell who's *not* going to make it. But when a scout tells you a player "can't miss," don't listen.

Sporting News, 1–17:4.

If it ever gets to the Supreme Court, the reserve clause undoubtedly will be thrown out; and the ballplayers may not know it, but that's going to be a sad day for them.

Interview, West Palm Beach, Fla./
The Dallas Times Herald, 2–27:B1.

Frank Robinson
Baseball player, Baltimore "Orioles"

Nowadays, it's rush to get to the golf course or out on a boat fishing. Baseball has become almost a sideline to the players now. Too much stock market, too much business, not enough dedication.

Interview, Miami/
The Dallas Times Herald, 3–11:B4.

Jackie Robinson
Former baseball player

The sport has come a long way for a man like the president of the New York *Yankees* to talk club ownership with a black. But he's in the minority. Most club owners are in the nineteenth century in their thinking.

Miami, Feb. 14/
San Francisco Examiner & Chronicle, 2–15:C4.

Anything that is one-sided is wrong in America. The reserve clause is one-sided in favor of the owners and should be modified to give the player some control over his destiny. Whenever there is a one-sided situation, you have a serious, serious problem. If the reserve clause is not modified, I think you will have a serious strike by the players.

At Curt Flood's "reserve clause" trial,
New York, May 21/
The New York Times, 5–22:22.

Chi Chi Rodriguez
Golfer

I think most of the rules of golf stink. They

were written by guys who can't even break a hundred.

Sporting News, 8–22:4.

Pete Rozelle
Commissioner of Football

I hope the next decade can become the stabilizing '70s for professional football. With all that happened in the '60s—expansion, the so-called "war" between the two leagues, the merger agreement, restructuring and realignment into a 26-team league—we are anxious to stabilize what we have. And paramount to stabilization would be getting our main emphasis back on the football field, to the playing of the game, to the on-the-field competition that has brought enjoyment to so many millions of people.

Sporting News, 1–24:14.

Johnny Sample
Former football player

Most of the people who play pro football came from underprivileged backgrounds—or at least they weren't too well off—and money is the driving factor. It's not for the love of it. You never see pro football players put on helmets and pads in the off-season and say, "Hey, let's play a little for the love of it." You see basketball players get together to shoot some baskets in the off-season, and baseball players get together; but not football players.

At Overseas Press Club, New York, Sept. 30/
The New York Times, 10–1:58.

Derek Sanderson
Hockey player, Boston "Bruins"

A hockey player must have three things planted in his head: hate, greed and jealousy. He must hate the other guy, he must be greedy for the puck and he must be jealous when he loses. Hockey players without those traits don't survive too long around here.

Sports Illustrated, 4–6:21.

Gene Sarazen
Golfer

The tour caddie must go. He is a menace

to golf. I have made this warning to Joe Dey (Golf Commissioner). I have told him that if we continue to allow the gypsy caddie in our big tournaments, we face the danger of a major scandal. We should avoid this iceberg before we smash into it . . . These touring caddies sign contracts with the players for a percentage of the winnings. Arnold Palmer, Bill Casper, Jack Nicklaus—all have their private caddies. I think this is a very dangerous thing. With this much money at stake and playing on 300 to 400 acres, in bushes and trees, what is to prevent a caddie from moving a ball or teeing it up to improve his man's lie? I say it's tempting and explosive.

Augusta, Ga., April 7/
The New York Times, 4–8:54.

Tom Seaver
Baseball player, New York "Mets"

The victorious clubhouse after a World Series win and the awards, if any, that would come my way were always what I dreamed would be the greatest satisfaction I could imagine. But now that I have experienced the pandemonium and the joy of the victorious clubhouse, I realize I was wrong. The ultimate thrill for me now in baseball is the game . . . the actual competition. That is much more important than all the awards I could possibly win. Standing out there on the mound and actually pitching to the batter has replaced for me the thrill that I thought all these awards would bring. I guess it is the same as the hunt to the hunter . . . the actual competition.

Interview, Fresno, Calif./
Sporting News, 1–31:33.

William (Bill) Shoemaker
Jockey

(About his tying the all-time mark of 6,032 wins held by Johnny Longden): To tell you the truth, I'm a little sorry, in a way. That record's the most important thing in the world to Johnny Longden, so I have a little sad feeling about equaling it. The perfect thing would have been if I could

have gone on winning races, hundreds and hundreds of races, but Johnny could somehow have held onto his record. That would have been beautiful.

Sports Illustrated, 9–14:29.

O.J. Simpson
Football player, Buffalo "Bills"

Basketball is tougher for a player, than football, in one respect. Everything he does is visible to the fans. You have to be good in basketball, because everything you do is in the open. In football, few people in the stands know the assignments of the players. If you blow one play that isn't obvious, not too many people who are watching will be aware of it.

Sporting News, 5–9:4.

Duke Sims
Baseball player, Cleveland "Indians"

The biggest thing I've learned is that it doesn't take any particular talent to play this game, except behind the plate and out on the mound. The catcher and the pitcher are the only guys who earn their pay. Hell, anybody who plays first base is stealing money . . . As long as you're not timid, you can be a pretty good baseball player.

Interview, Cleveland/Sporting News, 8–22:12.

George Sisler, Jr.
President, International (Baseball) League

Without the reserve clause, there will be no minor leagues at any level. It's really quite simple. The major league teams will not spend all that money to develop a player if they can't count on that player from one year to the next. Oh, there are a few cities that could support baseball by themselves, but the major leagues simply will not go to all that expense if they can't dictate where the players will be . . . Actually, the players benefit by the reserve clause. Their salaries would not be as high without it because everything would be helter-skelter from one year to the next. Speaking as the president of the International League, I don't think

(GEORGE SISLER, JR.)

(Curt) Flood's suit (to abolish the reserve clause) has any merit as far as the good of the game is concerned.

Rochester, N.Y./Sporting News, 6–13:35.

Dick Smothers
Entertainer; Race car driver

Racing is where it is today. The youth of today—and I include myself in that class—is car-oriented. We grew up in cars, and we respond to them. Cars give young people a chance to be free, to get away. Racing is the ultimate challenge of cars. In not too many years, I think, it will be the ultimate in sports.

Interview, Los Angeles, April 8/
Los Angeles Times, 4–9:(3)9.

Sam Steiger
United States Representative, R-Ariz.

. . . there's a need in athletics—in professional athletics particularly—to be scrupulous about image. Pro football and pro baseball have recognized this, and I think properly so. (Horse) racing, by its very nature, is going to be suspect; I suspect a majority of the population automatically assumes there's something wrong with racing. Therefore, racing ought to be more concerned about its image than any sport. Frankly, they've done a lousy job.

Washington/The Washington Post, 3–9:D8.

Casey Stengel
Former baseball manager, New York "Mets" and New York "Yankees"

When a fielder gets a pitcher into trouble, the pitcher has to pitch himself out of a slump he isn't in.

The Christian Science Monitor, 9–10:11.

Jackie Stewart
Auto racing driver

I don't get my kicks from flirting with death. I flirt with life. It's not that I enjoy the risks, the dangers and the challenge of a race. I enjoy the life it gives me. When I finish a race, the sky looks bluer, the grass looks greener, the air feels fresher. It's so much better to be alive.

Interview, New York/
The Dallas Times Herald, 9–27:B4.

A racing driver synchronizes his mind and body to the elements he is competing against. He reduces the blut in front of him to slow motion, approaching a corner, braking, changing gear, lining up the car, hitting the apex and leaving the corner with a calculated and unhurried action. You've got the track, the car, the speed, and you've got to merge them all into one, so that all of you are on the same wave-length. To do it exactly right is a wonderful sensation. I get a tremendous thrill from driving a car fast and properly and proving that I can do it—proving that I can go faster than anyone else.

Interview/Family Weekly, 12–13:15.

Hank Stram
Football coach, Kansas City "Chiefs"

The style of pro football is changing. Blocking, tackling and execution will still win games, but the people we're working with are getting bigger and faster and smarter—so it follows that we should use them with increased imagination. I also believe a football team reflects the personality of its coach. So, variety is the style of the Kansas City *Chiefs*. Some people like to wear just one suit and one pair of shoes. I like a lot of shoes and a lot of suits.

New York/Los Angeles Herald-Examiner,
9–20:D4.

Jim Sweeney
Football coach, Washington State University

The approach may be different, but I think the role of the coach is the same now that it's always been. We still teach the Spartan attitude, leadership, preparation for life's challenges. If a boy learns anything from football, he learns that to lead he first has to learn to follow. After he has gone through adversity, and leaves the program, he learns that discipline is necessary for survival. A boy wouldn't be in football if he didn't want discipline. But I don't think any coach wants to make an automaton out of a boy. Rather, he wants someone who is a thinking, responsible person who is not afraid to express himself, but at the same time doesn't turn away from the accepted methods of change. Law and order still is basically the answer. A kid learns that he is penalized for holding or for an illegal formation, then he also learns things that will lead to a better team and a better community. To me, football and athletics are a fortress that has held the wall against radical elements. I look for them to continue to play that same role.

Los Angeles Times, 9–30:(3)7.

John Unitas
Football player, Baltimore "Colts"

Football players today should be better because of their physical attributes and improved coaching. But they're not. Few young players coming into the game now have the proper attitude or desire. When it comes to dedication and self sacrifice, forget it. A lot of young players seem to have more on their minds than what they're being paid for. They don't want to spend any time and effort to improve. The majority seem satisfied just to make the team.

Baltimore, Feb. 3 /
Los Angeles Herald-Examiner, 2–4:C7.

Bill Veeck
Manager, Suffolk Downs racetrack; Former owner, Chicago "White Sox" baseball club

Racing gives you nine excitements a day, whereas you're lucky to get more than one or two in an average ball game . . . Baseball, in general, has lost it. Once upon a time, it was the only game in town. Then our people got greedy and let pro football come into their ball parks, and baseball's monopoly of the sports page began dying then and there. People ask me if I miss baseball and want back in. I don't.

Los Angeles Herald-Examiner, 2–13:A14.

Harry Walker
Baseball manager, Houston "Astros"

I think the most exciting hit in baseball is the triple. The action is sustained as the batter runs around the bases and the fielder chases the ball. Then there's the climax—the slide into third, with the ball and runner arriving at the same time. The excitement builds upon any extra-base hit. You usually have two or three men handling the ball; and, if everything fits together, the runner is flagged down in a close play. On doubles and triples, several men must contribute. On a home run, one man does it all.

Interview /
The Christian Science Monitor, 4–28:6.

Ted Williams
Baseball manager, Washington "Senators"

I hope they leave it (the reserve clause) alone. You know I'm for the ballplayer; I was one myself for 24 years. But even in modification there would be loopholes; there would be weaknesses. I'm against anything that even comes close to jeopardizing baseball. Any change at all in the clause could damage the structure of baseball. Why tamper with the rules of the game that has prospered for so long—in which both player and club have prospered?

Boston / The Christian Science Monitor, 1–28:7.

Baseball is the toughest sport for a rookie to crack—with no other sport even close . . . Everybody knows there will be some players just out of college who will make it big in the National Football League, and some of the big winners in pro golf are youngsters you've never heard of. In baseball, you have to learn to play before you get to the big leagues, even if you have all the physical ability in the world.

Interview, Washington / Sporting News, 8–22:22.

. . . the entire concept of pitching has changed in baseball. You expect to go to your bullpen in every game. It's a rare day when you don't have to . . . What is any manager trying to prove when he lets a tiring

WHAT THEY SAID IN 1970

starter try to go the distance? What difference does it make how many pitchers are used as long as you win? Winning is the name of the game . . . There's no sense to letting a starting pitcher struggle through the late innings when you've got a fresh, strong arm ready in the bullpen. When your pitcher is struggling, so is everybody else. The manager is up and down on the bench; you're giving body English to every pitch; your fielders are restless. If you've got a good bullpen—if you've got experienced men who can come in and get the ball over—you'd better use them.

Interview/
The Christian Science Monitor, 10–5:12.

Jonathan Winters
Actor, Comedian

I rap golf every chance I get . . . My major objection to golf courses is that they take up more space than cemeteries. If anyone wants to picket golf courses, I'll carry a placard. It's not a cheap little hobby. It costs a fortune to join a private club, rent a golf cart, buy the bag, clubs, balls and drinks after the game. And that's another thing: Golfers replay every hole all day long and into the night. I love to fish, but I never talk about fishing except to another fisherman. But golfers will make you sit there and listen to how they got a birdie on that long par-5 three long years ago.

Interview, Los Angeles/
San Luis Obispo Telegram-Tribune, 8–22:13.

John Wooden
Basketball coach, UCLA "Bruins"

I tell my athletes that youth today is fine. But I also tell them that there is something to be said for experience. A team must have leadership, and I'm the leader. I tell my players they needn't follow me blindly. All they need do is follow me. I never preach religion to my players, but I won't tolerate profanity. This isn't for moral reasons. Profanity to me symbolizes loss of control—and self-discipline is absolutely necessary to winning basketball.

Interview, Los Angeles/
Los Angeles Herald-Examiner, 3–25:C1.

Carl Yastrzemski
Baseball player, Boston "Red Sox"

To me, the ridiculous part of this whole thing is the claim that abolishing the reserve clause would help the little guy. I don't buy that. The little guy is going to get hurt. If it turns out that players in the future can jump from club to club for the best offer, then the stars are the ones who will benefit most. The bidding teams will go after the stars, not the little guys. So what will happen? They'll give a big contract to get a superstar to jump to their club. All teams operate on a budget. In order to make the budget balance, they'll have to cut the little guy because the big guy is getting the money.

Boston/Sporting News, 1–31:36.

United Nations

Arthur J. Goldberg
*Former United States Ambassador
to the United Nations*

We realize that the UN, with all its faults, is absolutely indispensable. There is no other way to preserve the human race from self-destruction in this last and decisive third of the 20th century.

*At UN 25th anniversary observance, New York/
The Christian Science Monitor, 5–25:5.*

Edvard Hambro
*Norwegian Ambassador to the
United Nations*

Many people thought at the beginning that it (the United Nations) would usher in an era of peace and understanding. But those of us who were taking part in the undertaking in San Francisco did not entertain any such hopes . . . However, you must keep in mind the fact that this organization has done much more than we expected in the fields of social and economic development. It has also made great strides in decolonization . . . As to whether it has served as keeper of the peace, remember that it would have been extremely difficult to decolonize without getting embroiled in colonial wars, had it not been for the United Nations.

*Interview, New York/
Los Angeles Times, 1–5:(1)20.*

Edvard Hambro
*President, United Nations
General Assembly*

Those who observe the United Nations from the outside may have experienced deeper disappointments over the last 25 years than those of us who work within the organization, who see the cautious progress and the small triumphs that give us the en-couragement to carry on. It is our task to re-kindle the enthusiasm of the public and restore the confidence of the millions who have placed their hopes in our work.

*Inauguration address as president,
United Nations, N.Y., Sept. 15/
Los Angeles Herald-Examiner, 9–16:A15.*

. . . the chief danger of the United Nations is to be by-passed by the great powers and that they fail to realize that they ought to use the organization as an instrument of their foreign policy. It is exactly that attitude of the major powers that destroyed the League of Nations. We should be aware of that. We should be realistic. But one of the main differences between the two organizations is, of course, the near-universal membership of the present-day organization, which makes it a much more live organization than the League of Nations was, even in its heyday.

*Interview, Meet the Press,
National Broadcasting Company, Oct. 18.*

I think we all ought to be aware of the fact that an international organization in reality only represents the possible maximum of international collaboration at any given time. You can't take more out of an organization than the states are willing to bring into the organization, and the only way to make the United Nations the chief instrument of world organization and world policy, as it ought to be, is for the great powers to treat it as such—and if the super powers do not understand this, are not willing to do it, the United Nations can never be the most important agent for peaceful collaboration between major states.

*Interview, Meet the Press,
National Broadcasting Company/Oct. 18.*

(EDVARD HAMBRO)

The world is not only ready for the United Nations, but the world is desperately in need of the United Nations. When you ask the question are we ready, you probably mean that the United Nations is aiming too high and that is not realistic. I think we must aim high. We must realize that it is not true to say that politics is the art of the possible. Politics is the art of making possible tomorrow what is not possible today.

Interview, Meet the Press,
National Broadcasting Company, 10–18.

Let us (in the UN) foster all that unites us and not that which divides us. Let us give the world cause to say: These were dedicated men; they did not posture and postpone, but strove humbly and honestly to lighten the afflictions that weigh so heavily on mankind.

San Francisco Examiner, 11–20:36.

Alexei N. Kosygin
Premier of the Soviet Union

We attach great importance to the United Nations, and we shall spare no efforts to ensure jointly with other peace-loving states that UN activity proceeds along the road outlined for it 25 years ago. The shortcomings and weak spots of the UN are explained not by some imperfections of its character, but by the fact that certain circles of the Western powers seek to undermine the basic principles of the charter so that it would be easier for them to use the UN for suppressing national liberation movements of the people.

Moscow/Daily World, 6–20:3.

Haile Selassie
Emperor of Ethiopia

Those of us who have a sad recollection of the crippled inaction of the League of Nations at the moment of its most acid test are compelled to view the predicaments of the United Nations with the gravest concern and apprehension.

Quote, 11–22:481.

Howard K. Smith
News commentator, American
Broadcasting Company

Reluctantly, but irresistibly, one is driven to the judgment that U Thant of Burma, as Secretary-General of the UN, is the wrong man in the wrong place during the wrong period of history.

Dallas Morning News, 1–26:D2.

U Thant
Secretary-General of the United Nations

Like many institutions, the United Nations is today facing a crisis of confidence. It has been the lot of institutions throughout history to have their usefulness questioned from time to time by the people. This process serves a useful purpose in keeping institutions up to the mark. In our time, this disillusionment has undoubtedly reached a new pitch. The United Nations, as a relatively young institution, faces a crisis of confidence without ever having emerged, as some older institutions have, from relative impotence to a position of accepted power and authority. If we are to respond to this challenge, nations—especially the great nations—must improve and change the quality and performance of the United Nations and the way it is used. There can be no question of taking the easy but suicidal way out by consigning the United Nations, along with other institutions, to the dusty attic of history. In an age where physical conservation has become an important issue, a degree of institutional conservation may also be in order.

At 25th anniversary of U.N. Charter signing,
San Francisco, June 26/
Vital Speeches, 8–15:652.

. . . no one can accuse me of having been impatient during my eight and a half years of service with the United Nations. Some have even accused me of being too patient. I have made every effort in the privacy of my functions to be of help and to bring people and their points of view closer together. I will continue this task in the same manner until the end of my mandate. But on this solemn occasion, when the eyes of the world are focused on us, I must emphatically warn nations not to pursue their present outmoded and fraticidal course. Time is running short. People are getting impatient. We need a fresh start; we need a fresh look. Governments must be able, once again, to lift themselves to the same high level of determination and vision as that of the authors of the (United Nations) Charter.

At 25th anniversary of U.N. Charter signing,
San Francisco, June 26/
Vital Speeches, 8–15:654.

There are times when I believe that the UN has not been faring so badly; that we have had an uneasy peace during the last 25 years, and that we have at least avoided an atomic conflagration; that nearly a billion people have gained their independence, without the bloodshed and struggle which other nations had to endure. But there are other times when I believe that with the will, support and enlightened vision of governments, especially the major ones, the United Nations could have fared infinitely better and done more during this period.

Time, 9–28:30.

The United Nations—this hesitant, almost reluctant instrument of nations for world peace and security—can only succeed if its constituent members support it, love it and give it their best and want it to succeed. It will fail if governments scoff at it and continue to tread their isolated, divisive and selfish paths.

At United Nations, N.Y., Oct. 14/
Los Angeles Times, 10–15:(1)4.

(The UN has helped) to prevent local conflicts from turning into worldwide conflagrations. It has assisted 1,000 million people to gain their independence. It has proclaimed the inalienable rights of the human person. It has revealed and helped to heal the great economic and social inequalities that prevail on earth. It has condemned and fought colonialism, discrimination and racism in all its forms. It has defended the dignity of man and the integrity of our environment . . . But the UN has not done well enough. Is it not high time for the leaders of this world to turn radically away from the errors of the past and to realize that understanding, love and tolerance are the highest forms of interest on our small and interdependent planet?

At United Nations, N.Y., Oct. 14/
The Christian Science Monitor, 10–17:3.

Earl Warren
Former Chief Justice of the United States

Twenty-five years ago, the UN emerged from the storms of world conflict as mankind's hope of saving "succeeding generations from the scourge of war." The vision persists. But . . . the rule of law still eludes a world ominously threatened with nuclear catastrophe and the passions of human deprivation . . . We must reaffirm our moral commitment to achieving world stability within the family of nations because the UN still remains the rallying point in the pursuit of peace.

At UN 25th anniversary observance,
New York/The Christian Science Monitor,
5–25:5.

Robert Welch
President, John Birch Society

The UN was dreamed up by the Communists, founded by the Communists, has supported Communist purposes and is the . . . framework by which the Communists will take over the world.

San Francisco Examiner & Chronicle
(This World), 1–25:2.

Charles W. Yost
United States Ambassador
to the United Nations

I believe that none of us is under the illusion that the forthcoming 25th anniversary of the UN should be a time for self-congratulation and complacency. On the contrary, it must be a time for soul-searching and for candid recognition of how far we have fallen short of the purposes of the UN charter and of effective means of carrying them out.

Los Angeles Herald-Examiner, 2–1:A15.

War and Peace

Richard Armour
Author

. . . we (the United States) have had 11 wars, including the French and Indian War. Increasingly, we have fought for idealism. We don't fight for land any more. We believe so strongly in democracy that we cherish it for other people in the world. Yes, we come to the aid of people.

Interview/
Los Angeles Herald-Examiner, 4–12:A17.

Errol W. Barrow
Prime Minister of Barbados

Expressions such as "local wars," "preemptive strikes," "small-scale interventions" and "wars of national liberation" are employed to absolve this organization (UN) from taking the effective measures which its charter clearly requires. But . . . man cannot live by semantics alone. For each new phrase that is minted by the public relations men in the war departments of belligerent nations, another twenty to thirty thousand die in some struggling developing country . . . We, the proletariat of primary producers; we who manufacture neither tanks nor planes, far less defoliants; we who sweat in the cane fields and the rice paddies and the coffee plantations; it is we, in Asia and Africa and Latin America, who are the inevitable victims of international violence.

At United Nations, N.Y., Oct. 14/
The Washington Post, 10–15:A17.

George Brown
Deputy leader, British Labor Party; Former Foreign Minister of the United Kingdom

Every Englishman will fight to the last Frenchman; every Kuwaiti will fight to the last Egyptian; and every western Jew will fight to the last Israeli.

The Dallas Times Herald, 2–19:A2.

Pablo Casals
Cellist

Before I leave New York, I will see U Thant at the United Nations. I'm not sure what I'll say to him, but I would very much like to talk about small children. When a child is eight or nine, he discovers the miracle of his senses—that he can see, taste, hear and smell. He learns the law of variety, that no two things are alike. At that age, a child should be taught to ask, "Being such a marvel, how can I kill? It's wrong and it's savage." Wars arise only from material thoughts, and people fight because they are ordered to fight. We are pacifists or we are savages.

New York, April 14/
The Washington Post, 4–16:D1.

Chou En-lai
Premier of Communist China

The people desire revolution and the times are progressing. This is the irresistible current of history. It is absolutely impossible for one or two superpowers to succeed in their wild attempts to divide the world and rule the fate of mankind.

Sept. 30/San Francisco Examiner, 10–1:6.

B.A. Clark
Deputy Secretary, External Affairs
Ministry of Nigeria

There are no victors in a civil war. Not when the people you have been fighting have been classmates or your friends or the man who used to work at the next desk or maybe even your cousin. All wars are bad, but civil wars are hideous.

Time, 1–26:18.

James B. Conant
Author; Former president,
Harvard Universiy

I have never been one of those who thought the use of atomic energy for peaceful purposes held such potential benefits for the human race that we should all rejoice at the discovery of atomic fission. To my mind, the potentialities for destruction are so awesome as to outweigh by far all the imaginable gains that may accrue in the distant future when atomic power plants may exist all over the world.

San Francisco Examiner & Chronicle
(This World), 3–15:2.

Abba Eban
Foreign Minister of Israel

There are no solutions without peace, and there are no problems which peace cannot resolve.

Before General Assembly, United Nations,
N.Y., Sept. 28/Daily World, 9–29:7.

Anthony Eden
Former Prime Minister of the
United Kingdom

There cannot be for any one of us any refuge in isolation. If we were to indulge in such false hopes, you (the U.S.), with your great responsibilities, and we (the British), with our lesser ones, would be increasing the dangers of a third world war. Our course must be the opposite to this, to work out together what each can do. If the free nations will make the effort collectively, they can achieve much more than they realize today, not only in their own interest, but in the service of this troubled and dislocated world.

At Hoover Institution on War, Revolution
and Peace/The Christian Science Monitor,
2–17:20.

Don Edwards
United States Representative, D-Calif.

Today it is not considered a war crime or atrocity to kill 1,000 civilians with a bomb or napalm, although it is still considered such a crime or atrocity to kill one civilian with a pistol . . . Rules of conduct during armed conflict have been discarded and nations throughout the world, instead of policing their own conduct, have played the game, "Your war crime is bigger than mine."

At Conference on War and National
Responsibility, Washington, Feb. 20/
The Washington Post, 2–21:A10.

Barry M. Goldwater
United States Senator, R-Ariz.

There is no way to pass a law which could make all men forever noble . . . by the same token, it is impossible to expect all nations—friendly and unfriendly—to be swayed by our belief in the value of peace and the foolishness of war.

At Norwich University commencement,
Northfield, Vt., June 7/
Los Angeles Herald-Examiner, 6–8:A4.

Edvard Hambro
President, United Nations
General Assembly

. . . it seems to me absolutely incredible that the voters of the world permit the race of arms to go on. We spend, I think, about $200 billion a year on arms, and it is quite impossible to get as much as a tenth of that for help to developing countries. I would suggest that the only people who can stop this are the electors of the world, in particular what we call the "free" nations. I think that the race of armaments, particularly of nuclear arms, today can only be qualified as collective insanity of the nations, and if anybody should live to write the history of this period, this will certainly be considered the ultimate folly of mankind. But only the electors can stop that, and here all the nations in the United Nations could help also in bringing pressure on the great powers

567

(EDVARD HAMBRO)

year by year, more and more strongly. That is the only way it can be done, and if we would not believe in the force of public opinion, nationally or internationally, I think there is very little that can be done.

Interview, Meet the Press,
National Broadcasting Company, Oct. 18.

Edward Heath
Prime Minister of the United Kingdom

We must recognize a new threat to the peace of the nations, indeed to the very fabric of society. It is the growth in the last few years of a cult of political violence, preached and practiced not so much between states as within them. Increasingly, the use of violence has become not the last resort of the desperate, but the first resort of those whose simple, unconstructive aim is anarchy. That we must all surely resist. Anarchy is not a prescription for peace, justice and progress. It achieves nothing but the suffering of innocent men and women . . . It is a somber thought, but it may be that in the 1970s civil war, not war between nations, will be the main danger we will face.

Before 25th anniversary session of
United Nations General Assembly,
New York, Oct. 23 /
Los Angeles Herald-Examiner, 10–27:A10.

Bruce K. Holloway
General, United States Air Force;
Commander-in-Chief, Strategic Air
Command

Our leaders work to make agreements which are meaningful and verifiable. Their actions are methodical and cautious—no more from a sense of distrust than we apply distrust when we assign referees to supervise athletics. They expect that the agreements which we all desire will be a long time in coming. Meantime, they know that the muscle of our nuclear deterrence holds a checkrein of safety all over the world. And this world—all of it—knows that it is protected by a society which for over a quarter

century has been, in the words of Andre Malraux, former French Minister of Culture, "The only nation that has waged war but not worshipped it, that has won the greatest power in the world but not sought it, that has wrought the greatest weapon of death but has not wished to wield it . . . May it inspire men with dreams worthy of its action."

At Texas A & M University, Jan. 17 /
Vital Speeches, 2–15:264.

Richard H. Ichord
United States Representative, D-Mo.

One salient truth has emerged from Vietnam, and that is that a war must be fought to win or not fought at all.

Before Veterans of Foreign Wars,
Miami Beach, Aug. 20 /
Memphis Commercial Appeal, 8–21:5.

Franklyn A. Johnson
President, William H. Donner Foundation;
Visiting Professor of Government,
John Jay College, New York

War is not only hell, it often is futile. That is what many say about Vietnam, and, with marvelous 20/20 hindsight, tell us it was all a horrible mistake. Looking back over this century's wars, we recall that World War I was fought to "make the world safe for democracy." It actually paved the way for a new despotism, Nazism. World War II was fought to end aggression by Nazism and "old despotism," Japanese militarism. It actually promoted an even older despotism, Communism. The Korean action was fought to turn back a further conquest by one element of that Communist tyranny. We still maintain U.S. and allied soldiers in South Korea to deter further attack, with a recent reminder in the form of the tragic *U.S.S. Pueblo*, of Communist potential for confounding us. All recent wars have their elements of error, ill-timing, inadequacy of resources, and other human miscalculations. No one will ever know what *would have happened* if the U.S., with generally generous and non-self-seeking motives, had *not* plunged into these caldrons of conspiracy—and then bound up the wounds of its enemies in completely unprecedented fashion. You must each guess for yourselves what the world would have looked like. For myself, I judge it to have been colored Red in far greater area than the old British Empire. And thus I believe and hope that 40,000 American men have died *for* freedom and justice, imperfect as it is, in Vietnam. They certainly died *against* the system, the institution, which buries women and children alive in Hue, which contemptuously seizes ships and planes in the open seas and skies, which brutally overruns a neighbor that opens a bit of freedom of press and politics, which consistently stirs the pot in the Middle East, which furtively conceals its space exploration and the military results thereof, and which has since 1917 segregated billions from ideas behind iron curtains, Berlin Walls and mined fields. War is hell, yes, and especially nuclear war. But there is something worse: slavery.

> *At Rutgers University, Feb. 4 /*
> *Vital Speeches, 4–1:372.*

Herman Kahn
Director, Hudson Institute

I believe we're in for a period of relative calm, like 1815-1914. For the first time in the 20th century, I think, you can go out and buy a map and it should still be pretty accurate at the end of the century.

> *Before House Science and Astronautics*
> *Committee, Washington /*
> *The Washington Post, 1–29:D3.*

Asa S. Knowles
President, Northeastern University

That "war is hell' was once known only to those who fought on the battlefront. Today, children of all ages can see the gory details in living color as they sit in the comfort of their living rooms to watch the dinner-hour news. Unlike World War II, this is not an era of rationing, victory gardens, parades, patriotic movies and radio broadcasts from London. It is an age of napalm, televised

executions in Saigon square, heated political debate over our military involvement and nightly televised news of the battlefront. Understandably, this has had an impact on the current generation. One can only speculate: Have modern communications media made war a firsthand experience for the entire population to the extent that the sacrifice of human lives will no longer be tolerated?

> *At Edison Electric Institute, Boston /*
> *The Wall Street Journal, 6–15:12.*

Alexei N. Kosygin
Premier of the Soviet Union

Commitments renouncing the proliferation of nuclear weapons are becoming one of the most important standards of international law. Those states who are not participating in the (non-proliferation) treaty cannot disregard the rule of international law. On them also lies the responsibility of seeing that a limit is set on the proliferation of nuclear weapons.

> *Moscow, March 5 /*
> *The Washington Post, 3–6:A9.*

Our delegation went to Vienna (to the SALT talks) with Soviet government directives to hold serious talks with the U.S.A. on . . . halting and reducing the possibility of atomic armament. Of course, everything in those talks is built on trust, and at a time when agreements are broken . . . of course, this puts us on our guard, and one must say that these actions by the U.S.A. (in Cambodia) do not strengthen mutual trust, without which it is very difficult to hold the talks.

> *News conference, Moscow, May 4 /*
> *The New York Times, 5–5:2.*

We approach the (strategic arms limitation) talks . . . with the utmost seriousness. The Soviet Union believes that the achievement of a mutually acceptable understanding on this question would be an important step in curbing the arms race, which is a matter of interest for the peoples of the world at large. As far as it concerns the Soviet side, despite the complexity of the prob-

(ALEXEI N. KOSYGIN)

lem, we intend to continue the talks and seek ways of checking the strategic arms.

Interview, Moscow/Milwaukee Journal, 8–10:4.

The Soviet Union is undertaking a number of steps to influence the world situation in the interests of strengthening peace . . . Our policy is to promote a detente in the world, to eliminate current armed conflicts and do our utmost to prevent the reappearance of conflicts between nations.

Interview, Moscow/
Memphis Commercial Appeal, 8–10:7.

Melvin R. Laird
Secretary of Defense of the United States

I believe that a policy of realistic deterrence places the major emphasis on avoiding war and maintaining peace.

News conference, Washington/
The Dallas Times Herald, 12–29:A2.

Li Hsien-nien
Vice Premier of Communist China

(The United States and the Soviet Union are) stepping up their mutual collusion and mutual contention in a vain attempt to stamp out the raging revolutionary flames of the peoples of various countries and re-divide the world . . . Both in Indochina and the Middle East, they are trying in a thousand and one ways to peddle a so-called "peaceful settlement," contriving Munich plots to sell out the interests of the people.

Peking/Los Angeles Times, 9–4:(1)5.

Lester G. Maddox
Governor of Georgia

Troops can fight the battles, but it takes a nation to win a war.

Washington, April 4/
The Washington Post, 4–5:A8.

Mao Tse-tung
Chairman, Communist Party of China

U.S. imperialism, which looks like a huge monster, is in essence a paper tiger, now in the throes of its death-bed struggle . . . U.S. imperialism . . . fears the people of the world. It becomes panic-stricken at the mere rustle of leaves in the wind. A weak nation can defeat a strong one; a small nation can defeat a big nation. The people of a small country can certainly defeat aggression by a big country if only they dare to rise in struggle, take up arms and grasp in their own hands the destiny of their country.

Radio broadcast, Peking, May 20/
Los Angeles Times, 5–21:(1)22.

John W. McCormack
United States Representative, D-Mass.

I saw what appeasement did in the '30s, when Britain and France let Hitler get away, first with the Rhineland—thinking he'd be satisfied—then Austria. Some of us in America saw to what this arrogant aggression was leading. Winston Churchill in England certainly saw what it meant, but he was like a voice crying in the wilderness. In those days before World War II, nobody agreed with Nazism or Hitler, but so many people in England and the rest of Europe and even in America said: "Well, we can live with him." Today, I find that there is a tendency in America to misread the significance of international Communism and its designs upon our own country. Arrogant aggression—whether under Nazism or under international Communism—isn't something Americans can ignore and live with.

Interview, Washington/
U.S. News & World Report, 7–27:58.

Robert S. McNamara
President, International Bank for
Reconstruction and Development

. . . it is tragic and senseless that the world today is spending $175 billion a year on armaments—a sum so huge that it is 25 times larger than the total spent in all foreign assistance programs. What is even worse is that defense spending is increasing by some 6% a year—a growth rate in destructive power that is greater than the growth rate of the world's total production of all goods and services. And the final irony in this litany of irrationalities is that arms-spending in the less-developed countries is rising at the rate of 7.5% a year, as against the world average of 6%. Prudent military preparedness has its place. Prodigal military proliferation is human folly at its worst.

At Columbia University Conference on International Economic Development, New York, Feb. 20/Vital Speeches, 2–15:340.

Vernon Mwanaga
Zambian Ambassador to the United Nations

It is obvious to me that the word "peace" does not hold the same meaning for the superpowers as it does for the ordinary major powers or the ordinary run of nations like my own—Zambia. For the superpowers, peace means quite simply the absence of a deadly world-wide confrontation with a whole range of nuclear overtones. Only in this context can we say that we have managed to preserve international peace and security for 25 years.

Before Women's Society of Christian Service and Wesleyan Service Guild, Houston/ Quote, 8–9:130.

Richard M. Nixon
President of the United States

No goal could be greater than to make the next generation the first in this century in which America was at peace with every nation in the world.

State of the Union address, Washington, Jan. 22/ Los Angeles Times, 1–23:(1)20.

When our astronauts returned safely to earth last Friday, the whole world rejoiced with us. We could have had no more eloquent demonstration of a profound truth: that the great force working for peace in the world today is the fact that men and women everywhere—regardless of differences in race, religion, nationality or political philosophy —value the life of a human being. We were as one when we thought of those brave men,

their wives, their children, their parents.

Radio-TV address, San Clemente, Calif., April 20/U.S. News & World Report, 5–4:62.

. . . if there is a war between the Soviet Union and the United States, there will be no winners. There will be only losers. The Soviet Union knows this, and we know that. That is the reason why it is vitally important, in areas like the Mideast, that we attempt to avoid, to the greatest extent possible, being dragged into a confrontation by smaller powers.

News conference, Los Angeles, July 30/ The Dallas Times Herald, 7–31:A6.

I can assure you that the greatest purpose and the greatest goal the American people have is to play a role to bring peace not only to America but to all the world. The armies and navies and air forces of the United States of America exist for the purpose of preventing war and building peace. They are peace forces, and that is the purpose of our policy.

Dublin, Oct. 5/ The Washington Post, 10–6:A16.

Since the end of World War II, there has always been a war going on somewhere in the world. The guns have never stopped firing. By achieving a cease-fire in Indochina, and holding firmly to the cease-fire in the Middle East, we could hear the welcome sound of peace throughout the world for the first time in a generation. We would have some reason to hope that we had reached the beginning of the end of war in this century. We might then be on the threshold of a generation of peace.

Radio-TV address, Washington, Oct. 7/ Los Angeles Times, 10–8:(1)27.

I invite the leaders of the Soviet Union to join us in taking that new road—to join a peaceful competition, not in the accumulation of arms, but in the dissemination of progress; not in the building of missiles, but in waging a winning war against hunger and

(RICHARD M. NIXON)

disease and human misery in our own countries and around the globe. Let us compete in elevating the human spirit, in fostering respect for law among nations and in promoting works of peace. In this kind of competition, no one loses and everyone gains ... There is no greater contribution which the United States and the Soviet Union could make than to limit the world's capacity for self-destruction.

At 25th anniversary session of United Nations
General Assembly, New York, Oct. 23/
Los Angeles Times, 10–25:A1.

One of the paramount problems of our time is that we must transcend the old patterns of power politics, in which nations sought to exploit every volatile situation for their own advantage or to squeeze the maximum advantage for themselves out of every negotiation. The profoundest national interest of our time—for every nation—is not immediate gain, but the preservation of peace.

At 25th anniversary session of United Nations
General Assembly, New York, Oct. 23/
The New York Times, 10–25:(4)4.

Nicholas Nyaradi
Director, School of International Studies,
Bradley University, Peoria, Ill.; Former
Finance Minister of Hungary

... the only language those people (Communists) understand is the language of iron determination. Everything else they mistake for weakness. The best way to maneuver ourselves into the horrors of World War III is to create the false impression ... that we are weak, that we are divided and that we want peace at any price.

Before Rotary Club, Memphis, Aug. 11/
Memphis Commercial Appeal, 8–12:32.

Paul VI
Pope

Poor peace! So abandoned, so necessary, so acclaimed; and still, today, so feigned, offended and betrayed.

The Dallas Times Herald, 3–23:A2.

John R. Platt
Biophysicist, University of Michigan

We continue to live under the daily threat not only of local wars but of nuclear escalation with overkill and megatonnage enough to destroy all life on earth. The danger is not so much that of the unexpected—such as a radar error or even a new nuclear dictator—as it is that our present systems will work exactly as planned!—from border testing, strategic gambles, threat and counterthreat, all the way up to that second-strike capability that is already aimed, armed and triggered to wipe out hundreds of millions of people in a 3-hour duel. Every year or two, there is a confrontation between nuclear powers—Korea, Laos, Berlin, Suez, Quemoy, Cuba, Vietnam, etc. Five or ten more such confrontations in this game of "nuclear roulette" might indeed give us only a 50-50 chance of living until 1980 or 1990. All our medical increases in length of life are meaningless, as long as our nuclear lifetime is so short.

Los Angeles Times, 4–23:(2)7.

Galo Plaza (Lasso)
Secretary-General, Organization of
American States

Revolution, in order to be successful, must be home-grown. It is a commodity which seldom lends itself to export.

News conference, Los Angeles, Feb. 17/
Los Angeles Herald-Examiner, 2–18:A15.

Georges Pompidou
President of France

The extensive means of destruction invented by science, the crime against mankind that a nuclear war would constitute, compel us to make peace our first and permanent goal. And because you (the United States) are the most powerful nation on earth, you more than any other are responsible for peace. Never has any nation borne so heavy a responsibility. But there is no nobler mission for a people than to follow the age-old words of Antigone: "My vocation is not hatred, but love"—not war, but peace.

Before Congress, Washington, Feb. 25/
The New York Times, 2–26:12.

Ronald Reagan
Governor of California

To blame the military for war makes about as much sense as suggesting that we get rid of cancer by getting rid of doctors.

At University of California at Los Angeles,
June 7/Los Angeles Herald-Examiner, 6–8:A3.

Stanley R. Resor
Secretary of the Army of the United States

Neither we nor the Soviets can use strategic nuclear weapons against each other without grave risk of being ourselves destroyed in the exchange. In this new era of nuclear parity, nuclear weapons cannot be the answer to all hostile acts . . . In this changed environment, conventional forces emerge as an increasingly effective means for exerting either military or diplomatic pressure . . . In an age of nuclear parity, conventional forces are the most credible deterrent to war.

October/National Observer, 11–30:18.

Abraham A. Ribicoff
United States Senator, D-Conn.

I have never known a President of the United States that would ever tell the people of this country the truth about matters involving war and peace.

Before American Society of Newspaper Editors,
San Francisco/The Dallas Times Herald,
5–14:A2.

Donald W. Riegle, Jr.
United States Representative, R-Mich.

. . . it is ironic that we must build items of war in order to insure the peace, that we must arm ourselves in order to lessen the chances that arms will be needed, that we must stand ready to fight in order to avoid a fight. But as long as suspicions and divisions exist between men and nations, and when the capacity for aggression is held by those whose motives are in doubt and who are unwilling to negotiate mutual safeguards, we are left no choice but to be strong and vigilant. We must be equal to any challenge that can present itself, just as we must be equally ready to lay down our armaments and work together the moment a mutual agreement can be reached which insures equitable world order.

At commissioning of "U.S.S. Detroit,"
Bremerton, Wash., March 28/
Congressional Record, 4–2:E2774.

Carlos P. Romulo
Foreign Secretary of the Philippines

No nation can say it really believes in workable peace if it enters into the making of peace with mental reservations. No nation can call for control of the terrible twin killers of fission and fusion if it says to itself that it will never really submit to complete inspection and enforceable safeguards. No nation can hold up the vision of a world free from individual misery if it shrinks from supporting, with money and men, the kind of total world cooperative effort necessary to bring this about. Finally, no nation can say it fully supports the cause of the United Nations if it goes outside the United Nations whenever it serves its purpose to do so.

At United Nations 25th anniversary celebration,
San Francisco/
San Francisco Examiner & Chronicle, 6–28:A7.

Maurice Cardinal Roy
President, Pontifical Commission for
Justice and Peace, The Vatican

Unless the '70s can reverse the widening gap between rich and poor, both within domestic society and in the world at large, it is all but impossible to believe that mankind can reach, in peace, the end of this troubled century.

Rome, Nov. 19/
Los Angeles Times, 11–20:(1)17.

Dean Rusk
Former Secretary of State of the
United States

I added eight years to the period in which no nuclear weapon was fired in anger . . . We now have 25 years since the military use of a nuclear weapon—a substantial achievement to pass on to the next generation. If they can add 25 years to that, they'll be doing very well.

Interview, Athens, Ga./
The Dallas Times Herald, 10–16:A20.

Robert C. Seamans, Jr.
Secretary of the Air Force of the
United States

. . . national pride and security are not incompatible with a peaceful international community; in fact, they are essential. All nations must develop pride and effectiveness in managing their own realms before they can feel secure in the presence of each other.

Before World Affairs Council of Orange
County, Los Angeles, Nov. 20/
Vital Speeches, 12–15:135.

Vladimir S. Semyonov
Head of Soviet delegation to Strategic
Arms Limitation Talks

. . . the Soviet Union unswervingly pursues the policy of peace and cooperation among states and peoples. We stand for peaceful coexistence of states irrespective of their social systems, as well as for stronger international security and disarmament. It is from these positions of principle that we also approach curbing the strategic arms race, the intensification of which serves the interests of aggressive imperialist circles. It is evident that effective measures toward curbing the strategic arms race would make a substantial contribution to stronger peace and facilitate progress in the field of disarmament. This would meet the interests of the peoples of all countries.

At opening of SALT talks, Vienna, April 16/
The New York Times, 4–17:3.

Jean-Jacques Servan-Schreiber
Journalist; Member, French National
Assembly

The old forms of power don't work now. Power today comes from industry and political ideas that serve people. Military conquest brings no rewards.

News conference, Washington/
The Christian Science Monitor, 8–7:2.

U Thant
Secretary-General of the United Nations

Contrary to the hopes entertained by the framers of the Charter, the UN collective-security system has not functioned well enough to make it unnecessary for governments to rely on the residual provisions for individual and collective self-defense, provided for in Article 51 of the Charter. This fact does not, however, prove either the permanence of the traditional alliance system or its wisdom.

Tokyo/The Christian Science Monitor, 4–17:15.

Josip Broz Tito
President of Yugoslavia

. . . the post-war development has clearly shown that stable peace and cooperation cannot rest on the balance of strength and terror . . . Any conflict, any crisis, has global repercussions. The whole experience of the post-war period testifies to the fact that universal peace and stability cannot be achieved by the big powers alone.

Zagreb, Yugoslavia, Sept. 30/
Washington Star, 10–1:A6.

Of course, we are not pro-American. But we support a balance of power that would make it impossible for one superpower to gain total supremacy. For this would end either in a new war, or in a division of the world into two distinctly-separated spheres. One power could hold total supremacy in one part of the world, and the other power similar supremacy in the other. This would be even worse than the already undesirable division of the world into spheres of influence.

The Washington Post, 11–16:B11.

Thomas J. Watson, Jr.
Chairman, International Business Machines

Are we still aiming at eliminating Communism? Well, we'd better think again. It's a happy, comfortable thought to believe that we can indeed make ourselves relatively safe and the Soviet Union relatively unsafe with anti-missile missiles and so forth. But think a little deeper. Our efforts might leave 50 million survivors here at home instead of 25 when the holocaust is over, while we kill two-thirds of the Russians instead of only half. This, to me, is only half-thinking and, if we set our national goals on this basis, we'll be following an impossible path.

Before Bond Club, New York, Jan. 7/
Vital Speeches, 3–1:302.

John J. Williams
United States Senator, R-Del.

First we sell arms to a country. Then we send advisers to show them how to use the arms. Then we send troops to protect the advisers. And that's how America gets into wars these days.

Before the Senate, Washington, June 12/
San Francisco Examiner & Chronicle
(This World), 6–21:2.

Ralph W. Yarborough
United States Senator, D-Tex.

We prepare for war at a rate that practically forces us to look for a war to use our material.

San Francisco Examiner & Chronicle, 8–30:C9.

Hideki Yukawa
Physicist

Only love for humanity will serve as the springboard for mankind to make his great leap toward a warless world . . . This is no time for mankind to consume its energies in international conflicts. (Instead) every man in the world should devote himself to the salvation of humanity by humanity.

Before World Conference on Religion and
Peace, Kyoto, Japan, Oct. 19/
The Dallas Times Herald, 10–19:B19.

The Indexes

Index to Speakers

A

Aaron, Hank, 548
Abed, Mawlid Kamal, 389
Abel, Elie, 420
Abernathy, Ralph D., 51, 269
Abram, Morris B., 269
Achebe, Chinua, 293
Acheson, Dean, 158, 365
Ackley, Gardner, 118, 187
Adams, Edie, 479, 500
Adams, Ruth M., 98, 118, 500
Adamson, Joy, 138
Adler, Mortimer, 98
Afolabi, Peter, 293
Agnelli, Giovanni, 365
Agnew, Spiro T., 33–34, 51–52, 88, 98, 118–119, 158–159, 171, 187, 206, 219, 230, 247–251, 269, 311, 323–325, 413, 420–421, 441, 472, 513, 537
Aichi, Kiichi, 311
Aiken, George D., 159, 325
Akar, John Joseph, 52, 513
Akwei, Richard M., 293
Albee, George W., 270, 441
Albert, Carl, 187–188, 230, 252
Aldrich, Robert, 452
Alexander, Clifford, 52
Alexander, Myrl E., 88
Ali, Muhammad (Cassius Clay), 513, 548
Alinsky, Saul, 52, 88, 270
Alioto, Joseph L., 53, 188
Allen, Dwight W., 100
Allen, George, 513, 548
Allen, James B., 53, 206
Allen, James E., Jr., 98–99
Allen, Rich, 549
Allende (Gossens), Salvador, 301–302, 513
Alliluyeva, Svetlana, 514
Allon, Yigal, 389
Allott, Gordon, 119, 171
Amalrik, Andrei, 365
Amory, Cleveland, 389
Anderson, Don, 549
Anderson, Robert, 230

Anderson, Sparky, 549
Andretti, Mario, 500, 549
Andrews, George W., 71
Annigoni, Pietro, 500
Anouilh, Jean, 479
Arafat, Yasir, 389–390
Archibald, Samuel, 252
Arden, Eve, 500
Arikpo, Okoi, 293
Arkin, Alan, 452
Arkoff, Samuel Z., 452
Armour, Richard, 436, 566
Arnold, Eddy, 472
Aron, Raymond, 88, 159, 325, **514**
Arrowsmith, William A., 100
Ashley, Elizabeth, 500, 514
Ashley, Thomas L., 390
Aspinall, Wayne N., 138
Atalla, Anton, 390
Attassi, Nureddin al, 390
Atwell, Robert H., 119
Aubrey, James T., Jr., 452, **487**
Auden, W. H., 34, 436, 500
Austin, J. Paul, 138
Aznavour, Charles, 501, 514

B

Bacall, Lauren, 501
Bailey, F. Lee, 206–207
Bailey, Stephen K., 120
Baker, Carroll, 501
Baker, Howard H., 188, 365, 421
Ball, Joseph A., 207
Ball, Lucille, 514
Bandaranaike, Felix Dias, 311
Banowsky, William S., 100
Barber, Alden G., 270
Barnard, Christiaan, 441
Barnes, Ben, 219
Barnett, Frank E., 277
Barnett, Larry, 138
Barre, Raymond, 366

H

O

P

Index to Subjects

C